001524

Bob
ABAIR JR

Ext 308

18 6

WESTERN CIVILIZATION

Volume II: From the 1600s

Houghton Mifflin Company   Boston
Dallas   Geneva, Illinois   Hopewell, New Jersey
Palo Alto   London

WESTERN

MARVIN PERRY

Baruch College, City University of New York

Myrna Chase

Baruch College, City University of New York

James R. Jacob

John Jay College of Criminal Justice, City University of New York

Margaret C. Jacob

Baruch College, City University of New York

Theodore H. Von Laue

Clark University

George W. Bock, Editorial Associate

Volume II: From the 1600s

CIVILIZATION

A Concise History

The following authors are members of The Institute for
Research in History: Marvin Perry, Myrna Chase, James
R. Jacob, and Margaret C. Jacob.

Printed in the U.S.A.

Library of Congress Catalog Card Number: 80-85255

ISBN: 0-395-29315-4

Cover Photograph
Ernst Ludwig Kirchner. German, 1880–1938
Dodo and Her Brother (detail). 1908/1920
Oil on canvas, 67⅛ × 37⁷⁄₁₆" (170.5 × 94.1 cm)

Smith College Museum of Art, Northampton,
Massachusetts
Purchased 1955

Chapter Opening Photographs
Chapter 16: Art and Architecture Division of the New
York Public Library, Astor, Lenox and Tilden Foundations
Chapter 17: Burndy Library, Norwalk, Conn. *Chapter 18:*
Detail, *Empress Maria Theresa;* Ringling Museum of Art,
Sarasota, Fla. *Chapter 19:* Courtesy National Museums of
France *Chapter 20:* Alinari/Editorial Photo Archives
Chapter 21: Detail, *Whirlwind of Lovers;* National
Gallery of Art, Washington, D. C.; Gift of W. G. Russell
Allen *Chapter 22:* Brown Brothers *Chapter 23:* BBC
Hulton Picture Library, London *Chapter 24:* The Mansell
Collection *Chapter 25:* The Mansell Collection *Chapters
26 and 28:* Historical Pictures Service, Inc., Chicago
Chapter 27: Detail, *Sunday Afternoon on the Island of La
Grande Jatte;* Collection of the Art Institute of Chicago;
Helen Birch Bartlett Memorial Collection *Chapter 29:*
National Gallery of Art, Washington, D. C.; Rosenwald
Collection *Chapter 30:* Sovfoto *Chapter 31:* Wide World
Photos *Chapters 32 and 33:* United Press International
Chapter 34: Tass from Sovfoto *Chapter 35:* Paul Arnaud

Contents

16
The Growth of the Nation-States: Transition to the Modern State   345

17
The Scientific Revolution: The Mechanical Universe   381

21

**Ferment of Ideas: Romanticism,
Conservatism, Liberalism,
Nationalism**   472

22

**Europe, 1815–1848: Revolution and
Counterrevolution**   489

Western Imperialism: Global Dominance   588

The Enlightenment Challenged: The Problem of Irrationalism   614

Art Essay: Early Masters of Modern Art   after 624

WORLD WARS AND TOTALITARIANISM: THE WEST IN CRISIS/1914–1945

The Road to World War I: Failure of the European State System   633

32

World War II: Western Civilization in the Balance   724

VI

**THE CONTEMPORARY WORLD: THE
GLOBAL AGE/SINCE 1945**

33

**Western Europe Since 1945: Recovery
and Realignment**   753

34

35

Preface

Western civilization is a grand but tragic drama. The West has forged the instruments of reason that make possible a rational comprehension of physical nature and human culture, conceived the idea of political liberty, and recognized the intrinsic worth of the individual. But the modern West, though it has unravelled nature's mysteries, has been less successful at finding rational solutions to social ills and conflicts between nations. Science, the great achievement of the Western intellect, while improving conditions of life, has also produced weapons of mass destruction. Though the West has pioneered in the protection of human rights, it has also produced totalitarian regimes that have trampled on individual freedom and human dignity. And although the West has demonstrated a commitment to human equality, it has also practiced brutal racism.

Despite the value that Westerners have given to reason and freedom, they have shown a frightening capacity for irrational behavior and a fascination for violence and irrational ideologies, and they have willingly sacrificed liberty for security or national grandeur. The world wars and totalitarian movements of the twentieth century have demonstrated that Western civilization, despite its extraordinary achievements, is fragile and perishable.

Western Civilization: A Concise History examines the Western tradition—those unique patterns of thought and systems of values that constitute the Western heritage. While focusing on key ideas and important issues, the text also provides a balanced treatment of economic, political, and social history for students in Western civilization courses.

The text contains several pedagogical features. Chapter introductions provide comprehensive overviews of key themes and give a sense of direction and coherence to the flow of history. Many chapters contain concluding essays that treat the larger meaning of the material. Facts have been carefully selected to illustrate key relationships and concepts and to avoid overwhelming students with unrelated and disconnected data. Appropriate quotations, many not commonly found in texts, have been integrated into the manuscript. Three essays link crucial periods in the history of art to their wider cultural setting. Each chapter contains an annotated bibliography and review questions that refer students to principal points.

The text is written with the conviction that history is not a meaningless tale. Without a knowledge of history, men and women cannot fully know themselves, for all human beings have been shaped by institutions and values inherited from the past. Without an awareness of the historical evolution of reason and freedom, the dominant ideals of Western civilization, commitment to these ideals will diminish. Without a knowledge of history, the West cannot fully comprehend or adequately cope with the problems that burden its civilization and the world.

In attempting to make sense out of the past, the authors have been careful to avoid superficial generalizations that oversimplify historical events and forces and arrange history into too neat a structure. But we have striven to interpret and to synthesize in order to provide students with a frame of reference with which to comprehend the principal events and eras in Western history.

Western Civilization: A Concise History is available in both one- and two-volume editions. Volume I of the two-volume edition treats the period from the first civilizations in the Near East through the Age of Enlightenment in the eighteenth century (18 chapters). Volume II covers the period from the growth of nation-states in the seventeenth century to the contemporary age (20 chapters). Because some instructors start the second half of their course with the period prior to the French Revolution, Volume II incorporates the last three chapters of Volume I: "The Growth of the Nation-States," "The Scientific Revolution," and "The Age of Enlightenment." Volume II also contains a comprehensive introduction that surveys the ancient world, the Middle Ages, and the opening centuries of the modern era; the introduction is designed particularly for students who did not take the first half of the course. An *Instructor's Manual* accompanies the text. In addition to enumerating the main concepts for each chapter, the *Manual* contains approximately a thousand questions: essay and discussion, multiple-choice, and matching.

The text represents the efforts of several authors. Marvin Perry, general editor of the project, wrote Chapters 1–12, 19–23, 27–29, 31, 32, and the sections on socialism and anarchism in Chapter 24. Theodore H. Von Laue is the author of Chapters 30, 33–35, and the section on Russia in Chapter 25. Myrna Chase wrote Chapters 24–26, with the exceptions just noted. Margaret C. Jacob provided Chapters 14, 16, 17, and 18. James R. Jacob is the author of Chapters 13 and 15. The three art essays were written by Katherine Crum. Marvin Perry and George Bock edited the manuscript for clarity and continuity.

The authors would like to thank the following instructors for their critical reading of sections of the manuscript:

Douglas Adler, *Utah State University*
Jack Balcer, *Ohio State University*
Phillip Bebb, *Ohio University*
Werner Braatz, *University of Wisconsin, Oshkosh*
Michael Dols, *California State University, Hayward*
Mary Gibson, *Brown University*
Stanley Grossman, *Ball State University*
Edward Gulick, *Wellesley College*
Robert Gutchen, *University of Rhode Island*
Jackson Hershbell, *University of Minnesota*
Lyle Linville, *Prince George's Community College*
James Powell, *Syracuse University*
Charles Rearick, *University of Massachusetts at Amherst*
Norman Rich, *Brown University*
Barry Rothaus, *University of Northern Colorado*
Julius Ruff, *Marquette University*
Joshua Stein, *Roger Williams College*
Thomas Turley, *University of Santa Clara*
Donald J. Wilcox, *San Diego State University*
Many of their suggestions were incorporated into the final version. We are also grateful to the staff of Houghton Mifflin Company who lent their considerable talents to the project. I would like to express my personal gratitude to George Bock who assisted in the planning of the text from its inception and who read the manuscript with an eye for major concepts and essential relationships.

M.P.

Introduction

The Foundations of Western Civilization

Western civilization is a blending of two traditions that emerged in the ancient world: the Judeo-Christian and the Greco-Roman. Before these traditions took shape, the drama of civilization was well advanced, having arisen some five thousand years ago in Mesopotamia and Egypt.

Religion was the central force in these first civilizations in the Near East. Religion provided explanations for the operations of nature, justified traditional rules of morality, and helped people to deal with their fear of death. Law was considered sacred, a commandment of the gods. Religion united people in the common enterprises needed for survival, such as the construction of irrigation works. Religion also promoted creative achievements in art, literature, and science. In addition, the power of rulers, who were regarded as gods or as agents of the gods, derived from the religious outlook. The many achievements of the Egyptians and the Mesopotamians were inherited and assimilated by both the Greeks and the Hebrews, the spiritual ancestors of Western civilization. But Greeks and Hebrews also rejected and transformed elements of the older Near Eastern traditions and conceived a new view of God, nature, and the individual.

THE HEBREWS

By asserting that God was one, sovereign, transcendent, and good, the Hebrews effected a religious revolution that separated them forever from the world-views of the Mesopotamians and Egyptians. This new conception of God led to a new awareness of the individual. In confronting God, the Hebrews developed an awareness of *self*, or *I*. The individual became conscious of his or her moral autonomy and personal worth. The Hebrews believed that God had bestowed on his people the capacity for moral freedom—they could choose between good and evil. Fundamental to Hebrew belief was the insistence that God had created human beings to be free moral agents. God did not want people to grovel before him, but to fulfill their moral potential by freely making the choice to follow, or not to follow, God's law. Thus, the Hebrews conceived the idea of moral freedom—that each individual is responsible for his or her own actions. Inherited by Christianity, this idea of moral autonomy is central to the Western tradition.

The Hebrew conception of ethical monotheism, with its stress on human dignity, is one source of the Western tradition. The other source derives from the ancient Greeks; they originated scientific and philosophic thought and conceived both the idea and the practice of political freedom.

THE GREEKS

In the Near East, religion dominated political activity, and following the mandates of the gods was a ruler's first responsibility. What made Greek political life different from that of earlier civilizations—and gives it enduring significance—was the Greeks' gradual realization that community problems were caused by human beings and required human solutions. The Greeks came to understand law as an achievement of the rational mind, rather than as an edict imposed by the gods. In the process, they also originated the idea of political freedom and created democratic institutions.

Greece was comprised of small, independent city-states. In the fifth century B.C., the city-state *(polis)* was in its maturity. A self-governing community, it expressed the will of free citizens, not the desires of gods, hereditary kings, or priests. The democratic orientation of the city-states was best exemplified by Athens, which was also the leading cultural center of Greece. In the Assembly, which was open to all adult male citizens, Athenians debated and voted on key issues of state.

In addition to the idea of political freedom, the Greeks conceived a new way of viewing nature and human society. The first speculative philosophers emerged during the sixth century B.C. in Greek cities located in Ionia in Asia Minor. Curious about the basic composition of nature and dissatisfied with earlier legends about creation, the Ionians sought physical, rather than mythico-religious, explanations for natural occurrences.

During this search, these philosophers arrived at a new concept of nature and a new method of inquiry. They maintained that nature was not manipulated by arbitrary and willful gods and that it was not governed by blind chance. The Ionians said that underlying the seeming chaos of nature were principles of order, that is, general rules that could be ascertained by human minds. This discovery marks the beginning of scientific thought. It made possible theoretical thinking and the systematization of knowledge. This is distinct from the mere observation and collection of data. Greek mathematicians, for example, organized the Egyptians' practical experience with land measurements into the logical and coherent science of geometry. In another instance, the Greeks used the data collected by Babylonian priests, who observed the heavens because they believed that the stars revealed their gods' wishes. The Greeks' purpose was not religious—they sought to discover the geometrical laws underlying the motion of heavenly bodies. Because of the philosophers' work, Greek doctors could examine human illness rationally. By the fifth century the Greek mind had applied reason to the physical world and to all human activities. This emphasis on reason marks a turning point for human civilization.

In their effort to understand the external world, early Greek thinkers had created the tools of reason. Greek thinkers now began a rational investigation of the human being and the human community. The key figure in this development was Socrates.

Socrates' central concern was the perfection of individual human character, the achievement of moral excellence. Excellence of character was achieved, said Socrates, when individuals regulated their lives according to objective standards arrived at through rational reflection, that is, when reason became the formative, guiding, and ruling agency of the soul. Socrates wanted to subject all human beliefs and behavior to the clear light of reason and in this way to remove ethics from the realm of authority, tradition, dogma, superstition, and myth. He believed that reason was the only proper guide to the most crucial problem of human existence—the question of good and evil.

Plato, Socrates' most important disciple, used his master's teachings to create a comprehensive system of philosophy that embraced the world of nature and the social world. Socrates had taught that there were universal standards of right and justice and that these were arrived at through thought. Building on the insights of his teacher, Plato insisted on the existence of a higher world of reality, independent of the world of things experienced every day. This higher reality, he said, is the realm of Ideas or Forms—unchanging, eternal, absolute, and universal standards of beauty, goodness, justice, and so forth. Truth resides in this world of Forms and not in the world revealed through the human senses.

Aristotle, Plato's student, was the leading

expert of his time in every field of knowledge, with the possible exception of mathematics. Aristotle objected to Plato's devaluing of the material world. Possessing a scientist's curiosity to understand the facts of nature, Aristotle appreciated the world of phenomena, of concrete things, and respected knowledge obtained through the senses. Like Plato, Aristotle believed that understanding universal principles is the ultimate aim of knowledge. But unlike Plato, Aristotle held that to obtain such knowledge, the individual must study the world of facts and objects revealed through sight, hearing, and touch. Aristotle adapted Plato's stress on universal principles to the requirements of natural science.

By discovering theoretical reason, by defining political freedom, and by affirming the worth and potential of human personality, the Greeks broke with the past and founded the rational and humanist tradition of the West. "Had Greek civilization never existed," says poet W. H. Auden, "we would never have become fully conscious, which is to say that we would never have become, for better or worse, fully human."[1]

THE HELLENISTIC AGE

By 338 B.C., Philip of Macedonia, a kingdom to the north of Greece, had extended his dominion over the Greek city-states. After the assassination of Philip in 336 B.C., his twenty-year-old son Alexander succeeded to the throne. Fiery, proud, and ambitious, Alexander sought to conquer the vast Persian Empire. Winning every battle, Alexander's army carved an empire that stretched from Greece to India. In 323 B.C., Alexander not yet thirty-three years of age, died of a fever. His generals engaged in a long and bitter struggle to succeed him. As none of the generals or their heirs could predominate

Alexander's empire was fractured into separate states.

The period from the early city-states that emerged in 800 B.C. until the death of Alexander the Great in 323 B.C. is called the *Hellenic Age.* The next stage in the evolution of Greek civilization *(Hellenism)* is called the *Hellenistic Age.* It ended in 30 B.C. when Egypt, the last major Hellenistic state, fell to Rome.

Although the Hellenistic Age had absorbed the heritage of classical (Hellenic) Greece, its style of civilization changed. During the first phase of Hellenism, the polis had been the center of political life. The polis had given the individual identity, and it was believed that only within the polis could a Greek live a good and civilized life. During the Hellenistic Age, this situation changed. The city-state was eclipsed in power and importance by kingdoms. While cities retained a large measure of autonomy in domestic affairs, they had lost their freedom of action in foreign affairs. No longer were they the self-sufficient and independent communities of the Hellenic period.

Hellenistic society was characterized by a mingling of peoples and an interchange of cultures. As a result of Alexander's conquests, tens of thousands of Greek soldiers, merchants, and administrators settled in eastern lands. Greek traditions spread to the Near East, and Mesopotamian, Hebrew, and Persian traditions—particularly religious beliefs—moved westward. Cities were founded in the east patterned after the city-states of Greece. The ruling class in each Hellenistic city was united by a common Hellenism that overcame national, linguistic, and racial distinctions.

During the Hellenistic Age, Greek scientific achievement reached its height. Hellenistic scientists attempted a rational analysis of nature, engaged in research, organized knowledge in logical fashion, devised procedures for mathematical proof, separated medicine from magic, grasped the theory of experiment, and applied scientific principles to mechanical devices. Hellenistic science, says historian Benjamin Farrington, stood "on the threshold of the modern world. When modern science began in the sixteenth century, it took up where the Greeks left off."[2]

Hellenistic philosophers preserved the rational tradition of Greek philosophy. Like their Hellenic predecessors, they regarded the cosmos as governed by universal principles intelligible to the rational mind. The most important philosophy in the Hellenistic world was Stoicism. By teaching that the world constituted a single society, Stoicism gave theoretical expression to the world-mindedness of the age. Stoicism with its concept of a world-state offered an answer to the problems of the loss of community and the alienation caused by the decline of the city-state. By stressing inner strength in dealing with life's misfortunes, Stoicism offered an avenue to individual happiness in a world fraught with uncertainty.

At the core of Stoicism was the belief that the universe contained a principle of order: the *logos* (reason). This ruling principle permeated all things; it accounted for the orderliness of nature. Because people were part of the universe, said the Stoics, they also shared in the logos that operated throughout the cosmos. Since reason was common to all, human beings were essentially brothers and fundamentally equal.

Stoicism had an enduring impact on the Western mind. To some Roman political theorists, their Empire fulfilled the Stoic ideal of a world community in which people of different nationalities held citizenship and were governed by a worldwide law that accorded with the law of reason and by natural law that operated throughout the universe. Stoic beliefs—such as all human beings are members of one family; each person is significant; distinctions of rank are of no account; and human law should not conflict with natural law—were incorporated into Roman jurisprudence, Christian thought, and modern liberalism. There is continuity between Stoic thought and the principle of inalienable rights stated in the Declaration of Independence.

ROME

Rome, conqueror of the Mediterranean world and transmitter of Hellenism, inherited the universalist tendencies of the Hellenistic Age and embodied them in its law and institutions. Roman history falls into two periods: the Republic, which began in 509 B.C. with the overthrow of the Etruscan monarchy; and the Empire, which started in 27 B.C. when Octavian became, in effect, the first Roman emperor.

The Roman Republic

The history of the Roman Republic was marked by three principal developments: the struggle between patricians and plebeians, the conquest of Italy and the Mediterranean world, and the civil wars. At the beginning of the fifth century B.C., Rome was dominated by *patricians* (the landowning aristocrats). The *commoners* (plebeians), had many grievances; these included enslavement for debt, discrimination in the courts, prevention of intermarriage with patricians, lack of political representation, and the absence of a written code of laws.

Resentful of their inferior status, the plebeians organized and waged a struggle for political, legal, and social equality. They were resisted every step of the way by the patricians, who wanted to preserve their dominance. The plebeians had one decisive weapon: their threat to secede from Rome, that is, not to pay taxes, work, nor serve in the army. Realizing that Rome, which was constantly involved in warfare on the Italian peninsula, could not endure without plebeian help, the pragmatic patricians begrudgingly made concessions. Thus the plebeians slowly gained legal equality.

Although many plebeian grievances were resolved and the plebeians gained the right to sit in the Senate, the principal organ of government, Rome was still ruled by an upper class. Power was concentrated in a ruling oligarchy consisting of patricians and influential plebeians who had joined forces with the old nobility.

By 146 B.C., Rome had become the dominant power in the Mediterranean world. Roman expansion occurred in three main stages: the uniting of the Italian peninsula, which gave Rome the manpower that transformed it from a city-state into a great power; the struggle with Carthage, from which Rome emerged as ruler of the western Mediterranean; and the subjugation of the Hellenistic states of the eastern Mediterranean, which brought Romans into close contact with Greek civilization.

A crucial consequence of expansion was Roman contact with the legal experience of other peoples. Roman jurists, demonstrating the Roman virtues of pragmatism and common sense, selectively incorporated elements of the legal codes and traditions of these nations into Roman law. Thus Roman jurists gradually and empirically fashioned the *jus gentium,* the law of nations or peoples.

Roman jurists then identified the jus gentium with the natural law *(jus naturale)* of the Stoics. The jurists said that law should accord with rational principles inherent in nature—universal norms capable of being discerned by rational people. The law of nations—Roman civil law (the law of the Roman state) combined with principles drawn from Greek and other sources— eventually replaced much of the local law in the Empire. This evolution of a universal code of law that gave expression to the Stoic principles of common rationality and humanity was the great achievement of Roman rule.

Another consequence of expansion was increased contact with Greek culture. Gradually the Romans acquired knowledge about scientific thought, philosophy, medicine, and geography from Greece. Adopting the humanist outlook of the Greeks, the Romans came to value human intelligence and eloquent and graceful prose and oratory. Rome creatively assimilated the Greek achievement and transmitted it to others, thereby extending the orbit of Hellenism.

During Rome's march to empire, all its classes had demonstrated a magnificent spirit in fighting foreign wars. With Carthage and Macedonia no longer threats to Rome, this cooperation deteriorated. Rome became torn apart by internal dissension during the first century B.C.

Julius Caesar, a popular military commander, gained control of the government. Caesar believed that only strong and enlightened leadership could permanently end the civil warfare destroying Rome. Rome's ruling class feared that Caesar would destroy the Republic and turn Rome into a monarchy. Regarding themselves as defenders of republican liberties and senatorial leadership, aristocratic conspirators assassinated Caesar in 44 B.C. The murder of Caesar plunged Rome into renewed civil war. Finally, in 31 B.C., Octavian, Caesar's adopted son, defeated his rivals and emerged as master of Rome. Four years later, Octavian, now called Augustus, became in effect the first Roman emperor.

The Roman Empire

The rule of Augustus signified the end of the Roman Republic and the beginning of the Roman Empire, the termination of aristocratic politics and the emergence of one-man rule. Under Augustus the power of the ruler was disguised; in ensuing generations, however, emperors would wield absolute power openly.

Augustus was by no means a self-seeking tyrant, but a creative statesman. His reforms rescued a dying Roman world and inaugurated Rome's greatest age. For the next two hundred years the Mediterranean world enjoyed the blessings of the *pax Romana,* the Roman peace.

The ancient world had never experienced such a long period of peace, order, efficient administration, and prosperity. The Romans called the pax Romana a "Time of Happiness." It was the fulfillment of Rome's mission—the creation of a world-state that provided peace, security, ordered civilization, and the rule of law. The cities of the Roman Empire served as centers of Greco-Roman civilization, which spread to the furthest reaches of the Mediterranean. Roman citizenship, gradually granted, was finally extended to virtually all free men by an edict in A.D. 212.

In the third century, the ordered civilization of the pax Romana ended. The Roman Empire was plunged into military anarchy, as generals supported by their soldiers fought for the throne. Germanic tribesmen broke through the deteriorating border defenses to raid, loot, and destroy. Economic problems caused cities, the centers of civilization, to decay. Increasingly people turned away from the humanist values of Greco-Roman civilization and embraced Near Eastern religions that offered a sense of belonging, a promise of immortality, and relief from earthly misery.

The emperors Diocletian (285–305) and Constantine (306–337) tried to contain the forces of disintegration by tightening the reins of government and squeezing more taxes out of the citizens. In the process they divided the Empire into eastern and western halves, and transformed Rome into a bureaucratic, regimented, and militarized state.

Diocletian and Constantine had given Rome a reprieve, but in the last part of the fourth century, the problem of guarding the frontier grew more acute. At the end of 406, the borders finally collapsed; numerous German tribes overran the Empire's western provinces. In 410 and again in 455, Rome was sacked by Germanic invaders. German soldiers in the pay of Rome gained control of the government and dictated the choice of emperor. In 476, German officers overthrew the Roman Emperor Romulus and placed a fellow German on the throne. This act is traditionally regarded as the end of the Roman Empire in the West.

EARLY CHRISTIANITY

When the Roman Empire was in decline, a new religion, Christianity, was sweeping across the Mediterranean world. Christianity was based on the life, death, and teachings of Jesus, a Palestinian Jew who was executed by the Roman authorities. Jesus was heir to the ethical monotheism of the Hebrew prophets. He also taught the imminent coming of the reign of God and the need for people to repent their sins—to transform themselves morally in order to enter God's kingdom. People must love God and their fellow human beings.

In the time immediately following the crucifixion of Jesus, his followers were almost exclusively Jews, who could more appropriately be called Jewish-Christians. To the first members of the Christian movement, Jesus was both a prophet who proclaimed God's power and purpose and the Messiah whose coming heralded a new age. To Paul, another Jewish-Christian, Jesus was the redeemer who held out the promise of salvation to the entire world and the savior-god who took on human flesh and atoned for the sins of humanity by suffering death upon the cross. And Saint Paul carried this message to Jews and especially to non-Jews (Gentiles).

The Christian message of a divine Savior, a concerned Father, and brotherly love inspired men and women who were dissatisfied with the world of here-and-now, who felt no attachment to city or Empire, who derived no inspiration from philosophy, and who suffered from a profound sense of loneliness. Christianity offered the individual what the city and the Roman world-state could not: a personal relationship with God, a promise of eternal life, and membership in a community of the faithful (the church) who cared for each other.

Unable to crush Christianity by persecution, Roman emperors decided to gain the support of the growing number of Christians within the Empire. By A.D. 392, Theodosius I had made Christianity the state religion of the Empire and declared the worship of pagan gods illegal.

The Judeo-Christian and Greco-Roman traditions are the two principal components of Western civilization. Both traditions valued the individual. For classical humanism, individual worth derived from the human capacity to reason, to shape character and life according to rational standards. Christianity also places great stress on the individual. It teaches that God cares for each person, and that He wants people to behave righteously and made them morally autonomous.

Despite their common emphasis on the individual, the two traditions essentially have different world-views. With the victory of Christianity, the ultimate goal of life shifted away from achieving excellence in this world through the full and creative development of human talent, toward attaining salvation in a heavenly city. For Christians, a person's worldly accomplishments counted very little if he or she did not accept God and his revelation.

Greek classicism held that there was no authority higher than reason; Christianity taught that without God as the starting point, knowledge is formless, purposeless, and error-prone.

But Christian thinkers did not seek to eradicate the rational tradition of Greece. Rather, they sought to fit Greek philosophy into a Christian framework. In doing so, Christians performed a task of immense historical significance—the preservation of Greek philosophy.

THE MIDDLE AGES

The triumph of Christianity and the establishment of Germanic kingdoms on once-Roman lands constituted a new phase in Western history: the end of the ancient world and the beginning of the Middle Ages. In the ancient world the locus of Greco-Roman civilization was the Mediterranean Sea. The heartland of medieval civilization shifted to the north, to regions of Europe that Greco-Roman civilization had barely penetrated.

The Early Middle Ages

During the Early Middle Ages (500–1050), a common civilization evolved with Christianity at the center, Rome as the spiritual capital, and Latin as the language of intellectual life. The opening centuries of the Middle Ages were marked by a decline in trade, townlife, central authority, and learning. The Germans were culturally unprepared to breathe new life into classical civilization. A new civilization with its own distinctive style was taking root, however. It consisted of Greco-Roman survivals, the native traditions of the Germans, and the Christian outlook.

Christianity was the integrating principle of the Middle Ages, and the church its dominant institution. People came to see themselves as participants in a great drama of salvation. There was only one truth—God's revelation to humanity. There was only one avenue to heaven—the church. To the medieval mind, society without the church was as inconceivable as life without the Christian view of God. By teaching a higher morality, the church tamed the warrior habits of the Germanic peoples. By copying and preserving ancient texts, monks kept alive elements of the high civilization of Greece and Rome.

One German people, the Franks, built a viable kingdom with major centers in France and the Rhine Valley of Germany. Under Charlemagne, who ruled from 768 to 814, the Frankish empire reached its height. On Christmas day in the year 800, Pope Leo crowned Charlemagne as "Emperor of the Romans." The title signified that the tradition of a world empire still survived, despite the demise of the Roman Empire three hundred years earlier. Because the pope crowned Charlemagne, this act meant that the emperor had a spiritual responsibility to spread and defend the faith.

The crowning of a German ruler as emperor of the Romans by the head of the church represented the merging of German, Christian, and Roman elements—the essential characteristic of medieval civilization. This blending of traditions was also evident on a cultural plane, for Charlemagne, a German warrior-king, showed respect for classical learning and Christianity, both non-Germanic traditions. During his reign, a distinct European civilization took root, but it was centuries away from fruition.

Charlemagne's successors could not hold the empire together, and it disintegrated. As central authority waned, large landowners began to exercise authority over their own regions. Furthering this movement toward localism and decentralization were simultaneous invasions by Muslims, Vikings from Scandinavia, and Magyars originally from Central Asia. They devastated villages, destroyed ports, and killed many people. Trade was at a standstill, coins no longer circulated, and untended farms became wastelands. The European economy collapsed, the political authority of kings disappeared, and cultural life and learning withered.

During these times, large landowners, or lords, wielded power formerly held by kings over their subjects, an arrangement called *feudalism*. Arising during a period of collapsing central authority, invasion, scanty public revenues, and declining commerce and town life, feudalism attempted to provide some order and security. A principal feature of feudalism was the practice of *vassalage*, in which a man in a solemn ceremony pledged loyalty to a lord. The lord received military service from his vassal, and the vassal obtained land, called a *fief*, from his lord.

Feudalism was built on an economic foundation known as *manorialism*. A village community (manor), consisting of serfs bound to the land, became the essential agricultural arrangement in medieval society. In return for protection and the right to cultivate fields, serfs owed obligations to their lords, and their personal freedom was restricted in a variety of ways.

Manorialism and feudalism presupposed an unchanging social order with a rigid system of estates, or orders—clergy who prayed, lords who fought, and peasants who toiled. The revival of an urban economy and the re-emergence of the king's authority in the High Middle Ages (1050–1270) would undermine feudal and manorial relationships.

The High Middle Ages

By the end of the eleventh century, Europe showed many signs of recovery and vitality.

The invasions of Magyars and Vikings had ended, and kings and powerful lords imposed greater order in their territories. Improvements in technology and the clearing of new lands increased agricultural production. More food, the fortunate absence of plagues, and the limited nature of feudal warfare contributed to a population increase.

Expanding agricultural production, the end of Viking attacks, greater political stability, and a larger population revived commerce. In the twelfth and thirteenth centuries, local, regional, and long-distance trade gained such a momentum that some historians describe the period as a commercial revolution that surpassed commerce in the Roman Empire during the pax Romana.

In the eleventh century, towns re-emerged throughout Europe, and in the next century became active centers of commerce and intellectual life. Socially, economically, and culturally, towns were a new and revolutionary force. Towns contributed to the decline of manorialism because they provided new opportunities for commoners, apart from food-producing.

A new class, the middle class, of merchants and artisans appeared; unlike the lords and serfs, the members of this class were not affiliated with the land. Townspeople possessed a value system different from that of lords, serfs, or clerics. Whereas the clergy prepared people for heaven, the feudal lords fought and hunted, and the serfs toiled in small villages, townspeople engaged in business and had money and freedom. Townspeople were freeing themselves from the prejudices of both feudal aristocrats, who considered trade and manual work degrading, and the clergy, who cursed the pursuit of riches as an obstacle to salvation. Townspeople were critical, dynamic, and progressive—a force for change.

Other signs of growing vitality in Latin Christendom (western and central Europe) were the greater order and security provided by the emergence of states. While feudalism fostered a Europe that was split into many local regions, each ruled by a lord, the church envisioned a vast Christian commonwealth, *Respublica Christiana*, guided by the pope. During the High Middle Ages, the ideal of a universal Christian community seemed close to fruition. Never again would Europe possess such spiritual unity.

But forces were propelling Europe into a different direction. Aided by educated and trained officials who enforced royal law, tried people in royal courts, and collected royal taxes, kings enlarged their territories and slowly fashioned strong central governments. Gradually, subjects began to transfer their prime loyalty away from the church and their lords to the person of the king. In the process the foundations of European states were laid. Not all areas followed the same pattern. England and France achieved a large measure of unity during the Middle Ages; Germany and Italy remained divided into numerous independent territories.

Accompanying economic recovery and political stability in the High Middle Ages was a growing spiritual vitality. This vigor was marked by several developments. The common people showed greater devotion to the church. Within the church, reform movements attacked clerical abuses, and the papacy grew more powerful. Holy wars against the Muslims drew the Christian community closer together. During this period, the church with great determination tried to make society follow divine standards, that is, to shape all institutions according to a comprehensive Christian outlook.

European economic and religious vitality was paralleled by a cultural flowering in philosophy, literature, and the visual arts. Creative intellects achieved on a cultural level what the papacy accomplished on an institutional level—the integration of society around a Christian viewpoint. The High Middle Ages saw the restoration of some learning of the Ancient World, the rise of universities, the emergence of an original form of architecture (the Gothic), and the creation of an imposing system of thought (scholasticism).

Medieval theologian-philosophers called *scholastics* fashioned Christian teachings into an all-embracing philosophy that represented the spiritual essence of medieval civilization. They achieved what Christian thinkers in the Roman Empire had initiated and what learned men of the Early Middle Ages were groping for: a synthesis of Greek philosophy and Christian revelation.

The Late Middle Ages

By the opening of the fourteenth century, Latin Christendom had experienced more than 250 years of growth, but during the Late Middle Ages, roughly the fourteenth and early fifteenth centuries, medieval civilization declined. The fourteenth century, an age of adversity, was marked by crop failures, famine, population decline, plagues, stagnating production, unemployment, inflation, devastating warfare, abandoned villages, and violent rebellions by the disadvantaged of towns and countryside, who were ruthlessly suppressed by the upper classes. This century witnessed flights into mysticism, outbreaks of mass hysteria, and massacres of Jews; it was an age of pessimism and general insecurity. The papacy declined in power, heresy proliferated, and the synthesis of faith and reason erected by Christian thinkers during the High Middle Ages began to disintegrate. All these developments were signs that the stable and coherent civilization of the thirteenth century was drawing to a close.

In innumerable ways the modern world is linked to the Middle Ages. European cities, the middle class, the state system, English common law, universities—all had their origins in the Middle Ages. During the

Middle Ages, important advances were made in business practices, such as double-entry bookkeeping and the growth of credit and banking facilities. By translating and commenting on the writings of Greek philosophers and scientists, medieval scholars preserved a priceless intellectual heritage without which the modern mind could never have evolved. During the Middle Ages, Europeans began to lead the rest of the world in the development of technology.

Believing that God's law was superior to the decrees of states, medieval philosophers provided a theoretical basis for opposing tyrannical kings who violated Christian principles. The idea that both the ruler and the ruled are bound by a higher law would become a principal element of modern liberal thought. The Christian stress on the sacred worth of the individual and on the higher law of God has never ceased to influence Western civilization. The Christian commandment to "love thy neighbor" has permeated modern reform movements.

Feudalism contributed to the history of liberty. The idea evolved that law should not be imposed by an absolute monarch, but requires the collaboration of king and subjects; that a king too should be bound by the law; and that lords should have the right to resist a monarch who violates agreements. Related to this development was the emergence of representative institutions, notably the English Parliament. The king was expected to consult its members on matters concerning the realm's affairs.

Despite these concrete elements of continuity, the characteristic outlook of the Middle Ages is much different from that of the modern world. Religion was the integrating feature of the Middle Ages, whereas science and secularism determine the modern outlook. Medieval thought began with the existence of God and the truth of his revelation as interpreted by the church, which set the standards and defined the purposes for human endeavor.

The medieval mind rejected the fundamental principle of Greek philosophy and modern thought—the autonomy of reason. Without the guidance of revealed truth, reason was seen as feeble. Unlike either ancient or modern thinkers, medieval schoolmen believed ultimately that reason alone could not provide a unified view of nature or society. To understand nature, law, morality, or the state, it was necessary to know its relationship to a supernatural order, a higher world.

In the modern view, both nature and the human intellect are self-sufficient. Nature is a mathematical system that operates without miracles or any other form of divine intervention. To comprehend nature and society, the mind needs no divine assistance; it accepts no authority above reason. The modern mind finds it unacceptable to reject conclusions of science on the basis of clerical authority and revelation, or to base politics, law, and economics on religion. It rejects the medieval division of the universe into a heavenly realm of perfection and a lower earthly realm. Almost ruthlessly, scientific and secular attitudes have driven Christianity and faith from their central position to the periphery of human concerns.

EARLY MODERN EUROPE

From the Italian Renaissance of the fifteenth century through the Age of Enlightenment of the eighteenth century, the outlook and institutions of the Middle Ages disintegrated, and distinctly modern forms emerged. This radical change in European civilization could be seen on every level of society. On the economic level, commerce and industry expanded greatly, and capitalism largely replaced medieval forms of economic organization. In politics, central government grew stronger at the expense of feudalism.

On the religious level, the unity of Christendom became fragmented by the rise of Protestantism. In society, the prosperous people in both city and country were gaining in numbers and strength and demanded a greater share in the political and cultural leadership of the various European states. In consequence, the clergy lost its monopoly over learning, and the otherworldly orientation of the Middle Ages gave way to a secular outlook in literature and the arts. Theology, the queen of the sciences in the Middle Ages, surrendered its crown to mathematics and the study of nature.

The Renaissance

Many new tendencies manifested themselves dramatically during the Renaissance, a period beginning about 1350 and lasting for two centuries. The word *renaissance* means rebirth, and it is used to refer to the attempt by artists and thinkers to recover and apply the learning and standards of ancient Greece and Rome. The Renaissance was an age of transition during which the medieval outlook was rejected, classical cultural forms were revived, and modern attitudes emerged. The Renaissance was not a complete and sudden break with the Middle Ages; many medieval ways and attitudes persisted. Nevertheless, the thesis that the Renaissance represents the birth of modernity has much in its favor.

New economic, political, and social conditions presented new challenges for which the old order of priest and feudal lord provided no answers. So the men—and women—of the Renaissance reached back beyond the feudal order, which they said belonged to the "Dark Ages," to classical antiquity where all seemed light, refinement, and civilization. They consciously modeled themselves on the standards set by ancient Greece and Rome. They ransacked monastic libraries for manuscript records of ancient wisdom and studied ancient ruins as examples of architectural and artistic perfection. They identified much more with the urban and urbane culture of antiquity than they did with the more recent and to their minds, barbarous past.

The Renaissance started in the independent city-states of northern Italy in the fourteenth century; during the fifteenth and sixteenth centuries, its ideas spread to other lands in Europe. In the developed urban centers of Italy, commercial elites enjoyed the leisure and freedom that came with the wealth procured by trade. The wealthy Italian city-states acted as magnets. They attracted men of talent in every field—the military, government, business, the arts, and education—because of the riches available to those who succeeded. Renaissance society was marked by a growing *secular outlook*. To be sure, the people were neither nonbelievers nor atheists. Increasingly, however, religion had to compete with worldly concerns. Members of the urban upper class did not allow religion to interfere with their quest for the full life. This worldliness found concrete expression in Renaissance art and literature.

Individualism was another hallmark of Renaissance society. Operating in the competitive marketplace taught the urban elite to assert their own personalities, to demonstrate their unique talents, and to fulfill their ambitions. Often employed by this elite, Renaissance artists in turn sought to capture individual character and achievement in their works. At the same time, explorers ventured into uncharted seas, conquerors carved out empires in the New World, and merchant-capitalists amassed fortunes.

The most characteristic intellectual movement of the Renaissance was *humanism*, an educational program based on the study of ancient Greek and Roman literature. Renaissance humanists valued

ancient literature for its clear and graceful style and for its insights into human nature. In contrast to medieval scholastic philosophers who used Greek philosophy to prove the truth of Christian doctrines, Italian humanists read classical literature to nourish their new interest in the worldly life.

A new curriculum was devised, aimed primarily at instructing not the clergy—as was the case in the Middle Ages—but the sons (rarely the daughters) of nobles and merchants. The new curriculum emphasized training in those skills of writing, speaking, politics, and ethics that were most in demand at the Renaissance courts and that one had to master for a career in the expanding civil service. This educational ideal took such hold on the imagination of the European elite that it served until the twentieth century as the standard of what it meant to be educated.

The Renaissance wedded its vision of antiquity to its contemporary concerns. In the process, an entirely new culture was created, as different from the ancient world as it was from the Middle Ages. Thus, in art, the human form and rules of perspective were recovered from antiquity, but were employed to represent a Christian idealism and a cult of the individual that were not antique. In politics, the ancient history of Greece and Rome was studied for clues to solve the problems of the Renaissance city-state, such as internal turmoil, mercenary armies, rivalry between city-states, and menace of powerful foreign monarchies like France and Spain. Out of this intense political life came a rich experimentation in forms of government. Perhaps the most important were the efforts of Florentines and Venetians, who tried for centuries to preserve the conditions of republican government and laid the theoretical foundations for modern republicanism.

The principal effect of this ferment was the gradual destruction of the medieval view that the world was static and the individual's place within it, whether as priest, warrior or peasant, fixed. Instead, Renaissance culture emphasized the human creative powers of an educated elite and the right of princes, as well as artists and merchants, to shape their own destiny. And embedded in this idea lay the germ of a completely new notion that was neither medieval nor ancient, but distinctly modern: the idea of progress.

The Reformation

Like the Renaissance, the Reformation marked a breaking away from the Middle Ages. Whereas the Renaissance turned away from medieval art and literary forms, the Reformation broke with the medieval religious outlook and ended the religious unity of the Middle Ages.

With entrepreneurial activity and curiosity spawned by Renaissance learning, a much more sophisticated and independent urban elite developed. By the early sixteenth century, that elite became increasingly alienated from the traditional moral authority exercised by the church. Of course the church had always had its dissenters, such as the medieval opponents of papal authority who favored placing ecclesiastical power into the hands of the church councils, or the late fourteenth century followers of the Oxford don, John Wycliffe, who attacked church corruption and repudiated certain church doctrines. Not until the early sixteenth century, however, did church critics gather enough strength to challenge successfully the rule of the papacy and the moral authority of Catholic doctrines.

The Reformation began in German cities and spread throughout western Europe. Only in countries like Spain and Italy, where ecclesiastical authority was firmly entrenched, did the church repel the Protestant advance. At the vanguard of the Reformation were Martin Luther and Ulrich Zwingli, angry young clerics. They used the newly invented printing press to appeal to that urban elite and also to the traditional nobility who had long coveted church lands and tax revenues. During the brief period from Luther's initial confrontation with a papal representative and seller of indulgences in 1517 until the death of Henry VIII in England in 1547, nearly a quarter of the western European population had embraced one version or another of Protestantism.

Two doctrines formed the basis of this new version of Christianity: salvation comes to the believer as a result of divine mercy and not from the church's practices and rituals, and the essence of Christianity lies in the Bible. Religion is, therefore, accessible to any literate person, and in matters of salvation, all believers act as priests over their own spiritual fate. The motives of the thousands of Europeans who embraced a Protestant creed were many: anger at the corrupt life-styles of some clergy, a restlessness with traditional authority coupled with the desire to search Scripture for themselves, the wish to bring about a social transformation that would indeed allow the poor to inherit the earth, and perhaps the need for a religion that glorified worldly activity rather than the cloister and its clergy.

Just as new energy revitalized European intellectual life during the Renaissance, and in the process discarded the medieval preoccupation with theology, a new religious outlook, personal faith, marked the Reformation. Personal faith, not adherence to the doctrines of the church, became central to the religious life of European Protestants. Like the Renaissance humanists, some Protestant leaders were trained in ancient learning, but they gave humanism a religious meaning. They wanted to restore the spirit of early Christianity, in which faith seemed purer, believers more sincere, and the clergy uncorrupted by luxury and power.

The Reformation shattered the religious unity of Europe, the chief characteristic of the Middle Ages, and weakened the church, the principal institution of medieval society. The church's moral authority was rejected by millions of Europeans, and its political power was curtailed.

By strengthening the power of kings at the expense of religious bodies, the Reformation furthered the growth of the modern state. Protestant rulers repudiated the pope's claim to temporal power and extended their authority over Protestant churches in their lands. In Catholic lands, the church in reaction to Protestantism tended to support, rather than to challenge, monarchs. Protestantism did not create the modern secular state; it did, however, help to free the state from subordination to religious authority, an essential feature of modern political life.

The Reformation also promoted individualism. Protestants sought a direct and personal relationship with God and interpreted the Bible for themselves. They developed an inner confidence and assertiveness. This individualism may also have been expressed in a work ethic that was compatible with capitalist forms of economic activity.

The Commercial Revolution

One of the most decisive changes occurring between 1450 and 1750 was the Commercial Revolution. This transformation saw the breakdown of the largely self-sufficient agrarian economy, based on the manor, that was characteristic of the Middle Ages. In its place came increased production and commercial activity. Perhaps the most dramatic change was that for the first time in human history the problem of providing an adequate food supply was solved in a few places (England, Holland, and British North America) by the late seventeenth century.

The Commercial Revolution was the product of two processes—overseas expansion and the price revolution. Western European monarchies carved out empires in other parts of the world—the Portuguese in Africa, India, and the East Indies in the fifteenth and early sixteenth centuries; the Spanish in Latin America in the sixteenth century; the French, the Dutch, and the English in North America, the East and West Indies, and India in the seventeenth and eighteenth centuries. Wherever they went, Europeans overcame armed opposition due to superior fire power in the form of the cannon, the musket, and especially the gunned sailing ship. For four hundred years, one small part of the globe, western Europe, dominated and exploited much of the rest of the planet. Only in this century were the western European powers forced to relinquish their empires.

Overseas colonies played a vital role in the Commercial Revolution. They furnished raw materials, gold, and silver to stoke European economies; they also furnished protected markets for products made in Europe. Finally, colonies produced materials at low cost because of slave labor, which was widely used on plantations until the nineteenth century. Out of the colonies came immense profits to invest in further economic development.

The rapid and unprecedented rise in prices (inflation) throughout the sixteenth century was known as the *price revolution*. This inflation can be traced to two causes: an unexplained and perhaps inexplicable increase in population beginning in the second half of the fifteenth century, and the influx of silver into western Europe from the mines of Mexico and Peru. There were more and more mouths to feed in the fifteenth and sixteenth centuries. Agricultural production expanded to meet this new demand, but never expanded rapidly enough. So prices, especially for primary products like wool and grain, shot up. The flooding of western Europe with silver from New World mines probably was also highly inflationary in an economy of scarcity. The money supply in the form of silver coin increased faster than the supply of goods, so prices rose faster.

The effect of the price revolution can hardly be overestimated. For the first time since the thirteenth century, demand was steadily rising. Investment in increased production was bound to yield increased profits, an enormous incentive to invest and reinvest.

In early modern Europe the largest industry by far was agriculture, thus the greatest investment was in land, and the most important changes that investment produced took place on the land. Driven by the desire for profit, landlords saw that it would be necessary to reorganize their farms in order to increase production for an expanding market. The old manorial agriculture, based on the three-field system, was geared to the needs of the manor, and not those of the market. The characteristic manorial pattern of farming in strips and of having communal access to common land was inefficient. So enterprising landlords denied their peasants the use of the commons and drove them from the manor. Having eliminated peasant holdings, the landlords tore down hedges and filled in ditches dividing the strips, in this way consolidating the fields into single units, which they often let—if they themselves did not have the areas cultivated—at high rents to the most efficient producers.

This process of consolidation was know as *enclosure,* and its consequences were momentous. More and more land was turned over to commercial agriculture and returned increasing yields and profits. Those peasants who had lost their customary use of the land either became agricultural laborers working for very low wages, or left to find work in the towns or in the colonies overseas. Rural poverty and violence increased because of this displacement of the peasants.

This ruthless transformation of agriculture was matched by a comparable process in trade and industry. As commercial activity increased, the medieval guilds, essentially restrictive of production and exchange, became obsolete. The initiative passed to rich merchants whose operations were not local like the guilds, but regional, national, and sometimes even international in scale. They exploited cottage industry by monopolizing raw materials.

Raw wool, for example, was put out by merchants to be processed by peasants in country villages (outside of towns where guild restrictions did not apply). This procedure saved money on overhead by using the peasants' own cottages and on labor by paying low piece rates to peasants, who were only too glad to find work. The merchants then sold the finished product where it would fetch the best price. In industry as in farming, the effect was the same: increasing profits, investment, economic expansion, and a widening gap between the rich and the poor.

The Commercial Revolution represented a crucial stage in the development of modern capitalism. It ushered in a world economy, and led to an earth dominated by Europeans, a situation that would endure until the twentieth century. We shall now examine other movements that helped shape the modern world: the growth of national states, the Scientific Revolution, and the Enlightenment.

Notes

1. W. H. Auden, ed., *The Portable Greek Reader* (New York: Viking, 1952), p. 38.
2. Benjamin Farrington, *Greek Science* (Baltimore: Penguin Books, 1961), p. 301.

WESTERN CIVILIZATION

Volume II: From the 1600s

CHAPTER 16

The Growth of the Nation-States: Transition to the Modern State

FROM THE THIRTEENTH to the sixteenth century a unique form of political organization emerged in the West: the nation-state. Without it, Western preponderance in world history would be unimaginable. The nation-state channeled and organized violence and the search for power around a central authority and directed the energies of the ruling elite into national service and international competition. The nation-state created relative domestic stability, while at the same time it encouraged, and indeed at various moments required military service in foreign wars and competition with other states and territories for foreign lands and markets. As a result, the history of the major nation-states of Europe was oftentimes bloody.

At every turn the pivotal figures in the nation-states' development were the kings. Europeans, whether landed or urban, grudgingly gave allegiance to these ambitious authority figures because, in general, they seemed the only alternative to the even more brutal pattern of war and disorder so basic to the governing habits of the feudal aristocracy. In the process of increasing their own power, the kings of Europe not only subordinated the aristocracy to their needs and interests, but they also gained firm control over the Christian churches in their territories. Gradually, religious zeal was made compatible with, and largely supportive of national goals, and not of papal dictates or even of universal Christian aspirations.

Any working definition of the nation-state embodies various components, although all are not necessarily present in the early stages of the state's development. One component was a strong standing army, composed not of foreign mercenaries, but of sometimes forcibly conscripted nationals. The army became the instrument by which kings enforced their wills over warring feudal lords, as well as over other states and unprotected territories. By the seventeenth century in France, England, and Spain (the three most highly developed nations in Europe), domestic armies, often used in conjunction with foreign mercenaries, had become essential to the maintenance and extension of state power. These states achieved a high degree of unity also because of common languages and recognized borders— with national armies guarding and extending those frontiers. A vast bureaucracy coordinated and administered the activities of the central government and its army. The creation of a strong central government required a struggle between the monarch and localized systems of power, feudal aristocrats, bishops, and even occasionally representative assemblies.

Where early modern European monarchs succeeded in subduing, destroying, or reconstituting local aristocratic and ecclesiastical power systems, nation-states were formed. Where the monarchs failed, as they did in the Holy Roman Empire and Italy, the creation of viable states was delayed until well into the nineteenth century. Those failures derived from independent authority of local princes or city-states, and in the case of Italy from the decentralizing influence of papal authority. In the Holy Roman Empire, feudal princes found allies in the newly formed Protestant communities, and in such a situation, religion worked as a decentralizing force. Successful early modern kings had to bring the churches under their authority. They had to subordinate religion to the needs of the state. They did this not by separating church and state (as was done in the United States), but rather by linking their subjects' religious identity and the national identity. For example, in England by the seventeenth century a true Protestant was seen to be a true English subject, while in Spain the same equation operated for the Catholic (as opposed to the Moslem or the Jew, who came to be regarded as non-Spanish.)

All these elements that make up the early modern nation-state evolved slowly and at first haltingly. In the thirteenth century, most Europeans still identified themselves with their localities: their villages, manors, or towns. They gave political allegiance to their local lord or bishop. They knew little, and probably cared less about the activities of the king and his court, except when taxes or military service were demanded or needed. By the late seventeenth century, by extreme contrast, aristocrats in many European countries defined the extent of their political power in terms of their relationship to king and court. By then the lives of very ordinary people were being affected by national systems of tax collection, by the doctrines and practices of national churches, and by conscription.

Increasingly prosperous town dwellers, the bourgeoisie, also realized that their prosperity hinged, in part, on the foreign and domestic policies formulated by bureaucrats chosen by the king and answerable to him. If the king assisted their commercial ventures, the bourgeoisie gave their support to the growth of a strong central state. Only in two states, England and the Netherlands, did the striking fortunes of the bourgeoisie create a form of centralized government that by the late seventeenth century had managed to redistribute political power so that it could be shared by monarchy (or a social oligarchy) and a powerful representative assembly.

THE GROWTH OF FRENCH POWER

When Hugh Capet became king of France in 987, he was, in relation to other great feudal lords, merely first among equals. He could demand military service from his vassals (only forty days a year) and was regarded as the protector of the church. But he only ruled over a small area around Paris, and the succession of his heirs to the kingship was by no means secure. Yet even at this early date, his title and his person were regarded as sacred. He was God's anointed, and his power, such as it was, descended on him from divine authority.

From this small power base, more symbolic than real, the successors of Hugh Capet extended their territory and dominion at the expense of feudal lords' power. By 1328 when the Capetian family became extinct and the crown passed to the Valois family, the Capetians had made the French monarchy the ruler of areas as distant from Paris as Languedoc in the south and Flanders in the north. To administer their territories the Capetians established an efficient bureaucracy composed of townsmen and trustworthy lesser nobles who, unlike the great feudal lords, owed their wealth and status directly to the king. These royal officials, an essential element of monarchical power, collected the king's feudal dues and administered justice. At the same time, French kings emphasized that they had been selected by God to rule, a theory known as the divine right of kings. This theory gave monarchy a sanctity that various kings used to enforce their commands over rebellious feudal lords and to defend themselves against papal claims of dominance over the French church.

Yet medieval French kings never imagined nor sought absolute power. Not until the seventeenth century was the power base of the French monarchy consolidated to the extent that kings and their courts could attempt to rule without formal consultations with their subjects. In the Middle Ages the French monarchs recognized the rights of, and consulted with the various local assemblies, the *Estates.* These were representative assemblies (whether regional or national) composed of deputies drawn from the various elites: the clergy, the nobility, and the leadership of cities and towns in a given region. The Estates met as circumstance—wars, taxes, local disputes— warranted, and the nationally representative assembly, the *Estates General*, was always summoned by the king. For example, in 1302 when Philip the Fair called an Estates General, he sought counsel and revenues. Most important, he also acknowledged that the *villes* (towns), as well as the great lords, had a role to play in national government. In general, medieval French kings consulted these assemblies to give legitimacy to their demands and credi-

bility to their administration. They also recognized that the courts—especially the highest court, the Parlement of Paris—had the right to administer the king's justice with a minimum of royal interference. Medieval kings did not see themselves as originators of law; they were its guarantors and administrators.

War also served the interests of a monarchy bent on consolidating its power and authority. As a result of the Hundred Years' War (1338– 1453), the English were eventually driven from France, and their claims to the French throne dashed. In the process of war and taxation to meet its burden, the French monarchy grew richer. The necessities of war enabled the French kings to levy new taxes, often enacted without the consent of the Estates General, and to maintain a large standing army under royal command. The Hundred Years' War also provoked allegiance to the king as the visible symbol of France. The war heightened the French sense of national identity; the English were a common enemy, discernibly different in manners, language, dress, and appearance.

With revenue and an army at their disposal, the French kings subsequently embarked on territorial aggrandizement. Charles VIII (1483–1498) invaded Italy in 1494. A shrewd assessor of the implications of power, Italian philosopher Machiavelli observed that Italy's weakness derived from its lack of unity, and that the power of this new nation-state of France derived in large measure from the strength of its prince and his huge and mostly native-born army. Though the French gained little territory from the Italian campaign, they did effectively challenge Spanish power in Italy and intimidate an already weakened papacy.

Religion and the French State

In every emergent nation-state, tension existed between national monarchs and the papacy. At issue was control over the church within that territory—over its personnel, wealth, and, of course, its pulpits from which an illiterate majority learned what their leaders believed they should know, not only in matters of religious belief but also about questions of obedience to civil authority. The monarch's power to make church appointments could ensure a complacent church. A church that was willing to preach about the king's divine right and was tractable on matters of taxes was especially important in France because the church was in the legal position of not having to pay taxes, only of giving donations to the crown. Centuries of tough bargaining with the papacy paid off when, in 1516, Francis I (1515–1547) concluded the Concordat of Bologna; Pope Leo X permitted the French king to nominate, and therefore effectively to appoint men of his choice to all the highest offices in the French church.

The Concordat of Bologna laid the foundation for what became known as the *Gallican church*, a term signifying the immense power and authority of the Catholic church in France, which was sanctioned and overseen by the French kings. By the early sixteenth century, religious homogeneity had strengthened the central government at the expense of papal authority and of traditional privileges enjoyed by local aristocracy. This ecclesiastical and religious settlement lay at the heart of monarchical authority. Consequently, the Protestant Reformation threatened the very survival of France as a nation-state. Throughout the early modern period the French kings had assumed that their states must be governed by one king, one faith, and one set of laws. Any alternative to that unity offered local power elites, whether aristocratic or cleric, the opportunity to channel religious dissent into their service. Once linked, religious and political opposition to any central government could be extremely dangerous.

Francis I (1515–1547) perceived that Protestantism in France would undermine the sacredness of his office, challenge his authority, and diminish his control over church officials.

JOOS VAN CLEVE (1485–1540): FRANCIS I OF FRANCE
Francis I was a true Renaissance prince, power-hungry yet a patron of the arts. The aged Leonardo da Vinci ended his days at Francis's court at Amboise as guest of the French king. Francis was also a brilliant politician who helped found the Gallican Church through his Concordat of Bologna with Pope Leo X. Henceforth, the French monarchs alone were to appoint men of their choice to church offices in France. (The Cincinnati Art Museum; bequest of Mary M. Emery)

In 1534 the king, in conjunction with the court of Paris (the Parlement), declared Protestant beliefs and practices illegal and punishable by fine, imprisonment, and even execution. The Protestant reformer Calvin and his friends fled from Paris and eventually to Geneva (see Chapter 14), but they never abandoned the hope of converting Francis and France to the Protestant cause.

During the decades that followed, partly through the efforts of the Huguenot underground and partly because the French king and his ministers vacillated in their efforts at persecution, the Protestant minority grew in strength and dedication. By challenging the authority of the Catholic church, Protestants were also inadvertently challenging royal authority, for the French church and the French monarchy supported each other. Protestantism became the basis for a political movement of an increasingly revolutionary nature.

From 1562 to 1598, France experienced waves of religious wars that cost the king control over vast areas of the kingdom. Protestantism became for some adherents a vehicle for expressing their rage against the French church and the increasing power of the Valois kings. The great aristocratic families, the Guise for the Catholics and the Bourbons for the Protestants, drew up armies that scourged the land, killing and maiming their religious opponents. Local grievances, when entwined with religion, proved for a time capable of dismantling the authority of the central government. In Protestant urban centers, townsmen asserted their right to control local government as well as to worship publicly in the Protestant manner. They allied with those aristocrats who would convert to the Reformation, for whatever reasons. The French Catholics, on the other hand, turned to the House of Guise for protection, a vivid reminder of the strength of feudal elites centuries after feudalism as an institution had ceased to be the main expression of political authority.

In 1579, extreme Huguenot theorists published the *Vindiciae contra Tyrannos*. This was the first theoretical statement combined with a call to action to be found in early modern times that justified rebellion against, and even the execution of an unjust king. European monarchs might claim power and divinely sanctioned authority, but by the late sixteenth century, their subjects had available the moral justification, based on Scripture and religious conviction, to oppose by force, if necessary, their monarch's will. Significantly, this same treatise was translated into English in 1648, a year before Parliament publicly executed Charles I, king of England.

The Valois kings floundered in the face of this kind of politico-religious opposition. The era of royal supremacy instituted by Francis I came to an abrupt end during the reign of his successor Henry II (1547–1559). Wed to a member of a powerful Italian banking family, Catherine de Medici, Henry occupied himself not with the concerns of government, but with the pleasures of the hunt. The sons who succeeded Henry—Francis II (1559–1560), Charles IX (1560–1574), and Henry III (1574–1589)—were uniformly weak. In this power vacuum, their mother Catherine emerged as virtual ruler—a queen despised for her foreign and nonaristocratic lineage, for the fact that she was a woman, and for her propensity for dangerous intrigue. One of the most hated figures of her day, Catherine de Medici defies dispassionate assessment. She ordered the execution of thousands of Protestants by royal troops in Paris—the infamous St. Bartholomew's Day Massacre (1572). Within a week, first in Paris and later throughout the country, soldiers and then ordinary citizens murdered Protestants wherever they could be found. The blood bath became both a symbol and a legend in subsequent European history: a symbol of the excesses of religious zeal and a legend of Protestant martyrdom that gave renewed zeal to the cause of international Protestantism.

The civil wars begun in 1562 were renewed in the massacre's aftermath. They dragged on until the death of the last Valois king in 1589. The Valois failure to produce a male heir to the throne placed Henry, duke of Bourbon and a Protestant, in line to succeed to the French throne. Realizing that the overwhelmingly Catholic population would not accept a Protestant king, Henry (apparently without much regret) renounced his adopted religion and embraced the church. His private religious beliefs may never be known, but outward conformity to the religion of the Catholic majority was the only means to effect peace and re-establish political stability. Under the reign of Henry IV (1589–1610) the French throne acquired its central position in national politics. Henry granted to his Protestant subjects and former followers a degree of religious toleration through the Edict of Nantes (1598), but they were never welcomed in significant numbers into the royal bureaucracy. Throughout the seventeenth century, every French king attempted to undermine Protestant regional power bases and ultimately to destroy their religious liberties.

The Consolidation of French Monarchical Power

The defeat of Protestantism as a national force set the stage for the final consolidation of the French state in the seventeenth century under the great Bourbon kings, Louis XIII and Louis XIV. Louis XIII (1610–1643) realized that his rule depended on an efficient and trustworthy bureaucracy, an ever-replenishable treasury, and constant vigilance against the localized claims to power by the great aristocracy and by the Protestant cities and towns, many of which were capable of taking military action against the central government or even of forming alliances with foreign princes. Cardinal Richelieu, who served as Louis XIII's chief minister from 1624 to 1642, became the great architect of French absolutism.

Richelieu was the king's loyal servant; in this way he served the state. His morality rested on one sacred principle embodied in the phrase he invented: *raison d'état*, "reason of state." For Richelieu the state's necessities and the king's absolute authority were synonymous; one was inconceivable without the other. In accordance with his political philosophy, Richelieu brought under control the disruptive and antimonarchical elements within French society. He increased the power of the central bureaucracy, attacked the power of independent and often Protestant towns and cities, and persecuted the Huguenots. Above all, he humbled the great nobles by limiting their effectiveness as councilors to the king and by prohibiting their traditional privileges,

like dueling rather than court action as a means to settle grievances.

Reason of state also guided Richelieu's foreign policy. Since the treaty of Cateau-Cambrésis (1559) that ended nearly a century of French-Spanish rivalry, both countries had ceased their armed hostilities to concentrate on the threat posed to internal order by the Protestant Reformation. This relative peace had enhanced Spanish power at the expense of the French, yet both were Catholic powers, interrelated by aristocratic marriages. When Richelieu came to power at the French court in 1624, the king and his mother were operating a policy of appeasement toward the Spanish. But reason of state, as Richelieu saw it, necessitated that France turn against Spain and enter the war that was raging at the time in the Holy Roman Empire on the Protestant and hence anti-Spanish side. Richelieu led France into the Thirty Years' War (1618–1648) allied with the Protestants, and the outcome produced a decided victory for French power on the Continent.

At his death in 1642, Richelieu had established certain practices and policies that were continued by his successors to great effect. First, Cardinal Mazarin, who took charge during the minority of Louis XIV (who was five years old when Louis XIII died) continued Richelieu's policies. Then Louis XIV (1643–1715), himself, continued the work of his father's minister. The growth of royal absolutism produced a severe reaction among its victims: peasants who paid the burden of the state's taxes; aristocrats who bitterly resented their loss of power; and judges in the royal courts, the parlements, who resented the king and his minister's attempt to bypass their authority.

After his death, Richelieu's policies, especially as they had been administered by his corrupt successor Mazarin, produced a rebellious reaction (the *Fronde*) that lasted from 1648 to 1653. Centered in Paris and supported by the great aristocracy, the courts, and Paris's poorer classes, the Fronde (a series of street riots that eventually cost the government

VERSAILLES: PRINT OF THE PALACE AND GROUNDS The palace of Versailles is an architectural expression of Louis XIV's absolutism. The ordered gardens, coupled with the vast scale and richness of the palace, reflect the power and glory of its monarch, the Sun King. Within Versailles, nobles performed rituals dictated by Louis XIV's daily habits. (Art and Architecture Division of the New York Public Library, Astor, Lenox and Tilden Foundations)

control over Paris) threatened to develop into a full-scale uprising. But for one crucial factor: its leadership was fundamentally divided. Court judges (lesser nobility who had oftentimes just risen from the ranks of the bourgeoisie) deeply distrusted the great nobility and refused in the end to make common cause with them. And both groups feared disorder among the urban masses. The discontented elites could not unite, and as a result they could offer no viable alternative except disorder to the rule of absolute kings and their ministers.

When Louis XIV finally assumed responsibility for governing in 1661, he vowed that the events he witnessed as a child during the Fronde would never be repeated. In the course of his reign, he achieved the greatest degree of monarchical power ever witnessed during the early modern period. Indeed, no absolute monarch in western Europe, before or possibly since, held so much personal authority or commanded such a vast and effective military and administrative machine. Louis XIV's reign represents the culmination of a process of increasing monarchical authority that had been underway for centuries. Yet Louis himself possessed such qualities of intelligence and cunning, coupled with a unique understanding of the capacities of his office, that some attention must be paid to this man who became the envy of his age.

Louis XIV's education had been practical, rather than theoretical. He knew that a hardworking monarch could dispense with chief ministers while still maintaining the effectiveness of his administration. Louis XIV worked long hours at being king, and he never undertook a venture without an eye to his personal grandeur. The sumptuous royal palace at Versailles was built for that reason; similarly, etiquette and style were cultivated there on a scale never before seen in any European court. A lengthy visit to Versailles, a necessity for any aristocrat who wanted his views and needs attended to, could bankrupt the less well-to-do.

Perhaps the most brilliant of Louis XIV's many policies was his treatment of the aristocracy. He dispensed with their services as influential advisors; indeed, Louis XIV would not have any minister assume the power that his father had accorded to Richelieu. He treated the aristocrats to elaborate rituals, feasts, processions, displays, and banquets, but amid all the clamor, their political power dwindled. The wiser of the aristocracy stayed home and managed their estates; others made their way at court as minor functionaries and basked in the glory of the "Sun King."

Louis XIV's domestic policies centered around his incessant search for new revenues. Not only the building of Versailles, but also wars cost money, and Louis XIV waged them to excess. He used the services of Jean Baptiste Colbert, a brilliant administrator who improved methods of tax collecting, promoted new industries, and encouraged international trade. Such ambitious national policies were possible because Louis XIV had inherited an efficient system of administration introduced by Richelieu. Instead of relying on the local aristocracy to collect royal taxes and to administer royal policies, Richelieu had appointed the king's own men as *intendants*, functionaries dispatched with wide powers into the provinces. At first, their missions had been temporary and their success minimal, but gradually they became a permanent feature of royal administration. During the reign of Louis XIV the country was divided into thirty-two districts, controlled by intendants. Operating with a total bureaucracy of about a thousand officials and no longer bothering even to consult the parlements or Estates, Louis XIV ruled in an absolute fashion.

Why did such a system of absolute authority work? Did the peasants not revolt? Why did the old aristocracy not rise in rebellion? For the aristocrats, the loss of political authority was not accompanied by a comparable loss in wealth and social position; indeed, quite the contrary was true. Throughout the seventeenth century the French nobility—2 percent of the population—controlled approximately 20 to 30 percent of the total national income. While there were peasant upheavals throughout the century, the sheer size of the royal army and police—over 300,000 by the end of Louis's reign—made successful revolt nearly impossible. When in the early 1700s a popular religious rebellion led by Protestant visionaries broke out in the south, royal troops crushed it in a matter of months. Thus, absolutism rested on the complicity of the old aristocracy, the self-aggrandizement of government officials, the church's doctrines, the revenues squeezed out of the peasantry, and the power of a huge military machine.

Yet Louis XIV's system was fatally flawed. Without any effective check on his power and dreams of international conquest, there was no limit imposed on the state's capacity for making war. Louis XIV coveted vast sections of the Holy Roman Empire; also, he sought to check Dutch commercial prosperity and had designs on the Spanish Netherlands. By the 1680s, his domestic and foreign policies took on a violently aggressive posture. In 1685, he revoked the Edict of Nantes and effectively forced the expulsion of the remaining Protestants from the country. In 1689, he embarked upon a military campaign to secure territory from the Holy Roman Empire. And in 1701, he tried to bring Spain under the control of the Bourbon dynasty. Yet Louis XIV had underestimated the power of his northern rivals, England and the Netherlands. He viewed the apparent chaos of English politics during much of the seventeenth century as an inherent weakness of the English state. The combined power of England and the Netherlands in alliance with the Holy Roman Empire and the Austrians brought defeat to Louis XIV's ambitions.

Due to these long wars, Louis XIV emptied the royal treasury. By the late seventeenth century, taxes had risen intolerably. They were essentially levied on those least able to pay—the peasants. By the 1690s the combination of taxes, bad harvests, and plague led to widespread poverty, misery, and starvation in large areas of France. Thus, for the great majority of French people, absolutism meant a decline in living standards and a significant increase in mortality rates. Absolutism also meant increased surveillance over the population through the censorship of books, the spying on heretics, Protestants, and freethinkers, and even the torture and execution of opponents of state policy.

By 1715, France was a tightly governed society whose treasury was bankrupt. Protestants had been exiled or forced to convert. Strict censorship laws closely governed publishing, causing a brisk trade in clandestine books and manuscripts to develop. Direct taxes burdened the poor and were legally evaded by the aristocracy. Critics of state policy within the church had been effectively silenced. And foreign wars had brought no significant gains.

In the France of Louis XIV, the nation-state had reached maturity and had begun to display some of its classic characteristics: centralized bureaucracy; royal patronage to enforce allegiance; a system of taxation universally, but inequitably applied; suppression of political opposition either through the use of patronage or, if necessary, through force; and the cultivation of the arts and sciences by the state as a means of increasing national power and prestige. These policies enabled France and its monarchs to achieve political stability, to enforce a uniform system of law, and to channel the country's wealth and resources into the service of the state as a whole.

Yet at his death in 1715, Louis XIV left his successors a system of bureaucracy and taxation vastly in need of overhaul, still locked into the traditional social privileges of the church and nobility to an extent that made reform virtually impossible. The pattern of war, excessive taxation of the lower classes, and expenditure in excess of revenues had severely damaged French finances. Failure to reform the system led to the French Revolution of 1789.

THE GROWTH OF LIMITED MONARCHY IN ENGLAND

England achieved national unity earlier than any other major European state. Its fortuitous geography separated it from the border disputes that plagued emerging states on the Continent. By an accident of fate, its administrative structure also developed in such a way as to encourage centralization. In 1066, William, duke of Normandy and vassal to the French king, had invaded and conquered England, acquiring at a stroke the entire kingdom. In contrast, the French kings took centuries to bring the territory of France under their domain.

MAP 16.1   EUROPE, 1648 ▶

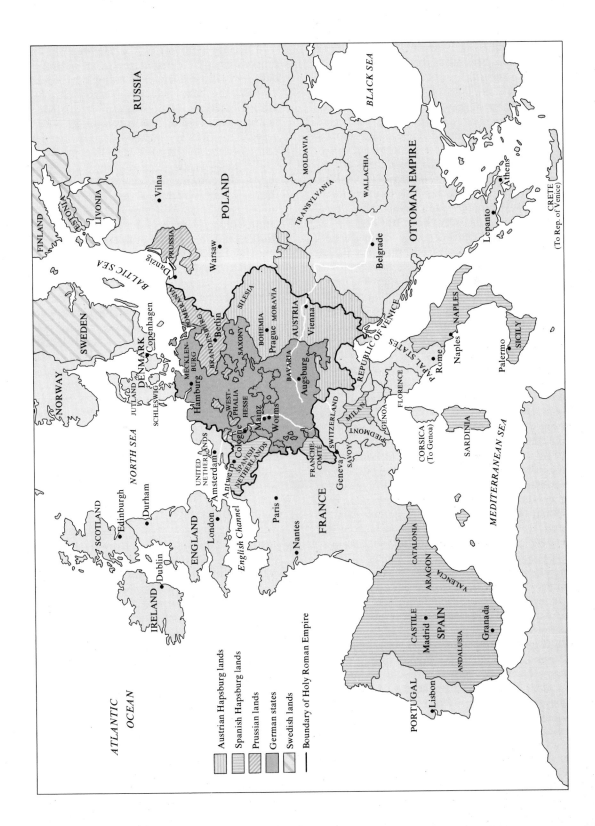

ATLANTIC OCEAN

RUSSIA

BLACK SEA

FINLAND

SWEDEN

NORWAY

LIVONIA

ESTONIA

• Vilna

POLAND

• Warsaw

BALTIC SEA

PRUSSIA

Danzig

POMERANIA

MECKLEN-BURG

DENMARK

Copenhagen

JUTLAND

SCHLESWIG

Hamburg

BRANDENBURG

Berlin

SAXONY

SILESIA

BOHEMIA

Prague

MORAVIA

AUSTRIA

Vienna

MOLDAVIA

TRANSYLVANIA

WALLACHIA

Belgrade

OTTOMAN EMPIRE

NORTH SEA

WEST-PHALIA

HESSE

Mainz

Worms

BAVARIA

Augsburg

REPUBLIC OF VENICE

PAPAL STATES

NAPLES

• Naples

Rome •

Naples

SICILY

Palermo

CRETE
(To Rep. of Venice)

Lepanto

Athens

SCOTLAND

• Edinburgh

• Durham

UNITED NETHERLANDS

Antwerp

Amsterdam

Cologne

SPANISH NETHERLANDS

SWITZERLAND

MILAN

Geneva

SAVOY

FRANCHE-COMTÉ

PIEDMONT

GENOA

FLORENCE

CORSICA
(To Genoa)

SARDINIA

MEDITERRANEAN SEA

IRELAND

Dublin

ENGLAND

London •

English Channel

• Paris

• Nantes

FRANCE

PORTUGAL

• Lisbon

CATALONIA

ARAGON

VALENCIA

CASTILE

Madrid •

SPAIN

ANDALUSIA

Granada •

Austrian Hapsburg lands

Spanish Hapsburg lands

Prussian lands

German states

Swedish lands

Boundary of Holy Roman Empire

The conquering Norman kings and their followers represented a distinct minority in England. Eventually they intermarried and merged with the larger population. In the first century of their rule the Norman kings frequently lived in France for long periods and depended therefore on an efficient bureaucracy and on their own knowledge of the English kingdom to maintain their power.

Out of necessity, these medieval Norman kings consulted with their powerful subjects, archbishops, bishops, earls, and barons. These consultations, or *parlays*, by the middle of the thirteenth century came to be called *parliaments*. Gradually the practice grew of inviting to these parliaments representatives from the shires, knights, and burgesses. These lesser than noble, but often wealthy and prominent representatives of the counties grew to see Parliament as a means of self-expression, of redressing their grievances. In turn, the later medieval kings saw Parliament as an effective means of exercising control and of raising taxes. By 1297 the Lords and Commons (as the lower house was called) had obtained the king's agreement that no direct taxes could be levied without their consent. By the fourteenth century, Parliament had become a permanent institution of government. Its power was entirely subservient to the Crown, but its right to question royal decisions had been established.

The medieval Parliament possessed two characteristics that distinguished it from its many Continental counterparts, such as the various French Estates. The English Parliament was national and not provincial, and more important, its representatives were elected across caste lines, with voting rights dependent on property and not on noble birth or status. These representatives voted as individuals, not collectively as clergy, nobles, or commoners, that is, as Estates. In the Middle Ages, Parliament and monarchy were interdependent; they were seen not as rivals but as complementary forms of centralized government. Yet that very interdependence would ultimately lead to conflict.

Also emerging during the Middle Ages in England was the constitution, a set of precedents, laws, or royal acts, which came to embody the basic principles of government. This theoretical foundation—up to this time not written as a single constitution—grew out of legal practices and customs described under the generic title *common law*. In contrast to feudal law, which applied only to a local region, the common law extended throughout the realm and served as a force for unity.

The strength of the monarchy during the later Middle Ages received dramatic expression in English victories against France during the Hundred Years' War. The power of the English kings enabled them to rally the nobility, who in turn benefited enormously from pillaging France. Only after the revitalization of the French monarchy and its subsequent victories was the English aristocracy forced to take its skills and taste for war back home. The consequences of their return were devastating. Civil war ensued—the Wars of the Roses (1453–1485)—and the medieval war machine turned inward. Gangs of noblemen with retainers roamed the English countryside, and lawlessness prevailed for a generation. Only in 1485 did the Tudor family emerge triumphant.

The Tudor Achievement

The Tudor dynasty begun by Henry VII (1485–1509) came to power through military victory in these civil wars. Henry and his successors strove to secure their power by remaking and revitalizing the institutions of government. Henry VII's goal was to bring an unruly nobility into check. He brought commoners into the government; these commoners, unlike the great magnates, could be channeled into royal service because the king was prepared to give them financial rewards and elevated social status. Commoners were brought into his inner circle, the Privy Council, the courts, and eventually into all the highest offices of the government. The strength and efficiency of Tudor government was shown during the Reformation when Henry VIII (1509–1547) made himself head of the English church. He was only able to take this giant step toward increasing royal power because his father had restored order and stability. But Henry VIII's step still entailed a struggle. (See Chapter 14.)

The Protestant Reformation in England was a revolution in royal, as well as ecclesiastical government. It attacked and defeated a main obstacle to monarchical authority, the power of the papacy. At the same time, the Reformation greatly enhanced the power of Parliament. Henry used Parliament to make the Reformation because he knew that he needed the support of the lords, the country gentry, and the merchants. No change in religious belief and practice could be instituted by the monarchy alone. Parliament's participation in the making of this Reformation gave it a greater role and sense of importance than it had ever possessed in the past. Yet the final outcome of this administrative revolution was to enhance monarchical power. By the end of his reign, Henry VIII easily possessed as much power as his French rival, Francis I. Indeed, up to the early seventeenth century the history of monarchical power in England, with its absolutist tendencies, was remarkably similar to the Continental pattern.

At Henry's death the Tudor bureaucracy and centralized government was strained to its utmost, and it survived. The government weathered the reign of Henry's sickly son, Edward VI (1547–1553), along with the extreme Protestantism of some of his advisors, and it survived the brief and deeply troubled reign of Henry's first daughter, Mary (1553–1558), who attempted to return England to Catholicism. At Mary's death, England had come dangerously close to the religious instability that undermined the French kings during the final decades of the sixteenth century.

Henry's second daughter, Elizabeth I (whose mother was Anne Boleyn), became queen in 1558. The Elizabethan period was characterized by a heightened sense of national identity. The English Reformation enhanced that sense, as did the increasing fear of foreign invasion by a Catholic power intent on returning England to the papacy. Such was the threat posed by Spain, a nation-state with twice England's population and in possession of a vast colonial empire. The fear was real enough and was only abated by the defeat—more psychologically than militarily crippling—of the Spanish Armada in 1588. In the seventeenth century, Englishmen would look back on Elizabeth's reign as a golden age. It was the calm before the storm, a time when a new commercial class was formed that, in the seventeenth century, would demand a greater say in government operations.

The Elizabethan age's capitalistic social and economic changes can be shown in microcosm with the Durham region in northern England from 1580 to 1640. A new coal-mining industry developed there through the efforts of entrepreneurs, gentlemen with minor lands whose industry and skill enabled them to exploit these mineral resources. The wool trade also prospered. By 1600, social and political tensions had developed between wool merchants along with the entrepreneurial gentry, who demanded a greater say in governing the region, and the traditional leaders of Durham society, who were the bishops and the dozen or so aristocratic families with great lands and access to the court in London.

This split is described as one between court and country. *Court* refers to the traditional aristocratic magnates, the hierarchy of the church, and royal officialdom. *Country* denotes a loose coalition of merchants and rising agricultural and industrial entrepreneurs from the prosperous gentry class, whose economic worth far exceeded their political power. The pattern found in Durham was repeated in other parts of the country, generally where industry and commerce grew and prospered. In the seventeenth century, these social and economic tensions would help foster revolution. The agricultural and industrial bourgeois who grew in social status and wealth in the period after 1560 constituted a potentially dangerous opposition to any king who ignored their economic interests and their desire for political power, both local and national. Such disregard was precisely what the Stuart kings, James I (1603–1625) and his son, Charles I (1625–1649), attempted.

By the early seventeenth century in England the descendents of the old feudal aristocracy differed markedly from their Continental counterparts. Their insular isolation from the great wars of the Reformation had produced an aristocracy less military and more commercial in orientation. Furthermore, the lesser ranks of the land-owning nobility, gentlemen without titles (the gentry), had prospered significantly in Tudor times. In commercial matters they were often no shrewder than the great landed magnates, but they had in Parliament, as well as in their counties, an effective and institutionalized means of expressing their political interests. The great aristocrats, on the other hand, had largely abandoned the sword as the primary expression of their political authority without putting anything comparable in its place. Gradually, political initiative was slipping away from the great lords into the hands of a gentry that was commercially and agriculturally innovative, as well as fiercely protective of its local base of political power.

Religion played a vital role in this realignment of political interests and forces. The old aristocracy clung to the Anglicanism of the Henrican Reformation, and in some cases to Catholicism. The newly risen gentry found in the Protestant Reformation of Switzerland and Germany a form of religious worship more suited to their independent and entrepreneurial spirit. Why should they not appoint their own preachers, and why should not the church reflect local tastes and beliefs, rather than a series of doctrines and ceremonies inherited from a discredited Catholicism? In late Tudor times the fusion of gentry and merchant interests with Puritanism produced a political-religious vision with dangerous potential for launching a coherent opposition to

established authority, even for fueling a political revolution.

The English Revolution

None of the opposing forces were understood by the first two Stuart kings. Both James I and Charles I believed, as did their Continental counterparts, in royal absolutism. Essentially, these Stuart kings tried to do in England what Louis XIII and later Louis XIV were to do in France: to establish court and Crown as the sole governing bodies within the nation-state. What the Stuarts lacked, however, was an adequate social and institutional base for absolutism. They did not possess the vast independent wealth of their French counterparts.

These kings had preached, through the established church, the doctrine of the divine right of kings. James I conducted foreign policy without consulting Parliament. Both tried to revitalize the old aristocracy and to create new peers to revitalize the feudal base of monarchical authority. After 1629, Charles brought his hand-picked advisers into government in the hope that they would purge the church of Puritans and the political nation of his opponents. Charles disbanded Parliament and attempted to collect taxes without its consent. These policies ended in disaster.

The English Revolution broke out in 1640 because Charles I needed new taxes to defend the realm against a Scottish invasion. Parliament, finally called after an eleven-year absence, refused his request unless he granted certain basic rights: Parliament to be consulted in matters of taxation, trial by jury, *habeas corpus,* and a truly Protestant church responsive to the beliefs and interests of its laity. Charles refused, for he saw these demands as an assault on royal authority. The ensuing civil war was directed by Parliament, financed by the merchants, and fought by the New Model Army led by Oliver Cromwell (1599–

ANTHONY VAN DYCK (1599–1641): PORTRAIT OF CHARLES I
Van Dyck painted three views of Charles I to assist
Bernini to sculpt a bust of the English sovereign.
Charles I sought the absolutism that Louis XIV
achieved. (The Mansell Collection, London)

1658). The New Model Army was unmatched
by any ever seen before in Europe. It was
financed by Parliament's rich supporters, led
by gentlemen farmers, and staffed by religious
zealots, as well as by the usual cross section
of poor artisans and day laborers. This army
brought defeat to the king, his aristocratic
followers, and the Anglican church's hierarchy.

In January 1649, Charles I was publicly
executed by order of Parliament, and for the
next eleven years the country was governed as
a republic with power in the hands of a Puritan
Parliament and the army. In the distribution of
power between the army and the Rump Parliament, so called because it was composed of a
faction of the old Parliament that had been
purged of royalists by the army, Cromwell

proved to be a key element. He had the support of the army's officers and some of its rank and file, and had been a member of Parliament for many years. His control over the army had only been secured, however, after its rank and file had also been purged not of royalists, but of radical groups. Some of these wanted to level society, that is, to redistribute property and give the vote to all male citizens. In the context of the 1650s, Cromwell was a moderate republican who also believed in religious toleration; yet history has painted him, somewhat unjustly, as a military dictator.

The English Revolution was begun by an agricultural and commercial bourgeoisie, urban merchants as well as primarily landed gentry, imbued with the strict Protestantism of the Continental Reformation. But in the 1650s the success of their revolution was nearly jeopardized by growing discontent from the bottom half of society, from the poor or less prosperous who had made up the rank and file of the army and who demanded that their economic and social grievances be rectified. The radicals of the English Revolution, men like Gerrard Winstanley, the first theoretician of social democracy in modern times, and John Lilburne, the Leveller, demanded a redistribution of property, voting rights for the vast majority of the male population, and the abolition of religious and intellectual elites whose power and ideology supported the interests of the ruling classes. The radicals rejected Anglicanism, moderate Puritanism, and even in some cases the lifestyle of the middle class; they opted instead for libertine and communistic beliefs and practices. The radicals terrified even devoted Puritans like Cromwell. By 1660 the country was adrift, without effective leadership.

Parliament, having secured the economic interests of its constituency (gentry, merchants, and some small landowners), chose to return to court and Crown, and invited the exiled son of the executed king to return to the kingship. Having learned the lesson his father spurned, Charles II (1660–1685) never instituted royal absolutism, although he did try to minimize Parliament's role in the government. His court was a far more open institution than his father's had been, for Charles II feared a similar death.

But Charles's brother James II (1685–1688) was foolishly fearless, a Catholic, and an admirer of French absolutism. James gathered at his court a coterie of Catholic advisers and supporters of royal prerogative, and attempted to bend Parliament and local government to the royal will. James's Catholicism was the crucial element in his failure. The Anglican church would not back him, and political forces similar to those that had gathered against his father, Charles I, in 1640, descended on him. The ruling elites, however, had learned their lesson back in the 1650s: civil war would produce social discontent from the masses. They wanted to avoid open warfare and preserve the monarchy as a constitutional, but not as an absolute authority. Puritanism with its sectarian fervor and its dangerous association with republicanism was allowed to play no part in this last English revolution.

In early 1688, Anglicans and opponents of royal prerogative (Whigs) formed a conspiracy against James II. Their purpose was to invite his son-in-law, William of Orange, *stadholder* of the Netherlands and husband of James's Protestant daughter Mary, to invade England and rescue its government from James's control. It was hoped that the final outcome of that invasion would be determined by William and his conspirators, in conjunction with a freely elected Parliament. This dangerous plan succeeded because William and the Dutch desperately needed English support against the threat of a French invasion; because James had lost the loyalty of key men in the army, powerful gentlemen in the counties, and the Anglican church; and because the political elite was committed and united in its intentions. James II fled the country, and William and Mary were declared king and queen by act of Parliament.

The bloodless revolution—commonly called the Glorious Revolution—created a new political and constitutional reality. Parliament secured its rights to assemble regularly and to vote on all matters of taxation; the rights of habeas corpus and trial by jury (for men of property and social status) were secured. These rights were in turn legitimated in a constitutionally binding document, the Bill of Rights (1689). All Protestants, regardless of their sectarian bias, were granted toleration. The Revolution Settlement of 1688–89 resolved the profound constitutional and social tensions of the seventeenth century and laid the foundations of English government until well into the nineteenth century. The revolution, says historian J. H. Plumb, established "the authority of certain men of property, particularly those of high social standing either aristocrats or linked with aristocracy, whose tap root was in land but whose side roots reached out to commerce, industry and finance."[1] Throughout the eighteenth century England was ruled by kings and Parliaments that represented the interests of an oligarchy whose cohesiveness and prosperity insured social and political stability.

The revolutions of the seventeenth century secured English parliamentary government and the rule of law, and they also provided for a significant degree of freedom for the propertied class. Whereas absolutism had triumphed in France, limited monarchy emerged victorious in England. The Revolution of 1688–89 was England's last revolution. In the nineteenth and twentieth centuries, parliamentary institutions would be gradually and peacefully reformed to express a more democratic social reality. The events of 1688–89 have rightly been described as "the year one," in that they fashioned a resilient system of government not only in Britain, but one also capable of being adopted with modification elsewhere. The British system became a model for other forms of bourgeois representative government that were adopted in France and former British colonies, beginning with the United States.

WILLIAM AND MARY IN TRIUMPH: PORTION OF A CEILING PAINTING AT ROYAL NAVAL COLLEGE, ENGLAND The Glorious Revolution of 1688–89 ousted James II, a monarch in search of the absolutism enjoyed by Louis XIV. The English Parliament gained major legal powers delineated in the Bill of Rights of 1689. The new monarchs William III and Mary II were received triumphantly. (By permission of The Admiral President, Royal Naval College, Greenwich, London)

THE RISE AND DECLINE OF HAPSBURG SPAIN

The Spanish political experience of the sixteenth century stands as one of the most extraordinary in the history of modern Europe. Spanish kings built a nation-state that burst through its frontiers and encompassed Portugal, part of Italy, the Netherlands, and enormous areas in the New World. Spain became an intercontinental empire, the first in the West since Roman times.

In the eighth and ninth centuries, the Muslims controlled all Spain except for some tiny Christian kingdoms in the far north. Beginning in the ninth century, the Christian states began a 500-year struggle—the Reconquest—to drive the Muslims from the Iberian Peninsula. By the middle of the thirteenth century, Granada in the south was all that remained of Muslim lands in Spain.

Hispania as a concept and geographical area existed in Roman times, and citizens of Portugal, Castile, Aragon, Catalonia, and Andalusia, to name only the larger and more important areas of the peninsula, recognized a certain common identity—no more, no less. Until 1469, Spain had not existed as a political entity, and even after the unification of Castile and the Crown of Aragon, relations among the various and fiercely independent provinces of Spain were often tense. Yet, in that year, Ferdinand, heir to the throne of Aragon, married his more powerful and prosperous cousin, Isabella, heiress of Castile.

Rich from the wool trade and more populous, Castile became the heart of Spain. But the Crown of Aragon (Catalonia, Aragon, and Valencia) supplied commercial expertise to the union, as well as control over the western Mediterranean. Ferdinand's Aragon also contributed a vibrant tradition of constitutional government characterized by a concern for individual and class rights as distinct from the rights of kings. Perhaps no territory in Europe possessed a more vital set of representative and judicial institutions. Aragonese independence is best summed up in the famous oath said to be taken by its nobility to the king: "We who are as good as you swear to you who are no better than we to accept you as our king and sovereign lord, provided you observe all our liberties and laws; but, if not, not."[2] Obviously any monarch set upon increasing royal authority in Aragon would have to proceed cautiously.

Ferdinand and Isabella

Ferdinand and Isabella displayed extraordinary statecraft in managing the various areas within their newly formed land. The success of their rule (1479–1516) laid the foundations for Spanish empire and Spanish domination of European affairs throughout the sixteenth century. They used Castile as their power base and set about ridding it of its military caste—those aristocrats who, in effect, operated from their fortified castles like private kings waging at will their private wars. In contrast, Ferdinand and Isabella "rationalized and modernized" the Spanish state.

Beginning in the late fifteenth century, Castilian dominance over government and administration was recognized and continually preserved, yet Aragonese rights were left more or less intact. Ferdinand and Isabella never established a unified state: there was no common currency, no single legal or tax system. Commonality of interests, rather than of administration and law, united Spain, and certain policies of Ferdinand and Isabella contributed decisively to this unity. They sought the reconquest of Spanish territory still held by the Muslims, and concomitantly they sought to assert the uniquely Christian character of the peninsula, to bring the Spanish church into alliance with the state.

Given the territorial and legal divisions within Spain, it is understandable why the church became the only universal institution in Spain, and why its legal arm, the Inquisition, played such a vital role in the intellectual and religious life of this most disparate of kingdoms. Most important for the development of strong monarchy, the Spanish rulers managed to bring the church's interests in line with their own. Ferdinand and Isabella's alliance with the church and their war against the Muslims were interrelated. The reconquest of the southern portion of the peninsula, Granada, required a popular commitment, a crusade against the Muslim infidel; this presupposed an energetic church and a deep and militant Catholicism. While other Europeans, partly under the impact of the Renaissance, questioned the church's leadership and attacked its corruption, the Catholic Kings (as Ferdinand and Isabella were called) reformed the church, making it responsive to their needs and also invulnerable to criticism. Popular piety and royal policy lead in 1492 to a victory over Granada, the last Muslim-ruled territory in Spain.

The five-hundred-year struggle for Christian hegemony in the Iberian Peninsula left the Spanish fiercely religious and strongly suspicious of foreigners. Despite centuries of intermarriage with non-Christians, by the early sixteenth century purity of blood and orthodoxy of faith became necessary for, and synonymous with Spanish identity. In 1492 the Jews were physically expelled from Spain or forced to convert, while the Muslims were likewise either expelled or forcibly converted. This process of detection and conversion was supervised by the church, or more precisely, the Inquisition. Run by clerics but responsive to state policies, the Inquisition existed to enforce religious uniformity and to ferret out the increasing numbers of Muslims and Jews who ostensibly converted to Catholicism but who remained secretly loyal to the religion of Muhammad or to Judaism. The Inquisition developed extremely sophisticated systems of interrogation, used its legal right to torture as well as to burn heretics, and eventually extended its authority to Christians as well. The

Inquisition represented the dark side of Spanish genius at conquest and administration, and its shadow stretched down through the centuries well into the twentieth.

The wars against the Muslims gave the Spanish invaluable military experience and rendered their army one of the finest in Europe. The wars also created a pattern in the growth of the Spanish empire: its victories always lay in the south—in Italy, against the Turks, and in Latin America—while its defeats and setbacks occurred in the north—in the Netherlands, against England, and in opposition to the Lutheran Reformation in the Holy Roman Empire. In possession of a superior army, with the great magnates pacified, and with the church and the Inquisition under monarchical control, the Catholic Kings expanded their interests and embarked on an imperialist foreign policy in Europe and abroad that had extraordinary consequences.

The imperialist foreign policy of Ferdinand and Isabella ultimately made Spain dominant in the New World. Ferdinand and Isabella gambled on Columbus's voyage and they won. Then, beginning in 1519, the conquistador Cortés defeated the Aztec nation with 600 foot soldiers and 16 horses, a feat that cannot be explained simply by citing the superior technology of the Spanish. This conquest rested primarily on the character and achievements of a particular segment of Spanish society, the hidalgos, as the lesser gentry were called. The willingness of the hidalgos to serve Crown and church was equaled or surpassed only by their desire to get rich. Lured by gold and land, they made excellent soldiers and explorers in foreign lands; while at home they entered governmental and ecclesiastical service where they formed the core of a loyal civil service, responsive to the needs of monarchy and distrustful of, and resentful toward the *grandees*, the great nobles. Spanish bureaucracy in the sixteenth century became a primary vehicle for social mobility, and the foreign and domestic policies initiated by Ferdinand and Isabella and continued by their successors received their greatest support from the gentry.

The Reign of Charles V: King of Spain and Holy Roman Emperor

Dynastic marriage constituted another crucial part of Ferdinand and Isabella's foreign policy. They strengthened their ties with the Austrian and Flemish (or Burgundian) kings by marrying one of their children, Juana (called *the Mad* for her insanity) to Philip the Fair, son of Maximilian of Austria. Their son Charles (1516–1556) inherited the kingdom of Ferdinand and Isabella; through his other grandparents, he also inherited the Netherlands, Austria, Sardinia, Sicily, the kingdom of Naples, and Franche Comté. In 1519 he was also elected Charles V, Holy Roman Emperor. Charles became the most powerful ruler in Europe, but his reign also saw the emergence of political, economic, and social problems that eventually led to Spain's decline.

Charles's inheritance was simply too vast to be governed effectively, but that apparently self-evident fact was only dimly perceived at the time. The Lutheran Reformation proved to be the first successful challenge to Hapsburg power. It was the first phase of a religious and political struggle between Catholic Spain and Protestant Europe that would dominate the last half of the sixteenth century.

Charles established a court filled with foreigners and spent much of his time in the northern provinces while still collecting taxes in Castile. These policies produced a full-scale revolt in the Castilian towns in 1520 and 1521. Led by artisans and merchants the revolt took on elements of a class war against the landed nobility. The nobles in turn rallied around Charles's royal army and eventually the revolt was crushed. But the event and its outcome reveals much about the nature of Spanish absolutism. It relied on its aristocracy (unlike the French kings who tried to suppress them), and it never encouraged the growth of a bourgeoisie.

The achievements of Charles V's reign rested on the twin instruments of army and bureaucracy. The Hapsburg empire in the New World was vastly extended and, on the whole, effectively administered and policed. Out of this sprawling empire with its newly enslaved native populations came the largest flow of gold and silver ever witnessed by Europeans. Constant warfare in Europe coupled with the immensity of the Spanish administrative network required a steady intake of capital. However, this easy access to capital appears to have been detrimental in the long run to the Spanish economy. There was no incentive for the development of domestic industry. Moreover, constant war engendered and perpetuated a social order geared to the aggrandizement of a military class, rather than to the development of a commercial class. The Spanish social and economic system, which never encouraged home-based industry for bourgeois entrepreneurs, lacked resilience and incentives for commerce and industry. And while war expanded Spain's power, it also increased the national debt. The weak economic foundation of Spanish power in the sixteenth century combined with numerous expensive wars sowed the seeds for the financial crises of the 1590s and beyond, and for the eventual decline of Spain as a world power.

Philip II

In 1556, Charles V abdicated in favor of his son, Philip, to whom he bequeathed an empire that was governed effectively, yet burdened by the specters of bankruptcy and heresy. Philip II (1556–1598) dedicated himself to the imposition of orthodoxy in Spain. He bided his time with foreign infidels and heretics, awaiting the day when the Crown would possess the revenue necessary to launch an offensive against the Turks and against international Protestantism.

To Philip II, being truly Spanish meant being Christian in faith and blood; the racist tendencies, already evident in the later fifteenth century, gained full expression during his reign. Increasingly the country came to be ruled by an exclusive class of old Christians who claimed to be untainted because for centuries they had refused to marry Muslims or Jews. Traditional in their thinking and control over the church, the religious orders, and the Inquisition, the Old Christians tried to preserve an imperial system badly in need of reform.

Melancholic and cold by temperament, Philip II worked arduously and declined most of life's enjoyments. He pored over his ministers' reports, editing and commenting, yet in the end he was strangely indecisive. Some problems remained unsolved for years, as frustrated advisers begged in vain for the king to take action. A zeal for Catholicism ruled his private conduct and infused his foreign policy. That zeal led to Spain's most psychologically upsetting defeat of the century—the destruction of the Spanish Armada in 1588.

Far more serious than the loss of Spanish ships, however, was the loss of the Netherlands, the industrial and commercial heartland of the Spanish empire. Buoyed by the victory over the Turks at the battle of Lepanto in 1571, Philip had longed to strike a devastating blow against his intractable Protestant subjects in the Netherlands. The Netherlands yielded large tax revenues; its ships serviced the empire; nearly half of the Spanish export trade, especially in wool, went to the Netherlands, which in turn sent a third of its exports back to Spain. The growth of Protestantism, particularly in the northern provinces, fundamentally threatened Spanish rule. Anti-Spanish feeling in the Netherlands—fostered by unemployment, high taxation, and bureaucratic delays—made the Dutch sympathetic to the Reformation. Protestant propaganda and ministers from Geneva found a receptive audience among Spain's Flemish and Dutch subjects who had become increasingly disillusioned with Spanish heavy-handedness and inefficiency. The revolt of the Netherlands began in the 1560s after Philip launched a brutal military campaign to suppress the "rebels and heretics." This army of some 65,000 troops, unprecedented in size for a force maintained in a foreign territory for years, failed miserably in its goals. Repression inspired new conversions to Protestantism, and this vital economic center of the Hapsburg empire was engulfed in a revolution led by Calvinist rebels.

The revolt in the Netherlands dealt a devastating blow to the Spanish economy, as well as to its northern defenses against France. By the 1580s, Philip's foreign policy was overextended in every direction: the campaign against England was matched by unsuccessful attempts to intervene on the side of the Guise in the French wars of religion. Meanwhile, the military campaign in the Netherlands wrought a terrible destruction. In 1576 the Spanish themselves were forced to flood and sack Antwerp, their leading commercial and banking city in northern Europe. Antwerp's trade gradually moved to Amsterdam, a Protestant stronghold, which replaced its southern rival as an international capital and as the center of the new Dutch nation-state.

At every turn in northern Europe, Philip II's policies proved futile. One dramatic event came to symbolize this malaise in the Spanish mind: the defeat of the powerful Armada by England, widely believed to be an inferior power. Spain had regarded an assault on England as a holy crusade against the "heretic and bastard" Queen Elizabeth. Some Spanish officials had reasoned that a successful invasion would signal a Catholic uprising by (vastly overestimated) numbers of English Catholics. Philip II had longed for the opportunity to conquer England; it was the main Protestant power in Europe, and its assistance to Dutch rebels had been particularly resented.

Outfitted in Lisbon harbor and constantly delayed by shortages of equipment, the Armada was composed of 130 ships, only a fourth of the originally planned fleet. These main ships and numerous smaller vessels carried 22,000 seamen and soldiers. The English fleet numbered less than 75. Sailing from Lisbon in May 1588, the Armada was poorly equipped. Its ships were too large and cumbersome to negotiate the treacherous English Channel, where the English sailing ships easily outmaneuvered them. The English sent fire ships against the Armada, which broke its formation; a Spanish army to be launched from Flanders failed to make its rendezvous; and perhaps most decisively, strong winds drove the Armada out of striking position. The victory went to the English, and both sides believed it to be a sign from God.

The psychological effect of this defeat on the Spanish was enormous. They openly pondered what they had done to incur divine displeasure. Protestant Europe, on the other hand, hailed this victory as a sign of its election, and the "Protestant wind" stirred by divine intervention entered the mythology of many a proud Englishman. In the rise and fall of nations, self-confidence has played a crucial, if inexplicable, role.

The Decline of Spain

After the defeat of the Armada, Spain gradually and reluctantly abandoned its imperial ambitions in northern Europe. Although the administrative structure built by Charles V and Philip II proved immensely vital throughout the seventeenth century, nevertheless by the first quarter of the century, enormous weaknesses had surfaced in Spanish economic and social life. In 1596, Philip II was bankrupt, his vast wealth overextended by the cost of foreign wars. Bankruptcy reappeared at various times in the seventeenth century, while the agricultural economy, at the heart of any early modern nation, stagnated. The Spanish in their golden age had never devoted enough attention to increasing domestic production.

Although Spain retained vast portions of its empire during the seventeenth century, vital pieces broke away. In 1609 the northern Netherlands secured its virtual independence. From 1606 to 1650, Spanish trade with the Americas dropped by 60 percent. In 1640, Portugal successfully revolted, as did Catalonia, although Catalonia was eventually brought back into the empire.

Despite these setbacks, Spain was still capable of taking a very aggressive posture during the Thirty Years' War (1618–1648). The Austrian branch of the Hapsburg family joined forces with their Spanish cousins, and neither the Swedes and Germans nor the Dutch could stop them. Only French participation in the Thirty Years' War on the Protestant side tipped the balance decisively against the Hapsburgs. Spanish aggression brought no victories, and with the Peace of Westphalia (1648), Spain officially recognized the independence of the Netherlands and severed its diplomatic ties with the Austrian branch of the family. The latter signed a separate treaty with the French. Austria itself would develop under this central European branch of the Hapsburg dynasty as a vital nation-state, but not until the eighteenth century.

Spain had only one great statesman in the seventeenth century, Gaspar de Guzmán, count of Olivares (d. 1645), whose skill and efficiency matched his craving to restore Spain's imperial glory. He served Philip IV for over twenty years until his aggressive foreign and domestic policies brought ruin. One strength of the Spanish monarchy had been its ability to favor Castile, yet to respect the liberties and privileges of the provinces, Aragon and Catalonia in particular. Olivares attempted to bring their laws and participation in Spanish affairs into conformity with those of Castile. Clearly neither the provincial assemblies, the *Cortes*, nor the provincial aristocrats wished to undo the status quo, and Olivares's policies led to revolt in Catalonia.

By 1660 the imperial age of the Spanish Hapsburgs had come to an end. The rule of the Protestant princes had been secured in the Holy Roman Empire; the Protestant and Dutch Republic flourished; Portugal and its colony of Brazil were independent of Spain; and dominance over European affairs had passed to France. The quality of material life in Spain deteriorated rapidly, and the ever-present gap between rich and poor widened even more drastically. The traditional aristocracy and the church retained their land and power, but failed conspicuously to produce effective leadership.

In the second half of the seventeenth century, Spanish leadership markedly grew worse. Palace intrigue replaced diplomacy and statesmanship. The reign of Charles II (1665–1700), whose Hapsburg parents were related as uncle and niece, witnessed the total administrative and economic collapse of Castile. What vitality remained in Spain could be found in its periphery, in Catalonia and Andalusia. At his death in 1700, Charles II (whose marriages had been childless) declared in favor of a French successor, Philip of Anjou, Louis XIV's grandson.

Charles's act, coupled with Louis XIV's designs on the kingdom of Spain, provoked another European war. The War of the Spanish Succession (1701–1713) pitted the Holy Roman Empire, England, and the Netherlands against France. Its outcome defeated Louis's desire to unite Spain and France under the Bourbons. Philip V, although king of Spain, was forced to renounce his claim to the French throne. Spain retained its political independence, but the Hapsburg dynasty had come to an end. From 1700 until very recently the Spanish state has been ruled by dictators or Bourbons.

Of all the nation-states of Europe to emerge in the early modern period, Spain presents the greatest set of paradoxes. Spain was the least centralized of all the states of the sixteenth and seventeenth centuries. In that fact lay its strength and its weakness. In the sixteenth century, Castile led the nation without crippling it. Spanish achievements in that century are nothing short of extraordinary in art, literature, navigation, exploration, administration, and even religious zeal. Then came the gradual and almost inexplicable decline in the seventeenth century from which Spain is yet to recover.

By the Spanish experience, two observations in the history of the European nation-state can be illustrated. First, the nation-state as empire could only survive and prosper if the domestic economic base remained vital. The Spanish reliance on bullion from its colonies and its failure to cultivate industry and reform the taxation system spelled disaster. Second, states that housed a vital and aggressive bourgeoisie flourished at the expense of societies where aristocracy and church dominated and controlled society and its mores—Spain's situation. The latter social groups tended to despise manual labor, profit taking, and technological progress. Although the major nation-states were originally created by kings and dynastic families, after 1700 they were increasingly nurtured by the economic activities of the bourgeoisie. Bureaucracies drawn from the lesser aristocracy, however, still governed the states.

THE NETHERLANDS: A BOURGEOIS REPUBLIC

The Netherlands, or Low Countries (Holland and Belgium), had been part of Hapsburg territory since the fifteenth century. When Charles V, a Hapsburg, ascended to the Spanish throne in 1516, the Netherlands became an increasingly important economic lynchpin of the Spanish empire. Spain exported wool and bullion to the Low Countries in return for manufactured textiles, hardware, grain, and

**PETER DE HOOGH (1629–AFTER 1684): THE GAME OF SKITTLES
(DETAIL)** Dutch painting in the 1600s stressed genre
paintings—music lessons, kitchen labors, games of
skittles—and landscapes. The calm and joy that
permeates these works attest to the prosperity of the
only republican nation-state to endure throughout
the seventeenth century. (The Cincinnati Art Museum; gift of Mary Hanna)

naval stores. Flanders, with Antwerp as its
capital, was the manufacturing and banking
center of the Spanish empire.

The Spanish monarchy exploited its colonies in both the old and new worlds in order to
finance wars against the Turks, the Italian
city-states, and by the 1540s, its crusade
against Protestant Germany. This tax burden
along with administrative inefficiency and
religious repression created, in the northern
Low Countries especially, the conditions that
sparked the first successful bourgeois revolution in history.

During the reign of Philip II, a tightly
organized Calvinist minority, with its popular
base in the cities and its military strategy
founded on sea raids, at first harassed and then
aggressively challenged Spanish power. In the
1560s the Spanish responded by trying to
export the Inquisition into the Netherlands
and by sending an enormous standing army
under the Duke of Alva. It was a classic

example of overkill; thousands of once-loyal Flemish and Dutch subjects turned against the Spanish Crown. The people either converted secretly to Calvinism or aided the revolutionaries. Led by William the Silent (1533–1584), head of the Orange Dynasty, the seven northern provinces (Holland, Zeeland, Utrecht, Gelderland, Overijssel, Friesland, and Groningen) adhered to the Union of Utrecht (1579) for protection against Spanish aggression. Their determined resistance, coupled with the serious economic weaknesses of the overextended Spanish empire, eventually produced unexpected success.

By 1609 the seven northern provinces were effectively free of Spanish control and loosely connected under a republican form of government. Seventeenth-century Netherlands became a prosperous bourgeois state. Rich from the fruits of trade and manufacture—everything from flower bulbs to ships—the Dutch merchants ruled their cities and provinces with a fierce pride. By the early seventeenth century, this new nation of a mere one and a half million souls possessed the most vital commercial and financial techniques in Europe.

In this fascinating instance, capitalism and Protestantism fused to do the work of princes, so the nation-state emerged without, and indeed in opposition to absolute monarchy. From that experience the ruling Dutch oligarchy retained a deep distrust of hereditary monarchy. The exact position of the House of Orange remained a vexing constitutional question until well into the eighteenth century. The oligarchs and their party, the Patriots, favored a republic without a single head, ruled by them through the Estates General. The Calvinist clergy, old aristocrats, and a vast section of the populace—all for very different reasons—wanted the head of the House of Orange to govern as stadholder (head) of the provinces, in effect as a limited monarch in a republican state. These unresolved political tensions prevented the Netherlands from developing a form of republican government that might have rivaled the stability of the British system of limited monarchy. The Dutch achievement came in other areas.

Calvinism had provided the ideology of revolution and national identity. Capital, in turn, created a unique cultural milieu in the Dutch urban centers of Amsterdam, Rotterdam, Utrecht, and The Hague. Wide toleration without a centralized system of censorship made the Dutch book trade, serviced often by refugees from the Spanish Inquisition and later by French Protestants, the most vital in Europe right up to the French Revolution. And not least, the sights and sounds of an active and prosperous peasantry, coupled with a politically engaged and rich bourgeoisie, fed the imagination as well as the purses of various artistic schools. Rembrandt van Rijn, the Brueghels, Frans Hals, Jan Vermeer, Jan van de Velde are at the top of a long list of great Dutch artists—many of them also refugees—who have left timeless images portraying the people of the first and only republican nation-state to endure throughout the seventeenth century.

THE HOLY ROMAN EMPIRE: THE FAILURE TO UNIFY GERMANY

In contrast to the French, English, Spanish, and Dutch experiences in the early modern period, the German failure to achieve national unity produced a legacy of frustration and antagonism toward the other powerful European states. The German failure to unify is tied to the history of the Holy Roman Empire. That union of various distinct central European territories was created in the tenth century when Otto I, in a deliberate attempt to revive Charlemagne's empire, was crowned Emperor of the Romans. Later the title was changed to Holy Roman Emperor, with the kingdom consisting of mostly German-speaking principalities.

Most medieval emperors busied themselves not with administering their territories, but with attempting to secure control over the rich Italian peninsula and with challenging the rival authority of various popes. In the meantime the German nobility extended and consolidated their rule over their peasants and over various towns and cities. Their aristocratic power remained a constant obstacle to German unity. Only by incorporating the nobility into the fabric of the state's power, into the court and the army, and by sanctioning their oppressive control over the peasants, would German rulers manage to create a unified German state. But that process of assimilation only commenced (first in Prussia) during the eighteenth century.

In the medieval and early modern periods the Holy Roman emperors were dependent on their most powerful noble lords—including an archbishop or two—because the office of emperor was an elected one, not the result of hereditary succession. German noble princes—some of whom were electors—such as the archbishops of Cologne and Mainz, the Hohenzollern elector of Brandenburg, the landgrave of Hesse, and the duke of Saxony— were fiercely independent. All belonged to the empire, yet all regarded themselves as autonomous powers. These decentralizing tendencies were highly developed by the fifteenth century when the emperors gradually realized that the outer frontiers of their empire were slipping away. The French had conducted a successful military incursion into northern Italy and on the western frontier of the empire. Hungary had fallen to the Turks, while the Swiss were hard to govern and, given their terrain, impossible to beat into submission. At the same time the Hapsburgs maneuvered themselves into the position of monopolizing the imperial elections. The Empire became increasingly German and Hapsburg, with Worms as the seat of imperial power.

The Holy Roman Empire in the reigns of the Hapsburg emperors Maximilian I (1493–1519) and Charles V (1519–1556) might have achieved a degree of cohesion comparable to that in France and Spain. Certainly the impetus of war—against France and against the Turks—required, as it did in the newly formed nation-states, the creation of a large standing army and the taxation to maintain it. Both additions could have worked to the benefit of a centralized, imperial power. But the Protestant Reformation, begun in 1517, played into the already well developed tendencies to local independence and, as a result, destroyed the last hope of Hapsburg domination and German unity. The German nobility were all too ready to use the Reformation as a vindication of their local power, and indeed Luther made just such an appeal to their interests.

At precisely the moment, in the 1520s, when Charles V had to act with great determination to stop the spread of Lutheranism, he was at war with France over its claims to Italian territory. Charles had no sooner won his Italian territories, particularly the rich city-state of Milan, when he had to make war against the Turks, who in 1529 beseiged Vienna. Not until the 1540s was Charles V in the position to attack the Lutheran princes. By then they had had considerable time to solidify their position and had united for mutual protection in the Schmalkaldic League.

The ensuing war raged in Germany between the Protestant princes and the imperial army led by Charles V. In 1551, Catholic France entered the war on the Protestant side, and Charles V had to flee for his life. Defeated and exhausted, Charles abdicated and retired to a Spanish monastery. The Treaty of Augsburg (1555) conferred on every German prince the right to determine the religion of his subjects. The Reichstag, or Diet, creaked on throughout the early modern period, but it was as powerless as the emperors themselves. The princes had won their territories, and a German nation-state was never constructed by the Hapsburgs.

When Emperor Charles V abdicated in 1556, he gave his kingdom to his son Philip and his brother. Philip inherited Spain and its colonies and Ferdinand acquired the Austrian territories. Two branches of the Hapsburg family were thus created, and well into the late seventeenth century, they defined their interests in common and often waged war accordingly. The enormous international power of the Hapsburgs was checked only by their uncertain control over the Holy Roman Empire. Throughout the sixteenth century the Austrian Hapsburgs barely managed to control these sprawling and deeply divided German territories. Protestantism, as protected by the Treaty of Augsburg, and the particularism and provinciality of the German nobility continued to prevent the creation of a German nation-state.

The Austrian Hapsburg emperors, however, never missed an opportunity to further the cause of the Counter Reformation and to court the favor of local interests opposed to the nobility. No Hapsburg was ever more fervid in that regard than the Jesuit-trained Archduke Ferdinand II, who ascended to the throne in Vienna in 1619. He immediately embarked on a policy of religious intolerance and used Spanish officials as his administrators. His policies provoked a war within the empire that engulfed the whole of Europe.

The Thirty Years' War (1618–1648) began when the Bohemians, whose anti-Catholic tendencies can be traced back to the Hussite reformation, attempted to put a Protestant king on their throne. The Austrian and Spanish Hapsburgs reacted by sending an army into the kingdom of Bohemia, and suddenly the whole empire was forced to take sides along religious lines. The Bohemian nobility, after centuries of enforcing serfdom, failed to rally the rural masses behind them, and victory went to the emperor. Indeed, Bohemia suffered an almost unimaginable devastation; three-fourths of its towns were sacked and burned, and its aristocracy practically exterminated.

Until the 1630s, it looked as if the Hapsburgs would be able to use the war to enhance their power and to promote centralization. But the intervention of Protestant Sweden, led by Gustavus Adolphus and encouraged by France, wrecked Hapsburg ambitions. The ensuing military conflict devastated vast areas of northern and central Europe. The civilian population suffered untold hardships: soldiers raped women and pillaged the land, and thousands of refugees took to the roads and forests. Partly because the French directly intervened, the Spanish Hapsburgs finally emerged from the Thirty Years' War with no benefits. At the Treaty of Westphalia (1648), their Austrian cousins reaffirmed their right to govern the eastern states of the kingdom with Vienna as their capital. Austria took shape as a nation, while the German territories in the empire languished under the independent interests of their largely unreformed feudal nobility.

THE EMERGENCE OF AUSTRIA AND PRUSSIA

Austria

As a result of the settlement at Westphalia, the Austrian Hapsburgs gained firm control over Hungary and Bohemia, where they installed a virtually new and foreign nobility. At the same time, they strengthened their rule in Vienna. In one of the few spectacular successes achieved by the Counter Reformation, the ruling elites in all three territories were forcibly, or in many cases willingly, converted back to Catholicism. At long last, religious predominance could be used as a force—long delayed in eastern Europe because of the Protestant Reformation—for the creation of the Austrian nation.

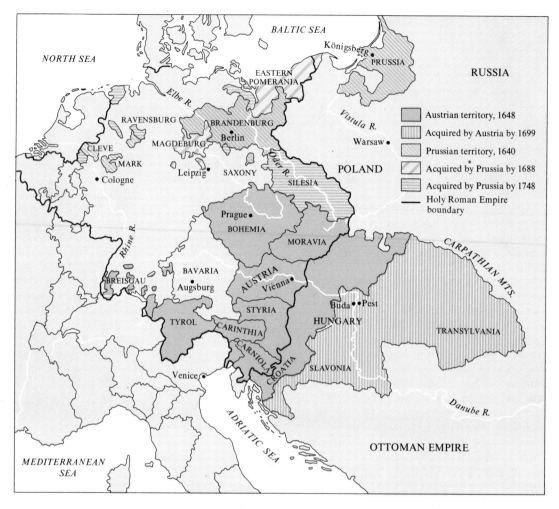

MAP 16.2 THE GROWTH OF AUSTRIA AND BRANDENBURG-
PRUSSIA, c. 1650–1750

One severe obstacle to territorial hegemony remained: the military threat posed by the Turks, who sought to control much of Hungary. During the reign of Austrian Emperor Leopold I (1658–1705), warfare against the Ottoman Empire—a recurrent theme in Hapsburg history beginning with Charles V—once again erupted. In 1683 the Turks actually beseiged the gates of Vienna. Yet the Ottoman Empire no longer possessed its former strength and cohesiveness. A Catholic and unified Austrian army, composed of a variety of peoples from that kingdom, and assisted by the Poles, managed to defeat the Turks and recapture the whole of Hungary, Transylvania, and part of Croatia. Austria's right to govern was firmly accepted by the Turks at the Treaty of Karlowitz (1699).

The Austrian Hapsburgs and their victorious army had now entered the larger arena of European power politics. In 1700 at the death of the last Spanish Hapsburg, Leopold I sought to place his second son, Archduke Charles, on the Spanish throne. But this brought Leopold into a violent clash with Louis XIV. Once again Bourbon and Hapsburg rivalry, a dominant theme in early modern history, provoked a major European war.

In the War of the Spanish Succession the Austrians, with their army led by the brilliant Prince Eugene of Savoy, joined forces with the English and the Dutch. This war brought rewards in western Europe to the Austrian Hapsburgs who acquired the Spanish Netherlands (Belgium today), as well as Milan and small holdings in Italy. But the Hapsburgs did not succeed in capturing the Spanish throne.

In the reign of Emperor Charles VI (1711–1740), Austria emerged as a major European power. Vienna became a cultural center in its own right. Austria's vast but loosely governed territories in the east, however, were not matched by territories in western and southern Europe.

Up to the early eighteenth century the Austrian Hapsburgs struggled to achieve territorial hegemony and to subdue the dissident religious groups (Protestant and Turkish Muslim), which in very different ways threatened to undermine their authority. Warfare and the maintenance of a standing army had taken precedence over administrative reform and commercial growth. Yet military victory created the conditions within which centralization could occur.

The Austrian achievement of the eighteenth century, which placed it as a major force in European affairs, derived in large measure from the administrative reforms and cultural revival initiated by Charles VI, assisted militarily by Eugene of Savoy, and continued by his successors, Maria Theresa and Joseph II. These eighteenth-century monarchs embraced a style of government sometimes described as *enlightened*. They sought through education and liberal policies to catch up with the more established and older nation-states of Europe.

Prussia

By the seventeenth century in northern Europe, the nation-state governed by absolute monarchs (or by bourgeois oligarchs as in the Netherlands) had replaced feudalism as a system of government. Serfdom had disappeared in western Europe by the late sixteenth century, although it remained in parts of central and eastern Europe. The feudal aristocracy recouped their losses, however. No longer free to play at war or to control the lives of their peasants, progressive aristocrats improved their agricultural systems or sought offices and military commands in the service of the absolutist state. On the whole, western European aristocracy did not fare too badly under absolutism, but in the course of the early modern period, their power independent of the state was decisively checked.

Prussia was different. Prussia was a state within the Holy Roman Empire that had emerged very late in northern Europe (the late seventeenth century). Like Austria, Prussia displayed certain unique characteristics. Though Prussia did develop an absolute monarchy like France, its powerful aristocracy only acquiesced to monarchical power in exchange for guarantees of their feudal privileges over the peasantry. In 1653 the Prussian nobility granted the elector power to collect taxes for the maintenance of a powerful army only after he issued decrees rendering serfdom permanent.

The ruling dynasty of Prussia, the Hohenzollern, had a most inauspicious beginning in the later Middle Ages. These rulers were little more than dukes in the Holy Roman Empire until in 1415 the Emperor Sigismund made one of them an imperial elector with the right to choose imperial successors. For centuries the Hohenzollern claims to territory in northern Germany had been legally weak. The Hohenzollerns finally achieved control over Prussia and certain other smaller principalities by claiming the inheritance of one wife (1608) and by single-minded, ruthless aggression.

The most aggressive of these Hohenzollerns, who played a key role in forging the new Prussian state, was the Elector Frederick William (1640–1688). Frederick William had inherited the territories of the beleaguered Hohenzollern dynasty whose main holding, Brandenburg in Prussia, was very poor in natural resources. Indeed, Prussia had barely survived the devastation wrought by the Thirty Years' War, especially the Swedish army's occupation of the electorate.

A distaste for foreign intervention and its accompanying humiliation and excessive taxes prompted the *Junker* class (the landed Prussian nobility) to support national unity and strong central government—provided that their economic power over their lands and peasants would be preserved. By 1672 the Prussian army led by Junker officers was strong enough to enter the Franco-Dutch war on the Dutch side. The war brought no territorial gains, but allowed the elector to raise taxes. Once again the pattern of foreign war, taxes, and military conscription led to an increase in the power of the central government. But in Prussia, unlike in western lands, the bureaucracy was entirely military in nature. No clerics or rich bourgeois shared power with this Junker class. The pattern initiated by the Great Elector (Frederick William) would be continued in the reigns of his successors: Frederick I (d. 1713), Frederick William I, and Frederick the Great.

The alliance between aristocracy and monarchy was especially strengthened in the reign of Frederick William I (1713–1740). In the older nation-states, absolute monarchs in every case tried to dispense with representative institutions once they were regarded as no longer necessary. So, too, did Frederick William undercut the Prussian provincial assemblies, the *Landtage,* which still had power over taxation and army recruitment. Only by incorporating the landowning Junker class into the machinery of government—especially into the army—and by keeping the tax-paying peasants in the status of serfs, was this monarch able gradually to render the Landtage superfluous.

In a nation where representative institutions in the twentieth century have struggled, often unsuccessfully, for survival, it is interesting to note that such institutions did exercise considerable influence in Prussia up to the early eighteenth century. Like Austria during the eighteenth century, the Prussians also embarked on a program of modernization, which has occasionally been described as "enlightened."

RUSSIA

Although remote from developments in western Europe, Russia's development in the early modern period took on some characteristics remarkably similar to those of western European nation-states. Russia also relied on absolute monarchy reinforced by a feudal aristocracy whose power to wreak havoc had to be checked and its energies channeled into the state's service. But the Russian pattern of absolutism breaks with the Western model and resembles that adopted in Prussia where serfdom increased as the power of centralized monarchy grew. The award of peasants was the bribe by which the aristocrats' cooperation in the state's growth was secured.

Russian absolutism experienced a false start under Ivan IV (1547–1584; called "The Terrible"). Late in the sixteenth century Ivan sought to impose tsarist autocracy. He waged a futile war against Sweden and created an

MAP 16.3 THE EXPANSION OF RUSSIA, 1300–1725 ▶

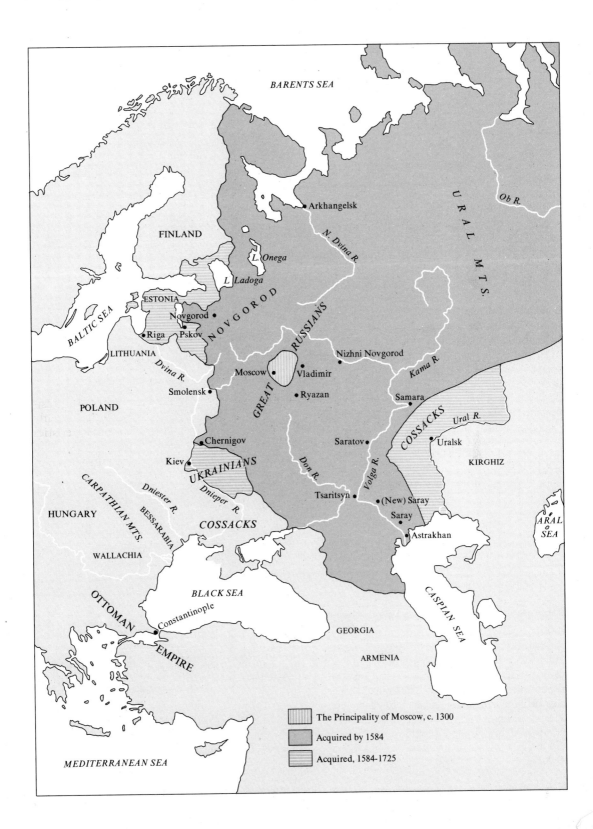

BARENTS SEA

URAL MTS.

Ob R.

Arkhangelsk

FINLAND

N. Dvina R.

L. Onega

L. Ladoga

ESTONIA

NOVGOROD

GREAT RUSSIANS

Novgorod

Riga

Pskov

LITHUANIA

Nizhni Novgorod

Dvina R.

Moscow

Vladimir

Kama R.

Smolensk

Ryazan

Samara

POLAND

Chernigov

Saratov

COSSACKS

Uralsk

Ural R.

Kiev

UKRAINIANS

Don R.

Volga R.

KIRGHIZ

CARPATHIAN MTS.

Dniester R.

Dnieper R.

COSSACKS

Tsaritsyn

(New) Saray

HUNGARY

BESSARABIA

Saray

ARAL SEA

WALLACHIA

Astrakhan

CASPIAN SEA

BLACK SEA

OTTOMAN

Constantinople

GEORGIA

EMPIRE

ARMENIA

MEDITERRANEAN SEA

BALTIC SEA

The Principality of Moscow, c. 1300

Acquired by 1584

Acquired, 1584–1725

CHRONOLOGY 16.1   THE RISE OF THE NATION-STATES

1453	The Hundred Years' War ends
1453–1485	The War of Roses in England between rival nobles
1469	Ferdinand and Isabella begin rule of Castile and Aragon
1485	Henry VII begins the reign of the Tudor dynasty in England
1517	The Protestant Reformation begins in Germany
1519	Charles V of Spain becomes Hapsburg emperor of the Holy Roman Empire
1553–1558	Queen Mary attempts to return England to Catholicism
1556–1598	Philip II of Spain persecutes Jews and Muslims
1559	The Treaty of Cateau-Cambrésis between France and Spain
1560s–1609	The Netherlands revolts from Spanish rule
1562–1598	Religious wars in France
1572	The St. Bartholomew's Day Massacre—Queen Catherine of France orders hundreds of Protestants executed
1579	*Vindiciae contra Tyrannos*, published by Huguenots, justifies regicide
1588	The Spanish Armada is defeated by the English fleet
1590s	Boris Gudonov leads a reaction in Russia against Ivan IV, "The Terrible"
1593	Henry IV of France renounces his protestantism to restore peace in France

internal police force that was entrusted with the administration of central Russia. His failure in war and an irrational policy of repression (fueled in part by Ivan's mental instability) doomed his premature attempt to impose absolutism. In the 1590s the landed magnate Boris Godunov led a reaction against Ivan's policies, although he did little to alleviate the oppression imposed on the peasantry during Ivan's reign.

In 1613 the Romanov dynasty gained the support of the aristocracy. The accession of Michael Romanov as tsar marks the emergence of a unified Russian state. Of that dynasty, by far the most important ruler was Peter the Great (1689–1725). He ruthlessly

1598	The French Protestants are granted religious toleration by the Edict of Nantes
1624–1642	Cardinal Richelieu, Louis XIII's chief minister, determines royal policies
1640	The Portuguese revolt successfully against Spain
1640–1660	The English Revolution
1648	The Peace of Westphalia ends the Thirty Years' War
1648–1653	The Fronde, a rebellious reaction centered in Paris
1649	Charles I, Stuart king of England, having disbanded Parliament, is executed by an act of Parliament
1649–1660	England is co-ruled by Parliament and the army under Oliver Cromwell
1660	Charles II returns from exile and becomes king of England
1681	The Turks attack Vienna and are defeated; the Austrians recapture Hungary, Transylvania, and parts of Croatia
1685	Louis XIV of France revokes the Edict of Nantes
1688–89	The Glorious Revolution
1701	Louis XIV tries to bring Spain under French control
1702–1713	The War of the Spanish Succession
1740	Frederick the Great of Prussia invades Silesia, starting war with Austria
1789	The French Revolution begins

suppressed the independent aristocrats, while inventing new titles and ranks for those loyal to the court. Both nobility and gentry were brought into the army by universal service obligations. The peasants were made the personal property of their lords, to be sold at will; thus, the distinction between serf and slave was obliterated. Finally, Peter brought the church under the control of the state by establishing a new office called the Holy Synod; its head was a government official, not a cleric.

From 1700 to 1707, taxes on the peasants multiplied five times over. Predictably, the money went toward the creation of a professional army along European lines and to making war. The preparation led this time to victory over the Swedes.

Peter succeeded in wedding the aristocracy to the absolutist state, and the union was so successful that strong Russian monarchs in the eighteenth century, like Catherine the Great, could embrace enlightened reforms without jeopardizing the stability of their regimes. Once again, repression and violence in the form of taxation, serfdom, and war had led to the creation of a nation-state, one that proved the least susceptible to reform, eventually to be dismantled in 1917 by the Russian Revolution.

THE STATE AND MODERN POLITICAL DEVELOPMENT

By the early seventeenth century, Europeans had developed the concept of a *state*—a distinctive political entity to which its subjects owed duties and obligations. With that concept the foundations of the modern science of politics had been laid. The one essential ingredient of the Western concept of the state, as it emerged in the early modern period, was the notion of *sovereignty*, that is, within its borders the state was supreme, and all corporations and organizations—by implication even the church—were allowed to exist by the state's permission.

The modern concept of the state first developed not in Renaissance Italy, as might be expected, but in France and England in the mid-1500s. In every instance where early modern theorists—with the exception of Calvinist revolutionaries—discussed a state, it was to instruct the prince in its governance. These theorists were responding to a new political reality. Princes had become significantly more powerful than any other single group within a country. But simultaneously an entity larger than its component parts and even more important than its rulers had emerged; the state seemed increasingly to possess its own

EQUESTRIAN MONUMENT OF PETER THE GREAT BY FRENCH SCULPTOR FALCONNET, LENINGRAD Peter the Great singlehandedly and ruthlessly forged the modern Russian state, which wrenched Russia out of the Middle Ages and endured until 1917. He suppressed independent aristocrats and created new lords faithful to his aims. The Church was brought under control by a new office, the Holy Synod, whose leading official was a secular government official. The peasants were made the property of their lords. (Sovfoto)

reason for existence. The art of government entailed molding the ambitions and powers of rulers into their state's service. The nation-state, its power growing through war and taxation, had become the basic unit of political authority in the West.

Significantly, the concept of human liberty, now so basic to Western thought, was not articulated first in the nation-states of Europe. Rather, it was largely an Italian creation, discussed with great vehemence by the Italian theorists of the later Middle Ages and the Renaissance. These humanists lived and wrote in the independent city-states, and they often aimed their treatises against the encroachments of the Holy Roman Emperor—in short, against princes and their search for absolute power. In the sixteenth and seventeenth centuries, the idea of liberty was generally found only in the writings of Calvinist opponents of absolutism. Not until the mid-seventeenth century in England was there a body of political thought arguing that human liberty could be ensured within the confines of a powerful nation-state—one governed by mere mortals and not by divinely sanctioned and absolute kings. Despite the English developments, in general, absolutism in its varied forms (Spanish, French, Prussian) dominated the political development of early modern Europe.

Not until the European Enlightenment of the eighteenth century did the republican ideal—first articulated in the Italian republics and then enacted briefly in England and more durably in the Netherlands—gain acceptance as a viable critique of absolutism. In the democratic and republican revolutions of the late eighteenth century, western Europeans and Americans repudiated monarchical systems of government in response to that ideal. By then, princes and the aristocratic elites had outlived their usefulness in many parts of Europe. The states they had created, in large measure to further their own interests, had indeed become larger than their creators. Eventually the nation-states of western Europe, as well as of the Americas, proved capable of surviving and prospering without kings or aristocrats, while they retained the administrative and military mechanisms so skilfully and relentlessly developed by early modern kings and their court officials.

Suggested Reading

Anderson, Perry, *Lineages of the Absolutist State* (1974). An excellent survey, written from a Marxist perspective.

Elliott, J. H., *Imperial Spain, 1469–1716* (1963). An excellent survey of the major European power of the early modern period.

Goubert, Pierre, *Louis XIV and Twenty Million Frenchmen* (1966). An important reappraisal of the "Sun King," emphasizing the effects of his policies on the lives of ordinary French people.

Hill, Christopher, *God's Englishman* (1970). A biography of Oliver Cromwell.

Koenigsberger, H. G., and Mosse, G. L., *Europe in the Sixteenth Century* (1968). Some excellent chapters on the monarchies, the Dutch revolt, and the Hapsburgs.

Parker, Geoffrey, *Spain and The Netherlands, 1559–1659* (1979). A good survey of a complex relationship.

Plumb, J. H., *The Growth of Political Stability in England, 1675–1725* (1967). A basic book, clear and readable.

Shennan, J. H., *The Origins of the Modern European State* (1974). An excellent brief introduction.

Wedgwood, C. V., *William the Silent* (1944). A good biography of one of the founders of the Dutch republic.

Zagorin, Perez, *The Court and the Country: The Beginning of the English Revolution* (1969). An indispensable introduction to the fundamental issue in seventeenth-century English political history.

Notes

1. J. H. Plumb, *The Growth of Political Stability in England: 1675–1725* (London: Macmillan, 1967), p. 69.
2. J. H. Elliott, *Imperial Spain, 1469–1716* (New York: St. Martin's Press, 1963), p. 18.

Review Questions

1. What role did the aristocracy play in the formation of the nation-state?
2. In what ways did early modern kings increase their power?

3. Discuss the differences between the treatment of the peasants in eastern Europe and the treatment of those in western Europe.

4. What made the Dutch state so different from its neighbors? Describe the differences.

5. Why did England move in the direction of parliamentary government, while most countries on the Continent embraced absolutism? Describe the main factors.

6. What role did religion play in creating the nation-state?

7. What were the strengths and weaknesses of the Spanish state?

8. What is meant by *raison d'état*?

9. What makes the Prussian, Russian, and Austrian experiences of statehood roughly comparable?

10. Government has sometimes been described as being, in the final analysis, organized violence. Is that an adequate description of early modern European governments?

CHAPTER 17

The Scientific Revolution:
The Mechanical Universe

STARTING IN the late fourteenth century, the cohesive medieval world began to disintegrate, a process lasting to the late seventeenth century. Not only did the basic medieval institutions like feudalism weaken, but also the medieval view of the universe became transformed into the modern and scientific understanding of nature. Three historical movements during the early modern period made this intellectual transformation, called the *Scientific Revolution,* possible. The Italian Renaissance created new literary and artistic styles that sought to portray people and nature as they are, and this curiosity fostered investigation into physical phenomena. Then the Reformation shattered the unity of Christendom, and a different religious person, one intent on finding personal salvation without the assistance of priests or sacraments, came into existence. Protestant cities and countries inevitably found themselves in opposition to the Roman church and its teaching authority; very gradually the practitioners of the new science found a more congenial atmosphere for work in those Protestant centers. Both the Renaissance and the Reformation encouraged a sense of confidence in human ability to arrive at new truths about the physical environment. Finally, feudalism and manorialism were replaced by the nation-state and commercial capitalism. And by the late seventeenth century the leaders of those states actively encouraged scientific knowledge as a key to increasing human control over the environment. They saw that with such control, particularly through agricultural experiments, might come increased prosperity.

Before governments and the scientific academies they fostered could dream about the possible benefits from scientific inquiry, a new understanding of the physical universe had to be accepted. In other words, Westerners had to believe that nature could be mastered. The unique contribution of the Scientific Revolution to the making of the modern world lies in its new mechanical conception of nature, which enabled Westerners to discover and to explain the laws of nature mathematically. They came to see nature as composed solely of matter whose motion, occurring in space and measurable by time, was governed by laws of force. This philosophically elegant construction renders the physical world knowable and even possibly manageable.

The Scientific Revolution also entailed the discovery of a new, scientific methodology. Because of the successful experiments performed by scientists and natural philosophers such as Galileo Galilei (1564–1642), William Harvey (1578–1657), Robert Boyle (1627–1691), and Isaac Newton (1642–1727), Western science acquired its still-characteristic methodology of observation and experimentation. By the late seventeenth century, no one could entertain a serious interest in any aspect of the physical order without actually doing experiments or without observing, in a rigorous and systematic way, the behavior of physical phenomena. The mechanical concept of nature coupled with a rigorous methodology gave modern scientists the means to unlock and explain the secrets of nature.

Mathematics increasingly became the language of the new science. For centuries, Europeans had used algebra and geometry to explain certain physical phenomena. With the Scientific Revolution came a new mathematics, the calculus, but even more important, philosophers became increasingly convinced that all nature—physical objects as well as invisible forces—was capable of mathematical expression. By the late seventeenth century, even geometry had become so complex that a gifted philosopher like John Locke (1632–1704), a friend and contemporary of Isaac Newton, could not understand the sophisticated mathematics used by Newton in the *Principia*. A new scientific culture had been born, which during the eighteenth-century Enlightenment (see Chapter 18) achieved great importance as a model for progress in both the natural and human sciences.

MEDIEVAL COSMOLOGY

To understand the unique character of the modern scientific outlook, it should be contrasted with what went before it, with the medieval understanding of the natural world and its physical properties. That understanding rested on a blending of Christian thought with theories derived from ancient Greek writers like Aristotle and Ptolemy. The explanations given by Aristotle (384–322 B.C.) for the motion of heavy bodies permeated medieval scientific literature. In trying to understand motion, Aristotle had argued simply that it was in the nature of things to move in certain ways. A stone falls because it is absolutely heavy; fire rises because it is absolutely light. Weight is an absolute property of a physical thing; therefore, motion results from the properties of bodies, and not from the forces or laws of motion at work in nature. It follows (logically but incorrectly) that if the medium through which a body falls is taken as a constant, then the speed of its fall could be doubled if its weight were doubled. Only rigorous experimentation could refute this erroneous concept of motion; it was many centuries before such experimentation was undertaken.

Aristotle's physics fitted neatly into his cosmology, or world picture. The earth, being the heaviest object, lay stationary and suspended at the center of the universe. The sun, the planets, and the moon revolved in circles, or in combinations of circles, about the earth. Aristotle presumed that since the planets were round themselves, always in motion and seemingly never altered, the most fitting or "natural" motion for them should be circular.

Aristotle's physics and cosmology were unified. He could put the earth stationary at the center of the universe because he presumed its absolute heaviness; all other heavy bodies that he had observed do fall toward it. He presumed that the planets were made of a

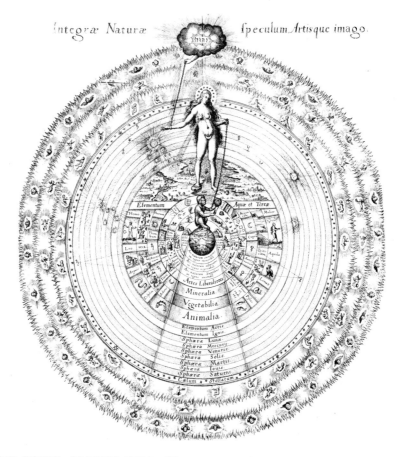

Integræ Naturæ   *Speculum.Artisque imago.*

UTRIUSQUE COSMI HISTORIA, BY ROBERT FLUDD: THE UNIVERSE This engraving from the early seventeenth century illustrates the persistence of the medieval view of the universe. Christian theology had reinterpreted classical models from Aristotle and Ptolemy. Here the hand of God is connected by a chain to the goddess Nature, who stands upon the earth, the center of the universe. (By permission of the Houghton Library, Harvard University)

kind of luminous ether and were held in their circular orbits by luminous spheres, or "tracks." They possessed a certain reality, though invisible to human beings, and hence they came to be known as the crystalline spheres.

Aristotle believed that everything in motion has been moved by another object that is itself in motion. By inference, this belief leads back to some object or being that began the motion. Christian philosophers of the Middle Ages argued that Aristotle's Unmoved Mover must be the God of Christianity, but for Aristotle, a pagan philosopher, such an identification would have been meaningless. He assumed an eternal universe filled with a continuing chain of movers and moved. For Aristotle, nature was filled entirely with matter of some sort, and nature abhorred a vacuum.

Although Aristotle's cosmology never obtained the stature of orthodoxy among the ancient Greeks, by the second century A.D. in Alexandria, Greek astronomy became codified and then rigid. Ptolemy of Alexandria produced the *Almagest* (A.D. 150), a handbook of Greek astronomy based on the theories of Aristotle. Central to that work was the assumption that the earth is at the center of the universe (although some ancient Greeks had disputed the notion) and that the planets move about it in a series of circular orbits interrupted by epicycles. By the Late Middle Ages, Ptolemy's handbook, because of the support it lent to Aristotelian cosmology, had come to embody standard astronomical wisdom. As late as the second half of the seventeenth century, over one hundred years after Polish astronomer Nicolaus Copernicus had argued mathematically that the sun was the center of the universe, educated Europeans in most universities still believed that the earth had that central position.

In the thirteenth century, mainly through the philosophical efforts of Thomas Aquinas (1225–1274), Aristotle's thought was adapted, often in tortured ways, to Christian beliefs. Aquinas emphasized that order pervaded nature, that every physical effect had a physical cause, but he denied that these causes could be stretched back to eternity or to infinity. Instead, he insisted that nature proves God's existence, that in the end God is the First Cause of all physical phenomena. The tendency in Aquinas's thought and that of his followers, the scholastics, was to search for these causes—again to ask why things move, rather than how they move. Despite the scholastic adaptations of Aristotle the church still re-garded Christian Aristotelianism with some suspicion, and in 1277, many of Aristotle's theories were condemned. That condemnation indirectly served to keep medieval science from falling totally under the influence of scholastic teachings.

Medieval thinkers integrated the cosmology of Aristotle and Ptolemy into a Christian framework that drew a sharp distinction between the world beyond the moon and an earthly realm. Celestial bodies were composed of the divine ether, a substance too pure, too spiritual to be found on earth; heavenly bodies, unlike those on earth, were immune to all change and obeyed different laws of motion than earthly bodies did. The universe was not homogeneous, but was divided into a higher world of the heavens and a lower world of earth. Earth could not compare with the heavens in spiritual dignity; nevertheless, God had situated it in the center of the universe. Earth deserved this position of importance, for only here was performed the drama of salvation. This vision of the universe would ultimately be shattered by the Scientific Revolution.

A NEW VIEW OF NATURE

Renaissance Background

Beginning in Italy in the late fourteenth century a new breed of intellectual began to challenge medieval assumptions about human beings and nature, and they were armed with a collection of newly discovered ancient Greek and Roman texts (see Chapter 13). The philosophy of Plato was seized on as an alternative to medieval scholasticism.

The great strength of Plato's philosophy lay in his belief that one must look beyond the appearance of things to an invisible reality that is simple, rational, and capable of coherent, mathematical explanation. Plato did not spurn observation, but he did urge the search for a fundamental nonphysical reality. That plea was heard more clearly during the Renaissance, and all the new scientists stood to some degree indebted to Plato.

The Renaissance Neo-Platonists interpreted Plato from a Christian perspective, and they believed that the Platonic search for truth about nature, about God's work, was but another aspect of the search for knowledge about God. The universities of Italy, as well as the independent academies founded in Italian cities, became centers where the Neo-Platonists taught, translated, and wrote commentaries about Plato's philosophy. These humanists tried to study the invisible world of Ideas and Forms that Plato claimed to be the essence of reality. Music and mathematics, they believed, provided contact with this universal, eternal, and unchanging higher reality. The leading thinkers of the Scientific Revolution found inspiration in the Platonic tradition that nature's truths apply universally and possess the elegance and simplicity of mathematics.

The search for invisible forces, for the most basic underlying principles of nature, had been an ideal proposed by some ancient philosophers. Plato had offered one approach; the ancient mathematician Pythagoras (fl. 532 B.C.) and his followers had offered another, more mystical, understanding of scientific inquiry. They believed that fundamental knowledge about the universe would lead to a sacred knowledge and that the true philosopher was like a priest of nature. The road to sacred knowledge often entails the belief that shortcuts are possible. At its very foundations in ancient learning, Western science was strongly tied to magic, to the belief that the individual possessing special power can arrive at sacred knowledge about nature simply by exercising that power.

In the first and second centuries A.D. when classical civilization was subjected to intense political and intellectual challenges, the mystical and magical approach to nature was elaborated on by varied practitioners and writers. Many of these anonymous students of magic were in contact with the Hermetic tradition. They believed that there had once been an ancient Egyptian priest, Hermes Trismegistus, who had possessed secret knowledge about nature's processes and the ultimate forces at work in the universe. In the second century A.D., this magical tradition was written down in a series of mystical dialogues about the universe. When Renaissance Europeans rediscovered these second-century writings, they erroneously assumed the author to be Hermes and his followers. Hence the writings seemed to be even older than the Bible.

This Hermetic literature glorified both the mystical and the magical. It prescribed that true knowledge comes from a contemplation of the One, or the Whole—a spiritual reality higher than, yet significantly for the development of science, embedded in nature. Some of these ancient writings argued that the sun was the natural symbol of this Oneness, and these writings seemed to give weight to a heliocentric picture of the universe. The Renaissance followers of Hermes indulged in what would now be called magic, as well as in what would be called science, without seeing any fundamental distinction between them. The route that the searcher for nature's wisdom took did not matter as much as the quest did. As a result, in early modern Europe the practitioners of alchemy and astrology could also be mathematicians and astronomers.

The Hermetic approach to nature also resembled Platonism in certain important ways. Both strove for perfection and a higher, spiritual reality, but the *magus*, or Hermetic magician, took certain shortcuts. The magus presumed that study and mental discipline were important, but that ultimate wisdom could come to its seeker through *gnosis*, an immediate, overpowering insight into the One, or God, or Nature. Important contributors to the Scientific Revolution, notably Johannes Kepler and Isaac Newton, grasped at the promise of such wisdom. Kepler believed in astrology, and Newton was profoundly interested in alchemy.

The Renaissance revival of ancient learning contributed a new approach to nature, one that was simultaneously mathematical, experimental, and magical. While the achievements of modern science depend on experimentation and mathematical logic, the compelling impulse to search for nature's secrets presumes a degree of self-confidence best exemplified and symbolized by the magician. Eventually the main practitioners of the new science would repudiate magic, largely because of its secretive quality and because of its associations with popular culture and religion. But the demise of magic, one of the important by-products of the Scientific Revolution, should not obscure its initial role as a stimulus for scientific inquiry.

The Copernican Revolution

From the Italian city-states of the Renaissance, Neo-Platonism took root and spread throughout Europe. The young Copernicus, born in Poland in 1473, journeyed to Italy to study in the universities of Bologna and Padua. The impact of Italian Neo-Platonism on Copernicus was highly formative.

Although Copernicus's studies ranged widely, his interests centered on mathematics and astronomy. Both were of immediate practical interest because of projects being undertaken to reform the calendar. His studies meant that inevitably Copernicus had to come to terms with the geocentric model of the universe proposed by Aristotle. What bothered Copernicus about the Aristotelian-Ptolemaic model of the universe was its mathematical complexity. As a Platonist, Copernicus was convinced that simplicity and intellectual elegance were symptomatic of truth as Plato had defined it. Furthermore, as a student of the Renaissance, Copernicus had learned about ancient astronomical and philosophical views that directly contradicted Aristotle and Ptolemy.

Toward the end of his stay in Italy, Copernicus became convinced that the sun lay at the center of the universe. So he set out on a lifelong task to work out mathematical explanations of how the heliocentric universe operated. Because he did not want to engage in controversy with the followers of Aristotle, Copernicus published his findings only in 1543 in a work entitled *On the Revolutions of the Heavenly Spheres*. He died that year, and legend says that his book, which in effect began the Scientific Revolution, was brought to him on his deathbed.

The treatise retained some elements of the Aristotelian-Ptolemaic system. Copernicus never doubted Aristotle's basic notion of the perfect circular motion of the planets, or the existence of crystalline spheres within which the stars revolved, and he retained many of Ptolemy's epicycles. What Copernicus was trying to do was to propose a heliocentric model of the universe that was mathematically simpler than Ptolemy's earth-centered universe. In this effort, Copernicus partially succeeded, for his system eliminated a significant number of Ptolemy's epicycles and cleared up some problems that had troubled astronomers.

Copernicus's genius was expressed in his ability to pursue an idea, a sun-centered universe, and to bring to that pursuit lifelong dedication and brilliance in mathematics. By removing the earth from its central position and by giving it motion, that is, by making the earth just another planet, Copernicus undermined the system of medieval cosmology and made the birth of modern astronomy possible.

But committed to the Aristotelian-Ptolemaic system and to Biblical statements that supported it, most thinkers rejected Copernicus's conclusions. They also raised specific objections. The earth, they said, is too heavy to move. How, they asked, can an object falling from a high tower land directly below the point from which it was dropped if the earth is moving so rapidly?

THE LAWS OF PLANETARY MOTION

The most gifted astronomer in the generation after Copernicus, Tycho Brahe (1546–1601), never accepted the Copernican system. He did, however, realize more fully than any contemporaries the necessity for new observations. Aided by the king of Denmark, Tycho built the finest observatory in Europe.

In 1572 he observed a new star in the heavens, a discovery that offered a direct and serious challenge to the Aristotelian assumption that the heavens are unalterable, fixed, and perfect. To this discovery of what eventually proved to be an exploding star, Tycho added his observations on the comet of 1577. He demonstrated that it moved unimpeded through the areas between the planets, that it passed right through the crystalline sphere. This discovery raised the question of whether such spheres existed. Once again Aristotelian science was weakened. Although his devotion to a literal reading of the Bible led Tycho to reject the Copernican sun-centered universe, he did propose an alternative system in which the planets revolved around the sun, but the sun moved about a motionless earth.

Tycho's fame ultimately rests on his skill as a practicing astronomer. He bequeathed to future generations precise calculations about the movements of heavenly bodies, which proved invaluable. These calculations were put to greatest use by Johannes Kepler (1571–1630), a German, who was Tycho's collaborator during his final years. After Tycho's death, Kepler inherited his astronomical papers, and he brought to this data a scientific vision that was both experimental and mystical.

Kepler searched persistently for harmonious laws of planetary motion. He did so because he believed profoundly in the Neo-Platonic and Pythagorean vision: Nature is a spiritual force infusing the physical order; and beneath appearances are harmony and unity; and the human mind can begin to comprehend that unity only through gnosis—that is, a direct and mystical realization of unity—and through mathematics. Kepler believed that both approaches were compatible, and he managed to combine them. He believed in, and practiced astrology (as did Tycho), and throughout his lifetime, Kepler tried to contact an ancient but lost and secret wisdom.

In the course of his studies and observations of the heavens, Kepler discovered the three basic laws of planetary motion. First, that the orbits of the planets are elliptical, not circular as had been assumed, and that in the heliocentric universe the sun is one focus of the ellipse. Unlike Tycho, Kepler accepted Copernicus's theory and provided proof for it. Kepler's second law demonstrated that the velocity of a planet is not uniform, as had been believed, but increases as its distance from the sun decreases. Kepler's third law—that the squares of the times taken by any two planets in their revolutions around the sun are in the same ratio as the cubes of their average distances from the sun—brought the planets together into a unified mathematical system.

The significance of Kepler's work was immense. He gave sound mathematical proof to Copernicus's theory, eliminated forever the use of epicycles that had saved the appearance of circular motion, and demonstrated that mathematical relationships can describe the planetary system. But Kepler left a significant question unresolved: what kept the planets in their orbits? Why did they not fly out into space or crash into the sun? The answer would be supplied by Isaac Newton, who synthesized the astronomy of Copernicus and Kepler with the new physics developed by Galileo.

EXPERIMENTAL PHYSICS

At the same time that Kepler was developing a new astronomy, his contemporary Galileo Galilei (1564–1642) was breaking with the older physics of Aristotle. A Pisan by birth, Galileo lived for many years in Padua where he conducted some of his first experiments on the motion of bodies. Guided by the dominant philosophy of the Italian Renaissance—the revived doctrines of Plato—Galileo believed that beyond the visible world lay universal truths, subject to mathematical verification. Galileo insisted that the study of motion entails not only the use of logic (as Aristotle had believed), but also the application of mathematics. For this Late Renaissance natural philosopher, mathematics became the language of nature. Galileo also believed that only after experimenting with the operations of nature can the philosopher formulate the harmonious laws of the universe and give them mathematical expression.

In his mechanical experiments, Galileo discovered that uniform force applied to bodies of unequal weights would produce, all other things being equal, a uniform acceleration. He demonstrated that bodies fall with arithmetic regularity. Motion could, therefore, be treated mathematically.

Galileo came very close to perceiving that inertia governs the motion of bodies, but his concept of inertia was flawed. He believed that inertial force was circular. For instance, said Galileo, "a ship . . . once having acquired some impetus in a calm sea would continue to move around our Earth without ever stopping."[1] He did not grasp what Newton would later proclaim, that bodies move in a straight line at a uniform velocity unless impeded. But Galileo's effect was enormous; he had suggested that terrestrial objects could in theory stay in motion forever.

Galileo established a fundamental principle of modern science—the order and uniformity of nature. There are no distinctions in rank or quality between the heavens and earth; heavenly bodies are not perfect and changeless as Aristotle had believed. In 1609, Galileo built a telescope through which he viewed the surface of the moon. In the next year in a treatise called *The Starry Messenger*, he proclaimed to the world that the moon "is not smooth, uniform, and precisely spherical as a great number of philosophers believe it and the other heavenly bodies to be, but is uneven, rough, and full of cavities . . . being not unlike the face of the earth, relieved by chains of mountains and deep valleys."[2] With his telescope, Galileo also saw spots on the sun, providing further evidence that heavenly objects, like earthly objects, undergo change. There are no higher and lower worlds; nature is the same throughout.

Through his telescope Galileo also saw moons around Jupiter, a discovery that served to support the Copernican hypothesis. If Jupiter had moons, then what about the Ptolemaic view that all heavenly bodies orbited the earth? The moons of Jupiter removed a fundamental criticism leveled against Copernicus and opened up the possibility that indeed the earth with its own moon might be just like the planet Jupiter—and both might in turn revolve around a central point, the sun.

Both as an experimenter and as a propagandist for the new science, Galileo was the boldest scientist of his generation. But in southern and Counter Reformation Europe the religious politics of the early seventeenth century called for discretion, not boldness. Galileo aggressively defended his discoveries and openly mocked his detractors—some of whom also happened to be powerful churchmen. The Italian church had already watched with horror the uses to which Copernican ideas could be put by such reformers as Giordano Bruno (1548–1600), and the Inquisition had burned Bruno at the stake for heresy. Such was the intellectual atmosphere within which Galileo lived, worked, and possibly, although the record is not clear, engaged in local church politics. His forcefulness coupled with his attack on scholasticism brought him into direct confrontation with the Inquisition, and he was silenced in 1633.

To this day, his trial has been interpreted as a classic confrontation between religion and science, between tradition and progress, between authority and freedom of inquiry. In historical terms the trial of Galileo represented the struggle waged by the Counter Reformation church against the Reformation and the latter's emphasis on knowledge and learning encouraged by the lay people and intended for their use. Due to Galileo's trial and the repressive controls imposed on the printing press in Catholic Europe, the new science became an increasingly Protestant and northern European phenomenon.

THE NEWTONIAN ACHIEVEMENT

By the middle of the seventeenth century largely because of the work of Copernicus, Kepler, and Galileo, Aristotle and Ptolemy had been dethroned. A new philosophy of nature and a new science had come into being, whose essence lay in the mathematical expression of physical laws that describe matter in motion. Yet what was missing was an overriding law that could explain the motion observed in the heavens and on earth. This law was supplied by Isaac Newton.

Isaac Newton was born in 1642 in Lincolnshire, England, the son of a modest yeoman. He acquired a place at Trinity College at Cambridge University not by virtue of his social status, but because of his intellect. There he came under the influence of Isaac Barrow, a mathematician and Anglican churchman, and Newton's mathematical ability became evident. In 1666, Cambridge was forced to close because of an outbreak of the plague, and Newton retreated to the countryside. During this period of solitude he was, as he later said in a letter to a friend, "in the prime of my life for invention and minded mathematics and philosophy more than at any time since." In a period of less than eighteen months, Newton formulated the law of universal gravitation and, after a series of rigorous experiments, determined the nature of light.

For many years, Newton never published his discoveries, partly because even he did not see the immense significance of his work.

Finally, another mathematician and friend, Edmund Halley, persuaded him to publish under the sponsorship of the Royal Society. The result was the *Principia Mathematica* of 1687. In 1704, Newton published his *Opticks* and revealed his theory that light was corpuscular in nature and that it emanated from luminous bodies in such a way as to produce waves.

Of the two books, both monumental achievements in the history of science, the *Principia* made the greater impact on contemporaries. Newton not only formulated universal mathematical laws, but offered a philosophy of nature that sought to explain the essential structure of the universe: matter is always the same; it is atomic in structure, and in its essential nature it is dead or lifeless; and it is acted upon by forces that are placed in the universe by God. Newton said that the motion of matter could be explained by three laws: inertia, that a body remains in a state of rest or continues its motion in a straight line unless impelled to change by forces impressed upon it; acceleration, that the change in the motion of a body is proportional to the force acting upon it; and that for every action there is an equal and opposite reaction.

Newton argued that these laws apply not only to observable matter but they also apply to the motion of planets in their orbits. He showed that planets did not remain in their orbits because circular motion was "natural" or because crystalline spheres kept them in place, as the Aristotelian-Ptolemaic system held. Rather, said Newton, planets keep to their orbits because every body in the universe exercises a force on every other body, a force that he called *universal gravitation*. Gravity is proportional to the product of the masses of two bodies and inversely proportional to the square of the distance between them. It is operative throughout the universe, whether on earth or in the heavens, and it is capable of mathematical expression. Newton was building his theory on the work of other scientific giants, notably Kepler and Galileo, yet no one before him possessed the breadth of vision, mathematical skill, and dedication to rigorous observation to combine this knowledge into one grand synthesis.

With Newton's discovery of universal gravitation, the Scientific Revolution reached its culmination. Physics and astronomy had reached a new level of maturity; and the theory of the nature of the universe had been transformed. The universe could now be described as matter in motion, governed by invisible forces that operated everywhere, both on earth and in the heavens, and were capable of mathematical expression. The medieval picture of the world as closed, earthbound, and earth-centered had been replaced by a universe seen to be infinite, governed by universal laws, and containing the earth as simply another planet.

But what was God's role in this new universe? Newton and his circle labored to create a mechanical world-picture dependent on the will of God, and in those efforts they were largely successful. Newton retained a central place for a providential deity who operates constantly in the universe; at one time he believed that gravity was simply the will of God operating on the universe. As Newton said in the *Opticks*, the physical order "can be the effect of nothing else than the wisdom and skill of a powerful ever-living agent."[3] Because of his deeply held religious convictions, Newton allowed his science to be used in the service of the established Anglican church. Newton, a scientific genius, was also a deeply religious thinker, who was committed to Protestant government.

BIOLOGY, MEDICINE, AND CHEMISTRY

The spectacular advances made in physics and astronomy in the sixteenth and seventeenth centuries were not matched in the biological sciences. Indeed, the day-to-day practice of medicine throughout western Europe changed little in the period from 1600 to 1700. Much of the medical practice relied heavily on astrology, which proved slow to absorb the discoveries of the new physics.

Doctors clung stubbornly to the teachings of the ancient practitioners Galen and Hippocrates. In general, Galenic medicine paid little attention to the discovery of specific cures for particular diseases. As a follower of Aristotle, Galen emphasized the elements that make up the body—he called their manifestations *humors*. A person with an excess of blood was sanguine; a person with too much bile was choleric. Health consisted of a restoration of balances among these various elements, so Galenic doctors often prescribed purges of one sort or another. The most famous of these was bloodletting, but sweating was also a favorite remedy. These methods were often as dangerous as the diseases they sought to cure, but they were taught religiously in the medical schools of Europe.

Despite the tenacity of Galenic medicine, innovators and reformers attempted during the sixteenth and seventeenth centuries to challenge and overturn medical orthodoxy. With an almost missionary zeal Paracelsus (1493–1541), the Swiss-German physician and Hermeticist, introduced the concept of diagnostic medicine. He argued that particular diseases can be differentiated and are related to chemical imbalances. His treatments relied on chemicals and not on bloodletting or the positions of the stars (although he did not discount such influences), and he proclaimed an almost ecstatic vision of human vitality and longevity. In most universities the faculties of medicine bitterly opposed his views, but by the mid-seventeenth century in England and in the latter part of that century in France, Paracelsian ideas had many advocates. Support for Paracelsian medicine invariably accompanied an attack on the traditional medical establishment and its professional monopoly, and it often indicated support for the new science in general. The struggle between Galenists and Paracelsians quickly took on a social dimension, as the innovators saw themselves pitted against a medical elite that, in their opinion, had lost its commitment to medical research and existed solely to perpetuate itself.

Victory came very slowly to the Paracelsians. In late-seventeenth-century France, the king himself intervened to allow medical students at the Sorbonne to read the writings of the medical reformers. Paracelsian medicine was not really accepted until the eighteenth century. The universities like Leiden's in the Netherlands adopted a new chemical approach to medicine, and a new generation of doctors was produced who were capable of advancing daily medical practice beyond a slavish following of the ancient texts. Simultaneously, there was an upgrading in the social position of surgeons who had been seen until then as lowly handworkers, quite separate from, and beneath the medical practitioners. Gradually during that century, enlightened doctors became skilled in both chemistry and surgery.

The medical reforms of the eighteenth century did not rest solely on the Paracelsian approach; they also relied heavily on the experimental breakthroughs made in the science of anatomy. A pioneer in this field was the Belgian surgeon Andreas Vesalius (1514–1564), who published *The Structure of the Human Body* in 1543. Opposing Galenic practice, Vesalius argued for observation and anatomical dissection as the keys to knowing how the human body works. By the late seventeenth century, doctors had a great deal new to learn about the human body, its structure and its chemistry, and this new learning owed much to Paracelsus and Vesalius.

This study of anatomy yielded dramatic results. In 1628, William Harvey (1578–1657) announced that he had discovered the circulation of the blood. Harvey compared the functioning of the heart to that of a mechanical pump, and once again this tendency to mechanize nature, so basic to the Scientific Revolution in physics, led to a significant discovery. Yet the acceptance of Harvey's work was very slow, and the practical uses of his discovery were not readily apparent.

The mechanization of the world-picture entailed more than the destruction of the cosmology advanced by Aristotle and Ptolemy. What was also at stake were the explanations offered for everyday physical events. In the Aristotelian and medieval outlook, bodies moved because it was in their nature to do so. Aristotle had postulated "forms" at work in nature; through Latin translations and scholastic commentaries, these forms were spirits, invisible forces at work in nature that produced changes as diverse as the growth in plants, the fall of heavy objects to the earth, or even (according to Catholic theologians) the transformation of bread and wine into the body and blood of Christ. The dethroning of Aristotle and Aristotelian spirits assaulted whole systems of knowledge, often of a theological nature, that went to the heart of medieval belief about the nature of creation and God's relation to it.

Predictably, the final assault on the Aristotelian world view came from Protestant England. By the seventeenth century, English scientific reformers had begun to equate Aristotle with Catholic teachings. Robert Boyle (1627–1691), the father of modern chemistry, believed that Aristotle's physics amounted to little more than magic. Boyle wanted to abolish the spirits on which Catholic theology rested; he advocated that scientists adopt the zeal of the magicians without their secretive practices and their conjuring with spirits. As an alternative to spirits, Boyle adopted the atomic explanation of matter, that it is made up of small, hard, indestructible particles that behave with regularity to explain changes in gases, fluids, and solids, without recourse to Aristotle's four elements or his forms.

Boyle pioneered in the experimental method with such exciting and accurate results that by the time of his death, no serious scientist could attempt chemical experiments without following his guidelines. Thus, the science of chemistry acquired its characteristic experimentalism; it was also based on an atomic theory of matter. But not until late in the eighteenth century was chemistry applied to medical research.

PROPHETS AND PROPONENTS OF THE NEW SCIENCE

The spectacular scientific discoveries necessitated a complete rethinking of the social and intellectual role of scientific inquiry. Science needed prophets and social theorists to give it direction and to assess its implications. During the early modern period, three major reformers attempted in disparate ways to channel science into the service of specific social programs: Giordano Bruno (1548–1600), Francis Bacon (1561–1626), and René Descartes (1596–1650).

Bruno

Giordano Bruno's life is one of the most fascinating and tragic to be found in the turbulent world of the Reformation and Counter Reformation. Born in Italy, Bruno began his mature years as a monk and was burned at the stake by the church. What led him to this cruel fate was his espousal of new religious ideas, which were in fact as old as the second century A.D., but which threatened the beliefs of the church. Bruno found in Hermetic philosophy, which he believed to be confirmed by Copernicus's heliocentric theory, the foundation of a new universal religion. He proposed that religion should be based on the laws found in nature and not on supernaturally inspired doctrines taught by the clergy.

Bruno was one of those Late Renaissance reformers who believed that the Hermetic philosophy with its mystical approach to God and nature held the key to true wisdom. In the Hermetic philosophy the sun is accorded a special symbolic role since it infuses life into nature. On the basis of his belief, Bruno accepted Copernicus's sun-centered concept of the universe and began to write and preach about it all over Europe. Indeed, Bruno's fertile imagination, fired by Hermetic mysticism and the new science, led him to be one of the first Europeans to proclaim that the universe is infinite, filled with innumerable worlds. He also speculated that there might be life on other planets.

All of these notions were regarded by the church as dangerous. Bruno was in effect posing the Hermetic philosophy coupled with the new science as an alternative religious vision to either Protestantism or Catholicism. His sense of awe and enchantment with the natural order is similar to that found among eighteenth-century freethinkers, who saw the scientific study and contemplation of nature, along with a vague sense of the Creator's majesty, as an alternative to organized religious worship. Bruno is a prophet of modern science to the extent that he saw the discoveries of the new science as confirming his belief that creation was in itself so wondrous that it too could be worshiped—that the natural world could replace the supernatural as a fitting object for human curiosity and glorification. Bruno was burned at the stake as a heretic for those beliefs.

Bacon

In contrast to Bruno's mysticism stands the decidedly practical and empirical mind of Francis Bacon, the most important English proponent, although not the most important practitioner, of the new science. Unlike Bruno, Bacon became profoundly suspicious of magic and the magical arts not because they might not work, but because he saw secrecy and arrogance as characteristic of their practitioners. Bacon was Lord Chancellor of England under James I, and he wrote about the usefulness of science partly in an effort to convince the Crown of its advantages.

No philosopher of modern science has surpassed Bacon in elevating the study of nature into a humanistic discipline. In the *Advancement of Learning* (1605), he wrote:

In Mathematics I can report no deficiency, except it be that men do not sufficiently understand the excellent use of Pure Mathematics, in that it does remedy and cure many defects in the wit and faculties intellectual. For if the wit be too dull, it will sharpen it; if too wandering, it will fix it.[4]

Bacon argued that science must be open and free and all ideas must be allowed a hearing. Science must have human goals: the improvement of humanity's material condition and the advancement of trade and industry, but not the making of war nor the taking of lives. Bacon also preached the necessity for science to possess an inductive methodology grounded on experience; the scientist should first of all be a collector of facts.

Although Bacon was rather vague about how the scientist as a theorist actually works, he knew that preconceived ideas imposed on nature seldom yield positive results. An opponent of Aristotle, Bacon argued that university education should move away from the ancient texts and toward the new learning. As a powerful civil servant, Bacon was not afraid to attack the guardians of tradition. The Baconian vision of progress in science leading to an improvement of the human condition inspired much scientific activity in the seventeenth century, particularly in England.

Descartes

René Descartes, a French philosopher of the first half of the seventeenth century, went to the best French schools and was trained by the Jesuits in mathematics and scholastic philosophy. Yet in his early twenties, he experienced a crisis in confidence. He felt that everything he had been taught was irrelevant and meaningless.

Descartes began to search within himself for what he could be sure was clear and distinct knowledge. All he could know with certainty was the fact of his existence, and even that he knew only because he experienced not his body, but his mind: "I think, therefore I am." From this point of certitude, Descartes deduced God's existence. God exists because Descartes had in his mind an idea of a supreme, perfect being which, he reasoned, could only have been put there by such a being, not by any ordinary mortal. Therefore, God's existence means that the physical world must be real, for no Creator would play such a cruel trick and invent a vast hoax.

Descartes thus found confidence in the fact of his own existence and in the reality of the physical world, which he reasoned could best be understood through observation and mathematics. Scientific thought for Descartes meant an alternative to the chaos of conflicting opinions and the tyranny of truths learned, but not experienced, for oneself. Descartes, possibly as a result of knowing Bacon's ideas, also believed that "it is possible to attain knowledge which is very useful in life, and that, instead of that speculative philosophy which is taught in the schools, we may find a practical philosophy by means of which . . . we can . . . thus render ourselves the masters and possessors of nature"[5] (*Discourse on Method*).

Descartes has rightly been called the father of modern philosophy and one of the first prophets of modern science. He recognized the power that can come to individuals who ground knowledge not on the fact of God's existence, but on a willful assertion of their own ability as thinkers and investigators. Solely by applying their human minds to the world around them, human beings can achieve scientific knowledge that will make them the masters and possessors of nature. Descartes believed so fully in the power of unaided human reason that his practical science was largely deductive and not sufficiently based on rigorous experimentation. He thought that the scientist, aided by mathematics, could arrive at correct theories without necessarily testing them against experience.

The prophetic visions of Bruno, Bacon, and Descartes brought for the first time in the

West the realization of just how important scientific knowledge could become. Science could become the foundation of a new religiosity, one grounded on the practical study of nature and one that was eventually used by Enlightenment reformers to displace the authority of traditional religion. At the same time, science could also serve the needs of humanity. It could give to its practitioners a sense of power and self-confidence unimagined even by Renaissance proponents of individualism.

THE SOCIAL CONTEXT OF THE SCIENTIFIC REVOLUTION

The Scientific Revolution reached its culmination during the second half of the seventeenth century in England at a time when that society was torn by revolution and civil war. That revolutionary context profoundly affected the direction of modern science. In the society that produced Boyle and Newton, the dreams of Bacon and Descartes were never actualized in ways they would have recognized because social and political events intervened to shape science in ways they could not have expected.

By the 1640s in England, due to the influence of the writings of Kepler, Galileo, Bacon, and Descartes, it was clear that a new science had been created, with mechanical principles, mathematical theorems, and universal forces replacing the old world view. Just as the new science was developing as a recognized body of learning, political revolution erupted. In opposition to absolute monarchy and the established church, the Puritans sought social and political reform, the rule of Parliament, and a church governed by true Calvinists rather than by bishops. This Puritan Revolution played a crucial role in the formation of modern science.

The Puritan reformers championed the new science and encouraged young experimental-

LOUIS XIV VISITING THE FRENCH ACADEMY OF SCIENCES The seventeenth century saw the formation of numerous scientific academies and a scientific community that stretched throughout western Europe, though with no formal structure. Great Britain was the first country to channel the practical applications of the new science into areas directly useful to the state. (Courtesy Burndy Library, Norwalk, Conn.)

ists to follow Bacon's call to put science in the service of humanity. The Puritan encouragement of science made it socially respectable, as well as religiously wholesome; the fear that mechanical notions might separate Creator from creation seemed irrelevant. The Puritan promoters of science encouraged young gentlemen like Robert Boyle and his circle at Oxford to experiment and to use science to reform the university and improve the human condition, both material and spiritual.

As victory came to the Puritan side with the execution of Charles I in 1649, the revolution began to take a turn never intended by the Puritan reformers. The victorious army was dangerously close to becoming an independent force, and its ranks were made up of religious and political radicals. As representatives of the lower classes, they demanded a share in the reforms initiated by the Puritan landowners. They also questioned the social uses of the new science and advocated in its place the introduction of scientific learning closer to the folk practices and needs of the poor. Boyle and his scientific associates grew increasingly alarmed by these demands, and they in turn advocated their understanding of science as an alternative to the science and magic proposed by the radicals. Suddenly, the new science assumed a social and political meaning never imagined by its earliest proponents, yet similar to its role in modern industrial society.

Science, Boyle argued, must be conducted by cautious experimentation, and its benefits should be determined by scientists who are supported by the state. Despite Bacon's dreams, Boyle and his circle argued that science should not be primarily a means of redressing human ills, but should serve the interests of commerce and industry. They said that science should focus on unraveling the mysteries of the universe and that the practical application of these theoretical insights, although desirable, should not be given highest priority. Finally, the understanding of nature, or natural philosophy, underlying scientific research should be compatible with the truths of Christianity. Boyle and his associates reacted violently against versions of the mechanical philosophy, as found in Descartes, threatening to divorce science from religion.

The English Revolution anticipated a development that would become common: the channeling of science in interest of the state and existing social arrangements. The Puritan reformers gave England a lead over much of Europe in scientific innovation. By the second half of the seventeenth century, many major scientific discoveries of the Scientific Revolution, particularly Newton's work, occurred within the intellectual milieu created by the English Revolution.

Newton approached problems in a rigorous, experimental way, adopting techniques first advocated by Boyle and his associates. He believed that the will of God gave uniformity to nature; his religious convictions enhanced his theoretical insights, so he believed it was possible to search for universal laws. And where Newton and his followers saw any practical application for the new science, it was largely in the service of commerce and industry as well as in support of the established church.

Newton's followers argued that the Newtonian universe stands as a model for human society. Just as God controls matter, they said, people should control natural resources, trade, and industry and use nature for their own self-aggrandizement. If the universe is an ordered place, then society and government must be ordered; obedience should be the first and only duty of the citizen. To challenge the social and political order would be, in effect, to challenge the harmony intended by God for both the human and the natural worlds.

In his later years, Newton acquired immense power in English intellectual life. After his death, his science received almost universal acceptance on the Continent. He saw to it that his friends and supporters obtained key positions in the scientific faculties of the major universities; Newton and his followers were honored and rewarded by the state. His achievements became "institutionalized," and the new science served to increase the wealth and power of the English state.

THE MEANING OF THE SCIENTIFIC REVOLUTION: THEN AND NOW

Perhaps because today science in its many branches has become a dominant element in Western civilization, and because fears for the world's survival hinge on the destructive aspects of atomic science, some historians have emphasized the fear experienced by early modern Europeans as they came to terms with the new science. The seventeenth-century English poet and social conservative, John Donne, provides some evidence for that interpretation. His poem *An Anatomy of the World (The First Anniversary)* (1611), about the effects of the new science, related the dislocation of the sun to the new social forces that were threatening traditional and hierarchical English society:

And new Philosophy calls all in doubt
The Element of fire is quite put out;
The Sun is lost, and th' earth, and no man's
*　　wit*
Can well direct him where to looke for it.
And freely men confesse that this world's
*　　spent,*
When in the Planets, and the Firmament
They seeke so many new; then see that this
Is crumbled out againe to his Atomies.
'Tis all in peeces, all cohaerence gone;
All just supply, and all Relation:
Prince, Subject, Father, Sonne, are things
*　　forgot,*
For every man alone thinkes he hath got
To be a Phoenix, and that then can bee
None of that kinde, of which he is, but hee.[6]

Donne responded fearfully to the new science, although he was nevertheless fascinated by its discoveries.

In Catholic countries, where the Scientific Revolution began, by the early seventeenth century there is a noticeably increasing hostility toward scientific ideas. The Counter Reformation had hardened the church into pursuing an all-out assault on heresy, and this mentality of censorship enabled lesser minds to exercise their fears and arrogance against any idea they regarded as suspicious. Galileo was caught in this hostile environment, and the Copernican system was condemned by the church in 1616.

As a result, by the second half of the seventeenth century, science had become an increasingly Protestant phenomenon. The major Protestant countries like England and the Netherlands accorded such natural philosophers as Boyle and Descartes greater intellectual freedom to pursue their scientific and philosophical studies. Their presses were relatively free to publish their findings, a most important factor in their spread. In its latter stages, science proved to be more compatible with the Protestant mind with its emphasis on individual striving.

Because science in the course of the seventeenth century was harnessed into the service of the state and commercial and industrial interests, its meaning in the twentieth century, and therefore the meaning of the Scientific Revolution, have become matters of considerable concern. Increasingly, historians are questioning the role of science, given its social history, as a liberator of the human spirit. Knowledge about the uses to which science was put by its earliest proponents, by Boyle and Newton among others, reveals that science, like every other aspect of human endeavor, can serve a variety of masters. As a historical and institutional reality, scientific knowledge has frequently supported established authorities, churches as well as states, and has served commercial and military elites. Science may offer liberation as an abstract ideal, but in practice the pursuit of that ideal depends on the social values and political interests of scientists, their allies, and their governments.

Unquestionably the new science played a crucial historical role in reorienting Western thought away from medieval theology and metaphysics and toward the study of physical and human problems. In the later Middle Ages, most men of learning were Aristotelians and theologians. But by the mid-eighteenth century, knowledge of Newtonian science and the dissemination of useful learning had become the goal of the educated classes. In place of the Latin textbooks of the schools and universities came the encyclopedia, written in the vernacular and often by a variety of scholars, with the aim of providing a wide range of information. All knowledge, it was believed, could imitate scientific knowledge; it could be systematic and progressive. At every turn the advocates of this new approach to learning hailed the scientists of the sixteenth and seventeenth centuries as proof that no institution or dogma had a monopoly on truth—only experience and experimentation would yield knowledge that might, if properly applied, produce a new and better age.

Notes

1. Quoted in Stephen Toulmin and June Goodfield, *The Fabric of the Heavens* (New York: Harper, 1965), p. 224.
2. Excerpted in Stillman Drake, ed., *Discoveries and Opinions of Galileo* (New York: Doubleday, 1957), p. 28.
3. Excerpted in *Newton's Philosophy of Nature*, H. S. Thayer, ed. (New York: Hafner, 1953), p. 177.
4. Excerpted in Francis Bacon, *Selected Writings*, Hugh G. Dick, ed. (New York: Modern Library, 1955), p. 262.
5. Excerpted in Norman Kemp Smith, ed., *Descartes' Philosophical Writings* (New York: Modern Library, 1958), pp. 130–131.
6. Charles M. Coffin, ed., *The Complete Poetry and Selected Prose of John Donne* (New York: Modern Library, 1952), p. 191.

Suggested Reading

Andrade, E. N. da Costa, *Sir Isaac Newton* (1954). A concise biography.

Briggs, Robin, *The Scientific Revolution of the Seventeenth Century* (1969). A clearly written survey with documents.

Butterfield, Herbert, *The Origins of Modern Science* (1957). A highly regarded analysis of the emergence of modern science.

Cohen, I. B., *The Birth of a New Physics* (1960). Authoritative, but difficult for the novice.

Drake, Stillman, ed., *Discoveries and Opinions of Galileo* (1957). A good place to start to learn Galileo's most important ideas.

Jacob, James R., *Robert Boyle and the English Revolution* (1977). Deals with the relationship between Boyle's science and the English Revolution.

Jacob, Margaret C., *The Newtonians and the English Revolution* (1976). Deals with the social meaning of Newton's science.

Kearney, Hugh, *Science and Social Change, 1500–1700* (1971). Includes a discussion of the social setting of the Scientific Revolution.

Koestler, Arthur, *The Watershed: A Biography of Johannes Kepler* (1960). A fascinating biography of a founder of modern science and a practitioner of magic.

Kuhn, Thomas, *The Structure of Scientific Revolutions* (1970). One of the first non-Marxist attempts to show that science has social implications.

Whitehead, Alfred North, *Science and the Modern World* (1960). An early and important meditation on the meaning of modern science.

Review Questions

1. What was the difference between the scientific understanding of the universe and the medieval understanding of it?
2. Describe the major achievements of Copernicus, Kepler, Galileo, and Newton.
3. How did the practice of medicine change during the Scientific Revolution? Describe the changes.
4. What were Bruno's differences with the church? Describe what happened.
5. Does modern science conform to Francis Bacon's ideals? List these ideals and discuss why each does/does not conform.
6. In what ways did the English Revolution shape modern science?
7. How did early modern Europeans perceive the new science as it was developing?

CHAPTER 18

The Age of Enlightenment: Reform Without Revolution

BY THE EIGHTEENTH CENTURY in northern Europe a new culture had captured the imagination of the educated elite. This culture was heavily indebted to the discoveries of the Scientific Revolution, to the experimental method pioneered by Galileo, Boyle, and Newton, and also and most important, to the scientific picture of the universe formed during the seventeenth century. The Scientific Revolution seemed to show that order and mathematically demonstrable laws were at work in the physical universe. Might it not be possible, reformers argued, to examine *human* institutions with the intention of imposing a comparable order and rationality?

This new culture relied heavily on the printing press as an agent of propaganda. Reformers could address the increasingly large audiences found in the major European cities, London, Amsterdam, and Paris, in particular. Thanks to the power of the printed word, the Enlightenment became a movement agitating for reform, which was able to address an educated and urban lay audience directly.

Late in the eighteenth century, a moderate leader of the Enlightenment, Immanuel Kant (1724–1804) was asked to define the Enlightenment. This German and Christian philosopher argued that it was the bringing of "light into the dark corners of the mind," the dispelling of ignorance and superstition. Kant went to the heart of one aspect of the Enlightenment, that is, its insistence that each individual should reason independently without recourse to the authority of the schools, churches, and universities.[1]

Kant believed that this call for self-education meant no disruption of the political order. In general, modern liberal and enlightened culture aimed at a gradual evolutionary transformation of the human condition; only a few radical thinkers during the eighteenth century were prepared to envision an immediate political disruption of the traditional authority of monarchy, aristocracy, and church. The mainstream of the Enlightenment was politically moderate, worshipful of the new science, critical of the clergy and all rigid dogma, tolerant in religious matters, and even loyal to enlightened monarchs who were prepared to keep the clerical censors away from the new books.

The leaders of the new culture acquired the name *philosophes;* these thinkers with a practical and reforming mission were not profoundly original, but bold in their criticisms of existing institutions, especially the churches and clergy. Philosophes were found most commonly in the major European cities, with Paris during the 1770s becoming the center of the Enlightenment. These embattled reformers developed a new style of writing philosophy, one that tried to make it understandable and even simple, if not entertaining. In the process the philosophes became journalists, propagandists, and in some cases brilliant literary stylists who made their various languages more readable for literate laymen and the growing number of literate women.

The proponents of Enlightenment gave close scrutiny to the learning of the clergy and the universities. They judged that accepted wisdom to be obsolete, even superstitious and reactionary. In essence, the philosophes were condemning medieval culture in all its aspects. Inevitably, modern liberal thought as initiated by the Enlightenment emerged as hostile to scholastic learning, priests, and eventually in some quarters, Christianity itself.

THE SCIENCE OF RELIGION

No single thread had united Western culture more powerfully than Christianity. Until the eighteenth century, educated people, especially rulers and servants of the state—however un-Christian their actions—had to give allegiance to one or another of the Christian churches. Undoubtedly in centuries past there had been some unrecorded individuals, often without formal education, who paid their church taxes while doubting much or all of what the clergy taught them. But these earlier anti-Christian tendencies made little impact on the educated and powerful classes. The Enlightenment's importance lies in the fact that it produced the first widely read and systematic assault on Christianity launched from within the ranks of the educated.

The leaders of the Enlightenment sought, by constant recourse to the printed word, to render traditional Christianity obsolete and to put in its place a "rational" system of ethics and philosophy, based on scientific truths. Various alternatives were offered during the eighteenth century. Some moderate philosophes called this new system of ethics a *religion of nature,* without specifying if it would retain any basic Christian doctrines. The more daring philosophes called for *deism,* while the most radical thinkers argued for *pantheism* or *materialism.*

Moderate philosophes like Kant wanted simply to put a basic belief in God's existence and his providence in place of the formal dogmas of the Christian churches. The deists wanted God to be so removed from his creation as to be irrelevant to everyday human concerns. The pantheists or materialists wanted people to acknowledge Nature as if it were God and at a stroke to eliminate any form of religious belief and worship that remotely resembled Christianity. This last group were labeled atheists by their enemies. Whatever the remedy proposed, the effect was the same: the clergy of every Christian denomination conducted a counteroffensive against the philosophes that went on throughout the eighteenth century.

In the last decade of the seventeenth century, the Enlightenment was well underway in England and in the Netherlands. Two factors were crucial in creating this new intellectual milieu: the Revolution of 1688–1689 (see Chapter 16) and the relative freedom of the press found in both countries. The Revolution of 1688–1689 weakened the power of the established church in England. The church lost the right to prosecute heretics and to control the licensing of books. The Revolution also united England and the Netherlands in a war against French aggression and the absolutist regime of the French king, Louis XIV (d. 1715). Suddenly it seemed to educated people on both sides of the English Channel that the unchecked power of kings, supported as they were in every European country by established churches firmly in their control, was the most serious abuse of all time. It seemed as though only in those countries where the power of the clergy had been weakened, would true intellectual inquiry occur.

Skeptics

The earliest examples of "enlightened" thinking show the importance of both the Revolution of 1688–1689 and the war against France. Enlightened propagandists of the 1690s challenged the wisdom of an entrenched clergy to guide people, to instill in them what these critics labeled as superstition. Pierre Bayle (1647–1706), a French Protestant forced by Louis XIV's persecution of Protestants to flee to the Netherlands, was one such propagandist. While there, he published the *Historical and Critical Dictionary* in 1697. An encyclopedia of sorts, it brought together alphabetically arranged subjects and tried to give the most recent learning concerning them.

In the *Dictionary*, Bayle never missed an opportunity to cast doubt on the doctrines taught by the clergy. Although, in the final analysis, Bayle himself was a Christian, his skepticism was used as a tool against the power of the clergy and became one hallmark of the enlightened mind. Rigorous questioning of accepted ideas was to be used as a method for arriving at new truths. And as Bayle noted in his *Dictionary:* "it is therefore only religion that has anything to fear from Pyrrhonism [i.e., skepticism]."[2] In this same critical spirit, Bayle compared Louis XIV to Goliath in his dictionary article entitled "David." The message was clear enough: great tyrants and the clergy who prop them up should beware of self-confident, independently minded citizens who are skeptical of the claims of authority made by kings and churches and are eager to use their own minds in the search for truth.

Partly through Bayle's writings, *skepticism* became an integral part of the Enlightenment's approach to religion. In the middle of the eighteenth century, Scottish philosopher and historian David Hume (1711–1776) also used skepticism to reject revealed religion and to arrive at a natural religion of universal reason and common sense. In *An Enquiry Concerning Human Understanding* (1748), Hume argued that what is called *cause and effect* is not that at all. He said that the human mind associates events or ideas; they have no inherent association, and they were not designed by some outside force to be causes and effects.

The implications of skepticism as articulated by Bayle and Hume were clear: randomness, and not the providential design argued by the clergy, governs human events, and it is the individual's job to impose order where none exists. All should be skeptical of assertions that "God ordains" certain human actions. Skepticism dealt a serious blow to revealed religion and seemed to point in the direction of "natural" religion, that is, toward a system of beliefs and ethics designed by rational people on the basis of their own needs.

Freethinkers

By the 1690s, skepticism was not the only challenge offered to traditional Christian belief. In England a postrevolutionary generation of radicals championed what they called *natural religion*. The clergy of the 1690s labeled these opponents as deists or even atheists. These early representatives of the Enlightenment in England preferred to call themselves *freethinkers*, by which they meant that they were capable of thinking for themselves and had little use for the churches' doctrines. One freethinker, who went further than Bayle's skepticism to embrace pantheism, was John

Toland (1670–1722). In 1696 he published a tract called *Christianity Not Mysterious,* in which he argued that any religious doctrine that seemed to contradict reason or common sense—for example, Jesus' resurrection or the miracles of the Bible—ought to be discarded. Toland also attacked the clergy's power; in his opinion the Revolution of 1688–1689 had not gone far enough in undermining the power of the established church and the king. Toland, and his freethinking associates, Anthony Collins and Matthew Tindal, wanted to see England be a republic governed by "reasonable" people who worshiped, as Toland proposed, not a mysterious God but intelligible Nature.

From science combined with skepticism and anticlericalism, thoughtful critics could find ample reason for abandoning all traditional authority. By 1700 a general crisis of confidence in established authority had been provoked by reading the works of Bayle and the freethinkers or of some seventeenth-century philosophers such as Descartes. Once started in England and the Netherlands, the Enlightenment almost immediately became international.

Voltaire the Philosophe

Although the French possessed a vital tradition of intellectual skepticism going back to the late sixteenth century, as well as a tradition of scientific rationalism easily identified with Descartes, in the early eighteenth century the French found it difficult to gain access to the new literature of Enlightenment because the French printing presses were the most tightly controlled and censored in Europe. As a result a brisk but risky traffic developed in clandestine books and manuscripts subversive of authority.

As a poet and writer struggling for recognition in Paris, the young Voltaire (1694–1778) encountered some of the new ideas that were being discussed in private gatherings (called *salons*) in Paris. Care had to be taken in the

BUST OF VOLTAIRE BY JEAN-ANTOINE HOUDON, 1781 Voltaire (born François Marie Arouet) was the internationally famous supporter of the Enlightenment. He was poet, journalist, essayist, and utopian thinker. Superstition, organized religion, and authoritarian government were the constant targets of his critical pen. (Permission of the Fine Arts Museums of San Francisco)

French capital by those educated people who wanted to read books and discuss ideas hostile to the church or to the Sorbonne, the clerically controlled university. Individuals had been imprisoned for writing or publishing or owning books hostile to Catholic doctrine. Though Voltaire learned something of the new enlightened culture in Paris, in 1726 when he journeyed to London, Voltaire the poet became Voltaire the philosophe.

In England, Voltaire became acquainted with the ideas of John Locke (1632–1704) and Isaac Newton. From Newton, Voltaire learned the mathematical laws that govern the universe; he witnessed the power of human reason to establish general rules that seem to explain the behavior of physical objects. From Locke, Voltaire learned that people should believe only those ideas received from the senses. Locke's theory of learning, his epistemology, impressed many of the proponents of the Enlightenment. Voltaire was only the first among the famous philosophes to champion Locke's ideas. Again the implications for religion were most serious: if people believe only those things that they experience, how can they accept mysteries and doctrines simply because they are taught by churches and the clergy? Voltaire encountered a new and self-confident scientific culture in England, and he also experienced considerable freedom of thought and religious toleration that stood in stark contrast to the absolutism of the French kings and the power of the French clergy.

Throughout his life Voltaire was a fierce supporter of the Enlightenment and a bitter critic of churches and the Inquisition. Although his own books were banned in France, he probably did more there than any other philosophe to popularize the Enlightenment and to mock the authority of the clergy. In *Letters Concerning the English Nation* (1733), Voltaire wrote about his experiences in England. He offered constitutional monarchy, new science, and religious toleration as models to be followed by all of Europe. In the *Letters* he praised English commerce and the more free and tolerant atmosphere that he found in London, in contrast to that in Paris.

Voltaire never ceased to mock the purveyors of superstition and blind obedience to religious authority. In such works as *Candide* (1759) and *Micromegas* (1752), Voltaire castigated the clergy, as well as the other philosophical supporters of the status quo who would have people believe that this was the best of all possible worlds. And like all reformers, Voltaire postulated utopian worlds, and in his ideal society, human greed, war, and the clergy were eliminated. By the middle of the eighteenth century, Voltaire had become internationally famous, and the movement he represented had spread as far as Berlin and St. Petersburg.

Freemasons

The Enlightenment's search for a new foundation of religious belief inevitably meant that some seekers would attempt to found new clubs or societies that tried to fulfill social and intellectual needs no longer being met by the traditional churches. In 1717 a group of London gentlemen, many of them very interested in the new science and in the spread of learning in general, founded the Grand Lodge, a collection of various Masonic lodges that had met in pubs around the city. From that date can be traced the origins of European Freemasonry and its spread into almost every European country.

The old Masonic lodges, some dating back to medieval times, had been nothing more than local guilds for masons, craftsmen who were often skilled in practical architecture and mathematics. Late in the seventeenth century, largely for financial reasons, they began to admit nonmasons, generally prosperous businessmen. Within a generation the businessmen took over many lodges, particularly in London. The tradition of secret meetings held by artisans was transformed into private gatherings where devotees of the new learning could fraternize. The earliest leaders of the London Grand Lodge were followers of Newtonian science, and the lodges became places where men with ordinary learning could acquire some grounding in the new science.

Freemasonry as an institution was never

MAP 18.1 EUROPE, 1715 ▶

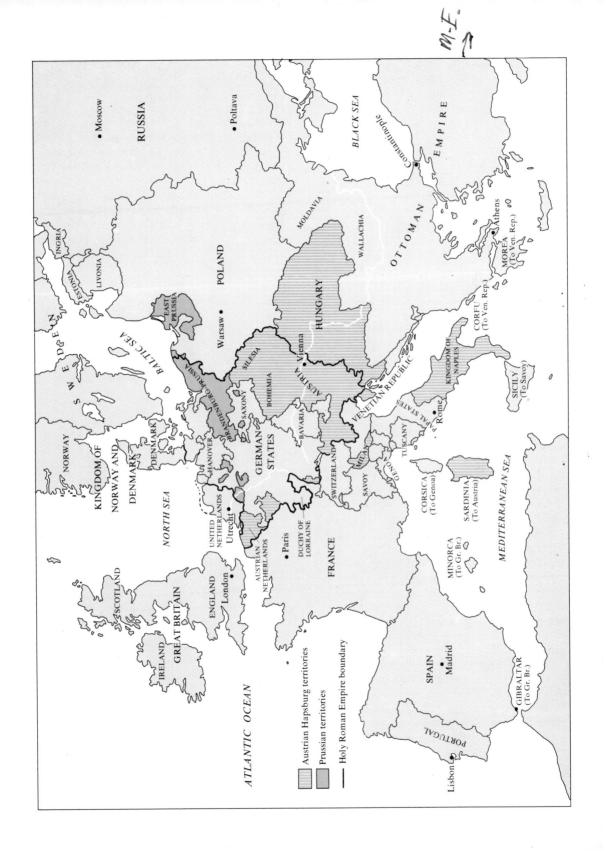

intended to rival the churches. Nevertheless, the lodges became, especially on the Continent, alternative meeting places for men interested in the Enlightenment. Some French philosophes joined lodges in Paris, as did some clergy. In Vienna at the time of Mozart, who was a Freemason, and in Berlin during the reign of Frederick the Great, Masonic membership came to denote support for enlightened and centralized government, often in opposition to the local power of the clergy and the old aristocracy. Freemasonry became, in Austria, for example, a way of expressing loyalty to enlightened monarchs. For a few extreme rationalists bent on destroying the Christian churches, the Masonic lodges also seemed to function as an alternative form of religion, complete with ritual, charitable funds, and sense of community. By the middle of the eighteenth century, perhaps as many as 50,000 men belonged to Masonic lodges in just about every major European city and in many towns as well.

Women were excluded from the lodges except in very middle-class and enlightened towns like The Hague, which was one of the publishing capitals of Europe. Records there indicate the existence of a women's lodge from as early as 1751. Although all early leaders of the Enlightenment were men (and a few of them Freemasons), the new culture they preached was never open solely to men, a policy that prevailed in church hierarchy and universities. During the eighteenth century, some philosophes attacked the appallingly low standard of education available to most women. By the end of the century, their literacy rates, as well as their access to the printing press, had significantly increased, and women began to demand a share in the process of Enlightenment.

But what implications did the Enlightenment's search for new forms of religious expression have? If the power of monarchs and ruling elites received vital support from the clergy and their pronouncements, what implications did Enlightenment thought have politically?

POLITICAL THOUGHT

With the exception of Machiavelli in the Renaissance and Hobbes and the republicans during the English Revolution, the Enlightenment produced the greatest originality in political thought witnessed in the West up to that time. Three major European thinkers and a host of minor ones wrote treatises on politics that remain relevant to this day: John Locke, *Two Treatises on Government* (1689), Montesquieu, *The Spirit of the Laws* (1748), and Jean Jacques Rousseau, *The Social Contract* (1762). All repudiated the notion of the divine right of kings and were concerned to check the power of monarchy; each offered different formulas for achieving that goal. These major political theorists of the Enlightenment were also aware of the writings of Machiavelli and Hobbes and, although often disagreeing with them, borrowed some of their ideas.

Machiavelli had analyzed politics in terms of power, fortune, and the ability of the individual ruler. He did not call in God to justify the power of princes or to explain their demise. Machiavelli had also preferred a republican form of government to that of monarchy, and his republican vision never lost its appeal during the Enlightenment. Very late in the century, most liberal theorists recognized that the republican form of government, or at the least the virtues practiced by citizens in a republic, was the only alternative to the corruption and repression associated with absolutist monarchy.

Enlightenment political thinkers also knew the writings of Thomas Hobbes (1588–1679), although they were ambivalent toward much of his writing. All liked the fact that he championed self-interest as a valid reason for engaging in political activity, and that he produced a secular theory of politics, refusing to bring God into his system to justify the power of kings. Hobbes said that their power rested not on divine right but on a contract made with their subjects. But Enlightenment thinkers found that the problem with Hobbes was that he made that contract unbreakable—once established, the power of the government, whether king or parliament, was absolute.

Hobbes published his major work, *Leviathan*, in 1651 when England was torn by civil war; as a result he was obsessed with the issue of political stability. He feared that left to their own devices, men would kill one another; the "war of every one against everyone"[3] would prevail without the firm hand of the sovereign to stop it. All of the Enlightenment theorists, beginning with John Locke, denied that governments possessed absolute power over their subjects, and to that extent they repudiated Hobbes. Later in the eighteenth century, Rousseau also took issue with Hobbes's dark vision of human nature; Hobbes had argued that life governed by men's passions would be nasty, brutish, and short. Rousseau argued that the passions were good and that society corrupted people's reasonableness and virtue.

Hobbes was often read during the eighteenth century, not because of his belief in absolute government but because of his secular interpretation of political power and his attack on the clergy. Hobbes would reduce the clergy to the status of civil servants; he also had little use for established religion—"the whole kingdom of fairies and bugbears,"[4] he called it. Enlightenment thinkers ignored his prescriptions for absolute government and concentrated on his ideas about religion and also on his interest in the new science.

Hobbes took the new science and its mechanical view of nature further than Newton or Boyle. To their horror, he argued that the universe could be explained by matter in motion, without reference to God's existence at all. This philosophy of materialism had an enormous impact on Enlightenment thought. In late eighteenth-century Paris, all the major philosophes were materialists and in some cases they got their ideas either from reading Hobbes directly or from reading clandestine books and manuscripts popularizing his ideas.

Locke

Probably the most widely read political philosopher during the first half of the eighteenth century was John Locke. His *Two Treatises on Government* (1689) were seen to have justified the Revolution of 1688–1689 and the notion of government by consent of the people. Locke had written his treatises before the Revolution, but in the Enlightenment that fact was unknown.

Locke's theory, in its broad outlines, stated that the right to govern derived from the consent of the governed. When people gave their consent to a government, they expected it to govern justly, to protect their property, and to ensure certain liberties for the propertied. If a government attempted to rule absolutely and arbitrarily, if it violated the natural rights of the individual, it forfeited the loyalty of its subjects. Such a government could be legitimately overthrown. Locke believed that a constitutional government that limited the power of rulers was the best defense of property and individual rights.

Late in the eighteenth century, Locke's ideas were used to justify liberal revolutions both in Europe and in America. Indeed, the most important feature of Locke's political philosophy was not simply his recourse to contract theory as a justification of constitutional government; it was also his assertion that the community may take up arms against its sovereign to secure a just contract and to protect private property.

Montesquieu

Baron de la Brède et de Montesquieu (1689–1755) was a French aristocrat who, like Voltaire, visited England late in the 1720s and who knew the writings of Locke. Montesquieu had little use for revolutions, but he did approve of constitutional monarchy. His primary concern was to check the unbridled authority of the French kings. In opposition to the old regime, Montesquieu proposed a balanced system of government where an executive branch was balanced by a legislature whose members were drawn from the landed and educated elements in society. It may be said that Montesquieu was giving free reign to the landed aristocracy, but that would oversimplify his writings. Montesquieu genuinely believed that the aristocracy possessed a natural and sacred obligation to rule, and that their honor called them to serve the community. Montesquieu was also concerned to fashion a government that channeled the interests and energies of its people, not a government that was bogged down in corruption and inefficiency. His writings, particularly *The Spirit of the Laws*, established Montesquieu as a major philosophe and critic of the Old Regime, whose philosophy possessed republican tendencies. Once again, innovative political thinking highlighted the failures of absolutist government and pointed to the need for some kind of representative assembly in every European country.

Rousseau

Not until the 1760s did democracy find its champion in Jean Jacques Rousseau (1712–1778). Rousseau based his politics on contract theory, that is, the belief that the people choose their government and, in so doing, they effectively give birth to civil society. But Rousseau went further than any other thinker of his day and demanded that the contract be constantly renewed, and that government be made immediately and directly responsible to the will of the people. *The Social Contract* opened with this stirring cry for reform: "Man is born free; and everywhere he is in chains," and it went on to ask, how can that be changed? Freedom is in the very nature of man; "to renounce liberty is to renounce being a man, to surrender the rights of humanity and even its duties."[5]

Rousseau argued that true liberty can only be found in small city-states where individuals can directly influence their governments. But his followers would see otherwise: they applied his ideas to the French state. No philosopher of the Enlightenment was more dangerous to the Old Regime than Rousseau. His ideas were perceived as truly revolutionary, as a direct challenge to the power of kings, churches, and aristocrats. Although Rousseau thought that many leaders of the Enlightenment had been corrupted by easy living and salon life, Rousseau nevertheless earned an uneasy place in the ranks of the philosophes. In the French Revolution, his name would be invoked to justify democracy and representative government, and of all the philosophes, Rousseau would probably have been least horrified by the early phase of that revolutionary upheaval.

Rousseau also saw society as the corrupter of human beings who, left to their own devices, were inherently virtuous and freedom loving. A wide spectrum of opinion in the Enlightenment also saw society if not as corrupting, then at least as needing constant reform. Some enlightened critics were prepared to work with those in power in an effort to bring about concrete social reforms. Other philosophes believed that the key to reform lay not in social and political institutions, but in a change in mentality brought about by education and propaganda. Still others placed their faith in an engine of change that had just begun to be seen as all-embracing: the working of a capitalist economy.

SOCIAL THOUGHT

Psychology and Education

Once enlightened propagandists, like Voltaire, had accepted Locke's notion that human knowledge was attained through the senses, the theoretical foundations had been established for an unprecedented interest in education and psychology. "Locke has unfolded to man the nature of human reason," Voltaire wrote in his *Letters*. For the Enlightenment the proper study of humanity became not simply people, but the process by which people can and do know. Locke had said that individuals take the data produced by their senses and reflect on it; in that way they arrive at complex ideas. Education obviously requires the active participation of students and an environment that promotes learning. Faith in knowledge not tested by their own sense experience is inadequate. Later philosophes, like the Frenchman Étienne Condillac (1715–1780), argued that knowledge is really nothing more than sense data. In this approach the Enlightenment came close to equating knowledge with instinct and pleasure. Although there was little experimentation on the senses of people and animals during the eighteenth century, it is easy to understand how that aspect of modern psychology developed from the theories of Condillac, among others.

More treatises were written on education during the eighteenth century than in all previous centuries combined. On the Continent where many schools and all universities were controlled by the clergy, the educated laity began to demand state regulation and inspection of all educational facilities. This was one practical expression of the growing discontent with the clergy and their independent authority. By the second half of the century, new schools and universities in Prussia, Belgium, Austria, and Russia attempted to teach practical subjects suited to the interests of the laity. Predictably, science was given a special place in these new institutions. Yet in 1762, one French author estimated that less than one-tenth of all school-age boys in France received a proper education. France was one of the more advanced European countries; by 1789 probably about half of the men and about 20 percent of the women were literate.

Prussia and Scotland excelled in the field of education, but for very different reasons. In Prussia, Frederick the Great decreed universal public education for boys as part of his effort to surpass the level of technical expertise found in other countries. His educational policy was another example of his using the Enlightenment to increase the power of the central government. In Scotland the improvements in education were largely sponsored by the established and Calvinist church. The heirs of the Protestant Reformation with its emphasis on the Bible and hence on the printed word were fully capable of sponsoring policies that in Catholic countries required the Enlightenment for their execution.

In the teaching of medicine the University of Leiden in the Netherlands became the most advanced institution in Europe in the eighteenth century. Indeed, its scientific faculty presented Newtonian physics and the latest chemistry to a generation of doctors and engineers assembled from all over Europe. A new medical school was also founded in Vienna. Many Scottish students, often trained in Leiden, brought their knowledge home to make Edinburgh University a major center for medical students. Again, in concrete ways, the impact of Locke's idea that knowledge comes primarily through experience is discernible.

Locke's doctrine found its most extreme expression in the writings of Rousseau on education. In *Émile* (1762), Rousseau argued that individuals learn from nature, from people, or from things. Indeed Rousseau wanted the early years of a child's education to be centered on developing the senses, not to be spent chained to a schoolroom desk. Later, attention would be paid to intellectual pursuits, then finally to morality. He appealed especially to women to protect their children from social convention, that is, to teach their children about life. On the one hand, Rousseau would render the family into the major educational force; on the other, he wanted its products to be cosmopolitan and enlightened, singularly free from superstition and prejudice. In the process, women (whom Rousseau would confine to the home) would bear the burden of instilling enlightenment, though they had little experience of the world beyond that of the family. Rousseau's contradictions sprang in large measure from his desperate search for an alternative to the formal educational systems that existed in his day. In the field of education the reality of most European schools fell far below the ideal put forward by the philosophes.

Humanitarianism

Crime and Punishment

If education of children in the eighteenth century was poor, the treatment of criminals was appalling. Conditions differed little whether an individual was imprisoned because of unpaid debts or whether he was a bandit or murderer. Prisoners were often starved or exposed to disease, or both. On the Continent where torture was still legal, prisoners could be subjected to brutal interrogation or to random punishment—treatment comparable to anything found today in many dictatorships. In 1777 an English reformer, John Howard, published a report on the state of the prisons in England and Wales: "the want of food is to be found in many country gaols. In about half these, debtors have no bread; although it is granted to the highwayman, the house-breaker, and the murderer; and medical assistance, which is provided for the latter, is withheld from the former." Although torture was illegal in England, except in cases of treason, the prison conditions were often as harmful to the physical and mental health of their inmates as torturers were.

Although there is something particularly reprehensible about the torturer, his skills were consciously applauded in many countries during the eighteenth century. Fittingly, the most powerful critique of the European system of punishment came from Italy, from the peninsula where the Inquisition and its torture chambers had reigned with little opposition for centuries. In Milan during the early 1760s, the Enlightenment had made very gradual inroads, and in a small circle of reformers the practices of the Inquisition and the relation-

TORTURE BY WEIGHTS, EIGHTEENTH-CENTURY PRINT The torturer was still applauded in some quarters during the eighteenth century. Crimes were punished because they were the manifestation of sin. Cesare Beccaria, in his *Of Crime and Punishment* (1764), stressed that the state should punish, but only with the goal of reintegrating the offender with society. His treatise was acclaimed by Parisian philosophes. (The Bettmann Archive Inc.)

ship between church and state in the matter of criminal justice were avidly discussed.

Out of that intellectual ferment came one of the most important books of the Enlightenment, *Of Crime and Punishment* (1764) by the Milanese reformer Cesare Beccaria (1738–1794). For centuries, sin and crime had been wedded in the eyes of the church; the function of the state was to punish the second because it was a manifestation of the first. Beccaria cut through that thicket of moralizing and argued that the church should concern itself with sin; it should abandon its prisons and courts. The state should concern itself with crimes against society, and the purpose of punishment should be to reintegrate the individual into society.

Beccaria also went further and inquired into the causes of crime. Abandoning the concept of sin, Beccaria, rather like Rousseau who saw injustice and corruption in the very fabric of society, regarded private property as the root of social injustice and hence at the root of crime. Pointedly he asked: "What are these laws I must respect, that they leave such a huge gap between me and the rich? Who made these laws? Rich and powerful men. . . . Let us break these fatal connections. . . . let us attack injustice at its source."[6]

Beccaria's attackers labeled him a *socialist* —the first time (1765) that that term was used—by which they meant that Beccaria paid attention only to people as social animals and that he wanted a society of free and equal citizens. In contrast, the defenders of the use of torture and capital punishment, and the necessity of social inequality argued that Beccaria's teachings would lead to chaos and to the loss of all property rights and legitimate authority. What these critics had sensed was the utopian aspect of Beccaria's thought. His humanitarianism was not directed toward the reform of the criminal justice system alone; he sought to restructure society in such a way as to render crime far less prevalent and, whenever possible, to re-educate its perpetrators.

When Beccaria's book and then the author himself turned up in Paris, the philosophes greeted them with universal acclaim. By the 1760s, Paris had become the center of the Enlightenment, and that period is commonly called the High Enlightenment. All the leaders of the period—Voltaire, Rousseau, Diderot, and the atheist d'Holbach—embraced one or another of Beccaria's views. But if the criminal justice system as well as the schools were subject to scrutiny by enlightened critics, what did the philosophes have to say about slavery, the most pernicious of all Western institutions?

Slavery

On both sides of the Atlantic during the eighteenth century there was growing criticism of slavery. At first it came from religious thinkers like the Quakers whose own version of religious enlightenment predated that European-wide phenomenon by several decades. The Quakers were born out of the turmoil of the English Revolution, and their strong adherence to democratic ideas grew out of their conviction that the light of God's truth works in every man and woman. Many philosophes on both sides of the Atlantic knew Quaker thought, and Voltaire, who had mixed feelings about slavery, and Benjamin Franklin, who condemned it, admired the Quakers and their principles.

On the problem of slavery the Enlightenment was strangely ambivalent. In an ideal world—just about all philosophes agreed—slavery would not exist. But such was not the world, and given human wickedness, greed, and lust for power, Voltaire thought that slavery might be inevitable: "the human race," Voltaire wrote in his *Philosophical Dictionary* (1764), "constituted as it is, cannot subsist unless there be an infinite number of useful individuals possessed of no property at all."[7] Denis Diderot (1713–1784) thought that slavery was probably immoral, but given the fact that the French empire subsisted in part on its slaves, their rights could not be discussed, he argued, in a monarchy. Indeed, not until 1794 after the first years of the French Revolution and only after agonized debate, did the French government, no longer a monarchy, finally abolish slavery.

It must be remembered that Enlightenment political thinkers, among them Locke (who condoned slavery) and Montesquieu (whose ideas were used to condone it), rejected God-given political authority and argued for the rights of property-holders and for social utility as the foundations of good government. Those criteria, property and utility, played right into the hands of the proslavery apologists. They particularly cited Montesquieu, who had said

DIDEROT'S ENCYCLOPEDIA, THE DRAWLOOM The *Encyclopédie* embodied revolutionary concepts: knowledge was valuable for its own sake; human beings could obtain all knowledge through their own efforts. The *Encyclopédie* also condemned slavery. This widely circulated work was the French Enlightenment's most influential publication. (Historical Pictures Service, Inc., Chicago)

that in tropical countries where sloth was "natural," slavery might be useful and even necessary to force people to work. Likewise, Montesquieu had argued that in despotisms the individual would lose little by willingly choosing enslavement. The proslavery propagandists also argued that since most African tribes were despotic, the slaves in European colonies were in effect better off.

Yet the Enlightenment must also be credited with bringing the problem of slavery into the forefront of public discussion in Europe and in the American colonies. The utility argument cut both ways. If the principle held, as so many philosophes argued, that human happiness was the greatest good, how could slavery be justified? In his short novel *Candide*, Voltaire has his main character, Candide, confront the spectacle of a young

Negro who has had his leg and arm cut off merely because it is the custom of a country. Candide's philosophical optimism is shattered as he reflects on the human price paid by this slave who harvested the sugar that Europeans enjoyed so abundantly. Throughout the eighteenth century the emphasis placed by the Enlightenment on moral sensibility produced a literature of shock that emphasized over and over again, and with genuine revulsion, the inhumanity of slavery.

By the second half of the century, again in that ferment of intellectual creativity described as the High Enlightenment, strongly worded attacks on slavery were issued by a new generation of philosophes. With Rousseau in the vanguard, they condemned slavery as a violation of the natural rights of man. In a volume issued in 1755 the great *Encyclopedia* of the Enlightenment, edited by the Parisian philosophe, Diderot, condemned slavery in no uncertain terms: "There is not a single one of these hapless souls . . . who does not have the right to be declared free . . . since neither his ruler nor his father nor anyone else had the right to dispose of his freedom."[8] That statement made its way into thousands of copies and various editions of an encyclopedia that was probably the most influential publication resulting from the French Enlightenment. Its wide circulation (about 25,000 copies were sold before 1789), often despite the vigorous efforts of censors to stop it, probably tipped the scales to put the followers of the Enlightenment in the antislavery camp. But that victory for humanitarian principles must be seen as clouded by much ambiguous language, coming straight from the pens of some of Europe's supposedly most enlightened thinkers, and downright prejudice against the Negro as a non-European.

Women

Predictably, given their ambiguity about the rights of those different from themselves, the men of the Enlightenment also had some ambiguous things to say about women. Not entirely unlike slaves, women had few property rights within marriage and their physical abuse by husbands was widely regarded as beyond the purview of the law. Women's education was slighted, and social theorists had for centuries regarded them as inferior. The origins of that sexual inequality intrigued the earliest political theorists, Hobbes and Locke, whose ideas made such an enormous impact on the Enlightenment. Both saw that neither nature nor Scripture gave the father dominion in the household. As Hobbes said in *Leviathan*, "in the state of nature, if a man and woman contract so, as neither is subject to the command of the other, the children are the mother's."[9] Yet this perception was never taken up by any of the major philosophes, and indeed Hobbes and Locke themselves both proceeded to deal with society as they saw it. Neither concerned himself with correcting the legal inferiority of women.

Yet by the middle of the eighteenth century, many French philosophes had begun to think about the condition of women and, in the case of Voltaire and Diderot, had taken up with women, outside of marriage, who were in several areas their intellectual equals. Diderot fretted, as a result, about the poor education accorded to women; yet, on the other hand, he distrusted their apparent commitment to the old religiosity. By the 1750s in Paris, rich women had become the organizers of fashionable salons where writers and enlightened reformers gathered for free and open conversation; Diderot attended such a salon. But Baron d'Holbach, who led the most famous gathering of the 1770s, specifically excluded women because he believed that they lowered the tone and seriousness of the discussion. Jean Jacques Rousseau, who had little use for Paris and its fashionable salons, also disdained elegant women of the drawing rooms.

Rousseau's own conception of women specifically excluded them from the social contract, in that he saw nature as having given men dominion over women and children. Outside the family in civil society, that dominion is never absolute; it rests on the will of the majority (presumably of men because in *The Social Contract* Rousseau never mentions women as a part of civil society). In *A Discourse on Political Economy* (1755), Rousseau insists that the patriarchical structure of the family is natural; the primary function of the family is to "preserve and increase the patrimony of the father."[10] Yet Rousseau does allot to women the education of children, and at the end of the eighteenth century, many women saw Rousseau as an ally because his views would lead to an improvement in their domestic status and conceivably in their educational benefits.

With his characteristic skepticism, Hume saw all this ambiguity about women as resulting from men's desire to preserve their power and patrimony. Since men had no guarantees that the children their wives bore were in fact fathered by them, the only recourse was to try to repress women sexually. According to Hume the necessity "to impose a due restraint on the female sex"[11] led to the sexual inequality. But Hume was never troubled sufficiently by that inequality to discuss the point in any detail. And Kant, who defined the Enlightenment so eloquently, argued that the differences between men and women were simply natural. In *Observations on the Feeling of the Beautiful and Sublime* (1764), Kant argued with characteristic idealism that "women have a strong inborn feeling for all that is beautiful, elegant, and decorated . . . they love pleasantry and can be entertained by trivialities." Predictably, Kant concluded that "laborious learning or painful pondering, even if a woman should greatly succeed to it, destroys the merits that are proper to her sex." In that treatise, Kant came dangerously close to denying women any need to know the new science or to speculate: "her philosophy is not to reason, but to sense."[12] This major philosophe almost denied women a right to enlightenment.

Only late in the century, after the French Revolution had begun, did any thinker representative of the Enlightenment challenge

ADAM SMITH In the *Wealth of Nations* (1776), Adam Smith advocated a capitalist system that is still prevalent. He called for laissez-faire, a free market governed by self-interest. He saw the monetary value of labor as a key factor in this capitalist economy. (Culver Pictures, Inc.)

Rousseau's views on women. Educated in enlightened circles and familiar with radical philosophes like the American revolutionary Thomas Paine, the English feminist Mary Wollstonecraft (1759–1797) extended the principles of the Enlightenment to the position and status of women. With devastating logic, her *Vindication of the Rights of Woman* (1792) called for "a revolution in female manners—time to restore to them their lost dignity—and make them, as part of the human species, labor by reforming themselves, to reform the world." She mocked the notion of sexual virtues, such as the beauty and modesty of which Kant had written. She believed, somewhat in the manner of Rousseau, only without his one-sex conclusions, that society had corrupted women: "from the tyranny of man the greater part of female follies proceed." Wollstonecraft viewed this corruption as analogous

to the evils stemming from property rights and the vast inequalities in privilege and opportunity between the rich and the poor. True to Enlightenment ideals, Wollstonecraft did not attack property rights as such, but she did urge a significant reduction in the gap between the wealthy and the poor. Again in keeping with enlightened prescriptions, she urged that equal public education be made available to both men and women. For Wollstonecraft, feminism brought with it a commitment to universal human values, to excellence in learning—which she had never had the opportunity to pursue—and to "the power of generalizing ideas, of drawing comprehensive conclusions from individual observations."[13] Although she explicitly wrote for middle- and upper-class women, Wollstonecraft's *Vindication* became a text on which nineteenth-century reformers and socialists could and did build.

ECONOMIC THOUGHT

The Enlightenment's emphasis on property as the foundation for individual rights and its search for uniform laws inspired by Newton's scientific achievement led to the development of the science of economics. Appropriately, that intellectual achievement occurred in the most advanced capitalistic nation in Europe, Great Britain. Not only were the British in the vanguard of capitalist expansion, by the third quarter of the eighteenth century that expansion had brought on the start of the Industrial Revolution. Its new factories and markets for the manufacture and distribution of goods provided a natural laboratory where theorists, schooled in the Enlightenment's insistence on observation and experimentation, could observe the ebb and flow of capitalist production and distribution. In contrast to the harsh criticisms leveled against existing institutions and old elites, the Enlightenment was on the whole approving of the independent businessman, the entrepreneur. And there was no one more approving than Adam Smith (1732–1790) whose *Wealth of Nations* (1776) became a kind of bible for those who would have capitalist activity stand as uniformly worthwhile, never to be inhibited by outside regulation.

Throughout the seventeenth century in England there had been a long tradition of economic thought and ideology that stressed independent initiative and the freedom of market forces to determine the value of money and the goods it can buy. By 1700, English economic thought was already well ahead of what could be found on the Continent, with the exception of some Dutch writings. That sophistication undoubtedly reflected the complexity of market life in cities like London and Amsterdam. One important element in seventeenth-century economic thought, as well as in the most advanced thinking on ethics, was the notion that self-interest, far from being crude or socially dangerous, was in fact a good thing, to be accepted and even encouraged. In the mid-seventeenth century, Hobbes took the view that self-interest lay at the root of political action, and by the end of the century, Locke argued that government, rather than primarily restraining the extremes of human greed and the search for power, should first reflect the interests of its citizens. By the middle of the eighteenth century, enlightened theorists all over Europe—especially in England, Scotland, and France—had decided that self-interest was the foundation of all human actions and that at every turn government should assist people in expressing their interests and thus in finding true happiness.

Of course in the area of economic life, government had for centuries regulated most aspects of the market. The classic economic theory behind such regulation was called *mercantilism*. Mercantilists believed that a constant shortage of riches—bullion, goods, whatever—existed, and that governments must so direct economic activity in their states as to compete successfully with other nations for a share of the world's scarce resources. There was also another assumption implicit in mercantilist theory: that money has a "real" value, which governments must protect. Its value is not to be determined solely by market forces.

It required enormous faith in the inherent usefulness of self-interest to assert that government should cease regulating economic activity, that the market should be allowed to be free. That doctrine of *laissez faire*—to leave the market to its own devices—was made the centerpiece of Adam Smith's massive economic study on the origins of the wealth of nations.

As a professor in Glasgow, Scotland, Smith actually went out and observed factories at work; he was one of the first theorists to see the importance of the division of labor in making possible the manufacture of more and cheaper consumer goods. Smith viewed labor as the critical factor in a capitalist economy: the value of money, or of an individual, for that matter, rested on the ability to buy labor or the by-products of labor, namely goods and services. According to *The Wealth of Nations*, "Labor is the real measure of the exchangeable value of all commodities."[14] The value of labor is in turn determined by market forces, by supply and demand. Before the invention of money or capital, labor belonged to the laborer, but in the money and market society that had evolved since the Middle Ages, labor belongs to the highest bidder.

Smith was not distressed by the apparent randomness of market forces. Beneath this superficial chaos he saw order. Just as Smith saw order in physical nature due to his understanding of the new science, he postulated the same order at work in commercial society. He used the metaphor of "the invisible hand" to explain the source of this order; by that he probably meant Newton's regulatory God, made very distant by Smith who was a deist. That hand would invisibly reconcile self-interest to the common or public interest. With that image of the invisible hand, Smith expressed his faith in the rationality of commercial society and laid the first principle for the modern science of capitalist economics. He did not mean to license the oppression of the poor and the laborer. Statements in *The Wealth of Nations* such as: "Landlords, like all other men, love to reap where they never sowed," or "Whenever there is great property, there is great inequality,"[15] reveal Smith to be a moralist. Yet he knew of no means to stop the exploitation of labor. He believed that its purchase at market value ensures the working of commercial society and assumed that the supply of cheap labor was inexhaustible.

The thought of Adam Smith includes an extreme version of two tendencies within Enlightenment thought. The first was the search for laws of society that would imitate the laws postulated by the new science. The second, which was not shared by all philosophes, was an unshakable belief in progress: "In the progress of society . . . each individual becomes more expert in his own peculiar branch, more work is done upon the whole, and the quantity of science is considerably increased by it." (*The Wealth of Nations*) Knowledge is progressive, and by implication, the human condition also yields to constant improvement. Smith ignored the appallingly low life-expectancy rates in the new factory towns, and in the process bequeathed a vision of progress wedded to capitalism that remains powerful in some quarters to this day.

ENLIGHTENED DESPOTISM

Although some of the enlightened prescriptions for the operation of modern society, such as laissez faire, remain current, one ideal commonly discussed and occasionally advocated by the philosophes has long since fallen by the wayside. It was extinguished in large measure by the democratic revolutions of the late eighteenth century. *Enlightened despotism*, although apparently a contradiction in terms, was used as a phrase by the French philosophe Diderot as early as the 1760s. Wherever this phrase is used by the philosophes, it refers to an ideal shared by many of them: the strong monarch who would imple-

ment rational reforms. He would remove obstacles to freedom and allow the laws of nature to work, particularly in trade, commerce, and book censorship.

When historians use the term *enlightened despotism*, they generally are describing the reigns of specific European monarchs and their ministers—Frederick the Great in Prussia; Catherine the Great in Russia; Charles III of Spain; Maria Theresa and, to a greater extent, her son, Joseph II, in Austria; and Louis XV of France. These eighteenth-century monarchs did institute specific reforms in education, trade, and commerce and against the clergy. This type of enlightened government must be understood in the context of the late development of these countries relative to the older nation-states of Europe. Prussia, Austria, and Russia had to move very quickly if they were to catch up to the degree of centralization achieved in England and France. And when monarchies in France and Spain also occasionally adopted techniques associated with enlightened despotism, they generally did in order to compete against a more advanced rival—for example, France against England and Spain against France.

Austria

In the course of the eighteenth century, Austria became a major state due to the reforms of Charles VI and his successors (see Chapter 16). Although Catholic and devout at home, Charles allied with Protestant Europe abroad against France. In the newly acquired Austrian Netherlands, he supported the progressive and reforming elements in the nobility which opposed the old aristocracy and clergy.

This pattern was continued by his daughter, Maria Theresa (1740–1780), and the Aus-

MAP 18.2 EUROPE, 1789 ▶

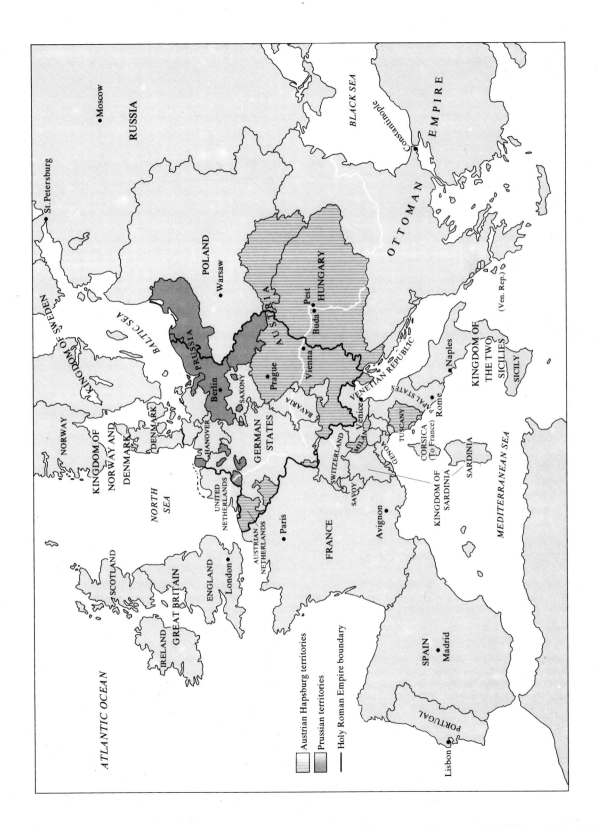

ATLANTIC OCEAN

RUSSIA
• Moscow

St. Petersburg

KINGDOM OF SWEDEN

BALTIC SEA

POLAND
• Warsaw

PRUSSIA
Berlin •

SAXONY

AUSTRIA

BLACK SEA

Constantinople •

OTTOMAN EMPIRE

Pest •
Buda • HUNGARY

Prague • Vienna •

NORWAY

KINGDOM OF NORWAY AND DENMARK

DENMARK

NORTH SEA

HANOVER

GERMAN STATES

BAVARIA

SWITZERLAND

SAVOY

UNITED NETHERLANDS

AUSTRIAN NETHERLANDS

• Paris

FRANCE

Avignon •

MILAN
Venice •
VENETIAN REPUBLIC
(Ven. Rep.)

GENOA

TUSCANY

CORSICA
(To France)

PAPAL STATES

Rome •

KINGDOM OF SARDINIA

SARDINIA

Naples •

KINGDOM OF THE TWO SICILIES

SICILY

MEDITERRANEAN SEA

SCOTLAND

IRELAND

GREAT BRITAIN

ENGLAND

London •

SPAIN
Madrid •

PORTUGAL

Lisbon •

Austrian Hapsburg territories

Prussian territories.

——— Holy Roman Empire boundary

trian administration became one of the most innovative and progressive to be found in the ancient regime. Paradoxically, many leading ministers, like the Comte du Cobenzl in the Netherlands or Gerard van Swieten, Joseph II's (Maria Theresa's son) great reforming minister, were Freemasons. This new and secret universalist religion of the eighteenth century glorified progress in the arts and the sciences, and often attracted progressive Catholics (as well as Protestants and freethinkers) who despised what they regarded as the medieval outlook of the traditional clergy.

Dynastic consolidation and warfare did contribute decisively to the creation of the Austrian state. But in the eighteenth century, the intellectual and cultural forces known as the Enlightenment enabled the state to establish an efficient system of government and a European breadth of vision, and therefore to rival (and to surpass Spain) the older, more established nation-states in Europe. Frustrated in their German territories, the Austrian Hapsburgs concentrated their attention increasingly on their eastern states. Vienna gave them a natural power base, while Catholic religiosity gradually united the ruling elites in Bohemia and Hungary with their Hapsburg kings. Hapsburg power created a nation-state in Austria, yet all efforts to consolidate the western Empire and to establish effective imperial rule met with failure. The unification of Germany would proceed very slowly and come from somewhat unexpected quarters.

Prussia

Under the most famous and enlightened Hohenzollern of the eighteenth century, Prussian absolutism (see Chapter 16) acquired some unique and resilient features. Frederick II (the Great; 1740–1786) initiated a policy of religious toleration and, in so doing, attracted French Protestant refugees, who had manufacturing and commercial skills. Intellectual dissidents, such as Voltaire, were also attracted to Prussia. Voltaire eventually went home disillusioned with this new Prussian "enlightened despotism," but not before Frederick had used him and in the process acquired a reputation for learning. By inviting various refugees from French clerical oppression, Frederick gave Berlin a minor reputation as a center for Enlightenment culture. But along with Frederick's courtship of the French philosophes with their enlightened ideals, there was the reality of Prussian militarism and the servitude of its peasants.

Yet the Hohenzollern dynasty succeeded in creating a viable state built by the labor of its serfs and the power of its Junker-controlled army, a state that managed to survive as a monarchy until the First World War. By the middle of the eighteenth century, this small nation of no more than 2.5 million inhabitants exercised inordinate influence in European affairs because of its military prowess.

In 1740, Frederick the Great was sufficiently confident of his army and resources to launch an aggressive foreign policy against neighboring states—the Austrian state of Silesia, in particular. The forces of the new Austrian queen, Maria Theresa, were powerless to resist this kind of military onslaught. In two years, Prussia had acquired what was probably the largest territory captured by any Continental European state in that era. Silesia augmented the Prussian population by 50 percent, and Frederick also acquired a relatively advanced textile manufacturing area. The Austrians never forgave his aggression. In 1756, Maria Theresa embarked on a "diplomatic revolution" and formed an alliance with France against Prussia. The ensuing Seven Years' War (1756–1763) involved every major European power, but it failed to weaken the Prussians. Indeed, by 1763, Prussian dominance in Germany was clear as was the gradual retreat of Austria from central and western German affairs.

Prussian absolutism rested on the army and the Junker class, and its economy was state-directed and financed. Its court expenses were held to a minimum—most state expenditures

went into maintaining an army of 200,000 troops, the largest in relation to population for all Europe.

Russia

Russia during the eighteenth century made significant strides toward joining the European state system under various monarchs. During the reign of Peter I (1682–1725), strong diplomatic ties were created in almost every European capital. In addition, the Russian metal industry became vital to European development. The English, who lacked the forest lands and wood necessary to fire smelting furnaces, grew dependent on Russian-produced iron.

Catherine the Great (1762–1796) consciously pursued policies intended to reflect her understanding of the Enlightenment. These presented contradictions. She entered into respectful correspondence with philosophes, but at the same time she extended serfdom to the entire Ukraine. She promulgated a new, more secular, educational system and sought at every turn to improve Russian industry, but her policies rested on the aggrandizement of the agriculturally based aristocracy. The Charter of Nobility in 1785 forever guaranteed the aristocracy's right to hold the peasants in servitude. The Enlightenment, as interpreted by this shrewd monarch, completed the tendency to monarchical absolutism that had been well underway since the sixteenth century.

The Effects of Enlightened Despotism

Insofar as the enlightened monarchs used the Enlightenment's principles to enhance the central government's power and thereby their own, it may be said that enlightened despotism existed. These eighteenth-century monarchs knew, in ways their predecessors had not known, that knowledge is power; they saw that application of learned theories to policy can produce useful results.

But did these enlightened despots try to create more humanitarian societies in which individual freedom flourished on all levels? In this area, enlightened despotism must be pronounced a shallow deployment of Enlightenment ideals. For example, Frederick the Great decreed the abolition of serfdom in Prussia, but had no means to force the aristocracy to conform because he desperately needed their support. And in the 1780s, Joseph II instituted liberalized publishing laws in Austria, until he heard of artisans reading pamphlets about the French Revolution. He quickly retreated and reimposed censorship. In the 1750s, Frederick the Great had also loosened the censorship laws, and writers were free to attack traditional religion, but they never were allowed to criticize the army, the key to Frederick's aggressive foreign policy. Catherine the Great gave Diderot a pension, but she would hear of nothing that compromised her political power, and her ministers were expected to give unquestioning service to her.

Finally, if the Enlightenment means the endorsement of reason over force, peace and cosmopolitan unity over ruthless competition, then the foreign policies of these enlightened despots were uniformly despotic. Evidence of this lies in a long series of aggressions: Frederick's invasion of Silesia in 1740, Austria's secret betrayal of the northern alliance and the ensuing Seven Years' War, the one-sided Russo-Turkish war of 1768–1774, and Austria's attempt in the 1770s to claim Bavaria. In short, the Enlightenment proved useful in providing a theory around which central and eastern European states only recently unified could organize their policies. The theory also justified centralization over the power of local elites, long grown comfortable through centuries of unopposed authority. There were no major philosophes who did not grow disillusioned with those monarchs on the rare occasions when their actions could be observed at close range. The Enlightenment did provide new principles for the organization of centralized monarchical power, but centralization and economic rationalization and management did not make their practitioners or beneficiaries any more enlightened.

THE HIGH ENLIGHTENMENT

More than any other political system in western Europe, the Old Regime in France was directly threatened by the doctrines and reforming impulse of the Enlightenment. The Catholic church was deeply entrenched in every aspect of life—landownership, control over universities and presses, and access to both the court and, through the pulpit, the people. For decades the church had brought its influence to bear against the philosophes, yet by 1750 the Enlightenment had penetrated learned circles and academies in Paris and the provinces. After 1750, censorship of the press was relaxed by a new censor deeply influenced by Enlightenment ideals. In fact, censorship had produced the opposite of the desired effect: the more irreligious and atheistic the book or manuscript was, the more attractive and sought-after it became.

By the 1740s the fashion among proponents of the Enlightenment was to seek an encyclopedic format for presenting their ideas. This form of writing partly came from Bayle's *Dictionary*; it partly was the natural by-product of the Enlightenment's desire to encompass all learning. The first successful encyclopedia was published in England by Ephraim Chambers in 1728, and before too long a plan was underway for its translation into French. A leading Freemason in France, the Chevalier Ramsay, even advocated that all the Masonic lodges in Europe should make a financial contribution to this effort, but few, if any, responded to the call.

The task of translating the encyclopedia fell to four aggressive Parisian publishers. One of them had had some shady dealings in clandestine literature and knew the more irreligious and daring philosophes in Paris, among them the young Denis Diderot (1713–1784). Out of that consortium of publishers and philosophes came the most important book of the Enlightenment, Diderot's *Encyclopedia*, published in 1751 and in succeeding years and editions. It initiated a new stage in the history of Enlightenment publishing, and brought to the forefront pantheistic and materialistic ideas that until that time only the most radical freethinkers in England and the Netherlands had openly written about. This new era is called the *High Enlightenment.* It permeated exclusive Parisian society, and it was characterized by a truly violent attack on the church's privileges and the very foundations of Christian belief. From the 1750s to 1780s, Paris became the capital of the Enlightenment. The philosophes, who had been a persecuted minority (Diderot had spent six months in jail for his philosophical and libertine writings), became cultural heroes. The *Encyclopedia* had to be read by anyone claiming to be educated.

In his preface to the *Encyclopedia*, Diderot's collaborator, Jean d'Alembert (c. 1717–1783), summed up the principles on which it had been compiled. In effect, he wrote a powerful summation of the Enlightenment's highest ideals. He also extolled Newton's science and gave a short description of its universal laws. The progress of geometry and mechanics in combination, d'Alembert wrote in his preface, "may be considered the most incontestable monument of the success to which the human mind can rise by its efforts."[16] In turn, he urged that revealed religion should be reduced to a few precepts to be practiced; religion should, he implied, be made scientific and rational. In the preface to the *Encyclopedia*, d'Alembert also praised the psychology of Locke: all that is known, is known through the senses. He added that all learning should be catalogued and made easily and readily available, that the printing press should serve the needs of Enlightenment, and that literary societies should be set up that encourage men of talent. D'Alembert added that "they should banish all inequalities that might exclude or discourage men who are endowed with talents that will enlighten others."[17]

During the High Enlightenment, reformers dwelt increasingly on the inequalities in the Old Regime that seemed to stifle men of talent. The privileges of the aristocracy and the clergy—not always talented and seldom the agitators for enlightenment and reform—seemed increasingly less rational. By the 1780s, Paris had spawned a new generation of philosophes for whom Voltaire, Diderot, and Rousseau were aged or dead heroes. But these young authors found the life of the propagandist to be poor and solitary, and they looked at society's ills from the perspective of victims rather than reformers. They gained firsthand knowledge of the injustices catalogued so brilliantly by Rousseau in *The Social Contract*.

The High Enlightenment's systematic, sustained, and occasionally violent attacks on the clergy and the irrationality of privilege link that movement with the French Revolution. The link did not lie in the comfortable heresies of the great philosophes, ensconced as they were in the fashionable Parisian salons. But it lay in the way those heresies were interpreted by a new generation of reformers, Marat and Robespierre among them, who in the early days of the Revolution used the Enlightenment as a mirror against which they reflected the evils of the old order.

THE ENLIGHTENMENT AND MODERN THOUGHT

The political philosophies of Locke, Montesquieu, and Rousseau held an entirely new and modern concept of the relationship between the state and the individual: states should exist not to accumulate power unto themselves, but to enhance human happiness. From that perspective, monarchy and even oligarchy began to seem increasingly less useful. And if happiness be a goal, then some sort of progress must be possible in history.

The Enlightenment has often been accused of advocating a blind faith in progress, but that is an oversimplification of its sophisticated sense of history. More commonly, the Enlightenment saw a struggle between instincts for happiness and benevolence and the greed of powerful leaders and entrenched elites. Occasionally the philosophes pronounced instincts for happiness to be the inevitable victors over greed—but that would occur sometime in a future order. The main point is that the philosophes insisted that people plan for that

CHRONOLOGY 18.1   THE ENLIGHTENMENT

1685	Revocation of the Edict of Nantes; persecution of Protestants in France
1687	Publication of Newton's *Principia*
1688–89	Revolution in England; weakening of the clergy's power and loosening of censorship
1690	Publication of Locke's *Second Treatise of Civil Government*
1717	Founding of the Grand Lodge, London; the beginning of organized Freemasonry
1733	Voltaire publishes *Letters Concerning the English Nation*
1740	Frederick the Great invades Silesia; the War of Austrian Succession ensues
1748	Hume publishes *An Enquiry Concerning Human Understanding*; Montesquieu publishes *The Spirit of the Laws*
1749–50	French advocates of the Enlightenment become increasingly critical of their government
1751	Publication of Diderot's *Encyclopedia* in Paris
1762	Rousseau publishes *Émile*
1768–1774	The Russo-Turkish War
1775	The American Revolution begins
1776	Adam Smith publishes *Wealth of Nations*
1785	The Russian Charter of Nobility; the servitude of the peasants is guaranteed
1789	The French Revolution begins

future victory by education, judicial reform, political maturity, and even the creation of new religions that would be more civil than godly and more interested in humanity and nature than in heaven or sectarian dogmas.

On the issue of how to achieve that future victory, the philosophes wavered. They wanted a liberal society, but they feared the masses and their potential for revolutionary action. In place of such action the philosophes offered science as the universal improver of the human condition. Faith in reform without the necessity of revolution proved to be a doctrine for the elite of the salons.

In that sense the French Revolution can be said to have repudiated the essential moderation of philosophes like Voltaire, d'Alembert, and Kant. Yet in some of its earliest literature, the Enlightenment established a vision of humanity so independent of Christianity and so focused on the needs and abuses of present society that no established institution, once grown corrupt and ineffectual, could long withstand its penetrating critique. The Enlightenment speaks only to the world of people in society; it renders the systems of theologians and the inherited privileges of the untalented irrelevant to the pressing matters of knowledge, education, and reform.

Notes

1. "An Answer to the Question: 'What Is Enlightenment?'" in Hans Reiss, ed., *Kant's Political Writings* (Cambridge, England: Cambridge University Press, 1970), pp. 54–60.
2. Pierre Bayle, *Historical and Critical Dictionary*, Richard H. Popkin, ed. (New York: Bobbs-Merrill, 1965), p. 195.
3. Thomas Hobbes, *Leviathan*, C. B. Macpherson, ed. (Harmondsworth, England: Penguin Books, 1977), p. 189.
4. Ibid., p. 174.
5. Jean Jacques Rousseau, *The Social Contract and Discourses* (New York: Dutton, 1950), pp. 3, 9.
6. Quoted in Franco Venturi, *Utopia and Reform in the Enlightenment* (Cambridge, England: Cambridge University Press, 1971), p. 101.
7. Voltaire, *Philosophical Dictionary*, Theodore Besterman, ed. (Harmondsworth, England: Penguin, 1974), p. 183.
8. Quoted in David B. Davis, *The Problem of Slavery in Western Culture* (Harmondsworth, England: Penguin, 1970), p. 449.
9. Quoted in Rosemary Agonito, ed., *History of Ideas on Women: A Source Book* (New York: G. P. Putnam's Sons, 1977), p. 101.
10. Ibid., p. 118.
11. Ibid., p. 124.
12. Ibid., p. 130.
13. Ibid., pp. 154–155.
14. Excerpted from Adam Smith, *The Wealth of Nations*, George Stigler, ed. (New York: Appleton, 1957), p. 3.
15. Ibid., p. 38.
16. Jean Le Rond d'Alembert, *Preliminary Discourse to the Encyclopedia of Diderot*, trans. by Richard N. Schwab (New York: Bobbs-Merrill, 1963), p. 22.
17. Ibid., pp. 101–102.

Suggested Reading

Anderson, M. S., *Europe in the Eighteenth Century, 1713–1783* (1961). A good general survey of the century with excellent chapters on cultural and intellectual life.

Becker, Carl, *The Heavenly City of the Eighteenth-Century Philosophers* (1932). Still a provocative assessment of the Enlightenment's relation to Christianity.

Cassirer, Ernst, *The Philosophy of the Enlightenment* (1951). A classic and basic account of Enlightenment philosophy; difficult reading.

Goldmann, Lucien, *The Philosophy of the Enlightenment: The Christian Burgess and the Enlightenment* (1968). Intended as a corrective to Cassirer, by a prominent European Marxist historian.

Hazard, Paul, *The European Mind, 1680–1715* (1963). Indispensable for the early period of the Enlightenment.

Hirschman, Albert O., *The Passions and the Interests: Political Arguments for Capitalism Before Its Triumph* (1977). Focuses on economic thought just prior to and during the Enlightenment.

Jacob, Margaret, *The Radical Enlightenment: Pantheists, Freemasons and Republicans*

(1980). A study of the radical materialists and their contribution to the Enlightenment, especially in the first half of the century.

Venturi, Franco, *Utopia and Reform in the Enlightenment* (1971). A difficult but rewarding book, focussed on the more extreme reformers of the age.

Wangermann, Ernst, *The Austrian Achievement, 1700–1800* (1973). An excellent case study of the strengths and weaknesses of the most enlightened of European monarchies.

Review Questions

1. How do skepticism, deism, and materialism differ?

2. Define a *philosophe* and briefly discuss the writings of two of the major philosophes.

3. Where did the Enlightenment begin? How did it spread?

4. Why was Freemasonry important in the eighteenth century?

5. What are the major characteristics of enlightened political thought? Did enlightened despotism fulfill those characteristics?

6. How did the enlightened philosophes come to terms with the status of slaves, criminals, and women?

7. The philosophes approved of capitalism. Defend or refute this statement.

8. What made the High Enlightenment different from what went before it? Describe how it differed.

9. The Enlightenment was a cause of the French Revolution. Defend or refute this statement.

10. Why were the major philosophes so reluctant to call for revolutionary action to correct existing abuses?

PART IV

Modern Europe:
From Certainty to Doubt
1789–1914

CHAPTER 19

The French Revolution:
Affirmation of Liberty
and Equality

THE OUTBREAK of the French Revolution in 1789 stirred the imagination of Europeans. Both participants and observers sensed that they were living in a pivotal age. On the ruins of the Old Order founded on privilege and despotism, a new era was forming that promised to realize the ideals of the Enlightenment. These ideals included the emancipation of the human personality from superstition and tradition, the triumph of liberty over tyranny, the refashioning of institutions in accordance with reason and justice, and the tearing down of barriers to equality. It seemed that the natural rights of the individual, hitherto a distant ideal, would now reign on earth, ending centuries of oppression and misery. Never before had people shown such confidence in the power of human intelligence to shape the conditions of existence. Never before had the future seemed so full of hope.

This lofty vision kindled emotions akin to religious enthusiasm and attracted converts throughout the Western world. "If we succeed," wrote the French poet André Chénier, "the destiny of Europe will be changed. Men will regain their rights and the people their sovereignty."[1] The editor of the Viennese publication *Wiener Zeitung* wrote to a friend: "In France a light is beginning to shine which will benefit the whole of humanity."[2] British reformer John Cartwright expressed the hopes of reformers everywhere: "Degenerate must be that heart which expands not with sentiments of delight at what is now transacting in . . . France. The French . . . are not only asserting their own rights, but they are asserting and advancing the general liberties of mankind."[3]

THE OLD REGIME

The causes of the French Revolution reach back into the aristocratic structure of society in the Old Regime. Eighteenth-century French society was divided into three orders, or Estates: the clergy constituted the First Estate; the nobility the Second Estate; and everyone else (about 96 percent of the population) belonged to the Third Estate. The clergy and nobility, totaling about 400,000 out of a population of 26 million, enjoyed special privileges. The semifeudal social structure of the Old Regime, based on inequalities sanctioned by law, produced the tensions that precipitated the Revolution.

The First Estate

The powers and privileges of the French Catholic church made it a state within a state. As it had done for centuries, the church registered births, marriages, and deaths; collected tithes (a tax on products from the soil); censored books considered dangerous to religion and morals; operated schools; and distributed relief to the poor. Since it was illegal for Protestants to assemble together for prayer, the Catholic church enjoyed a monopoly on public worship. Although it owned an estimated 10 percent of the land, which brought in an immense revenue, the church paid no taxes. Instead it made a "free gift" to the state—the church determined the amount—which was always smaller than direct taxes would have been. Critics denounced the church for promoting superstition and obscurantism, for impeding reforms, and for being more concerned with wealth and power than with the spiritual message of Jesus.

The clergy reflected the social divisions in France. The upper clergy shared the attitudes and way of life of the nobility from which they sprang. The parish priests, commoners by birth, resented the haughtiness and luxurious living of the upper clergy. In 1789, when the Revolution began, many priests sympathized with the reform-minded people of the Third Estate.

The Second Estate

Like the clergy, the nobility was a privileged order. Nobles held the highest positions in the church, army, and government. They were exempt from most taxes, collected manorial dues from peasants, and owned approximately 20 percent of the land. All nobles were not equal, however. There were gradations of dignity among the 200,000 to 250,000 members of the nobility.

Enjoying the most prestige were *nobles of the race*—families who could trace their aristocratic status back to time immemorial. (Of these, many were officers in the king's army and were called *nobles of the sword*.) The highest of the ancient nobles were engaged in the social whirl at Versailles and Paris, receiving pensions and sinecures from the king but performing few useful services for the state. Most nobles of the race, unable to afford the gilded life at court, remained on their provincial estates, the poorest of them barely distinguishable from prosperous peasants.

Alongside this ancient nobility, a new nobility had arisen, created by the monarchy. In order to obtain money, reward favorites, and weaken the old nobility, French kings had sold titles of nobility to members of the bourgeoisie and had conferred noble status on certain government offices bought by wealthy members of the bourgeoisie. Particularly significant were the *nobles of the robe*, whose ranks included many former bourgeois who had purchased judicial offices in the *parlements*, the high law courts. In the late eighteenth century the nobles of the robe championed the cause of aristocratic privilege.

Determined not to share his power and fearful of threats to the throne, Louis XIV (1643–1715) had allowed the nobility social prestige, but denied it a voice in formulating high policy. In the eighteenth century, nobles sought to regain the power that they had lost under Louis XIV. This resurgence of the nobility was led not by regenerated ancient aristocrats, but by the new nobility, the nobles of the robe. The parlements became obstreperous critics of royal policy and opponents of reform that threatened aristocratic and provincial privileges. This "feudal reaction" triggered the Revolution.

The Third Estate

The Third Estate was composed of the bourgeoisie, peasants, and urban laborers. While the bourgeoisie provided the leadership for the Revolution, its success depended on the support given by the rest of the Third Estate.

The Bourgeoisie

The bourgeoisie consisted of merchant-manufacturers, wholesale merchants, bankers, master craftsmen, doctors, lawyers, intellectuals, and government officials below the top ranks. Though the bourgeois had wealth, they lacked social prestige. A merchant, despite his worldly success, felt that his occupation denied him the dignity enjoyed by the nobility. "There are few rich people who at times do not feel humiliated at being nothing but wealthy," observed an eighteenth-century Frenchman.[4]

Influenced by the aristocratic values of the day, the bourgeoisie sought to erase the stigma of common birth by obtaining the most esteemed positions in the nation and by entering the ranks of the nobility, whose style of life they envied. Traditionally, some bourgeoisie had risen socially either by purchasing a judicial or political office that carried with it a title of nobility, or by gaining admission to the upper clergy and the officer ranks of the army. As long as these avenues of upward social mobility remained open, the bourgeoisie did not challenge the existing social structure, including the special privileges of the nobility.

But in the last part of the eighteenth century it became increasingly difficult for the bourgeois to gain the most honored offices in the land. The nobles, seeking to increase their power at the expense of the king and to protect their status from the encroachments of the bourgeoisie, closed their ranks to outsiders and monopolized the high positions. By 1788 not a single commoner headed a diocese or held a top rank in the army, and only one served as a minister to the king. This hardening of the class structure denied the bourgeois opportunities for social dignity, despite their education, wealth, talent, and ambition. Finding the road blocked in every direction, the bourgeois came to resent a social system that valued birth more than talent. Envy of the nobility turned to hatred; instead of aspiring to acquire noble status, the bourgeois, by 1789, sought to abolish the privileges of birth and to open careers to talent.

Practical considerations of social prestige and economic gain, however, do not alone explain the revolutionary mentality of the bourgeoisie. When they challenged the Old Regime, the bourgeois felt that they were fulfilling the ideals of the philosophes and serving all humanity. This idealism would inspire sacrifice and heroism.

By 1789 the bourgeois had many grievances. They wanted all positions in church, army, and state open to men of talent regardless of birth. They sought a parliament; a constitution that would limit the king's power and guarantee freedom of thought, a fair trial, and religious toleration; and administrative reforms that would eliminate waste, inefficiency, and interference with business. In effect, the bourgeois aspired to political power and social prestige in proportion to their economic power. Because the bourgeois were the principal leaders and chief beneficiaries of the French Revolution, historians view it, along with the English revolutions of the seventeenth century and the growth of capitalism, as "an episode in the general rise of the bourgeoisie."[5]

The Peasantry

The condition of the more than 21 million French peasants was a paradox. On the one hand, they were better off than peasants in Austria, Prussia, Poland, and Russia, where serfdom still predominated. In France, serfdom had largely disappeared; many peasants owned their own land, and some were even prosperous. On the other hand, most French peasants lived in poverty, which worsened in the closing years of the Old Regime.

Peasants owned between 30 and 40 percent of the land, but the typical holding was barely large enough to eke out a living. The rising birthrate (between 1715 and 1789 the population may have increased from 18 million to 26 million) led to the continual subdivision of farms among heirs. Moreover, many peasants did not own their own land but rented it from a nobleman or a prosperous neighbor. Others, too poor to own oxen, worked as sharecroppers, turning over to their creditors a considerable share of the harvest.

Unable to survive on their small holdings, many peasants tried to supplement their incomes. They hired themselves out for whatever employment was available in their region—agricultural day laborers, charcoal burners, transporters of wine, or textile workers in their own homes. Landless peasants tried to earn a living in such ways. The increasing birthrate resulted in an overabundance of rural wage earners. This worsened the plight of small landowners and reduced the landless to beggary. "The number of our children reduces us to desperation,"[6] was a common complaint of the peasants by 1789.

An unjust and corrupt system of taxation weighed heavily on the peasantry. Louis XIV had maintained his grandeur and financed his wars by milking ever more taxes from the peasants, a practice that continued throughout the eighteenth century. An army of tax collectors victimized the peasantry. In addition to royal taxes, peasants paid the tithe to the church and manorial dues to lords.

Although serfdom had ended in most parts of France, lords continued to demand obligations from peasants as they had done in the Middle Ages. In addition to performing labor services on the lord's estate, peasants still had to grind their corn in the lord's mill, bake their bread in his oven, press their grapes in his winepress, and give the lord part of the produce in payment. In addition, the lord collected a land rent from peasant proprietors, levied dues on goods at markets and fairs, and exercised exclusive hunting rights on lands tilled by peasants. The last was a particularly onerous right, for the lord's hunting parties damaged crops. Lords were determined to hold on to these privileges not only because of the income they brought, but because they were symbols of authority and social esteem. The peasants, on the other hand, regarded these obligations as odious anachronisms from the Middle Ages from which they derived no benefit.

In the last part of the eighteenth century, lords sought to exact more income from their lands by reviving manorial dues that had not been collected for generations, by increasing the rates on existing dues, and by contracting businessmen to collect payments from the peasants. These capitalists naturally tried to squeeze as much income as possible from the peasants, making the whole system of manorial obligations more hateful to them.

Inefficient farming methods also contributed to the poverty of the French peasants. In the eighteenth century, France did not experience a series of agricultural improvements comparable to those in England. Failure to invest capital in modernizing agricultural methods meant low yields per acre and a shortage of farm animals.

A rise in the price of necessities during the closing decades of the Old Regime worked hardship on those peasants who depended on wages for survival. With prices rising faster than wages, only the more prosperous peasants with produce to sell benefited. The great majority of peasants were driven deeper into poverty, and the number of beggars roaming the countryside increased.

A poor harvest in 1788–89 aggravated peasant misery and produced an atmosphere of crisis. The granaries were empty; the price of bread, the staple food of the French, soared; and starvation threatened. Hatred of the manorial order and worsening poverty sparked a spontaneous and autonomous peasant revolution in 1789.

Urban Laborers

The urban laboring class in this preindustrial age consisted of journeymen working for master craftsmen, factory workers in small-scale industries, and wage earners, such as day laborers, gardeners, handimen, deliverymen, who were paid by those they served. The poverty of the urban poor, like that of the peasant wage earners, had worsened in the late eighteenth century. From 1785 to 1789 the cost of living increased by 62 percent, while wages rose only 22 percent. For virtually the entire decade of the Revolution, urban workers struggled to keep body and soul together in the face of food shortages and rising prices, particularly the price of their staple food, bread. Material want drove the urban poor to acts of violence that affected the course of the Revolution.

Inefficient Administration and Financial Disorder

The administration of France was complex, confusing, and ineffective. The practice of buying state offices from the king, introduced as a means of raising money, resulted in many incompetent officeholders. "When his Majesty created an office," stated one administrator, "Providence called into being an imbecile to buy it."[7] Tariffs on goods shipped from one province to another and differing systems of weights and measures hampered trade. No single law code applied to all the provinces; instead, there were overlapping and conflicting law systems based on old Roman law or customary feudal law, which made the administration of justice slow, arbitrary, and unjust. To admirers of the philosophes, the administrative system was an insult to reason. The Revolution would sweep the system away.

Financial disorders also contributed to the weakness of the Old Regime. In the last years of the Old Regime the government could not raise sufficient funds to cover expenses. By 1787, it was still paying off the enormous debt incurred during the wars of Louis XIV. The costs of succeeding wars during the eighteenth century, particularly France's aid to the colonists in the American Revolution, increased the debt considerably. The king's gifts and pensions to court nobles and the extravagant court life further drained the treasury.

Finances were in a shambles not because France was impoverished, but because of an inefficient and unjust tax system. Few wealthy Frenchmen, including the bourgeois, paid their fair share of taxes. Because tax income came chiefly from the peasants, it was bound to be inadequate. Indirect taxes on consumer goods and excise duties yielded much-needed revenue in the last decades of the Old Regime. These additional funds, however, instead of replenishing the royal treasury, were pocketed by rich tax collectors who, for a fixed payment to the state, had obtained the right to collect these indirect taxes. The financial crisis, although serious, was solvable if the clergy, nobility, and bourgeoisie would pay their fair share of taxes. King Louis XVI (1774–1792) recognized the need for tax reform, but his efforts were resisted by nobles who clung tenaciously to their ancient privileges.

Mainly through the parlements, the high courts of justice, the nobles were able to thwart royal will. Many parlementaires were originally wealthy bourgeois who had purchased their offices from the state (nobles of the robe). Both the office and status of nobility remained within the family. The Paris parle-

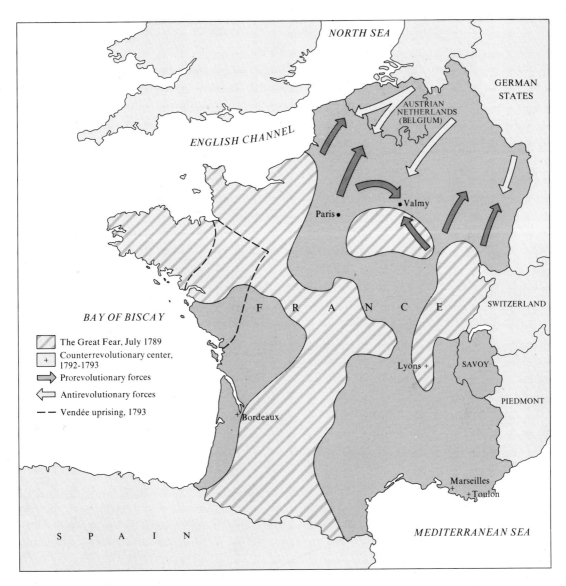

NORTH SEA

GERMAN STATES

ENGLISH CHANNEL

AUSTRIAN NETHERLANDS (BELGIUM)

Valmy

Paris

BAY OF BISCAY

F   R   A   N   C   E

SWITZERLAND

The Great Fear, July 1789

Counterrevolutionary center, 1792-1793

Prorevolutionary forces

Antirevolutionary forces

Vendée uprising, 1793

Lyons

SAVOY

PIEDMONT

Bordeaux

Marseilles

Toulon

S   P   A   I   N

MEDITERRANEAN SEA

MAP 19.1   THE FRENCH REVOLUTION, 1789–1793

ment and twelve provincial parlements reviewed the judgments of lower courts and registered royal edicts. The parlements had the right to *remonstrate*, that is, to pass judgment on the legality of royal edicts before registering them. If the courts considered the king's new laws at variance with previous legislation or ancient traditions, they would refuse to register them. The king could revise the edicts in accordance with the parlements' instructions, or force their registration by means of a *lit de justice*—a solemn ceremony in which the monarch appeared before the court. If the parlementaires persisted in their resistance, the king might order the arrest of their leaders. While the king could force his will on the parlements, their bold opposition embarrassed royal prestige.

With France on the brink of bankruptcy, the king's ministers proposed that the nobility and church surrender some of their tax privileges. The parlements, steadfast defenders of noble prerogative, protested and remonstrated, and the church insisted on the immunity of its property from taxation. Throughout the nation, members of the privileged orders united in their determination to preserve their social exclusiveness.

The resistance of the nobility forced the government in July 1788 to call for a meeting of the Estates General—a medieval representative assembly that had last met in 1614—in order to deal with the financial crisis. It was to convene in May 1789. Certain that they would dominate the Estates General, the nobles intended to weaken the power of the throne, protect their social status, and prevent the bourgeoisie from entering their ranks. Once in control of the government, they would introduce financial reforms. But the revolt of the nobility against the Crown had unexpected consequences; it opened the way for revolutions by the Third Estate that destroyed the Old Regime and with it the aristocracy and its privileges.

THE MODERATE STAGE, 1789–1791

The Clash Between the Nobility and the Third Estate

Frenchmen in great numbers went to the polls to elect deputies to the Estates General. Churchmen and nobles voted directly for their representatives. Most deputies of the clergy were parish priests, many of them sympathetic to reform. Though the majority of deputies of the Second Estate were conservative country nobles, there was a sizable liberal minority, including some who had fought in the American Revolution, that favored reform. The representatives from the Third Estate were elected indirectly with virtually all taxpaying males over age twenty-five eligible to vote. The delegates of the Third Estate consisted predominantly of bourgeois drawn from the professions, including many articulate lawyers.

Each Estate drew up lists of grievances and suggestions (cahiers de doleances). The cahiers from all three orders expressed loyalty to monarchy and church, recognized the sanctity of property rights, and called for a written constitution and an elected assembly. The cahiers drawn up by the bourgeoisie stressed guarantees of personal liberty; the cahiers of the nobility predictably insisted on the preservation of manorial rights and honorific privileges.

As the Estates General prepared to meet, reform-minded Frenchmen held great hopes for the regeneration of France and the advancement of liberty. But immediately it became clear that the hopes of reformers clashed with the intentions of the aristocracy. What had started as a struggle between the Crown and the aristocracy was turning into something far more significant, a conflict between the two privileged orders on one side and the Third Estate on the other. One pamphleteer, Abbé Sieyès (1748–1836), expressed the hatred the bourgeoisie held for the aristocracy. "The privileged order has said to the Third Estate: 'Whatever be your services, whatever be your talents, you shall go thus far and no farther. It is not fitting that you be honored.'" The higher positions in the land, said Sieyès, should be the "reward for talents," not the prerogative of birth. Without the Third Estate, "nothing can progress"; without the nobility, "everything would proceed infinitely better."[8]

APPROVAL OF THE TENNIS COURT OATH On June 17, 1789, the Third Estate declared itself the National Assembly. On June 20, they met on a nearby tennis court when they found their customary meeting hall locked. They vowed not to disband until a constitution had been drawn up for the entire nation. In this painting by Jacques Louis David, aristocrat, clergyman, and commoner embrace before a cheering National Assembly. (Courtesy National Museums of France)

Formation of the National Assembly

The Estates General convened at Versailles on May 5, 1789, but was stalemated by the question of procedure. Seeking to control the Estates General, the nobility insisted that the three Estates follow the traditional practice of meeting separately and voting by order. Since the two privileged orders were likely to stand together, the Third Estate would always be outvoted, two to one. But the delegates from the Third Estate, unwilling to allow the nobility and the higher clergy to dominate the Estates General, proposed instead that the three Estates meet as one body and vote by head. There were some 610 delegates from the Third Estate; the nobility and clergy together had an equivalent number. Since the Third Estate could rely on the support of sympathetic parish priests and liberal nobles, it would be assured a majority if all orders met together. The privileged orders therefore opposed deliberating with the common people of the Third Estate.

On June 10, the Third Estate broke the stalemate. It invited the clergy and nobility to join with it in a common assembly; if they refused, the Third Estate would go ahead without them. A handful of priests answered the roll call, but not one noble. On June 17, the Third Estate made a revolutionary move. It declared itself the National Assembly. On June 20, locked out of their customary meeting hall (apparently by accident), the Third Estate delegates moved to a nearby tennis court and took a solemn oath not to disband until a constitution had been drawn up for France. By these acts the bourgeois delegates had demonstrated their desire and determination to reform the state.

Louis XVI commanded the National Assembly to separate into orders, but the Third Estate held firm. The steadfastness of the delegates and the menacing actions of Parisians who supported the National Assembly forced Louis XVI to yield. On June 27 he ordered the nobility (some had already done so) and the clergy (a majority had already done so) to join with the Third Estate in the National Assembly. The Third Estate had successfully challenged the nobility and defied the king. It would use the National Assembly to institute reforms, including the drawing up of a constitution that limited the king's power.

But the victory of the bourgeoisie was not yet secure, for most nobles had not resigned themselves to a bourgeois-dominated National Assembly. Recognizing that France was on the threshold of a social revolution that threatened their status, the nobles, reversing their position of previous years, joined with the king in an effort to crush the National Assembly. Louis XVI, influenced by his wife, Queen Marie Antoinette, his brother Count Artois, and court aristocrats, ordered special foreign regiments to the outskirts of Paris and Versailles and replaced Necker, a reform-minded minister, with a nominee of the queen. It appeared that Louis XVI, overcoming his usual hesitancy and vacillation, had resolved to use force against the National Assembly and to stop the incipient bourgeois revolution. At this point, uprisings by the common people of Paris and peasants in the countryside saved the National Assembly and ensured the victory of the bourgeoisie.

Storming of the Bastille

In July 1789, the level of tension in Paris was high for three reasons. First, the calling of the Estates General had aroused hopes for reform. Second, the price of bread was soaring: in August 1788, a Parisian laborer had spent 50 percent of his income on bread; by July 1789 he was spending 80 percent. A third element in the tension was the fear of an aristocratic plot to crush the National Assembly. Fearful that royal troops would bombard and pillage the city, Parisians searched for weapons.

On July 14, eight hundred to nine hundred Parisians gathered in front of the Bastille, a fortress used as a prison and a despised symbol of royal despotism. They gathered primarily to obtain gunpowder and to remove the cannon that threatened a heavily populated working-class district. Fearing an attack, the governor of the Bastille, de Launay, ordered his men to fire into the crowd; they killed ninety-eight and wounded seventy-three of the people. When the tables were turned and five cannons were aimed on the main gate of the Bastille, de Launay surrendered. Although promised that no harm would come to him, de Launay and five of his men were killed, and their heads, placed on pikes, were paraded through the city.

Historians hostile to the French Revolution have long depicted the besiegers of the Bastille as a destructive mob composed of the dregs of society—smugglers, beggars, bandits, degenerates. However, recent scholarship[9] reveals that

ENGRAVING OF BASTILLE DAY About 900 Parisians gathered on July 14, 1789, in front of the Bastille to obtain gunpowder and remove a cannon threatening a populated working-class district. When fired upon, they attacked the ancient fortress and put its commander and five of his men to death. A hated symbol of absolutism had fallen to the Revolution. (Brown Brothers)

the Bastille crowd was not drawn from the criminal elements, but consisted almost entirely of small tradesmen, artisans, and wage earners—concerned citizens driven by hunger, fear of an aristocratic conspiracy, and hopes for reform.

The fall of the Bastille had far-reaching consequences: a symbol of the Old Regime had fallen; some court nobles hostile to the Revolution decided to flee the country; the frightened king told the National Assembly that he would withdraw the troops ringing Paris. The revolutionary act of the Parisians had indirectly saved the National Assembly and with it the bourgeois revolution.

The Great Fear

The uprising of the Parisians strengthened the hand of the bourgeoisie in the National Assembly. Revolution in the countryside also served the interests of the bourgeoisie. The economic crisis of 1788–89 had worsened conditions for the peasantry; the price of bread soared and the number of hungry beggars wandering the roads spreading terror multiplied. Also contributing to this revolutionary mentality were the great expectations unleashed by the summoning of the Estates General, for, like the urban poor, the peasants hoped that their grievances would be remedied. In the spring of 1789, peasants were attacking food convoys and refusing to pay royal taxes, tithes, and manorial dues. These revolutionary outbreaks intensified at the end of July 1789 as rumors spread that aristocrats were organizing bands of brigands to attack the peasants and steal their crops. Inflamed by hunger and fear, stimulated by the uprising of the Parisians, and suspicious of an aristocratic plot to thwart efforts at reform, the peasants in some regions panicked. When the mythical army of brigands did not materialize, the peasants let loose centuries of stored-up hatred against the nobles, raiding the chateaux, and burning manorial registers on which were inscribed their obligations to the lords.

Known as the Great Fear, this peasant upheaval in late July 1789, like the insurrection in Paris, worked to the advantage of the bourgeoisie. It provided the National Assembly with an opportunity to strike at noble privileges by putting into law what the peasants had accomplished with the torch—the destruction of feudal remnants. On the night of August 4, 1789, the National Assembly resolved that the nobles must surrender their special privileges—exclusive hunting rights, tax exemptions, monopoly of highest offices, manorial courts, and the right to demand labor services from peasants. The Assembly maintained that "the feudal regime had been utterly destroyed."*

*This was not entirely true. Some peasant obligations were abolished outright. However, for being released from other specified obligations, peasants were required to compensate their former lords. The peasants simply refused to pay, and in 1793 the Jacobins, recognizing reality, declared the remaining debt null and void.

In the decrees of August 5 and 11, the National Assembly implemented the resolutions of August 4. The National Assembly also declared that the planned constitution should be prefaced by a declaration of rights. On August 26, it adopted the Declaration of the Rights of Man and Citizen. The August Decrees and the Declaration of Rights marked the death of the Old Regime.

October Days

Louis XVI, cool to these reforms, postponed his approval of the August Decrees. It would require a second uprising by the Parisians to force the king to agree to the reform and to nail down the victory of the bourgeoisie.

On October 5, 1789, Parisian housewives marched twelve miles to Versailles to protest the lack of bread to the National Assembly and the king. A few hours later, 20,000 Paris Guard, sympathetic to the Revolution, also set out for Versailles in support of the women protesters. The king had no choice but to promise bread and to return with the demonstrators to Paris. Two weeks later the National Assembly abandoned Versailles for Paris.

Once again the "little people" had aided the bourgeoisie. Louis XVI, aware that he had no control over the Parisians and fearful of further violence, approved the August 4 Decrees and the Declaration of the Rights of Man and Citizen. Nobles who had urged the king to use force against the Assembly and had tried to block reforms fled the country in large numbers.

Reforms of the National Assembly

With resistance enfeebled, the National Assembly continued the work of reform begun in the summer of 1789. By abolishing the special privileges of the nobility and the clergy and promoting the interests of the bourgeoisie, the reforms of the National Assembly destroyed the Old Regime.

1. *Abolition of special privileges.* By ending the special privileges of the nobility and the clergy in the August 4 Decrees, the National Assembly pronounced the equality that the bourgeoisie had demanded. The aristocratic structure of the Old Regime, a remnant of the Middle Ages that had hindered the progressive bourgeoisie, had been eliminated.

2. *Statement of human rights.* The Declaration of the Rights of Man and Citizen expressed the liberal and universal goals of the philosophes and the particular interests of the bourgeoisie. To contemporaries it was a refutation of the Old Regime, a statement of ideals that, if realized, would end longstanding abuses and usher in a new society. In proclaiming the inalienable right to liberty of person and thought and to equal treatment under the law, the Declaration affirmed the dignity of human personality; it asserted that government belonged not to any ruler but to the people as a whole, and that its aim was the preservation of the natural rights of the individual. Because the Declaration stood in sharp contrast to the principles espoused by an intolerant clergy, a privileged aristocracy, and a despotic monarch, it has been called the death warrant of the Old Regime.

The Declaration expressed the view of the philosophes that people need not resign themselves to the abuses and misfortunes of human existence, but through reason, they could improve society. But in 1789 the Declaration was only a statement of intent; it remained to be seen whether its principles would be achieved.

3. *Subordination of church to state.* The National Assembly also struck at the privileges of the Roman Catholic church. The August 4 Decrees declared the end of tithes. To obtain badly needed funds, the Assembly in November 1789 confiscated church lands and put them up for sale. In 1790 the Assembly passed the Civil Constitution of the Clergy, which altered the boundaries of the dioceses, reduc-ing the number of bishops and priests, and transformed the clergy into government officials elected by the people and paid by the state. Almost all bishops and many priests opposed the Civil Constitution.

One reason was that reorganization deprived a sizable number of clergymen of their positions. Moreover, Protestants and nonbelievers could, in theory, participate in the election of Catholic clergy. In addition, the Assembly had issued the decree without consulting the pope or the French clergy as a body. When the Assembly required the clergy to take an oath that they would uphold the Civil Constitution, only about one-half would do so, and many believing Catholics supported the dissenting clergy. The Civil Constitution divided the French and gave opponents of the Revolution an emotional issue around which to rally supporters.

4. *Constitution for France.* In September 1791 the National Assembly achieved the goal at which it had been aiming since June 1789: a constitution limiting the power of the king and guaranteeing all Frenchmen equal treatment under the law. Citizens paying less than a specified amount in taxes could not vote. Probably about 30 percent of the males over age twenty-five were excluded by this stipulation, and only the more well-to-do citizens qualified to sit in the Legislative Assembly, a unicameral parliament that would succeed the National Assembly. Despite this restriction, suffrage requirements under the Constitution of 1791 were far more generous than in Britain.

5. *Administrative and judicial reforms.* The National Assembly aimed to reform the chaotic administrative system of France. It replaced the patchwork of provincial units with eighty-three new administrative units, or departments, approximately equal in size. The departments and their subdivisions were allowed a large measure of self-government.

Judicial reforms complemented the administrative changes. A standardized system of courts replaced the innumerable jurisdictions of the Old Regime, and the sale of judicial offices was ended. All judges were selected

JACQUES LOUIS DAVID (1748-1825): A WOMAN OF THE
REVOLUTION Although David portrayed royalty and
would go on to glorify Napoleon, he captured here
the obdurate woman of the Revolution. Driven by
hunger, she would demand bread and march twelve
miles to Versailles to state her case before National
Assembly and king on October 5, 1789. She would
favor social reforms and condone terror in order to
achieve the goals of the Revolution. (Museé des
Beaux-Arts, Lyons)

lished a uniform system of weights and measures, eliminated the guilds (medieval survivals
that blocked business expansion), and forbade
workingmen to form unions or to strike.

By ending absolutism, striking at the privileges of the nobility, and preventing the mass
of people from gaining control over the government, the National Assembly consolidated
the rule of the bourgeoisie. With one arm, it
broke the power of aristocracy and throne;
with the other, it held back the common
people. While the reforms benefited the bourgeoisie, it would be a mistake to view them
merely as a selfish expression of bourgeois
interests. The Declaration of the Rights of
Man was addressed to all and proclaimed
liberty and equality as the right of all and
called for citizens to treat each other with
respect. Both French and foreign intellectuals
believed that the Revolution would lead ultimately to the emancipation of humanity.
"The men of 1789," says Lefebvre, "thought of
liberty and equality as the common birthright
of mankind."[10] These ideals became the core
of the liberal-democratic credo that spread
throughout much of the West in the nineteenth century.

THE RADICAL STAGE, 1792–1794

The Sans-Culottes

Pleased with their accomplishments—equality before the law, careers open to talent, a
written constitution, parliamentary government—the bourgeoisie wished the Revolution
to go no further. But revolutionary times are
unpredictable. Soon the Revolution moved in
a direction neither anticipated nor desired by
the bourgeoisie, who had gained the ascendancy in this first and moderate stage of the
Revolution. A counterrevolution, led by irrec-

from graduate lawyers, and all courts based
their decisions on uniform law codes. In the
penal code completed by the National Assembly, torture and barbarous punishments were
abolished.

6. *Aid for business.* The National Assembly
abolished all tolls and duties on goods transported within the country, maintained a tariff
to protect French manufacturers, and insisted
that French colonies trade only with the
mother country. The Assembly also estab-

oncilable nobles and alienated churchmen and supported by socially unprogressive and strongly Catholic peasants, began to threaten the changes made by the Revolution, forcing the revolutionary leadership to resort to extreme measures.

Also propelling the Revolution in the direction of radicalism was the discontent of the *sans-culottes*—small shopkeepers, artisans, and wage earners. Although they had played a significant role in the Revolution, particularly in the storming of the Bastille and the October Days, they had gained little. The sans-culottes, says French historian Albert Soboul, "began to realize that a privilege of wealth was taking the place of a privilege of birth. They foresaw that the bourgeoisie would succeed the fallen aristocracy as the ruling class."[11] Inflamed by poverty and their hatred of the rich, the sans-culottes insisted that it was the government's duty to guarantee them the "right of existence," a policy that ran counter to the economic individualism of the bourgeoisie. They also demanded that the government increase wages, set price controls on food supplies, end food shortages, punish food speculators and profiteers, and deal severely with counterrevolutionaries.

Though most sans-culottes upheld the principle of private property, they wanted laws to prevent extremes of wealth and poverty. "A State is on the verge of ruin when you find extreme poverty and abundant wealth existing side by side," said a sans-culotte spokesman.[12] Socially, their ideal was a nation of small shopkeepers and small farmers. "No one should own more than one workshop or one store," read a sans-culotte petition.[13] Whereas the men of 1789 sought equality of rights, liberties, and opportunities, the sans-culottes expanded the principle of equality to include a narrowing of the gap between rich and poor. Politically, they favored a democratic republic in which the common man had a voice.

In 1789 the bourgeois had demanded equality with the aristocrats—the right to hold the most honored position in the nation and an end to the special privileges of the nobility. By the end of 1792 the sans-culottes were demanding equality with the bourgeois—political reforms that would give the poor a voice in the government and social reforms that would improve their lot.

Despite the pressures exerted by reactionary nobles and clergy on the one hand and discontented sans-culottes on the other, the Revolution might not have taken a radical turn had France remained at peace. The war that broke out with Austria and Prussia in April 1792 exacerbated internal dissensions, worsened economic conditions, and threatened to undo the reforms of the Revolution. It was under these circumstances that the Revolution moved from a moderate into a radical stage that historians refer to as the Second French Revolution.

Foreign Invasion

In June 1791, Louis XVI and the royal family, traveling in disguise, fled Paris for the northeast of France to join with *émigrés* (nobles who had left revolutionary France and were organizing a counterrevolutionary army) and to rally foreign support against the Revolution. Discovered at Varennes by a village postmaster, they were brought back to Paris as virtual prisoners. The flight of the king turned many Frenchmen against the monarchy, strengthening the position of radicals who wanted to do away with kingship altogether and to establish a republic. But it was foreign invasion that led ultimately to the destruction of the monarchy.

In the Legislative Assembly, the lawmaking body that had succeeded the National Assembly in October 1791, one group, called the *Girondins*, urged an immediate war against Austria, which was harboring and supporting the émigrés. The Girondins believed that a successful war would unite France under their leadership, and they were convinced that Austria was already preparing to invade France and destroy the Revolution. Moreover, regarding themselves as crusaders in the struggle of liberty against tyranny, the Girondins hoped to spread revolutionary reforms to other lands to provoke a war of the people against kings.

On April 20, 1792, the Legislative Assembly declared war on Austria. Commanded by the Duke of Brunswick, a combined Austrian and Prussian army crossed into France. French forces, short of arms and poorly led (about 6,000 of some 9,000 officers had abandoned their command), could not halt the enemy's advance. Food shortages and a counterrevolution in the south increased the unrest. Into an atmosphere already charged with tension, the Duke of Brunswick issued a manifesto declaring that if the royal family were harmed he would exact a terrible vengeance on the Parisians. On August 10, 1792, enraged Parisians and militia from other cities attacked the king's palace, killing several hundred Swiss guards.

In early September, as foreign troops advanced deeper into France, there occurred an event analogous to the Great Fear of 1789. As rumors spread that jailed priests and aristocrats were planning to break out of their cells to support the Duke of Brunswick, the Parisians panicked. Driven by fear, patriotism, and murderous impulses, they raided the prisons and massacred 1,100 to 1,200 prisoners. Most of the victims were not political prisoners but ordinary criminals.

On September 21–22, 1792, the National Convention (the successor to the Legislative Assembly) abolished the monarchy and established a republic. In December 1792, Louis XVI was placed on trial, and in January 1793, he was executed for conspiring against the liberty of the French people. The execution of Louis XVI intensified tensions between the revolutionaries and the crowned heads of Europe. The uprising of August 10, the September Massacres, the creation of a republic, and the execution of Louis XVI were all signs of a drift toward radicalism.

Meanwhile the war continued. Short of

LOUIS XVI EXECUTED Crowned heads of Europe looked on with horror as Louis XVI was tried and executed. The sans-culottes, who had become radical with the invasion of France by forces sympathetic to the king, cheered the beheading. (La Librairie Larousse/Société Encyclopédique Universelle, Goldner, Paris)

supplies, hampered by bad weather, and possessing insufficient manpower, the Duke of Brunswick never did reach Paris. Outmaneuvered at Valmy on September 20, 1792, the foreign forces retreated to the frontier, and the armies of the Republic took the offensive. By the beginning of 1793, French forces had overrun Belgium (then a part of the Austrian Empire), the German Rhineland, and the Sardinian provinces of Nice and Savoy. To the peoples of Europe the National Convention had solemnly announced that it was waging a popular crusade against privilege and tyranny, aristocrats and princes.

Frightened by these revolutionary social ideas, the execution of Louis XVI, and most importantly French expansion that threatened the balance of power, the rulers of Europe, urged by Britain, had formed an anti-French alliance by the spring of 1793. The allies' forces pressed toward the French borders. The Republic was endangered.

Counterrevolutionary insurrections further undermined the fledgling Republic. In the Vendée in western France, peasants who were protesting against taxation and conscription and were still loyal to their priests took up arms against the Republic. Led by local nobles, the peasants of Vendée waged a guerrilla war for religion, royalism, and their traditional way of life. In other quarters, federalists revolted in the provinces, objecting to the power wielded by the centralized government in Paris.

The Jacobins

As the Republic tottered under the weight of foreign invasion, internal insurrection, and economic crisis, the revolutionary leadership grew more radical. In June 1793, the Jacobins replaced the Girondins as the dominant group in the National Convention. Whereas the Girondins favored a government in which the departments would exercise control over their own affairs, the Jacobins wanted a strong central government with Paris as the center of power. Whereas the Girondins opposed government interference with business, the Jacobins would support temporary government controls to deal with the needs of war and economic crisis. This last point was crucial; it won the Jacobins the support of the sans-culottes.

Both Girondins and Jacobins came from the bourgeoisie, but some Jacobin leaders were more willing to listen to the economic and political demands of the hard-pressed sans-culottes. The Jacobins also sought an alliance with the sans-culottes in order to defend the Revolution against foreign and domestic enemies. The Jacobins had a further advantage in the power struggle: they were tightly organized, well-disciplined, and convinced that only they could save the Republic. On June 2, 1793, some 80,000 armed sans-culottes surrounded the Convention and demanded the arrest of Girondin delegates, an act that enabled the Jacobins to gain control of the government.

The problems confronting the Jacobins were staggering. They had to cope with civil war, economic distress, blockaded ports, and foreign invasion. They lived with the terrible dread that if they failed, the Revolution for liberty and equality would perish. Only strong leadership could save the Republic; it was provided by the Committee of Public Safety. Serving as a cabinet for the Convention, the Committee of Public Safety organized the nation's defenses, formulated foreign policy, supervised ministers, ordered arrests, and imposed the central government's authority throughout the nation. The twelve members of the committee, all veterans of revolutionary politics, constituted "a government of perhaps the ablest and most determined men who have ever held power in France."[14]

Jacobin Achievements

The Jacobins continued the work of reform. A new constitution, in 1793, expressed Jacobin enthusiasm for political democracy. It contained a new Declaration of Rights that affirmed and amplified the principles of 1789. By giving all adult males the right to vote, it overcame sans-culotte objections to the Constitution of 1791. However, due to the threat of invasion and the revolts, implementation of the Constitution of 1793 was postponed, and it never was put into effect. By abolishing slavery in the French colonies and imprisonment for debt and by making plans for free public education, the Jacobins revealed their humanitarianism and their debt to the philosophes.

Jacobin economic policies derived from the exigencies of war. To halt inflation and gain support of the poor—both necessary for the war effort—the Jacobins decreed the *law of the maximum*, which fixed prices on bread and other essential goods and raised wages. To win over the peasants, the Jacobins made it easier for them to buy the property of émigré nobles. To equip the Army of the Republic, the Committee of Public Safety requisitioned grain, wool, arms, shoes, and other items from individual citizens, required factories and mines to maximize production, and established state-operated armament and munition plants.

The Nation in Arms

To cope with foreign invasion, the Jacobins, in an act that anticipated modern conscription, drafted unmarried men between eighteen and twenty-five years of age. They mobilized all the resources of the nation, infused the army with a love for *la patrie* (the nation), and in a remarkable demonstration of administrative skill, equipped an army of more than 800,000 men. In creating the nation in arms, the Jacobins heralded the emergence of modern warfare. The citizen-soldiers of the Republic, commanded by officers who had proved their skill on the battlefield and inspired by the ideals of Liberty, Equality, and Fraternity, won decisive victories. In May and June of 1794, the French routed the allied forces on the vital northern frontier, and by the end of July, France had become the triumphant master of Belgium.

In demanding complete devotion to the nation, the Jacobin phase of the Revolution also heralded the rise of modern nationalism. In the schools, newspapers, speeches, and poems, on the stage and at rallies and meetings of patriotic societies, Frenchmen were told of the glory won by Republican soldiers on the battlefield and were reminded of their duties to la patrie. "The citizen is born, lives and dies for the fatherland."[15] These words were written in public places for all citizens to read and ponder. The soldiers of the Revolution fought not for money or for a king, but for the nation. "When *la patrie* calls us for her defense," wrote a young soldier to his mother, "we should rush to her. . . . Our life, our goods, and our talents do not belong to us. It is to the nation, to *la patrie*, to which everything belongs."[16] Could this heightened sense of nationality that concentrated on the special interests of the French people be reconciled with the Declaration of the Rights of Man, whose principles were addressed to all humanity? The revolutionaries themselves did not understand the implications of the new force that they had unleashed.

The Republic of Virtue and the Reign of Terror

Robespierre

At the same time that the Committee of Public Safety was forging a revolutionary army to deal with external enemies, it also waged war against internal opposition. The pivotal personality in this struggle was Maximilien Robespierre (1758–1794). Robespierre had served in the National Assembly and was an active Jacobin. Neither a brilliant orator nor a hero in appearance, he was, however, distinguished by a fervent faith in the rightness of his beliefs, a total commitment to republican democracy, and a pure integrity that earned him the name *the Incorruptible*.

Robespierre wanted to create a better society founded on reason, good citizenship, and patriotism. In his Republic of Virtue, there would be no kings or nobles; men would be free, equal, and educated; reason would be glorified and superstition ridiculed; there would be no extremes of wealth or poverty; man's natural goodness would prevail over vice and greed; laws would preserve, not violate, inalienable rights. In this utopian vision, an individual's duties would be "to detest bad faith and despotism, to punish tyrants and traitors, to assist the unfortunate, to respect the weak, to defend the oppressed, to do all the good one can to one's neighbor, and to behave with justice towards all men."[17]

A disciple of Rousseau, Robespierre conceived the national general will as ultimate and infallible. Its realization meant the establishment of a Republic of Virtue; its denial, the death of an ideal and a return to despotism. Certain that he and his colleagues in the Committee of Public Safety had correctly ascertained the needs of the French people and that they were the genuine interpreters of the general will, Robespierre felt duty-bound to ensure its realization. He pursued his ideal society with religious zeal. Knowing that the Republic of Virtue could not be established while France was threatened by foreign and civil war, Robespierre urged harsh treatment for enemies of the Republic. "Whoever makes war on a people in order to check the progress of liberty and annihilate the rights of man must be prosecuted by all not as ordinary enemies, but as rebels, brigands, and assassins."[18]

The Jacobin leadership, with Robespierre playing a key role, moved against enemies of the Republic—Girondins who challenged Jacobin authority, federalists who opposed a strong central government emanating from Paris, counterrevolutionary priests and nobles and their peasant supporters, and profiteers who hoarded food. The Jacobins even sought to discipline the ardor of the sans-culottes who had given them power. Fearful that sans-culotte spontaneity would undermine central authority and promote anarchy, Robespierrists brought about the dissolution of sans-culotte societies. Robespierrists also executed sans-culotte leaders known as *enragés,* who threatened insurrection against Jacobin rule and pushed for more social reforms than the Jacobins would allow. The enragés wanted to set limits on incomes and the size of farms and businesses and preached de-Christianization of France—policies considered far too extreme by the supporters of Robespierre.

To preserve republican liberty, the Jacobins made terror a deliberate government policy.

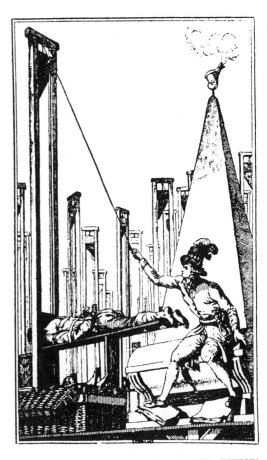

ROBESPIERRE: A CONTEMPORARY CARTOON WHEREIN ROBESPIERRE EXECUTES THE EXECUTIONER AFTER ALL OF FRANCE HAD BEEN EXECUTED BY THE JACOBIN LEADER'S ORDERS To create a Republic of Virtue where men would be free and equal, Maximilien Robespierre considered terror necessary. Robespierre lost favor with his own party and was himself guillotined. (University of Rochester Library, Rochester, New York)

Does not liberty, that inestimable blessing . . . have the . . . right to sacrifice lives, fortunes, and even, for a time, individual liberties? . . . Is not the French Revolution . . . a war to the death between those who want to be free and those content to be slaves? . . . There is no middle ground; France must be entirely free or perish in the attempt, and any means are justifiable in fighting for so fine a cause.[19]

Perhaps as many as 40,000 people perished during the Reign of Terror.

Robespierre and his fellow Jacobins did not resort to the guillotine because they were bloodthirsty or power mad. Instead, they sought to establish a temporary dictatorship in a desperate attempt to save the Republic and the Revolution. Deeply devoted to republican democracy, the Jacobins viewed themselves as bearers of a higher faith. Like all visionaries, Robespierre was convinced that he knew the right way, that the new society he envisaged would benefit all humanity, and that those who impeded its implementation were not just opponents, but sinners who had to be liquidated for the good of humanity.

The Jacobins did save the Republic. Foreign armies were expelled, federalist uprisings were crushed, counterrevolutionaries in the Vendée were contained, and anarchy was avoided. Without the discipline, order, and unity imposed on France by the Robespierrists, it is likely that the Republic would have collapsed under the twin blows of foreign invasion and domestic anarchy.

The Significance of the Terror

The Reign of Terror poses fundamental questions about the meaning of the French Revolution and the validity of the Enlightenment conception of man. To what extent was the Terror a reversal of the ideals of the Revolution as formulated in the Declaration of the Rights of Man? To what extent did the feverish passions and fascination for violence demonstrated in the mass executions in the provinces and in the public spectacles in Paris indicate a darker side of human nature beyond control of reason? Did Robespierre's religion of humanity revive the fanaticism and cruelty of

the Wars of Religion that had so disgusted the philosophes? Did the Robespierrists, who considered themselves the staunchest defenders of the Revolution's ideals soil and subvert these ideals by their zeal? By mobilizing the might of the nation, by creating the mystique of la patrie, by imposing temporary dictatorial rule in defense of liberty and equality, and by legalizing and justifying terror committed in the people's name, were the Jacobins unwittingly unleashing new forces that, in later years, would be harnessed by totalitarian ideologies consciously resolved to stamp out the liberal heritage of the Revolution? Did 1793 mark a change in the direction of Western civilization: a movement away from the ideals of the philosophes, and the opening of an age of violence and irrationalism that would culminate in the cataclysms of the twentieth century?

The Fall of Robespierre

The Terror had been instituted during a time of crisis and keyed-up emotions. By the summer of 1794, with the victory of the Republic seemingly assured, the fear of an aristocratic conspiracy had subsided, the will to punish "traitors" had slackened, and popular fervor for the Terror had diminished. As the need and enthusiasm for the Terror abated, Robespierre's political position weakened.

Opponents of Robespierre in the Convention, feeling the chill of the guillotine blade on their own necks, ordered the arrest of Robespierre and some of his supporters. On July 27, 1794, the ninth of Thermidor according to the new republican calendar, Robespierre was guillotined. Parisian sans-culottes might have saved him, but they made no attempt. With their political clubs dissolved, the organization needed for an armed uprising was lacking. Moreover, the sans-culottes' ardor for Jacobinism had waned; apparently the social legislation instituted by the Robespierrist leadership had not been sufficiently carried out to soothe sans-culotte discontent.

After the fall of Robespierre, the machinery of the Jacobin Republic was dismantled. Leadership passed to the property-owning bourgeois who had endorsed the constitutional ideas of 1789–1791, the moderate stage of the Revolution. The new leadership, known as *Thermidoreans* until the end of 1795, wanted no more of the Jacobins or of Robespierre's society. They had considered that Robespierre was a threat to their political power because he would have allowed the common people a considerable voice in the government, and a threat to their property because he would have introduced some state regulation of the economy to aid the poor.

The new republican government, called the *Directory*, at the end of 1795 was burdened by war, a sagging economy, and internal unrest. The Directory crushed uprisings by royalists seeking to restore the monarchy and by Parisian sans-culottes maddened by hunger and hatred of the rich. As military and domestic pressures worsened, power began to pass into the hands of generals. One of them, Napoleon Bonaparte, seized control of the government in November 1799, pushing the Revolution into yet another stage.

THE MEANING OF THE FRENCH REVOLUTION

The French Revolution has been described as a series of concurrent revolutions. In addition to the revolution of the bourgeoisie, there occurred an autonomous peasant revolution precipitated by increasing poverty, hatred of the manorial order, and rising hopes aroused by the calling of the Estates General. There also occurred a third uprising, that of urban journeymen, wage earners, and lesser bourgeois shopkeepers and craftsmen hard hit by food shortages and rising prices.

But bad conditions alone need not lead to revolution. "No great event in history," states Henri Peyre, a twentieth-century student of French culture, "has been due to causes chiefly economic in nature, and certainly not the French Revolution."[20] For centuries, Indian untouchables and Egyptian fellahin lived under the most wretched of conditions, bearing their misery without raising a voice in protest. In the eighteenth century, the peoples of Eastern and Central Europe were far worse off than the average Frenchman. Yet it was in France that the great revolution broke out.

Revolutions are born in the realm of the spirit. Revolutionary movements, says George Rudé, a historian of the French Revolution, require "some unifying body of ideas, a common vocabulary of hope and protest, something, in short, like a common 'revolutionary psychology'."[21] The philosophes were themselves not revolutionaries, asserts Peyre, but their ideas helped to create a revolutionary psychology.

Eighteenth-century philosophy taught the Frenchman to find his condition wretched, or in any case, unjust and illogical and made him disinclined to the patient resignation to his troubles that had long characterized his ancestors. . . . The propaganda of the "'Philosophes" perhaps more than any other factor accounted for the fulfillment of the preliminary condition of the French Revolution, namely discontent with the existing state of things.[22]

The American Revolution which gave practical expression to the liberal philosophy of the philosophes, helped to pave the way for the French Revolution. Did not the Declaration of Independence proclaim the natural rights of man and approve resistance against a government that deprived men of these rights? Had not the Americans set an example of social equality unparalleled in Europe? In the United States there was no hereditary aristocracy, no serfdom, and no state church. Liberal French aristocrats, such as the Marquis de Lafayette, who had fought in the American Revolution returned to France more optimistic about the possibilities of reforming French society.

The French Revolution was a decisive period in the shaping of the modern West. It implemented the ideology of the philosophes, destroyed the hierarchic and corporate society of the Old Regime, assured the ultimate ascendancy of the bourgeoisie, and speeded the growth of the modern state.

The French Revolution ended the dominance of the aristocracy. With their feudal rights, privileges, and titles eliminated, the lands of the émigrés confiscated, and their influence curtailed, the nobles became simply ordinary citizens. The church, having lost its courts, assemblies, property, and tithes, was no longer a state within a state, but merely a spiritual community.

The bourgeoisie led the Revolution and emerged the principal gainers. The principle of careers open to talent gave them access to the highest positions in the state. The destruction of feudal remnants, internal tolls, and the guilds speeded up the expansion of a competitive market economy. Possessing wealth, talent, ambition, and now opportunity, the bourgeoisie would dominate the future. Throughout the continent the reforms of the French Revolution served as a model for progressive bourgeois who, sooner or later, would challenge the Old Regime in their own lands.

The French Revolution transformed the dynastic state of the Old Regime into the modern state: national, liberal, secular, and rational. When the Declaration of the Rights of Man and Citizen stated that "the source of all sovereignty resides essentially in the nation," the concept of the state took on a new meaning. The state was no longer merely a territory or a federation of provinces; it was not the private possession of the king claiming to be God's lieutenant on earth. In the new conception, the state belonged to the people as a whole, and the individual, formerly a subject, was now a citizen with both rights and duties and was governed by laws that drew no distinction on the basis of birth.

The liberal thought of the Enlightenment found practical expression in the reforms of the Revolution. Despotism and divine right of monarchy, repudiated in theory by the philosophes, were invalidated by constitutions that set limits to the powers of government and by elected parliaments that represented the governed. By providing for equality before the law and the protection of human rights—habeas corpus, trial by jury, freedom of religion, speech, and the press—the Revolution struck at the abuses of the Old Regime. These gains seemed at times more theoretical than actual, because of violations and interruptions, but nevertheless, these liberal ideals reverberated throughout the Continent. During the nineteenth century the pace of reform would quicken. And with the demands of the sansculottes for equality with the bourgeois, political democracy, and social reform, the voice of the people in politics began to be heard. This phenomenon would become increasingly intensified with growing industrialization.

By disavowing any divine justification for the monarch's power and by depriving the church of its special position, the Revolution accelerated the secularization of European political life. Sweeping aside the administrative chaos of the Old Regime, the Revolution attempted to impose rational norms on the state. The sale of public offices that produced ineffective and corrupt administrators was eliminated, and the highest positions in the land were opened to men of talent, regardless of birth. The Revolution abolished manorial obligations of the peasantry that hampered agriculture, guilds that protected members but thwarted business expansion, internal duties and customs that increased the cost of land transport, and diverse systems of weights and measures that complicated financial transactions. The Revolution based taxes on income and streamlined their collection. In the nineteenth century, reformers in the rest of Europe would follow the lead set by France.

The French Revolution also unleashed two potentially destructive forces identified with the modern state: total war and nationalism.

CHRONOLOGY 19.1 THE FRENCH REVOLUTION

May 5, 1789	The Estates-General convene
June 20, 1789	The Tennis Court Oath
July 14, 1789	The storming of the Bastille
End of July–early August 1789	The Great Fear
August 4, 1789	Abolition of feudal privileges
August 26, 1789	Declaration of the Rights of Man and the Citizen
October 5, 1789	The march on Versailles
November 1789	The National Assembly confiscates church lands
June 1791	Flight of the royal family
September 1791	The constitution limits the king's power
April 1792	France declares war on Austria
August 10, 1792	King's palace in Paris is attacked
September 21–22, 1792	Abolition of the monarchy and creation of a republic
January 1793	Execution of King Louis XVI
June 1793	Jacobins gain control of the government
July 27, 1794	Robespierre is executed
October 1795–November 1799	Rule by the Directory
November 1799	Napoleon Bonaparte seizes power

These contradicted the rational and universal aims of the reformers as stated in the Declaration of the Rights of Man. Whereas eighteenth-century wars were fought by professional soldiers for limited aims, the French Revolution, says British historian Herbert Butterfield,

brings conscription, the nation in arms, the mobilization of all the resources of the state for unrelenting conflict. It heralds the age when peoples, woefully ignorant of one another, bitterly uncomprehending, lie in uneasy juxtaposition watching one another's sins with hysteria and indignation. It heralds Armageddon, the giant conflict for justice and right between angered populations each of which thinks it is the righteous one. So a new kind of warfare is born—the modern counterpart to the old conflicts of religions.[23]

The world wars of the twentieth century are

the terrible fulfillment of this new development in warfare.

The French Revolution also gave birth to modern nationalism. During the Revolution, loyalty was directed to the entire nation, not to a village or province or to the person of the king. The whole of France became the fatherland. Under the Jacobins, the French became converts to a secular faith preaching total reverence for the nation. "In 1794 we believed in no supernatural religion; our serious interior sentiments were all summed up in the one idea, how to be useful to the fatherland. Everything else . . . was, in our eyes, only trivial. . . . It was our only religion."[24] Few suspected that the new religion of nationalism was fraught with danger. Saint-Just, a young, ardent Robespierrist, was gazing into our own century when he declared: "There is something terrible in the sacred love of the fatherland. This love is so exclusive that it sacrifices everything to the public interest, without pity, without fear, with no respect for the human individual."[25]

The Revolution attempted to reconstruct society on the basis of Enlightenment thought. The Declaration of the Rights of Man, whose spirit permeated the reforms of the Revolution, upheld the dignity of the individual, demanded respect for the individual, attributed to each person natural rights, and barred the state from denying these rights. It insisted that society and state have no higher duty than to promote the freedom and autonomy of the individual. "It is not enough to have overturned the throne," said Robespierre; "our concern is to erect upon its remains holy Equality and the sacred Rights of Man."[26] The tragedy of the Western experience is that this humanist vision, brilliantly expressed by the Enlightenment and given recognition in the reforms of the French Revolution, would weaken in later generations. And, ironically, by spawning total war, nationalism, terror as government policy, and a revolutionary mentality that sought to change the world through violence, the French Revolution itself contributed to the shattering of this vision.

Notes

1. Quoted in G. P. Gooch, *Germany and the French Revolution* (New York: Russell & Russell, 1966), p. 39.

2. Quoted in Ernst Wangermann, *From Joseph II to the Jacobin Trials* (New York: Oxford University Press, 1959), p. 24.

3. Alfred Cobban, *The Debate on the French Revolution* (London: Adam & Charles Black, 1960), p. 41.

4. Quoted in Elinor G. Barber, *The Bourgeoisie in Eighteenth-Century France* (Princeton, N.J.: Princeton University Press, 1967), p. 57.

5. Georges Lefebvre, *The French Revolution from 1793 to 1799* (New York: Columbia University Press, 1964), 2: 360.

6. Quoted in C. B. A. Behrens, *The Ancien Regime* (New York: Harcourt, Brace and World, 1967), p. 43.

7. Quoted in Leo Gershoy, *The French Revolution and Napoleon* (New York: Appleton-Century-Crofts, 1933), p. 18.

8. John Hall Stewart, ed., *A Documentary Survey of the French Revolution* (New York: Macmillan, 1951), pp. 43–44.

9. See George Rudé, *The Crowd in the French Revolution* (New York: Oxford University Press, 1959).

10. Georges Lefebvre, *The Coming of the French Revolution* (Princeton, N.J.: Princeton University Press, 1967), p. 210.

11. Albert Soboul, *The Parisian Sans-Culottes and the French Revolution, 1793–94,* trans. by Gwynne Lewis (London: Oxford University Press, 1964), pp. 28–29.

12. Ibid., p. 63.

13. Ibid., p. 64.

14. Alfred Cobban, *A History of Modern France* (Baltimore: Penguin, 1961), 1: 213.

15. Quoted in Hans Kohn, *Nationalism: Its Meaning and History* (Princeton, N.J.: D. Van Nostrand, 1965), p. 25.

16. Quoted in J. H. Hayes, *The Historical Evolution of Modern Nationalism* (New York: Richard R. Smith, 1931), p. 55.

17. George Rudé, ed., *Robespierre* (Englewood Cliffs, N.J.: Prentice-Hall, 1976), p. 72.

18. Ibid., p. 57.
19. E. L. Higgins, ed., *The French Revolution* (Boston: Houghton Mifflin, 1938), pp. 306–307.
20. Henri Peyre, "The Influence of Eighteenth-Century Ideas on the French Revolution," *Journal of the History of Ideas*, 10 (1949): 72.
21. George Rudé, *Revolutionary Europe, 1783–1815* (New York: Harper Torchbooks, 1966), p. 74.
22. Peyre, "The Influence of Eighteenth-Century Ideas," p. 73.
23. Herbert Butterfield, *Napoleon* (New York: Collier Books, 1962), p. 18.
24. Quoted in Carlton J. H. Hayes, *The Historical Evolution of Modern Nationalism*, (New York: Russell & Russell, 1931), p. 55.
25. Quoted in Hans Kohn, *Making of the Modern French Mind* (New York: D. Van Nostrand, 1955), p. 17.
26. Quoted in Christopher Dawson, *The Gods of Revolution* (New York: New York University Press, 1972), p. 83.

Suggested Reading

Gershoy, Leo, *The Era of the French Revolution* (1957). A brief survey with useful documents.

Higgins, E. L., ed. *The French Revolution* (1938). Excerpts from contemporaries.

Kafker, F. A., and Laux, J. M., *The French Revolution: Conflicting Interpretations* (1976). Excerpts from leading historians.

Lefebvre, Georges, *The French Revolution*, 2 vols. (1962, 1964). A detailed analysis by a master historian.

———, *The Coming of the French Revolution* (1967). A brilliant analysis of the social structure of the Old Regime and the opening phase of the Revolution.

Palmer, R. R., *The Age of the Democratic Revolution*, 2 vols. (1959, 1964). The French Revolution as part of a revolutionary movement that spread on both sides of the Atlantic.

———, *Twelve Who Ruled* (1965). An admirable treatment of the Terror.

Rudé, George, *The Crowd in the French Revolution* (1959). An analysis of the composition of the crowds that stormed the Bastille, marched to Versailles, and attacked the king's palace.

———, *Robespierre: Portrait of a Revolutionary Democrat* (1976). A recent biography of the revolutionary leader.

Soboul, Albert, *The Sans-Culottes* (1972). An abridgment of the classic study of the popular movement of 1793–94.

Stewart, J. H., *A Documentary Survey of the French Revolution* (1951). A valuable collection of documents.

Review Questions

1. What privileges were enjoyed by clergy and nobility in the Old Regime?
2. What were the grievances of the bourgeoisie, the peasantry and the urban laborers?
3. Why was France in financial difficulty?
4. Analyze the causes of the French Revolution.
5. Identify and explain the significance of the following: Formation of the National Assembly, Storming of the Bastille, the Great Fear, and October Days.
6. Analyze the nature and significance of the reforms of the National Assembly.
7. What were the grievances of the sans-culottes?
8. Identify and explain the significance of the following: Flight of the King, the Brunswick Manifesto, and the September Massacres.
9. What were the principal differences between the Jacobins and the Girondins?
10. What were the accomplishments of the Jacobins?
11. Analyze Robespierre's basic philosophy.
12. Why was the French Revolution a decisive period in the shaping of the West?

CHAPTER 20

Napoleon: Destroyer and
Preserver of the Revolution

THE LOOSENING of the bonds of authority in a revolutionary age offers opportunities for popular and ambitious military commanders to seize power. History affords numerous examples of revolutions culminating in military dictatorships. The upheavals of the French Revolution made possible the extraordinary career of Napoleon Bonaparte. This popular general combined a passion for power with a genius for leadership. He was, said a contemporary, "the mightiest breath of life which ever animated clay."[1] Under Napoleon's military dictatorship, the constitutional government for which the people of 1789 had fought and the republican democracy for which the Jacobins had rallied the nation seemed lost. Nevertheless, during the Napoleonic era, many achievements of the Revolution were preserved, strengthened, and carried to other lands.

RISE TO POWER

Napoleon was born on August 15, 1769, on the island of Corsica, the son of a petty noble. After finishing military school in France, he became an artillery officer; the wars of the French Revolution afforded him an opportunity to advance his career. In December 1793, Napoleon's brilliant handling of artillery forced the British to lift their siege of the city of Toulon. Two years later he saved the Thermidorean Convention from a royalist insurrection by ordering his troops to fire into the riotous mob—the famous "whiff of grapeshot." In 1796 he was given command of the French Army of Italy. His star was rising.

In Italy, against the Austrians, Napoleon demonstrated a dazzling talent for military planning and leadership that earned him an instant reputation. Having tasted glory, he could never do without it; having experienced only success, nothing seemed impossible. He sensed that he was headed for greatness. Years later he recalled: "[In Italy] I realized I was a

PORTRAIT OF NAPOLEON This engraving idealizes the features of Napoleon. He is here reminiscent of Roman imperial busts and coinage. (Brown Brothers)

superior being and conceived the ambition of performing great things, which hitherto had filled my thoughts only as a fantastic dream."[2]

In November 1797, Napoleon was ordered to plan an invasion of England. Aware of the weakness of the French navy, he recommended postponement of the invasion, urging instead an expedition to the Near East to strike at British commerce with India. With more than 35,000 troops, Napoleon set out for Egypt, then a part of the Turkish empire. Although he captured Cairo, the Egyptian campaign was far from a success. At the Battle of the Nile (1798), the British, commanded by Admiral Nelson, annihilated Napoleon's fleet. Deprived of reinforcements and supplies, with his manpower reduced by battle and plague,

Napoleon was compelled to abandon whatever dreams he might have had of threatening India.

Meanwhile in France, political unrest, financial disorder, and military reversals produced an atmosphere of crisis. Napoleon knew that in such times people seek out a savior. A man of destiny must act. Without informing his men, he slipped out of Egypt, avoided British cruisers, and landed in France in October 1799.

Coup d'État

When Napoleon arrived in France, a conspiracy was already underway against the government of the Directory. Convinced that only firm leadership could solve France's problems, some politicians plotted to seize power and establish a strong executive. Needing the assistance of a popular general, they turned to Napoleon, whom they thought they could control. Although the hastily prepared coup d'état was almost bungled, the government of the Directory was overthrown. The French Revolution entered a new stage, that of military dictatorship.

Demoralized by a decade of political instability, economic distress, domestic violence, and war, most of the French welcomed the leadership of a strong man. The bourgeois, in particular, expected Napoleon to protect their wealth and the influence they had gained during the Revolution.

The new constitution (1799) created a strong executive. Though three Consuls shared the executive, the First Consul, Napoleon, monopolized power. Whereas Napoleon's fellow conspirators, who were political moderates, sought only to strengthen the executive, Napoleon aspired to personal rule. He captured the reins of power after the coup, and his authority continued to expand. In 1802 he was made First Consul for life with the right to name his successor. And on December 2, 1804, in a magnificent ceremony at the

JACQUES LOUIS DAVID: LE SACRE Napoleon crowned himself as emperor and Josephine as empress. But to French émigrés he was the "crowned Jacobin." He had risen from general to First Consul to emperor in five years. (Alinari/Editorial Photocolor Archives)

Cathedral of Notre Dame in Paris, Napoleon crowned himself Emperor of the French. General, First Consul, and then Emperor—it was a breathless climb to the heights of power. And Napoleon, who once said he loved "power as a musician loves his violin,"[3] was determined never to lose it.

The Character of Napoleon

What sort of man was it upon whom the fate of France and Europe depended? While Napoleon's personality, complex and mysterious, continues to baffle biographers, certain distinctive traits are evident.

Napoleon's intellectual ability was impressive. His mind swiftly absorbed details that his photographic memory classified and stored. With surgical precision he could probe his way to the heart of a problem while still retaining a grasp over peripheral considerations. Ideas forever danced in his head, and his imagination was illuminated by sudden flashes of insight. He could work for eighteen or twenty hours at a stretch, deep in concentration, ruling out boredom or tiredness by an act of will. Napoleon, man of action, warrior par excellence, was in many ways, says Georges

Lefebvre, "a typical man of the eighteenth century, a rationalist, a *philosophe* . . . [who] placed his trust in reason, in knowledge, and in methodical effort."[4]

Rationalism was only one part of his personality. There was also that elemental, irresistible urge for action, "the romantic Napoleon, a force seeking to expand and for which the world was no more than an occasion for acting dangerously."[5] This love of action fused with his boundless ambition. Continues Lefebvre:

His greatest ambition was glory. "I live only for posterity," he exclaimed, "death is nothing, but to live defeated and without glory is to die every day." His eyes were fixed on the world's great leaders: Alexander who conquered the East and dreamed of conquering the world; Caesar, Augustus, Charlemagne. . . . They were for him examples, which stimulated his imagination and lent an unalterable charm to action. He was an artist, a poet of action, for whom France and mankind were but instruments.[6]

He also exuded an indefinable quality of personality, a charismatic force that made people feel they were in the presence of a superior man. Contemporaries remarked that his large gray eyes, penetrating, knowing, yet strangely expressionless, seemed to possess a hypnotic power. He was capable of moving men to obedience, to loyalty, to heroism.

The rationalist's clarity of mind and the romantic's impassioned soul, the adventurer's love of glory and the hero's personal magnetism—these were the components of Napoleon's personality. There was also an aloofness, some would say callousness, that led him to regard people as pawns to be manipulated in the pursuit of his destiny. "All my life," he said, "I have sacrificed everything—comfort, self-interest, happiness—to my destiny."[7] He was also capable of sacrificing men, without hesitation and without regret. "A man like me," he once said, "troubles himself little about the lives of a million men."[8]

Napoleon's genius might have gone unheralded, his destiny unfulfilled, had it not been for the opportunities created by the French Revolution. By opening careers to talent, the Revolution enabled a young Corsican of undistinguished birth to achieve fame and popularity. By creating the nation in arms and embroiling France in war, it provided a military commander with enormous sources of power. By plunging France into one crisis after another, it opened up extraordinary possibilities for a man with a gift of leadership and an ambition "so intimately linked with my very being that it is like the blood that circulates in my veins."[9] It was the Revolution that made Napoleon conscious of his genius and certain of his destiny.

NAPOLEON AND FRANCE

Living in a revolutionary age, Napoleon had observed firsthand the precariousness of power and the fleetingness of popularity. A superb realist, he knew that his past reputation would not sustain him. If he could not solve the problems caused by a decade of revolution and war and bind together the different classes of French people, his prestige would diminish and his power collapse. The general must become a statesman, and when necessary, a tyrant. His domestic policies, showing the influence of both eighteenth-century enlightened despotism and the Revolution, affected every aspect of society and had an enduring impact on French history. They continued the work of the Revolution in destroying the institutions of the Old Regime.

Government: Centralization and Repression

In providing France with a strong central government, Napoleon continued a policy initiated centuries earlier by Bourbon monarchs. Although the Bourbons had not been able completely to overcome the barriers presented by provinces, local traditions, feudal remnants, and corporate institutions, Napoleon succeeded in giving France administrative uniformity. An army of officials, subject to the emperor's will, reached into every village, linking together the entire nation. This centralized state suited Napoleon's desire for orderly government and rational administration, enabled him to concentrate power in his hands, and provided him with the taxes and soldiers needed to fight his wars. To suppress irreconcilable opponents, primarily die-hard royalists and republicans, Napoleon used the instruments of the police state—secret agents, arbitrary arrest, summary trials, executions.

Napoleon also shaped public opinion in order to prevent hostile criticism of his rule and to promote popular support for his policies and person. In these actions, he was a precursor of twentieth-century dictators. Liberty of the press came to an end. Printers swore an oath of obedience to the Emperor, and newspapers were converted into government mouthpieces. Printers were forbidden to print, and booksellers to sell or circulate, "anything which may involve injury to the duties of subjects toward the sovereign or the interests of the state."[10] When Napoleon's secretary read him the morning newspapers, Napoleon would interrupt: "Skip it, skip it. I know what is in them. They only say what I tell them to."[11] These efforts at indoctrination even reached schoolchildren, who were required to memorize a catechism glorifying the ruler.

Q. What are the duties of Christians with respect to the princes who govern them, and what in particular are our duties toward Napoleon I, our Emperor?
A. Christians owe to the princes who govern them, and we owe in particular to Napoleon I, our Emperor, love, respect, obedience, fidelity, military service; . . . we also owe him . . . prayers for his safety. . . .
Q. Why are we bound to all these duties towards our Emperor?
A. First of all, because God, who creates
emperors and distributes them according to his will, in loading our Emperor with gifts, both in peace and in war, has established him as our sovereign. . . . To honor and to serve our Emperor is then to honor and to serve God himself.
Q. What . . . of those who may be lacking in their duty towards our Emperor?
A. . . . they would be resisting the order established by God himself and would make themselves worthy of eternal damnation.[12]

By repressing liberty, subverting republicanism, and restoring absolutism, Napoleon reversed some of the liberal gains of the Revolution. Though favoring equality before the law and equality of opportunity as necessary for a well-run state, Napoleon believed that political liberty impeded efficiency and threatened anarchy. He would govern in the interest of the people as an enlightened but absolute ruler.

Religion: Reconciliation with the Church

For Napoleon, who was a deist if not an atheist, the value of religion was not salvation, but social and political cohesion. It promoted national unity and prevented class war. He stated:

Society cannot exist without inequality of fortunes, and inequality of fortunes cannot exist without religion. When a man is dying of hunger alongside another who stuffs himself, it is impossible to make him accede to the difference unless there is an authority which says to him God wishes it thus; there must be some poor and some rich in the world, but hereafter and for all eternity the division will be made differently.[13]

This is what Napoleon probably had in mind when he said: "Men who do not believe in God—one does not govern them, one shoots them."[14]

Napoleon attempted to close the breach with the Catholic church that had emerged during the Revolution. Such a reconciliation would gain the approval of the mass of the French people who still remained devoted to their faith and would reassure those peasants and bourgeois who had bought confiscated church lands. For these reasons, Napoleon negotiated an agreement with the pope. The Concordat of 1801 recognized Catholicism as the religion of the great majority of the French, rather than as the official state religion (the proposal that the pope desired). The clergy were to be paid and nominated by the state, but consecrated by the pope.

In effect, the Concordat guaranteed the reforms of the Revolution. The church did not regain its confiscated lands nor its right to collect the tithe. The French clergy remained largely subject to state control. And by not establishing Catholicism as the state religion, the Concordat did not jeopardize the newly won toleration of Jews and Protestants. Napoleon had achieved his aim. The Concordat made his regime acceptable to Catholics and to owners of former church lands.

Law: The Code Napoleon

Under the Old Regime, France was plagued with numerous and conflicting law codes. Reflecting local interests and feudal traditions, these codes obstructed national unity and administrative efficiency. Efforts by the revolutionaries to draw up a unified code of laws bogged down. Recognizing the value of such a code in promoting effective administration throughout France, Napoleon pressed for the completion of the project. The Code Napoléon incorporated many principles of the Revolution: equality before the law, the right to choose one's profession, freedom of conscience, protection of property rights, the abolition of serfdom, and the secular character of the state.

The Code also had its less liberal side, denying equal treatment to workers in their dealings with employers, to women in their relations with their husbands, to children in their relations with their fathers. In assigning wives an inferior status to their husbands in matters of property, adultery, and divorce, the Code reflected both Napoleon's personal attitude and the general view of the times toward women and family stability. Of women, he once said that "the husband must possess the absolute power and right to say to his wife: 'Madam, you shall not go out, you shall not go to the theater, you shall not receive such and such a person: for the children you shall bear shall be mine!'"[15]

Adopted in lands conquered by France, the Code Napoléon contributed to the weakening of feudal privileges and institutions and clerical interference with the secular state. With justice, Napoleon could say: "My true glory is not to have won forty battles. . . . Waterloo will erase the memory of so many victories. . . . But what nothing will destroy, what will live forever, is my Civil Code."[16]

Education: The Imperial University

Napoleon's educational policy was in many ways an elaboration of the school reforms initiated during the Revolution. Like the revolutionaries, Napoleon favored a system of public education with a secular curriculum and a minimum of church involvement. For Napoleon, education served a dual purpose: it would provide him with capable officials to administer his laws and trained officers to lead his armies; and it would indoctrinate the young in obedience and loyalty. He established the University of France, a giant board of education that placed education under state control. To this day the French school system, unlike that in the United States, is strictly centralized, with curriculum and standards set for the entire state.

The emperor did not consider education for girls important, holding that "marriage is their whole destination."[17] Whatever education girls did receive, he believed, should stress religion. "What we ask of education is not that girls should think but that they should believe. The weakness of woman's brains, the instability of their ideas, the place they fill in society, their need for perpetual resignation . . . all this can only be met by religion."[18]

Economy: Strengthening the State

Napoleon's financial and economic policies were designed to strengthen France and enhance his popularity. To stimulate the economy and to retain the favor of the bourgeois who supported his seizure of power, Napoleon aided industry through tariffs and loans and fostered commerce (while also speeding up troop movements) by building or repairing roads, bridges, and canals. To protect the currency from inflation, he established the Bank of France, which was controlled by the nation's leading financiers. By keeping careers open to talent, he endorsed one of the key demands of the bourgeoisie during the Revolution. Fearing a revolution based on lack of bread, he provided food at low prices and stimulated employment for the working class. He endeared himself to the peasants by not restoring feudal privileges and by allowing them to keep the land they had obtained during the Revolution.

By preserving many social gains of the Revolution while suppressing political liberty, Napoleon showed himself as an heir of eighteenth-century enlightened despotism. Like the reforming despots, Napoleon admired administrative uniformity and efficiency, hated feudalism, religious persecution, and civil inequality, and favored government regulation of trade and industry. He saw in enlightened despotism a means of ensuring political stability, overcoming the confusion presented by feudal and corporative institutions, avoiding the dangers of democracy, which he equated with mob rule, and strengthening the state militarily. Napoleon belonged to the tradition of enlightened despotism; he did not identify with the republicanism and democracy of the Jacobins.

While Napoleon's domestic policies gained him wide support, it was his victories on the battlefield that mesmerized the French people and gratified their national vanity. Ultimately his popularity and his power rested on the sword.

NAPOLEON AND EUROPE

Napoleon, the Corsican adventurer, realized Louis XIV's dream of French mastery of Europe. Between 1805 and 1807, Napoleon inflicted decisive defeats on Austria, Prussia, and Russia, to become the virtual ruler of Europe. In these campaigns, as in his earlier successes in Italy, Napoleon demonstrated his greatness as a military commander.

Napoleon's Art of War

While foregoing a set battle plan in favor of flexibility, Napoleon was guided by certain general principles that comprised his art of war. He stressed the advantage of "a rapid and audacious attack" in preference to waging defensive war from a fixed position. "Make war offensively; it is the sole means to become a great captain and to fathom the secrets of the art."[19] Warfare could not be left to chance, but required mastering every detail and anticipating every contingency. "I am accustomed to thinking out what I shall do three or four months in advance, and I base my calculations on the worst of conceivable circumstances."[20] Every master plan contained numerous alternatives to cover all contingencies.

Surprise and speed were essential ingredients of Napoleonic warfare. Relying heavily on surprise, Napoleon employed various stratagems to confuse and deceive his opponents: providing newspapers with misleading information, launching secondary offensives, and placing a dense screen of cavalry ahead of marching columns to prevent penetration by enemy patrols. Determined to surprise and consequently demoralize the enemy by arriving at a battlefield ahead of schedule, he carefully selected the best routes to the chosen destination, eliminated slow-moving supply convoys by living off the countryside, and inspired his men to incredible feats of marching as they drew closer to the opposing army. In the first Italian campaign, his men drove 50 miles in thirty-six hours; in 1805, against Austria, they marched 275 miles in twenty-three days.

His campaigns anticipated the blitzkrieg, or lightning warfare, of the twentieth century. As the moment of battle neared, Napoleon would disperse his troops over a wide area; the enemy would counter by dividing its forces. Then, by rapid marches, Napoleon would concentrate a superior force against a segment of the enemy's strung-out forces. Here the hammerblow would fall. Employing some troops to pin down the opposing force, he moved his main army to the enemy's rear or flank, cutting off his supply line. Conducted with speed and deception, these moves broke the spirit of the opposing troops. Heavy barrages by concentrated artillery opened a hole in the enemy lines that was penetrated first by heavy columns of infantry and then by shock waves of cavalry. Unlike the typical eighteenth-century commander, who maneuvered for position and was satisfied with his opponent's retreat, Napoleon sought to annihilate the enemy army, thereby destroying its source of power.

The emperor thoroughly understood the importance of morale in warfare. "Moral force rather than numbers decides victory," he once said.[21] He deliberately sought to shatter his opponent's confidence by surprise moves and lightning thrusts. Similarly, he recognized that he must maintain a high level of morale among his own troops. By sharing danger with his men, he gained their affection and admiration. He inspired his men by appealing to their honor, vanity, credulity, and love of France. "A man does not have himself killed for a few halfpence a day or for a petty distinction," he declared. "You must speak to the soul in order to electrify the man."[22] This Napoleon could do. It was Napoleon's charisma that led the Duke of Wellington to remark: "I used to say of him that his presence on the field made a difference of 40,000 men."[23]

Despite his reputation, Napoleon was not essentially an original military thinker. His greatness lay rather in his ability to implement and coordinate the theories of earlier strategists. Eighteenth-century military planners had stressed the importance of massed artillery, rapid movement, deception, living off the countryside, and the annihilation of the enemy army. Napoleon alone had the will and ingenuity to convert these theories into battlefield victories.

Similarly, Napoleon harnessed the military energies generated during a decade of revolutionary war. The Revolution had created a mass army, had instilled in the republican soldier a love for la patrie, and had enabled promising young soldiers to gain promotions on the basis of talent rather than birth. Napoleon took this inheritance and perfected it. Here, too, he was not a creator but a brilliant practitioner.

The Grand Empire: Diffusion of Revolutionary Institutions

In 1802, Napoleon had made peace with Austria and Great Britain. But when the French ruler expanded his interests in Italy and the Rhineland, Britain organized another coalition against France. In 1805, Britain signed an

MAP 20.1   NAPOLEON'S EUROPE, 1810 ▶

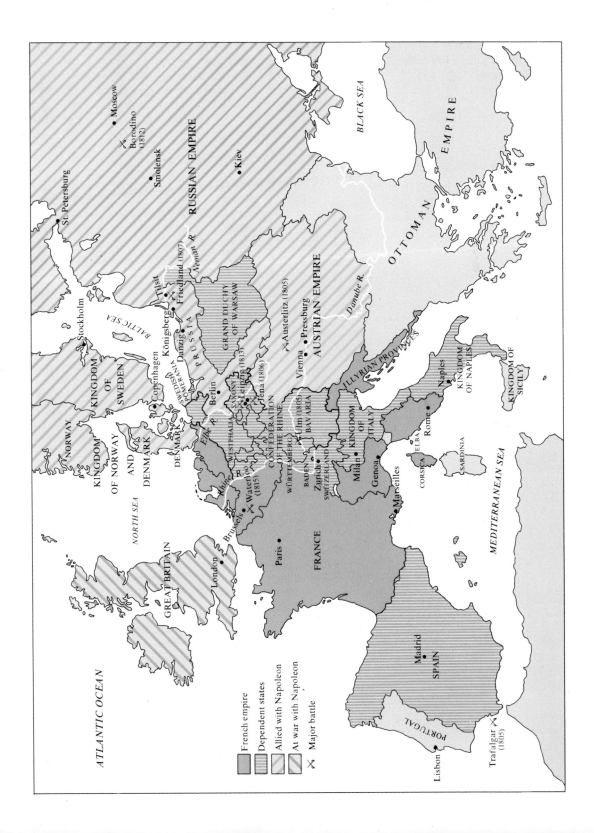

ATLANTIC OCEAN

BLACK SEA

OTTOMAN EMPIRE

RUSSIAN EMPIRE

Moscow
Borodino (1812)
Smolensk
Kiev
St. Petersburg

Stockholm
KINGDOM OF SWEDEN
BALTIC SEA
Tilsit
Friedland (1807)
Neman R.
Königsberg
Danzig
PRUSSIA
GRAND DUCHY OF WARSAW

NORWAY
KINGDOM OF NORWAY AND DENMARK
Copenhagen
DENMARK
SWEDISH POMERANIA
Berlin
Elbe R.
WESTPHALIA
SAXONY
Leipzig (1813)
Jena (1806)
CONFEDERATION OF THE RHINE
Ulm (1805)
BAVARIA
Austerlitz (1805)
Vienna
Pressburg
AUSTRIAN EMPIRE
Danube R.
ILLYRIAN PROVINCES

NORTH SEA

GREAT BRITAIN
London
Brussels
Waterloo (1815)
Rhine R.
WÜRTEMBERG
BADEN
Zurich
SWITZERLAND
KINGDOM OF ITALY
Milan
Genoa
Marseilles

Paris
FRANCE

Rome
ELBA
CORSICA
SARDINIA
Naples
KINGDOM OF NAPLES
KINGDOM OF SICILY

MEDITERRANEAN SEA

Madrid
SPAIN

PORTUGAL
Lisbon
Trafalgar (1805)

French empire
Dependent states
Allied with Napoleon
At war with Napoleon
Major battle

alliance with both Austria and Russia, and in the summer, Austrian and Russian armies advanced westward.

Napoleon acted swiftly. He outmaneuvered an Austrian army at Ulm in Bavaria (October 1805), forcing its surrender, and occupied Vienna. At Austerlitz (December 1805), he decimated a Russo-Austrian force. In the peace of Pressburg, Austria surrendered its Italian possessions to the Kingdom of Italy, a French satellite in northern Italy.

In October 1806, Napoleon decisively defeated the Prussians at Jena and entered Berlin. Another French victory at Friedland (June 1807) compelled the Russian tsar Alexander I to request an armistice. In 1807, two peace treaties were concluded at Tilsit, with Prussia and with Russia. Prussia's Polish territories became the duchy of Warsaw, a French protectorate ruled by the King of Saxony. Prussian territories west of the Elbe River became the Kingdom of Westphalia, ruled by Napoleon's youngest brother Jerome. These territorial losses reduced Prussia's population from ten to five million. Russia's territorial losses were slight, principally the Ionian islands. More important was the tsar's promise to side with France if Britain refused to make peace with Napoleon. In an incredibly short period of time, the terrible Corsican had routed the three leading Continental powers and established his domination over Europe.

Napoleon's Grand Empire consisted of an enlarged France, satellite kingdoms, and cowed allies. With varying degrees of determination and success, Napoleon extended the reforms of the Revolution to other lands. His administrators instituted the Code Napoléon, opened careers to talent, and equalized payment of taxes. They abolished serfdom and manorial payments, introduced a unified system of weights and measures, promoted public education, fought clerical interference with secular authority, and supported religious toleration. Napoleon had launched a European-wide social revolution that attacked the privileges of the aristocracy and clergy—who regarded him as that "crowned Jacobin"—and

worked to the advantage of the bourgeoisie. This diffusion of revolutionary institutions speeded up the social and political modernization of nineteenth-century Europe.

Napoleon's purpose in implementing these reforms was twofold: he wished to promote administrative efficiency and to win the support of conquered peoples. He explained his position to his brother Jerome:

What the people of Germany desire with impatience is that the individuals who are not nobles and who have talents have an equal right to your consideration and to positions; it is that every kind of serfdom and intermediary bonds between the sovereign and the lowest class of people be entirely abolished.[24]

Pleased by the overhauling of feudal practices and the diminishing of clerical power, many Europeans, particularly the progressive bourgeoisie, welcomed Napoleon as a liberator.

But there was another side to Napoleon's rule. Napoleon, the tyrant of Europe, turned conquered lands into satellite kingdoms, placed his relatives on the thrones, and exploited these lands for the benefit of France. Napoleon's policy of "France first" is revealed in the following letter to Prince Eugene, Viceroy of Italy:

All the raw silk from the Kingdom of Italy goes to England. I wish to divert it from this route to the advantage of my French manufacturers: otherwise my silk factories, one of the chief supports of French commerce, will suffer substantial losses. My principle is France first. You must never lose sight of the fact that . . . France should claim commercial supremacy on the continent.[25]

The satellite states and annexed territories were compelled to provide recruits for Napoleon's army and taxes for his war treasury. Opponents of Napoleon faced confiscation of property, the galleys, and execution.

These methods of exploitation and repression increased hatred against Napoleon and French rule. Subject peoples, including bourgeois liberals who felt that he had betrayed the ideals of the Revolution, came to view Napoleon as a tyrant ready for his downfall.

THE FALL OF NAPOLEON

In addition to the hostility of subject nationals, Napoleon had to cope with the determined opposition of Great Britain. Its subsidies and encouragement kept resistance to the emperor alive. But perhaps Napoleon's greatest obstacle was his own boundless ambition, which warped his judgment; the emperor's career slid downhill from defeat to dethronement to deportation.

Failure to Subdue England

Britain was Napoleon's most resolute opponent. It could not be otherwise, for any power that dominated the Continent could organize sufficient naval might to threaten British commerce, challenge its sea power, and invade the island kingdom. Britain would not make peace with any state that sought European hegemony, and Napoleon's ambition would settle for nothing less.

Unable to make peace with Britain, Napoleon resolved to crush it. Between 1803 and 1805 an invasion flotilla was assembled across the English Channel. But there could be no invasion of Britain while British warships commanded the channel. British naval power was demonstrated in 1805 at the battle of Trafalgar when Admiral Nelson devastated a combined French and Spanish fleet. Napoleon was forced to postpone his invasion scheme indefinitely.

Unable to conquer Britain by arms, Napoleon decided to bring what he called "the nation of shopkeepers" to its knees by damaging the British economy. His plan, called the *Continental System*, was to bar all countries under France's control from buying British goods. However, by smuggling goods onto the Continent and increasing trade with the New World, Britain, although hurt, escaped economic ruin. Moreover, the Continental System punished European lands dependent on British imports. Hundreds of ships lay idle in European ports. Industries closed down. The bourgeoisie, generally supportive of Napoleon's social and administrative reforms, turned against him because of the economic distress caused by the Continental System. Furthermore, Napoleon's efforts to enforce the system enmeshed him in two catastrophic blunders: the occupation of Spain and the invasion of Russia.

The Spanish Ulcer

An ally of France since 1796, Spain proved a disappointment to Napoleon. It failed to prevent the Portuguese from trading with Britain and contributed little military or financial aid to France's war effort. Napoleon decided to incorporate Spain into his empire. In 1808, while a French army moved toward Madrid, Charles IV, the aged and mentally feeble Spanish ruler, was forced to abdicate by his son, who proclaimed himself Ferdinand VII. The change in rulers pleased the Spanish people, but Napoleon had other plans. Determined to control Spain, he forced both Charles and Ferdinand to surrender their rights to the throne and designated his brother Joseph as king of Spain.

Napoleon believed the Spaniards would rally round the gentle Joseph and welcome his liberal reforms. This was a fatal illusion and perhaps Napoleon's worst blunder, for what appeared to be another French victory and the establishment of another satellite kingdom became, in Napoleon's words, "that miserable Spanish affair . . . [that] killed me."[26] Spanish nobles and clergy feared French liberalism; the overwhelmingly peasant population, illiterate and credulous, intensely proud, fanatically religious, and easily aroused by the clergy, viewed Napoleon as the Devil's agent. Loyal to Ferdinand and faithful to the church, the

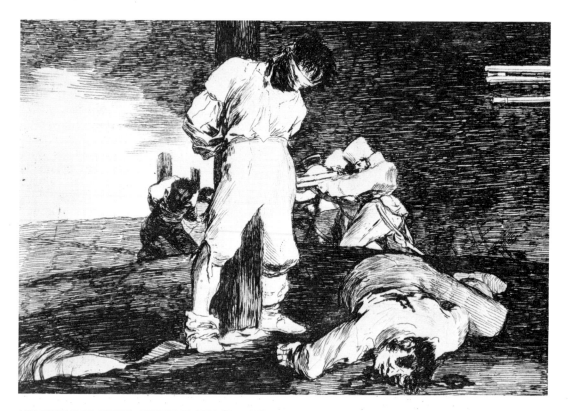

AND THERE IS NO REMEDY—ETCHING BY GOYA (1746–1828)
Napoleon could not understand the resistance of
Spain to his grand plan. Spaniards rejected Napoleon's gentle brother as their new monarch. Their
revolt was a "war to the knife." Executions and
repression followed. Napoleon would state, "that
miserable Spanish affair killed me." (Philadelphia
Museum of Art: Smithkline Corporation Collection)

Spaniards fought a "War to the Knife" against
the invaders.

The Peninsular War was fought with a
special cruelty. Wrote one shocked French
officer: "At La Carolina we established a
hospital and left 167 of our sick and wounded
men. That hospital was set afire . . . all were
burned alive or horribly massacred. The barbarians believed they had done a glorious thing
for God and religion!"[27] Guerrilla bands, aided
and encouraged by priests preaching holy war,
congregated in the mountain hideouts. Striking from ambush, they raided French convoys
and outposts, preventing the French from
consolidating their occupation and keeping
the French forces in a permanent state of
anxiety. An invisible army had spread itself
over Spain. The war waged by Spanish partisans foreshadowed a twentieth-century phenomenon—the inability of a great power,
using trained soldiers and modern weapons, to
subdue peasant guerrillas.

Seeking to keep alive the struggle against
Napoleon, Britain came to the aid of the

Spanish insurgents. The intervention of British troops commanded by Sir Arthur Wellesley, the future duke of Wellington, led to the ultimate defeat of Joseph in 1813. The "Spanish ulcer" drained Napoleon's treasury, tied down hundreds of thousands of French troops, enabled Britain to gain a foothold on the Continent from which to invade southern France, and inspired patriots in other lands to resist the French emperor.

The German War of Liberation

Anti-French feeling also broke out in the German states. Hatred of the French invaders evoked a feeling of national outrage among some Germans, who up to this time had thought in terms not of a German fatherland, but of their own particular state and prince.

The humiliation of defeat, combined with a flourishing national culture fashioned by talented writers using a common literary language, imbued some German intellectuals with a sense of national identity and national purpose. Using the emotional language of nationalism, these intellectuals called for a war of liberation against Napoleon and, in some instances, for the creation of a unified Germany. "How much longer will you be crushed beneath the heels of a proud conqueror?" demanded Friedrich Schlegel. "Awaken! Awaken, Germans, from the stupor of shame and ignominy! Awaken and act for the sake of German honor."[28] In urging Germans to seek vengeance against the conqueror, Ernst Moritz Arndt insisted that it was "the highest religion to love the Fatherland more clearly than lords and princes, fathers and mothers, wives and children."[29]

Other than this handful of intellectuals, however, few Germans were aroused by a desire for political unification. Nor did there occur anything like the general uprising that took place in Spain. Nevertheless, during the Napoleonic wars, German nationalism took shape and would continue to grow in intensi-ty, for students, professors, and poets had found a cause worthy of their idealism.

In addition to arousing a desire for national independence and unity, French domination of Germany stimulated a movement for reform and revitalization. The impact of revolutionary ideals, armies, and administration reached into Prussia, giving rise to a reform movement among members of the Prussian high bureaucracy and officer corps. The disastrous defeat of the Prussians at Jena (1806), the oppressive Peace of Tilsit (1807), the presence of a French army of occupation, and the weakening of the Prussian economy by Napoleon's policy of "France first" spurred the reform party to act. If Prussia were to survive in a world altered by the French Revolution, it would have to learn the principal lessons of the Revolution—that aroused citizens fighting for a cause make better soldiers than mercenaries and oppressed serfs, and that officers selected for daring and intelligence command better than nobles possessing only a gilded birthright.

To drive the French out of Prussia, it would be necessary to overcome the apathy of the Prussian people—so painfully demonstrated at Jena and in their passive responses to French occupation—and to bind the Prussians to the monarchy in a spirit of cooperation and loyalty. The heart of the Prussian nation must beat with that same national energy that spurred the armies of the Jacobin Republic against foreign invaders. This strengthening of the state, it was felt, could be accomplished only through immediate and far-reaching social and political reforms.

The reforms were largely the achievement of Baron vom Stein, who served for a while as first minister to King Frederick William III. Stein believed that the elimination of social abuses would overcome defeatism and apathy and encourage Prussians to serve the state willingly. A revitalized Prussia could then deal with the French. "The chief idea," said Stein, "was to arouse a moral, religious, and patriotic spirit in the nation, to instill into it again courage, confidence, readiness for every sacrifice in behalf of independence from foreigners and for the national honor, and to seize the first favorable opportunity to begin the bloody and hazardous struggle."[30]

Among the important reforms introduced in Prussia between 1807 and 1813 were the abolition of serfdom, the granting to towns of a large measure of self-administration, the awarding of army commissions on the basis of merit instead of birth, the elimination of cruel punishment in the ranks, and the establishment of national conscription. In 1813 the reform party forced King Frederick William III to declare war on France. The military reforms did improve the quality of the Prussian army. In the War of Liberation (1813), Prussian soldiers demonstrated far more enthusiasm and patriotism then they had at Jena in 1806, and the French were driven from Germany. The German War of Liberation came on the heels of Napoleon's disastrous Russian campaign.

Disaster in Russia

The unsuccessful invasion of Russia in 1812 diminished Napoleon's glory and hastened the collapse of his empire. Deteriorating relations between Russia and France led Napoleon to his fatal decision to attack the Eastern giant. Unwilling to permit Russia to become a Mediterranean power, the emperor resisted the tsar's attempts to acquire Constantinople. Napoleon's creation of the Grand Duchy of Warsaw irritated the tsar, who feared a revival of Polish power and resented French influence on Russia's border. Another source of friction between the tsar and Napoleon was Russia's illicit trade with Britain in violation of the Continental System. If the tsar were permitted to violate the trade regulations, Napoleon reasoned, other lands would soon follow and England would never be subdued. No doubt Napoleon's inexhaustible craving for power also compelled him to strike at Russia.

Napoleon assembled one of the largest armies in history, some 614,000 men, 200,000 animals, and 20,000 vehicles. Frenchmen comprised about half the *Grande Armée de la Russie*; the others, many serving under compulsion, were drawn from a score of nationalities. The emperor intended to deal the Russians a knockout blow, compelling Tsar Alexander I to sue for peace. But suppose the Russians avoided pitched battles, retreated eastward, and refused to make peace with the invader. How deeply into Russia could Napoleon go in pursuit of the enemy?

In June 1812, the Grand Army crossed the Neman River into Russia. Fighting only rearguard battles and retreating according to plan, the tsar's forces lured the invaders into the vast ocean of Russian space far from their lines of supply. In September the Russians made a stand at Borodino, some seventy miles west of Moscow. Although the French won, opening the road to Moscow, they lost 40,000 men and failed to destroy the Russian army, which withdrew in order. Napoleon still did not have the decisive victory with which he hoped to force the tsar to make peace. At midnight on September 14, the Grand Army, its numbers greatly reduced by disease, hunger, exhaustion, desertion, and battle, entered Moscow. Expecting to be greeted by a deputation of nobles, Napoleon found instead that the Muscovites had virtually evacuated their holy city.

Taking up headquarters in Moscow, Napoleon waited for Alexander I to admit defeat and come to terms. But the tsar remained intransigent. Napoleon was in a dilemma: to penetrate deeper into Russia was certain death; to stay in Moscow with winter approaching meant possible starvation. Faced with these alternatives, Napoleon decided to retreat westward to his sources of supply in Poland. On October 19, 1812, 95,000 troops and thousands of wagons loaded with loot left Moscow for the long trek back.

In early November came the first snow and frost. Army stragglers were slaughtered by Russian Cossacks and peasant partisans. Hun-

PRECIPITATE FLIGHT OF THE FRENCH THROUGH LEIPZIG
PURSUED BY THE ALLIED ARMIES, OCTOBER 19, 1813 The
combined forces of the four nations defeated Napoleon's green troops at Leipzig. His Grand Army had
been destroyed the previous year in the disastrous
attempt to conquer Russia. (The Mansell Collection,
London)

gry soldiers pounced on fallen horses, carving them up alive. The wounded were left to lie where they dropped. Some wretches, wrote a French officer, "dragged themselves along, shivering . . . until the snow packed under the soles of their boots, a bit of debris, a branch, or the body of a fallen comrade tripped them and threw them down. Then their moans for help went unheeded. The snow soon covered them up and only low white mounds showed where they lay. Our road was strewn with these hummocks, like a cemetery."[31]

In the middle of December, with the Russians in pursuit, the remnants of the Grand Army staggered across the Neman River into East Prussia. Napoleon had left his men earlier in the month and, traveling in disguise, reached Paris on December 18. Napoleon had lost his army; he would soon lose his throne.

Final Defeat

After the destruction of the Grand Army, the empire crumbled. Although Napoleon raised a new army, he could not replace the equipment, cavalry horses, and veterans squandered in Russia. Now he had to rely on schoolboys and overage veterans.

Most of Europe joined in a final coalition against France. In October 1813, allied forces from Austria, Prussia, Russia, and Sweden defeated Napoleon at Leipzig; in November, Anglo-Spanish forces crossed the Pyrenees into France. Finally, in the spring of 1814, the allies captured Paris. Napoleon abdicated and was exiled to the tiny island of Elba off the coast of Italy. The Bourbon dynasty was restored to the throne of France in the person of Louis XVIII, younger brother of the executed Louis XVI and the acknowledged leader of the émigrés.

Only forty-four years of age, Napoleon did not believe that it was his destiny to die on Elba. On March 1, 1815, he landed on the French coast with a thousand soldiers. Louis XVIII ordered his troops to stop Napoleon's advance. When Napoleon's small force approached the king's troops, Napoleon walked up to the soldiers who blocked the road. "If there is one soldier among you who wishes to kill his Emperor, here I am." It was a brilliant move by a man who thoroughly understood the French soldier. The king's troops shouted, "Long live the Emperor!" and joined Napoleon. On March 20, 1815, Napoleon entered Paris to a hero's welcome. He had not lost his charisma.

Raising a new army, Napoleon moved against the allied forces in Belgium. There the Prussians led by Field Marshal Gebhard von Blücher and the British led by the duke of Wellington defeated Napoleon at Waterloo in June 1815. Napoleon's desperate gamble to regain power—the famous "hundred days"— had failed. This time the allies sent Napoleon to St. Helena, a lonely island in the South Atlantic, a thousand miles off the coast of southern Africa. On this gloomy and rugged rock, Napoleon Bonaparte, emperor of France and would-be conqueror of Europe, spent the last six years of his life.

THE LEGEND AND THE ACHIEVEMENT

"Is there anyone whose decisions have had a greater consequence for the whole of Europe?" asks Dutch historian Pieter Geyl about Napoleon.[32] It might also be asked: Is there anyone about whom there has been such a wide range of conflicting interpretations? Both Napoleon's contemporaries and later analysts have seen Napoleon in many different lights.

Napoleon himself contributed to the historical debate. Concerned as ever with his reputation, he reconstructed his career while on St. Helena. His reminiscences are the chief source of the Napoleonic legend. According to this account, Napoleon's principal aim was to defend the Revolution and consolidate its gains. He emerges as a champion of equality, a supporter of popular sovereignty, a destroyer of feudalism, a restorer of order, an opponent of religious intolerance, and a lover of peace forced to take up the sword because of the implacable hatred of the reactionary rulers of Europe. According to this reconstruction, it was Napoleon's intention to spread the blessings of the Revolution to Germans, Dutch, Spanish, Poles, and Italians, and to create a United States of Europe, a federation of free and enlightened nations living in peace. Had Napoleon realized this vision of a socially modernized, economically integrated, rationally ruled, and politically unified western Europe, which already shared a common cultural tradition, he would have performed one of the great creative acts in human history.

Undoubtedly, Napoleon did disseminate many gains of the Revolution. Nevertheless, say his critics, this account overlooks much. It ignores the repression of liberty, the subverting of republicanism, the oppression of conquered peoples, and the terrible suffering resulting from his pursuit of glory. The reminiscences were another example of Napoleonic propaganda.

CHRONOLOGY 20.1 NAPOLEON'S MILITARY CAREER

1796	Napoleon gets command of French Army of Italy
1798	Battle of the Nile; the British annihilate Napoleon's fleet
November 10, 1799	He helps overthrow the Directory's rule, establishing a strong executive in France
1802	He becomes First Consul for life; peace is made with Austria and Britain
March 21, 1804	The Civil Code (called Code Napoléon in 1807)
December 2, 1804	He crowns himself Emperor of the French
October 1805	French forces occupy Vienna
October 21, 1805	The battle of Trafalgar—French and Spanish fleets are defeated by the British
December 1805	The battle of Austerlitz—Napoleon defeats Russo-Austrian force
1806	War against Prussia and Russia
October 1806	He defeats the Prussians at Jena and French forces occupy Berlin
June 1807	French victory over the Russians at Friedland
July 1807	The treaties of Tilsit
1808–1813	The Peninsular War—Spaniards, aided by the British, war against French occupation
September 14, 1812	The Grand Army reaches Moscow
October–December 1812	The Grand Army retreats from Russia
October 1813	Allied forces defeat Napoleon at Leipzig
1814	Paris is captured and Napoleon is exiled to Elba
March 20, 1815	Escaping, he enters Paris and begins a 100 days' rule
June 1815	Defeated at Waterloo, he is exiled to St. Helena

While the argument over Napoleon continues, historians agree on two points. First, his was no ordinary life. A self-made man who had harnessed the revolutionary forces of the age and imposed his will on history, Napoleon was right to call his life a romance. His drive, military genius, and charisma propelled him to the peak of power; his inability to moderate his ambition bled Europe, distorted his judgment, and caused his downfall. His overweening pride, the hubris of the Greek tragedians, would have awed Sophocles; the dimensions of his mind and the intricacies of his personality would have intrigued Shakespeare; his cynicism and utter unscrupulousness would have impressed Machiavelli. Secondly, historians agree that by spreading revolutionary ideals and institutions, Napoleon made it impossible for the traditional rulers to restore the Old Regime intact after the emperor's downfall. The destruction of feudal remnants, the secularization of society, the transformation of the dynastic state into the modern national state, and the ascendancy of the bourgeoisie were assured.

The new concept of warfare and the new spirit of nationalism also became an indelible part of the European scene. In the course of succeeding generations, the methods of total warfare in the service of a belligerent nationalism would shatter Napoleon's grandiose vision of a united Europe and subvert the liberal humanism that was the essential heritage of the French Revolution.

Notes

1. Quoted in Felix Markham, *Napoleon and the Awakening of Europe* (New York: Collier Books, 1965), p. 148.
2. Ibid., p. 27.
3. J. Christopher Herold, ed., *The Mind of Napoleon* (New York: Columbia University Press, 1965), p. 260.
4. Georges Lefebvre, *Napoleon* (New York: Columbia University Press, 1969), 2: 65.
5. Ibid., 2: 67.
6. Ibid., 2: 66.
7. Herold, *The Mind of Napoleon*, p. 40.
8. Quoted in David Chandler, *The Campaigns of Napoleon* (New York: Macmillan, 1966), p. 157.
9. Maurice Hutt, ed., *Napoleon* (Englewood Cliffs, N.J.: Prentice-Hall, 1972), p. 3.
10. David L. Dowd, ed., *Napoleon: Was He the Heir of the Revolution?* (New York: Holt, Rinehart, and Winston, 1966), p. 42.
11. Quoted in Felix Markham, *Napoleon* (New York: Mentor Books, 1963), p. 100.
12. Frank Malloy Anderson, ed., *The Constitution and Other Select Documents Illustrative of the History of France* (Minneapolis: H. W. Wilson, 1908), pp. 312–313.
13. Quoted in Robert B. Holtman, *The Napoleonic Revolution* (Philadelphia: J. B. Lippincott, 1967), pp. 123–124.
14. Quoted in ibid., p. 121.
15. Quoted in Markham, *Napoleon*, p. 97.
16. Dowd, *Napoleon*, p. 27.
17. Quoted in Holtman, *The Napoleonic Revolution*, p. 143.
18. Hutt, *Napoleon*, pp. 49–50.
19. Quoted in Chandler, *The Campaigns of Napoleon*, p. 145.
20. Ibid.
21. Ibid., p. 155.
22. Ibid.
23. Ibid., p. 157.
24. Quoted in Jacques Godechot, Beatrice F. Hyslop, and David L. Dowd, *The Napoleonic Era in Europe* (New York: Holt, Rinehart, and Winston, 1971), pp. 170, 172.
25. Dowd, *Napoleon*, p. 57.
26. Quoted in Owen Connelly, *Napoleon's Satellite Kingdoms* (New York: The Free Press, 1965), p. 223.
27. Quoted in Owen Connelly, *The Gentle Bonaparte* (New York: Macmillan, 1968), pp. 110–111.
28. Quoted in Boyd C. Shafer, *Nationalism: Myth and Reality* (New York: Harcourt, Brace, 1955), p. 138.
29. Quoted in ibid., p. 139.
30. Quoted in Gordon A. Craig, *The Politics of*

the Prussian Army, 1640–1945 (New York: Oxford University Press, 1964), p. 40.

31. Quoted in J. Christopher Herold, *The Age of Napoleon* (New York: Dell, 1963), p. 320.

32. Pieter Geyl, *Napoleon For and Against* (New Haven: Yale University Press, 1964), p. 16.

Suggested Reading

Chandler, David, *The Campaigns of Napoleon* (1966). An exhaustive analysis of Napoleon's art of war.

Connelly, Owen, *Napoleon's Satellite Kingdoms* (1965). Focuses on the kingdoms in Naples, Italy, Holland, Spain, and Westphalia that were created by Napoleon and ruled by his relatives.

Cronin, Vincent, *Napoleon Bonaparte* (1972). A recent highly acclaimed biography.

Geyl, Pieter, *Napoleon For and Against* (1949). A critical evaluation of French writers' views of Napoleon.

Herold, J. C., ed., *The Mind of Napoleon* (1961). A valuable selection from the written and spoken words of Napoleon.

———, *The Horizon Book of the Age of Napoleon* (1965). Napoleon and his times.

Holtman, R. B., *The Napoleonic Revolution* (1967). Napoleon as revolutionary innovator who influenced every aspect of European life; particularly good on Napoleon the propagandist.

Hutt, Maurice, ed., *Napoleon* (1972). Excerpts from Napoleon's words and the views of contemporaries and later historians.

Lefebvre, Georges, *Napoleon*, 2 vols. (1969). An authoritative biography.

Markham, Felix, *Napoleon* (1963). A first-rate short biography.

———, *Napoleon and the Awakening of Europe* (1965). Napoleon's influence on other lands.

Review Questions

1. What made it possible for Napoleon to gain power?

2. What personality traits did Napoleon possess?

3. What principles underlay Napoleon's domestic reforms?

4. What was Napoleon's "art of war"? Describe his tactics.

5. Napoleon both preserved and destroyed the ideals of the French Revolution. Discuss this statement.

6. What factors led to Napoleon's downfall?

7. What were Napoleon's greatest achievements? What were his greatest failures?

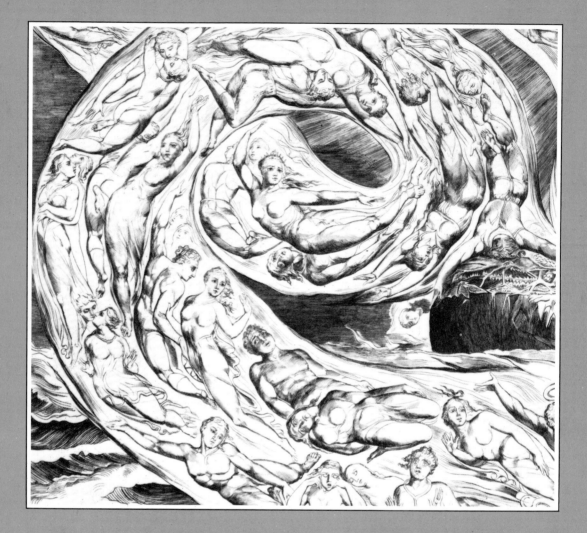

CHAPTER 21

Ferment of Ideas:
Romanticism, Conservatism,
Liberalism, Nationalism

Napoleon's Exile

IN 1815 THE ARMIES of France no longer marched across the Continent, and Napoleon was imprisoned on an island a thousand miles off the coast of Africa. The traditional rulers of Europe, some of them just restored to power, were determined to protect themselves and society from future Robespierres who organized reigns of terror and Napoleons who obliterated traditional states. As defenders of the status quo, they attacked the reformist spirit of the philosophes that had produced the Revolution. In *conservatism*, which championed tradition over reason, hierarchy over equality, and the community over the individual, they found a philosophy to justify their assault on the Enlightenment and the French Revolution.

But the forces unleashed by the French Revolution had penetrated European consciousness too deeply to be eradicated. One force for revolution was *liberalism*, which aimed to secure the liberty and equality proclaimed by the French Revolution. Another was *nationalism*, which called for the liberation of subject peoples and the unification of broken nations.

The postrevolutionary period also saw a new cultural orientation. *Romanticism*, with its plea for the liberation of human emotions and the free expression of personality, challenged the Enlightenment stress on rationalism. Although primarily a literary and artistic movement, Romanticism also permeated philosophy and political thought, particularly conservatism. Thus, conservatism, liberalism, nationalism, and romanticism—these were the motivating forces in the decades following the fall of Napoleon.

ROMANTICISM: A NEW CULTURAL ORIENTATION

The Romantic Movement, which began in the closing decades of the eighteenth century, dominated European cultural life in the first half of the nineteenth century. Historians recognize the prominence of romanticism in nineteenth-century cultural life, but they cannot agree on a definition of romanticism, so complex was the movement, so innumerable were the differences among the various romantic writers, artists, and musicians. Romantics were both liberals and conservatives, revolutionaries and reactionaries; some were preoccupied with religion and God, while others paid little attention to faith.

Most of Europe's leading cultural figures came under the influence of the Romantic Movement. Among the exponents of romanticism were the English poets Shelley, Wordsworth, Keats, and Byron, the French novelist Victor Hugo and the Catholic philosopher Chateaubriand, the German writers A. W. and Friedrich Schlegel and philosophers Schiller and Schelling. Caspar David Friedrich in Germany and John Constable in England expressed the romantic mood in art, and the later Beethoven, Schubert, Chopin, and Wagner expressed it in music.

Exalting Imagination and Feelings

Romantics

Perhaps the central message of the romantics was that the imagination of the individual should determine the form and content of an artistic creation. This outlook ran counter to the rationalism of the Enlightenment, which itself had been a reaction against the otherworldly Christian orientation of the Middle Ages. The Romantic Movement reacted against the dominant ideas of the Enlightenment. The philosophes had attacked faith because it thwarted and distorted reason; romantic poets, philosophers, and artists now denounced the rationalism of the philosophes because it crushed the emotions and impeded creativity. The philosophes, said the romantics, had turned flesh-and-blood human beings into soulless thinking machines and vibrant nature into lifeless wheels, cogs, and pulleys. The reign of reason had separated individuals

from their feelings; it had prevented them from realizing their human nature; it had deadened their hearts and paralyzed their wills. To restore human beings to their true nature, to make them whole again, they must be emancipated from the tyranny of excessive intellectualizing; the feelings must be nourished and expressed.

The philosophes had concentrated on people in general—those elements of human nature shared by all people. Romantics, on the other hand, emphasized human uniqueness—those distinctive traits that set one human being apart from others. Each person yearns to discover and to express his or her true self. Each plays his or her own music; each writes his or her own poetry; each paints his or her own personal vision of nature. Each experiences love and suffering in his or her own way. In the opening lines of his autobiography, *Confessions*, Jean Jacques Rousseau, a romantic in an age of reason, expressed the intense subjectivism that characterized the Romantic Movement.

I am commencing an undertaking, hitherto without precedent and which will never find an imitator. I desire to set before my fellows the likeness of a man in all the truth of nature, and that man myself. Myself alone! I know the feelings of my heart, and I know men. I am not made like any of those I have seen. I venture to believe that I am not made like any of those who are in existence. If I am not better, at least I am different.[1]

Whereas the philosophes had regarded the feelings as an obstacle to clear thinking, to the romantics they were the human essence. People could not live by reason alone, said the romantics. They agreed with Rousseau, who wrote: "For us, to exist is to feel and our sensibility is incontestably prior to our reason."[2] For the romantics, reason was cold and dreary, its understanding of people and life meager and inadequate. Reason could not comprehend or express the complexities of human nature nor the richness of human

WILLIAM BLAKE (1757–1827): THE WHIRLWIND OF LOVERS
(DETAIL) Romantic writers and painters celebrated
emotions and passions. Blake illustrated this episode from Dante's *Divine Comedy* probably because
he sympathized with, rather than condemned, the
lovers. (National Gallery of Art, Washington, D.C.;
Gift of W. G. Russell Allen)

experience, said the romantics. By always dissecting and analyzing, by imposing deadening structure and form, and by demanding adherence to strict rules, reason crushed inspiration and creativity and barred true understanding. "The Reasoning Power in Man," said William Blake, the British poet, artist, and mystic, is "an incrustation over my immortal Spirit."[3]

For the romantics, the avenue to truth was not the intellect, but spontaneous human emotions. By cultivating instincts and imagination, individuals could experience reality and discover their authentic selves. The ro-

mantics wanted people to feel and to experience—to "bathe in the waters of life," said Blake.[4] Or as Johann Goethe, Germany's greatest poet, wrote in *Faust:* "My worthy friend, gray are all theories,/And green alone Life's golden tree."[5]

For this reason, the romantics insisted that imaginative poets had a greater insight into life than analytical philosophers did. Poetry is a true philosophy, the romantics said; it can do what rational analysis and geometric calculations cannot—clarify life's deepest mysteries, participate in the eternal, and penetrate to the depths of human nature. "I am certain of nothing but of the holiness of the Heart's affections and the truth of Imagination," wrote John Keats. "O for a Life of Sensations rather than of Thoughts."[6] For reason to function best, it must be nourished by the poetic imagination.

The Enlightenment mind had been clear, critical, and controlled. It had adhered to standards of esthetics thought to be universal that had dominated European cultural life since the Renaissance. That mind stressed technique and form and tended to reduce the imagination to mechanical relationships. "Analysis and calculation make the poet, as they make the mathematician," wrote Étienne Condillac, a prominent French philosophe. "Once the material of a play is given, the invention of the plot, the characters, the verse, is only a series of algebraic problems to be worked out."[7] Following in this tradition, Népomucène Lemercier determined that there were twenty-six rules for tragedy, twenty-three for comedy, and twenty-four for the epic; he proceeded to manufacture plays and epics according to this formula.

Romantic poets, artists, and musicians broke with the traditional styles and austere rules and created new cultural forms and techniques. "We do not want either Greek or Roman Models," said Blake, but should be "just and true to our own Imaginations."[8] For the romantics, persons did not learn how to write poetry or paint pictures by following textbook rules; they could not comprehend the poet's or artist's intent by judging works according to fixed standards. "It is the beginning of poetry," wrote Friedrich Schlegel, "to abolish the law and the method of the rationally proceeding reason and to plunge us once more into the ravishing confusion of fantasy, the original chaos of human nature."[9] Only by trusting to their own feelings could individuals fulfill their creative potential and achieve self-realization. The most beautiful works of art, for example, were not photographic imitations of nature, but authentic and spontaneous expressions of the artist's feelings, fantasies,

and dreams. Similarly, the romantics were less impressed by Beethoven's constructions than by the intensity and fury that the music embodied.

The romantics explored the inner life of the mind that Freud would later call _the unconscious_. It was this layer of the mind, mysterious, primitive, more elemental and more powerful than reason, the wellspring of creativity, that the romantics yearned to revitalize and release.

Nature, God, History

The philosophes had viewed nature as a lifeless machine, a giant clock all of whose parts worked together in perfect precision and harmony. Its laws, operating with mathematical certainty, were uncovered by the methodology of science. To the romantics, nature was alive and vital, suffused with God's presence. Nature stimulated the creative energies of the imagination; it taught human beings a higher form of knowledge, as William Wordsworth wrote:

One impulse from a vernal wood
May teach you more of man,
Of moral evil and of good,
Than all the sages can.[10]

For the romantics, nature did not consist of mechanical parts, but of trees, lakes, mountains, clouds, and stars that one experienced in an emotional way and with which one sought mystical union. Not the mathematician's logic, but the poet's imagination unlocked nature's most important secrets.

The philosophes had seen God as a great watchmaker, an idle observer of a self-operating mechanical universe, and tried to reduce religion to a series of scientific propositions. Many romantics viewed God as a spiritual force that inspired people, and they deplored the decline of Christianity. The cathedrals and ceremonies, poetic and mysterious,

JEAN FRANÇOIS MILLET (1814–1875): PLANTING POTATOES
(DETAIL) For the romantic, the peasant and his lowly
occupation became fit subjects for literature and
painting. The emotions of a beggar were now seen as
important as those of an emperor. (Courtesy Museum of Fine Arts, Boston)

satisfied the esthetic impulse: Christian moral
commands, compassionate and just, elevated
human behavior to a higher level. The romantics condemned the philosophes for weakening Christianity by submitting its dogmas to
the test of reason. For the Romantics, religion
was not science and syllogism, but a passionate and authentic expression of human nature.

The philosophes had viewed the Middle
Ages as an era of darkness, superstition, and
fanaticism and regarded surviving medieval

institutions and traditions as barriers to progress. The romantics, on the other hand, revered the Middle Ages. The wars of the French
Revolution, Napoleon, and the breakdown of
political equilibrium had produced a sense of
foreboding about the future. Some sought
spiritual security by looking back to the Middle Ages when Europe was united by a single
faith. Then, said romantics, no rationalist's
blade dissected and slashed Christian mysteries; no wild-eyed revolutionaries tore apart the
fabric of society. To the romantic imagination,

JOHN CONSTABLE (1776–1837): SALISBURY CATHEDRAL FROM
THE BISHOP'S GARDEN Romantics admired Christianity and the Middle Ages. Cathedrals and ceremonies,
they felt, satisfied an esthetic impulse. (The Frick
Collection, New York)

the Middle Ages abounded with heroic deeds,
noble sentiments, and social harmony.

Romantics and philosophes held differing
conceptions of history. For the philosophes,
history served a didactic purpose by providing
examples of human folly. Such knowledge
assisted people in preparing for a better future.
The thinkers of the eighteenth century says
philosopher-historian Ernst Cassirer, "never
studied history in order to satisfy a merely
intellectual curiosity. They saw in it a guide to
action, a compass that could lead them to a
future and better state of human society."[11] To

the romantics, a historical period, like an
individual, was a unique entity with its own
soul. They wanted the historian to portray and
analyze the bewildering variety of nations,
traditions, and institutions that constituted
the historical experience. The romantic command to study and comprehend the concrete
and specific productions of history is the
foundation of modern historical scholarship.

Searching for universal principles, the philosophes had dismissed the folk traditions of a
people as peasant superstitions and impediments to progress. The romantics, on the other

hand, rebelling against the standardization of culture, saw native languages, songs, and legends as unique creations of a people, the deepest expression of national feeling. In this way, romanticism was instrumental in the shaping of modern nationalism.

The Impact of the Romantic Movement

The romantic revolt against the Enlightenment had an important and enduring impact on European history. By focusing on the creative capacities inherent in the emotions, the romantics shed light on a side of human nature that the philosophes had often overlooked or undervalued. By encouraging personal freedom and flexibility in art, music, and literature, they greatly enriched European cultural life. Future artists, writers, and musicians would proceed along the path paved by the romantics. Modern art, for example, owes much to the Romantic Movement's emphasis on the legitimacy of human feeling and its exploration of the hidden world of dreams and fantasies. The romantic emphasis on feeling sometimes found expression in humanitarian movements that fought slavery, child labor, and poverty. By recognizing the distinctive qualities of historical periods, peoples, and cultures, the romantics helped to create the modern historical outlook. By valuing the nation's past, romanticism contributed to modern nationalism and conservatism.

But there was a potentially dangerous side to the Romantic Movement. By waging their attack on reason with excessive zeal, the romantics undermined the rational foundations of the West. The romantic idealization of the past and glorification of ancient folkways, native soil, and native language introduced a highly charged, nonrational component into political life. In the decades to come, romanticism, particularly in Germany, fused with political nationalism and "created a general climate of inexact thinking, an intellectual . . . dream world and an emotional approach to problems of political action to which sober reasoning should have been applied."[12]

CONSERVATISM: THE VALUE OF TRADITION

To the traditional rulers of Europe—kings, aristocrats, clergy—the French Revolution was a great evil that had inflicted a near-fatal wound on civilization. Did not the revolutionaries execute Louis XVI, confiscate the land of the church, destroy the special privileges of the aristocracy, and institute the Reign of Terror? Did not the Revolution give rise to Napoleon, who deposed kings, continued the assault on the aristocracy, and sought to dominate Europe? Disgusted and frightened by the revolutionary violence, terror, and warfare, the traditional rulers sought to refute the philosophes' world-view that had spawned the Revolution. To them, natural rights, equality, the goodness of man, and perpetual progress were perverse doctrines that had produced the Jacobin "assassins." In conservatism they found a political philosophy to counter the Enlightenment ideology.

Edmund Burke's *Reflections on the French Revolution* (1790) was instrumental in shaping conservative thought. Burke (1729–1797), a British philosopher and statesman, wanted to warn his countrymen of the dangers inherent in the ideology of the revolutionaries. Although writing in 1790, Burke astutely predicted that the Revolution would lead to terror and military dictatorship. To Burke, fanatics armed with pernicious principles—abstract ideas divorced from historical experience—had dragged France through the mire of revolution. Burke developed a coherent political philosophy that served as a counterweight to the ideology of the Enlightenment and the Revolution.

Hostility to the French Revolution

The philosophes and French reformers, entranced by the great discoveries in science, had believed that the human mind could also transform social institutions and ancient traditions according to rational models. Progress through reason became their faith. Dedicated to creating a new future, the revolutionaries abruptly dispensed with old habits, traditional authority, and familiar ways of thought.

To conservatives, who like the romantics venerated the past, this was supreme arrogance and wickedness. They regarded the revolutionaries as presumptuous men who recklessly severed society's links with ancient institutions and traditions and condemned venerable religious and moral beliefs as ignorance. Moreover, the revolutionaries forgot—or never knew—that the traditions and institutions they wanted to destroy did not belong solely to them. Past generations and indeed future generations had a claim to these creations of French genius. By attacking time-honored ways, the revolutionaries had deprived French society of moral leadership and had opened the door to anarchy and terror. "You began ill," said Burke of the revolutionaries, "because you began by despising everything that belonged to you. . . . When ancient opinions and rules of life are taken away, the loss cannot possibly be estimated. From that moment we have no compass to govern us; nor can we know distinctly to what port we steer."[13]

The philosophes and French reformers had expressed unlimited confidence in the power of the human intellect to understand and to change society. While appreciating human rational capacities, conservatives also recognized the limitations of reason. They saw the Revolution as a natural outgrowth of an arrogant Enlightenment philosophy that overvalued reason and sought to reshape society in accordance with abstract principles. Conservatives condemned radical social change imposed by utopian thinkers with grandiose blueprints.

For conservatives, human beings were not by nature good. Human wickedness was not due to a faulty environment, as the philosophes had proclaimed, but was at the core of human nature, as Christianity taught. Evil was held in check not by reason, but by tried and tested institutions, traditions, and beliefs. Without these habits inherited from ancestors, said conservatives, the social order was threatened by sinful human nature.

Because monarchy, aristocracy, and the church had endured for centuries, argued the conservatives, they had worth. The clergy taught proper moral values; monarchs preserved order and property; aristocrats guarded against despotic kings and the tyranny of the common people. All protected and spread civilized ways. However, by despising and uprooting these ancient institutions, the revolutionaries had hardened the people's hearts, perverted their morals, and caused them to commit terrible outrages upon each other and society.

Conservatives detested attempts to transform society according to a theoretical model. They felt that human nature was too intricate and that social relations were too complex for such social engineering. For conservatives, the revolutionaries had reduced people and society to abstractions divorced from their historical settings; consequently, they had destroyed ancient patterns that seemed inconvenient and had drawn up constitutions based on the unacceptable principle that government derives its power from the consent of the governed.

For conservatives, God and history were the only legitimate sources of political authority; states were not made, but were an expression of the nation's moral, religious, and historical experience. No legitimate or sound constitution could be drawn up by a group assembled for that purpose. Scraps of paper with legal terminology and philosophic visions could not produce an effective government; instead, a sound political system evolved gradually and inexplicably in response to circumstances. For this reason, conservatives admired the English constitution. It was not a product of abstract thought; no assembly had convened to fashion it. Because it grew imperceptibly out of the historical experience and needs of the English people, it was durable and effective.

For conservatives, society was not a machine with replaceable parts, but a complex and delicate organism. Tamper with its vital organs, as the revolutionaries had done, and it would die.

The Quest for Social Stability

The liberal philosophy of the Enlightenment and the French Revolution started with the individual. The philosophes and the revolutionaries envisioned a society in which the individual was free and autonomous. Conservatives believed that society was not a mechanical arrangement of disconnected individuals, but a living organism held together by centuries-old bonds. Alone, a person would be selfish, unreliable, frail; it was only as a member of a social group—family, church, or state—that one acquired the ways of cooperation and the manners of civilization. By exalting the individual, the revolutionaries had threatened to dissolve society into disconnected parts. Individualism would imperil social stability, destroy obedience to law, and fragment society into self-seeking isolated atoms.

Holding that the community was more important than the individual, conservatives rejected the philosophy of natural rights. Rights were not abstractions that preceded an individual's entrance into society and pertained to all people everywhere. Rather, the state, always remembering the needs of the entire community and its links to past genera-

tions, determined what rights and privileges its citizens might possess. There were no "rights of man," only rights of the French, the English, and so forth, as determined and allocated by the particular state.

Conservatives viewed equality as another pernicious abstraction that contradicted all historical experience. For conservatives, society was naturally hierarchical, and they believed that some men by virtue of their intelligence, education, wealth, and birth were best qualified to rule and instruct the less able. They said that by denying the existence of a natural elite and uprooting a long-established ruling class that had learned its art through experience, the revolutionaries had deprived society of effective leaders, brought internal disorder, and prepared the way for a military dictatorship.

Whereas the philosophes had attacked Christianity for promoting superstition and fanaticism, conservatives saw religion as the basis of civil society. An excess of liberty and the weakening of religion had brutalized people and shattered the foundations of society. Catholic conservatives in particular held that God had constituted the church and monarchy in order to check sinful human nature. "Christian monarchs are the final creation of the development of political society and of religious society," said Louis de Bonald, a French émigré. "The proof of this lies in the fact that when monarchy and Christianity are both abolished society returns to savagery."[14]

Conservatism pointed to a limitation of the Enlightenment. It showed that human beings and social relationships are far more complex than the philosophes had imagined. People do not always respond to the rigorous logic of the philosopher and are not eager to break with ancient ways, however illogical they appear to the intellect. They often find familiar customs and ancestral religions more satisfying guides to life than the blueprints of the philosophers. The granite might of tradition remains an obstacle to all the visions of reformers.

LIBERALISM: THE VALUE OF THE INDIVIDUAL

The period from 1815 to 1848 saw a spectacular rise of the bourgeoisie. Talented and ambitious bankers, merchants, manufacturers, professionals, and officeholders wanted to break the stranglehold that the landed nobility held on political power and social prestige and to eliminate restrictions on the free pursuit of profits.

Liberalism was most commonly the political philosophy of the bourgeoisie. While conservatives sought to strengthen the foundations of traditional society, liberals wanted to alter the status quo and to carry out the promise of the Enlightenment and the French Revolution. Conservatives concentrated on the community, but liberals gave central concern to individual freedom. Conservatives tried to preserve a hierarchic society that gave prominence to an inherited aristocracy, but liberals insisted that a person's value was measured not by birth but by achievement. Conservatives held that the state rests on ancient traditions or divine authority, but liberals sought the rational state in which political institutions and procedures were based on intelligible principles. Regarding human nature as inherently evil, conservatives wanted individuals to obey their betters. Liberals, on the other hand, had confidence in the capacity of the individuals to control their own lives.

The Sources of Liberalism

In the long view of Western civilization, liberalism is an extension and development of the democratic practices and rational outlook that originated in ancient Greece. Also flowing into the liberal tradition is a Judeo-Christian respect for the individual. But the immediate historical roots of liberalism extend back to seventeenth-century England. At that time, the struggle for religious toleration by English Protestant dissenters established the principle of freedom of conscience, which is easily transferred into freedom of opinion and expression in all matters. The Glorious Revolution of 1688 set limits on the power of the English monarchy. In that same century the natural-rights philosophy of John Locke declared that the individual was by nature entitled to freedom and justified revolutions against rulers who deprived citizens of their lives, liberty, or property.

The French philosophes were instrumental in the shaping of liberalism. From Montesquieu, liberals derived the theory of the separation of powers and checks and balances that sought to guard against autocratic government. The philosophes had supported religious toleration and freedom of thought, expressed confidence in the capacity of the human mind to reform society, maintained that human beings are essentially good, and believed in the future progress of humanity—all fundamental principles of liberalism.

The American and French revolutions were crucial phases in the history of liberalism. The Declaration of Independence gave expression to Locke's theory of natural rights; the Constitution of the United States incorporated Montesquieu's principles and demonstrated that people could create an effective government; the Bill of Rights protected the person and rights of the individual. In destroying the special privileges of the aristocracy and opening careers to talent, the French National Assembly of 1789 had implemented the liberal ideal of equality under the law. They also drew up the Declaration of the Rights of Man and Citizen, which affirmed the dignity and rights of the individual, and a constitution that limited the king's power. Both the American and French revolutions explicitly called for the protection of property rights, another basic consideration of liberals.

Individual Liberty

The central concern of liberals was the enhancement of individual liberty. They agreed with German philosopher Immanuel Kant that every person exists as an end in himself or herself and not as an object to be used arbitrarily by others. Uncoerced by government and churches and properly educated, a person could develop into a good, creative, and self-directed human being. Every individual could make his or her own decisions, base actions on universal moral laws, and respect others' rights.

Liberals rejected a legacy of the Middle Ages, the classification of the individual as a commoner or aristocrat on the basis of birth. They held that a person was not born into a certain station in life, but made his way through his own efforts. Taking their cue from the French Revolution, liberals called for an end to all privileges of the aristocracy.

In the tradition of the philosophes, liberals stressed the pre-eminence of reason as the basis of political life. Unfettered by ignorance and tyranny, the mind could eradicate evils that had burdened people for centuries and begin an age of free institutions and responsible citizens. For this reason, liberals supported the advancement of education. They believed that educated people apply reason to their political and social life, that they act in ways beneficial to themselves and society, and are less likely to submit to tyrants.

Liberals attacked the state and other authorities that prevented the individual from exercising the right of free choice, that interfered with the right of free expression, and that prevented the individual from self-determination and self-development. They agreed with John Stuart Mill, the British philosopher, who declared that "over his own body and mind, the individual is sovereign. . . . that the only purpose for which power can be rightfully exercised over any member of a civilized community, against his will, is to prevent harm to others."[15]

The great question that confronted nineteenth-century liberals was the relationship between state authority and individual liberty. To guard against the absolute and arbitrary authority of kings, liberals demanded written constitutions that granted freedom of speech, the press, and religion; freedom from arbitrary arrest; and the protection of property rights. To prevent the abuse of political authority, liberals called for a freely elected parliament and the distribution of power among the various branches of government. Liberals held that a government that derived its authority from the consent of the governed as given in free elections was least likely to violate individual freedom. A corollary of this principle was that the best government was one that governs least—that is, one that is least involved in the private lives of its citizens.

Liberals held that the economy, like the state, should proceed according to natural laws rather than the arbitrary fiat of rulers. Adopting the laissez-faire theory of Adam Smith, they maintained that a free economy, in which private enterprise would be unimpeded by government regulations, was as important as political freedom to the well-being of the individual and the community. When people acted from self-interest, the liberals said, they worked harder and achieved more; self-interest spurred economic activity, which ultimately would benefit the entire nation. For this reason, the government must not block free competition nor deprive individuals of their property. The state contributed to the nation's prosperity when it maintained domestic order; it endangered economic development when it tampered with the free pursuit of profits. Believing that individuals were responsible for their own misfortunes, liberals were often unmoved by the misery of the poor and considered social reforms to alleviate poverty as an unwarranted and dangerous meddling with the natural laws of supply and demand.

Liberalism and Democracy

The French Revolution presented a dilemma for liberals. They supported the reforms of the moderate stage—the destruction of the special privileges of the aristocracy, the drawing up of a declaration of rights and a constitution, the establishment of a parliament, the opening of careers to talent—but they repudiated Jacobin radicalism. Liberals were frightened by the excesses of the Jacobin regime—its tampering with the economy, which liberals felt violated the rights of private property; its appeal to the "little people," which they felt invited mob rule; its subjection of the individual to the state, which they regarded as the denial of individual rights; its use of the guillotine, which awakened the basest human feelings.

Though many liberals still adhered to the philosophy of natural rights, some who were disturbed by the Jacobin experience discarded the theory underlying the reforms of the Revolution. These liberals feared that abstract theories led to endless revolutions; they feared social disorder as much as conservatives did. In the hands of the lower classes the natural-rights philosophy was too easily translated into the democratic creed that all people should share in political power, a prospect that the bourgeois regarded with horror. To them, participation of commoners in politics meant a vulgar form of despotism and the end to individual liberty. The masses, uneducated, unpropertied, inexperienced, and impatient, had neither the ability nor the temperament to maintain liberty and protect property.

In this new age, said Alexis de Tocqueville, a French political theorist, the masses had a passion for equality, not liberty. They demanded that the avenue to social, economic, and political advancement be opened to all; they no longer accepted disparity in wealth and position as part of the natural order. They would willingly sacrifice political liberty in order to improve their material well-being. Looking to the state as the guarantor of equality, said de Tocqueville, the people would grant it ever more power. The state then would regulate its citizens' lives, crush local institutions impeding centralized control, and impose the beliefs of the majority on the minority. Liberty would be lost not to the despotism of kings, but to the tyranny of the majority.

Because bourgeois liberals feared that democracy could crush personal freedom as ruthlessly as any absolute monarch could, they called for property requirements for voting and officeholding. They wanted political power to be concentrated in the hands of a safe and reliable—that is, a propertied and educated—middle class. Such a government would prevent revolution from below, a prospect that caused anxiety among bourgeois liberals.

Early nineteenth-century liberals engaged in revolutions, to be sure, but their aims were always limited. Once they had destroyed absolute monarchy and gained a constitution and a parliament or a change of government, they quickly tried to terminate the revolution. When the fever of revolution spread to the masses, liberals quickly turned counterrevolutionary, for they feared the stirrings of the multitude.

Although liberalism was the political philosophy of the middle class (generally hostile to democracy), the essential ideals of democracy flowed logically from liberalism. Democracy was a later stage in the evolution of liberalism, because the masses, their political power enhanced by the Industrial Revolution, would press for greater social, political, and economic equality. Thus, by the early twentieth century, many European states had introduced universal suffrage, abandoned property requirements for officeholding, and improved conditions for workers.

But the fears of nineteenth-century liberals were not without foundation. In the twentieth century, the participation of common people in politics has indeed threatened freedom. Impatient with parliamentary procedures, the masses, particularly when troubled by economic problems, in some instances have turned to demagogues who promised swift and decisive action. The granting of political participation to the masses has not always made people more free. The confidence of democrats has been shaken in the twentieth century by the seeming willingness of the common people to trade freedom for authority, order, economic security, and national power.

NATIONALISM: THE SACREDNESS OF THE NATION

Nationalism is an awareness shared by a group of people who feel strongly attached to a particular land and who possess a common culture and common history marked by shared glories and sufferings. Nationalism is accompanied by a conviction that one's highest loyalty and devotion should be directed to the nation. Nationalists exhibit great pride in their people's history and traditions and often feel that their nation has been specially chosen by God or history. Like a religion, nationalism provides the individual with a sense of community and with a cause worthy of self-sacrifice.

Thus, in an age when Christianity was in retreat, nationalism became the dominant spiritual force in nineteenth-century European life. Nationalism provided new myths, martyrs, and "holy" days that stimulated reverence; it offered membership in a community, which satisfied the overwhelming psychological need of human beings for fellowship and identity. And nationalism gave a mission, the advancement of the nation, to which people could dedicate themselves.

The Emergence of Modern Nationalism

The essential components of nationalism emerged at the time of the French Revolu-

FRANÇOIS RUDE (1784–1855): LA MARSEILLAISE The nineteenth century saw the emergence of modern nationalism. The romantics' explorations of myths and folk traditions provided roots and cultural bases for nationalistic feelings. (French Press and Information Service, New York)

tion. The Revolution asserted the principle that sovereignty derived from the nation, the people as a whole—the state was not the private possession of the ruler, but the embodiment of the people's will. The nation-state was above king, church, estate, guild, province; it superseded all other loyalties. Frenchmen must view themselves not as subjects of the king, not as Bretons or Normans, not as nobles or bourgeois, but as citizens of a united fatherland, *la patrie*. These two ideas—the people possessing unlimited sovereignty and the people united into a nation—were crucial in the fashioning of a nationalist outlook.

As the revolution moved from the moderate to the radical stage, French nationalism gained in intensity. In 1793–1794, when the Republic was threatened by foreign invasion, the Jacobins created a national army, demanded ever greater allegiance to and sacrifice for the nation, and called for the expansion of the borders to the Alps and the Rhine. With unprecedented success, the Jacobins used every means—press, schoolroom, rostrum—to instill a love of country.

The Romantic Movement also awakened nationalist feelings. By examining the language, literature, and folkways of their people, romantic thinkers instilled a sense of national pride in their countrymen. Johann Gottfried Herder (1744–1803) conceived the idea of the *Volksgeist*, the soul of the people. For Herder, each people was unique and creative; each expressed its genius in language, literature, monuments, and folk traditions. Herder did not make the theoretical jump from a spiritual or cultural nationalism to political nationalism; he did not call for the formation of states based on nationality. But his emphasis on the unique culture of a people stimulated a national consciousness among Germans and the various Slavic peoples who lived under foreign rule. The Volksgeist led intellectuals to investigate the past of their own people, to rediscover their ancient traditions, and to extol their historic language and culture. From this cultural nationalism it was only a short step to a political nationalism that called for national liberation, unification, and statehood.

The romantics were the earliest apostles of German nationalism. They restored to consciousness memories of the German past and emphasized the peculiar qualities of the German folk and the special destiny of the German nation. The romantics glorified medieval Germany and valued hereditary monarchy and aristocracy as vital links to the nation's past. They saw the existence of each individual as inextricably bound up with folk and fatherland, and found the self-realization for which they yearned by identifying their own egos with the national soul. To these romantics, the national community was a vital force which gave the individual both an identity and a purpose to life. The nation stood above the individual; the national spirit bound isolated souls into a community of brethren. In unmistakably romantic tones, Ernst Moritz Arndt urged Germans to unite against Napoleon:

German man, feel again God, hear and fear the eternal, and you hear and fear also your Volk [people], you feel again in God the honor and dignity of your fathers, their glorious history rejuvenates itself in you, their firm and gallant virtue reblossoms in you, the whole German Fatherland stands again before you in the august halo of past centuries. . . .

No longer Catholics and Protestants, no longer Prussians and Austrians, Saxons and Bavarians, Silesians and Hanoverians, no longer of different faith, different mentality, and different will—be Germans, be one, will to be one by love and loyalty, and no devil will vanquish you.[16]

Most German romantics expressed hostility to the liberal ideals of the French Revolution. They condemned the reforms of the Revolution for trying to reconstruct society by separating individuals from their national past, for treating them as isolated abstractions. They held that the German folk spirit should not be polluted by foreign French ideas.

To the philosophes, the state was a human creation that provided legal safeguards for the individual. To the romantics, the state was something holy, the expression of the divine spirit of a people; it could not be manufactured to order by the intellect. The state's purpose was not the protection of natural rights nor the promotion of economic well-being, as the philosophes had conceived it; rather, the state was a living organism that linked each person to a sacred past and imbued private individuals with a profound sense of community.

Nationalism and Liberalism

In the early nineteenth century, liberals were the principal leaders and supporters of nationalist movements. They viewed the struggle for national rights—the freedom of a people from foreign rule—as an extension of the struggle for the rights of the individual. There could be no liberty, said nationalists, if people were not free to rule themselves in their own land. People must be liberated not only from despotic kings and narrow-minded priests, but they must also be emancipated from foreign oppression and subjugation.

Liberals called for the unification of Germany and Italy, the rebirth of Poland, the liberation of Greece from Turkish rule, and the granting of autonomy to the Hungarians of the Austrian Empire. Liberal nationalists envisioned a Europe of independent states based on nationality and popular sovereignty. Free of foreign domination and tyrant princes, these newly risen states would protect the rights of the individual and strive to create a brotherhood of nationalities in Europe.

In the first half of the nineteenth century, few intellectuals recognized the dangers inherent in nationalism or understood the fundamental conflict between liberalism and nationalism. For the liberal, the idea of the rights of man transcended all national boundaries; it was a universal principle that applied to everyone. Inheriting the cosmopolitanism of the Enlightenment, liberalism emphasized what all people had in common, called for all individuals to be treated equally under the law, and preached toleration. Manifesting the particularist attitude of the in-group and the tribe, nationalists regarded the nation as the essential fact of existence. Consequently, they often willingly subverted individual liberty for the sake of national grandeur. Whereas the liberal sought to protect the rights of all within the state, the nationalist often ignored or trampled on the rights of individuals and national minorities. Whereas liberalism grew out of the rational tradition of the West, nationalism derived from the emotions. Because it fulfilled an elemental yearning for community and kinship, nationalism exerted a powerful hold over human hearts. Liberalism ruthlessly attacked traditions and

institutions that seemed to oppose reason and demanded objectivity in analyzing society and history, but nationalism evoked a mythic and romantic past that often distorted history.

In the last part of the nineteenth century, the irrational and mythic quality of nationalism would intensify. By stressing the unique qualities and history of a particular people, nationalism would promote hatred between nationalities. By kindling deep love for the past, including a longing for ancient borders, glories, and power, nationalism would lead to wars of expansion. By arousing the emotions to a fever pitch, nationalism would shatter rational thinking, drag the mind into a world of fantasy and myth, and introduce extemism into politics. Love of nation would become an overriding passion that threatened to extinguish the liberal ideals of reason and freedom.

Notes

1. Jean Jacques Rousseau, *The Confessions* (New York: Modern Library, 1950), p. 2.
2. Quoted in H. G. Schenk, *The Mind of the European Romantics* (Garden City, N.Y.: Doubleday, 1969), p. 4.
3. William Blake, *Milton*, 40. 34–35.
4. Ibid., 41. 1.
5. Goethe, *Faust*, trans. by Bayard Taylor (New York: Modern Library, 1950), pt. 1, sc. 4.
6. Letter of Keats, November 22, 1817, in Hyder E. Rollins, ed., *The Letters of John Keats* (Cambridge, Mass.: Harvard University Press, 1958), 1: 184–185.
7. Quoted in John Herman Randall, Jr., *The Career of Philosophy* (New York: Columbia University Press, 1965), 2: 80.
8. William Blake, *Milton*, Preface.
9. Quoted in Ernst Cassirer, *An Essay on Man* (New York: Bantam Books, 1970), p. 178.
10. From "The Tables Turned," in *The Poetical Works of Wordsworth*, Thomas Hutchinson, ed., rev. by Ernest de Selincourt (London: Oxford University Press, 1936), p. 377.

11. Ernst Cassirer, *The Myth of the State* (New Haven: Yale University Press, 1946), p. 181.

12. Horst von Maltitz, *The Evolution of Hitler's Germany* (New York: McGraw-Hill, 1973), p. 217.

13. Edmund Burke, *Reflections on the Revolution in France* (New York: Liberal Arts Press, 1955), pp. 40, 89.

14. Quoted in Frederick B. Artz, *Reaction and Revolution, 1814–1832* (New York: Harper Torchbooks, 1963), p. 73.

15. John Stuart Mill, *On Liberty*, Currin V. Shields, ed. (Indianapolis: Bobbs-Merrill, 1956), ch. 1.

16. Quoted in Hans Kohn, *Prelude to Nation-States* (Princeton, N.J.: D. Van Nostrand, 1967), p. 262.

Suggested Reading

Bullock, Alan, and Shock, Maurice, eds., *The Liberal Tradition* (1956). Selections from the works of British liberals, preceded by an essay on the liberal tradition.

Epstein, Klaus, *The Genesis of German Conservatism* (1966). An analysis of German conservative thought as a response to the Enlightenment and the French Revolution.

Hayes, Carlton J. H., *Historical Evolution of Modern Nationalism* (1931). A pioneering work in the study of nationalism.

Kohn, Hans, *The Idea of Nationalism* (1961). A comprehensive study of nationalism from the ancient world through the eighteenth century by a leading student of the subject.

———, *Prelude to Nation-States* (1967). The emergence of nationalism in France and Germany.

Ruggiero, Guido de, *The History of European Liberalism* (1927). A classic study.

Schapiro, J. S., *Liberalism: Its Meaning and History* (1958). A useful survey with readings.

Schenk, H. G., *The Mind of the European Romantics* (1966). A comprehensive analysis of the Romantic Movement.

Shafer, B. C., *Faces of Nationalism* (1972). The evolution of modern nationalism in Europe and the non-European world, containing a good bibliography.

Smith, A. D., *Theories of Nationalism* (1972). The relationship between nationalism and modernization.

Weiss, John, *Conservatism in Europe, 1770–1945* (1977). Conservatism as a reaction to social modernization.

Review Questions

1. The Romantic Movement was a reaction against the dominant ideas of the Enlightenment. Discuss this statement.

2. What was the significance of the Romantic Movement?

3. What were the attitudes of the conservatives toward the philosophes and the French Revolution?

4. "It is with infinite caution that any man ought to venture upon pulling down an edifice which had answered in any tolerable degree for ages the common purposes of society." How does this statement by Burke represent the conservative viewpoint?

5. Why did conservatives reject the philosophy of natural rights?

6. What were the sources of liberalism?

7. The central concern of liberals was the enhancement of individual liberty. Discuss this statement.

8. What were the attitudes of liberals toward the state, the economy, the Middle Ages, and democracy?

9. Define nationalism.

10. How did the French Revolution and Romanticism contribute to the rise of modern nationalism?

11. What is the relationship between nationalism and liberalism?

CHAPTER 22

Europe, 1815–1848: Revolution
and Counterrevolution

A CLASH between the forces unleashed by the French Revolution and the traditional outlook of the Old Regime took place during the years 1815 through 1848. The period opened with the Congress of Vienna, which drew up a peace settlement after the defeat of Napoleon, and closed with the revolutions that swept across most of Europe in 1848. Much of the Old Regime outside of France had survived the stormy decades of the French Revolution and Napoleon. Monarchs still held the reins of political power. Aristocrats, particularly in central and eastern Europe, retained their traditional hold over the army and administration, controlled the peasantry and local government, and enjoyed tax exemptions.

The French Revolution had shown the masses how absolutism and feudal privileges could be destroyed and the lands of the church and the nobility confiscated. Determined to smother the liberal ideals of the Revolution and to enforce respect for traditional authority among the peasants, the conservative ruling elites resorted to censorship, secret police, and armed force. Inspired by the revolutionary principles of liberty, equality, and fraternity, liberals and nationalists continued to engage in revolutionary activity.

THE CONGRESS OF VIENNA

Metternich: Arch-Conservative

After the defeat of Napoleon, a congress of European powers met at Vienna (1814–1815) to draw up a peace settlement. The pivotal figure at the Congress of Vienna was Prince Klemens von Metternich (1773–1859) of Austria, who had organized the coalition that had triumphed over Napoleon. Belonging to the old order of courts and kings, Metternich hated the new forces of nationalism and liberalism. He regarded liberalism as a dangerous disease carried by middle-class malcontents,

How many Napoleans Can you See In This pitcher?

JEAN BAPTISTE ISABEY (1767–1855): CONGRESS OF VIENNA, 1815 The delegates to the Congress of Vienna in 1815 sought to re-establish many features of the Europe that existed before the French Revolution and Napoleon. They can be called shortsighted; nevertheless, the balance of power that they formulated preserved international peace. (New York Public Library; Astor, Lenox, and Tilden Foundations)

and believed that domestic order and international stability depended on rule by monarchy and respect for aristocracy. The misguided liberal belief that society could be reshaped according to the ideals of liberty and equality, said Metternich, had led to twenty-five years of revolution, terror, and war. To restore stability and peace, the old Europe must suppress liberal ideas and quash the first signs of revolution. If the European powers did not destroy the revolutionary spirit, they would be devoured by it.

Metternich also feared the new spirit of nationalism. As a multinational empire, Austria was particularly vulnerable to nationalist unrest. If its ethnic groups—Poles, Czechs, Magyars, Italians, South Slavs, Rumanians—became infected with the nationalist virus, they would shatter the Hapsburg Empire. A highly cultured, multilingual, and cosmopolitan aristocrat, Metternich considered himself the defender of European civilization. He felt that by arousing the masses and setting people against people, nationalism could undermine the foundations of the European civilization that he cherished.

Metternich's critics accuse him of short-sightedness. Instead of harnessing and directing the new forces let loose by the French Revolution, he thought that he could stifle them. Instead of trying to rebuild and remodel, he thought only of propping up dying institutions. Regarding any attempt at reform as opening the door to radicalism and revolution, he refused to make any concessions to liberalism.

Metternich sought to return to power the ruling families deposed by more than two decades of revolutionary warfare, and to restore the balance of power so that no one country could be in a position to dominate the European continent as Napoleon had. Metternich was determined to end the chaos of the Napoleonic period and restore stability to Europe. There must be no more Napoleons who obliterate states, topple kings, and dream of European hegemony. While serving the interests of the Hapsburg monarchy, Metternich also had a sense of responsibility to Europe as a whole. He sought a settlement that would avoid the destructiveness of a general war.

Representing Britain at the Congress of Vienna was Robert Stewart Viscount Castlereagh (1769–1822), the British Foreign Secretary, who was realistic and empirical-minded. Although an implacable enemy of Napoleon, Castlereagh demonstrated mature statesmanship in his attitude toward defeated France: "it is not our business to collect trophies, but to try . . . to bring the world back to peaceful habits. I do not believe this to be compatible with any attempt . . . to affect the territorial character of France . . . neither do I think it a clear case . . . that France . . . may not be found a useful rather than a dangerous member of the European system."[1]

Tsar Alexander I (1777–1825) attended the Congress himself. Showing signs of mental instability and steeped in Christian mysticism, the Russian tsar wanted to create a European community based on Christian teachings. Influenced by Baroness von Kruedener, a religious fanatic, Alexander regarded himself as the savior of Europe, an attitude that caused other diplomats to regard him with distrust.

Representing France was Prince Charles Maurice de Talleyrand-Périgord (1754–1838), who had served Napoleon as foreign minister, but when the Emperor's defeat seemed imminent, worked for the restoration of the Bourbon monarchy. A devoted patriot, Talleyrand sought to remove from France the stigma of the revolution and Napoleon.

The aging Prince Karl von Hardenberg (1750–1822) represented Prussia. Like Metternich, Castlereagh, and Talleyrand, the Prussian statesman believed that the various European states, in addition to pursuing their own national interests, should concern themselves with the well-being of the European community as a whole.

Crisis over Saxony and Poland

Two interrelated issues threatened to disrupt the conference and enmesh the Great Powers in another war. One was Prussia's intention to annex the German kingdom of Saxony; the other was Russia's demand for Polish territories. The tsar wanted to combine the Polish holdings of Russia, Austria, and Prussia into a new Polish kingdom under Russian control. Both Britain and Austria regarded such an extension of Russia's power into central Europe as a threat to the balance of power. Metternich declared that he had not fought Napoleon to prepare the way for the tsar. Britain agreed that Russia's westward expansion must be checked.

Prince Talleyrand of France suggested that Britain, Austria, and France conclude an alliance to oppose Prussia and Russia. This clever move by Talleyrand restored France to the family of nations. Now France was no longer the hated enemy, but a necessary counterweight to Russia and Prussia. Threatened with

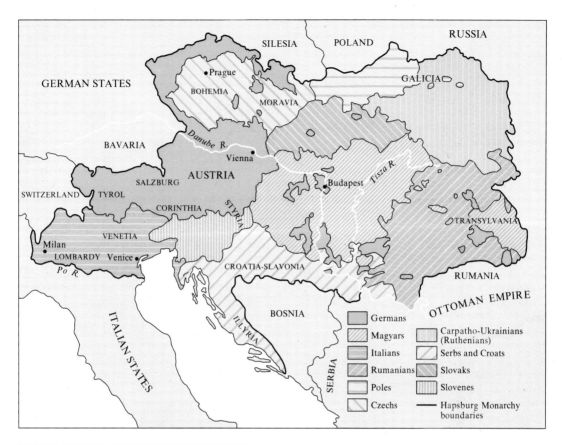

MAP 22.1 PEOPLES OF THE HAPSBURG MONARCHY, 1815

war, Russia and Prussia moderated their demands and the crisis ended.

The Settlement

After months of discussion, quarrels, and threats, the delegates finished their work. Resisting Prussia's demands for a punitive peace, the allies did not punish France severely. They feared that a humiliated France would only prepare for a war of revenge. Moreover, Metternich needed France to balance the power of both Prussia and Russia. France had

to pay a large indemnity over a five-year period and submit to allied occupation until the obligation was met.

The peace settlement changed the borders throughout Europe. Though it lost most of its conquests, France emerged with somewhat more land than it possessed before the Revolution. To guard against a resurgent France, both Prussia and Holland received territories on the French border. Holland obtained the southern Netherlands (Belgium), while Prussia gained the Rhineland and part of Saxony, but not as much as Prussia had desired. Nevertheless, Prussia emerged from the settlement significantly larger and stronger. Russia obtained

Finland and a considerable part of Polish territories, but not as much as the tsar had anticipated. The Congress prevented further Russian expansion into central Europe. The north Italian province of Lombardy was restored to Austria, who also received adjacent Venetia. England obtained strategic naval bases: Helgoland in the North Sea, Malta and the Ionian Islands in the Mediterranean, the Cape Colony in South Africa, and Ceylon in the Indian Ocean. Germany was organized into a confederation of thirty-eight (later thirty-nine) states. Norway was given to Sweden. The legitimate rulers, who had been displaced by the revolution and the wars of Napoleon, were restored to their thrones in France, Spain, Portugal, the Kingdom of the Two Sicilies, the Papal States, and many German states.

The conservative delegates at the Congress of Vienna have often been criticized for ignoring the liberal and nationalist aspirations of the different peoples and turning the clock back to the Old Regime. Critics have castigated the Congress for dealing only with the rights of thrones and not the rights of peoples. But, after the experience of two world wars in the twentieth century, some historians today are impressed with the peacermakers' success in restoring a balance of power that effectively stabilized international relations. No one country was strong enough to dominate the Continent; no Great Power was so unhappy that it resorted to war to undo the settlement. Not until the unification of Germany in 1870–1871 was the balance of power upset; not until World War I in 1914 did Europe have another general war of the magnitude of the Napoleonic wars.

REVOLUTIONS, 1820–1829

Russia, Austria, Prussia, and Great Britain agreed to act together to preserve the territorial settlement of the Congress of Vienna and the balance of power. After paying its indemnity, France was admitted into this Quadruple Alliance, also known as the *Concert of Europe*. Metternich intended to use the Concert of Europe to maintain harmony between nations and internal stability within nations. Toward this end, Metternich and his fellow conservatives in their respective countries censored books and newspapers, imprisoned liberal activists, and suppressed liberal and national uprisings.

But repression could not contain the liberal and nationalist ideals unleashed by the French Revolution; the transformation of European society could not be halted. The first revolution to stir conservative rulers during the restorations of legitimate rulers occurred in Spain in 1820. The uprising was essentially a military revolt by infrequently paid and poorly fed soldiers who were being sent to Latin America to win back Spain!s colonies. King Ferdinand VII attempted to appease the soldiers by reinstating the liberal constitution of 1812, which had been promulgated during the struggle against Napoleon and revoked two years later. Both Metternich and Tsar Alexander were alarmed. Fearing that the Spanish uprising, with its quasi-liberal overtones, would inspire revolutions in other lands, the Concert of Europe empowered France to intervene. In 1823, 100,000 French troops crushed the revolution. King Ferdinand dismissed the liberal constitution and brutally punished the leaders of the insurrection.

Revolutionary activity in Italy also frightened the Concert of Europe. In 1821 it authorized Austria to extinguish a liberal uprising in the Kingdom of the Two Sicilies. The Austrians also crushed an uprising in Piedmont, in northern Italy. Rulers in other Italian states jailed and executed liberal leaders, and several thousand Italians went into exile.

In both instances, Britain strongly opposed the actions of the alliance; it interpreted the alliance differently from the way that Austria, Prussia, and Russia did. The three eastern powers wanted the alliance to smother in the cradle all subversive movements that threatened the old order. To Metternich the central problem of the age was suppressing revolutions that undermined the foundations of society; therefore, he regarded the alliance as a means of preserving the status quo against revolution. Britain, however, viewed the alliance solely as a means of guarding against renewed French aggression. It had no desire to intervene in the domestic affairs of other nations.

A revolution also failed in Russia. During the Napoleonic wars and the occupation of France, Russian officers were introduced to French ideas. Contrasting French liberal ideas and ways with Russian autocracy, some officers resolved to change conditions in Russia. Like their Western counterparts, they organized secret societies and disseminated liberal ideas within Russia. When Alexander I died, these liberal officers struck. But representing only a fraction of the aristocracy and with no mass following among the soldiers, they had no chance of success. Their uprising in December 1825 was easily smashed by the new tsar, Nicholas I, and the leaders were severely punished. To prevent Western ideas from infiltrating into his realm, Nicholas imposed rigid censorship and organized the Third Section, a secret police force that spied on suspected subversives. The Decembrists had failed, but their courage would inspire future opponents of tsarist autocracy.

The revolutions in Spain, Italy, and Russia failed, but the Concert of Europe also suffered setbacks. Stimulated by the ideals of the French Revolution, the Greeks revolted against their Turkish rulers in 1821. Although the Turkish sultan was the legitimate ruler, France, England, and Russia aided the Greek revolutionaries. Pro-Greek sentiments were very strong among educated western Europeans who had studied the literature and history of ancient Greece. Were not the Greeks struggling to regain the freedom of their ancient forebears? Not only the pressure of public opinion but fear of Russian motives led Britain to intervene. If Russia carried out its intention of aiding the Christian Greeks to secure independence from the Muslim Turks, no doubt

the Russian bear would never release Greece from its hug. Britain could not permit this extension of Russian power in the eastern Mediterranean. Despite Metternich's objections, Britain, France, and Russia took joint action against the Turks.

In 1829, Greece gained its independence. The Metternich system, which aimed to preserve the territorial settlements made at Vienna and to protect traditional and legitimate rulers against liberal and nationalist revolutions, had been breached. The success of the Greeks heartened liberals in other lands.

REVOLUTIONS, 1830–1832

After the defeat of Napoleon, a Bourbon king, Louis XVIII (1814–1824), ascended the throne of France. Louis XVIII's heart belonged to the Old Regime, but his intellect told him that twenty-five years of revolutionary change could not be undone. Recognizing that the French people would not accept a return to the old order, Louis XVIII pursued a moderate course. Although his pseudoconstitution, the Charter, declared that the king's power rested on divine right, it also stipulated that citizens possess fundamental rights—freedom of thought and religion and equal treatment under the law—and set up a two-house parliament. But peasants, urban workers, and most bourgeois could not meet the property requirements for voting.

Louis XVIII was resisted by diehard aristocrats, called *ultras*. These aristocrats, many of them returned émigrés, wanted to erase the past twenty-five years of French history and restore the power and privileges of church and aristocracy. Their leader was the king's younger brother, the Comte d'Artois. Aided by competent ministers and committed to a policy of moderation, Louis governed effectively. After his death in 1824, the Comte d'Artois ascended the throne as Charles X (1824–1830).

HONORÉ DAUMIER (1808–1879): RUE TRANSNONAIN, APRIL, 15, 1834 Throughout Europe, cartoonists began to champion the poor and the oppressed working classes. This poor family had been the victims of a brutal police action. Government repression was always swift and harsh during this time of unrest. (Philadelphia Museum of Art; Bequest of Fiske and Marie Kimball)

The new government aroused the hostility of the bourgeoisie by indemnifying the émigrés for the property they had lost during the Revolution, by censoring the press, and by giving the church greater control over education. In the election of 1830, the liberal opposition to Charles X won a decisive victory. Charles responded with the July Ordinances, which dissolved the newly elected chamber; the Ordinances also deprived most bourgeois of the vote and severely curtailed the press.

The bourgeois, students, and workers rebelled. They engaged in street demonstrations and drew up barricades and were joined by army regiments that had deserted Charles. In the fighting that followed, some 2,000 Parisians were killed.

The insurgents hoped to establish a republic, but the wealthy bourgeois who took control of the revolution feared republican radicalism. They offered the throne to the Duc d'Orléans; Charles X abdicated and went into exile in England. The new king, Louis Philippe (1830–1848), never forgot that he owed his throne to the rich bourgeois. And the Parisian workers who had fought for a republic and economic reforms to alleviate poverty felt betrayed by the outcome.

The Revolution of 1830 in France set off shock waves in Belgium, Poland, and Italy. The Congress of Vienna had assigned Catholic Belgium to Protestant Holland; from the outset the Belgians had protested. Stirred by the events in Paris, Belgian patriots proclaimed their independence from Holland. The Dutch could not suppress the insurgents, and the Quadruple Alliance did not act, largely because Russia was tied down by a revolution in Poland. Thus, liberal government was established in Belgium.

Inspired by the uprisings in France and Belgium, Polish students, intellectuals, and army officers took up arms against their Russian overlord. The peasants refused to join the insurrection because the revolutionaries did not promise land reform. The revolutionaries wanted to restore Polish independence, a dream that poets, musicians, and intellectuals had kept alive. Polish courage, however, was no match for Russian might, and Warsaw fell in 1831. The tsar took savage revenge on the revolutionaries; those who failed to escape to the West were executed. The tsar's government made strenuous efforts to impose Russian language and culture on Polish students.

In 1831–32, Austrian forces again extinguished a revolution in Italy. Here, too, revolutionary leaders had failed to stir the great peasant masses to the cause of Italian independence and unity.

THE REVOLUTIONS OF 1848: FRANCE

Eighteen-forty-eight is often called *the year of revolution,* for throughout Europe, uprisings for political liberty and nationhood took place.

Political and national unrest was intensified by the economic crisis of the previous two years. Food riots broke out in many places. The decimation of the potato crop by disease and the grain harvest by drought had caused terrible food shortages. Also, a financial crisis precipitated by overspeculation had caused business failures, unemployment, and reduced wages. The common people blamed their governments for their misery and sought a redress of their grievances. Though the economic hardships aggravated discontent with the existing regimes, nevertheless, concludes historian Jacques Droz, "it was the absence of liberty which . . . was most deeply resented by the peoples of Europe and led them to take up arms."[2]

The February Revolution

An uprising in Paris set in motion the revolutionary tidal wave that was to engulf much of Europe in 1848. The Revolution of 1830 had broken the back of the ultras in France. There would be no going back to the Old Regime.

But King Louis Philippe and his ministers, moderates by temperament and philosophy, had no intention of going forward to democracy. A new electoral law broadened the franchise from less than 100,000 voters to 248,000 by 1846. Even so, only about 3 percent of the adult males qualified to vote. The government of Louis Philippe was run by a small ruling elite consisting of wealthy bourgeois bankers, merchants, professors, and lawyers, and aristocrats who had abandoned the hope of restoring the Old Regime. This ruling elite championed the revolutionary ideas of equal treatment under the law and of careers open to talent, but feared democracy and blocked efforts to broaden the franchise. When the poorer bourgeoisie protested against the limited franchise that excluded professionals and small tradesmen, François Guizot, the leading minister, arrogantly proclaimed: "Get rich, then you can vote." The ruling elite had become a selfish and entrenched oligarchy, unresponsive to the aspirations of the rest of the nation. Articulate intellectuals denounced the government for its narrow political base and voiced strong republican sentiments. To guard against republicanism and as a reaction to repeated attempts to assassinate the king, the government cracked down on radical societies and newspapers.

Radical republicans, or democrats, wanted to abolish monarchy and grant all men the vote. They had fought in the Revolution of 1830, but were disappointed with the results. Patriots and romantics who looked back longingly on the glory days of Napoleon also hated Louis Philippe's government. These Frenchmen complained that the king, who dressed like a businessman and pursued a pacifistic foreign policy, was not fit to lead a nation of patriots and warriors. Under Louis Philippe, they said, France could not realize its historic mission of liberating oppressed nationalities throughout Europe.

The strongest rumblings of discontent, but barely detected by the ruling elite, came from the working class. Many French workers, literate and concerned with politics, read the numerous books and newspapers that denounced social injustice and called for social change. Artisans and their families had participated in the great revolutionary outbreaks of 1789 and had defended the barricades in 1830. Like their sans-culottes forebears, they favored a democratic republic that would aid the common people. These people felt betrayed by the regime of Louis Philippe, which had brought them neither political representation nor economic reform.

A poor harvest in 1846 and an international financial crisis in 1847, which drastically curtailed French factory production, aggravated the misery of the working class. Factory workers (still few in number) and artisans in small workshops were growing attracted to socialist thinkers who attacked capitalism and called for state programs to deal with poverty.

Louis Blanc, a particularly popular socialist theorist, denounced capitalist competition and demanded that the government establish cooperative workshops. Owned by the workers themselves, these workshops would assure employment for the jobless. Prevented by law from striking, unable to meet the financial requirements for voting, and afflicted with unemployment, the urban workers wanted relief from their misery. "I believe that we are at this moment sleeping on a volcano," said Alexis de Tocqueville prophetically.[3]

Discontent with the regime had been mounting for years, but the government refused to pass electoral reforms to appease the middle class or to initiate social reforms to ease the burden of the poor. Middle-class opponents of the government had gathered at large banquets to hear speakers attack the government and to demand electoral reforms. When the government foolishly tried to block future banquets, students and workers took to the streets in February 1848, denouncing Guizot and demanding reforms. Barricades began to go up. Attempting to defuse an explosive situation, Louis Philippe dismissed the unpopular Guizot. But the barricades, commanded by republicans, did not come down, and the antigovernment demonstrations continued. When soldiers, confused by a shot that had perhaps gone off accidentally, fired directly into a crowd and killed fifty-two Parisians, the situation got out of hand. Unable to pacify the enraged Parisians, Louis Philippe abdicated. France became a republic, and the people of Paris were jubilant.

The June Days: Revolution of the Oppressed

The new bourgeois liberal leaders of France favored political democracy, but not social democracy. Drawn almost exclusively from the middle class, they had little comprehension of, nor sympathy for the plight of the laboring poor; they regarded socialist ideas as a threat to private property. Though they attacked the inherited privileges of aristocracy, these leaders never questioned the privileges that derived from inherited wealth.

These bourgeois liberals passionately denounced oppressive rulers, but they could not grasp that to the working class, *they* had become the oppressors. They considered it a sacred duty to fight for the rights of the individual, but they did not include freedom from hunger and poverty among these rights. Thus, the republican leadership had little to offer the urban poor, who pressed for social legislation to ease their punishing poverty. Workers labored twelve and fourteen hours a day under brutalizing conditions. In some districts, one out of three children died before the age of five, and everywhere in France, beggars, paupers, prostitutes, and criminals were evidence of the struggle to survive.

By occupation and wealth, the middle class considered itself to be apart from the working class. To the bourgeoisie, the workers were dangerous creatures, "the wild ones," "the vile mob." But the inhabitants of the urban slums could no longer be ignored. They felt as de Tocqueville stated,

that all that is above them is incapable and unworthy of governing them; that the distribution of goods prevalent until now . . . is unjust; that property rests on a foundation which is not an equitable one.[4]

The urban poor were desperate for jobs and bread. Socialist intellectuals, sympathetic to the plight of the worker, proposed that the state organize producer cooperatives run by workers. Some wanted the state to take over insurance companies, railroads, mines, and other key industries. To the property owners of all classes, such schemes smacked of madness.

The middle-class leaders of the new republic gave all adult males the vote and abolished censorship; however, its attempts to ease the distress of the working class were insincere and halfhearted. The government limited the workday to ten hours and legalized labor unions, but failed to cope effectively with unemployment. Socialists demanded that the new government guarantee employment for the city poor. The republic responded by establishing national workshops. Drawn by the promise of work, tens of thousands of laborers left the provinces for Paris, swelling the ranks of the unemployed. The national workshops provided work, food, and medical benefits for some of the unemployed. To the workers, this was a feeble effort to deal with their monumental distress. To the property-owning peasantry and bourgeoisie, the national workshops were a hateful concession to socialism and a waste of government funds. They viewed the workshops as nests of working-class radicalism, where plans were being hatched to change the economic system and seize their property.

For their participation in the February uprising against Louis Philippe, the workers had obtained meager benefits. When the government closed the workshops, working-class hostility and despair turned to open rebellion. Again barricades went up in the streets of Paris.

The June Revolution in Paris was unlike previous uprisings in France. It was a revolt against poverty and a cry for the redistribution of property; as such, it foreshadowed the great social revolutions of the twentieth century. The workers stood alone. To the rest of the nation, they were barbarians attacking civilized society. Aristocrats, bourgeois, and peasants feared that no one's property would be safe if the revolution succeeded. From hundreds of miles away, Frenchmen flocked to Paris to crush what they considered to be the madness within their midst.

Although they had no leaders, the workers showed remarkable courage. Women and children fought alongside men behind the barricades. After three days of vicious street fighting and atrocities on both sides, the army extinguished the revolt. Some 1,460 lives had been lost, including four generals. The June

Days left deep scars in French society. For many years, workers would never forget that the rest of France had united against them; the rest of France would remain terrified of working-class radicalism.

In December 1848, the French people in overwhelming numbers elected Louis Napoleon, nephew of the great emperor, as president of the Second Republic. They were attracted to the magic of Louis Napoleon's name, and they expected him to prevent future working-class disorders. The election, in which all adult males could vote, demonstrated that most Frenchmen were socially conservative; they were unsympathetic to working-class poverty and deeply suspicious of socialist programs.

THE REVOLUTIONS OF 1848: GERMANY, AUSTRIA, AND ITALY

Like an epidemic, the fever of the revolution that broke out in Paris in February raced across the Continent. Liberals, excluded from participation in political life, fought for parliaments and constitutions; many liberals were also nationalists who wanted unity or independence for their nations. Some liberals had a utopian vision of a new Europe of independent and democratic states. In this vision, reactionary rulers would no longer stifle individual liberty; no longer would a people be denied the right of nationhood.

The German States: Liberalism Discredited

After the Congress of Vienna, Germany consisted of a loose confederation of thirty-nine independent states, of which Austria and Prussia were the most powerful. Jealous of their independence and determined to preserve their absolute authority, the ruling

princes detested liberal and nationalist ideals. In 1819, Metternich urged the other states to institute the Karlsbad Decrees, which called for strict control over the press and education. In the southern German states, which had been more influenced by the French Revolution, princes did grant constitutions and establish parliaments to retain the loyalty of their subjects. But even in these states the princes continued to hold the reins of authority.

German nationalism emerged during the era of the French Revolution. The French occupation had sparked nationalist feelings among German intellectuals, who called for a war of liberation against the hated Napoleon. The call for German unity gained in intensity during the restoration (the post-Napoleonic period), as intellectuals insisted that Germans who shared a common language and culture should also be united politically. German nationalism was profoundly influenced by romanticism, which glorified German traditions and history. During the restoration, the struggle for German unity and liberal reforms was waged primarily by students, professors, writers, lawyers, and other educated people. The great mass of people, knowing only loyalty to their local prince, remained unmoved by appeals for national unity.

The successful revolt against Louis Philippe, hostility against absolute princes, and the general economic crisis combined to produce uprisings in the capital cities of the German states in March 1848. Throughout Germany, liberals clamored for constitutions, parliamentary government, freedom of thought, and an end to police intimidation. Some called for the creation of a unified Germany governed by a national parliament and headed by a constitutional monarch. The poor of town and countryside joined the struggle. The great depression of the 1840s had aggravated the misery of the German peasant and urban masses, and as the pressures of

MAP 22.2 EUROPE, 1815 ▶

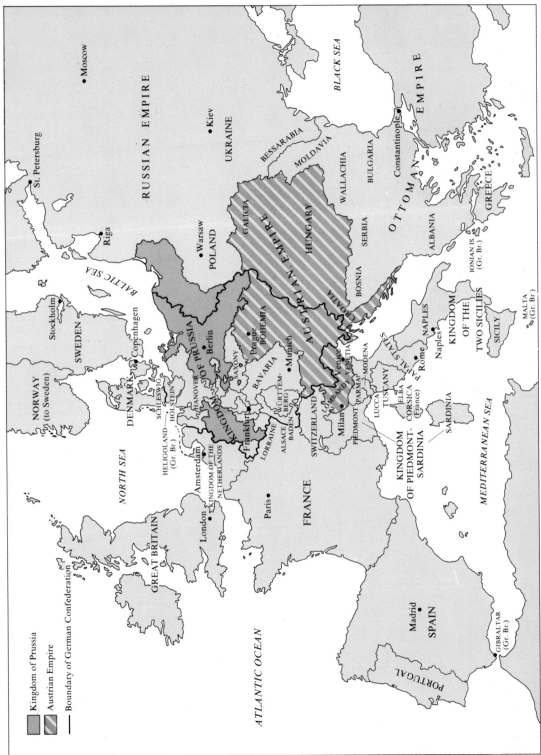

Kingdom of Prussia

Austrian Empire

Boundary of German Confederation

RUSSIAN EMPIRE

• Moscow

St. Petersburg •

• Kiev

UKRAINE

BLACK SEA

OTTOMAN EMPIRE

• Constantinople

Riga •

• Warsaw
POLAND

BESSARABIA

MOLDAVIA

WALLACHIA

BULGARIA

GALICIA

HUNGARY

SERBIA

BALTIC SEA

AUSTRIAN EMPIRE

BOSNIA

ALBANIA

GREECE

IONIAN IS.
(Gr. Br.)

Stockholm •

SWEDEN

CROATIA

Copenhagen

BOHEMIA

Prague

MALTA
(Gr. Br.)

NORWAY
(to Sweden)

DENMARK

SCHLESWIG

HOLSTEIN

KINGDOM OF PRUSSIA

Berlin •

SAXONY

• Munich

BAVARIA

Venice
LOMBARDY-VENETIA

MODENA

PARMA

Rome •
PAPAL STATES

NAPLES

KINGDOM
OF THE
TWO SICILIES

SICILY

Naples •

NORTH SEA

HANOVER

WÜRTTEM-
BERG

Frankfurt •

LORRAINE

ALSACE

BADEN

SWITZERLAND

Milan •
PIEDMONT

LUCCA

TUSCANY

ELBA

CORSICA
(France)

SARDINIA

HELIGOLAND
(Gr. Br.)

Amsterdam •

KINGDOM OF THE
NETHERLANDS

London •

GREAT BRITAIN

• Paris

FRANCE

KINGDOM
OF PIEDMONT-
SARDINIA

MEDITERRANEAN SEA

ATLANTIC OCEAN

Madrid •
SPAIN

GIBRALTAR
(Gr. Br.)

PORTUGAL

hunger and unemployment worsened, their discontent exploded into revolutionary fervor.

In the spring of 1848, downtrodden artisans, who faced severe competition from the new factories that mass-produced goods, served as the revolution's shock troops. Without their support, bourgeois liberals could not challenge the Throne nor wrest power from the aristocrats. Unable to compete with the new machines, artisans saw their incomes fall and their opportunities for work decrease. For example, skilled weavers at home earned far less than factory hands did, and some jobless craftsmen were forced to take factory jobs, which they regarded as a terrible loss of status. These craftsmen wanted to restrict the growth of factories, curtail capitalist competition, and restore the power of the guilds, survivals of the Middle Ages that gave them security and status. Having lost hope that the absolute princes would aid them, craftsmen gave their support to bourgeois liberals. In many German states the actions of the embittered urban craftsmen determined the successful outcome of the insurrection. (The factory workers in the emerging industries, on the other hand, showed no enthusiasm for revolution, despite the appeals of radical socialists.) Adding to the discomfort of the ruling princes was the rioting in the countryside by peasants goaded by crop failure, debt, and oppressive demands from the aristocracy.

Terrified that these disturbances would lead to anarchy, the princes made concessions to the liberals whom they previously had censored, jailed, and exiled. During March and April 1848, the traditional rulers in Baden, Württemberg, Bavaria, Saxony, Hanover, and other states replaced reactionary ministers with liberals, eased censorship, established jury systems, framed constitutions, formed parliaments, and ended peasant obligations to lords.

In Prussia, Frederick William IV was slow to make concessions, and his troops treated the Berliners with contempt. As tension in Berlin mounted, the king proclaimed reforms on March 18. The Berliners gathered in the palace square to applaud Frederick William's decision. But the hostilities between civilians and soldiers led to pushing and the unintentional firing of two shots by two soldiers. The enraged Berliners, who had a long-standing hatred for the army quartered in their city, armed themselves and hurriedly constructed barricades from anything they could find— barrels, pavement stones, fire pumps, bedding, sacks of flour, and fruit stalls. Most insurgents were artisans, but merchants and students also participated in the fighting. Unable to subdue the insurgents, the army urged bombarding the city with artillery. Frederick William opposed the idea and ordered the troops to leave Berlin. The insurgents had won the first round.

The jubilant Berliners paraded the bodies of the fallen fighters in the palace courtyard, demanding that the king come to the window. Frederick William removed his hat and the queen fainted. Recalling that day, the king would later remark: "We all crawled on our stomachs." The military monarchy had surrendered ingloriously to the popular uprising. The Prussian king, like the other German princes, had to agree to the formation of a parliament and the admission of prominent liberals into the government.

But the triumph of the liberals in Prussia and the other German states was not secure. Though reforms liberalized the governments of the German states, the ruling dynasties had not been toppled. Moreover, the alliance between the bourgeois and the artisans, which had brought victory, was tenuous. The violence of the artisans frightened the property-owning middle class, which sought only moderate political reforms through peaceful means. In addition, restoration of the guild system, desired by the artisans, was to the middle class a reactionary economic measure.

Liberals took advantage of their successes in Prussia and other German states to form a national assembly charged with the task of creating a unified and liberal Germany. Repre-

BARRICADES, BERLIN, 1848 During the revolutions of 1848, barricades went up in many European cities. But the revolutionaries ultimately proved no match for the armed forces of conservative rulers. (Brown Brothers)

sentatives from all the German states attended the assembly, which met at Frankfurt. The delegates, including many articulate lawyers and professionals, came predominantly from the educated middle class; only a handful were drawn from the lower classes. After many long debates, the Frankfurt Assembly approved a federation of German states. The German union would have a parliament and would be headed by the Prussian king. Austria, with its many non-German nationalities, would be excluded from the federal union. Some radical democrats wanted to proclaim a German republic, but they were an ineffective minority.

Most delegates were moderate liberals who feared that universal (male) suffrage and the abolition of monarchy would lead to plebeian rule and the destruction of the social order. The deputies selected Frederick William as emperor of the new Germany, but the Prussian king refused; he would never wear a crown given to him by common people during a period of revolutionary agitation.

While the delegates debated, the ruling princes recovered from the first shock of revolution and ordered their armies to crush the revolutionaries. The February Revolution in Paris had shown European liberals that

FRANKFURT PARLIAMENT, 1848 This was a year of revolutions. The Frankfurt assembly approved a federation of German states, but Frederick William of Prussia refused to accept a crown from liberals. While the liberals debated, conservative German princes crushed liberal parliaments with military force. (Historical Pictures Service, Inc., Chicago)

authority could be challenged successfully; the June Days, however, had shown the authorities that revolutionaries could be beaten by professional soldiers. Moreover, the German middle class, frightened by lower-class agitation and unsympathetic to the artisans' demands to restrict capitalism and restore the authority of the old guilds, was losing enthusiasm for revolution—so, too, were the artisans. The disintegration of the alliance between middle-class liberals and urban artisans de-

prived the revolutionaries of mass support. A revived old order would not face much resistance.

In Prussia, a determined Frederick William IV ordered his troops to reoccupy Berlin. In March the citizens of Berlin had fought against the king's troops, but in November, no barricades went up in Berlin. Prussian forces also assisted the other German states in crushing the new parliaments. The masses of workers and peasants did not fight to save the liberal governments, which fell one by one. A small minority of democrats resisted, particularly in Baden; many of these revolutionaries died in the fighting or were executed.

German liberalism had failed to unite Germany or to create a constitutional government dominated by the middle class. Liberalism, never securely rooted in Germany, was discredited. In the following decades, many Germans, identifying liberalism with failure, abandoned liberal values and turned to authoritarian Prussia for leadership in the struggle for unification. The fact that authoritarians hostile to the spirit of parliamentary government eventually united Germany had deep implications for future German and European history.

Austria: Hapsburg Dominance

The Hapsburg Empire, the product of dynastic marriage and inheritance, had no common nationality or language; it was held together only by the reigning Hapsburg dynasty, its army, and its bureaucracy. The ethnic composition of the Empire was enormously complex. The Germans, who were concentrated principally in Austria and who constituted about 25 percent of the Empire's population, were the dominant nationality. The Magyars predominated in the Hungarian lands of the Empire. The great bulk of the population consisted of Slavs—Czechs, Poles, Slovaks, Slovenes, Croats, Serbs, Ruthenians. In addition, there were Italians in northern Italy and Rumanians in Transylvania. The Hapsburg dynasty, aided by the army and the German-dominated civil service, prevented the multinational Empire from collapsing into anarchy.

Metternich, it is often said, suffered from a "dissolution complex": he understood that the new forces of nationalism and liberalism could break up the Austrian Empire. Liberal ideas could lead Hapsburg subjects to challenge the authority of the emperor, and nationalist feelings could cause the different peoples of the Empire to rebel against German domination and Hapsburg rule. To keep these ideas from infecting Austrian subjects, Metternich's police imposed strict censorship, spied on professors, and expelled from the universities students caught reading forbidden books. Despite Metternich's political police, the universities still remained hotbeds of liberalism.

In 1848, revolutions spread throughout the Austrian Empire. In Vienna, German liberals pressed for a constitution. In Bohemia, Czech nationalists demanded a constitution for Bohemia and equal status (with German) for the Czech language in the schools and government agencies. In Hungary, the Magyars waged a war of liberation against Hapsburg domination. To the south, Italians tried to drive the Hapsburgs out of northern Italy.

Aroused by the abdication of Louis Philippe, Viennese liberals denounced Hapsburg absolutism and demanded a constitution, relaxation of censorship, and restrictions on the police. The government responded with hesitance and limited force to the demonstrations of students and workers, and many parts of Vienna fell to the revolutionaries. The authorities used force that was strong enough to arouse the insurrectionists and create martyrs, but not to subdue them. Confused and intimidated by the revolutionaries, the government allowed freedom of the press, accepted Metternich's resignation, and promised a constitution. The Constitutional Assembly was convened for that purpose and in August voted the abolition of serfdom. At the same time that the Viennese insurgents were tasting the heady wine of reform, revolts in other parts of the Empire—Bohemia, Hungary, northern Italy—added to the distress of the monarchy.

But the revolutionaries' victory was only temporary, and the defeat of the old order only illusory; the Hapsburg government soon began to recover its balance. The first government victory came with the crushing of the Czechs in Bohemia. In 1848, Czech nationalists wanted the Austrian Empire reconstructed along federal lines that would give the Czechs equal standing with Germans. The Czechs called for a constitution for Bohemia and equal status for the Czech language in all official business. In June, students and destitute workers engaged in violent demonstrations that frightened the middle and upper classes, both Czech and German. General Windischgrätz bombarded Prague, the capital of Bohemia, into submission and re-established Hapsburg authority.

In October 1848, the Hapsburg authorities ordered the army to bombard Vienna. Against the regular army the courageous, but disorganized and divided students and workers had little chance. Royal troops broke into the city, overcame resistance, and executed several of the revolutionary leaders. In March 1849, the Hapsburg leaders replaced the liberal constitution drafted by the popularly elected Constitutional Assembly with a more conservative one drawn up by its own ministers.

The most serious threat to the Hapsburg realm came from the Magyars in Hungary. Some 12 million people lived in Hungary, 5 million of whom were Magyars. The other nationalities consisted of South Slavs (Croats and Serbs) and Rumanians. The upper class consisted chiefly of Magyar landowners, who enjoyed tax exemptions and other feudal privileges. Drawn to liberal and modern ideas and fearful of peasant uprisings, some Hungarian nobles pressed for an end to serfdom and the tax exemptions of the nobility. The great landowners, determined to retain their ancient privileges, resisted liberalization. Louis Kossuth (1802–1894), a member of the lower nobility, called for both social reform and a deepening of national consciousness.

Led by Kossuth, the Magyars demanded local autonomy for Hungary. Hungary would remain within the Hapsburg Empire, but would have its own constitution and national army and would control its own finances. The Hungarian leadership introduced liberal reforms—suffrage for all males who could speak Magyar and owned some property, freedom of religion, freedom of the press, the termination of serfdom, and the end of the privileges of nobles and church. Within a few weeks, the Hungarian parliament changed Hungary from a feudal to a modern liberal state.

But the Hungarian leaders' nationalist dreams towered above their liberal ideals. The Magyars intended to incorporate lands inhabited by Serbs, Slovaks, and Rumanians into their kingdom and transform these people, whom they regarded as ethnic inferiors, into Hungarians. As historian Hugh Seton-Watson has written,

Kossuth and his friends genuinely believed that they were doing the non-Hungarians a kindness by giving them a chance of becoming absorbed in the superior Hungarian culture. To refuse this kindness was nationalist fanaticism; to impose it by force was to promote progress. The suggestion that Rumanians, Slovaks, or Serbs were nations, with a national culture of their own, was simply ridiculous nonsense.[5]

In the spring of 1849, the Hungarians renounced their allegiance to the Hapsburgs and proclaimed Hungary an independent state with Kossuth as president.

The Hapsburg rulers took advantage of the ethnic animosities inside and outside Hungary. They encouraged Rumanians and South Slavs to resist the new Hungarian government. When Hapsburg forces moved against the Magyars, they were joined by an army of South Slavs whose nationalist aspirations had been flouted by the Hungarians. The new Hapsburg emperor, Francis Joseph, also appealed to Tsar Nicholas I for help. Fearing that a successful revolt by the Hungarians might lead the Poles to rise up against their Russian overlords, the tsar complied. The Russians invaded Hungary from the east. The Hungarians fought with extraordinary courage but were overcome by superior might. Kossuth and other rebel leaders went into exile; about one hundred rebel leaders were executed. Thus, through division and alliance, the Hapsburgs had prevented the disintegration of the Empire.

Italy: Continued Fragmentation

Italian nationalists, eager to end the humiliation of Hapsburg occupation and domination and to unite the disparate states into a unified and liberal nation, rose in rebellion in 1848. Revolution broke out in Sicily six weeks before the February Revolution in Paris. Bowing to the revolutionaries' demands, King Ferdinand II of Naples granted a liberal constitution. The Grand Duke of Tuscany, King Charles Albert of Piedmont-Sardinia and Pope Pius IX as ruler of the Papal States also felt compelled to introduce liberal reforms.

Then the revolution spread to the Hapsburg lands in the north. The citizens of Milan built barricades and stood ready to fight the Austrian oppressor. When the Austrian soldiers attacked, they were fired upon from nearby windows. From rooftops, Italians hurled stones and boiling water. After "Five Glorious Days" (March 18–22) of street fighting, the Austrians withdrew. The people of Milan had liberated their city. On March 22, the citizens of Venice declared their city free from Austria and set up a republic. King Charles Albert, who hoped to acquire Lombardy and Venetia, declared war on Austria. Intimidated by the insurrections, the ruling princes of the Italian states and Hapsburg Austria had lost the first round.

But soon everywhere in Italy the forces of reaction recovered and reasserted their authority. The Austrians defeated the Sardinians and reoccupied Milan, and Ferdinand II crushed the revolutionaries in the south. Revolutionary disorders in Rome had forced Pope Pius IX to flee in November 1848, and in February 1849 the revolutionaries proclaimed Rome a republic. Heeding the call of Pope Pius for assistance, Louis Napoleon attacked Rome, destroyed the infant republic, and allowed Pope Pius to return. The last city to fall to the reactionaries was Venice, which the Austrians subjected to a merciless bombardment. After six weeks, the Venetians, weakened by starvation and cholera, surrendered. Reactionary princes still ruled in Italy, the Hapsburg occupation persisted; Italy was still a fragmented nation.

THE REVOLUTIONS OF 1848: AN ASSESSMENT

The Revolutions of 1848 began with much promise, but they all ended in defeat. The initial success of the revolutionaries was due less to their strength than to the governments'

CHRONOLOGY 22.1   REVOLUTION AND REACTION

1820	Military revolt in Spain
1821	Austria crushes revolts in Italy
1823	French troops crush revolt in Spain
1825	Uprising in Russia crushed by Nicholas I
1829	Greece gains its independence from Turkey
1830	The July Ordinances in France are followed by a revolution led by Adolph Thiers
August 1830	The Belgian revolution
October 1830	Belgians declare their independence from Holland, establishing a liberal government
1831	The Polish revolution fails
1831–1832	Austrian forces crush a revolution in Italy
1848	The year of revolutions
February 1848	Revolution in Paris—Louis Philippe abdicates, and France becomes a republic

hesitancy to use their superior force. The reactionary leaders of Europe overcame their paralysis, however, and moved decisively to smash the revolutions. The courage of the revolutionaries was no match for regular armies. Thousands were killed and imprisoned; many fled to America.

Class divisions weakened the revolutionaries. The union between middle-class liberals and workers, which brought success in the opening stages of the revolutions, was only temporary. Bourgeois liberals favoring political reforms—constitution, parliament, and protection of basic rights—grew fearful of the laboring poor, who demanded social reforms—jobs and bread. To the bourgeois, the workers were an uneducated mob driven by dark instincts. When the working class en-

gaged in revolutionary action, a terrified middle class deserted the cause of revolution, or joined the old elites in subduing the workers.

Intractable nationalist animosities helped to destroy all the revolutionary movements against absolutism in central Europe. In many cases the different nationalities hated each other more than they hated the reactionary rulers. When German liberals at the Frankfurt Convention debated the boundary lines of a united Germany, the problem of Prussia's Polish territories emerged. In 1848, Polish patriots wanted to re-create the Polish nation, but German delegates at the Convention by an overwhelming majority opposed returning the Polish lands seized by Prussia in the late eighteenth century. Hungarian revolutionaries dismissed the nationalist yearnings of the

March 1848	Uprisings in capital cities of the German states; liberal reforms follow
March 18–22, 1848	"Five Glorious Days" in Milan
March 22, 1848	Citizens of Venice declare their freedom from Austria and establish a republic
June 1848	June Days of Paris—revolutionaries are beaten by professional soldiers
August 1848	The Constitutional Assembly meets in Vienna; serfdom is abolished
October 1848	Vienna is bombarded by Hapsburg forces, and the revolutionaries are overcome
November 1848	Pope Pius XI flees Rome because of revolutionaries
December 1848	Louis-Napoleon is elected President of the Second Republic of France
August 1849	The Hungarians' bid for independence is crushed by the Hapsburg forces, aided by Russian troops

Serbs and Rumanians living in Hungary, who in turn helped the Hapsburg dynasty to extinguish the nascent Hungarian state. The Germans of Bohemia resisted Czech demands for self-government and the equality of the Czech language with German.

Before 1848, democratic idealists envisioned the birth of a new Europe of free people and liberated nations. The revolutions in central Europe showed that nationalism and liberalism were not natural allies, that nationalists were often indifferent to the rights of other peoples. Disheartened by these nationalist antagonisms, John Stuart Mill, the English liberal statesman and philosopher, lamented that "the sentiment of nationality so far outweighs the love of liberty that the people are willing to abet their rulers in crushing the liberty and independence of any people not of their race or language."[6]

The liberal and nationalist aims of the revolutionaries were not realized, but liberal gains were not insignificant. All French men obtained the right to vote; the labor services of peasants were abolished in Austria and the German states; parliaments, dominated to be sure by princes and aristocrats, were established in Prussia and other German states. In the decades to come, liberal reforms would become more widespread. These reforms would be introduced peacefully, for the failure of the Revolutions of 1848 convinced many people, including liberals, that popular uprisings were ineffective ways of changing society. The Age of Revolution initiated by the French Revolution of 1789 had ended.

Notes

1. Henry A. Kissinger, *A World Restored* (New York: Grosset & Dunlap, The Universal Library, 1964), p. 183.
2. Jacques Droz, *Europe Between Revolutions, 1815–1848* (New York: Harper Torchbooks, 1968), p. 248.
3. *The Recollections of Alexis de Tocqueville*, trans. by Alexander Teixeira de Mattos (Cleveland: Meriden Books, 1969), p. 12.
4. Ibid., pp. 11–12.
5. Hugh Seton-Watson, *Nations and States* (Boulder, Colo.: Westview Press, 1977), p. 162.
6. Hans Kohn, *Nationalism: Its Meaning and History* (Princeton, N.J.: D. Van Nostrand, 1965), pp. 51–52.

Suggested Reading

Artz, F. B., *Reaction and Revolution* (1963). Part of the multi-volume series *The Rise of Modern Europe*, this work concentrates on the period 1814–1832.

Droz, Jacques, *Europe Between Revolutions* (1967). A fine survey of the period 1815–1848.

Duveau, Georges, *1848: The Making of a Revolution* (1967). A valuable history of the two revolutions in France in 1848.

Fasel, George, *Europe in Upheaval: The Revolutions of 1848* (1970). A good introduction.

Fejtö, François, ed., *The Opening of an Era: 1848* (1973). Contributions by nineteen eminent European historians.

Hobsbawm, E. J., *The Age of Revolution 1789–1848* (1964). Interprets the many changes in Europe resulting from the impact of the French and Industrial revolutions.

Kissinger, Henry A., *A World Restored* (1964). A study of the statesmen and their statesmanship during, and immediately after the Congress of Vienna.

Langer, W. L., *Political and Social Upheaval, 1832–1852* (1969). Another volume in *The Rise of Modern Europe* series by its editor. Rich in data and interpretation; contains a valuable bibliographical essay.

Robertson, Priscilla, *Revolutions of 1848* (1960). Vividly portrays the events and the personalities involved.

Talmon, J. L., *Romanticism and Revolt* (1967). The forces shaping European history from 1815 to 1848.

Review Questions

1. What was Metternich's attitude toward the French Revolution? What was his attitude toward Napoleon?

2. How did the Congress of Vienna violate the principle of nationalism? What was the principal accomplishment of the Congress?

3. Between 1820 and 1832, where were revolutions suppressed, and how? Where were revolutions successful, and why?

4. What were the complaints of the urban poor to the new French government after the February Revolution in 1848? What was the significance of the June Days in French history?

5. Why did the Revolutions of 1848 fail in the German states, in the Austrian Empire, and in Italy?

6. What were the liberal gains of the Revolutions of 1848? Why were liberals and nationalists disappointed with the results of the Revolutions of 1848?

CHAPTER 23

The Surge of Nationalism: Italy, Germany, and the Hapsburg Empire

THE REVOLUTIONS of 1848 ended in failure, but nationalist energies were too powerful to contain. In 1867, Hungary gained the autonomy it had sought in 1848; by 1870, the unification of both Italy and Germany had been realized. Growing increasingly resentful of Magyar and German domination, the Slavic minorities of the Hapsburg Empire agitated for recognition of their national rights. Once Germany was unified, Pan-Germans sought to incorporate Germans living outside the Reich into the new Germany and to build a vast overseas empire. Russian Pan-Slavs dreamed of bringing the Slavs of eastern Europe under the control of "Mother Russia." Gaining in intensity in the last part of the nineteenth century, nationalism was to become the dominant spiritual force in European life. In the process, nationalism broke with liberalism and became increasingly belligerent, intolerant, and irrational—threatening both the peace of Europe and the liberal-humanist tradition of the Enlightenment.

THE UNIFICATION OF ITALY

In 1848, liberals had failed to drive the Austrians out of Italy and to unite their nation. By 1870, however, Italian unification had been achieved. The movement for Italian unification faced many obstacles.

Forces For and Against Unity

In 1815, Italy consisted of several separate states. In the south, a Bourbon king ruled the Kingdom of the Two Sicilies; the pope governed the Papal States in Central Italy; Hapsburg Austria ruled Lombardy and Venetia in the north; Hapsburg princes subservient to Austria ruled the duchies of Tuscany, Parma, and Modena. Piedmont in the northwest and the island of Sardinia were governed by an Italian dynasty, the House of Savoy.

Besides all these political divisions, Italy was divided economically and culturally. Throughout Italy, attachment to the local region was stronger than devotion to national unity. Economic ties between north and south were weak; inhabitants of the northern Italian cities felt little closeness to Sicilian peasants. Except for the middle class, most Italians clung to the values of the Old Regime. Holding that society was ordered by God, they accepted without question rule by prince and pope and rejected the values associated with the French Revolution and the Enlightenment— parliamentary government, equality, and freedom of thought. To these traditionalists, national unity was also hateful. It would deprive the pope of his control over central Italy, introduce liberal ideas that would undermine clerical and aristocratic authority, and depose legitimate princes.

During the wars of the French Revolution, France had occupied Italy. The French eliminated many barriers to trade among the Italian states: they built roads that improved links between the various regions, and introduced a standard system of law over most of the land. The French had also given the Italian states constitutions, representative assemblies, and the concept of the state as a community of citizens.

The Italian middle class believed that the expulsion of foreign rulers and the forging of national unity would continue the process of enlightened reform initiated by the French occupation, and this would promote economic growth. Merchants and manufacturers wanted to abolish taxes on goods transported from one Italian state to another; they wanted roads and railways built to link the peninsula together; they wanted to do away with the numerous systems of coinage and weights and measures that complicated business transactions. Italians who had served Napoleon as local officials, clerks, and army officers resisted the restoration of clerical and feudal privileges that denied them career opportunities.

An expanding intellectual elite, through novels, poetry, and works of history, awakened interest in Italy's glorious past. They asked: Should a people who had built the Roman Empire and had produced the Renaissance remain weak and divided, their land occupied by Austrians? These sentiments appealed particularly to university students and the middle class. But the rural masses, illiterate and preoccupied with the hardships of daily life, had little concern for this struggle for national revival.

Failed Revolutions

Secret societies kept alive the hopes for liberty and independence from foreign rule in the period after 1815. The most important of these societies was the Carbonari, which had clubs in every state in Italy. In 1820 the Carbonari, its members drawn largely from the middle class and the army, enjoyed a few months of triumph in the Kingdom of the Two Sicilies. Supported by the army and militia, they forced King Ferdinand to grant a constitution and a parliamentary government. But Metternich, fearing that the germs of revolution would spread to other countries, would not permit this. Supported by Prussia and Russia, Austria suppressed the constitutional government in Naples and another revolution that broke out in Piedmont. In both cases, Austria firmly fixed an absolute ruler on the throne. In 1831–32, the Austrians suppressed another insurrection by the Carbonari in the Papal States. During these uprisings the peasants had given little support; indeed, they seem to have sided with the traditional rulers.

After the failure of the Carbonari, a new generation of leaders emerged in Italy. One of them, Giuseppi Mazzini (1805–1872), dedicated his life to the creation of a united and republican Italy, a goal he pursued with extraordinary moral intensity and determination. Mazzini was both a romantic and a liberal. As a liberal, he fought for republican and constitutional government and held that national unity would enhance individual liber-

Legend:
- Kingdom of Sardinia before 1859
- To Kingdom of Sardinia, 1859
- To Kingdom of Sardinia, 1860
- To Kingdom of Italy, 1866, 1870

SWITZERLAND

AUSTRIAN EMPIRE

SAVOY
To France
1860

FRANCE

Po R.

PIEDMONT

From Austria
LOMBARDY
• Milan

From Austria
VENETIA
(1866)
Venice •

PARMA

Genoa •

MODENA

Bologna
ROMAGNA

OTTOMAN EMPIRE

NICE
To France 1860
• Nice

Florence
• Pisa

THE MARCHES

Tiber R.

A D R I A T I C

TUSCANY

PAPAL STATES

CORSICA
(France)

(1870)
• Rome

S E A

SARDINIA

Naples •

M E D I T E R R A N E A N

KINGDOM OF THE TWO SICILIES

• Palermo

SICILY

Straits of Messina

S E A

MAP 23.1   UNIFICATION OF ITALY, 1859–1870

ty. As a romantic, he sought truth through heightened feeling and intuition and believed that an awakened Italy would lead to the regeneration of humanity. Just as Rome had provided law and unity in the ancient world, and the Roman pope had led Latin Christendom during the Middle Ages, Mazzini believed that a third Rome, a newly united Italy, would usher in a new age of free nations, personal liberty, and equality. This era would represent a great progress for humanity: peace, prosperity, and universal happiness would replace conflict, materialism, and self-interest. Given to religious mysticism, Mazzini saw a world of independent states founded on nationality, republicanism, and democracy as the fulfillment of God's plan.

After his release from prison for participating in the insurrection of 1831, Mazzini went into exile and founded a new organization—Young Italy. Consisting of dedicated revolutionaries, many of them students, Young Italy was intended to serve as the instrument for the awakening of Italy and the transformation of Europe into a brotherhood of free peoples. This sacred struggle, said Mazzini, demanded heroism and sacrifice.

Mazzini believed that a successful revolution must come from below, from the people moved by a profound love for their nation. They must overthrow the Hapsburg princes and create a democratic republic. The Carbonari had failed, he said, because they had staged only local uprisings and had no overall plan for the liberation and unification of Italy. This could be achieved only by a revolution of the masses. Mazzini had great charisma, determination, courage, and eloquence; he was also a prolific writer. His idealism attracted the intelligentsia and youth and kept alive the spirit of national unity. He infused the *Risorgimento*, the movement for Italian unity, with spiritual intensity.

Mazzini's plans for a mass uprising against Austria and the princes failed. In 1834, a band of Mazzini's followers from bases in Switzerland attempted to invade Savoy. But every-thing went wrong, and the invasion collapsed. Other setbacks were suffered in 1837, 1841, and 1843–1844. During the Revolutions of 1848, Italian liberal-nationalists had enjoyed initial successes (see Chapter 22). In Sicily, revolutionaries forced King Ferdinand to grant a liberal constitution. The rulers of Tuscany and Piedmont-Sardinia promised constitutions. After five days of fighting, revolutionaries drove the Austrians out of Milan in Lombardy. The Austrians were also forced to evacuate Venice, where a republic was proclaimed. The pope fled Rome, and Mazzini was elected to an executive office in a new Roman Republic. However, the forces of reaction led by Hapsburg Austria regained their courage and their authority, and one by one, they crushed the revolutionary movements. Louis Napoleon's troops dissolved the infant Roman Republic and restored Pope Pius IX to power. Italy remained divided, and Austria still ruled the north.

Cavour and Victory over Austria

The failure of the Revolution of 1848 contained an obvious lesson: Mazzini's approach—an armed uprising by aroused masses—did not work. The reasons for failure lay in the fact that the masses were not deeply committed to the nationalist cause, and that the revolutionaries were no match for the Austrian army. Italian nationalists now hoped that the Kingdom of Piedmont-Sardinia, ruled by an Italian dynasty, would expel the Austrians and lead the drive for unity. Count Camillo Benso di Cavour (1810–1861), the Chief Minister of Piedmont-Sardinia, became the architect of Italian unity.

Cavour, unlike Mazzini, was neither a dreamer nor a speechmaker, but a cautious and practical politician who realized that mass uprisings could not succeed against Austrian might. Moreover, mistrusting the common people, he did not approve of Mazzini's goal of a democratic republic. Cavour had no precise blueprint for unifying Italy. His immediate aim was to increase the territory of Piedmont by driving the Austrians from northern Italy and incorporating Lombardy and Venetia into Piedmont-Sardinia. But this expulsion could not be accomplished without allies, for Austria was a great power and Piedmont a small state. To improve Piedmont's image in foreign affairs, Cavour launched a reform program to strengthen the economy. He reorganized the currency, taxes, and the national debt; in addition, he had railways and steamships built, fostered improved agricultural methods, and encouraged new businesses. Within a few years, Piedmont had become a progressive modern state.

In 1855, Piedmont joined England and France in the Crimean War against Russia. Cavour had no quarrel with Russia, but sought the friendship of Britain and France and a chance to be heard in world affairs. At the peace conference, Cavour was granted an opportunity to denounce Austria for occupying Italian lands.

After the peace conference, Cavour continued to encourage anti-Austrian feeling among Italians and to search for foreign support. He found a supporter in Napoleon III, (1852–1870) the French emperor, who hoped that a unified northern Italy would become an ally and client of France.

In 1858, Cavour and Napoleon III reached an agreement. If Austria attacked Sardinia, France would aid the Italian state. Sardinia would annex Lombardy and Venetia and parts of the Papal States. For its assistance, France would obtain Nice and Savoy from Sardinia. With this agreement in his pocket, Cavour cleverly maneuvered Austria into declaring war, for it had to appear that Austria was the aggressor.

Supported by French forces and taking advantage of poor Austrian planning, Piedmont conquered Lombardy and occupied Milan. But Napoleon III quickly had second thoughts. If Piedmont took any of the pope's territory, French Catholics would blame Napoleon III. Even more serious was the fear that Prussia, which had already undergone mobilization, would aid Austria. For these reasons Napoleon III, without consulting Cavour, signed an armistice with Austria. Piedmont would acquire Lombardy, but no more. An outraged Cavour demanded that Piedmont continue the war until all northern Italy was liberated, but King Victor Emmanuel of Piedmont accepted the Austrian peace terms.

The Sardinian victory, however, proved greater than Cavour had anticipated. During the conflict, patriots in Parma, Modena, Tuscany, and Romagna (one of the Papal States) had seized power. These new revolutionary governments voted to join with Piedmont. Neither France nor Austria would risk military action to thwart Piedmont's expansion. In return for Napoleon III's acquiescence, Sardinia ceded Nice and Savoy to France.

Garibaldi and Victory in the South

Sardinia's success spurred revolutionary activity in the Kingdom of the Two Sicilies. In the spring of 1860, some one thousand red-shirted adventurers and patriots led by Giuseppe Garibaldi (1807–1882) landed in Sicily. They were determined to liberate the land from its Bourbon ruler.

An early supporter of Mazzini, Garibaldi had been forced to flee Italy to avoid arrest for his revolutionary activities. He spent thirteen years in South America, where he participated in revolutionary movements. There he learned the skills of the revolutionary's trade, and toughened his body and will for the struggle that lay ahead.

Garibaldi held exceptional views for his day. He supported the liberation of all subject nationalities, female emancipation, the right of workers to organize, racial equality, and the abolition of capital punishment. But the cause of Italian national unity was his true religion. Whereas Cavour set his sights primarily on extending Piedmont's control over northern

VICTOR EMMANUEL AND GARIBALDI AT THE BRIDGE OF TEANO, 1860 The unification of Italy was the work of the romantic liberal Giuseppe Mazzini, the practical politician Count Cavour, and the seasoned revolutionary Giuseppe Garibaldi. Selflessly, Garibaldi turned over his conquests in the south to Victor Emmanuel in 1861. (Alinari/Editorial Photocolor Archives)

Italy, Garibaldi dedicated himself to the creation of a unified Italy.

Garibaldi returned to Italy just in time to fight in the Revolution of 1848. He was an extraordinary leader who captivated the hearts of the people and won the poor and illiterate to the cause of Italian nationality. A young Italian artist who fought beside Garibaldi in 1849 said of his commander: "I shall never forget that day when I first saw him on his beautiful white horse. He reminded us of . . . our Savior . . . everyone said the same. I could not resist him. I went after him; thou-

sands did likewise. He only had to show himself. We all worshipped him. We could not help it."[1]

After the liberation of Sicily, Garibaldi invaded the mainland. He occupied Naples without a fight and prepared to advance on Rome. In this particular instance, Garibaldi's success confirmed Mazzini's belief that a popular leader could arouse the masses to heroic action.

Cavour feared that an assault on Rome by Garibaldi would lead to French intervention. Napoleon III had pledged to defend the pope's

CHRONOLOGY 23.1 UNIFICATION OF ITALY

1821	Austria suppresses a rebellion by the Carbonari
1831–32	Austria suppresses another insurrection by the Carbonari
1832	Mazzini forms the Young Italy
March 1848	Austrians are forced to withdraw from Milan and Venice
November 1848	Pope forced to flee Rome
1848–49	Austria reasserts its authority in Milan and Venice; Louis Napoleon crushes revolutionaries in Rome
1858	Napoleon III agrees to help Sardinia against Austria
1859	Austro-Sardinian War; Sardinia obtains Lombardy from Austria; Parma, Modena, Tuscany, and Romagna vote to join with Sardinia
1860	Garibaldi invades the Kingdom of Two Sicilies
March 17, 1861	Victor Emmanuel of Sardinia is proclaimed king of Italy
1866	Italy's alliance with Prussia against Austria results in annexation of Venetia by Italy
1870	Rome is incorporated into the Italian state and unity is achieved

lands, and a French garrison had been stationed in Rome since 1849. Moreover, Cavour considered Garibaldi too impulsive and rash, too attracted to republican ideals, too popular to lead the struggle for unification.

Cavour persuaded Napoleon III to approve a Sardinian invasion of the Papal States in order to head off Garibaldi. A papal force offered only token opposition, and the Papal States of Umbria and the Marches soon voted for union with Piedmont, as did Naples and Sicily. Refusing to trade on his prestige with the masses to fulfill personal ambition, Garibaldi turned over his conquests to the Sardinian king, Victor Emmanuel, who was declared king of Italy in 1861.

Italian Unification Completed

Two regions still remained outside the control of the new Italy: the city of Rome, ruled by the pope and protected by French troops; and Venetia, occupied by Austria. Cavour died in 1861, but the march toward unification continued. During the conflict between Prussia and Austria in 1866, Italy sided with the victorious Prussians and was rewarded with Venetia. During the Franco-Prussian War of 1870, France withdrew its garrisons from Rome; Italian troops, much to the anger of the pope, marched in, and Rome was declared the capital of Italy.

THE UNIFICATION OF GERMANY

In 1848, German liberals and nationalists, believing in the strength of their ideals, had naively underestimated the power of the conservative old order. Some disenchanted revolutionaries retained only a halfhearted commitment to liberalism, or had embraced conservatism; others fled the country, weakening the liberal leadership. All liberals came to doubt the effectiveness of revolution in transforming Germany into a unified state; all gained a new respect for the realities of power. Abandoning idealism for realism, liberals now thought that German unity would be achieved through Prussian arms, not liberal ideals.

Prussia, Agent of Unification

What type of state was Prussia, in which German nationalists were placing their hopes? During the late seventeenth and eighteenth centuries, Prussian kings had fashioned a rigorously trained and disciplined army. The state bureaucracy, often staffed by ex-soldiers, perpetuated the military mentality. As the chief organizations in the state, the army and the bureaucracy drilled into the Prussian people a respect for discipline and authority.

The Prussian throne was supported by the Junkers in the 1700s. They owned vast estates farmed by serfs, were exempt from most taxes, and dominated local government in their territories. The Junkers' commanding position made them officers in the royal army, diplomats, and leading officials in the state bureaucracy. The Junkers knew that a weakening of the king's power would lead to the loss of their own aristocratic prerogatives.

In late-eighteenth-century France, a powerful and politically conscious middle class had challenged aristocratic privileges. The Prussian monarchy and the Junkers had faced no

such challenge, for the Prussian middle class was small and without influence. The idea of the rights of the individual did not deeply penetrate Prussian consciousness nor undermine the Prussian tradition of obedience to military and state authority.

Reforms from Above

In 1806, Napoleon had completely routed the Prussians at Jena. Distressed by the military collapse and the apathy of the Prussian population, high bureaucrats and military men demanded reforms that would draw the people closer to their country and king. These leaders had learned the great lesson of the French Revolution: a devoted citizen army fights more effectively than oppressed serfs. To imbue all classes with civic pride, the reformers abolished hereditary serfdom, gave the urban middle class a greater voice in city government, laid the foundations for universal education, and granted full citizenship to Jews. To improve the army's morale, they eliminated severe punishments and based promotions on performance rather than birth.

But the reformers failed to give Prussia a constitution and parliamentary institutions. The middle class still had no voice in the central government; monarchical power persisted, and the economic, political, and military power of the Junkers remained unbroken. Thus, liberalism had an unpromising beginning in Prussia. In France, the bourgeoisie had instituted reforms based on the principles of liberty and equality; in Prussia, the bureaucracy introduced reforms to strengthen the state, not to promote liberty. A precedent had been established: reform would come from conservative rulers, not from the efforts of a middle class aroused by liberal ideals.

In 1834, under Prussian leadership, the German states established the *Zollverein*, a customs union that abolished tariffs between the states. Attracted by the prospects of free trade, the German states, with the notable exception of Austria, entered the Zollverein. The customs union stimulated economic activity and promoted a desire for greater unity. Businessmen particularly felt that political unity would promote economic expansion and that having thirty-nine states in Germany was an obstacle to economic progress. The Zollverein provided the economic foundations for the political unification of Germany, and it led many Germans to view Prussia, not Austria, as the leader of the unification movement.

Failure of Liberals

During the restoration the ideas of legal equality, political liberty, and careers open to talent found favor with the Prussian bourgeoisie. Like the French bourgeois of the Old Regime, Prussian bankers, manufacturers, and lawyers found intolerable a system that denied them social recognition and political influence and rewarded idle sons of the nobility with the best positions. They also denounced government regulations and taxes that hampered business and hated the rigorous censorship that stifled free thought. The peasants and artisans—concerned with economic survival, respectful of tradition, and suspicious of new ideas—had little comprehension of, nor sympathy for liberal principles.

During the Revolution of 1848, bourgeois liberals failed to wrest power from the monarchy and aristocracy and to create a unified Germany. Frederick William IV (1841–1861) had refused the crown offered him by the Frankfurt Assembly (see Chapter 22). The Prussian monarch could not stomach a German unity created by a revolution of commoners. But a German union fashioned and headed by a conservative Prussia was different and attractive to Frederick. In 1849, Prussia initiated a diplomatic campaign toward this end. Austria resisted this maneuver because it was determined to retain its pre-eminence in German affairs. Faced with Hapsburg resistance, Prussia renounced its plans for a German

union and agreed to the re-establishment of the German Confederation. This political humiliation taught Prussia an obvious lesson: before Prussia could extend its hegemony over the other German states, Austrian influence in German affairs would have to be eliminated.

Bismarck and the Road to Unity

In 1858, Frederick William IV, by then mentally deranged, surrendered control of the government to his brother, who became William I (1861–1888), King of Prussia, when Frederick William died. William also regarded Austria as the principal barrier to the extension of Prussian power in Germany. This was one reason why he called for a drastic reorganization of the Prussian army. But the liberals in the lower chamber of the Prussian parliament blocked passage of the army reforms, for they feared that the reforms would greatly increase the power of the monarchy and the military establishment. Unable to secure passage, William withdrew the reform bill and asked the lower chamber for additional funds to cover government expenses. When parliament granted these funds, he used the money to institute the army reforms. Learning from its mistake, the lower chamber would not approve the new budget in 1862 without an itemized breakdown.

A conflict had arisen between the liberal majority in the lower chamber and the Crown. If the liberals won, they would, in effect, establish parliamentary control over the king and the army. At this critical hour, King William asked Otto von Bismarck to lead the battle against parliament.

Descended on his father's side from an old aristocratic family, Bismarck was a staunch supporter of the Prussian monarchy and the Junker class, and a devout patriot. He yearned to increase the territory and prestige of his beloved Prussia and to protect the authority of the Prussian king who, Bismarck believed, ruled by the grace of God. Liberals were

DENMARK

BALTIC SEA

NORTH SEA

SCHLESWIG

• Königsberg

• Kiel

HOLSTEIN

• Danzig   EAST PRUSSIA

POMERANIA

WEST PRUSSIA

Hamburg •   MECKLENBURG

Elbe R.

OLDENBURG

HANOVER   BRANDENBURG

• Berlin

• Hanover

POSEN

Vistula R.

RUSSIAN EMPIRE

WESTPHALIA

Oder R.

POLAND

BELGIUM

Ruhr R.

• Cologne

Leipzig •

Dresden •

SILESIA

Rhine R.

RHINE PROVINCE

Weimar •   SAXONY

Sadowa
1866

Sedan
1870

Frankfurt •

Main R.

Prague •

BOHEMIA

Luxembourg

Nuremberg •

MORAVIA

LORRAINE

BAVARIA

AUSTRIAN EMPIRE

• Stuttgart

ALSACE   WÜRTTEMBERG

Danube R.

BADEN

FRANCE

Munich •

Vienna •

SWITZERLAND

German Confederation boundary,
1815–1866

– – – Bismarck's German Empire

Prussia before 1866

Conquered by Prussia, 1866

Austrian territories excluded from
German Confederation, 1867

Joined with Prussia to form
German Confederation, 1867

South German States joining to
form German Empire, 1871

Conquered from France, 1871

✕ Major battle

ITALY

MAP 23.2 UNIFICATION OF GERMANY, 1866–1871

outraged by Bismarck's domineering and authoritarian manner and his determination to preserve monarchical power and the aristocratic order. Determined to continue with the reorganization of the army and not to bow to parliamentary pressure, Bismarck ordered the collection of taxes without parliament's approval, an action that would have been unthinkable in Britain or the United States.

When the lower chamber continued to withhold funds, Bismarck took action. He dismissed the chamber, imposed strict censorship on the press, arrested outspoken liberals, and fired liberals from the civil service. Prus-

OTTO VON BISMARCK Between 1862 and 1871, Bismarck worked tirelessly to unite Germany under the Prussian monarchy. Bismarck's wars against Denmark, Austria, and France led to the unification of Germany and earned him the admiration of the German people. He expanded Prussian power and authoritarianism. (Brown Brothers)

sian liberals protested against these arbitrary and unconstitutional moves, but did not use force. Since the army fully supported the government, and there was no significant popular support for challenging the government, an armed uprising would have failed. What led to a resolution of the conflict was Bismarck's extraordinary success in foreign affairs.

Wars with Denmark and Austria

To Bismarck a war between Austria and Prussia seemed inevitable, for only by removing Austria from German affairs could Prussia extend its dominion over the other German states. Bismarck's first move, however, was not against Austria but against Denmark. The issue that led to the war in 1864 was enormously complex. Simplified, the issue was that Bismarck wanted to obtain the two duchies of Schleswig and Holstein from Denmark, while Austria hoped to prevent Prussia's annexing these duchies by fighting as Prussia's ally. What Austria wanted was a joint Austrian and Prussian occupation of the disputed regions. After Denmark's defeat, Austria and Prussia tried to decide the ultimate disposition of the territory. But the negotiations broke down. Bismarck used the dispute to goad Austria into war. The Austrians, on their side, held that Prussia must be defeated in order that Austria retain its influence over German affairs.

In 1866, with astonishing speed, Prussia assembled its forces and overran Austrian territory. At the battle of Sadowa (or Königgrätz), Prussia decisively defeated the main Austrian forces, and the Seven Weeks' War ended. Prussia took no territory from Austria. Austria agreed to Prussia's annexation of Schleswig and Holstein and a number of smaller German states. Prussia organized a Confederation of North German States from which Austria was excluded. In effect, Austria was removed from German affairs, and Prussia became the dominant power in Germany.

The Triumph of Nationalism and Conservatism over Liberalism

The Prussian victory had a profound impact on political life within Prussia. Bismarck was the man of the hour, the great hero who had extended Prussia's power. Most liberals forgave Bismarck for his authoritarian handling of parliament. The liberal press that had previously denounced Bismarck for running roughshod over the constitution embraced him as a hero. Prussians were urged to concentrate on the glorious tasks ahead and to put aside the constitutional struggle, which in contrast appeared petty and insignificant.

Bismarck recognized the great appeal of nationalism and used it to expand Prussia's power over other German states and to strengthen Prussia's voice in European affairs. By heralding Prussia as the champion of unification, Bismarck gained the support of nationalists throughout Germany. In the past, the nationalist cause had been the property of liberals, but Bismarck appropriated it to promote Prussian expansion and conservative rule.

Prussia's victory over Austria, therefore, was a triumph for conservatism and nationalism and a defeat for liberalism. The liberal struggle for constitutional government in Prussia collapsed. The Prussian monarch retained the right to override parliamentary opposition and act on his own initiative. In 1848, Prussian might had suppressed a liberal revolution; in 1866, liberals, beguiled by Bismarck's military triumphs, gave up the struggle for responsible parliamentary government. They had traded political freedom for Prussian military glory and power.

The capitulation of Prussian liberals demonstrated the essential weakness of the German liberal tradition. German liberals displayed a diminishing commitment to the principles of parliamentary government, and a growing fascination with force, military triumph, and territorial expansion. Bismarck's words, written in 1858, turned out to be prophetic: "Exalt his self-esteem toward foreigners and the Prussian forgets whatever bothers him about conditions at home."[2] The liberal dream of a united Germany had been pre-empted by conservatives. Enthralled by Bismarck's achievement, many liberals abandoned liberalism and threw their support behind the authoritarian Prussian state. And Germans of all classes acquired an adoration for Prussian militarism and the power-state with its Machiavellian guideline that all means are justified if they result in the expansion of German power. In 1848, German liberals had called for "Unity and Freedom." What Bismarck gave them was unity and authoritarianism.

War with France

Prussia emerged from the war with Austria with additional territory and the position as the leading power in the North German Confederation; the Prussian king controlled the armies and foreign affairs of the states within the confederation. To complete the unification of Germany, Bismarck would have to draw the South German states into the new German confederation. But the South German states, Catholic and hostile to Prussian authoritarianism, feared being absorbed by Prussia.

Bismarck hoped that a war between Prussia and France would ignite the nationalist feelings of the South Germans, causing them to overlook the differences that separated them from Prussia. If war with France would serve Bismarck's purpose, it was also not unthinkable to Napoleon III, the emperor of France. The creation of a powerful North German Confederation had frightened the French, and the prospect that the South German states might one day add their strength to the new Germany was terrifying. Both France and Prussia had their parties that advocated war.

A cause for war arose over the succession to the vacated Spanish throne. Under strong consideration was Prince Leopold of Hohenzollern-Sigmaringen, a distant relative of King William of Prussia. France vehemently opposed the candidacy of Leopold, for his accession might lead to Prussian influence being extended into Spain. William, seeking to preserve the peace, urged Prince Leopold to withdraw his name from consideration.

PROCLAMATION OF WILLIAM I AS GERMAN EMPEROR, **1871** The Franco-Prussian War brought the southern German states into the nationalistic fold. After the decisive defeat of the French, patriotic German princes granted the title of kaiser to Frederick William of Prussia, who became Kaiser William I of Germany. (BBC; Hulton Picture Library, London)

The French ambassador then demanded that William give formal assurance that no Hohenzollern would ever again be a candidate for the Spanish crown. William refused. In a telegram sent from Ems to Berlin, he informed Bismarck of his conversation with the French ambassador. With the support of high military leaders, Bismarck edited the telegram. The revised version gave the impression that the Prussian king and the French ambassador had insulted each other. Bismarck wanted to inflame French feeling against Prussia and arouse German opinion against France. He succeeded. In both Paris and Berlin, crowds of

people, gripped by war fever, demanded satisfaction. When France declared general mobilization, Prussia followed suit, and Bismarck had his war.

With the memory of the great Napoleon still strong, the French expected a quick victory. But the poorly prepared and incompetently led French army could not withstand the powerful Prussian military machine. The South German states, as Bismarck had anticipated, came to the aid of Prussia. Quickly and decisively routing the French forces and capturing Napoleon III, the Prussians went on to besiege Paris. Faced with starvation, Paris

CHRONOLOGY 23.2   UNIFICATION OF GERMANY

1815	Formation of the German Confederation
1834	Establishment of the Zollverein under Prussian leadership
1848	Failure of the liberals to unify Germany
1862	Bismarck becomes chancellor of Prussia
1864	Austria and Prussia defeat Denmark in a war over Schleswig-Holstein
1866	Seven Weeks' War between Austria and Prussia; Prussia emerges as the dominant power in Germany
1866	Formation of North German Confederation under Prussian control
1870–71	Franco-Prussian War
January 18, 1871	William I becomes German kaiser

surrendered in January 1871. France was compelled to pay a large indemnity and to cede to Germany the border provinces of Alsace and Lorraine, a loss that French patriots could never accept.

The Franco-Prussian War completed the unification of Germany. On January 18, 1871, in the Palace of Versailles built by Louis XIV, the German princes granted the title of German kaiser (emperor) to William I. A powerful nation had arisen in central Europe. Its people were educated, disciplined, and efficient; its industries and commerce were rapidly expanding; its army was the finest in Europe. Vigorous, confident, and intensely nationalistic, the new German Empire would be eager to play a greater role in world affairs. No nation in Europe was a match for the new Germany. Metternich's fears had been realized—a Germany dominated by Prussia had upset the balance of power. The unification of Germany created fears, tensions, and rivalries that would culminate in world war.

NATIONALITY PROBLEMS IN THE HAPSBURG EMPIRE

In Italy and Germany, nationalism had led to the creation of unified states; in Austria, nationalism eventually caused the destruction of the centuries-old Hapsburg dynasty. A mosaic of different nationalities, each with its own history and traditions, the Austrian Empire could not survive in an age of intense nationalism. England and France had succeeded in unifying peoples of different ethnic backgrounds, but they did this during the Middle Ages when ethnic consciousness was still rudimentary. The Austrian Empire, on the other hand, had to weld together and reconcile antagonistic nationalities when the temperature of nationalism was high. Its collapse in the final stages of World War I marked the end of decades of antagonism between the different peoples of the Empire.

In the first half of the nineteenth century, the Germans, constituting less than one-quarter of the population, were the dominant national group in the Empire. But Magyars, Poles, Czechs, Slovaks, Croats, Rumanians, Ruthenians, and Italians were experiencing national self-awareness. Poets and writers who had been educated in Latin, French, and German began to write in their mother tongues and extol their splendor. By searching their past for glorious ancestors and glorious deeds, writers kindled pride in their native history and folklore and aroused anger against past and present injustices.

In 1848–1849 the Hapsburg monarchy extinguished a Magyar bid for independence, a Czech revolution in Prague, and uprisings in the Italian provinces of Lombardy and Venetia. Gravely frightened by these revolutions, the Austrian power structure resolved to resist the pressures for political rights by strengthening absolutism and tightening the central bureaucracy. German and Germanized officials took over administrative and judicial duties formerly handled on a local level. An expanded secret police stifled liberal and nationalist expressions. The various nationalities, of course, resented these efforts at centralization and repression.

Magyarization

Defeats by France and Piedmont in 1859 and by Prussia in 1866 cost Austria its two Italian provinces. The defeat by Prussia in the Seven Weeks' War of 1866 forced the Hapsburg monarchy to make concessions to the Magyars, the strongest of the non-German nationalities, for without a loyal Hungary the Hapsburg monarchy would suffer other humiliations. The Settlement of 1867 split the Hapsburg territories into Austria and Hungary. The two countries retained a common ruler, Francis Joseph (1848–1916), who was emperor of Austria and king of Hungary. Hungary gained complete control over its internal affairs—the administration of justice and education. Foreign and military affairs and common financial concerns were conducted by a ministry consisting of delegates from both lands.

With the Settlement of 1867, Magyars and Germans became the dominant nationalities in the Empire. The other nationalities felt that the German-Magyar political, economic, and cultural domination blocked their own national aspirations. Nationality struggles in the half-century following the Settlement of 1867 consumed the energies of the Austrians and Hungarians. In both lands, however, the leaders failed to solve the minority problems, a failure that ultimately led to the dissolution of the Empire during the last weeks of World War I.

The nationality problems in Hungary differed substantially from those in Austria. Constituting slightly less than half the population of Hungary, the Magyars were determined to retain their hegemony over the other minorities—Rumanians, Slovaks, Ruthenians, Serbs, Croats, and Jews. In the first phase of their national struggle, the Hungarians had sought to liberate their nation from German domination. In the second phase, after 1867, the landholding aristocracy that ruled Hungary tried to impose the Magyar language and traditions on the other nationalities. Non-Magyars who learned the Magyar language and considered themselves Hungarians could participate as equals in Hungarian society. Those who resisted were viewed as traitors and conspirators and faced severe penalties. Non-Magyars were largely excluded from voting and virtually barred from government jobs, which were reserved for Magyars or those who had adopted Magyar language and culture.

The government tightly controlled the non-Magyar peoples. It suppressed the cultural organizations and newspapers of the nationalities. The great majority of public schools, even those located in predominantly non-Magyar regions, carried on instruction largely in Magyar. Because of limited suffrage, the manipulation of districts, and threats of violence, non-Magyars were barely represented in the Hungarian parliament. Protests by the nationalities against this forced Magyarization often led to jail sentences. The repressive measures strengthened the hatred of Slavs and Rumanians for the regime. On the other hand, Magyarization brought economic and cultural opportunities. Jews in particular accepted the Magyar government and took advantage of what it offered.

But nationality movements within Hungary constituted less of a threat to the preservation of the Austro-Hungarian Empire than Magyar nationalism itself did. The Independence Party, whose influence grew after 1900, began to demand a complete severance of the link with Austria and the "cursed common institutions."

German versus Czech

The Austrian population of the Dual Monarchy was made up of Germans (one-third) and Slavs (two-thirds). Hungary tried to forge a unified state by assimilating the non-Magyars; Austria, on the other hand, made no deliberate effort to Germanize the Slavic nations. No attempt was made to make German the official language of the state or to dissociate non-Germans from their native traditions. In Austria, elementary school students were usually taught in their mother tongues. The state acknowledged the equal right of all the country's languages in the schools, in administration, and in public life.

But the nationality problem was aggravated by the haughty attitude of the German Austrians, who considered themselves culturally superior to the Slavic peoples. The Germans believed that they had a historic mission to retain their dominance over the Slavic nations, an attitude that clashed with the growing national consciousness of the Slavs. This antagonism between Slav and German marred Austrian political life. Neither the Germans nor the Magyars would allow the Czechs and the South Slavs the same control over domestic affairs that had been granted the Magyars in the Settlement of 1867. Could the Germans retain their dominant position in Austria when the Slavic masses were not only aroused by nationalism but, with the spread of liberal-democratic ideas, were also gaining the vote?

The most serious conflict occurred in Bohemia between Germans and Czechs, the largest of the Slavic nations. Championed by a growing middle class that had made considerable economic and cultural gains, nationalism among the Czechs of Bohemia gained in intensity in the final decades of the nineteenth century. The Czechs had the highest literacy rate in the Dual Monarchy, and Bohemia had become the industrial heartland of the Empire. The emergence of a Czech university and Czech youth associations and the growth of Czech literature stimulated a national consciousness. Between the Czechs and the Germans, who constituted one-third of the population of Bohemia, there was great animosity.

Concentrated primarily in the Sudetenland, the German Bohemians regarded themselves as culturally and morally superior to the Czechs and wanted to preserve their predominance in the government's administration. Considering the Czech language fit only for peasants and servants, the Sudeten Germans felt it ridiculous that Czech be placed on an equal level with the German tongue. The two groups argued over whether street signs and menus should be written in German or Czech. Czech nationalists wanted the same constitutional independence that had been granted to the Hungarians; Sudeten Germans demanded that Austria remain a centralized state governed by a German-dominated bureaucracy. Violent demonstrations, frenzied oratory, and strident editorials fanned the flames of hatred between Czechs and Germans. A growing resentment against the Czechs and a growing admiration for the new Germany created by

Bismarck led some Austrian Germans, particularly the Sudeten Germans, to seek union with Germany. Georg von Schönerer, the leader of the Austrian Pan-German movement, denounced both Slavs and Jews as racial inferiors, and called for the creation of a Greater Germany.

The clash between Czech and German grew uglier when in 1897 a new prime minister, Count Casimir Badeni, required government officials in Bohemia to know both the German and Czech languages. This requirement was no hardship for Czech officials, since most of them already knew German. Few German officials, however, knew Czech or cared to learn it. Riots broke out in various cities, German and Czech deputies in parliament engaged in fist fights, and the emperor was forced to dismiss Badeni. Eventually the reform was dropped, but Czech-German hostilities remained intense.

South Slavs

The problem of the South Slavs—Serbs, Croats, Slovenes—differed from that of the Czechs. No Czech state served as a magnet for the Czechs living within Austria, whereas in the Kingdom of Serbia (which gained full independence from the Ottoman Turks in 1878), the South Slavs had a foreign power to encourage their nationalist hopes. Serbian nationalists dreamed of extending their rule over their ethnic cousins, the South Slavs of Austria-Hungary. The Hapsburg monarchy viewed this vision of a Greater Serbia as a threat to its existence. This conflict between Serbia and Austria-Hungary was to trigger World War I.

The awakening of nationalism in the multiethnic Austro-Hungarian Empire raised the specter of dissolution. Could the forces of unity—the army, the bureaucracy, and loyalty to the Hapsburg dynasty—contain the centrifugal forces that threatened to shatter the Empire into separate parts? A restructuring of

the Dual Monarchy into a federated state that would give equality to the Slavs might have eased the pressures within the Empire, particularly since only extremists among the minorities were calling for independence. But the leading statesmen resisted the demands of the Slavs. At the end of World War I, the Empire was fractured into separate states based on nationality.

FROM LIBERAL TO RACIAL NATIONALISM

In the first half of the nineteenth century, nationalism and liberalism went hand in hand. Liberals sought both the rights of the individual and national independence and national unification. They demanded that the rights of the individual be protected from oppressive governments and that a people sharing a common culture, language, and history should rule itself in its own land. Liberal nationalists believed that a unified state free of foreign subjugation was in harmony with the principle of natural rights, and insisted that love of country led to love of humanity. "With all my ardent love of my nation," said Francis Palácky, the Czech patriot, "I always esteem more highly the good of mankind and of learning than the good of the nation."[3] Addressing the Slavs, Mazzini declared: "We who have ourselves arisen in the name of our national right, believe in your right, and offer to help you to win it. But the purpose of our mission is the permanent and peaceful organization of Europe."[4] Liberal nationalists believed that national freedom would lead to greater personal liberty within the nation and to peace between the states. As nationalism grew more extreme, however, its profound difference with liberalism became more apparent.

Concerned exclusively with the greatness of the nation, nationalists rejected the liberal emphasis on political liberty. This they regarded as an obstacle to national power and maintained that authoritarian leadership was needed to meet national emergencies. Nationalists also rejected the liberal ideal of equality. Placing the nation above everything, nationalists became increasingly intolerant of minorities within the nation's borders and hateful of other peoples. In the name of national power and unity, they persecuted minorities at home and stirred up hatred against other nations. In the pursuit of national power, nationalists increasingly embraced militaristic, imperialistic, and racial doctrines. Interpreting politics with the logic of emotions, they insisted that they had a sacred mission to regain lands once held in the Middle Ages, to unite with their kinfolk in other lands, or to rule over peoples considered inferior. Loyalty to the nation-state was elevated above all other allegiances. The ethnic-state became an object of religious reverence; the spiritual energies that formerly had been dedicated to Christianity were now channeled into the worship of the nation-state. In 1902, Friedrich Paulsen, a German philosopher, stated:

A supersensitive nationalism has become a very serious danger for all the peoples of Europe; because of it, they are in danger of losing the feeling for human values. Nationalism, pushed to an extreme, just like sectarianism, destroys moral and even logical consciousness. Just and unjust, good and bad, true and false, lose their meaning; what men condemn as disgraceful and inhuman when done by others, they recommend in the same breath to their own people as something to be done to a foreign country.[5]

Volkish Thought

Extreme nationalism was a general European phenomenon, but it was especially dangerous in Germany. Bismarck's triumphs lured Germans into a dreamworld. Many started to yearn for the extension of German power throughout the globe. The past, they said, belonged to France and Britain; the future, to Germany.

The most ominous expression of German nationalism, and a clear example of mythical thinking, was *Volkish* thought.[6] (*Volk* means folk or people.) German Volkish thinkers sought to bind together the German people through a deep love of their language, traditions, and fatherland. These thinkers felt that Germans were animated by a higher spirit than that found in other peoples. To Volkish thinkers the Enlightenment and parliamentary democracy were foreign ideas that corrupted the pure German spirit. With fanatical devotion, Volkish thinkers embraced all things German—the medieval past, the German landscape, the simple peasant, the village— and denounced the liberal-humanist tradition of the West as alien to the German soul.

Volkish thought attracted Germans frightened by all the complexities of the modern age—industrialization, urbanization, materialism, class conflicts, alienation. Seeing their beloved Germany transformed by these forces of modernity, Volkish thinkers yearned to restore the sense of community that they attributed to the preindustrial age. Only by identifying with their sacred soil and sacred traditions could modern Germans escape from the evils of industrial society. Only then could the different classes be banded together in an organic unity.

The Volkish movement had little support from the working class, which was concerned chiefly with improving its standard of living. It appealed mainly to farmers and villagers who regarded the industrial city as a threat to native values and a catalyst for foreign ideas, to small artisans and shopkeepers threatened by big business, and to scholars, writers, teachers, and students who saw in Volkish nationalism a cause worthy of their idealism. The schools were leading agents for the dissemination of Volkish ideas.

Volkish thinkers looked back longingly to the Middle Ages, which they viewed as a period of social and spiritual harmony and reverence for national traditions. They also

RICHARD WAGNER (1813–1833), DETAIL OF PORTRAIT BY AUGUST FRIEDRICH PECHT Wagner was a crucial figure in the shaping of German romanticism. His operas, glorifying a mythic German past, contributed to the Volkish outlook. (The Metropolitan Museum of Art; Gift of Frederick Loeser, 1889)

glorified the ancient Germanic tribes that overran the Roman Empire; they contrasted their courageous and vigorous German ancestors with the effete and degenerate Romans. A few tried to harmonize ancient Germanic religious traditions with Christianity.

Such attitudes led Germans to see themselves as a heroic people fundamentally different from, and better than the English and French. It also led them to regard German culture as unique—innately superior to, and in opposition to the humanist outlook of the Enlightenment. Volkish thinkers, like their romantic predecessors, held that the German people and culture had a special destiny, a unique mission. They pitted the German soul against the Western intellect, feeling and spirit against a drab rationalism. To be sure, the Western humanist tradition still had its supporters in Germany, but the counter-ideology of Volkish thought was becoming increasingly widespread.

Volkish thinkers were especially attracted to racial doctrines. Racial thinkers held that race was the key to history, and that not only physical features, but moral, esthetic, and intellectual qualities distinguished one race from another. In their view, a race demonstrated its vigor and achieved greatness when it preserved its purity; intermarriage between races was contamination that would result in genetic, cultural, and military decline. Like their Nazi successors, Volkish thinkers claimed that the German race was purer and, therefore, superior to all other races. Its superiority was revealed in such physical characteristics as blond hair, blue eyes, and fair skin, all signs of inner qualities lacking in other races. German racists claimed that Germans were descendants of ancient Aryans.* They held that the Aryans were a superior race and the creators of European civilization, and that the Germans had inherited their superior racial qualities.

Volkish thinkers embraced the ideas of Houston Stewart Chamberlain (1855–1927), an Englishman whose fascination for Germanism led him to adopt German citizenship. In *The Foundations of the Nineteenth Century*, published in 1899, Chamberlain, in pseudoscientific fashion, asserted that the inner quali-

---

*The Aryans emerged some 4,000 years ago, probably between the Caspian Sea and the Hindu Kush Mountains. An Aryan tongue became the basis of most European languages. Intermingling with other peoples, the Aryans lost their identity as a people.

ties of a people were related to such physical characteristics as the size of the skull. Germans had a superior physical form; consequently they were esthetically, morally, and intellectually superior and the bearers of a higher culture—in short, members of a master race. Chamberlain's book was enormously popular in Germany; the Kaiser read it aloud to his children.

German racial nationalists insisted that as a superior race Germans had a national right to dominate other peoples, particularly the "racially inferior" Slavs of the East. The Pan-German Association, whose membership included professors, schoolteachers, journalists, lawyers, and aristocrats, spread racial and nationalist theories and glorified war as an expression of national vitality.

Anti-Semitism

German racial nationalists singled out Jews as a particularly wicked race and a deadly enemy of the German people. Anti-Semitism, which was widespread in late-nineteenth-century Europe, provides a striking example of the perennial appeal, power, and danger of mythical thinking. Anti-Semitic organizations and political parties that sought to deprive Jews of their civil rights and anti-Semitic publications proliferated. Holding that all the ills of France were due to the Jews, the journalist Edouard Drumont demanded their expulsion from France. Karl Lueger, the mayor of Vienna, exploited anti-Semitism to win elections. Rumania barred most Jews from voting and holding office, and Russia restricted their admission into secondary schools and universities. The Russian government permitted and even encouraged pogroms (mob violence) against Jews. But in Germany, hatred of Jews developed into a systematic body of beliefs. As historian Hans Kohn says, "Germany became the fatherland of modern anti-Semitism; there the systems were thought out and the slogans

coined. German literature was the richest in anti-Jewish writing."[7]

Anti-Semitism had a long and bloodstained history in Europe, stemming both from an irrational fear and hatred of outsiders with noticeably different ways and from the commonly accepted myth that the Jews as a people were collectively and eternally cursed for rejecting Christ. Christians saw Jews as the murderers of Christ, an image that promoted terrible anger and hatred.

During the Middle Ages, people believed and spread incredible tales about Jews. They accused Jews of torturing and crucifying Christian children in order to use their blood for religious ceremonies, of poisoning wells to kill Christians, and of worshiping the Devil. Christians considered the Jews to be demons in human form, agents of Satan who had organized a secret government that conspired to destroy Christianity. Jews were thought to be physically different from other people—they were said to have tails, horns, and a distinctive odor. Serving to propagate the myth of the Jew as a different form of humanity was the decision of the Fourth Lateran Council (1215) that required Jews to wear a distinguishing mark. In Latin countries, Jews had to sew a disk on their clothing; in German lands, they wore a distinctive hat.

This image of the Jew as a deicide, an infidel, a demon, and a conspirator would persist in the popular mentality well into the modern age. While medieval popes and bishops condemned these fables and sought to protect Jews from mob violence, the lower clergy and popular preachers spread them to the receptive masses. Periodically mobs humiliated, tortured, and massacred Jews, and rulers expelled them from their kingdoms. Often barred from owning land and excluded from the craft guilds, medieval Jews concentrated in trade and moneylending, occupations that often earned them greater hostility. By the sixteenth century, Jews in a number of lands were forced by law to live in separate quarters of the town called *ghettos*.

In the nineteenth century, under the impact of the liberal ideals of the Enlightenment and the French Revolution, Jews gained legal equality in most European lands. They could leave the ghetto and participate in many activities that had been closed to them. Traditionally an urban people, the Jews were concentrated in the leading cities of Europe. Taking advantage of this new freedom and opportunity, many Jews achieved striking success as entrepreneurs, bankers, lawyers, journalists, doctors, scientists, scholars, and performers. For example, in 1880, Jews, who constituted about 10 percent of the population of Vienna, accounted for 38.6 percent of the medical students and 23.3 percent of the law students in Vienna. Viennese cultural life before World War I was to a large extent shaped by Jewish writers, artists, musicians, critics, and patrons. All but one of the major banking houses was Jewish.

But most European Jews—peasants, pedlars, and laborers—were quite poor. Perhaps 5,000 to 6,000 Jews of Galicia in Austria-Hungary died of starvation annually, and many Russian Jews fled to the United States to escape from desperate poverty. But the anti-Semites saw only "Jewish influence," "Jewish manipulation," and "Jewish domination." Aggravating anti-Semitism among Germans was the flight of thousands of Russian Jews into Austria and Germany. Poor, speaking a different language (Yiddish), and having noticeably different customs, these Jews offended Germans and triggered primitive fears and hates.

Those Jews who were members of the commercial and professional classes, like other bourgeois, gravitated toward liberalism. Moreover, as victims of persecution, they naturally favored societies that were committed to the liberal ideals of legal equality, toleration, the rule of law, and equality of opportunity. As strong supporters of parliamentary government and the entire system of values associated with the Enlightenment, the Jews became targets for conservatives and Volkish thinkers who repudiated the humanist

and cosmopolitan outlook of liberalism. German historian Karl Dietrich Bracher concludes: "Anti-Semitism was a manifestation of a rejection of the 'West' with which the Jews were identified . . . because the Enlightenment and democracy were essential preconditions for their acceptance and progress."[8]

Anti-Semites blamed the Jews for all the social and economic ills caused by the rapid growth of industries and cities and for all the new ideas that were undermining the old order. Their anxieties and fears concentrated on the Jews, to whom they attributed everything that was repellent to them in the modern age, all that threatened the German Volk. In the mythical world of the Volkish thinkers, the Jews were regarded as evil entrepreneurs and financiers who exploited hardworking and decent Germans, manipulated the stock exchange, and caused depressions; as international socialists who were dragging Germany into class war; as democrats who were trying to impose an alien system of parliamentary democracy on Germany; as intellectuals who undermined traditional German culture; as city people who had no ties to or love for the German soil; as materialists who were totally without German spiritual qualities; as foreign intruders who could never be loyal to the fatherland; as racial inferiors whose genes could infect and weaken the German race; and as international conspirators who were plotting to dominate Germany and the world. This last accusation was a secularized and updated version of the medieval myth that Jews were plotting to destroy Christendom. In an extraordinary display of mythical thinking, Volkish thinkers held that Jews throughout the world were gaining control over political parties, the press, and the economy in order to dominate the planet.

In the Middle Ages, Jews had been persecuted and humiliated primarily for religious reasons, but in the nineteenth century, national-racial considerations were the decisive force behind anti-Semitism. Christian anti-Semites believed that through conversion, Jews could

ANTI-SEMITISM: BODIES OF JEWISH FUGITIVES, SHOT WHILE CROSSING THE DNIESTER BETWEEN THE UKRAINE AND RUMANIA In Russia, the government encouraged and supported anti-Semitic outrages. (Brown Brothers)

escape the curse of their religion. But to racial anti-Semites, Jews were indelibly stained and eternally condemned by their genes. Their evil and worthlessness derived not from their religion, but from inherited racial characteristics. As one anti-Semitic deputy stated in a speech before the German Reichstag in 1895:

If one designates the whole of Jewry, one does so in the knowledge that the racial qualities of this people are such that in the long run they cannot harmonize with the racial qualities of the Germanic peoples and that every Jew who at this moment has not done anything bad may nevertheless under the proper conditions do precisely that, because his racial qualities drive him to do it. . . . the Jews . . . operate like parasites . . . the Jews are cholera germs.[9]

The Jewish population of Germany was quite small: in 1900 there were only about 497,000, or 0.95 percent of the total population of 50,626,000. Jews were proud of their many contributions to German economic and intellectual life, considered themselves patriotic Germans, and regarded Germany as an altogether desirable place to live—a place of refuge in comparison to Russia, where Jews lived in terrible poverty, and the government instigated violent attacks against them.

German anti-Semitic organizations and political parties had failed to get the state to pass anti-Semitic laws, and by the early 1900s these groups had declined in political power and importance. But the mischief had been done. In the minds of many Germans the image of the Jew as an evil and dangerous creature had been firmly planted, even in respectable circles. It was perpetuated by the schools, youth groups, the Pan-German Association, and an array of racist pamphlets and books. Late nineteenth-century racial anti-Semites had constructed an ideological foundation on which Hitler would later build his movement. In words that foreshadowed Hitler, Paul de Lagarde (1827–1891) said of the Jews: "One does not have dealings with pests and parasites; one does not rear them and cherish them; one destroys them as speedily and thoroughly as possible."[10]

It is, of course, absurd to believe that a nation of 50 million was threatened by a half million citizens of Jewish birth, or that the 12 million Jews of the world had organized to rule the planet. The Jewish birthrate in Germany was low, the rate of intermarriage high, and the desire for complete assimilation into German life great. Within a few generations the Jewish community in Germany might well have disappeared. Moreover, despite the paranoia of the anti-Semite, the German Jews and indeed the Jews in the rest of Europe were quite powerless. There were scarcely any Jews in the ruling circles of governments, armies, civil services, or heavy industries. As events were to prove, the Jews, with no army or state and dwelling among people who despised them, were the weakest of peoples. But the race mystics, convinced that they were waging a war of self-defense against a Satanic foe, were impervious to rational argument.

Thus, racial nationalists attacked and undermined the Enlightenment tradition. They denied equality, scorned toleration and cosmopolitanism, and made myth and superstition a vital force in political life. That many people believed these racial theories was an ominous sign for Western civilization. It showed how tenuous the Enlightenment tradition of reason was, how receptive the mind was to myths, and how powerful the attraction of precivilized standards of conduct could be.

Notes

1. Quoted in Christopher Hibbert, *Garibaldi and His Enemies* (Boston: Little, Brown, 1965), p. 45.
2. Otto Pflanze, *Bismarck and the Development of Germany: The Period of Unification* (Princeton, N.J.: Princeton University Press, 1963), p. 232.
3. Hans Kohn, *Pan-Slavism* (Notre Dame, Ind.: University of Notre Dame Press, 1953), pp. 66–67.
4. Ibid., p. 44.
5. Cited in Friedrich Meinecke, *The German Catastrophe* (Boston: Beacon Press, 1963), pp. 23–24.
6. This discussion is based largely on the works of George L. Mosse, particularly *The Crisis of German Ideology* (New York: Grosset & Dunlap Universal Library, 1964).
7. Hans Kohn, *Nationalism: Its Meaning and History* (Princeton, N.J.: D. Van Nostrand, Anvil Books, 1965), p. 77.
8. Karl Dietrich Bracher, *The German Dictatorship*, trans. by Jean Steinberg, (New York: Praeger, 1970), p. 36.
9. Quoted in Raul Hilberg, *The Destruction of the European Jews* (Chicago: Quadrangle, 1967), pp. 10–11.
10. Quoted in Helmut Krausnick, Hans Buchheim, Martin Broszat, and Hans-Adolf Jacobsen, *Anatomy of the SS State*, trans. by Richard Barry et al. (London: William Collins Sons, 1968), p. 9.

Suggested Reading

Beales, Derek, *The Risorgimento and the Unification of Italy* (1971). A comprehensive overview followed by documents.

Hamerow, T. S., *Restoration, Revolution, Reaction* (1958). An examination of economics and politics in Germany, 1815–1871, stressing the problems caused by the transition from agrarianism to industrialism.

———, ed., *Otto von Bismarck* (1962). A collection of readings from leading historians.

Hibbert, Christopher, *Garibaldi and His Enemies* (1965). A vivid portrait of the Italian hero.

Jászi, Oscar, *The Dissolution of the Hapsburg Monarchy* (1961). Originally published in 1929, this volume examines how nationalist animosities contributed to the dissolution of the Hapsburg monarchy.

Kohn, Hans, *Nationalism: Its Meaning and History* (1955). A concise history of modern nationalism by a leading student of the subject.

Pauley, B. F., *The Hapsburg Legacy, 1877–1939* (1972). A good brief work on a complex subject.

Pflanze, Otto, *Bismarck and the Development of Germany* (1963). An excellent study of the political history of Germany during the period 1815–1871.

———, ed., *The Unification of Germany, 1848–1871* (1968). Excerpts from the works of leading historians.

Smith, D. M., ed., *Garibaldi* (1969). A collection of readings; Garibaldi as he saw himself, how his contemporaries saw him, how nineteenth- and twentieth-century historians have viewed him; preceded by a valuable introduction.

Whyte, A. J., *The Evolution of Modern Italy* (1965). A study of the Risorgimento, its origins and its leaders.

Review Questions

1. What forces worked for and against Italian unity?

2. Mazzini was the soul, Cavour the brains, and Garibaldi the sword in the struggle for the unification of Italy. Discuss their participation in, and contributions to the struggle.

3. Why is it significant that Prussia served as the agent of German unification, rather than the Frankfurt Assembly in 1848?

4. Prussia's victory over Austria was a triumph for conservatism and a defeat for liberalism. Discuss this statement.

5. What was the significance of the Franco-Prussian War for European history?

6. In the Hapsburg Empire, nationalism was a force for disunity. Discuss this statement.

7. To whom did Volkish thought appeal? Describe why.

8. Why is racial nationalism a repudiation of the Enlightenment tradition and a regression to mythical thinking?

9. Summarize some of the basic reasons for medieval and modern anti-Semitism.

CHAPTER 24

The Industrial Revolution:
The Transformation of
Society

I N THE SECOND HALF of the eighteenth century, forces at work in the European economy and society gained momentum—forces destined to have at least as great a significance for humanity as the events and achievements of the French Revolution. Experimentation in agriculture and new forms of organizing labor and capital, along with a rapidly growing population, had so startling an impact that French observers in the 1820s gave the developments a name—*industrialism*, or *the Industrial Revolution.* These developments occurred first in England, but within a short time, this "English system" spread to Europe and the United States, bringing changes of immense importance to the entire world.

The term *Industrial Revolution* refers to the shift from an agrarian, handicraft economy to one dominated by machine manufacture in factories in urban areas. For contemporaries of the Industrial Revolution, the application of inventions to human tasks seemed the most significant change taking place in England. Today, that period's new and more efficient ways of organizing tasks that made them simple enough for children to do and that greatly increased productivity seem as impressive as the early inventions, many of which were simple alterations of existing tools. This application of invention to human tasks and the organization of labor into teams in factories had enormous consequences for society. Technological change appealed to the hopes of progressive men and women, offering a promise of alleviating poverty, want, and harsh labor. But rapid industrialization and urbanization also created immense problems for the individual and the state.

Industrial progress did not proceed everywhere at the same pace. The changes in production, distribution, and organization of business, commerce, and labor that can be dated from the middle of the eighteenth century in England did not start in France until the French Revolution. The changes were, in fact, fostered by the Code Napoléon, perhaps even by the military needs of the Napoleonic Wars. French industrialization accelerated after the Revolution of 1848. In central Europe, industrial growth began as late as the 1840s. The social disruption of that era originated in the hardships that artisans and craftsmen faced, comparable to those faced by their class in England a generation earlier. Commerce and development also lagged because the German states were not united under one government. Though German industrial growth was phenomenal after unification, even up to the First World War the German economy was full of contradictions. Archaic and traditional economic forms and customs persisted alongside very modernized sectors. Industrialization proceeded slowly in Italy, too, where it was hampered by the sharp economic divisions between north and south, the comparatively poor natural resources, and late unification. In the last half of the nineteenth century the United States was also industrializing by leaps and bounds. In eastern Europe, the beginnings of industrialization were delayed to the very last decade of the nineteenth century. As for the Balkans, it may be said that industrialization did not begin until the end of the Second World War.

THE RISE OF THE INDUSTRIAL AGE

Why Western Europe?

The Industrial Revolution began in western Europe earlier than the rest of the world for a number of reasons. On the eve of industrialization, western Europe was wealthier than most of the world, and its wealth was spread across more classes of people. Some wealth came from the rapid expansion of trade, both overseas and Continental, over the previous two centuries, an expansion that built on the capitalist practices of medieval and Renaissance bankers and merchants. Also, wealth

had slowly accumulated over the centuries, despite devastating setbacks of famine, plague, and war.

Western agriculture differed from that of the Orient in many ways, which contributed to the coming of an industrial age in Europe. Western agriculture was thrifty of land, capital, and human labor. Grain crops, rather than rice, were grown in the West; they were planted by scattering seed. Each individual seed of rice, on the other hand, had to be planted; rice fields were covered with water. More varied lands, differing in fertility and contour, could be used for grain, which did not require the costly irrigation ditches, dams, and canals that the growth of rice demanded and that characterized the growth of state power in China and ancient Egypt. Europeans were also quick to accept new foodstuffs from other continents, like potatoes. This acceptance enabled them to feed more people, releasing some workers for other economic activities. Over the centuries, the decline of serfdom and manorial obligations released people for new forms of labor in western Europe.

The growth of centralized states and a system of states that competed for markets, for territory, and for prestige also contributed to economic expansion. States that centralized power in the hands of a strong monarch, such as Spain, Portugal, England, and France, were able to claim territorial and trading privileges with much of the rest of the world. Engaged in fierce military and commercial rivalries, the states actively promoted industries to manufacture weaponry, uniforms, and ships, and encouraged subjects to engage in trade.

The Growth of Population

One precondition for industrialization was population growth, for an expanding population provided industry with both markets and labor. There was an enormous expansion of Europe's population in the eighteenth century. Most of this growth took place after the middle of the century, and continued into the nineteenth century. In the Europe of 1800, there were about 190 million people (only the United States took an accurate census at that time); by 1914 there were 460 million people in Europe and about 200 million Europeans elsewhere in the world.

The population expanded rapidly for several reasons. First, the number of deaths from war and from plagues declined during the eighteenth century. A more important reason for growth was the reduction of famine, which meant better health, more births, and fewer deaths. The signs of better health and nutrition included height—the average man was five feet six inches tall in 1900, compared to five feet a century earlier—and the age at which girls began to menstruate, which dropped by several years in the course of the eighteenth century. Also, the number of births actually increased due to a lower age for marriage and a longer period of childbearing.

This population growth might have sunk Europeans into famine, disease, and misery once again; in fact, signs of rural destitution were apparent by the end of the eighteenth century. However, major changes in agriculture not only increased productivity enough to feed the greater population, but also improved the diet of many Europeans.

In the eighteenth century, farming became more and more a capitalist enterprise, that is, production was undertaken for a market, rather than for self-subsistence. Land began to be used more efficiently; by rotating crops, all the fields could be cultivated, rather than some land lying fallow as had been the practice for several centuries. In some areas, however, within every country (particularly in central and eastern Europe), the three-field system continued well into the nineteenth century. After 1750 the British and Dutch practice of selective breeding of animals became more widespread. Mixed farming, which combined pasture for livestock, root crops (such as the potato, turnip, and sugar beet), and cereals, became more common. These changes greatly increased efficiency and production.

In the nineteenth century, traditional patterns of farming began to break up, and capitalist practices started to be applied to agriculture. Land freed from traditional obligations became just another commodity to be bought and sold and traded. Peasants freed from the obligations of serfdom became entrepreneurs or tenants or wage laborers—all farming for a market. Land formerly used by villagers was enclosed for private use. This sometimes resulted in more production, when large landowners applied the latest and most efficient methods of agriculture. But grasping landlords who wanted to maximize their profits immediately, rather than to build a future of greater profits, were often as much the enemy of experimentation as the peasantry who held on to traditional ways. The improvement of methods, crops, and livestock gradually extended to the peasantry; they too learned to diversify crops, use better hand-tools (the scythe instead of the sickle, for example), shift from oxen to horses, and use fertilizer.

By the middle of the nineteenth century the application of technical ingenuity to farming brought improved plows, reapers, horse-drawn rakes, and threshers; these vastly increased productivity, although peasants did not usually own even these simple machines until the end of the century. Due to these agricultural changes, fewer men and women were needed to produce food and raw materials, leaving greater numbers to work in industry.

Industrialization in Britain

Great Britain was the first country to industrialize, although it was not the only country with many of the prerequisites for industrialization. In the eighteenth century, England had serious economic competition from France, which was wealthier and more populous and possessed an empire equal to England's in importance for trade. The French had a skilled populace; their government, if anything, was more responsive than the British to the need

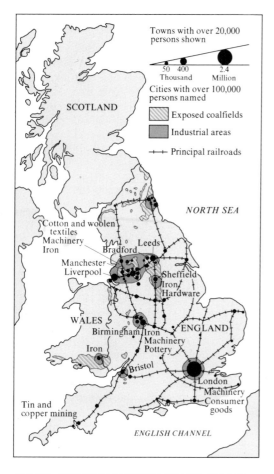

Towns with over 20,000 persons shown

50 400   2.4
Thousand   Million

Cities with over 100,000 persons named

Exposed coalfields

Industrial areas

Principal railroads

SCOTLAND

NORTH SEA

Cotton and woolen textiles
Machinery
Iron

Leeds

Bradford

Manchester
Liverpool

Sheffield
Iron
Hardware

WALES

Birmingham Iron
Machinery
Pottery

ENGLAND

Iron

Bristol

London
Machinery
Consumer
goods

Tin and copper mining

ENGLISH CHANNEL

MAP 24.1 INDUSTRIAL GROWTH IN ENGLAND, MID-1800s

for transportation and communication. The French early had instituted schools for technicians and fostered civil engineers for public works such as water works, canals, roads, and bridges.

But the French seemed less willing to change traditional ways, methods of agriculture, for instance. Moreover, much of the French economy produced luxury items rather than goods for mass consumption. In France, as in England, the people had enough wealth to make an effective demand for products at home. Well into the nineteenth century, however, the French economy continued to produce fine goods by hand for the few, rather than cheap goods by machine for the many. A more serious obstacle to French industrialization, which German and Italian states faced later, was internal tariffs—at least until the French Revolution abolished them. Britain did not have these obstacles to the free flow of goods within the country, and with the union of Scotland and Britain in 1707, Scotland was able to trade freely within the British system.

The French Revolution, which gave so much political freedom and opportunity and in many ways brought France alongside Britain, in other ways had the effect of maintaining traditional agricultural and commercial practices. Peasants who acquired land in the Revolution often gained small plots where new methods of farming were difficult to apply. They continued using old methods, trying to restrict their needs and even the size of their families to hold onto their land.

Like France, the Dutch Republic had sufficient wealth to support industrialization. For almost a century, the Dutch had developed techniques of finance and commerce that every nation tried to imitate. They also had a good transportation system. The Dutch lacked natural resources, however, and they continued to put their efforts into finance throughout the eighteenth century, rather than into expansion of manufacturing and trade.

Britain possessed several advantages that put it first in industrializing. Its large and easily developed supplies of coal and iron had given the British a long tradition of metallurgy and mining. Britain's natural transportation system of rivers was supplemented by canals and roads in the early stages of industrialization. In addition, Britain had a labor pool of farmers in both England and Ireland whose labor was no longer needed on the land because of the enclosures of common pasture or new crops or new farming methods. By providing law, order, and protection of private property, the state aided industrialization. Also, there was in Britain a remarkable freedom of

A COTTON MILL The movement from cottage to factory as the place of manufacture occurred during the late eighteenth and early nineteenth centuries. Until reform acts protected workers from exploitation, women and children worked long hours for extremely low wages. (The Mansell Collection)

entry into economic activity and far less restriction by monopolies, charters, and guilds than in other countries.

Changes in Technology

The Industrial Revolution involved a change from hand to machine manufacture and from human or animal power to other forms of energy, such as steam or the combustion engine. The first stages of development in a particular industry, however, often resulted from simple changes made by workers as they plied their craft, sometimes without altering the power source. The development of British textile manufacture, a pioneer in the Industrial Revolution, is a good example of how industrialization began.

Long the home of an important wool trade, Britain jumped ahead in the production of cotton, the industry that first showed the possibility of unprecedented growth rates. The quantity of British cotton expanded tenfold between 1760 and 1785, and another tenfold between 1785 and 1825. Several inventions helped produce these increases. In 1733, long before expansion started, a simple invention, John Kay's flying shuttle, was developed; it doubled a weaver's output. This shuttle, which could be used in the home, was an adaptation of other machines that had been used in the wool trade for generations. Then, James Hargreaves' spinning jenny, perfected by 1768, allowed an operator to work several spindles at once (still using only human power). Richard Arkwright's water frame (spinning machine, 1769) could be moved by water or animal power, an enormous advantage, and Samuel Crompton's spinning mule (1779) at first powered many spindles by human power, then by animal and water power. These changes in spinning improved productivity so much that bottlenecks in weaving developed until Edmund Cartwright's power loom of 1787. Several other inventors perfected the application of power to weaving.

These inventions were not complex and were made by weavers and spinners, not by technicians or inventors or scientists. They were fashioned after models of machines already in use. These simple inventions did not begin cotton's explosive expansion—that expansion was directed by social and economic demands. Once begun, however, the expansion was so great and the demand so urgent that it called for more and more complicated technology. A role emerged for the engineer, an expert in building and adapting machines.

The steam engine, which James Watt developed in the 1760s, was used to power machinery in the textile mills. Women and children, who earned less than men, could easily tend steam-powered machinery. Entrepreneurs who had many laborers available did not always shift quickly to steam power or to women and children workers because male labor was also cheap. But over the long run they did. Then expansion became even more rapid.

No other industry grew as fast as the cloth and clothing industry did, but the iron industry, which developed much more slowly, made enormous impact on the entire process of industrialization. The first step in increasing production of high-quality iron came when Abraham Darby produced coke-smelted cast iron in 1709. Experimenters had found it difficult to get the right match of ore and coal

and their correct proportions, and this breakthrough took several decades of trial and error. By the mid-eighteenth century the quality of cast iron was so high that it began to replace wood in construction. Another major advance was turning cast iron into wrought iron, which was the most widely used metal until steel was cheaply produced in the 1860s.

The iron industry made great demands on the coal mines to fuel its furnaces. Steam engines enabled miners to pump water from the mines more efficiently and at a much deeper level, which meant that the limits of mining reached in the seventeenth century could be greatly surpassed. The production of coal, which powered Britain's industrial growth, kept pace with that expansion and rose from 16 million tons at the end of the Napoleonic Wars to 30 million in 1836 and to 65 million tons in 1856. Coal could be used for industry and for powering the railroad and the steamboat when they came into wide use in the mid-1800s.

Hand in hand with greater productivity in coal went the improvement of iron smelting. Then in 1856, Henry Bessemer developed a process for converting pig iron into steel by removing the impurities in the iron. In the 1860s, William Siemens and Emile and Pierre Martin developed the open-hearth process, which could handle much greater amounts of metal than Bessemer's converter could. Producing steel became so cheap that it quickly replaced iron in industry because of its greater tensile strength and durability.

Each of these changes called for further changes in other industries and in transportation and communications. Transportation was revolutionized rapidly, providing a network that could support major changes in many other areas of the economy. Major road-building activity took place in the eighteenth century in England and in France, and later in the rest of Europe. Canals were constructed in Britain and the United States between 1760 and 1820. Steam-powered engines replaced horses as the power source for railroads in the 1820s. Governments licensed and encouraged

THE CRYSTAL PALACE The Great Exhibition of 1851 was held in London at Hyde Park in the Crystal Palace, constructed for the occasion using the new technology. Prosperity was its theme, and all Western nations exhibited. (Historical Pictures Service, Inc., Chicago)

the early railroads, hoping that they would fill in the transportation network where canals or roads were inadequate.

Steamboats could not be widely used in Britain for internal navigation because the rivers are small, but in the United States where many rivers are broad, there was a boom in steamboats in the first part of the nineteenth century. For long journeys, however, such as transatlantic crossings, steamboats could not compete with the sail-powered clipper ships of the 1850s. These ships were faster and their holds could be entirely filled with cargo, while the steamboats' holds had space taken by coal for the engine.

Continental European states were slower in adopting steam transport because they lacked capital and skilled civil engineering, not because they were unwilling to experiment with new forms. Roads, canals, railways, and steamships in Britain were financed by private enterprise, which invested unprecedentedly large amounts of capital for profit. All these building projects required Parliament's approval, but were undertaken by private entrepreneurs. The capital flow from western Europe, particularly France, to central and even eastern Europe in the mid-nineteenth century contributed to development of transportation systems that could support capitalist export agriculture and domestic industry. In these lands the state played a much greater role in economic development than in the United States or Britain. This was particularly the case in transport; Prussia and Austria-Hungary sponsored roads, canals, and railroads for the state's military needs. Military leaders soon devised strategies to make use of improved transport, and railroads played a significant role in the American Civil War and in the German and Italian wars of unification.

Communications changed as spectacularly as transportation did. Britain inaugurated the penny post in 1840, making it possible to send a letter to any part of the kingdom for one cent. The cost of postage in most places in Europe then was so high that letters were rarely written; many letters of the time cover every space to get the most on a single sheet of paper. But business, particularly across widespread markets, needed cheaper communication. The telegraph was an astonishing breakthrough in communications. Though certainly not cheap for some time, the telegraph was quickly employed by business. The first telegraphic message was sent from Baltimore to Washington, D.C., in 1844. Seven years later the first submarine cable under the English Channel was laid, and by 1866, transatlantic cable was in operation.

Financing Industrialization

The first steps of industrialization—the use of new crops and tools in agriculture and the first changes in spinning and weaving—did not require much capital. Subsequent growth—the establishment of new means of transportation and communication, the growth of machine industry organized in factories, the extensive application of machinery to agriculture, the expansion of mining and construction in cities—all required the investment of enormous capital. Railroads and steamship lines were often so expensive that only governments could finance them; even in Belgium,

where they were privately financed at first, the king was the major investor. Funding the steel industry required large investments. The building of canals, the Suez or the Panama for example, was a gigantic undertaking needing international investment.

Estimating the rate of saving from 1760 to 1860 in the United States, Britain, or France is very difficult, but it is known to be very high. In the earliest stages of industrialization, the saving for individual company growth was generally done by the family-owners, for the family firm dominated the field. The demand for capital was very great indeed, and it rose steadily from 1760 to the end of the First World War. In Britain, for example, wealthy merchants and landlords provided investment capital, and low interest rates encouraged borrowing. On the Continent the supply of capital was limited, and the British became international investors of the first rank, furnishing much of the capital for the industrialization of other nations.

One major difficulty was the lack of a form of organization that would enable a number of people to pool their capital without taking on individual responsibility for all the debts of an enterprise. The joint-stock company had a bad name in France and England because of financial scandals at the beginning of the eighteenth century. But more and more individuals joined together in this manner, keeping the right to transfer their shares without the consent of the other stockholders. England finally repealed the laws against this practice in 1825, and permitted incorporation in 1844. Incorporation was the practice of creating an organization that would be treated as one party before the law, though it actually was comprised of a number of individuals joined together for commerce. In the 1850s, limited liability was applied to the stock of most English businesses, and a little later it was extended to banks and insurance companies. This change meant investors could invest safely, endangering only the actual amount of their stock, not all the funds they possessed. In 1844, after nearly a century of industrial progress, England had almost a thousand such companies with a stock value of 345 million pounds, compared to 260 similar companies in France. By the 1860s the French, Germans, and all the American states permitted limited liability.

Several important banking families contributed to Europe's industrialization, including the Barings of London and the Rothschilds of France, England, and Germany. The family unit again provided the loyalty to join together amounts of capital for an investment bank. Banking was risky business in the nineteenth century, and dozens of banks failed in every financial crisis. Without insurance for deposits and possessing limited resources, banks could not protect their investors. To avoid the risk of losing everything in the failure of a single industry, banks diversified their investments, but in any given country the number of industries with resources to borrow substantial amounts of capital was limited.

THE TRANSFORMATION OF SOCIETY

The changes in agricultural production, business organization, technology, and the uses of power had revolutionary consequences for society and politics. People were drawn into cities from the countryside and from one country to another. Traditional ways of life for Europeans and eventually for non-Westerners changed. Industrialism made the world smaller; the whole world was drawn into commerce and manufacturing at a dizzying speed.

European society before the Industrial Revolution was based on kinship. Property in land was the base of social power and social class, and was usually exercised on a local or provincial level. Industrialization brought a new world in which there were many forms of property and several kinds of power, and the nation had become more important than the local area. In this new world, individuals were

increasingly important—before the law, in trade, and in political theory—but they came to feel small and cut adrift as they tried to make their way. Perhaps the family or the town had less control over individuals than before, but it was also less supportive to them in time of need, such as unemployment or illness.

Contemporaries saw the Industrial Revolution as a sudden and complete break with the past, the shattering of traditional moral and social patterns. Historians view the Industrial Revolution as a process, a period of gradual but sustained growth over 150 years.

While the foundations of new socioeconomic patterns were being laid, much of the old life persisted. In the nineteenth century, monarchs still reigned, landed property was still the principal form of wealth, and large landowners continued to exercise political power. From England to Russia, families of landed wealth continued to constitute the social elite. European society remained overwhelmingly rural; only England in the middle of the century was half urban. But to the people of that era, the new industrial society elicited so powerful a response that they found it hard to remember how much stayed the same.

The Condition of the Poor

One of the most hotly debated issues today about the history of industrialization, especially that of England, is the "standard of living controversy," which contemporaries first posed as the "condition of the poor." Poverty became an issue with the onset of industrialization. There had always been poor people, but with industrialization the economic and psychological hardships borne by the work force became a special concern. If machines could produce so much wealth and so many products, many wondered why there were so many poor people.

The effects of industrialization differed from country to country in their severity and

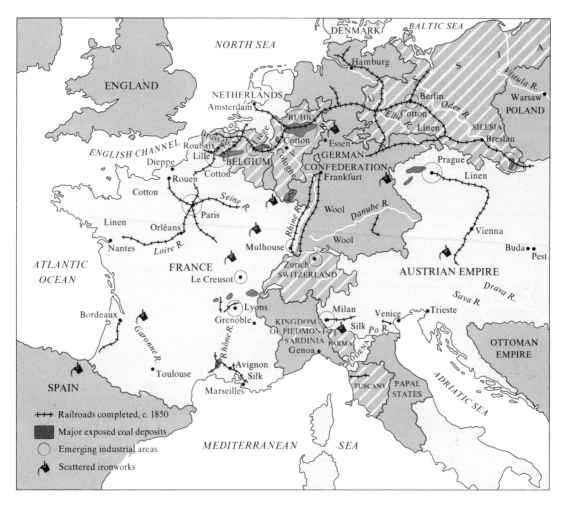

MAP 24.2 INDUSTRIAL GROWTH ON THE CONTINENT, MID-1800s

benefits. There were also differences from class to class in a country and from time to time. The feeling that conditions had deteriorated ran high in Britain. Why was this so? In Britain in the eighteenth century the agricultural classes seem to have had a higher standard of living than those in rural areas of other states. Britain was the first to undergo rapid industrialization and urban crowding; other countries learned from Britain's painful expe-

rience, though workers of all industrializing nations faced the cruel conditions of factories and slums. Moreover, committed to a policy of laissez faire (absence of restrictions on trade and capital), the British government introduced fewer reforms and regulations than other governments did during the early stages of industrialization.

Deterioration in the quality of life among the working classes seemed greatest among the artisans, especially handweavers; factory workers may actually have improved their standard of living in the first years of industrialization. The general instability of conditions contributed to a widespread discontent, reflected in the Chartist movement in England (see page 567) or in the strikes in the 1830s in France. When examined closely, this discontent seems to have been strongest among the artisans, who had more education, organization, and greater expectations than the factory workers, who were former farm laborers.

Parliamentary reports and the investigations of civic-minded citizens documented the suffering for all to read. These parliamentary "blue books" aimed at making reforms, and they did (for example, the Factory Acts, which tried to control the employment conditions of women and children). Historians still debate whether this "testimony" was true or representative of the conditions of most workers. They generally conclude that, although these were periods of acute distress for most workers, the standard of living was higher and improving over the eighteenth and nineteenth centuries. Exceptions to this improvement included craft workers, faced with competition from machines, and Irish farm laborers, whose families faced hunger and deprivation. Emigration to England, Britain's colonies, or the United States might mean that workers did not starve, but they lived desperately hard lives. Many historians argue that statistical evidence showing an increase in the *quantity* of goods received by workers does not reveal much about the deprivations in the *quality* of life that men, women, and children experienced as they moved from rural communities to urban factories, slums, and daily insecurity.

Urbanization

Due to industrialization, cities grew in number, size, and population. Before 1800, about 10 percent of the European population lived in cities, with Great Britain and the Netherlands leading the way to urbanization with 20 percent of their populations in cities. A mere forty-five cities in the world had more than 100,000 people. But even halfway through the nineteenth century, when 52 percent of the British were living in cities, only 25 percent of the French did, 36 percent of the Germans, 7 percent of the Russians, and only 10 percent of the inhabitants in the United States. The enormous shift from rural to urban dwelling both in Europe and in the United States has taken place in the twentieth century.

Industrial cities in the nineteenth century, particularly in England, grew rapidly, without planning or much regulation. A long period of industrial growth took place in Britain, with few attempts to control or regulate that growth. Civic pride and private patronage were the only forces to combat the effects of unregulated private enterprise. On the European continent where industrialization came later, there was more concern for planning. Continental states were more willing to regulate both industry and urban development.

So much growth with so little planning or control led to cities with little sanitation, no lighting, wretched housing, poor transportation, and little security. Rich and poor alike suffered in this environment of disease, crime, and ugliness, though the poor obviously bore the brunt. Government and business were often reluctant to use taxation to remedy these conditions. Almost universally, those who wrote about industrial cities like Manchester, Leeds, Liverpool, and Lyon describe the stench, the filth, the inhuman crowding, the poverty, and the immorality. Novelists Charles Dickens, Victor Hugo, and Émile Zola captured the horrors of industrial life and the plight of the poor. Alexis de Tocqueville described the cesspool of Manchester: "from this foul drain the greatest stream of human industry flows out to fertilize the whole world. From this filthy sewer pure gold flows. Here humanity attains its most complete development and its most brutish, here civilization works its miracles and civilized man is turned almost into a savage."[1] Many people could see no remedy to the inhuman existence of the urban workers. Others, excited by the potential for progress of the productive capacities of factories, regarded the terrible conditions as temporary phenomena that would pass away.

Changes in the Social Structure

The social result of industrialization is clear. The shift from a rural, agricultural society to an urban, industrial, and commercial society was truly revolutionary. Industrial areas grew in each country—the Midlands in England, the Lowlands in Scotland, the northern plains in France, the German Rhineland, the northeastern section of the United States and parts of northern Italy. Industrialization sharpened the distinction between the middle class (bourgeoisie) and the laboring class (proletariat).

Defining the *middle class*, the bourgeoisie, presents problems. Contemporaries often referred to these people as a plural unit—not a class but classes. The middle class were the people of common birth, that is, not noble. But they were not laboring people either, as they were engaged in trade and other capitalist ventures. The middle class was characterized by its virtues of work, thrift, ambition, and caution, or by the perversion of these virtues into materialism, selfishness, callousness, harsh individualism, and cultural Philistinism. These characteristics influenced their business practices, their political beliefs (which were frequently "liberal"), and their personal lives.

Over the century the social changes resulting from the Industrial Revolution brought the bourgeoisie greater political power and social respectability. By the end of the century, bourgeois politicians held the highest offices in much of western Europe and shared authority with aristocrats, whose birth no longer guaranteed them the only political and social power in the nation. As industrial wealth became more important in the modern world,

the middle class became more influential, and the aristocracy moved aside either to share or to yield political and social power.

Defining the *laboring class,* or proletariat, is equally difficult. Even in cities there were many gradations of workers. There were artisans who practiced a craft, factory workers who were the newest and most rapidly growing social group, and servants who made up great numbers of the urban dwellers, especially in capital cities.

The artisans were the largest group in the cities for at least half of the nineteenth century, and in some places much longer. They worked in construction, in printing, in clothing and textiles (in small tailoring or dressmaking establishments), in preparation and processing of food, and in special, luxury-producing crafts such as furniture making, jewelry, and lace making. Artisans as a group were distinct from factory workers; their technical skills were difficult to learn, and traditionally their crafts were acquired in guilds, which were both social and economic organizations. Artisans were usually educated, lived in one city or village for generations, and maintained stable families, often securing places for their children in their craft.

Artisans were threatened by the increase in the numbers of factory workers and the extension of machinery into their world. To compete with cheap factory-produced goods, artisans began to downgrade their skills by dropping apprenticeship training or by forcing journeymen to work longer hours on shoddy materials. In Britain and in France by the nineteenth century, the guilds had lost their special status and remained primarily as social organizations, sometimes as mutual aid or educational societies. In central Europe, guilds fared better; in 1848, artisans were at the forefront of the revolutionary movement as they tried to save themselves from the effects of the Industrial Revolution. Artisans, rather than factory workers, seem to have been the center of the political and economic protest against industrialization and for political representation. Certainly, they were at the heart of worker discontent in 1848 in France and Germany (see Chapter 22). Their guild organizations were the models for many early socialists, and artisans were generally in the front ranks of supporters of utopian movements.

Factory workers differed from artisans in many ways. First, they generally had recently come from agricultural areas, driven off the land where they may have been day laborers or perhaps owned a marginal plot. These workers had no special craft skills or traditions of working together with others of their craft. Frequently, factory workers came to the city factories without their families, until they could support them, or else the workers were single men or women who could find no jobs as servants or farm laborers in their home neighborhoods. These people entered rapidly growing industries where long hours—sometimes fifteen a day—were not unusual; farming had meant long hours, too, but the pace of the machine and the routine made factory work more oppressive. Sometimes the pay was good, and their standard of living rose, though working conditions were still oppressive. They often lived in overcrowded conditions, usually with members of the same sex if they were unmarried.

In general, the factory workers' lives were depressing because they had so little connection with their surroundings. Like immigrants to a new country, they were immigrants to the cities and lived with deprivation. They had left villages in which they were poor but perhaps connected to family, church, and even to local landlords. In cities, factory workers were usually employed in places with twenty to a hundred workers, so they had little contact with their employers. Instead, foremen were hired to make them work hard and efficiently. The workers had few roots in the city, and churches rarely reached out to them; the established church usually seemed formidable. They possessed no tools as journeymen did, so they had only their labor to sell. In fact, they had few of the artisans' advantages for

meeting the impact of industrialization. Thus, factory workers were torn from their traditions, had no organization or sense of comradeship, little education, little experience with city living, and often no family to support them when times were bad.

But factory workers did make lives for themselves. They married a little younger than artisans did, or entered into some relationship, and they had more children on the average than other classes did. One reason for this increase was the fact that children were an economic asset because they worked to help the family. Factory workers frequented churches that did try to reach them, such as the Methodists and other Dissenters in England. They developed a life around the pub, or its equivalent, where there were drinks and games and the gossip and news of the day. On Sundays, their one day off, many played sports, and some social organizations developed around their sporting games. Also on Sundays some workers drank and danced, with the result that absenteeism was so great on Monday that the day was called *holy Monday*. In short, factory workers developed a culture of their own, a culture often deplored by middle-class reformers.

For the first forty years or so of industrialization, factory workers did not show much organized discontent. They rarely broke machines in factories as was done by workers in rural areas. They did join with artisans in movements like the Chartists for political rights. Their attempts to form trade unions were crushed by employers or the law, but their associations for mutual benefit or self-help did develop. After the middle of the nineteenth century in England and western Europe, trade unions made economic and political progress in protecting their members from unemployment and dangerous working conditions. But strikes were rarely successful; they were usually misunderstood by the general public, imbued with individualist principles, and often suppressed by force. Not until the 1870s and 1880s, following a great depression in 1873 and a major drive toward heavy industrialization, was widespread discontent expressed by militant trade unions.

A third group, the servants, formed a substantial group of city workers. In many cities like Paris and London, where the number of factories was not great even in the nineteenth century, there were more servants than factory workers. Working in a middle- or upper-class household, servants were separated from factory workers and artisans. They were often women who had come to the city from the country, where they might also have been servants. They were completely at the command of their employers; they might be exploited or they might be treated decently, but they had little recourse when they were abused. Some worked their entire lifetime as servants; others left service to marry working-class men. Servants usually had some education. If they married and had children, they taught them reading and writing and sometimes the manners of the households in which they had worked. Many historians believe that these women passed on to their children their own deference to authority and their aspiration to bourgeois status; such an education could limit social discontent and radical political activity.

MOVEMENTS OF REFORM AND PROTEST

Intellectuals and political leaders struggled with the new and immense problems posed by rapid industrialization and urbanization—the crowding, the rootlessness, the poor working conditions, the poverty. What was to be done? Some believed industrialization could remedy social distress either through increasing economic capacity or through better organization of industry and government. In their minds, poverty was no longer a question of the will of God, but a social evil for which there was a rational solution.

But would the economy expand and benefit the lowliest of workers by itself, or did it need direction from the state? In much of Europe, people accepted the idea that the state could interfere with the market more readily than they did in Britain; further, most states in Europe had larger bureaucracies to carry out relief measures. Some reformers felt that they must do something to alleviate human distress because it was their Christian duty or their duty to humanity. But could this relief be adequate to the new conditions? How was it to be given—in individual acts of Christian charity, through the government, or through voluntary, religious and humanitarian agencies? Many workers and radicals believed that the only hope for workers was self-help through trade unions, mutual-aid societies, cooperatives, or political organizations. Still others believed that government efforts at reform would only make matters worse. They reasoned that people who relied on charity, whatever its sources, would not labor to provide for their families and would always be a drain on the economy and the society.

Some humanitarians—whether Christian, conservative, or liberal—agreed that women and children, having no political rights, needed protection from the harsh realities of long hours, low pay, and dreadful conditions in factories and mines. In England there were statutes protecting children as early as 1802 and 1819, but these laws lacked inspection provisions and penalties against those who broke the law. England did not have a powerful state bureaucracy—much local governing was done by unpaid local gentry—so enforcing regulations was difficult. The very people who were concerned for the well-being of children were often afraid of the state's power and unwilling to increase it. Workers themselves were not in favor of child-labor legislation because their family livelihood often depended on the contributions of children who worked by their side in the factories and mines. The workers thought that any interference was likely to lower their income and their ability to survive. Manufacturers also opposed supervision of the way that they conducted business. But by 1842, reformers carried the day in Britain with legislation forbidding the employment of women and children in the mines and containing inspection provisions and penalties for evasion of the law. One after another, industries were brought under the state's supervision to protect the helpless.

Another way to protect children and, it was hoped, to emancipate them from harsh conditions was to educate them. The first compulsory-education provisions of the English law (which did not provide the schools) often resulted in children working ten or twelve hours and then going to school to learn the rudiments of reading and writing. As difficult as that must have been for the children, the principle was established that the state could and should intervene to protect labor and to place limitations on employers' rights to exploit labor. Thereafter, a series of measures trying to regulate hours, conditions of labor and safety, the ages of the workers, and similar improvements were passed across the century. In France, compulsory education existed, as it did in some German states, but miserly governments often failed to provide adequate funds for schools.

The Transformation of Liberalism

Many English liberal thinkers supported the laissez-faire doctrines of Adam Smith (see pages 414–416). They felt that economic growth would follow naturally from removing restrictions on trade and capital, not just in Britain but in the whole world. They thought that people were especially competitive creatures, and that if all barriers to the free movement of capital, labor, and commodities were ended, then natural competitive impulses would ensure the production of more and better commodities at the lowest possible price for the greatest good of all—at least in the long run.

This optimistic doctrine required of government that it preserve law and order, enforce contracts and protect property, defend the nation, and undertake only those projects too costly for an individual or group of individuals. Laissez faire won many converts in many nations and became an integral part of liberal doctrine.

Economics also fostered a doctrine less optimistic than laissez faire, one that tended to have more impact on the lives of workers and the thought of reformers. English economist Thomas Malthus (1766–1834) wrote *An Essay on the Principle of Population* in which he cast doubt on the possibility of beneficial economic growth. Malthus argued that population increase would outstrip the increase in food production, which suggested that the poverty of the working class was permanent. Malthus reasoned that if wages were raised, workers' families would grow, and the extra wages would be used to support the added members. This new doctrine was called Malthusianism. Fellow economist David Ricardo (1772–1823) used Malthus's idea to form another theory that also made poverty seem inevitable. Wages, said Ricardo, tended to remain at the minimum needed to maintain workers. An increase in wages encouraged laborers to increase their families. As the supply of workers increased, competition for jobs also increased, causing wages to decline. Ricardo's disciples made his law inflexible— an Iron Law of Wages.

Many people considered the arguments of economists like Malthus and Ricardo irrefutable. But there were two attitudes in these principles: one optimistic, hoping for the expansion of human productive capacities and the end of want; and the other pessimistic, predicting a cycle of increasing pressure on scarce resources and deepening competition among workers for the necessities of life. The arguments supplied "scientific" justification for opposing governmental action to aid the poor, for poverty was an iron law of nature, the result of population pressure on resources.

Many workers argued that the liberals were only concerned with their class and national interests, that they were passive, hard, and callous to the sufferings of the poor. The liberals responded that the cure for the evils of industrialization was more industrialization.

But there were many avenues to liberalism, not just economic principles. In England the Nonconformists or Dissenters who argued for political and religious freedom were also Christian humanitarians with a social and moral purpose. They were suspicious of government, viewing it as a threat to liberty and as the tool of the privileged establishment of church and class. These humanitarians advocated voluntary charity, rather than state aid, to help the destitute.

These liberal reformers were often joined by a most unlikely group of allies, the utilitarians. They were disciples of English philosopher Jeremy Bentham (1748–1832). Unlike the Nonconformists, they did not worry about the state's power over the individual. In fact, they argued for state action according to the principle of "utility," or "the greatest good for the greatest number."

The utilitarians were radical reformers who supported legislation about factories protecting women and children and who argued for sanitation reform to improve the conditions in the cities, but who at the same time ardently championed the New Poor Law of 1834. This law's purpose was to make relief for the poor so unpleasant that every able-bodied worker would be forced to get a job to support his or her family. Relief would be given only inside the workhouse, where families were broken up, where food was meager and distasteful, and where the work was hard. This system would force all who were able to work to do so, and yet provide subsistence for the blind, maimed, very young, and severely handicapped. The poor hated these workhouses so much that they called them *bastilles*, after the infamous prison of the French Revolution, and rioted in districts in northern England when the law's enforcement was attempted. The New Poor Law assumed that work was always available if a person was willing to work. But this was a false assumption, inadequate to the new economic conditions. In a world market economy being shaped by industrialization, unemployment resulted from cycles of boom and bust over which the worker had no control.

Among liberals there had always been those who found it difficult to reconcile their ethical concerns and beliefs with the science of economics. The most eminent of these was John Stuart Mill (1806–1873). Mill was an English radical, a disciple of Bentham and of his father, James Mill, in that he accepted utilitarian propositions of the greatest good for the greatest number as well as Malthusianism. He supported the then-radical idea of contraception and the schemes for colonization of New Zealand and Australia to alleviate population pressure in Great Britain.

Mill defended mass education and the right to vote for all, men and women. He believed that men and women were much more equal in abilities than any of his contemporaries did. Mill argued that differences between the sexes and between the classes were much more products of education than the result of inherent inequalities. Believing that the goal of society was the fullest development of free and happy individuals, Mill thought that all men and women should be able to develop their talents and interests as fully as they could. He was one of the most ardent champions of free speech and free thought that the world has known, and his essay *On Liberty* (1859) remains the classic defense of individual freedom.

Early in the nineteenth century, liberals feared that state interference in the economy in order to redress social evils would threaten individual rights and the free market, which they thought was essential to personal liberty. In time the liberals modified their position, first supporting government action to provide education or opportunity for all and then accepting the principle of state aid to the poor because justice required some protection against the economy's ravages. From begin-

JOHN STUART MILL Although labeled a utilitarian, John Stuart Mill fits no category exactly. He concerned himself with most of the major issues of industrialization, including the definition of productive and unproductive labor, the distribution of gains from international commerce, and the precise relationship between profits and wages. (Historical Pictures Service, Inc., Chicago)

ning to end, the rights of the individual—particularly political, economic, and intellectual freedom—were the central concern of liberals.

Early Socialism

A new group called *socialists* went further than the liberals, demanding the creation of a new society based on a spirit of cooperation, rather than competition. Distressed by the unsettling conditions caused by industrialization, socialists sought a new socioeconomic system. In it, the production and distribution of goods would be planned for the general good of society. The most influential socialist thinker of the nineteenth century was German philosopher and economist Karl Marx. His works, written in collaboration with Friedrich Engels, provided the theoretical foundation for European socialist parties, both revolutionary and evolutionary. Some early socialists predating Marx wanted to establish planned, noncompetitive societies of men and women who would voluntarily withdraw from capitalist society. Believing that people can reform society through reason, these utopian socialists drew up blueprints for a better world. The principal early socialist thinkers were Saint-Simon, Fourier, and Owen.

Saint-Simon

Descended from a distinguished French aristocratic family, Henri Comte de Saint-Simon (1760–1825) renounced his title during the French Revolution. The central idea of Saint-Simon's thought was that contemporary society was defective and in need of reorganization. The critical philosophy of the eighteenth century had helped to shatter the old order, said Saint-Simon, but it had not provided a guide for reconstructing society. He believed that he had a mission to set society right by providing a clear understanding of the new age being shaped by science and industry.

Religion had provided social unity and stability during the Middle Ages; a new unity was now required, but it must rest on scientific knowledge, said Saint-Simon. Scientific principles would replace religious dogma as the binding force of society, and scientists, industrialists, bankers, artists, and writers would replace clergy and aristocrats as the ruling elite. In this new industrial age, Saint-Simon believed, the control of society must pass to those who actually produce, particularly the bankers, who as financiers of industry would best be able to engage in economic planning.

This industrial-scientific elite, said Saint-Simon, would harness technology for the betterment of humanity. In accordance with his philosophy, Saint-Simon's disciples championed the building of great railway and canal systems, including the Suez Canal. Saint-Simon's vision of a scientifically organized society led by trained experts—economists, scientists, industrialists, and administrators—is very much alive today.

Like the philosophes, Saint-Simon valued science, had confidence in the power of reason to improve society, and believed in the certainty of progress. In the spirit of the philosophes, he envisioned the creation of a science of humanity based on laws of social development. Also like the philosophes, he attacked the clergy for clinging to superstition and dogma at the expense of concern for people. Traditional Christianity must be recast to make it suitable for scientific-industrial society, insisted Saint-Simon. The essence of Christianity, he said, was the Golden Rule—the sublime command that people should treat each other like brothers and sisters. According to Saint-Simon, the traditional clergy, having placed dogma above the moral law, had forfeited their right to lead Europe in this new age, and a new clergy, fully abreast of scientific knowledge, would instruct the faithful to love one other. A new Christianity would serve as an antidote to nationalism, uniting spiritually and morally all the peoples of Europe. Like the Christian Middle Ages, the new society would be unified by a universal religion, one divested of myth and dogma to fit the new age of science.

Fourier

Another early French socialist was Charles Fourier (1772–1837), a salesman and an eccentric. Fourier believed that the conflict between the natural needs of human beings and the present arrangement of society was responsible for human misery. He wanted to rearrange society so that it would satisfy people's desire for pleasure and satisfaction. Whereas Saint-Simon and his followers had elaborate plans to reorganize society on a grand scale—large industries and giant railway and canal systems—Fourier sought to create small communities to allow men and women to enjoy simple pleasures and to satisfy their true human needs—a situation impossible in the existing society.

These communities, called *phalanxes*, each would consist of about 1,600 people and be organized according to the unchanging needs of human nature. In phalanxes, men and women could engage in pleasure, and would not be subject to coercion or thwarting of innocent human drives. Everyone would work at tasks that interested them and would produce things that brought themselves and others pleasure. Money and goods would not be equally distributed; those with special skills and responsibilities would be rewarded accordingly. This, too, accorded with human nature, said Fourier, for people have a natural desire to be rewarded for their achievements.

Fourier supported female equality. Women as well as men would select their jobs. He saw marriage as pure brutality, for he said that it denied the sexual needs of most men and women whose natures rebelled against strict monogamy. Because married women had to devote all their strength and time to household and children, they had no time or energy left to enjoy life's pleasures. Married life also harmed the husband, making him care only for his own family and not for other human beings. Fourier wanted people to escape boredom not only by changing occupations but also by changing lovers. He did not call for the outright abolition of the family, but he did hope that it would disappear of its own accord as men and women found new ways to fulfill sexual needs and the community undertook the responsibility for rearing children. In the 1840s, about twenty-nine Fourierist communities were established in the United States, but their duration was short.

Owen

In 1799, Robert Owen (1771–1858) became part owner and manager of the New Lanark cotton mills in Scotland. Distressed by the widespread mistreatment of workers, Owen resolved to improve the lives of his employees. He raised wages, upgraded working conditions, refused to hire children under ten, and provided workers with neat homes, food, and clothing at reasonable prices. He also provided educational opportunities for children, and initiated a program of adult education.

Owen demonstrated that a humane treatment of workers was not inconsistent with profits, as healthier, happier workers would produce more than less fortunate workers. He held that the environment was the principal shaper of character, that the ignorance, alcoholism, and crime of the poor derived from bad living conditions. Public education and factory reform, said Owen, would make better citizens of the poor. Owen eventually believed that the entire social and economic order must be replaced by a new system based on harmonious group living, rather than competition. He established a model community at New Harmony, Indiana, but the experiment ended in failure.

Marxism

Karl Marx (1818–1883) was born of German-Jewish parents (both descendants of prominent rabbis). In order to advance his career, Marx's father, a lawyer, converted to Protestantism. Enrolled at a university to study law, Marx switched to philosophy. In 1842, Marx was editing a newspaper that was soon suppressed by the Prussian authorities for its outspoken ideas. Leaving his native Rhineland, Marx went to Paris where he met another German, Friedrich Engels (1820–1895), who was the son of a prosperous textile manufacturer. Marx and Engels entered into a lifelong collabora-

tion and became members of socialist groups. In February 1848, they published the *Communist Manifesto*, which called for a working-class revolution to overthrow the capitalist system. Forced to leave France for his political views in 1849, Marx moved to London where he spent the rest of his life.

Marx believed that human history, like the operations of nature, was governed by scientific law. Marx was a strict materialist; rejecting all religious and metaphysical interpretations of both nature and history, he sought to fashion an empirical science of society. He viewed religion as a human creation, a product of people's imagination and feelings, a consolation for the oppressed; and the happiness it brought as an illusion. Real happiness would come, said Marx, not by transcending the natural world, but by improving it. Rather than deluding oneself by seeking refuge from life's misfortunes in an imaginary world, one must confront the ills of society and reform them.

The world could be rationally understood and changed, said Marx. People were free to make their own history, but to do so effectively, they must comprehend the inner meaning of history, the laws governing human affairs in the past and operating in the present. To Marx, history was not an assortment of unrelated and disconnected events, but, like the growth of a plant, proceeded according to its own inner laws. Marx claimed to have uncovered these laws. He said that economic and technological factors—the way in which goods are produced and wealth is distributed—were the moving forces in history. They accounted for historical change and were the basis of all culture—politics, law, religion, morals and philosophy.

Material technology—the methods of cultivating land and the tools for manufacturing goods—determined society's social and political arrangements and its intellectual outlooks, said Marx. For example, the hand mill and similar means of production had given rise to a feudal society, whereas power-driven machinery had led to a capitalist society. As material technology expanded, it came into conflict with established economic, social, and political forms—a tension that produced change. Thus, feudal patterns could not endure when power machinery had become the dominant mode of production, for they hindered the factory system. Consequently, Marx said, the expansion of technology had necessitated and triggered a change from feudal social and economic relationships to capitalist ones. Ultimately, the change in economic-technological conditions would become the cause for great political changes.

This process was most clearly demonstrated by the French Revolution. Whatever their conscious intentions, said Marx, the bourgeois leaders of the French Revolution had scattered feudal remnants to the wind; they had promoted free competition and commercial expansion and transferred power from the landed aristocracy to the leaders of finance and industry. This change was necessary because the economic foundations of society had been radically altered since the feudal Middle Ages.

Throughout history, said Marx, there has been a class struggle between those possessing the means of production and those whose labor has been exploited to provide wealth for the upper class. This opposing tension between classes has pushed history forward into higher stages. In the ancient world, when wealth was based on land, the struggle was between master and slave, patrician and plebeian; during the Middle Ages, when land was still the predominant mode of production, the struggle was between lord and serf. In the modern industrial world, two sharply opposed classes were confronting each other—the capitalists owning the factories, mines, banks, and transportation systems, and the exploited wage earners (the proletariat).

The class with economic power also controlled the state, said Marx and Engels. That class used political power to protect and increase its property and to hold down the laboring class. "Thus the ancient State was above all the slaveowners' state for holding down the slaves," said Engels, "as a feudal State was the organ of the nobles for holding down the . . . serfs, and the modern representative State is the instrument of the exploitation of wage-labor by capital."[2]

The class that controlled material production also controlled mental production, that is, the ideas held by the ruling class became the dominant ideas of society. These ideas, presented as laws of nature or moral and religious standards, were regarded as the truth by oppressor and oppressed alike. In reality, however, these ideas merely reflected the special economic interests of the ruling class. Thus, said Marx, bourgeois ideologists would insist that natural rights and laissez faire were laws of nature having universal validity. But these "laws of nature" were born of bourgeois needs in their struggle to wrest power from an obsolete feudal regime and to protect their property from the state. Similarly, nineteenth-century slaveholders convinced themselves that slavery was morally right, that it had God's approval, and was good for the slave. While they may have defended slavery on universal principles thought to be true, in reality their defense rested on a simple economic consideration—slave labor was good for their pocketbooks.

Under capitalism, said Marx, the worker knew only poverty. He worked long hours for low wages, suffered from periodic unemployment, and lived in squalid overcrowded apartments. Most monstrous of all, he was forced to send his young children into the factories.

Children of nine or ten years are dragged from their squalid beds at two, three, or four o'clock in the morning and compelled to work for a bare subsistence until ten, eleven, or twelve at night, their limbs wearing away, their frames dwindling, their faces whitening, and their humanity absolutely sinking into a stone-like torpor, utterly horrible to contemplate.[3]

Capitalism also produced another kind of poverty, said Marx—poverty of the human spirit. Under capitalism the factory worker was reduced to a laboring beast, performing tedious and repetitive tasks in a dark, dreary, dirty cave, an altogether inhuman environment that deprived people of their human sensibilities. Unlike the artisans in their own shops, factory workers found no pleasure and took no pride in their work; they did not have the satisfaction of creating a finished product that expressed their skills. Work, said Marx, should be a source of fulfillment for people. It should enable people to affirm their personalities and develop their potential. Capitalism, by treating people not as human beings, but as cogs in the production process, alienated people from one another and dehumanized them.

Capitalist control of the economy and the government would not endure forever, said Marx. The capitalist system would perish just as the feudal society of the Middle Ages and the slave society of the ancient world had perished. From the ruins of a dead capitalist society a new economic-social system, socialism, would emerge.

Marx predicted how capitalism would be destroyed. Periodic unemployment would increase the misery of the workers and intensify their hatred of capitalists. Small businessmen and shopkeepers, unable to compete with the great capitalists, would sink into the ranks of the working class, greatly expanding its numbers. Society would become polarized into a small group of immensely wealthy capitalists and a vast proletariat, poor, embittered, and desperate. This monopoly of capital by the few would become a brake on the productive process. Growing increasingly conscious of their misery, the workers, aroused, educated, and organized by communist intellectuals, would revolt, smash the government assisting the capitalists in maintaining their dominance, confiscate the property of the capitalists, abolish private property, place the means of production in the workers' hands and organize a new society. The *Communist Manifesto* ends with a ringing call for revolution:

The Communists . . . openly declare that their ends can be attained only by the forcible overthrow of all existing social conditions. Let the ruling classes tremble at a Communist revolution. The proletarians have nothing to lose but their chains. They have a world to win.

Workingmen of all countries, unite![4]

Marx did not speculate in great depth about the new society that would be ushered in by the socialist revolution. With the destruction of capitalism, the distinction between capitalist and worker would cease and with it the class conflict. No longer would society be divided into haves and have-nots, oppressor and oppressed. Since this classless society would contain no exploiters, there would be no need for a state, which was merely an instrument for maintaining and protecting the power of the exploiting class. Thus, the state would eventually wither away. The production and distribution of goods would be carried out through community planning and communal sharing, replacing the capitalist system of competition. People would work at varied tasks, rather than being confined to one form of employment. No longer factory slaves, people would be free to fulfill their human potential, to improve their relationships on a basis of equality with others, and to work together for the common good.

Marxism had immense appeal for both downtrodden and intellectuals. It promised to end the injustices of industrial society; it claimed the certainty of science; it assured adherents that the triumph of their cause was guaranteed by history. In many ways, Marxism was a secular religion—the proletariat became a chosen class endowed with a mission to achieve worldly salvation for humanity.

Marx was a principal architect of the modern age. Both the socialist parties of western Europe, which press for reform through parliamentary methods, and the communist regimes in Russia and China, which came to power through revolution, claim to be heirs of

Marx. Marx's emphasis on economic forces has immeasurably broadened the perception of historians, who now explore the economic causes of great historical developments. This approach has greatly expanded an understanding of Rome's decline, the outbreak of the French Revolution and the American Civil War, and other crucial developments. Marx's theory of class conflict has provided social scientists with a useful tool for analyzing social conflict. His theory of alienation has been absorbed by sociologists and psychologists. Of particular value to social scientists is Marx's insight that the ideas people hold to be true and the values they consider valid often veil economic interests.

But critics point out serious weaknesses in Marxism. The rigid Marxist who tries to squeeze all historical events into an economic framework is at a disadvantage. Economic forces alone will not explain the triumph of Christianity in the Roman Empire, the Fall of Rome, the Crusades, the French Revolution, modern imperialism, World War I, or the rise of Hitler. Economic explanations particularly fall flat in trying to account for the emergence of modern nationalism, whose appeal, resting on deeply ingrained emotional needs, crosses class lines. The great struggles of the twentieth century have not been between classes, but between nations.

Many of Marx's predictions or expectations have not materialized. Workers in Western lands have not grown increasingly poorer. Instead of the oppressed and impoverished working class that Marx described in the mid-nineteenth century, contemporary Western workers, because of increased productivity and the efforts of labor unions and reform-minded governments, enjoy the highest standard of living in history. The tremendous growth of a middle class of professionals, civil service employees, and small businesspersons belies Marx's prediction that capitalist society would be polarized into a small group of very rich capitalists and a great mass of destitute workers. Marx believed that socialist revolutions would break out in the advanced industrialized lands. But the socialist revolutions of the twentieth century have occurred in underdeveloped, predominantly agricultural states. The state in communist lands, far from withering away, has grown more centralized, powerful, and oppressive. In no country where communist revolutionaries have seized power have people achieved the liberty that Marx desired. All these failed predictions and expectations seem to contradict Marx's claim that his theories rested on an unassailable scientific foundation.

Anarchism

Anarchism was another radical movement that attacked capitalism. Like Marxists, anarchists protested the exploitation of workers and called for an end to private property. Marxists preached the eventual withering away of the state after capitalism had been overthrown, but anarchists demanded the immediate destruction of the state. To achieve their ends, anarchists advocated revolutionary terror, particularly the assassination of heads of state.

Anarchists drew inspiration from Pierre Joseph Proudhon (1809–1865), a self-educated French thinker. Critical of social theorists who devised elaborate systems that conflicted with human nature, regimented daily life, and deprived people of their personal liberty, Proudhon desired a new society that maximized individual freedom. Proudhon looked back longingly to preindustrial society, free of exploitation and corruption and great manufacturers and financiers. He had great respect for the dignity of labor and wanted to liberate it from the exploitation and false values of industrial capitalism. An awakened working class would construct a new moral and social order. Proudhon believed that people would deal justly with each other, respect each other, and develop their full potential in a society of small peasants, shopkeepers, and artisans. Such a society would not require a govern-

GUSTAVE COURBET (1819–1877): PROUDHON AND HIS DAUGH-
TERS Pierre-Joseph Proudhon condemned the new
industrial society, which he believed restricted
workers and spread poverty. He sought a society that
would maximize individual freedom. His call for
freedom influenced many social thinkers and was
adopted by nineteenth-century anarchists. (Historical Pictures Service, Inc., Chicago)

ment that only fostered privilege and suppressed freedom:

*To be governed is to be watched over, inspect-
ed, spied on, directed, legislated at, regulated, docketed, indoctrinated, preached at,
controlled . . . censored, ordered about, by
men who have neither the right nor
the knowledge nor the virtue. To be governed means to be, at each operation, at
each transaction, at each movement . . .*
*registered, controlled, taxed . . . hampered,
reformed, rebuked, arrested. It is to be, on the
pretext of the great interest, taxed, drilled . . .
exploited . . . repressed, fined, abused. . . .
That's government, that's its justice, that's its
morality.[5]*

Proudhon was a theorist from whom anarchists derived basic principles.

Mikhail Bakunin (1814–1876) was a man of
action who organized revolutionary move-

ments, fought in revolutions, and set an example of revolutionary fervor. The son of a Russian nobleman, Bakunin left the tsar's army to study philosophy. His studies took him to Berlin in 1840, where he read socialist literature. He then went to Paris, where he became attracted to the ideas of Proudhon and the young Marx. Putting these ideas into practice, Bakunin was arrested for participating in the Revolution in Germany in 1848 and was handed over to the Russian authorities. He served six years in prison and was then banished to Siberia, but he escaped in 1861.

Bakunin devoted himself to organizing secret societies that would lead the oppressed to revolt. Whereas Marx held that revolution would occur in the industrial lands through the efforts of a class-conscious proletariat, Bakunin wanted the oppressed of all kinds, including the peasants, to revolt. Toward this end, he favored secret societies and terrorism.

Marx and Bakunin disagreed on one crucial issue of strategy. Marx wanted to organize the workers into mass political parties; Bakunin, on the other hand, held that revolutions should be fought by secret societies of fanatic insurrectionists. Bakunin feared that after the Marxists overthrew the capitalist regime and seized power, they would become the new masters and exploiters, using the state to enhance their own power. They would, said Bakunin, become a "privileged minority . . . of *ex-workers*, who, once they become rulers or representatives of the people, cease to be workers and begin to look down upon the toiling people. From that time on they represent not the people but themselves and their claims to govern the people."[6] Therefore, said Bakunin, once the workers capture the state, they should destroy it forever. Bakunin's astute prediction that a socialist revolution would lead to an intensification of state power rather than its disappearance has been borne out in the twentieth century.

Anarchists engaged in numerous acts of political terrorism, including the assassination or attempted assassination of heads of state and key ministers, but they never waged a successful revolution. They failed to reverse the trend toward the concentration of power in industry and government that would become characteristic of the twentieth century. But the motives that impelled them to challenge the values and institutions of modern society and to engage in acts of terror express an emotional need that has not disappeared with the waning of anarchism.

THE LEGACY OF THE INDUSTRIAL REVOLUTION

The changes in agriculture, business, labor, technology, and power that took place with industrialization were revolutionary. Some changes occurred over centuries, others over decades. But the end of the spread of industrialization is not in sight, nor likely to be in the foreseeable future.

In the long run, the Industrial Revolution was a great force for the democratization of human life. In the industrial world, social power is not limited to land owners, as it was in previous centuries. Even laborers have gained political and social rights, acquired education, and in most industrialized countries become consumers of goods previously reserved solely for the very wealthy. In the last half of the nineteenth century, workingmen gained the right to vote—in France as the result of the Revolution of 1848, in England through the Reform Bills of 1867 and 1884 (see pages 568–569), and in Prussia upon unification of Germany. But the gain of suffrage rights did not bring equality or even genuine political power to the masses. Though workers became a force to be reckoned with in every industrial state as they followed democratic or socialist parties and joined trade unions, sometimes they were also managed and manipulated by political leaders who had little concern for their conditions and interests.

Industrialization also contributed greatly to the secularization of society, that is, the movement away from belonging to a community of families united by religious belief and customary ceremony. The roles of the priest, the village, and the family in an individual's life changed drastically. A spiritual and communal vacuum emerged that for some would be filled by substitutes—the nation, the government, the political party, the professional or occupational association, or the fraternal, ethnic, or school club.

Due to industrialization, great numbers of men and women moved from rural to urban settings, or from one continent to another, which drastically altered their lives. Industrialization has changed relations between nations, between classes, between sexes, and between parents and children. Industrialization gave Western nations the power to dominate the globe at the beginning of the twentieth century. Many peoples became the subjects of Western lands, while others were drawn into the world market economy dominated by Western states. The rise of industry made nations more interdependent through trade, but it also encouraged conflict between states by adding economic competition to existing national antagonisms.

Industrialization made goods cheaper and more plentiful, raising the real standard of living and making it possible for people to have goods and services that had previously been reserved for the very few. Industrialization also made great numbers of people the victims of poor living and working conditions, subject to low wages, and periodically threatened with unemployment. Businessmen used their economic importance to gain a voice in political decisions and then persuaded governments to follow policies beneficial to business. This use of political power for economic purposes was imitated by the workers, who demanded the rights to organize unions, strike, and work, and sometimes even called for the end of capitalism and the advent of socialism.

Industrialization has freed humanity of many onerous tasks, raised the average standard of living, and offered the promise of an end to want. At the same time, technology has created tasks that seem trivial and meaningless to workers who derive no sense of pride from their work and do not know their part in the whole work process—or if they do know it, no longer care. The alienation of workers may be heightened if they feel powerless when confronted by faceless bureaucracies with reams of paper, red tape, and arbitrary rules.

A higher standard of living has been purchased at the cost of greater dependence on forces over which workers, their industry, and sometimes even their country have no power. The world money market, inflation, the control of energy by a few nations, and the multinational corporations—all elude individuals' and nations' attempts at control. And the technology that holds promises of new and better ways to do, to learn, and to make things contains, at the same time, horrifying possibilities of controlling human thoughts and behavior, even of world annihilation.

Notes

1. Alexis de Tocqueville, *Journeys to England and Ireland*, ed. J. P. Mayer (New Haven, Conn.: Yale, 1958), pp. 107–108.
2. Friedrich Engels, *The Origin of the Family, Private Property and the State*, in Emile Burns, *A Handbook of Marxism* (New York: Random House, 1935), p. 330.
3. Karl Marx, *Capital* (Chicago: Charles H. Kerr, 1912), 1:268.
4. Karl Marx, *The Communist Manifesto*, trans. by Samuel Moore (Chicago: Henry Regnery, 1954), pp. 81–82.
5. Quoted in James Joll, *The Anarchists* (New York: Grosset & Dunlap, 1964), pp. 78–79.
6. Excerpted in G. P. Maximoff, ed., *The Political Philosophy of Bakunin* (Glencoe, Ill.: The Free Press, 1953), p. 287.

Suggested Reading

The Cambridge Economic History of Europe, vol. 6 (1965). Includes several fine essays on industrialization by specialists in central and eastern Europe.

Cameron, Rondo, *France and the Economic Development of Europe, 1800–1914* (1975). Puts emphasis on France's role as investor in the development of the rest of Europe.

Clapham, J. H., *Economic Development in France and Germany, 1815–1914,* 4th ed. (1935). A classic work.

Deane, Phyllis, *The First Industrial Revolution, 1750–1850* (1965). An excellent introduction.

Fried, Albert, ed., *Socialist Thought* (1964). Selections from writings on socialist theorists.

Halévy, Elie, *The Growth of Philosophic Radicalism* (1928). The best work on utilitarianism, but difficult reading.

———, *A History of the English People in the Nineteenth Century,* vols. 1–3, rev. ed. (1949). A must for anyone who wants to know England's experience from 1815 to the 1840s.

Hamerow, Theodore, *Restoration, Revolution, Reaction: Economics and Politics in Germany, 1815–1871* (1958). Traces the economic and social developments that contributed to the failure to establish a liberal Germany.

Heilbroner, R., *The Worldly Philosophers,* rev. ed. (1972). A useful introduction to nineteenth-century economic thought.

Joll, James, *The Anarchists* (1964). A fine treatment of anarchists, their lives, and thought.

Landes, David, *The Unbound Prometheus: Technological Change and Industrial Development in Western Europe from 1750 to the Present* (1969). A classic treatment of a complex subject, beautifully and intelligently written.

McLellan, David, *Karl Marx: His Life and Thought.* A highly regarded biography (1977).

Ruggiero, G. de., *The History of European Liberalism* (1927). Survey of a subject that is usually treated by studies of individuals or politics. A good starting point.

Thompson, Edward P., *Making of the English Working Class* (1966). A very readable, dramatic, enormously influential and controversial book.

Webb, R. K., *Modern England from the Eighteenth Century* (1967 and 1980). A text that is balanced, well-written, well-informed, and up-to-date on historical controversies.

Review Questions

1. Why did England experience industrialization before the rest of Europe? What noneconomic political and social factors influenced industrialization in England?

2. What importance did the growth of population have in the process of industrialization?

3. What were the basic theories of economists Smith, Malthus, and Ricardo?

4. What factors promoted the growth of cities between 1800 and 1860? How did changes in European agriculture in the early nineteenth century reflect the impact of capitalism and of industrialization?

5. What groups were designated *middle class* in nineteenth-century Europe? What groups were designated *working class*, or lower orders, in nineteenth-century Europe?

6. How was Mill's liberalism a combination of radical measures and liberal ones?

7. Why are Saint-Simon, Fourier, and Owen regarded as early socialists? Discuss their ideas.

8. Summarize Marx's philosophy of history.

9. Why did Marx think that capitalism was doomed? How would its destruction happen?

10. Why is Marx regarded as a leading architect of the modern age? What criticisms have been levelled against Marxist theory?

11. In what ways did Bakunin and Marx differ?

CHAPTER 25

Industrial Europe:
The Challenge of
Modernization

THE PROCESS of industrialization overtook particular European nations at different times during the nineteenth century. States or areas were affected in varying ways, depending on their political and social institutions, as well as on the pace and extent of industrialization. Every nation had to adjust its traditional institutions that preceded industrialization and the French Revolution to the requirements of factories and industrial cities. The old structures of rural agrarian privileged society endured, though perhaps in altered forms, and shaped the political and social institutions of each country during its industrialization. The clash between traditional classes and institutions and the massive economic and political transformations brought on by the Industrial Revolution created a wide variety of problems throughout Europe. Each nation was reshaped by this interaction between traditional and modern.

GREAT BRITAIN, 1815–1914

In the nineteenth century, Great Britain was the model progressive nation, enjoying the benefits of a unified liberal government, social stability, and the prosperity of the Industrial Revolution. The British ability to absorb protest without succumbing to revolution and Parliament's ability to continue to govern constitutionally—came to be regarded by most Europeans as a miracle. Britain had waged war against French power and revolutionary ideas for a generation; at the same time, the British expanded their empire, developed their industry and prosperity, and maintained their Parliament, constitutional monarchy, and national church. Their success made even the British smug about their accomplishments.

After the middle of the nineteenth century, a general rise in prosperity benefited the British working class at the same time that it enriched the middle and upper classes. This development seemed to prove that the classical economists had been right: that the surest remedy for the birth pangs of industrialization was more industrialization. Though injustices and inequities existed, many believed that industrialization, rather than giving grounds for revolution, provided an economic base for governmental stability and for the reduction of class conflict. The political experience of the first half of the century laid the foundation for British parliamentary practices, which came to be the model of liberal, progressive, and stable politics. Britain was the symbol for all those who argued for reform and not revolution. Others argued that Britain's spirit of compromise maintained a two-class society.

The Rise of Reform

In the early decades of the nineteenth century, Britain was far from democratic. The vast majority of people could not vote. Many towns continued to be governed by corrupt groups. New towns that had developed from industrialization were not allowed to elect representatives to Parliament. Often the working classes had no voice in their government except the protest of riot and rampage. The landed aristocrats controlled both the House of Lords and the House of Commons—the House of Lords because they constituted its membership and the House of Commons because they patronized or sponsored men favorable to their interests. Since younger sons of aristocrats did not inherit titles, they were obliged to make careers in business, the military, the church, law, and even the House of Commons. Thus, the social separation of noble and commoner was not as complete in Britain as on the Continent. There was much mingling between the upper and middle classes, and the wealthiest merchants tended to buy lands, titles, and husbands for their daughters—all of which drew them closer to the aristocracy.

The two greatest political parties in Britain, the Whigs and the Tories, were separated not by class, but by ideas and values. Parliament, the courts, local government, the church, the monarch—all were a part of a social and political system dominated by aristocratic interests and values. The Whigs saw themselves as champions of civil, political, and religious liberties, as defenders of Parliament and the nation against tyranny of king and state. The Tories, on the other hand, defended royal authority, the established church, the empire, and imperial glory; they believed that some are born to rule and most to follow. Neither party was democratic, and at the end of the eighteenth century and the beginning of the nineteenth, a group of radical reformers criticized both parties as part of a corrupt oligarchy that deprived the people of ancient liberties and a voice in government.

In 1815, at the end of the Napoleonic Wars, when returning veterans found no work, Britain faced depression in the industrial areas and unrest in the rural districts. Both the Whigs and the Tories, afraid that the revolutionary ideas of the Jacobins had infected the English masses, urged strict measures repressing any agitation or violence. Crimes against property, such as the Luddites' burning of machinery, were severely punished. Workers were forbidden to organize.

In 1819, at St. Peter's Fields near Manchester, a meeting of radical reformers who wanted changes in the suffrage law ended when the troops and militia fired on workers who had gathered there. Nicknamed the "Peterloo Massacre" in derisive comparison to the great victory of Waterloo, the incident seemed to encourage the government to increase repression. Many radicals were imprisoned. Large meetings were forbidden, seditious libel was severely punished, and many political agitators were hastily tried without due process of law. Newspapers and pamphlets were taxed and homes searched. These measures of repression violated the English birthright—to speak and meet freely, to due process of law, and to privacy in one's own home. This repression differed little from that used in the autocratic states of Europe to stamp out the ideas of the French Revolution.

THE PETERLOO MASSACRE, MANCHESTER, AUGUST 16, 1819 British soldiers charged into a crowd of people gathered to hear a speech on parliamentary reform and repeal of the corn laws. The troops intended only to arrest the speaker, but several people were killed and hundreds injured. Soon after, a repressive code, the Six Acts, was passed to curtail public meetings. (Public Records Office, London)

Some limited measures of reform accompanied the repression, however, and these helped to take the edge off the discontent. Two traditions strengthened the reformers. One was the tradition carried on by liberal aristocrats committed to principles of political, religious, and civil liberties. Whigs often championed reform of the Parliament and of the established church. The other tradition was one of pragmatic politics, of dealing with specific problems in nonideological terms. Reforms in the criminal code and the prisons and the introduction of a police force gained the support of Whigs, radicals, and Tories alike. Even Tory politicians could initiate reforms. Thus, a liberal Tory statesman and prime minister, Robert Peel (1788–1850), might resolve a problem in the economy by removing a tax without discussing the general principles of free trade and mercantilism. Whigs and liberals could defend this action in terms of freedom, while conservatives and Tories could accept it because the particular measure would solve a problem. Both parties had beliefs, values, and institutions that they protected and encouraged, but there were many areas in which they could compromise. In such an atmosphere, skilled parliamentary politicians enacted many reforms, and their success contributed to a spirit of compromise.

Catholic emancipation (1829), or the removal of restrictions on Catholics, is a good example of a case that joined these two traditions. The liberal Whigs championed this legislation because it would end legal discrimination on the grounds of religious belief. The conservative Tories, defenders of the established Church of England, led by the Duke of Wellington (hero of Waterloo), and Robert Peel advocated Catholic emancipation as necessary to preserve order in Ireland, where the majority of the population was Catholic. Wellington and Peel were both deeply committed to the Anglican church, but in the face of great distress and unrest in Ireland, they accepted the reform as a necessary one. Both Roman Catholics and Nonconformist Protestants (emancipated by the repeal of the Test Acts) were now allowed to participate as equals to Anglicans in the nations' political life, voting and sitting in Parliament, though they still suffered from social discrimination.

Increasingly, reform centered on extending suffrage and redrawing boundaries of voting districts to enfranchise new industrial towns and the newly wealthy middle classes. Suffrage reform became an issue that joined the middle classes, who wanted representation, with the working classes, who thought the right to vote would enable them to gain measures that would lessen their distress. The Reform Bill of 1832 addressed this issue.

The very process of passing the Reform Bill of 1832 created a precedent for party politics and cabinet government for the remainder of the century. The House of Commons, dominated by the Whigs since 1830, passed the Reform Bill, to extend the suffrage by some 200,000 votes, almost double the number who were then entitled to vote. The House of Lords, however, refused to pass the bill. There were riots in many cities and mass meetings, which included both the workers and the middle class, all over the country. King William IV (1830–1837) became convinced, along with many Whig and even some Tory politicians, that the situation was potentially revolutionary. He threatened to increase the number of supporters of the bill in the House of Lords by creating new peers. This threat brought reluctant peers into line and the bill was passed. Thus, the House of Commons became more representative—many cities were represented that had not been—and the House of Lords somewhat more amenable to reforms. Suffrage did not extend to workers, however, since it limited voting rights to persons with fairly high property qualifications.

Workers found they remained outside the arena of politics. Those who wanted the suffrage extended further joined the Chartist movement. From the 1830s into the 1840s, Chartists agitated for several democratic demands, including universal manhood suffrage, a secret ballot, abolition of property qualifications for members of Parliament, salaries for members of Parliament, and annual meetings of Parliament. These demands remained the democratic reform program for the nineteenth century, long after the Chartists had declined in strength. The severe economic hardships of the "hungry forties" strengthened the Chartists, but leaders of the movement split into two groups, one favoring radical and revolutionary action and the other continuing to advocate peaceful tactics. Supporters spent their efforts on the Anti-Corn Law League, agitating to remove tariffs on grain in order to lower food prices and to strike a blow at the great landowners who dominated British political life. The League succeeded in repealing the Corn Laws in 1846, which established free trade for Britain. Still others devoted their efforts to trade unions, cooperatives, and mutual-aid societies. In 1848, when much of Europe burst into national and social revolution, Chartism died. A mass demonstration called by the Irish Chartist leader, Feargus O'Connor, presented a petition to Parliament with millions of signatures favoring their reform program, but the government ignored this Great Charter.

In a few years, however, labor discontent was channeled in new directions. An upturn in the economy had been accompanied by a shift by the workers away from politics to trade unionism as the way to improve their lives. Inside Parliament, the liberal reform movement accomplished a number of measures, some for principled reasons and others for pragmatic, which marked the 1830s and 1840s as the era of reform. In 1833, slavery was abolished within the British Empire and the owners of slaves were compensated for the loss of their property, so that humanitarians and pragmatists alike could champion the reform. Between 1815 and 1847, Parliament passed several measures regulating (or prohibiting) the employment of women and children in mills and mines, limiting the hours, and regulating the labor conditions. Tories, now called *Conservatives*, could support these measures because they believed that the state should protect the unfortunate. They opposed the laissez-faire view of the state held by *Liberals*, as the Whigs now called themselves. The Municipal Corporations Act (1835) granted towns and cities greater authority over their affairs, a first step toward ending corruption and beginning democratization of town government. The measure began to solve some problems of urbanization and industrialization; housing and public health measures followed.

Britain at Mid-Century

At mid-century, then, Great Britain symbolized the liberal, stable state with political practices, ideas, and values that made compromise and reform possible. A two-party system of Liberals and Conservatives, supported by a limited electorate, vied for leadership of the government. After the Crimean War (1854–56), two men emerged as the political actors of the epoch: William E. Gladstone (1809–1898), a pious, solid man and an orator who could inspire people over issues of taxes and revenues; and Benjamin Disraeli (1804–1881), a flamboyant personality, a novelist and dreamer, who talked of the greatness of empire. The competition between them and their parties in the House of Commons actually stimulated reform.

Such was the case in the passage of the Reform Bill of 1867. First, Gladstone led the Liberals with a measure to extend suffrage, which failed, forcing his resignation, according to the custom of cabinet responsibility. Then Disraeli introduced a bill that would give the vote to the great majority of city workers, far more than Gladstone had envisioned; this was passed. His Reform Bill doubled the electorate and suddenly the threat of democracy, which Liberals and Conservatives alike had feared, became a reality. Disraeli claimed that he was not afraid of the mass electorate and that Conservatives had a social program that would appeal to the masses. However, a number of his followers, and many Liberals as well, claimed that in his eagerness to win in the game of passing bills in the House of Commons, he had been "shooting Niagara" (a reference to the daredevil practice, then a fad, of going over Niagara Falls in a barrel).

The leaders decided it was imperative to educate the masses since they had political power. The religious controversies that had previously blocked educational reform became calm in the face of the prospect of uneducated workers voting. A bill was passed (the Education Act of 1870) to provide elementary education for all. Although real political power remained in the hands of the gentry, the middle classes, and the traditional aristocracy, the Second Reform Bill brought democracy closer. By 1884, Gladstone had enfranchised virtually all English*men*.

The rivalry between Gladstone and Disraeli was a political one carried on within Parliament in a nation of liberal customs and economic stability. The prosperity of the midcentury had enveloped all classes to some degree. To the Britons who were complacent, it seemed that all shared an ethic of individualism and competition, and though class divisions and social barriers existed, there was not the bitterness and hatred between the classes that existed on the Continent. Indeed, it was often said that Britain was a deferential society in which the lower orders respected their betters and the upper classes took responsibility for the care of their workers. If that situation had ever been true, it ended in 1873 when a Great Depression brought a halt to everonward-and-upward progress. Almost simultaneously the British realized that their rivals in industry, Germany and the United States, were very keen competitors. And labor armed with the vote became more and more strident in its demands for political and economic reform at the very moment that British confidence seemed to be shaken by economic depression, industrial rivalry, and the unresolvable Irish problem.

The Irish Problem

The suffering of the Irish during the great famine of 1846–47 in which as many as a million Irish died was climaxed by the hopeless uprising of 1848. The English response was callous repression; they combined the economic principles of laissez faire and Malthusianism with prejudice to justify their refusal to aid the Irish. Many of the Irish emigrated to America or English-speaking colonies to survive. Many Irish hated the union of their nation with England and Scotland, hated it as much as Czechs or Italians hated their connections with the Austrians. Out of this national hatred there arose a revolutionary force that threatened to disrupt British stability and parliamentary politics. The *Fenians*, a Republican brotherhood, was formed. This group, which aimed at Irish independence, committed acts of terrorism throughout the 1860s, financed by Irish-Americans and staffed by the unhappy youth of Ireland.

Gladstone staked his reputation and his party on the Irish question. He launched a series of reforms in the hope of reconciling the Irish to Britain and to parliamentary politics. He "disestablished" the Irish church, which meant there was no longer an official Protestant church supported by Catholic taxpayers. As a result, Irish Protestants no longer held privileges in the predominantly Catholic country. Gladstone also passed a land act that compensated poor tenant farmers, if they were evicted, for any improvements they had made on the land. This measure was calculated to prevent the steady decrease in Ireland's productivity (renters had no incentive to improve land or farm buildings if they could be evicted without compensation), as well as to bring justice to tenant croppers.

But Gladstone's efforts were too little and too late. In the 1880s the issue was Home Rule for Ireland. Under the leadership of the Protestant (but anti-English) Charles Stewart Parnell, the Irish formed a separate bloc in Parliament committed to Home Rule, with which both parties had to reckon. The Irish used every parliamentary tactic, and some extraparliamentary ones, to secure a separate legislature and executive for Ireland. Their bloc of votes also undermined the two-party system because the Liberals needed their support for a majority. Gladstone urged Home Rule, but his party refused to go along with the "grand old man," splitting the Liberal party.

At the end of his career, Gladstone knew he had failed at his most important task, the reconciliation of the Irish. And he knew that two-party politics, which he and Disraeli had practiced to perfection, was in danger because there were militant groups and important issues outside the political arena.

Social Unrest in the Later Nineteenth Century

At the turn of the twentieth century the young Liberals, Gladstone's heirs, welded together a majority from diverse groups—religious dissenters, humanitarians, and labor. They committed their party to a program of social and economic reform aimed at gaining labor support.

British labor had never been attracted to the doctrines of socialism, particularly not to Marxism, which exercised a powerful hold on the German working class. An Independent Labour Party had been founded in 1893, which offered a socialist program, but its supporters were as likely as not to be Christians. British labor used the political liberties and rights of their country more than the French did, and they possessed much greater freedom and more political power than the Germans.

Nonetheless, the end of the century was difficult for labor because economic and social conditions threatened to undermine British political harmony, real or mythical. Whatever wage gains the trade unions made were wiped out by inflation; the competition of foreign labor and industry seemed to threaten the future, and memories of the Great Depression hung on from the past. The Taff Vale decision (1901), which awarded damages to an employer picketed by a union, forced labor to more sustained and effective political action. If they did not pressure for legislation to legalize picketing, they would lose the economic gains of half a century. The Labour Representation Committee, made up of various socialists and trade union organizations, became the nucleus of a Labour Party. In the elections of 1906, in which the Liberals were returned overwhelmingly to the House of Commons, the new Labour party had gained twenty-nine members.

Between 1906 and 1911 the Liberals introduced a series of important social measures, spurred on by David Lloyd George (1863–1945) and Winston Churchill (then a Liberal) and aided by the Labour party. A program of old-age pensions, labor exchanges for the unemployed, unemployment and health insurance (a program deeply influenced by Bismarckian social legislation), and minimum wages for certain industries was enacted. The Taff Vale decision was overridden. But in the process of legislating these reforms, a constitutional crisis developed between the Liberals, with Labour support, and the Conservatives, who dominated the House of Lords.

When Lloyd George introduced the budget of 1909, the Lords refused to accept it, though the House of Commons was traditionally responsible for financial measures. The Liberals went to the voters determined to an all-out struggle with the Lords, many of whom earned the nickname "diehard" for their intransigence in defending their privileges. Many Lords saw their struggle as the defense of Britain and its Empire against the "socialist" campaign of the Liberals, a party of minorities. The procedure by which the Reform Bill of 1832 had been passed—that is, the king's threats to create peers to pass the bill—was again threatened and seemed likely to shake the parliamentary system—certainly to destroy the House of Lords. The campaign was a bitter one in which class antagonisms were expressed freely, but the bill was passed. After the Parliament Act of 1911, the Lords could only delay the passage of a bill that the Commons wanted, not prevent it.

Bitter as the struggle over social legislation and the taxation of land and income was, other issues also threatened parliamentary government and British liberal institutions during the last decade before the First World War. There was a wave of labor unrest, and the tactics of the new unions were increasingly militant. Strikes and violence swept England. The miners, the dock workers, and the railway workers made an alliance, urging a general strike for minimum wages. The tactics of the French syndicalists (militant trade unionists organized by industry, rather than by craft, who advocated the general strike as the method for obtaining substantial political and economic gains) appealed to great numbers of British laborers. The traditional trade-union movement and the new unions of unskilled industrial labor pushed each other to greater militancy. The spirit of compromise, which many Britons believed that their system exemplified, seemed to be dying.

An equally explosive issue was female suffrage, and the tactics and repressions steadily escalated in violence. Women were able to vote for school boards and for local government officials; in both institutions they had been very active—in fact, women were the backbone of school boards and charity organizations. Their importance in thousands of voluntary activities was a powerful argument against those who said that women did not have the reasoning capacity nor the political experience to vote intelligently for members of the House of Commons. But women were denied this suffrage, despite their petitions and influence with important members of the parliament. Therefore, the militants, led by a family of feminists, Emmeline Pankhurst and her daughters, Sylvia and Christabel, changed their tactics to demonstrations, invasions of the House of Parliament, destruction of property, and hunger strikes. One militant threw herself to her death under King Edward VII's horse at the Derby as a gesture of protest.

When feminists were arrested for a violation of the laws, they would stage hunger strikes—a tactic Gandhi would later use against the British in his struggle for India's independence. It was an ugly situation, with police force-feeding the demonstrators. Or the police would release imprisoned feminists, and, when they had recovered from starvation, reimprison them. A common argument at the time was that the use of such tactics proved women could not participate rationally and maturely in governing the country. Ridiculed, humiliated, and punished, the feminists refused to accept the passive role that a male-dominated society had assigned them. Their major part on the home front in the First World War changed the minds of the ruling elites and finally brought women the right to vote.

In addition to labor unrest and the struggle for female suffrage, the long and embittered struggle of the Irish for Home Rule added a third element to the explosive situation. The House of Lords used every tactic against Home Rule. But they could not prevent its passage because after the parliamentary crisis of 1911, they could only delay measures, not defeat them. Outside the Parliament, militant groups took the law into their own hands: Ulstermen (as northern Protestant Irish were called) and Catholics fought one another in the streets of Dublin and Belfast. Gangs smuggled guns, soldiers fired on demonstrators, violence bred violence, civil war was threatened. Tory leaders threatened mutiny, defying Parliament, and arming Ulster gangs, the government threatened to use force to carry out the law. At the very time of the assassination of the archduke of Austria-Hungary in 1914 and the declaration of war by Great Britain, Ireland was uppermost in everyone's minds and on the front page of all the newspapers. With the onset of war, women and labor suspended their militant campaigns, pledging their loyalty to king and country "for the duration."

Many Irish fought for Britain in World War I, but the deferred promise of Home Rule angered many others, who continued their struggle for independence. In 1916 the Irish insurrection, the Easter Rebellion led by Sir Roger Casement (see Chapter 26), was suppressed, and its leaders were executed. After the war, with ill will on all sides, Ireland was divided. The south gained independence and a republican government, and the six counties of the north remained in the United Kingdom.

FRANCE, 1848–1914

The Era of Napoleon III

In December 1848, less than a year after the revolution that had expelled Louis Philippe from the throne, Louis Napoleon Bonaparte (1808–1873), nephew of Napoleon I, was elect-

MAP 25.1 EUROPEAN CITIES OF 100,000 OR MORE, 1800 (left) AND 1900

ed president of the Second French Republic by an overwhelming majority. Within three years, in a December coup d'état, he had made himself dictator by force, though a plebiscite of the French people ratified his destruction of the Republic. Napoleon III's coup called an abrupt halt to the politics and the reforms of the revolutionary Republic. His declaration of the Second Empire signaled a shift to the right and the stabilization of France. The liberal and republican forces of France, including some of the finest and most talented minds such as Alexis de Tocqueville and Victor Hugo, were appalled and outraged. But after some relatively minor uprisings among workers and radicals, the remainder to the French seemed to accept and perhaps to be proud of the "little Napoleon."

The governments of Prussia, Austria, Russia, and Britain did not immediately see Napoleon as a force for stability. Between 1852 and 1870 the new emperor, descendant of a great military tradition, promised peace, but waged two successful wars: one humiliated Austria

for the unification of Italy, and one devastated Russia in the Crimea. Both humiliations seemed to be triumphs of the forces of progress over the forces of reaction. In the process, Bonaparte made friends with the English, whose enmity had plagued France for a century or more. He also won the Italians and the pope to the support of France, though he could not keep both on its side simultaneously. His adventurism in foreign affairs also involved French troops in a dangerous fiasco of imperial expansion in Mexico. Napoleon III tried unsuccessfully to place the Hapsburg archduke, Maximilian, on the Mexican throne, but managed to extricate French troops without too much cost to France (see Chapter 26). Similarly, he fostered French imperialism in the opening of China (with Britain) and in claims to portions of Africa; these moves, however, did not seem likely to upset the peace of Europe.

At home, France benefited from the inflation and economic growth that followed the discovery of gold in California and Alaska.

CLAUDE MONET (1840–1926): GARE ST. LAZARE, PARIS,
c. 1877 The fascination with railroads, visible in the
work of painters as diverse as realists, naturalists,
impressionists, and post-impressionists, is apparent
in Monet's treatment. The railroad boom in the
Second Empire was fostered by Napoleon III. (Fogg
Art Museum, Cambridge, Mass.; Bequest—
Collection of Maurice Wertheim)

The mid-century was a period of prosperity, confidence, and political apathy. Certainly for the period 1851 to 1860, politics under the authoritarian ruler was impossible; Napoleon kept strict control of the legislature, rarely convening it and always manipulating it. He censored the press and harassed his critics. His support came from property owners, including the mass of peasants, and from the Catholic church and businesses. They approved of the stability at home and abroad and of the program of economic development stimulated by railroad construction and the rebuilding of Paris. Of course, there was plenty of room for corruption by real-estate speculators and building firms, but many shared in the work (and in the corruption) and even more regarded the changes in the City of Light to be the requirements of progress and civilization. It was a period of enormous creativity in France—in the arts, the French had no equals, and in the sciences, they were major contributors.

In the first years of the Second Empire, Napoleon's advisors and administrators were his close personal friends; mostly the legitimate and illegitimate members of his large family, they seemed to have no particular political position other than loyalty to him. Napoleon III claimed that he was a socialist rather than a Bonapartist (an advocate of rule by a strong man). He did have some ideas of economic progress, which he insisted must be tempered by order. He expressed a sympathy for some of the Saint-Simonian ideas espoused by his supporters—grand schemes of canal and railroad building and of cheap credit from state-sponsored banks. He also talked of the plight of the workers. Few socialists were willing to claim this "Saint-Simonian on horseback," however. The first ten years of his rule were characterized by careful managing of elections and a search for people who were willing to accept the new order. It was personal and authoritarian rule by a strong man.

The Italian War of 1859 brought a turning point in Napoleon's successes. His luck seemed to have turned: He was faced with fiascos abroad and critics in government at home. Even the workers he had subsidized to go to a London exhibition returned filled with ideas of unionization; they promptly joined in the creation of the First International Workingmen's Association. French businessmen were sorry that they had allowed free trade to be established with Great Britain for the competition was still fierce, despite France's economic progress. The scandals involved in many of Napoleon's building activities became known when greater freedom of the press and speech in parliament was allowed in the 1860s. In 1864, strikes were legalized; in 1868, workers were given the right to unionize—but these reforms did not win workers' loyalty to the emperor. When many members of the Opposition were elected in

1869, Napoleon accepted a new constitution that made his role in government much like that of Queen Victoria—a symbol of the nation over a constitutional parliamentary monarchy, with liberal safeguards for individual liberties.

Was Napoleon III, after all, a sincere liberal who wanted first to establish his power and then give France reforms? Or was he the nephew of the great Napoleon, who was more concerned with his personal power and glory and who only succumbed to liberalism because he feared revolution? The question of Napoleon's goals still perplexes historians. But, in fact, the liberal government was not instituted because Napoleon's foreign policy drew France into war with Prussia in 1870.

Aftermath of the Franco-Prussian War

Defeat in the Franco-Prussian War brought down the empire of Napoleon III. In bitter frustration at the defeat by the invading Prussian armies, the people of Paris rose against the provisional government—the politicians had replaced Napoleon, who made the armistice and wanted to make peace. The uprising, known as the Paris Commune (1871), began as a patriotic refusal to accept the army's defeat, but became a rejection of the authority of the provisional government as well as that of the corrupt Second Empire. Ultimately, the actions of the Communards (as those who resisted the Prussians and the provisional government were called) were a challenge to the property owners. The resistance to the Prussian siege, which joined together French people of all classes, flared into flaming hostility toward landlords and creditors when the provisional government lifted the moratorium on rent and debts that had been declared during the war.

The Parisians held elections, and the revolutionary forces that had been gathering for a generation came to the fore. They included the followers of Proudhon, who were very influential among artisans and small entrepreneurs. The republican and socialist veterans of the Revolution of 1848 reappeared. There were also the disciples of Auguste Blanqui, an old insurrectionist who had spent much time in French prisons with brief interludes of glorious release when each new revolutionary wave proclaimed him a hero of the people. For two months in the spring of 1871 the revolutionaries ruled Paris, always guided by the heroic precedents of the Jacobins of 1793 and the radicals of June 1848. Then, Adolphe Thiers, the man who had accepted peace at the hands of Bismarck to lift the siege of France, ordered a siege of Paris. The French fought against the French. The fighting was bitter and desperate, with many acts of terrorism and violence. Both sides in this civil war set fires that destroyed large parts of the city. When apprehended, 20,000 Communards were executed without trial; those who were tried were given harsh sentences of death, transportation, and life imprisonment.

The Commune became legendary, and not just to the French. Across Europe, governing classes were terrified by what they imagined the passionate hatreds of the revolutionary masses to be. Many well-intentioned social reformers and sympathetic intellectuals made an about-face and became quite conservative in their attitudes. Few examined the facts of the case, which would have indicated that most Communards were ardent French patriots, not international revolutionaries; that their desperate economic plight had driven them to action, not some ideological commitment to the abolition of private property.

As for the international revolutionaries, both socialist and anarchist, they were encouraged by the radicalization that they thought they saw in the desperate actions of the Communards. They also took a hard look at the ruling classes and became convinced that, just as Thiers had used French troops against French people, the political leaders of other states would take similar actions to prevent the peaceful evolution of society toward socialism. The masses, said revolutionaries like Marx, must perfect their organizations for insurrections and violent seizure of power. Just as Thiers's methods had been ruthless, the workers must use every revolutionary method. Other radicals, appalled by the blood bath, argued for the ballot box and the organization of political parties; in their view, the power of the modern state was too great for insurrection to lead to revolution as it had in 1789, 1830, and 1848.

The Paris Commune and its brutal suppression did not create social and political differences among Frenchmen; it did dramatize existing differences and intensify the hatreds between the groups. The Empire defeated and the Commune suppressed, law and order were reestablished under the burden of a harsh peace treaty, which inflicted an indemnity and the loss of Alsace and part of Lorraine to Germany. How was France to rebuild and to regain its place in Europe? The first task was to move from the provisional government of national defense, headed by Adolphe Thiers, a monarchist, to a permanent government.

Emergence of the Third Republic

No individual of that time would have believed it possible that the government emerging from the next few years of political crises would be a republic, and the longest-lasting republic in the history of France (1870–1940). The monarchists were the most numerous and most powerful of the political groups in France. They seemed to offer stability and order without the dangers of radical or even liberal republicanism. But there were two groups of monarchists who would not compromise: the Legitimists, who supported the count of Chambord, the grandson of Charles X, who had fled France in the Revolution of 1830, and the Orléanists, who supported the grandson of the man who had replaced him, Louis Philippe. When the Orléanists finally agreed to compromise, the count of Chambord refused to accept the flag of red, white, and blue, the tricolor, which symbolized the liberties won in the French Revolution.

The disunity among the forces of the right—mainly monarchists in the first decade after the Franco-Prussian War—enabled France to become a republic by default. Not until 1879, however, did the French government become wholly republican in the legislative and executive branches of government. Until then, there were monarchist aspects to the constitution, but no king to carry them out.

The constitutional laws finally provided for a government of a powerful legislature and a prime minister who had to have the support of a majority of the Chamber of Deputies. There was some self-conscious imitation of the British system in this organization. The presidency became a figurehead in the hope that no new Napoleon would rise to overthrow the regime, but the result was an office that no talented politician wanted. Unlike the British two-party system, France had many political parties, which meant that the differences between the French were exaggerated, not modified, and were a force for instability. No one party had sufficient strength within parliament to provide strong leadership. Prime ministers resigned in rapid succession; cabinets rose and fell frequently, giving the impression of a state without direction. The skills of a politician who could keep fences mended in a local district were at a premium. The highly centralized bureaucracy went hand in hand with a very decentralized and local politics. Political life seemed to be one of wheeling and dealing. The Republic survived, but not without major crises.

The first generation of the Third Republic had times when dissatisfaction seemed to unite elements of the right and the left. In the 1880s, scandals among the defenders of the Republic—one of which centered on the sale of medals and honors as well as influence by the son-in-law of the president—threatened to overthrow the Republic. The opposition to the regime began to center around a dashing general, Georges Boulanger (1837–1891),

whose popularity frightened many French with fresh memories of Napoleon III. But Boulanger was a republican; more important, at the crucial moment of seizing power, either his nerve failed him or his personal life undermined him. The whole story never became known. The man who might have toppled the Third Republic fled to Belgium, where he was said to have committed suicide on the grave of his former mistress. The crisis forced the radicals and the moderates together in defense of the Republic.

Almost immediately, further scandals developed in the financing and building of the Panama Canal. Several radical republican deputies were implicated in a giant swindle in which people were sold stocks that constantly diminished in value. The deputies had taken bribes to permit their names to be used in the sale of stocks and bonds and tried to cover this up. The French were disgusted with the low level of political morality in the Third Republic.

The crisis that tore France in two for over a decade came closely on the heels of the Panama Canal scandals and the Boulanger affair. In 1894, Captain Alfred Dreyfus, an Alsatian-Jewish artillery officer, was wrongly accused of treason, of having sold secrets to the Prussians; he was condemned to life imprisonment on Devil's Island. Anti-Semitic elements joined with the Republic's opponents in the army, the church, among the monarchists, indeed throughout French society to denounce and block every attempt to clear Dreyfus of the charges against him. In the beginning, Dreyfus was defended by very few people and opposed by many, who felt that the honor of France and of the army was at stake. Then individuals came to his defense, including the writers Anatole France and Émile Zola, and Georges Clemenceau (the would-be radical republican leader), along with university students and other intellectuals. After many humiliations, Dreyfus was finally cleared (1906). The result of the victory of the radical republicans, however, was a fierce campaign to root out those opposing the

EDOUARD MANET (1832–1883): PORTRAIT OF ÉMILE ZOLA
Many intellectuals and students defended an Alsatian Jew, Captain Dreyfus, falsely convicted of treason. France was a battleground of demonstrations and riots over the Dreyfus Affair. Among the Dreyfusards were novelists Émile Zola, Anatole France, Marcel Proust, and Charles Péguy; painter Paul Cezanne; and politicians Georges Clemenceau and Jean Jaurès. (Alinari/Editorial Photocolor Archives)

Republic. The church was attacked, religious orders were expelled and their property confiscated, and a vigorous campaign was waged to replace the influence of the parish priest with that of the district schoolmaster. Complete separation of church and state was ordered. France became a secular state, and taxes no longer supported the parishes and schools.

As for socialism and trade unionism, the peculiar state of the French economy and the experiences of the working class led to a different history from that of Britain or Germany. Despite progress in the middle of the nineteenth century, French economic development lagged. France had fewer and smaller industries than Britain and Germany; more French people lived in rural areas or in small communities; and, in general, industry, trade unionism, and socialist groups tended to be decentralized rather than national and to be made up of artisans rather than proletarians. For a generation after the bitter suppression of the Paris Commune, French labor was markedly antipolitical. For a decade, its leadership was broken and dispersed within France or in exile. Labor argued that there could be no cooperation with the Republic or with any bourgeois government.

In the 1880s, however, both trade unionism and political parties with a socialist program began making headway and pressing for social reform by using the democratic parliamentary procedure of the Third Republic. But class bitterness was so deep that France was very slow to enact social measures, such as pensions, old-age insurance, conditions regulating the workplace and the wages and hours of workers, which Germany and Britain had enacted. Such measures, which might have ameliorated the lives of workers and other ordinary French people, were often regarded as sops to buy off their allegiance to socialism. As late as the First World War, any socialist who contemplated a seat in the cabinet was ostracized by his socialist and working-class following for collaboration with the bourgeois enemy. This deep feeling of alienation meant that political compromises were not often achieved.

GERMANY, 1870–1914

The German Empire that Bismarck created was in many ways exactly the empire that he had desired. Prussia dominated all the German states, the king of Prussia was emperor, and Bismarck was responsible only to the emperor. The act of unification, for all its hypocritical diplomacy, was received with enormous enthusiasm by most Germans. Bismarck, the Iron Chancellor, was the man of the hour—not just for conservatives, but for liberals as well.

The constitution that Bismarck had created for the Empire was hardly liberal. The Empire was *kleindeutsch* (little Germany), or Germany without the German-speaking and Catholic Hapsburg lands. The organizational structure was federal. Some powers were reserved for the member states, such as Bavaria, Baden, and Württemberg; other powers, particularly diplomacy and defense, were in the hands of the emperor and his appointee, Bismarck. There were no controls over Bismarck, except the ability of the Reichstag, the Lower House of Parliament, to refuse to pass the budget. There was no responsibility of the cabinet to the majority of representatives in the Reichstag, that is, the members of the cabinet did not have to maintain the support of the majority to keep their office. The German Empire did not have two-party government or guarantees of civil liberties. If the legislature disapproved of the chancellor, it could not remove him from office. The German kaiser, unlike the British monarch, had considerable control over lawmaking and foreign affairs and commanded the army and navy. Still, the Reichstag could discuss any issue, and its members were elected by universal male suffrage, which was unusual in the 1870s—only France had such an extensive electorate.

Impressed by Bismarck's leadership, German liberals did not struggle for basic political and civil liberties with enthusiasm. They tolerated evasions of principle and practice that their British liberal cousins would never have allowed. Germany never developed a truly parliamentary system, and certainly not a liberal society. The civil service was a separate corps with its own special spirit—high-minded and honest perhaps, but aloof and incapable of responding to either criticism or the demands of democracy. The military was not under the control of the parliament any more than the chancellor was. Furthermore, Bismarck's political practices strengthened illiberal elements, rather than liberal or democratic ones. Bismarck cared little for principle and regarded political parties as mere interest groups to be called on for support; he believed they were incapable of governing or making policy.

Bismarck versus Catholics and Socialists

In Bismarck's mind, two groups undermined the unity of his Reich: the Catholics and the socialists. Almost 40 percent of Germany's population was Catholic despite Austria's exclusion from the German Empire. Taking advantage of a split in the Catholic church over the question of papal infallibility, Bismarck initiated a systematic persecution of Catholics, the *Kulturkampf.* Embodied in the May laws of 1873, the Kulturkampf involved an attempt to subject the church to the state. The laws discriminated against the Jesuits and required state supervision of the church and the training of priests in state schools. Catholics were required to be married by the state. Churchmen who refused to accept these laws were imprisoned or exiled.

The effect of the Kulturkampf in the long run was exactly the opposite of the one Bismarck had intended, though not because the liberals defended the civil liberties of the Catholics. The Catholic Center party attracted more and more support, and persecution strengthened the German Catholics' faith. Prussian conservatives, Protestant in religion, resented Bismarck's policy for its anticlericalism, which could damage Lutherans as well as Catholics. With the succession of Leo XIII to the papacy in 1878, Bismarck quietly opened negotiations for peace with the church.

In the late 1870s, Bismarck turned against the socialists. Ferdinand Lassalle (1825–1864), a charismatic lawyer-reformer whose influence extended from workers and trade unionists to Bismarck himself, had formed a German Workers' Association. He was an ardent German nationalist who was convinced that the government could assist the workers. Marx opposed Lassalle's joining of socialism and nationalism. He detested Lassalle's dilettantism, but did not have his popularity with the workers or his organization. Other influential socialists, Wilhelm Liebknecht and August Bebel, were Marxists and opposed to any courting of the emperor or his Prussian military and bureaucracy. But they joined their forces with the Lassalleans in 1875 to create a German socialist party. Courting would have made little difference, however, because Bismarck was intent on winning the workers away from their leaders and on crushing the socialists and along with them the liberals.

Two attempts on the life of Emperor William I in 1878 gave Bismarck the excuse that the socialists were a threat to society and had to be suppressed. In reality, the socialists were not a threat—they were few in number and their immediate practical program was a demand for civil liberties and democracy in Germany. Only the narrowest of conservative views would have seen the socialists as a threat, but many in Germany had such a view. The conservative Junker class, which dominated Prussian political life, would not champion the socialists. The liberals, who should have defended the civil liberties of the socialists, just as they should have championed the Catholics in the Kulturkampf, did not oppose Bismarck's special legislation outlawing subversive organizations and authorizing the police to ban meetings and newspapers. But the Social Democratic party of Germany, like the Catholic Center party before, survived the Bismarckian persecution. It grew stronger and better disciplined as the liberals grew weaker, discredited by their unwillingness to act against the Iron Chancellor.

Bismarck tried to win the support of the workers through paternalistic social legislation. The problems of industrialization, which developed in Germany at a rapid pace in the 1850s and 1860s until the worldwide depression of 1873, disturbed him as they did conservative thinkers in every nation. Germany was the first state to enact a program of social legislation for the proletariat; it included insurance against sickness, disability, accidents, and old age. Bismarck's laws called for the employer to contribute along with the state and the worker. Although the German working class continued to support the Social Democratic party in elections, nonetheless, great numbers of German workers, who voted socialist and who belonged to the many socialist political, youth, athletic, and cultural organizations, felt that their government deserved their loyalty. Thus, the revolutionary fervor of French laborers, and the devotion to the trade unions that characterized British workers, were not emotions shared by the Germans.

Economic and Colonial Policies

Bismarck was a conservative in economics. Rejecting the laissez faire of the liberals, he placed tariffs on the importation of grain and industrial products, which pleased landowners and industrialists. After the crash of 1873, Germany's economic expansion was steady but moderate, not the great growth of the mid-century. By the end of the century, Germany and the United States were major industrial powers and serious rivals to Britain. Neither country had practiced laissez-faire economics as the British had. Their economies were characterized by the growth of monopolies and cartels that relied on their governments for support of their economic activity.

The German government backed the economic interests of its industries in many ways, including the colonial policy of the 1880s. At first, Bismarck had claimed Germany was a satiated power and did not need colonies, but increasingly in the 1880s, he responded to pressure groups for expansion by supporting the acquisition of minor colonies in the Pacific and in Africa. These were territories of little importance in terms of economics or the Empire, but ultimately of considerable importance in world affairs. These colonial interests joined with other pressure groups urging construction of a powerful German navy to make the Empire possible. Forces that endangered world peace were set in motion.

Kaiser William II (1889–1918) ascended the German throne. He was a brash, outspoken young man who alienated people in other nations. He dismissed Bismarck in 1890 and shifted to policies that led to the First World War. But before too much blame is placed on William II, two facts should be remembered: first, Germany was not as horrified by the young kaiser's behavior as foreigners were (or historians since); second, Bismarck prepared the way for William II. The colonial policy was Bismarck's—a man with his influence could have resisted the clamor for colonies. The alliance system, which played an important part in touching off the declaration of war in 1914, was Bismarck's. The German constitution—a peculiar mixture of aristocratic Prussian power in the Upper House, democratic universal male suffrage that was manipulated to illiberal ends, and an untouchable chancellor—was Bismarck's creation. Finally, the opportunistic maneuvers that Bismarck made in the Reichstag by attacking Catholics, liberals, and socialists undermined the development of a viable parliamentary government. The bureaucracy, the military, and the chancellor remained out of the reach of the voting populace. Indeed, in 1914, Germany, the most highly industrialized and powerful European nation, was subject to a political regime that preserved aspects of an absolute monarchy.

ITALY, 1870–1914

Italian nationalists expected greatness from the unification of their country, so long plundered, conquered, divided, and ruled by absolute princes. But it seemed that in every cause for rejoicing, Italians had to face a nagging doubt as well. Illiterate and impoverished people and their republican leaders expected much of the Italian state, much that would not be fulfilled for such reasons as the economic and political backwardness of the nation and of its politicians.

Italy, in addition, was split on the religious issue. Many Catholics in the overwhelmingly Catholic country had wanted to see a unified Italy, perhaps even an Italy where the pope played a less political role. But Pope Pius IX refused to accept this new Italy whose leaders had confiscated papal territories, closed religious houses, and taken church properties. Also, the liberal leaders wanted to create a secular state with civil marriage and public secular education, all of which was anathema to the church.

Another divisive factor was the long tradition of separate and often rival states. Some resisted unification under Victor Emanuel, the Piedmontese king. Many Italians argued for federalism, a government in which some powers—particularly those of defense and diplomacy, and perhaps even some areas of the economy such as railroad building—might be under the control of the central government. But in federalism, the important aspects of life, such as education, would remain in the hands of local governments. To Italians, there seemed to be no institutions that could safeguard the rights of local areas and no way to make sure that the central government would deal justly with every area.

Participation in the political system established in Italy was limited to the few. Of the 27 million citizens, only about 2 million could vote, even after the reforms of 1881, which tripled the size of the electorate. Liberals could point out that in a country plagued with illiteracy on a vast scale, 2 million meant that almost every literate male could vote, but this was small consolation to those whose efforts to unite Italy had not required literacy. The government was comprised of ministers responsible to the king (as in Germany), an Upper House (appointed members), and a Lower House (members elected by a narrow franchise). Italian political parties remained small groups gathered around a few personalities; parties and ideologies did not mean much when an ambitious politician wanted to take office. For example, a man might be elected as member of the Left, only to move to the Center in order to hold cabinet office. To many Italians, Parliament seemed to be a place where deals were made and corruption was prevalent.

Among Italian workers, cynicism about the government was so deep that they were attracted to the ideas of syndicalism and the general strike. Strong trade unions, socialist ideals, and a disgust with parliamentary government led them to believe that direct action would gain more than elections and parties. Many in labor were anarchists. In some rural areas, particularly in the south, the peasants were so isolated from the national political and economic life that traditional patterns of loyalty to the local landowner, now also a political leader, persisted. Catholic, loyal to their landlord, and bitterly discontent with their economic situation, they saw few signs of the new state other than taxation and conscription. Often their children migrated to the north to work in factories—or even further, to the New World.

Italy's difficult social and economic problems were brushed aside for issues more easily expressed to an inexperienced political nation: nationalism, foreign policy, and military glory. Italy's ambitions for Great-Power status became the justification for military expenditures beyond the capacity of the poor state. They furnished the rationale for its scramble for African and Mediterranean territories; this foreign policy of expansion was to provide the solution to all Italy's social ills. The profits from exploiting others would pay for badly needed social reforms, and the raw materials would fuel industrialization. None of these promises came true, which deepened the cynicism of a disillusioned people. As a foreign and as a domestic policy, this pursuit of glory was too costly for the fragile nation.

RUSSIA, 1825–1914

Nineteenth-century Russia differed considerably from the other major countries of Europe. Of far greater diversity and territorial sway than even the Hapsburg monarchy, Russia spread from the Prussian border to the Pacific Ocean, a Eurasian giant.

The huge borderlands and the diversity of peoples inhabiting them reaffirmed the autocratic tradition of the Russian state. It possessed neither a loyal and intelligent nobility of independent means nor an enterprising and well-to-do middle class; it also lacked the creative competition of free citizens. For several centuries the state itself had taken over the responsibility for mobilizing resources, growing all-powerful while reducing its subjects to pawns. Even in the early nineteenth century, only two classes of people were said to exist in the Russian Empire: the servitors of the tsar—army officers, officials, and the landed nobility from which they sprang—and the serfs who served the servitors. The urban people, merchants and craftsmen forcibly organized in the late eighteenth century into guilds, enjoyed little freedom; they were few in number and generally despised like the common folk by the nobility.

The servitors, Europeanized since the time of Peter the Great, constituted a small privileged minority. They were separated from the mass of the population by barriers of education, culture, and experience that were more profound than any class distinctions in Europe. No wonder they lived in fear of popular uprisings, like the tsar himself. The tsar had additional reasons for fear: the country suffered from external insecurity, especially in its relations with the Great Powers of Europe, which were better armed, more prosperous, and, above all, had popular support.

Russia's fortunes depended on its political order, centered, more than in western Europe, on the rulers. The tsarist government, its central institutions reorganized after Western models in the wake of the French Revolution, took a decidedly conservative turn after Napoleon had been defeated, and for good reason. Returning Russian officers, asking why Russia could not share the civilized life they had witnessed in western Europe, turned revolutionary. In December 1825, in the brief interlude between the death of Alexander I (1801–1825) and the accession of Nicholas I (1825–1855), a small group of conspirators staged an unsuccessful revolt, demanding a constitution. The Decembrist uprising determined the character of the reign of Nicholas I and of Russian governments thereafter.

Aware of the subversive influence of foreign ideas and conditions, Nicholas decreed an ideology of Russian superiority, called *official nationality.* The Russian people were taught to believe that the Orthodox creed of the Russian church, the autocratic rule of the tsar, and Russia's Slavic culture made the Russian Empire superior to the West. In order to enforce this fake invincibility, Nicholas I created a secret police to watch over the minds and the conduct of his subjects. In addition, he controlled access to his country from Europe, drawing toward the end of his reign a virtual iron curtain for keeping out dangerous influences. His ideal was a monolithic country run, like an army, by a vigorous administration centered on himself; all Russians were to obey his wise and fatherly commands.

The realities of Nicholas's reign, unfortunately, were different. Corruption and deceit pervaded the bureaucracy. Society stagnated except for intense intellectual agitation among small circles of students. Yet the tsar also promoted innovation. He ordered a railway built between St. Petersburg and Moscow; he opened schools and universities, vainly hoping to encourage Russian participation in the European advance of knowledge without encouraging subversive comparison with the West.

Nicholas I's ambition to make Russia victorious in all comparisons with western Europe collapsed in the Crimean War (1854–1856).

Russian threats to the Ottoman Empire and to Anglo-French domination of the eastern Mediterranean led to armed conflict fought on Russian soil. The English and French expeditionary forces defeated the Russian army. Thus began, in a mood of profound crisis, a new regime under Alexander II (1855–1881).

Alexander II was hailed as "tsar liberator," but suffered from an emotional instability that reflected the dilemma of his reign. On one hand, he was determined to preserve autocratic rule; his country lacked all prerequisites for constitutional government. On the other hand, he wanted Russia to achieve what had made western Europe strong; the energetic support and free enterprise of its citizens. Whether stimulating popular initiative was possible without undermining autocracy was the key puzzle for him and his successors to the end of the tsarist regime.

Alexander's boldest reform was the emancipation of the serfs in 1861. The serfs were liberated from bondage to the nobility and given land of their own, but not individual freedom. They remained tied to their village and to their households, which owned the land collectively. Emancipation did not transform the peasants into enterprising and loyal citizens.

For the nonpeasant minority, a package of other reforms brought new opportunities: limited self-government for select rural areas and urban settlements, an independent judiciary, and the rule of law. Trial by jury was introduced, as well as a novel profession—lawyers. Military service was also reformed, so that all male Russians, regardless of status, were drafted into a citizen army granting as much equality as Russian conditions would permit.

Meanwhile, the borders were reopened, allowing closer ties with Europe and westernizing Russian society. The rising class of business people and professional experts looked West and conformed to Western middle-class standards. There was some relaxation of the repression of non-Russian minorities. Railroads were constructed, which facili-

EXECUTION OF SOFIA PERONSKAIA Faced with the indifference of the masses and the repression of the Russian regime, the generation of the 1870s formed revolutionary groups. In 1881, a group of nihilists, including Sofia Peronskaia, assassinated Alexander II in the hope that destruction of the symbol of the autocratic regime might make way for the regeneration of Russia. (Culver Pictures, Inc.)

tated agricultural exports and permitted the import of Western goods and capital. For some years the economy boomed.

More significant in the long run was the flowering of Russian thought and literature. Since the late eighteenth century, the impact of Western culture on Russian life had created an extraordinary intellectual ferment; it came to a climax under Alexander II among a slowly growing group known as the *intelligentsia*. Its members were educated Russians whose minds were shaped by Western schooling and travel, yet who still were prompted by the "Russian soul." Caught between two conflicting cultures, their critical awareness was heightened by their alienation. They examined Russian life by Western sensibilities and the West by Russian sensibilities. They tried to escape from their sense of guilt through service to the common people (much idealized); at their best, they produced a brilliant literature that became a source of intense national pride and exerted a profound influence around the world. Fyodor Dostoyevsky and Leo Tolstoy wrote their greatest novels in the 1860s and 1870s. Intellectuals quarreled, with fierce sincerity, over the merits of making Russia superior by imitating the West or by cultivating their own Slavic genius, possibly through a Pan-Slavic movement. Even more than the tsars, the intelligentsia hoped for a glorious Russia that would outshine the West.

Yet how might this be done? The tsar would not permit open discussion likely to provoke rebellion (in 1863 he faced an uprising in his Polish lands). Liberals advocating gradual change were thwarted by censorship and the police. The 1860s saw the rise of self-righteous fanatics ready to match the chicanery of the police and foment social revolution. By the late 1870s, they organized themselves into a secret terrorist organization. In 1881, they assassinated the tsar. The era of reforms ended.

The next tsar, Alexander III (1881–1894), a firm if unimaginative ruler, returned to the principles of Nicholas I. In defense against the revolutionaries, he perfected the police state, adapting Western methods and even enlisting anti-Semitism in its cause. He updated autocracy and stifled dissent, but he also promoted the economy. Russia had relied too heavily on foreign loans and goods; it had to build up its own resources. It also needed more railroads to bind the huge country together, so in 1891 the tsar ordered the construction of the Trans-Siberian Railroad. Soon afterward, his Minister of Finance, Sergei Witte, used railroad expansion to boost heavy industry and industrialization generally. In 1900, he addressed a far-sighted memorandum to the young Nicholas II (1894–1917), who, hopelessly unprepared and out of tune with the times, had succeeded his father in 1894.

Russia more than any other country needs a proper economic foundation for its national policy and culture . . . International competition does not wait. If we do not take energetic and decisive measures so that in the course of the next decade our industry will be able to satisfy the needs of Russia and of the Asiatic countries which are—or should be—under our influence, then the rapidly growing foreign industries will . . . establish themselves in our fatherland and the Asiatic countries mentioned above . . . Our economic backwardness may lead to political and cultural backwardness as well.[1]

Yet forced industrialization also brought perils. It propelled the country into alien and often hated ways of life; it created a discontented new class of workers and it impoverished agriculture; it promoted mobility, literacy, and contact with western Europe, thereby increasing political agitation among the professional classes, intelligentsia, workers, peasants, and subject nationalities. Indispensable for national self-assertion and survival, industrialization strained the country's fragile unity to the utmost.

The first jolt, the Revolution of 1905, followed Russia's defeat by Japan in the Russo-Japanese War (see Chapter 26). Fortunately for the tsar, his soldiers stayed loyal, allowing the autocracy to survive, although now saddled with a parliament called the *Imperial Duma*, a concession to the Revolution. The new regime, inwardly rejected by Nicholas II, started auspiciously. Under its freedoms, Russian art and literature flourished and the economy progressed. Agrarian reforms introduced the incentives of private property and individual enterprise into the villages. The supporters of the constitutional experiment hoped for a liberal Russia at last, but the heightened insecurity as revealed in the pre-1914 international crises merely prepared the doom of tsarist Russia.

The rulers of Russia between 1825 and 1914 had labored under enormous difficulties in their efforts to match the power and prestige

CHRONOLOGY 25.1 EUROPE IN THE AGE OF INDUSTRIALIZATION

1815–1820	Economic depression in England fosters reform legislation
1828–1829	England's Test Act (against Nonconformist Protestants) is repealed, and the Catholic Emancipation Act is passed
1830s–1840s	Chartist movement in England
1830–1834	Liberal reform movement in England: Reform Bill of 1832 extending suffrage; New Poor Law of 1834
1846–1847	Great famine in Ireland
1848	Insurrection in England; France's Second Republic is established; nationalist uprising in German and Italian states; Czechs and Hungarians rebel against Hapsburg rule
1851	Louis Napoleon Bonaparte overthrows the Second Republic, becoming Emperor Napoleon III
1860s	Irish movement for republic form of government (the Fenians)
1861	Kingdom of Italy is formed; Alexander II, Russian tsar, emancipates the serfs and institutes reforms
1867	Second Reform Bill doubles the English electorate
1870	The Third French Republic is established
1870–1871	The Franco-Prussian War; the Paris Commune; creation of the German Empire with William I as kaiser and Bismarck as chancellor
1873	The Great Depression
1880s	Charles Stewart Parnell leads the Irish Home Rule movement in the British Parliament
1881	Tsar Alexander II is assassinated
1884	Reform Bill grants suffrage to virtually all English men
1894–1906	The Dreyfus Affair in France
1905	Revolution in Russia—Nicholas II grants the formation of the Imperial Duma

of the great states of Europe. Two of them (Alexander II and Nicholas II) came to violent ends; the other two died in weariness and failure. Although the fear that the tsars inspired was real, their splendor was hollow. Their tragedy was recognized neither by the liberal West nor by their critics among the intelligentsia, with whom they shared the vision of a superior Russia.

A GOLDEN AGE?

Europe at the Congress of Vienna in 1815 and Europe exactly one hundred years later, at the end of the first year of the First World War, seem two different worlds. The nineteenth century viewed from the vantage point of 1915 must have seemed a golden era, a period of unparalleled peace and progress, full of promise of liberal institutions and democratic movements, autonomous nations, scientific progress, and individual human development. It seemed a century of progress in the production of goods, alleviation of want, development of technology, and practice of constitutional and liberal government. Serfdom and feudal obligations had been abolished; so had slavery. Europeans had recognized self-government as a human right. The importance of democracy had been acknowledged. The world had become smaller, more interdependent and cosmopolitan, more educated, and probably better fed, housed, and clothed. It seemed, in short, so different from the twentieth-century realities of world war, mass destruction, national passions, and manipulation of humanity in the name of causes having little to do with daily lives and daily bread.

Yet something had gone wrong with all that promise of progress even during the nineteenth century. Perhaps it had taken place in the failures of the revolutions of 1848, failures to reconcile national and class conflict. Perhaps the ideals of free trade, liberal government, individual freedom, and national auton-

omy had been perverted in the bitter reaction to 1848 and in the brutal reality of the mid-century wars of unification. Perhaps the ideals had been wrong in the first place, ill suited to the realities of the time. But these ideals persisted, and in the twentieth century they presented major problems to the West—and the rest of the world—as people strove to achieve national self-determination, individual liberty, and economic progress.

Notes

1. Theodore H. Von Laue, *Sergei Witte and the Industrialization of Russia* (New York: Columbia University Press, 1963), p. 3.

Suggested Reading

Blake, R., *Disraeli* (1967). An excellent one-volume biography.

Chekhov, Anton, *Selected Stories,* especially "The Peasants," "Three Years," and "In Exile."

Dostoevsky, Fyodor, *Notes from the Underground.*

Eyck, Erich, *Bismarck and the German Empire* (1950). A very critical biography; an abridgment of a larger work.

Goldberg, Harvey, *The Life of Jean Jaurès* (1962). The most readily available work on this important man.

Gordon, Craig, *Politics of the Prussian Army* (1955). A very valuable study with important implications for German and European history.

Gorky, Maxim, *My Childhood.*

Holborn, Hajo, *History of Modern Germany, 1840–1945,* 3 vols. (1969). A definitive work.

Jellinek, Frank, *The Paris Commune of 1871* (1937).

Johnson, D., *France and the Dreyfus Affair* (1967). The best of many books on the controversial affair.

Joll, James, *Europe Since 1870* (1973). A valuable general survey, particularly good on socialism in the individual nations.

Kann, Robert, *The Multinational Empire: Nationalism and National Reform in the Hapsburg Monarchy, 1840–1918*, 2 vols. (1950–1964). A definitive text.

Mosse, W. E., *Liberal Europe, 1848–1875* (1974). A comparative history of Europe in the liberal era.

Noland, Aaron, *The Founding of the French Socialist Party, 1893–1905* (1956). A well-informed study of the origins of the socialist party in France.

O'Brien, C. C., *Parnell and His Party, 1880–90* (1957). A good book on this important Irish leader.

Seton-Watson, Christopher, *Italy from Liberalism to Fascism* (1967). Another excellent survey of Italian history.

Smith, Dennis Mack, *Italy: A Modern History*, rev. ed. (1969). Excellent survey with emphasis on the theme of the failure of Italy to develop viable liberal institutions or economic solutions.

Taylor, A. J. P., *The Hapsburg Monarchy, 1809–1918* (1965). A well-written, incisive, brief history.

———, *Bismarck: The Man and the Statesman* (1967). A brilliant portrait of a complicated man who dominated the second half of the nineteenth century.

Webb, R. K., *Modern England from the Eighteenth Century to the Present* (1968). A balanced, well-informed, readable book that is up-to-date on controversial issues.

Williams, Roger, *The World of Napoleon III*, rev. ed. (1965). An indispensable fresh look at the "Saint-Simonian on Horseback."

Wright, Gordon, *France in Modern Times*, 2nd ed. (1974). A good survey of the entire period.

Review Questions

1. How did the Reform Bill of 1832 modify the roles of the cabinet and the parties in the British Parliament?

2. What were the aims of the Chartists?

3. How did the Reform Bill of 1867 usher in a new era in British politics?

4. Why was Napoleon III able to overthrow the Second Republic? Who supported him and why?

5. In England the middle class and the workers often worked together for reform in the period from 1865 to 1914. Discuss why was this not done in France.

6. What was the general crisis of liberalism after 1870?

7. How did conservatives attempt to win over the masses after 1870?

8. What social problems did unified Italy fail to resolve?

9. On the eve of the First World War, most of the European states were threatened by a crisis, either political or social. Discuss the threat of revolution or social change in Britain, France, Germany, Italy, and Russia on the eve of the war.

10. There are several major figures in the period from 1870 to 1914 whose influence shaped historical developments. Discuss the impact of one of these individuals and support your choice.

11. What problems did the tsars from Nicholas I to Nicholas II face in ruling Russia? Given the conditions of their country, could they have become constitutional monarchs?

CHAPTER 26

Western Imperialism:
Global Dominance

IN THE LAST TWO DECADES of the nineteenth century, Europeans very rapidly claimed and conquered the lands in Asia and Africa. For almost three-quarters of the century, European influence over the rest of the world had grown. Masses of European immigrants had made new homes in North and South America, Australia, and New Zealand. World trade had greatly expanded as European nations industrialized. European economic penetration shifted somewhat abruptly from commerce to active conquest and exploitation of previously unclaimed territories.

From the long perspective, European history has been one of an expansionist society. Europeans conquered and settled substantial regions of the Americas. In a series of wars in the eighteenth century, Europeans competed with one another for the rights of trade and settlement in faraway lands. But by the end of the century the old slaving stations in Africa had decayed as had the production in Caribbean sugar islands and mines in Latin America. The settlements of the English, Spanish, and Portuguese grew and prospered until those in the New World rebelled, demanding independence from their mother countries.

For most of the nineteenth century, Europeans showed little interest in annexing parts of Asia and Africa to add to the remnants of the eighteenth-century empires. The American Revolution seemed to prove that colonies were too expensive a proposition, and that once independent, they would continue to trade with Europe. Free traders argued that commerce, rather than following the flag, would go to whichever country could produce the best goods most cheaply and that efforts to add colonies would be better expended in improving industry. Many in the nineteenth century thought the days of empire were over, that Europeans had grown too civilized to fight over trade networks. European liberals, in particular, believed that the interdependence of commerce precluded a major war because it would be too destructive of the livelihoods of too many people. But from the 1880s to

1914, in an era sometimes called the *new imperialism*, Europeans rapidly claimed and conquered Asia and Africa.

THE EMERGENCE OF THE NEW IMPERIALISM

The new imperialism (so-called to differentiate it from the "old colonialism" of settlement and trade in the sixteenth to eighteenth centuries) seemed a new, as well as potentially dangerous phenomenon. The Great Powers laid claim to African territories and began actively to encourage their nationals' trade activities in far-flung places.

But why was there this burst of expansion after at least a half century in which Europeans tended to their own affairs? Some historians see imperialism as an aspect of industrialization, of a new economic situation in which Europeans struggled for raw materials, markets for their commodities, and places to invest capital. In the nineteenth century, changing technology widened the gap between Europe and other areas, making European states for the first time clearly more powerful than the nations of Asia and Africa. The enormous powers of industry, new agriculture, military technology, and the European states, which could mobilize the support of all citizens, made it almost a foregone conclusion that in any conflict between a European state and a non-European country or people, the European would triumph. The same was true of the United States' strength.

Industrialization did more than create an enormous technological gap between Europe (and America), and the rest of the world. Economic growth in the nineteenth century became more international and then truly global by the end of the century. New markets, new technology, overseas trade, and investments increased enormously, creating a single world market economy. Western powers, even small ones like Belgium and the Netherlands and backward ones in eastern and southern Europe, were industrialized and exploited the raw materials and markets of the rest of the world.

The undeveloped areas of the world, in turn, found markets for their crops and were able to buy European commodities. But being part of the world market economy also made these areas subject to the smallest tremor on the European and American stock exchanges. Participation in the world market could bring wealth for a few people in these areas, but it meant hardship for many, as well as the loss of traditional customs and social relationships. It meant virtual slavery to the Indians who harvested rubber on the Orinoco River in South America or to the Africans who performed the same task on the Congo River. Increasing crop production to satisfy European markets often created problems. Producing coffee for export, or cattle, or indigo, meant turning land that had grown food for families over to export crops, thus reducing the food supply.

Economic interdependence operated to the great advantage of Europeans and Americans; the world economy enriched and eased the lives of these consumers at the beginning of the twentieth century. In this world, for example, a European or an American could be found well dressed in Egyptian cotton, Australian wool, and Argentinian leather, consuming Chinese tea or Colombian coffee in his home or office, which he had furnished in hardwoods from Burma, Malaya, or Africa and in silks and damasks of the Orient, carpets from the Middle East, and so on. He could purchase all these goods at a favorable price. He could travel anywhere without need of a passport (unless he was a Russian), using gold or easily available foreign currency exchanged at a rate almost always favorable to the dollar or the pound. He could invest his money in the raw materials or government debts of virtually any area of the world and expect a return as well as security for his investment, the safety of law and order and private property.

Captains of industry defended the new empires and predicted dire consequences if their state—England, for example—did not get its share of world markets. They argued that rivals would acquire the benefits that the English renounced, and that England would fall behind in the struggle for survival, that it would be surpassed by vital nations like Germany or the United States, which were already surpassing the English in production of such essential goods as coal, iron, and steel. Though England had had a head start, the industry leaders said, the advantages of this jump on empire and world trade were diminishing every day as other nations began competing. National competition was joined with economic competition as an argument for empire.

The images of youth and vitality, of survival and decay, of competition between the fit and the unfit, were part of the language of Social Darwinism (see page 618), whose advocates tried to apply a popular model of biological evolution to society. Frequently, in the popular mind, the concepts of evolution justified the exploitation by superior races of the "lesser breeds beneath the law." This language of race and conflict, of superior and inferior people, gave a particularly ugly cast to the extension of the world market and the expansion of European power. Often people who thought in these nationalistic and racist terms had little or no sense that other cultures and other peoples had merit and deserved respect. Their arrogant lack of consideration for other peoples was paralleled by their attitude toward unfortunate men and women in their own nations.

Not all advocates of empire were Social Darwinists, however. Other people believed that the extension of empire, law, order, and industrial civilization would raise "backward peoples" up the ladder of evolution and civilization. Still other Europeans believed it was their duty as Christians to set an example and to educate others. Christian missionaries were the first to meet and learn about many peoples and the first to develop writing for the languages of peoples without written language. Throughout the nineteenth century, missionaries had gone to regions unexplored by Westerners to preach and carry on the crusade against slavery, which the English in particular had long opposed as un-Christian. Missionaries like David Livingstone believed that the slave trade in those regions would end only when their own native land furnished law, order, and stability, and when the world market economy offered the peoples of those areas alternatives to the ancient occupations of war, pillage, and slavery.

An interest in exotic places contributed to the passion for imperialism. The explorations of Livingstone in the Congo Basin and of Richard Burton and John Speke (who raced with each other and with Livingstone to find the source of the Nile) fascinated many Europeans. The expeditions of the Scot Mungo Park on the Niger River or Stanley and the Frenchman Pierre Savorgnan de Brazza in the Congo were great adventures. Sponsored by national geographic and exploration societies and encouraged by their nation's military, explorers captured the imagination of Europeans and Americans in much the same way that space explorers do today. Individuals and nations competed to find the highest mountain, the longest river, the highest waterfall, the land unseen by white people.

All the superlatives called men and women away from humdrum lives to adventure—if not to experience it, at least to dream of it. The fiction of English authors Rudyard Kipling (1865–1936), H. Rider Haggard (1856–1925), and many inferior imitators stimulated the passion for faraway places and unknown peoples. Kipling wrote: "Take up the White Man's Burden—send forth the best ye breed—go bind your sons to exile to serve your captives' need."[1] He also wrote of the Indian Gunga Din whose faithful service to his white masters, some British soldiers in battle, won him their respect as a man. Writers told of heroism and sacrifice, the "burden" part of the "White

CHRISTIAN MISSIONARY IN TOGOLAND (GHANA)
Throughout the nineteenth century, Christian missionaries had gone to Asia, Africa, and Latin America to preach and to carry on the crusade against slavery. Many of these Christians devoted their lives to accomplish these goals; at the same time, many carried with them the ethnocentric values and judgments of their compatriots who thought that non-Europeans were backward and uncivilized. (Culver Pictures, Inc.)

Man's Burden," rather than the exploitation, cruelty, and abuse of empire.

Throughout the era of the new imperialism, there was a gradual shift from policies of economic penetration of Asia, Africa, and Latin America to a practice of establishing different degrees of political control. Some historians believe that increasing nationalism in Europe during the 1870s at least partially explains this shift. Certainly the unification of Germany and Italy altered the balance of power and diplomatic relations. Moreover, the

press and politics in England, France, Germany, Italy, and the United States involved increasing numbers of enthusiastic citizens in the imperial adventures of their governments. These enthusiasts often pressed for aggressive activity abroad.

Many historians believe that the antagonisms and power struggles between European states were simply extended to Africa and Asia. In this view, the master diplomat Bismarck had encouraged the French to expand in Africa knowing full well that this would bring the French into conflict with the Italians and English, who also had ambitions in Africa. He hoped that imperialism would weaken France further by dividing domestic French opinion into two camps: those who were champions of imperialism, and those who wanted to throw all of France's efforts into a war of vengeance for the loss of Alsace and Lorraine. Russia's imperial activity in Asia and in the Middle East brought it into conflict with the British and, by the turn of the twentieth century, with the Japanese. The British may have thought that they were not assertive or imperialistic, and were merely defending interests and empire already in their possession. However, nations with less empire or less desirable empire saw Britain as their primary rival for the spoils of imperialism. Germany's shift to colonialism called for its naval expansion; this move, in turn, caused Britain to ally with its rival, France.

Europeans established varying degrees of political control over much of the rest of the world. Control could mean outright annexation and the governing of a territory as a colony, such as German control of Tanganyika (East Africa) after 1886, or British rule in India after 1857. It could mean status as a protectorate, in which a local ruler who continued to rule was directed or protected by a Great Power, as was the case with British control of Egypt after 1882. There were also *spheres of influence* in which a European nation had special trading and legal privileges without any military or political involvement. Northern Persia became a sphere of Russian influence at the turn of the century and southern Persia was under British influence.

The resistance of non-Europeans to American and European economic penetration and control must not be underestimated. The history of every area differed according to its resistance to outside control. The Turks managed to play Europeans off against one another for the entire nineteenth century, maintaining control over their non-European territories, though they had lost their lands on the European continent. The Chinese emperor granted trading privileges, even control of cities, to Europeans as spheres of influence, but he kept his country under his rule. The Japanese, responding to European and American penetration, drastically changed their economy, their government, and even aspects of their social structure, but they kept their territory intact. Egypt, on the other hand, fell deeply in debt to Europeans and became a British protectorate. Indochina was directly annexed by France and was governed by French civil servants and soldiers. Annexation was a fate that befell much of Africa as well.

THE SCRAMBLE FOR AFRICA

The most rapid European expansion took place in Africa. As late as 1880, European nations ruled only a tenth of the continent. By 1914, Europeans had claimed all of Africa except Liberia, a small territory of freed slaves from the United States, and Ethiopia (Abyssinia), which had successfully held off Italian invaders at Aduwa in 1896. Most of the Great Powers were involved in the carving up of Africa, except for Russia, Austria-Hungary, and the United States.

There had been a few involvements of European powers in Africa earlier in the century. The French had moved into Algeria in 1830. In South Africa, the British during the Napoleonic Wars had gained Cape Town, a useful provisioning place for trading ships bound for India and the Far East. Dutch cattlemen and farmers (Boers), who had settled in Cape Town since the mid-seventeenth century, moved northward on the Great Trek (1835–1837) to get away from the British. The Boers made war on native tribes, the Kaffir and the Zulu, as they went. Aggressively asserting their independence from the British, by 1880 the Boers seemed likely to maintain their self-government and the territory that they had taken in the interior.

Thus, up to the 1870s, it seemed that Great Power interest in Africa was marginal and might decline even further. Then the astounding activities of Leopold II, king of Belgium, changed the picture. As a private entrepreneur, he formed the International Association for the Exploration and Civilization of Central Africa in 1876. Among others, Leopold sent Henry Stanley (1841–1904) to the Congo River Basin to establish trading posts, sign treaties with the chiefs, and claim the territory for the association. Stanley was an adventurer and newspaper reporter; he had fought on both sides of the American Civil War. Stanley had earlier led an expedition to central Africa in search of David Livingstone, the popular missionary-explorer who had not been heard of for some time. Stanley's rescue of Livingstone in 1871 was a human-interest story calculated to delight thousands of readers. Leopold's private development efforts promised profit and adventure for men like Stanley and other Europeans, and brutal exploitation for the Africans. The French responded to the news of Leopold's agents' acquisitions by immediately establishing their protectorate on the north bank of the Congo River. The scramble was on.

Bismarck and Jules Ferry, premier of France, called an international conference of the Great Powers in Berlin in 1884 to form some ground rules for the development of Africa south of the Sahara. Leopold (as an individual, not as the king of Belgium) was declared the personal ruler of the Congo Free State. The Congo Basin was made a free-trade zone for merchants of every nation.

The Berlin Conference established the rule that a European country had to occupy territory effectively in order to claim it. This led to a mad race to the interior of Africa; it was field day for explorers and soldiers. As Europeans rushed to claim territory, they ignored both natural and cultural frontiers. Even today the map of Africa reveals many straight boundary lines drawn with a ruler rather than irregular lines of natural boundaries such as rivers and mountains.

The Berlin Conference also agreed to stop slavery and the slave trade in Africa. Soon, however, the practices of the Congo Association, as it tried to turn a profit for Leopold and the stockholders, were as vicious as those of the African slave traders. At the turn of the twentieth century, Edward D. Morel, an English humanitarian, and Roger Casement, a hero of Irish nationalism who was at that time a British civil servant, waged a vigorous campaign against Leopold for the Aborigines' Protection Society. They produced evidence that slavery, mutilation, brutality, and murder were common practices in the Congo Free State as blacks were forced to work for the rubber plantations. In response to the outcry of public opinion, the Belgian Parliament declared the territory a Belgian colony in 1908, putting an end to Leopold's vicious private enterprise.

Great Britain's activities in Africa provide an excellent case study of the complicated motives, operations, and results of European imperialism. In the second half of the nineteenth century, Britain maintained a few outposts along the coast of West Africa. The British hold on South Africa looked as though it would loosen. The British navy, from time to time, interfered with slave traders in Africa. But there was little concern in the British government. Then, local conditions in Egypt resulted in British occupation, carried out by men who in principle rejected empire.

The Egyptian khedive had proclaimed Egypt's independence from Turkey. Strong khedives, with British and French support, maintained Egypt's autonomy. But foreign investment and influence grew in Egypt as successive khedives spent their treasuries lavishly in attempts to maintain their position and to turn their people into a modern nation. The building of the Suez Canal (1859–1869), in which the khedive, along with British and French capitalists, was a principal stockholder, brought Egypt to the verge of bankruptcy. The canal promised much in the long run for

MAP 26.1 AFRICA IN 1914 ▶

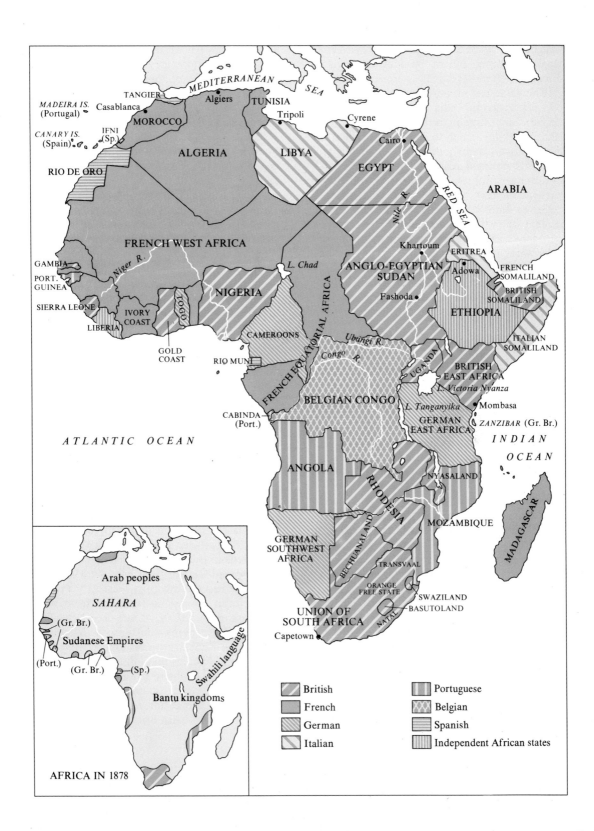

MEDITERRANEAN SEA

MADEIRA IS.
(Portugal)

TANGIER

Casablanca

Algiers

TUNISIA

Tripoli

Cyrene

CANARY IS.
(Spain)

IFNI
(Sp.)

MOROCCO

Cairo

ARABIA

ALGERIA

LIBYA

EGYPT

RIO DE ORO

Nile R.

RED SEA

FRENCH WEST AFRICA

Niger R.

L. Chad

ANGLO-EGYPTIAN
SUDAN

Khartoum

ERITREA

Adowa

FRENCH
SOMALILAND

GAMBIA

PORT.
GUINEA

SIERRA LEONE

IVORY
COAST

TOGO

NIGERIA

Fashoda

BRITISH
SOMALILAND

ETHIOPIA

LIBERIA

GOLD
COAST

CAMEROONS

RIO MUNI

FRENCH EQUATORIAL AFRICA

Ubangi R.

Congo R.

ITALIAN
SOMALILAND

CABINDA
(Port.)

BELGIAN CONGO

UGANDA

BRITISH
EAST
AFRICA

L. Victoria Nyanza

L. Tanganyika

Mombasa

ZANZIBAR (Gr. Br.)

ATLANTIC OCEAN

ANGOLA

GERMAN
EAST AFRICA

INDIAN
OCEAN

NYASALAND

GERMAN
SOUTHWEST
AFRICA

RHODESIA

MOZAMBIQUE

BECHUANALAND

MADAGASCAR

TRANSVAAL

ORANGE
FREE STATE

SWAZILAND

BASUTOLAND

UNION OF
SOUTH AFRICA

NATAL

Capetown

Arab peoples

SAHARA

(Gr. Br.)

Swahili language

Sudanese Empires

(Port.)

(Gr. Br.)

(Sp.)

Bantu kingdoms

AFRICA IN 1878

British

French

German

Italian

Portuguese

Belgian

Spanish

Independent African states

Egypt in terms of trade and contact with the world economy, but it brought immediate disaster.

The canal was important to the British as the waterway to India, but it was only a financial investment to the French. The British invited the French to join their invasion to protect investments, but they were unable for domestic political reasons. The French were deeply resentful that the British proceeded without them.

Prime Minister Gladstone, a "Little Englander" (one who opposed empire), promised to withdraw once stability in Egypt was assured. Every day that the British remained, Egyptian discontent and nationalistic feelings mounted against them, threatening the stability of markets and British investments and even of government. Furthermore, Egyptian opposition was of two irreconcilable minds. One group wanted to modernize or westernize their nation with a strong government and army in order to throw the British out. Another group hated all aspects of modernizing Egypt because it westernized the country and took Egypt further away from the Islamic nation that they wanted.

As the British became entrenched, resistance became more violent in vain attempts to dislodge the "protectors." Not only did they not withdraw from Egypt, the British also moved further south into the Sudan. There religious Muslims were carrying on a holy war against the Egyptians whom they accused of betraying the cause of Islam under the influence of the Christian Britons. In 1883, an English general, William Hicks, led 10,000 men for the Egyptian khedive against the Muslim leader in the Sudan, the Mahdi. The Egyptians were annihilated.

The English Liberals argued against further support of the khedive.

Egypt should no longer be hampered by the attempt to govern a piece of the world as large as Europe when she cannot find a Corporal's guard fit to fight . . . or . . . a hundred thou-

sand pounds to pay troops without plunging deeper into bankruptcy . . . we are not going to spend the lives of Englishmen or the natives of India in either supporting Egyptian rule in the Sudan or taking half of Africa for ourselves and trying to govern it.[1]

But the cost of the campaign made finances much worse in Cairo—occupation angered the French and occupation without control angered British financiers.

In 1885, Prime Minister Gladstone sent General Charles "Chinese" Gordon, who had won fame in suppressing the Taiping Rebellion, to the Sudan to see what could be done about the Mahdi. Gordon was killed at Khartoum; his head was severed and placed on a pike. Gladstone faced a storm of protest accusing him of martyring the famous hero by forbidding Gordon to wage war. Gladstone and the Liberals held out against demands to make war and annex the Sudan, but in 1898 when the Conservatives were in power there were further difficulties. General Herbert Kitchener was sent to the Sudan, and his men and machine guns mowed down charging Muslims at Omdurman. The casualties were reported to be 11,000 Muslims and 28 Britons, which many Britons felt was a suitable revenge for the death of Gordon.

But the battle of Omdurman was an ominous victory, and the year 1898 an ominous year in the history of the British Empire. Immediately after the battle there was confrontation between French and British forces at Fashoda in the Sudan. The French under the command of General Jean Baptiste Marchand had moved all the way from West Africa to the Sudan in an attempt to lay claim from West Africa to Somaliland on the Red Sea. The British were moving south from Egypt and north from Kenya into the same territory. In the diplomatic crisis that followed, Britain and France were brought to the brink of war and public passions were inflamed. Too divided by the Dreyfus Affair at home (see Chapter 25) to risk a showdown with Britain, France bitterly ordered Marchand to retreat to the French territory in West Africa. French statesmen began to negotiate with Britain to reconcile their claims with British ambitions. France did not have the resources to confront both Germany across the Rhine and Britain in Africa and Asia. The British, too, faced with conflict in the Sudan and mounting troubles in South Africa, realized their limitations. Their "splendid isolation" (a policy of refusing to make alliances with others) was now seen as a policy of risking the whole world as their enemy (with the possible exception of the United States, at that moment also isolated and involved with Spain in a war).

Nothing underlined Britain's isolation and the widespread distrust and disgust with Britain's hypocrisy more than the Boer War. British relations with the Boer settlers of the Transvaal and the Orange Free State, which had been difficult since the Great Trek, were aggravated by the discovery of rich mineral deposits of gold and diamonds. Paul Kruger (1825–1904), the Afrikaner president of the Transvaal, tried to gain independence, power, and access to the sea for the Boers or Afrikaners, and to restrict the foreigners who were flooding into Boer territory by the thousands in search of quick riches.

Adventurers from many lands descended upon the tiny Transvaal Republic, including Cecil Rhodes (1853–1902). This British subject soon made a fortune in diamonds and gold in South Africa. He became prime minister of Rhodesia, a sizable, wealthy territory that he had grabbed for his company and his country. Rhodes, who dreamed of the map of Africa from Cairo to the Cape of Good Hope, from north to south, colored red for British territory, plotted with powerful men in London and with foreigners who were denied citizenship and representation in the Transvaal.

In 1895, Cecil Rhodes's close friend, Leander Jameson, led about six hundred armed men into the Transvaal to stimulate an uprising against Kruger, which would give the British a pretext to invade. The raid failed and

Dr. Jameson and Rhodes were disgraced. The scandal reached all the way to Joseph Chamberlain, the imperialist colonial secretary in the British cabinet. Kaiser William II of Germany impetuously sent President Kruger a congratulatory telegram after the Boers had repulsed the Jameson raid. The British took this telegram as a symbol of their isolation.

Everything about the Boer War was unfortunate for the British. The Boers were formidable opponents, farmers by day and commandos by night. There was almost universal hatred for the British in the press of other European countries. The war was incredibly costly in money and lives. The British were aroused in a fever of patriotism. But, at the same time, anti-imperialism gained strength, and there was considerable outrage within Britain at the war and at the path that British policy had taken. Humanitarians in London found some British tactics shameful. The British won the major battles, but faced stiff guerrilla resistance. To deal with their stubborn foe, the British herded or "concentrated" whole settlements of Boers into wired compounds. The nasty war, which began in 1899, ended in 1902.

The British hoped to live together in peace with the Boers, to make a settlement of cooperation rather than revenge. The peace treaty gave many concessions to the Afrikaners, including the right to use Afrikaans, the language of the Boers (though English was the official language). Amnesty was given to any Boer who would swear allegiance to the British king. The Boers almost immediately gained control of the newly established government. By 1906, General Louis Botha, who had commanded the Boers, was elected the prime minister of the Transvaal.

But the settlement that appeared to be a generous and just dealing between enemies boded ill for other people who were not involved in the war. Justice, equality, and self-government for the Boers and the British did nothing for the black population of South Africa. In fact, the autonomy granted to the

Boers meant that the government in London could do little to protect the rights of black Africans in Boer territories. There were few safeguards for the blacks written into the treaty or into the constitution of the new Union of South Africa.

The wages of imperialism in Africa seemed slim not only to the British and French, but to other imperialists as well. Italian defeat at Aduwa (1896) at the hands of the Ethiopians did little to bolster their dreams of empire and national glory. Bismarck scoffed that the Italians had enormous appetites but very poor teeth. Neither defeat nor victory would have alleviated the Italian economic problems, though victory might have lessened political discontent. Germans also could take little heart from their African acquisitions—Southwest Africa (Namibia), Southeast Africa (Tanzania, but not Zanzibar, which was British), the Cameroons, and Togo (part of Ghana today). The German colonies were the most efficiently governed (critics said the most rigidly and ruthlessly organized), but they yielded few benefits other than pride of ownership and they were very costly to govern. Nor did Belgians gain prestige from the horrors of their colony, the Congo. Serious thinkers, contemplating the depths to which Leopold's search for fortune had brought Europeans, began to doubt European civilization and African barbarism. The Europeans seemed to be the moral barbarians, as the novelist Joseph Conrad and others pointed out. Honor was fleeting and profits illusory, for the most part, in these new African empires.

Furthermore, it appeared that Europeans might go to war with each other for those African lands. Such a war promised to be more deadly than the colonial conflicts between the technologically superior Europeans and Africans or Asians. Europeans came close to war over lands with few people and fewer resources. German aggressive imperialism, once Germany entered the race, infuriated England, where tempers flamed when Emperor William II gleefully congratulated the Boers on victor-

YORUBA CARVING OF A EUROPEAN This African artist has captured the spirit of the old colonialism and the new imperialism with the symbols of the European man with a gun and a horse. Aztecs, Chinese, Japanese, and Indian artists also conveyed in their works the sense of the intruder with power. (Courtesy of The American Museum of Natural History, New York)

ies in the field. British power, as well as national emotions, seemed threatened by Germany's decision to build a navy equal to its imperial ambitions. In a short time the "Teutonic cousins" eyed each other with deepening suspicions. The tensions arising from imperial conflicts contributed to the alliances that the

Great Powers made in the decade before the outbreak of the First World War.

EUROPEAN DOMINATION OF ASIA

The story of European imperialism in Asia is more complicated, because powerful kingdoms existed in India, Japan, and China when the Europeans arrived. These kingdoms possessed a sense of cultural unity provided by tradition and loyalty to Hinduism, Buddhism, or Islam. When the Europeans first arrived, the feeling of cultural unity was scarcely a conscious nationalism, but there was definitely animosity to Europeans.

China and Japan were hostile to Europeans whether they were Christian missionaries, traders, or soldiers and sailors. Wanting to preserve their traditional ruling classes, economies, and beliefs, at first they resisted Christianity, Western science, and secular ideologies. They successfully maintained their independence, though with considerable difficulty, against the onslaught of British, French, German, Russian, and American forces.

India was torn internally by religious conflict between Hindus and Muslims, as well as other religious beliefs and by the rivalries of native princes. India became the scene of an intense rivalry between British, Portuguese, Spanish, Dutch, and French traders and merchants in the seventeenth and eighteenth centuries. India became the brightest jewel in the British imperial crown when, one by one the British cleared out their European rivals in the mercantile and colonial wars of the eighteenth century. The British suppressed Hindu and Muslim resistance in the 1857–58 Sepoy Mutiny, which the Indians call the Great Rebellion. Parliament suppressed the East India Company (a private, chartered company which had a monopoly of trade there), and thereafter, ironically, the nation in which democracy and liberty had progressed rapidly after industrialization—Great Britain—ruled millions with little thought of liberties and rights and self-government.

China

The Chinese did not begin to trade with the West until they were defeated by the British in the Opium Wars of 1839–1842. Any commerce before this had been severely limited and entirely in the hands of monopolists granted trading privilege by the emperor. Aggressively demanding the right to trade opium, which was raised in their colony India, the British seized several trading cities along the coast.

Defeat in the war forced the emperor to change, and he did so by drawing on China's traditions and its elite. The mandarins, who were the traditional ruling elite, revitalized the Manchu bureaucracy and moved to strengthen China against the rapacious Westerners. The mandarins suppressed rebellion in the south, the Taiping uprising of 1850–1864, which was based on economic discontent, rejection of the emperor, and religious mysticism. For a time the Europeans seemed content with trading rights in coastal towns.

But China was not destined to follow the pattern of Japan, a pattern of reform under the traditional ruler to strengthen the nation against the Europeans' incursions. The Sino-Japanese War of 1894–95, in which Japan won an easy victory over the Chinese, only encouraged the Europeans to mutilate China. Britain, France, Russia, and Germany all scrambled for concessions and protectorates. The dowager empress Tzu Hsi watched helplessly as territories on the periphery (Indochina, Korea, Manchuria) that had once acknowledged the authority of China came under foreign powers. Treaty ports were given up to foreign control. The scramble might have followed the same course as that of Africa, but each European nation, more afraid of its rivals than of China, resisted any partition that might possibly give another European state an advantage. The United States proclaimed a policy of "Open Door"—that trade should be open to all and that the Great Powers should respect the territorial integrity of China—which some believe may have influenced Western powers to restrain annexations and partitions. Others believe the American policy was merely a way to ensure American interests in China and to continue to open China to the inroads of Western capitalism, whether the Chinese government liked it or not.

Chinese traditionalists organized secret societies whose aim was to expel foreigners and punish Chinese who accepted Christianity or in any way fostered Westernization. Usually these societies opposed both the Manchu Dynasty and the foreigners, but one of them, the Society of Righteous and Harmonious Fists (called the Boxers by Europeans), was encouraged by the empress who was sympathetic to its campaign against foreigners, particularly Christian missionaries. In 1900 the Boxers rebelled against the presence of foreigners in China. An allied army of Europeans and Americans suppressed the rebellion. China was forced to pay an indemnity and lost many national treasures when the capital was sacked and burned by Westerners.

Chinese unrest and discontent with the dynasty and the West deepened. When the Japanese defeated the Russians in 1905, many Chinese argued that the only way to protect China was to imitate the West as the Japanese had done. There were many signs of growing nationalism, particularly the widespread support given a Chinese boycott of American goods in 1905 to protest against the American exclusion of Chinese immigrants. In 1911 nationalistic antiforeign revolutionaries, who were particularly strong among the soldiers, workers, and students, overthrew the Manchu Dynasty and established a republic.

Espousing the Western ideas of democracy, nationalism, and social welfare, the republic struggled to establish its authority over China and to repel the imperialists who moved in immediately to lay claim to Mongolia (Russia) and to Tibet (England). China fell into civil war. Much of the north was controlled by powerful leaders who resisted any attempt to strengthen the republic against foreign imperialists because it might diminish their own authority. The south was more or less under the rule of Dr. Sun Yat-sen. A divided country, China continued to be the prey of imperialists.

Japan

Japan, like China, was opened to the West against its will in the nineteenth century. The Americans, in particular, refused to accept Japanese prohibitions on commercial and religious contacts with the West. And, like China, Japan succumbed to superior technological power. In 1853, Commodore Matthew C. Perry sailed to Japan, an American show of force that gave the Japanese little choice but to make treaties with the United States and others permitting trade.

Forced to reckon with the West, Japan experienced a flood of unrest. The warrior nobility, the *samurai*, attacked foreigners and murdered members of their own government. An allied fleet of American and European forces then attacked and destroyed important Japanese fortresses. The government was seized by a group of samurai determined to strengthen Japan to preserve its independence. The Meiji Restoration of 1867 returned power to the emperor, or *Meiji*, from the feudal military aristocracy that had ruled in his name for almost seven hundred years. Determined to modernize or Westernize, the new government refused to hang on to the traditional ways. It enacted a series of reforms that created a powerful unitary state from a feudal regime. The Japanese trained an army

MAP 26.2 ASIA IN 1914 ▶

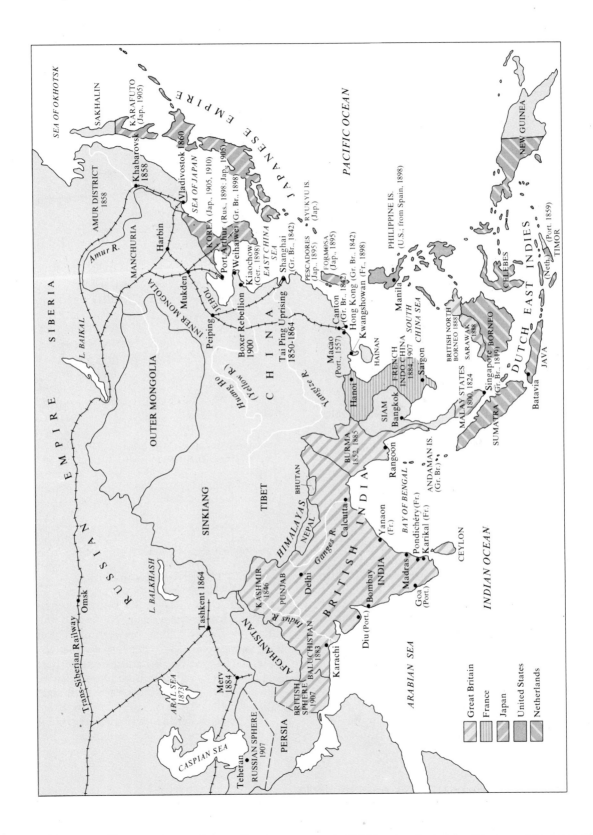

SEA OF OKHOTSK

SAKHALIN

KARAFUTO (Jap. 1905)

AMUR DISTRICT 1858

MANCHURIA

Khabarovsk 1858

Amur R.

Harbin

Vladivostok 1860

SEA OF JAPAN

KOREA (Jap. 1905, 1910)

Port Arthur (Rus. 1898: Jap. 1905)

Weihaiwei (Gr. Br. 1898)

Kiaochow (Ger. 1898)

Shanghai (Gr. Br. 1842)

EAST CHINA SEA

PESCADORES (Jap. 1895)

RYUKYU IS. (Jap.)

FORMOSA (Jap. 1895)

JAPANESE EMPIRE

PACIFIC OCEAN

NEW GUINEA

PHILIPPINE IS. (U.S.: from Spain. 1898)

Manila

DUTCH EAST INDIES

CELEBES

TIMOR (Port. 1859) (Neth.)

SIBERIA

RUSSIAN EMPIRE

Omsk

L. BAIKAL

L. BALKHASH

OUTER MONGOLIA

INNER MONGOLIA

JEHOL

Peiping

Mukden

Boxer Rebellion 1900

CHINA

Hwang Ho (Yellow R.)

Tai Ping Uprising 1850-1864

Yangtze R.

Canton (Gr. Br. 1842)

Hong Kong (Gr. Br. 1842)

Kwangshowan (Fr. 1898)

Macao (Port. 1557)

HAINAN

SOUTH CHINA SEA

FRENCH INDO-CHINA 1884-1907

Saigon

BRITISH NORTH BORNEO 1888

SARAWAK 1888

BORNEO

Singapore (Gr. Br. 1819)

JAVA

Batavia

SUMATRA

Trans-Siberian Railway

Tashkent 1864

ARAL SEA (1873)

Merv 1884

AFGHANISTAN

BALUCHISTAN

BRITISH SPHERE 1907

PERSIA

Teheran

RUSSIAN SPHERE 1907

CASPIAN SEA

SINKIANG

TIBET

HIMALAYAS

BHUTAN

NEPAL

KASHMIR 1846

PUNJAB

Indus R.

Delhi

Ganges R.

BRITISH INDIA

Karachi

Diu (Port.)

Bombay

INDIA

Goa (Port.)

Madras

Calcutta

Yanaon (Fr.)

Pondichéry (Fr.)

Karikal (Fr.)

CEYLON

BAY OF BENGAL

BURMA 1852, 1885

Rangoon

ANDAMAN IS. (Gr. Br.)

SIAM

Bangkok

Hanoi

MALAY STATES 1800, 1824

ARABIAN SEA

INDIAN OCEAN

Great Britain

France

Japan

United States

Netherlands

along the lines of the German and French. In place of the traditional economy, they introduced modern industry and economic competition.

By 1895 an aggressively imperialistic Japan had won a war with China over Korea. The intervention of the Great Powers, which forced the Japanese to return some of the spoils of victory, infuriated them, especially when the Europeans annexed cities from the defeated Chinese. Finally, in 1904, conflict over influence in Manchuria brought Japan and Russia to war, a war in which the Western power was defeated.

If Japan could fuse people together by nationalism and strong leadership and defeat the West, then other Asians believed they could do so, too. Anti-Western movements formed in China, Indochina, India, the Middle East, and among the Indians in South Africa.

India

Unlike the Chinese and Japanese, the peoples of India lost all semblance of independence after the Sepoy Mutiny. This popular uprising had combined with mutinies of sepoy troops and revolts of Hindu and Muslim chiefs for privileges the English had canceled. British losses were small, but a number of atrocities, including the massacre of about 200 women and children at Cawnpore, embittered the British against the Indians. The last of the Mogul rulers was deposed and exiled by the British for his part in the uprising. Parliament then passed the Government of India Act, which took control of India away from the East India Company (which had dominated India by indirect means), and began to rule it directly.

The British created an Indian civil service. At first, it was entirely white, its officials confident of their superiority to anyone or anything Indian. Later an elite of Indians educated in English and trained in administration and military tactics became part of the

JAPAN'S FIRST RAILROAD, 1872 With the Meiji Restoration of 1868, Japan launched a program of rapid Westernization. In 1895, it demonstrated that it had mastered the imperialists' power politics as well. In that year, Japan successfully waged war with China, to be blocked by the European powers, and in 1905, Japan defeated Russia. This success was a message to the victims of imperialism that Europe was not invincible. (Historical Pictures Service, Inc., Chicago)

civil service. It ruled over 300 million Indians of several languages, religions, races, and cultures, all the people of the territories that today are called India, Pakistan, and Bangladesh. In many areas Britain governed these peoples through the jurisdiction of native Indian princes, but in others a powerful state with a single system of law, administration, and language was created with little regard for the diversity of peoples that were ruled. They were so diverse that they undoubtedly could never have been fused into a nation without the impact of British imperialism. Britain made India into a nation by giving the subcontinent some political unity, an English-educated elite, and a focus for their discontent—Indians had in common their resentment of the Britons.

The British built a modern railroad and communications system and developed agriculture and industry to meet the needs of the world market. The railroad with its links to areas of food surplus reduced the incidence and impact of local famines, which had plagued India's history. British rule stopped the constant wars and disorder that had been part of the subcontinent's history, but resistance to the British replaced internal wars. Many people believed that the masses of Indians did not benefit from economic progress because an increase in population matched the increase in food. Rather than starvation for some, malnutrition for all became the reality of Indian life.

The elitism and racism that excluded the Indian elite from British clubs, hotels, social gatherings, and the top government positions alienated the leaders that British rule had created. Educated Indians, demanding equality and self-government, created the Hindu Indian National Congress in the 1880s. This organization was not Indian (only Hindu), not national (only Hindu upper class), and not a congress (because it had no representative authority). Despite its narrow membership, after World War II this group would free India. After the Russo-Japanese War, radicals among the Congress party demanded independence, though moderates would have been content with home rule. By 1912 the Muslims had founded a Muslim League. As the elite found some unity and grounds for cooperation, the masses continued to be divided by religion, class, and community differences.

The First World War would bring about greater solidarity among Indians, who were united in their opposition to British rule. In 1919 the British granted a Legislative Assembly to India representing almost one million of the 247 million in the subcontinent. An elaborate scheme allotted representation by groups (that is, to non-Muslims, Muslims, Europeans, Anglo-Indians) and by economic and social functions (that is, rural and urban, university, landholding, and commercial). Some powers were granted to this assembly, but many were reserved to the civil service. At the very moment that the reforms were granted, agitation and unrest became the most bitter. At Amritsar in Punjab, a British officer commanded his Gurkha troops to fire until their ammunition was exhausted, in the hope of terrorizing protesting Indians—379 died and 1,200 were wounded. The Amritsar Massacre of 1919 was a powerful stimulant to Indian nationalism.

Out of this maelstrom, Mohandas K. Gandhi (1869–1948) emerged as a gentle, but nonetheless revolutionary leader. His doctrine of noncooperation was based on a belief that the power of love and purity would ultimately overthrow the British *raj* (rule). Gandhi called on all Indians to give up privileges allotted by the British and resign their positions, to boycott British schools, and finally to boycott all foreign goods. Gandhi and his followers were willing to give up the privileges that an English education and employment in the civil service gave them. They were also willing to sacrifice the higher standard of living that an industrial economy could bring to India or that employment in such a capitalistic economy could bring to them personally.

Thus, Gandhi launched a campaign of civil disobedience—the peaceful refusal to acknowledge British courts, taxes, or administration. A Hindu himself, Gandhi worked with the Muslims, refusing to accept ancient hatreds that had alienated peoples of the subcontinent. When imprisoned, Gandhi and his followers fasted. This act forced British physicians to keep them alive, or else they would be adding to the martyrs of Amritsar. Gandhi, and India, had found the way to defeat British imperialism.

Southeast Asia

Most of Asia was either annexed or dominated by the Europeans. In Southeast Asia, the lands bordering China were separated and claimed by Europeans. The French warred in China from 1883 to 1885 to claim Indochina. The war led to the fall of the government of the imperialist Jules Ferry (see page 594), but France annexed the territory nonetheless. Indochina was a prosperous country, but of little benefit to the French because it traded mostly with Asia and very little with France. French expansion might have continued into Siam, just as the British might have expanded from their base in Burma. But Siam (Thailand) was fortunate in being situated between the colonies of the two Great Powers. It remained an area of conflict between them until the Entente Cordiale of 1904, when European politics dominated colonial interests. Britain's claims to the lands that are today Malaya and Singapore were recognized by the French in exchange for a province of Siam. Thus, Siam, like Turkey in the Middle East, was able to play the Great Powers off against one another and preserve some territorial integrity. Siam's history belied the claim of the imperialists that European rule improved the economies of backward countries, because Siam's prosperity increased much more than that of Burma or most of Indochina.

Elsewhere in Southeast Asia the dominance of Britain and France was challenged by the United States and Germany. During the Spanish-American War, the United States took the opportunity to seize and annex the Philippines. Once taken, the islands proved difficult to pacify. Germany, the United States, Britain, and France laid claim to islands in the South Pacific on which they built naval stations, symbols of their nations' presence in the Far East. And, all the while, the Netherlands maintained their holdings in the East Indies (Indonesia), the wealthy remnant of their once-great seventeenth-century empire.

Central Asia

The other border territories of China fell to the imperialists, bringing them into conflict as much with one another as with the weak Chinese dynasty. As the Japanese obtained Korea, the Russians moved into Port Arthur. Furthermore, the Russians moved south into Central Asia, dominating Mongolia and threatening Tibet and Afghanistan. In fact, of the three areas of Russian expansion in the last decades of the nineteenth century (southeastern Europe, Central Asia, and the Far East), two threatened territories that had once acknowledged Chinese sovereignty. All three brought Russia into conflict with a strong opponent: Russia and Japan went to war over Korea and Manchuria; Russia and Austria-Hungary as well as Germany fought over the Balkans and Turkish territory; and Russia and Britain opposed one another in Central Asia.

Central Asia was an area of steady conflict between Britain and Russia. This situation lasted until European alliances made the British willing to compromise, and the defeat of Russia in the Russo-Japanese War calmed Russian ambitions.

Russia's moves south into Afghanistan and into Persia (Iran) alerted the British to the potential threat to their holdings in India. After 1889, Britain and Russia vied in loaning money to the shah of Persia to build a railroad to Teheran. The Russians, were then borrowing money from the French, nonetheless were creating a dependency in Persia by proffering capital. The British took steps to stop the Russians, whose designs on the Persian Gulf to obtain a warm-water port brought them very near India. In 1878–81 and again in 1884–85, British and Russian troops were in Afghanistan.

During the Boer War the Russians moved into Persia and Tibet, as well as into Afghanistan. In 1904 the British moved on Tibet on the pretext that the Dalai Lama's tutor was negotiating special trade arrangements with the Russians. In the 1906–1908 negotiations between Russia and Britain but not Tibet's nominal suzerain, China, both powers agreed to stay out of Tibet. The Russians promised not to interfere with Britain's puppet, the ruler of Afghanistan. And Persia was divided into three zones: one in the north for the Russians, a smaller zone in the south for the British, and a neutral zone separating them.

This resolution of Central Asian difficulties made possible the British and Russian alliance in Europe, but it also had tremendous impact on Persia. The Persian shah, backed by the Russians, fought a civil war with the Nationalists, an elite of his own people, throughout the period from 1905 to 1925. The shah was deposed in 1909 for granting many favors to the Europeans, particularly the Russians, who dominated the northern portion of his country. Persia gained neither the precarious independence of Siam, nor the stability of Egypt under the imperialists. Torn by the conflicting interests of Britain and Russia, the situation in Persia was further complicated after World War I when its vast reserves of oil became valuable to the Great Powers. In the 1920s the new shah, Riza Khan of the Pahlavi family, called in the Americans rather than the British. He decided to trust foreigners whose interests seemed only economic, rather than both economic and geopolitical.

The Turkish Empire

Throughout the nineteenth century, Turkey and the Ottoman Empire were another arena of combat for Europeans. The Turks owned Balkan territories, which one after another became independent nations. The Russians pressured the Turks because they wanted a warm-water port and access to the Mediterranean. Also, the Russians liked to pose as the defenders of Orthodox Christians. The British tended to back the Turks in order to restrain the Russians and keep them away from the

Mediterranean, which the British regarded as their special sphere of influence. This was British policy in the Crimean War, and it continued once they were committed in the Suez Canal.

The development of Slavic nationalism and Austrian interest in the Balkans altered the picture somewhat. Attempts to reform the Ottoman Empire, westernize it, and give some autonomy to Slavic peoples aroused Turkish traditionalism. The new sultan, Abdul Hamid II (1876–1909), showed himself as harsh and autocratic as any Ottoman ruler before him. In 1876, having defeated the Serbs, he ordered the mass murder of some 12,000 Christian Bulgarians, which shocked all Europe.

British policy shifted abruptly toward intervention, but the Russians declared war and handed the Turks a treaty (the Treaty of San Stefano) so favorable to themselves that the Austrians immediately called an international conference in Berlin. There Bismarck, playing the "honest broker," redressed the balance of power in favor of Austria and Britain to avoid war in Europe. Britain, indicating that its true interests were in Egypt, and the Suez Canal, and the route to India, obtained Cyprus from Turkey.

At the turn of the twentieth century, Anglo-Russian rivalry over the "sick man of Europe" (as Turkey was called to indicate the Great Powers sitting around the deathbed waiting for their inheritance) was increasingly overshadowed by Anglo-German rivalry. The origins of the conflict seemed quite innocent, certainly not political. A group of German financiers proposed a railroad from central Turkey to Baghdad, with a connection down the Euphrates River to Basra and the Persian Gulf. A railroad already existed from Berlin through the Balkans to Constantinople and central Turkey. Because the railroad would open Turkey and Turkish dependencies to the world market, the Turkish government was enthusiastic and offered to subsidize the road by guaranteeing the bonds and profits to the syndicate. At the end of ninety-nine years the ownership would fall to the Turks. This was not at all an unusual practice; railroads had been built in China this way, and the Suez and Panama canals were similarly financed. The German backers of the railroad offered British and French investment groups each a 25 percent share, with 25 percent control going to the Turks; they retained the final quarter for themselves as entrepreneurs.

The British government refused to allow their citizens to invest. Politics dominated economics, and the British were afraid of German ascendancy in an area so close to both India and the Suez Canal. This action, together with German naval expansion, became a grievance between Germany and Britain. In World War I the Turks joined with the Germans, partly due to German influence over a generation of the Turkish elite and partly due to fear of Russian presence in the Caucasus and the Black Sea areas.

Throughout World War I the Allies (Britain, France, and Russia, then Italy and Greece) secretly negotiated the division of the Turkish empire. Britain sponsored Arab independence movements in the Arabian Peninsula and in the territories that are today Iraq, Syria, Lebanon, Jordan, and Israel in the hope of weakening the Turkish war effort through internal dissension. In the Balfour Declaration the British also promised the Zionists a homeland for the Jews in Palestine to gain their support against the Germans.

When the war was over the Turks, led by Kemal Atatürk, refused to accept the dismemberment of the Turkish-speaking territory, although they did accept the loss of the Arab lands and the Dodecanese Islands. The Turks drove the Allies out, declared a republic, and moved the capital to Ankara, far away from the Europeanized city of Constantinople (Istanbul). Turkey, which became a secular state, was no longer the spiritual leader of millions of Muslims. Atatürk (1923–1938) became president and ordered the end of many religious customs, such as veils for women, harems, and polygamy. European clothing style, education,

and ideas flourished in the new republic. The old conflict between those Turks who saw their country's future as a modern nation-state and those who wanted to preserve traditional Turkish leadership of a union of Muslims was resolved by war and revolution in favor of modern nationalism.

The developing Arab consciousness of a national identity did not mean that the Arabs desired political unity. Several forces around the time of the First World War fostered the desire for national self-determination, particularly the passions and politics of the war. But national consciousness and religious identity were often at cross-purposes, as they had been in Egypt and the Sudan and would be in many areas facing the impact of the West. After the war, the British schemed for a while to replace Turkish spiritual leadership over the world of Islam (which stretched from the Atlantic to Indonesia and the Philippines) with the caliph of Hejaz, their puppet, whose sons Britain made the princes of Iraq and Trans-Jordan. The Arab chiefs appreciated British aid against the Turks, but they deeply resented British intervention in their spiritual and local political affairs. Abdul Aziz ibn Saud (1932–1953), the Arab leader of a puritanical Muslim sect (the Wahabis), invaded Hejaz. He threw out the British puppet, and proclaimed himself the king of Arabia.

The conflict between the Great Powers did not diminish when oil, as well as strategic location, became a reason for their involvement in the area. And Europeans no longer had a free hand, because they faced the opposition of a new nationalism among the peoples of the Middle East. This nationalism, once encouraged against the Turks, could not be controlled when the Turks ceased to be a power. As nationalism developed, it often took a religious form, as the British learned from the Muslim movement in India and the Muslim-

MAP 26.3   THE MIDDLE EAST, POST–WORLD WAR I ▶

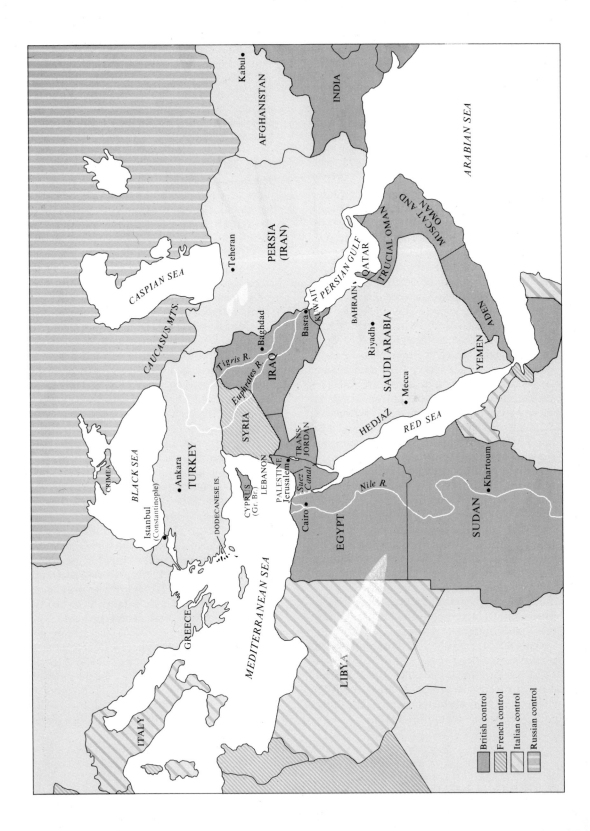

AFGHANISTAN

• Kabul

INDIA

ARABIAN SEA

PERSIA
(IRAN)

• Teheran

CASPIAN SEA

CAUCASUS MTS.

OMAN

MUSCAT AND

TRUCIAL OMAN

QATAR

PERSIAN GULF

KUWAIT

BAHRAIN

Basra •

Tigris R.

• Baghdad

IRAQ

Euphrates R.

SAUDI ARABIA

Riyadh •

• Mecca

YEMEN

ADEN

SYRIA

HEDJAZ

RED SEA

TRANS-
JORDAN

BLACK SEA

• Ankara
TURKEY

CRIMEA

LEBANON

CYPRUS
(Gr. Br.)

PALESTINE
Jerusalem •

*Suez
Canal*

Nile R.

• Khartoum

Cairo •

SUDAN

DODECANESE IS.

Istanbul
(Constantinople) •

EGYPT

GREECE

MEDITERRANEAN SEA

LIBYA

ITALY

	British control
	French control
	Italian control
	Russian control

Zionist conflict in Palestine. Both religious and nationalistic opposition plagued the imperialists between the two World Wars.

LATIN AMERICA

Latin America, like the United States, was conquered and settled by Europeans. In the nineteenth century, Argentina, Brazil, Chile, and other nations had the same types of immigrants as North America—Irish, Germans, Italians, some Spaniards, and eastern Europeans.

Some similarities with American history also are found. Early in the century, in the era of democratic revolution, Latin American colonists rebelled against Spain and gained their independence. They were encouraged by the British and the Yankees, who wanted a free hand for trade—British minister George Canning and U.S. President James Monroe both specifically warned Europeans against attempts at colonization of Latin America.

During the nineteenth century, Britain in particular cooperated commercially with local merchants. English banking houses financed Latin American commercial activity, established offices in port towns, and worked with English consuls to formulate treaties favorable to English merchants. Until the end of the century, England and, to a lesser degree, France dominated the business in the area. Much as they had invested heavily in North America, the English owned Argentine railroads, Brazilian gasworks, and steamships. Latin American farmers and merchants traded Argentine wheat and beef to feed Manchester's English workers, and Chilean mines and Peruvian guano islands supplied materials for Europe's munitions and fertilizers.

Was this heavy European investment in Latin America the same as the investment in the United States? Or is all investment abroad imperialism and exploitation? Latin America's parallel to American history reveals the problem of European economic dominance.

European cultural dominance also was present throughout the Western Hemisphere. A small, wealthy upper class benefited from a connection with Europe; they also imitated Europe. In the Amazon regions at Manaus, rich South Americans built an ornate opera house resembling Milan's La Scala from profits on rubber farms worked by enslaved Indians; wealthy Americans lived like the British gentry, using profits of cotton slavery. In Buenos Aires, Rio de Janeiro, and Santiago, merchants discussed the latest European intellectual fad. Upper-class South and North Americans sent their children to Europe to school.

The wealthy classes depended on Europe for more than culture: they especially depended on Europe for trade. They became indebted to Europeans for funds to support their governments and to build their railroads. The Europeans, for their part, were content to gain the profits from commerce without direct colonization. When the rules of free trade were violated, European vessels might blockade harbors or seize customs houses. But unlike the British in Egypt, Europeans usually withdrew their troops or ships as soon as they had enforced their will.

An exception to this general policy of nonintervention was Napoleon III's attempt to conquer Mexico and install an Austrian archduke to a bogus throne. The Mexicans, led by Benito Juárez (1806–1872), resisted the French invasion. Napoleon thought better of his dreams of easy glory and withdrew French troops. The Mexicans captured and executed Maximilian, the archduke-emperor.

Although Latin Americans were sheltered from European imperialism by the protection of Britain and the United States, they had no outside protection against the aggressions of the United States. Its quick victory in the Spanish-American War of 1898 signaled a new assertiveness in U.S. foreign policy, but it was not a new policy in Latin America. Its growing economic power allowed the United States to compete successfully with Britain in the Caribbean area as well as in South America. After

EDOUARD MANET (1832–1883): THE DEATH OF EMPEROR MAXIMILIAN Napoleon III, ruler of France, dabbled in Mexican politics and placed the Archduke of Austria on the Mexican throne. But an uprising of Mexicans led by Benito Juárez resisted French troops. The tragic, would-be emperor was executed. (Courtesy Museum of Fine Arts, Boston)

the war, the United States occupied Cuba and annexed Puerto Rico; it also restated the Monroe Doctrine, which prohibited colonization of the Americas by foreign nations, but did not inhibit expansionism by the United States. In the Roosevelt Corollary (1904) to the Monroe Doctrine, the United States announced that Europeans could not intervene in the Western Hemisphere to protect their citizens and business interests.

Americans organized the secession of Panama from Colombia in 1903 in order to build an interoceanic canal. For the next three decades the United States intervened repeatedly in the Caribbean, sending Marines to occupy the Dominican Republic, Haiti, Nicaragua, and the Mexican port of Veracruz. Seizing customs revenues for payment of debts and threatening Latin American governments, American "gunboat diplomacy" replaced English and French commercial power in northern Latin America. Like the British before them, the Americans used force while at the same time articulating a policy of free competition for trade and commerce, of open doors around the world including Latin America.

In many ways, American behavior resembled European imperialism. Like the Germans and Japanese who acquired bases in China, the Americans took Guantánamo Bay in Cuba, Fonseca in Nicaragua, and the Canal Zone in Panama, which was leased in perpetuity at first. The Americans, like the Europeans, invested so heavily in underdeveloped areas that they frequently controlled governments and ruling elites. In 1925, 43 percent of all American foreign investment went to Latin America, 27 percent to Canada, 22 percent to Europe (at a time when Americans were underwriting German recovery from the First World War), and 8 percent to all of Asia and Africa. The United States practiced "dollar diplomacy" just as the Europeans had in Morocco, Tunis, Egypt, Persia, Turkey, and China. The United States put the customs of Haiti (1915) and Santo Domingo (1904, 1916–1924) into receivership, just as the British and French did Egyptian customs. In Central America the Americans controlled the governments as puppet or client states, just as the Europeans had done in other parts of the world. And in the twentieth century, American relations with Mexico under the presidency of Porfirio Díaz (1876–1880, 1884–1911) were very similar to German and British controls over the Turks.

The presence of oil in Mexico and the attractiveness of railroads, mining, and other industries exercised an irresistible attraction to American capitalists. The 1911 revolution in Mexico was led by Emiliano Zapata, Victoriano Huerta, and Francisco (Pancho) Villa. Zapata aimed at division of the land for the good of the peasantry; Huerta, who was encouraged by the British, hoped to strengthen industry, with its concomitant foreign investment; and "Pancho" Villa angered the United States by killing several American engineers and carrying on a raid across the frontier. At that time, 1916, President Woodrow Wilson, who was advocating peaceful negotiation of differences among the warring European states, ordered American troops to pursue Villa.

The troubled relations between the United States and Latin America continued after World War I, indeed to the present day—a legacy of the distrust that developed from imperialism in the nineteenth and early twentieth centuries. This legacy is a bitter one because the United States, like Great Britain, paid tribute to human rights and to national self-determination. American and British arguments for free trade sounded suspiciously like defenses of their industrial and economic superiority and seemed calculated to maintain Latin American backwardness to ensure a source of raw materials for the West.

THE LEGACY OF IMPERIALISM

Almost a century after the rapid division of the world among the European and American powers and decades after the decolonization of most of the world, the results of imperialism persist. One result was the rapid spread of Western institutions and thought to millions of people. This Western expansion was religious, social, political, and economic; it affected institutions, customs, and beliefs. Westerners often destroyed local institutions, societies, and economies. As European trade, technology, and governments made demands on non-European labor, resources, culture, and institutions, confrontation and adaptation were inevitable. For better or for worse, "Westernization" of much of the world has occurred. Non-Europeans, reacting to their contacts

CHRONOLOGY 26.1   EXPANSION OF WESTERN DOMINANCE

1853	Commodore Perry with U.S. naval forces opens Japan to trade
1854–1856	The Crimean War
1857	The Sepoy Mutiny—Britain replaces the East India Company and governs India through a viceroy
1867	Mexicans led by Juárez execute Emperor Maximilian
1868	The Meiji Restoration in Japan
1874–1877	Stanley sets up posts in the Congo for Leopold II of Belgium
1878–1881	British and Russian troops occupy Afghanistan
1881	The French take control of Tunisia
1882	Britain occupies Egypt
1883–1885	The French fight the Chinese to claim Indochina
1886	The British establish a protectorate in Burma; Germany controls East Africa
1894–1895	Sino-Japanese War—the British, Russians, and French intervene to take away Japan's gains
1896	Ethiopians defeat Italian invaders
1898	The Spanish-American War—the United States annexes the Philippines and Puerto Rico
1899–1902	The Boer War
1900	The Boxers rebel against foreign presence in China
1904–1905	Russo-Japanese War—the Japanese defeat the Russians
1911–1912	The Manchu Dynasty is overthrown and a republic formed; Dr. Sun Yat-sen becomes president; civil war breaks out in China
1919	Britain grants a legislative assembly in India; Gandhi begins a passive resistance movement; the Amritsar Massacre

with the West, developed a sense of nationalism, borrowed the technology of the West, and shaped European ideas and values to their own needs.

Another result of imperialism may have been world war. Once it was assumed that economic competition, especially for colonies, was a cause of World War I. Now many historians would disagree, pointing out that the main areas of colonial conflict were resolved by diplomats several years before the war broke out over a Balkan question (and the Balkan nations, though economically underdeveloped, were not colonies). But undoubtedly, tensions and suspicions between the Great Powers deepened over issues of imperialism.

Imperialism has also left a legacy of deep animosity between peoples. The economic arguments that were advanced for imperial expansion—the need for raw materials, markets, and a place for investment—do not hold up. Most of the areas that were claimed by Europeans and Americans were not profitable sources of raw materials or wealthy enough to be good markets. Europeans and Americans primarily traded with and invested in one another. Perhaps individual businesses made profits, but certainly most colonies proved unprofitable for the Western taxpayers. Most colonies did not attract surplus population from a Western country—America tended to draw most of the European emigration. Aggressive nationalism, including the struggle for diplomatic and military gains far away from dangerous fields of conflict in Europe, seems to have been one of the strongest forces behind imperial activity.

Though most nations have political independence, the problems of economic, political, and cultural dominance of the vast majority of the world remain today. Most of the world is still poor and suffers from a lack of capital, skilled leaders, and stable governments. Parts of the world are strategic to the Great Powers or at least are areas of ideological conflict.

One of the most powerful ideological forces in the developing world today is the anti-imperialism of Leninism, which was first expressed as an analysis of imperialism on the eve of the First World War. Lenin argued that the capitalist nations were unable to maintain their economic and social organization because capitalism had become monopolistic in both production and finance. Monopoly capitalism was condemned to periodic depressions for lack of materials, markets, and capital, he said. Unless the governments of capitalist countries were able to ensure high wages and profits through the exploitation of colonial peoples, working-class revolutions would break out, or influential business people protecting their interests would push their governments to the verge of war. Imperialism or exploitation of other nations was essential to the well-being of capitalism, and was not a choice of their leaders, said Lenin. And at the same time, imperialism greatly speeded up the process of development of, as well as opposition to capitalism among the victims of imperialism in Asia, Africa, and Latin America. Many people in the non-Western world believe that Lenin's analysis explains the poverty of their nations and the rapaciousness of European and American business.

But the world's dependence on European industry and technology was not reduced. The world economy grew out of the Industrial Revolution and spread until every part of the world has been entangled in it. The dependence of all nations and peoples on forces beyond the control of any one country—for food, for manufactured goods, for energy, for technology—is greater than ever before. This dependence, complicated by the legacy of bitterness and distrust, is at the heart of many problems today.

Imperialism has been a source of great bitterness not only for its economic exploitation, but for the racism and callous disregard of other cultures that it fostered. And now, everywhere that Europeans and Americans would like to deal in the areas of economics and politics, they find nations, not disparate peoples, groups, or individuals—nations that imperialism called into being or at least into awareness of nationhood.

Notes

1. Lord Northbrook to Ripon, 13 Feb. 1884, quoted in R. E. Robinson, et al., *Africa and the Victorians: The Official Mind of Imperialism* (New York: Doubleday, 1968), p. 135.

Suggested Reading

Brodie Fawn, *Devil Drives: A Life of Sir Richard Burton* (1967). A fine biography of the great explorer.

Brunschwig, Henri, *French Colonialism: 1871–1914. Myths and Realities* (tr. 1964). His general thesis is similar to Robinson, Gallagher, and Denny; the best book on French imperialism.

Henderson, W. O., *Studies in German Colonial History* (1963). Several interesting essays on this topic, which is difficult to research in English sources.

Hobson, J. A., *Imperialism, A Study* (1902). This book and those of Luxemburg and Lenin (see below) are highly controversial and influential theoretical analyses.

Jeal, Jim, *Livingstone* (1974). A very readable biography of a fascinating life, with good background on Africa.

Langer, William, *European Alliances and Alignments, 1871–1890* and *Diplomacy of Imperialism, 1890–1902*, 2 vols. (1950). Indispensable sources for information about imperialism with a perspective of diplomatic history.

Lenin, V. I., *Imperialism: The Highest Stage in Capitalism* (1917).

Luxemburg, Rosa, *The Accumulation of Capital* (tr. 1963).

May, Ernest, *Imperial Democracy* (1961). American expansionism discussed more thoroughly and less controversially than is usual.

Porter, Bernard, *The Lion's Share, A Short History of British Imperialism, 1850–1970* (1975). A good survey history.

Robinson, R. E., John Gallagher, and Alice Denny, *Africa and the Victorians: The Official Mind of Imperialism* (1961). An essential book for this fascinating subject; well-written and controversial.

Thornton, A. P., *The Imperial Idea and Its Enemies: A Study in British Power* (1959). An interesting study of the ideas and policies of British imperialism.

Review Questions

1. Why did imperialism grow after 1880? What are the rationalizations for European expansion that were usually offered at the end of the nineteenth century?

2. Why did Bismarck believe Germany to be a satiated power and then change his mind?

3. How did imperialism fit in with the European alliance system? How did it cause it? How did imperialism undermine European stability under the alliance system?

4. What were the specific reasons for expansion of each of the Great Powers: Russia, Britain, France, Germany, and Italy?

5. Why were Japan and China able to withstand imperialist expansion?

6. Why was Africa divided up in such a brief time?

7. How did imperialism threaten world peace in the early twentieth century?

8. Why did England and France (which seemed on the verge of war in 1898) make peace and form an alliance?

9. How was Turkey able to maintain itself in the nineteenth century against the encroachments of Europeans? Why did it fail to do so in the twentieth century?

10. What problems in the Middle East and the Central Asia appear to have been resolved because Russia was defeated in World War I?

11. What were the obstacles preventing Indian independence?

CHAPTER 27

The Enlightenment
Challenged: The Problem
of Irrationalism

SCIENCE AS MODEL AND PROMISE

POSITIVISM

EVOLUTION

IRRATIONALISM

NIETZSCHE

BERGSON

SOREL

FREUD: A NEW VIEW OF HUMAN NATURE

SOCIAL THOUGHT: CONFRONTING THE IRRATIONAL AND THE COMPLEXITIES OF MODERN SOCIETY

DURKHEIM

PARETO

WEBER

ALTERING THE NEWTONIAN UNIVERSE

MOST NINETEENTH-CENTURY thinkers carried forward the spirit of the Enlightenment, particularly in its emphasis on science and its concern for individual liberty and social reform. In the tradition of the philosophes, nineteenth-century thinkers regarded science as humanity's greatest achievement and identified progress with the advance of science. The spread of parliamentary government and the extension of education along with the many advances in science and technology seemed to confirm the hopes of the philosophes in humanity's future progress.

But at the same time, the Enlightenment tradition was being undermined. In the early nineteenth century, the romantics revolted against the rational-scientific spirit of the Enlightenment. In the closing decades of the century the Enlightenment tradition was challenged by those who glorified violence and saw conflict between individuals and between nations as a law of nature. A number of thinkers, rejecting the Enlightenment view of people as fundamentally rational, held that subconscious drives and impulses govern human behavior more than reason. These thinkers urged celebrating and glorifying the irrational, which they regarded as the true essence of human beings.

Others, heirs to the rational tradition of the Enlightenment, sought to protect civilization from dangerous outbreaks of the irrational. Approaching the problem of the irrational in a scientific manner, they tried to resolve it in the interests of civilization. They sought to enlarge the tradition of the Enlightenment in order to encompass irrationalism, whose power the Enlightenment view of human nature had underestimated.

There was a growing conviction that reason was a puny instrument in comparison to the volcanic strength of nonrational impulses, that these impulses pushed people toward evil and made political life precarious, and that the nonrational did not bend very much to education. European thought was in crisis, a crisis accentuated by the increasing complexities of modern society, the breakdown of traditional Christian values, and the growing sense of the meaninglessness of life.

At the end of the nineteenth century an increasing number of intellectuals expressed disillusionment with the rational-scientific tradition and with bourgeois values. The Enlightenment tradition was in disarray, although few thinkers realized it. In the twentieth century, disoriented and disillusioned people would search for new certainties and new values in political ideologies that openly rejected reason, lauded violence, and scorned the inviolability of the human person. These currents began to form at the end of the nineteenth century, but World War I brought them together into a tidal wave that nearly obliterated reason and freedom.

SCIENCE AS MODEL AND PROMISE

Franklin L. Baumer refers to the core element of nineteenth-century thought as the New Enlightenment because "of its similarity, in mood and general intent, if not always in doctrine, to the Old Enlightenment of the eighteenth century."[1] The chief proponents of the New Enlightenment were liberals, socialists, scientists, positivists, and British utilitarians.

Positivism

In the nineteenth century, science and technology continued to make astonishing strides, leading many Westerners to believe that they were living in an age of progress and that a golden age was on the horizon. Viewing science as the highest achievement of the mind, many intellectuals sought to apply the scientific method to other areas of thought. They believed that this method was a reliable way to approach all problems. They insisted that history could be studied scientifically, and society reorganized in accordance with scientific laws of social development. Marxism was one attempt to fashion a science of society; another attempt was positivism.

Positivists held that whereas people's knowledge of nature was vastly expanding, their understanding of society was deficient. This lack could be remedied by applying a strict empirical approach to the study of society. The philosopher must proceed like a scientist, carefully assembling and classifying data and formulating general rules that demonstrate regularities in the social experience. Such knowledge based on concrete facts would provide the social planner with useful insights. Positivists rejected metaphysics, which in the tradition of Plato tried to discover ultimate principles through reason alone, rather than through observation of the empirical world. For the positivist, any effort to go beyond the realm of experience to a deeper reality would be a mistaken and fruitless endeavor. The positivist restricted human knowledge only to what could be experienced, and saw the method of science as the only valid approach to knowledge.

A leading figure in the emergence of positivism was Auguste Comte (1798–1857), an engineer with a thorough scientific training. Comte served as secretary to Saint-Simon (see page 553) until their association, punctuated by frequent quarrels, terminated in 1824. But much of Saint-Simon's thought found its way into Comte's philosophy. Like Saint-Simon (and Marx), Comte called for a purely scientific approach to history and society. Only by a proper understanding of the laws governing human affairs, said Comte, could society, which was in a state of intellectual anarchy, be rationally reorganized. Comte called his system *positivism* because it rested on knowledge derived from observed facts and was empirically verifiable. Like others of his generation, Comte believed that scientific laws underlay human affairs and that they were discoverable through the methods of the geologist and the chemist—that is, by the recording and systematizing of observable data. "I shall bring factual proof," he said, "that there are just as definite laws for the development of the human race as there are for the fall of a stone."[2]

One of the laws that Comte believed he had discovered was the "law of the three stages." Comte held that the human mind had progressed through three broad historical stages—the theological, the metaphysical, and the scientific. In the theological stage, the most primitive, the mind found a supernatural explanation for the origins and purpose of things, and society was ruled by priests. In the metaphysical stage, which included the Enlightenment, the mind tried to explain things through abstractions—"nature," "equality," "natural rights," "popular sovereignty"—that rested on hope and belief rather than on empirical investigation. The metaphysical stage was a transitional period between the infantile theological stage and the highest stage of society, the scientific or positive stage. In this culminating stage the mind breaks with all illusions inherited from the past, formulates laws based on careful observation of the empirical world, and reconstructs society in accordance with these laws. People remove all mystery from nature and base their social legislation on laws of society similar to the laws of nature discovered by Newton.

Because Comte advocated a scientific study of society he is regarded as a principal founder of sociology, but he influenced other fields as well. Comte's effort inspired many thinkers to collect and analyze critically all data pertaining to social phenomena. An English historian, Henry T. Buckle (1821–1862), for example, tried to make the study of civilization an exact science. Buckle saw human culture as a product of climate, soil, and food, so that the achievements of western Europe were due to a favorable environment, the backwardness of Russia and Africa to an unfavorable one. Buckle believed that rigorous laws operated in the social world and that they could be uncovered best through statistical studies.

Although Comte attacked the philosophes for delving into abstractions instead of fashioning laws based on empirical knowledge, he was also influenced by the spirit of eighteenth-century philosophy. Like the philosophes he valued science, criticized supernatural religion, and believed in progress.

Evolution

Science advanced relentlessly in the nineteenth century. Perhaps the most important scientific advance was the theory of evolution suggested by Charles Darwin (1809–1882), an English naturalist. Darwin did for biology what Newton had done for physics. By making biology an objective science based on general principles, Darwin initiated an intellectual revolution comparable to the one launched by Copernicus.

During the eighteenth century virtually all thinkers had adhered to the Biblical account of creation contained in Genesis according to which God had instantaneously created the universe and the various species of animal and plant life. God had given every river and mountain and each species of animal and plant a finished and permanent form. All this, it was believed, occurred some six thousand years ago.

Gradually this view was questioned. In 1830–1833 Sir Charles Lyell published his three-volume *Principles of Geology*, which showed that the planet had evolved slowly over many ages. In 1794, Erasmus Darwin, the grandfather of Charles Darwin, published *Zoonomia, or the Laws of Organic Life* which suggested correctly that the earth had existed for millions of years before the appearance of people and that animals experienced modifications that they passed on to their offspring. In the *Origin of Species* (1859) and *The Descent of Man* (1871), Charles Darwin provided massive empirical evidence that the wide variety of animal species was due to a process of development over many millennia, and he supplied a convincing theory that explained how evolution operates.

Darwin adopted the Malthusian idea (see page 551) that the population reproduces faster than the food supply causing a struggle for existence. Not all infant organisms grow to adulthood; not all adult organisms live to old age. The principle of *natural selection* determines which members of the species have a better chance for survival. The offspring of a lion, giraffe, or insect are not exact duplications of their parents. A baby lion might have the potential for being slightly faster or stronger than its parents; a baby giraffe might grow up to have a longer neck than its parents; an insect might have a slightly different color. These small variations gave the organism a crucial advantage in the struggle for food and against natural enemies. The organism favored by nature is more likely to reach maturity, to mate, and to pass on its superior qualities to its offspring, some of which will acquire the advantageous trait to an even greater degree than the parent. Over many generations the favorable characteristic becomes more pronounced and more widespread within the species. Over centuries, natural selection causes the death of old species and the creation of new ones. Very few of the species that dwelt on earth ten million years ago still survive today and many new ones, including human beings, have emerged. People themselves are products of natural selection, evolving from earlier, lower, nonhuman forms of life.

Like Newton's law of universal gravitation, Darwin's theory of evolution had revolutionary consequences in areas other than science. Evolution challenged the traditional religious belief that a fixed number of species was created instantaneously some six thousand years ago. Rather, said Darwin, the various species, including human beings, evolved gradually over millions of years and new species are constantly evolving. This theory challenged traditional Christian beliefs. Could one still believe in the infallibility of Scripture? Was the Bible indeed the Word of God? Darwin's theory touched off a great religious controversy between fundamentalists who defended a literal interpretation of Genesis and advocates of the new biology. In time, religious thinkers tried to reconcile evolution with the Christian view that there was a Creation and that it had a purpose. These Christian thinkers held that God was the creator and the director of the evolutionary processes.

Darwinism ultimately helped to bring to an end the practice of relying on the Bible as an authority in questions of science, completing a trend initiated by Galileo. Darwinism contributed to the waning of religious belief and a growing secular attitude that dismissed or paid scant attention to the Christian view of a universe designed by God and a soul that rises to heaven. For many the conclusion was inescapable. Nature contained no divine design or purpose, and the human species itself was a chance product of impersonal forces. The core principle of Christianity that people were children of God participating in a drama of salvation rested more than ever on faith rather than reason. People now openly talked about the death of God. The knowledge that people are sheer accidents of nature was shocking. Copernicus had deprived people of the comforting belief that earth had been placed in the center of the universe just for them; Darwin deprived people of the privilege of being God's special creation, thereby contributing to the feeling of anxiety that is characteristic of the twentieth century.

Darwin's theories were extended by others beyond the realm in which he had worked. Social thinkers, who recklessly applied Darwin's conclusions to the social order, produced theories that had dangerous consequences for society. Social Darwinists—those who transferred Darwin's scientific theories to social and economic issues—used the terms "struggle for existence" and "survival of the fittest" to buttress economic individualism and political conservatism. Successful businessmen, they said, had demonstrated their fitness to succeed in the competitive world of business. Their success accorded with nature's laws and therefore was beneficial to society; those who lost out in the struggle for existence had demonstrated their unfitness. Using Darwin's model of organisms evolving and changing slowly over tens of thousands of years, conservatives insisted that society too should experience change at an unhurried pace. Instant reforms conflicted with nature's laws and wisdom, and resulted in a deterioration of the social body.

The application of Darwin's biology to the social world where it did not apply also buttressed imperialism, racism, nationalism, and militarism. Social Darwinists insisted nations and races were engaged in a struggle for survival in which only the fittest survive and indeed only the fittest deserve to survive. Karl Pearson, a British professor of mathematics, wrote in *National Life from the Standpoint of Science* (1905):

History shows me only one way, and one way only in which a higher state of civilization has been produced, namely the struggle of race with race, and the survival of the physically and mentally fitter race. . . . The path of progress is strewn with the wrecks of nations; traces are everywhere to be seen of the hecatombs of inferior races, and of victims who found not the narrow way to perfection. Yet these dead people are, in very truth, the stepping stones on which mankind has arisen to the higher intellectual and deeper emotional life of today.[3]

"We are a conquering race," said U.S. Senator Albert J. Beveridge. "We must obey our blood and occupy new markets, and if necessary, new lands."[4] "War is a biological necessity of the first importance,"[5] exclaimed the Prussian General von Bernhardi in *Germany and the Next War* (1911).

Darwinian biology was used to promote the belief in Anglo-Saxon (British and American) and Teutonic (German) racial superiority. The growth of the British Empire, the expansion of the United States to the Pacific, and the extension of German power were all attributed to the racial qualities of these peoples. The domination of other peoples—American Indians, Africans, Asians, Poles—was regarded as the natural right of the superior race. British naturalist Alfred Russel Wallace, who arrived at the theory of evolution independently of Darwin, wrote in 1864:

The intellectual and moral, as well as the physical qualities of the European are superior; the same power and capacities which have made him rise in a few centuries from the condition of the wandering savage . . . to his present state of culture and advancement . . . enable him when in contact with savage man, to conquer in the struggle for existence and to increase at his expense.[6]

Social Darwinists undermined the Enlightenment tradition. Whereas the philosophes emphasized human equality, Social Darwinists divided humanity into racial superiors and inferiors. Whereas the philosophes believed that states would increasingly submit to the rule of law to reduce violent conflicts, Social Darwinists regarded racial and national conflict as a biological necessity, a law of history and a means to progress. In propagating a tooth-and-claw version of human and international relations, Social Darwinists dispensed with the humanitarian and cosmopolitan sentiments of the philosophes and corrupted the image of progress.

The theory of evolution was a great achievement of the rational mind, but in the hands of the Social Darwinists it served to undermine the Enlightenment tradition. Social Darwinist themes promoted territorial aggrandizement and military build-up and led many to welcome World War I. The Social Darwinist notion of the struggle of races for survival became a core doctrine of the Nazi party after World War I and provided the scientific and ethical justification for genocide.

IRRATIONALISM

The Enlightenment legacy was also being assaulted by thinkers who glorified the nonrational character of human nature. Some late-nineteenth-century thinkers challenged the basic premises of the philosophes and their nineteenth-century heirs. They repudiated the Enlightenment conception of human rationality, stressing instead the irrational side of human behavior. For these thinkers it seemed that reason exercised a very limited influence over human conduct; impulses, drives, instincts, all forces below the surface, determined behavior much more than did logical consciousness. Like the romantics, they placed more reliance on feeling and intuition than on reason. They belittled the intellect's attempt to comprehend nature and society, praised outbursts of the irrational, and in some instances exalted violence.

Nietzsche

The principal figure in the "dethronement of reason" and the glorification of the irrational was the German philosopher Friedrich Nietzsche (1844–1900). Nietzsche attacked the accepted views and convictions of his day as a hindrance to a fuller and richer existence for man. He denounced social reform, parliamentary government, and universal suffrage, ridiculed the vision of progress through science, condemned Christian morality, and mocked the liberal belief in man's essential goodness and rationality. Modern bourgeois society, said Nietzsche, was decadent and enfeebled, a victim of the excessive development of the rational faculties at the expense of will and

instinct. Against the liberal-rationalist stress on the intellect, Nietzsche urged recognition of the dark mysterious world of instinctual desires, the true forces of life. Smother the will with excessive intellectualizing and you destroy that spontaneity that sparks cultural creativity and ignites a zest for living. The critical and theoretical outlook destroyed the creative instincts. For man's manifold potential to be realized, he must forego relying on the intellect and nurture again the instinctual roots of human existence.

Christianity, with all its prohibitions, restrictions, and demands to conform, also crushes the human impulse for life, said Nietzsche. Christian morality must be obliterated for it is fit only for the weak, the slave. The triumph of Christianity in the ancient world, said Nietzsche, was a revolution of the meek to inherit the earth from the strong. Christian otherworldliness undermined man's will to control the world; Christian teachings saddled man with guilt, preventing him from expressing his instinctual nature. Christianity has imposed on man an asceticism that is contrary to human nature.

Although the philosophes had rejected Christian doctrines, they had largely retained Christian ethics. Nietzsche, however, did not attack Christianity because it was contrary to reason, as the philosophes had; he attacked Christianity because he said it gave man a sick soul. It was life-denying; it blocked the free and spontaneous exercise of human instincts and made humility and self-abnegation virtues and pride a vice; in short, Chrisianity ruined the spark of life in man. This spark of life, this inner yearning which is man's true essence, must again burn.

"God is dead," proclaimed Nietzsche. God is man's own creation; there are no higher worlds. Christian morality is also dead. The death of God and Christian values can mean the liberation of man, insisted Nietzsche. Man can surmount *nihilism* (the belief that moral and social values have no validity); he can create new values and achieve self-mastery.

FRIEDRICH NIETZSCHE Nietzsche was a classical scholar and philosopher. A bitter critic of Christian morality and bourgeois society, Nietzsche proclaimed that "God is dead" and urged man to create his own values. He wrote of the rise of a new man, the *overman.* Nazism was to distort Nietzsche's philosophy to support the belief in the German master race. (Historical Pictures Service, Inc., Chicago)

He can overcome the deadening uniformity and mediocrity of modern civilization. He can undo democracy and socialism, which have made masters out of cattlelike masses, and the shopkeeper's spirit, which has made man soft and degenerate. European society is without heroic figures; all belong to a vast herd but there are no shepherds. Europe can only be saved by the emergence of a higher type of man, the *superman* or *overman* who would not be held back by egalitarian values, by the rubbish of the equality of man preached by democrats and socialists, by a superficial and petty bourgeois culture. "It is necessary for *higher* man to declare war upon the masses," said Nietzsche, to end "the dominion of *inferior* men." Europe requires "the annihilation of universal suffrage—this is to say, that system by means of which the lowest natures prescribe themselves as a law for higher natures."[7] Europe needs a new breed of rulers, a true aristocracy of masterful men. The superman is a new kind of man who breaks with accepted morality and sets his own standards. He does not repress his instincts but asserts them. He destroys old values and asserts his prerogative as master. Free of Christian guilt he proudly affirms his own being; dispensing with Christian "thou shalt not" he instinctively says "I will." He dares to be himself. Because he is not like other people, traditional definitions of good and evil have no meaning for him. He does not allow his individuality to be stifled. He makes his own values, those that flow from his very being. He knows that life is meaningless but lives it laughingly, instinctively, fully. The masses, cowardly and envious, will condemn the superman as evil; this has always been their way.

The German philosopher Arthur Schopenhauer (1788–1860) had declared that beneath the conscious intellect is the will, a striving, demanding, and imperious force that is the real conductor of human behavior. Schopenhauer sought to repress the will. He urged stifling desires and retreating into quietude in order to escape from life's misfortunes. Nietzsche learned from Schopenhauer to appreciate the unconscious strivings that dominate human behavior, but Nietzsche called for the heroic and joyful assertion of the will in order to redeem life from nothingness.

Supermen are free of all restrictions, rules, and codes of behavior imposed by society. They burst upon the world propelled by that something that urges people to want, take, strike, create, struggle, seek, dominate. Supermen are people of restless energy who enjoy living dangerously, have contempt for meekness and humility, and dismiss humanitarian sentiments. At times Nietzsche declares that supermen, a new breed of nobles, will rule the planet; at other times he states that they will demonstrate their superiority by avoiding public life, ignoring established rules, and refraining from contact with inferiors.

The influence of Nietzsche's philosophy is still a matter of controversy and conjecture. Perhaps better than anyone else, Nietzsche recognized the ills of modern Western civilization and urged confronting these ills without hypocrisy or compromise. But he had no constructive proposals for dealing with the malaise of modern society. No social policy could be derived from his radical individualism. And his vitriolic attack on European institutions and values, immensely appealing to central European intellectuals, helped to erode the rational foundations of Western civilization. Many young people, attracted to Nietzsche's philosophy, welcomed World War I because they thought that it would clear a path to a new heroic age.

The Nazis regarded themselves as embodiments of Nietzsche's supermen. Nietzsche himself who detested German nationalism, militarism, and anti-Semitism, would have rejected Hitler, but his extreme and violent denunciation of Western values and his praise of power provided a breeding ground for violence.

Bergson

Another thinker who reflected the growing irrationalism of the age was Henri Bergson (1859–1941), a French philosopher of Jewish background. Originally attracted to positivism, Bergson turned away from the positivistic claim that science could explain everything and fulfill all human needs. Such an emphasis on the intellect, said Bergson, sacrifices spiritual impulses, imagination, and intuition and reduces the soul to a mere mechanism. The methods of science cannot reveal ultimate reality, Bergson insisted. European civilization must recognize the limitations of scientific rationalism. The method of intuition, whereby the mind strives for an immanent relationship with the object, becoming one with it, can tell us more about reality than the method of analysis employed by science. Entering into the object through an intuitive experience is the avenue to a truth that the calculations and measurements of science cannot obtain. Although not based on scientific procedures, Bergson insisted, the method of intuition is a superior avenue to knowledge. Science is not the only avenue to truth and the mind is not a collection of atoms operating according to mechanical principles. The mind is a stream of consciousness with extraordinary intuitive capacities. Bergson's philosophy pointed away from science toward religious mysticism.

Sorel

Nietzsche grasped that irrational forces constitute the essence of human nature; Bergson held that a nonrational intuition provided knowledge unavailable to the scientific mentality. Georges Sorel (1847–1922), who gave up engineering to follow intellectual pursuits, was a French syndicalist philosopher who showed the political potential of the nonrational. Like Nietzsche, Sorel was disillusioned with contemporary bourgeois society, which he considered decadent, soft, and unheroic. Whereas Nietzsche called for the superman to rescue society from decadence and mediocrity, Sorel placed his hopes in the proletariat whose position made them courageous, virile, and determined.

Sorel wanted the proletariat to destroy the existing order and make the workshop the model of a new society. This, said Sorel, would be accomplished through a *general strike*—a universal work stoppage that would bring down the government and give power to the workers. To Sorel the image of such a strike would stir the soul of the workers and increase their dedication to the cause of revolution.

The general strike had all the power of a great myth, said Sorel. What is important is not that the general strike will actually take place but that its image stirs all the anticapitalist resentments of the workers and inspires them to their revolutionary responsibilities. Sorel understood the extraordinary potency of myth for eliciting total commitment and inciting heroic action. Because they appeal to the imagination and feelings, myths are an effective way of moving the masses to revolt. By believing in the myth of the general strike workers would soar above the moral decadence of bourgeois society and bear the immense sacrifices that their struggle calls for.

Like Marx, Sorel believed that the goals of the worker could not be achieved through peaceful parliamentary means; he too wanted no reconciliation between bourgeois exploiters and oppressed workers. The only recourse for workers was direct action and violence which Sorel regarded as ennobling, heroic, and sublime, a means of restoring grandeur to a flabby world.

Sorel's exaltation of violence and mass action, his condemnation of liberal democracy, and his recognition of the power and political utility of fabricated myths would find concrete expression in the fascist movements after World War I. Sorel heralded the age of mass political movements and myths manufactured by propaganda experts.

SIGMUND FREUD WITH HIS FIANCÉE, MARTHA BERNAYS, 1885 Freud did not believe that human beings were inherently good and reasonable. Instead he found individuals to be driven by subconscious drives and aggressive tendencies. Freud believed, however, that through psychoanalysis, a scientific study of the subconscious, people could understand and control their behavior. (The Granger Collection, New York)

FREUD: A NEW VIEW OF HUMAN NATURE

In many ways Sigmund Freud (1856–1939), an Austrian-Jewish doctor who spent most of his adult life in Vienna, was a child of the Enlightenment. Like the philosophes Freud identified civilization with reason and regarded science as the avenue to knowledge. But unlike the philosophes, Freud focused on the massive power and influence of nonrational drives. Whereas Nietzsche glorified the irrational and approached it with a poet's temperament, Freud recognized its potential danger, sought to comprehend it scientifically, and wanted to regulate it in the interests of civilization. Unlike Nietzsche, Freud did not express contempt for the intellect or belittle the rational, but always sought to salvage respect for reason.

Freud held that people are not fundamentally rational; human behavior is governed primarily by powerful inner forces that are hidden from consciousness. These instinctual strivings and not rational faculties constitute the greater part of the mind. Freud's great achievement was to explore the world of the unconscious with the tools and temperament of a scientist. Freud considered not just the external acts of a person but the inner psychic reality that underlies human behavior. The key to the unconscious mind, said Freud, was the dream.

The *id*, the seat of the instincts, constantly demands gratification, said Freud. Unable to endure tension, it demands the termination of pain, sexual release, the cessation of hunger. When the id is denied an outlet for its instinctual energy, people become frustrated, angry, and unhappy. Its gratification is our highest pleasure. But the full gratification of instinctual demands is inimicable to civilized life.

Freud postulated a terrible conflict between the relentless strivings of our instinctual nature and the requirements of civilization. Civilization, for Freud, requires the renunciation of instinctual gratification and the mastery of animal instincts, a thesis he developed in *Civilization and Its Discontents* (1930). While Freud's thoughts in this work were no doubt influenced by the great tragedy of World War I, the main theme could be traced back to his earlier writings. Human beings derive their highest pleasure from sexual fulfillment, said Freud, but unrestrained sexuality drains off psychic energy needed for creative artistic and intellectual life. Hence society, through the family, the priest, the teacher, and the police, imposes rules and restrictions on our animal nature. But this is immensely painful. People are caught in a tragic bind. The denial of full instinctual gratification demanded by society causes terrible frustration; equally distressing,

the violation of society's rules under the pressure of instinctual needs evokes terrible feelings of guilt. Either way people suffer; civilized life simply entails too much pain for people. It seems that the price we pay for civilization is neurosis. Most people cannot endure the amount of instinctual renunciation that civilization requires. There are times when our elemental human nature rebels against all the restrictions and "thou shalt nots" demanded by society, all the misery and torments imposed by civilization.

"Civilization imposes great sacrifices not only on man's sexuality but also on his aggressivity,"[8] says Freud. People are not good by nature as the philosophes had taught; on the contrary, they are "creatures among whose instinctual endowments is to be reckoned a powerful share of aggressiveness." Their first inclination is not to love their neighbor but to "satisfy their aggressiveness on him, to exploit his capacity for work without compensation, to use him sexually without his consent, to seize his possessions, to humiliate him, to cause him pain, to torture and to kill him."[9] Man is wolf to man, concludes Freud. "Who has the courage to dispute it in the face of all the evidence in his own life and in history?"[10] Civilization "has to use its utmost efforts in order to set limits to man's aggressive instincts," but "in spite of every effort these endeavors of civilization have not so far achieved very much."[11] People find it difficult to do without "the satisfaction of this inclination to aggression."[12] When circumstances are favorable this primitive aggressiveness breaks loose and "reveals man as a savage beast to whom consideration towards his own kind is something alien."[13] For Freud, "the inclination to aggression is an original self-subsisting disposition in man . . . that . . . constitutes the greatest impediment to civilization." Civilization attempts "to combine single human individuals and after that families, then races, peoples and nations into one great unity. . . . But man's natural aggressive instinct, the hostility of each against all and of all against each, opposes this program of civilization."[14]

EARLY MASTERS OF MODERN ART

FIGURE 1   GAUGUIN: SOYEZ AMOUREUSES, VOUS SEREZ HEUREUSES
(Courtesy Museum of Fine Arts, Boston)

Toward the end of the nineteenth century, a small group of artists working in France and Germany began to re-evaluate the meaning and function of art. In the preceding century, art had lost many of its traditional functions. It had ceased to be an important method for recording the way things look because that job had been taken over by the camera. Artists now sought to isolate the special province of art, to define its own particular essence. Painters and sculptors joined other intellectuals in questioning classical standards based on rationalized patterns and generalized ideals. The world view of the 1890s had been so altered by the tumultuous changes of the nineteenth century that the cool, orderly classical figure style and static Renaissance compositions no longer seemed appropriate forms of expression.

Freed from the grip of classical values, artists began to recognize the power and effectiveness of non-Western art. A large number of artifacts and art objects from Asia, Africa, and the Pacific area came into European capitals as souvenirs of nineteenth-century imperialist ventures. Paul Gauguin (1848–1903) saw the beauty of carvings and fabrics made by such technologically backward people as the Marquesas islanders. He also discovered that art did not depend on skilled craftsmanship for its power. Very simple, even primitive means of construction could produce works of great beauty. Like many other intellectuals of his time, Gauguin was attracted to "primitive" people because they seemed uncorrupted by industrial society, closer to the earth, and more in tune with nature. The elemental force of nature, respect for non-European traditions, and the simple, "primitive" technique of woodcarving all appear in Gauguin's *Soyez Amoureuses* (Figure 1).

In 1886 the painter Vincent van Gogh (1853–1890) came from Holland to France, where he produced a revolution in the use of color. He used purer, brighter colors than artists had used before. He also recognized that color, like other formal qualities, could act as a language in and of itself. He believed that the local or "real" color of an object does not necessarily express the artist's experience. Artists, according to van Gogh, should seek to paint things not as they are, but as the artists feel them. In *Public Garden at Arles* (Figure 2), the colors of the pathway, the trees, and the sky are all far more intense and pure than the garden's real colors. Thus, van Gogh captures the whole experience of walking alone in the stillness of a hot afternoon.

Practically unknown in his lifetime, van Gogh's art became extremely influential soon after his death in 1890. One of the first artists to be affected by his style was a Norwegian artist named Edvard Munch (1863–1944), who discovered van Gogh's use of color in Paris. In *The Dance of Life* (Figure 3), Munch used strong, simple line and intense color to explore the unexpressed sexual stresses and conflicts that Sigmund Freud's studies were bringing to light.

In Germany the tendency to use color for its power to express psychological forces continued in the work of artists known as the German Expressionists. In Ernst Ludwig Kirchner's (1880–1938) *Reclining Nude* of 1909, strong, acid yellows and greens evoke feelings of tension, stress, and isolation (Figure 4). Kirchner also used bold, rapid lines to define flat shapes, a technique borrowed from folk art and from non-Western native traditions.

In France, Henri Matisse (1869–1954) also drew with forceful, rough strokes. He, too, painted broad areas of stunning color unrelated to the real colors of the subject. Yet, when Kirchner's nude is compared with Matisse's *Blue Nude* of 1907 (Figure 5), it is apparent that similar techniques produced paintings with different expressive results. While the Kirchner nude evokes a feeling of alienation, Matisse's *Blue Nude* leaves the viewer with a wordless sense of spontaneity, vitality, and joy.

Alongside the revolution in color, another revolution was occurring in the use of space. Ever since the Renaissance, European artists had treated the outside edges of paintings as window frames. The four sides of a frame bounded an imaginary cube of space—a three-dimensional world—in which figures and background were presented. From about 1880 on, Paul Cézanne (1839–1906) explored a new way of expressing the experience of seeing. He sought to create paintings with perfectly designed compositions, true both to the subject

FIGURE 2   VAN GOGH: PUBLIC GARDEN AT ARLES   (The Phillips Collection, Washington)

FIGURE 3   MUNCH: THE DANCE OF LIFE   (National Gallery, Oslo)

FIGURE 4   KIRCHNER: RECLINING NUDE   (Courtesy Museum of Fine Arts, Boston)

FIGURE 5   MATISSE: THE BLUE NUDE   (The Baltimore Museum of Art, The Cone Collection formed by Dr. Claribel Cone and Miss Etta Cone of Baltimore, Maryland)

FIGURE 6   CEZANNE: STILL LIFE WITH APPLES   (1895–98). Oil on canvas, 27×36½". (Collection, The Museum of Modern Art, New York; Lillie P. Bliss Collection)

matter and to his own perceptions. He also wanted to include and build upon tradition.

Cézanne's *Still Life with Apples* (Figure 6) has the solidity, monumentality, and balanced composition of a classical French painting from the seventeenth century. The space of the painting, however, is not treated as a block viewed from a stationary position. The space is compressed, and the fruit, tabletop, and drapery are each seen from a slightly different angle. The fluid viewpoint helps to convey time and movement, which are part of the visual experience. In looking at the painting, one is struck with its breadth, its order, and the intense concentration of Cézanne's vision.

Between 1909 and 1914, Pablo Picasso (1881–1973) and Georges Braque (1882–1963) worked together to develop a new style that is called *cubism*. Like Cézanne, they explored the interplay between the flat world of the art of painting and the three-dimensional world of visual perception. The two worlds influence each other, so that in art as in life, one confuses symbols or painted representations with the objects in the real world for which they stand. This observation about experience is explicit in a cubist work like *The Violin* (Figure 7). Illustrations of fruit cut from an actual book are pasted in the corner. These sheets are real objects introduced into a drawing, or symbol. But the illustrations are also printed reproductions of drawings that were based on real fruit.

In a typical Renaissance or baroque painting, objects are set inside an imaginary block of space, and they are represented from a single

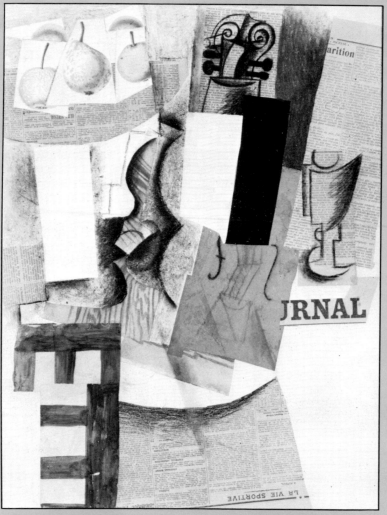

FIGURE 7   PICASSO: THE VIOLIN   (Philadelphia Museum of Art; the
A. E. Gallatin Collection)

stationary point of view. A cubist work is constructed on a different system, so that it re-creates the experience of seeing in a space of time. One can only know the nature of a volume by seeing it from many angles. Therefore, cubist art presents objects from multiple viewpoints. Furthermore, vision is conditioned by context, memories, juxtapositions, and events in time. In *The Violin*, some of the words cut from real newspapers refer ironically to an artist's life: *arition* suggests *apparition*, and *la vie sportive* means *the sporting*

life. The numerous fragmentary images of cubist art make one aware of the complex experience of seeing.

The colors used in early cubist art are deliberately banal, and the subjects represented are ordinary objects from everyday life. Picasso and Braque wanted to eliminate eye-catching color and intriguing subject matter so that their audiences would focus on the process of *seeing* itself.

Throughout the period from 1890 to 1914, avant-garde artists were de-emphasizing sub-

FIGURE 8   MONDRIAN: COMPOSITION 7   (Collection, The Solomon R. Guggenheim Museum, New York; photo by Robert E. Mates)

ject matter and stressing the expressive power of such formal qualities as line, color, and space. It is not surprising that some artists finally began to create work that did not refer to anything seen in the real world. Piet Mondrian (1872–1944), a Dutch artist, came to Paris shortly before World War I. There he saw the cubist art of Picasso and Braque. The cubists had compressed the imaginary depth in their paintings so that all the objects seemed to be contained within a space only a few inches deep. They had also reduced sub-

ject matter to insignificance. It seemed to Mondrian that the next step was to eliminate illusionistic space and subject matter entirely. His painting *Composition 7* (Figure 8), for example, seems entirely flat. Looking at Mondrian's paintings is a kinesthetic experience, as one senses the delicate interplay of balances and counterweights.

Mondrian, like several other early masters of modern art, was a philosophical idealist. He held that the objects of perception are actually manifestations of another independent and

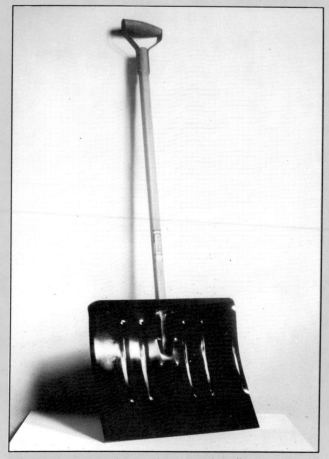

FIGURE 9 DUCHAMP: IN ADVANCE OF THE BROKEN
ARM (Yale University Art Gallery; gift of Katherine S.
Dreier for the Collection Société Anonyme)

changeless realm of essences. Art, he believed, should take its audience beyond the world of appearances into the other, more "real" reality. Logically, he eliminated from his paintings any references to the visible world.

Just before World War I, a young French artist named Marcel Duchamp (1887–1968) observed that things become art when the artist designates them as such, usually by placing them in an art context. *Art*, in other words, can be defined as a mode of perception. As the cubists had demonstrated, objects are always seen in relation to other objects in the environment. *In Advance of the Broken Arm* (Figure 9) is a real snow shovel purchased in a store. If it were seen in a hardware store, one would probably think only of its efficiency. But when seen in the Yale University Gallery, equipped with stand and label, one thinks of the shovel's sculptural form and notices, as Duchamp intended, that it is not a sensuous sculpture. Its title conjures up scenarios about shoveling snow, preventing broken arms, or having heart attacks. One then becomes conscious of perceiving the shovel in a special way unique to art.

The revolution in art that took place near the turn of the twentieth century is reverberating still. After nearly a hundred years, these masters of modern art continue to inspire their audiences with their passion and vision.

—KATHERINE CRUM

Aggressive impulses drive people apart, threatening society with disintegration. For Freud an unalterable core of human nature is ineluctably in opposition to civilized life. To this extent everyone is potentially an enemy of civilization.

Freud's awareness of the irrational and his general pessimism regarding people's ability to regulate it in the interests of civilization did not lead him to break faith with the Enlightenment tradition, for Freud did not celebrate the irrational. He was too aware of its self-destructive nature for that. Civilization was indeed a burden but people must bear it for the alternative was far worse. In the tradition of the philosophes Freud sought truth based on a scientific analysis of human nature and believed that reason was the best road to social improvement. Like the philosophes he was critical of religion, regarding it as a pious illusion, a fairy tale, in conflict with reason. Freud wanted people to throw away the crutch of religion, to break away from childhood dependency and stand alone. Also like the philosophes, Freud was a humanitarian who sought to relieve human misery by making people aware of their true nature, particularly their sexuality. He wanted society to soften its overly restrictive sexual standards because they were injurious to mental health. As a practicing psychiatrist, he tried to assist other people in dealing with emotional problems. Freud wanted to raise to the level of consciousness hitherto unrecognized inner conflicts that caused emotional distress.

Although Freud undoubtedly was a child of the Enlightenment, in crucial ways he differed from the philosophes. Regarding the Christian doctrine of original sin as myth, the philosophes had believed that people's nature was essentially good. If people took reason as their guide, evil could be eliminated. Freud, however, asserted, in secular and scientific terms, a pessimistic view of human nature. Freud saw evil rooted in human nature rather than a product of a faulty environment. Education and better living conditions will not eliminate evil, as the philosophes expected, nor will

abolition of private property, as Marx had declared. The philosophes venerated reason; it had enabled Newton to unravel nature's mysteries and would permit people to achieve virtue and reform society. Freud, who wanted reason to prevail, understood that its soft voice had to compete with the thunderous roars of the id. Freud broke with the optimism of the philosophes. His awareness of the immense pressures that civilization places on our fragile egos led him to be generally pessimistic about the future. Unlike Marx, Freud had no vision of utopia.

SOCIAL THOUGHT: CONFRONTING THE IRRATIONAL AND THE COMPLEXITIES OF MODERN SOCIETY

The great age of sociological thought was the end of the nineteenth and the beginning of the twentieth centuries. The leading thinkers of the period—Émile Durkheim, Vilfredo Pareto, and Max Weber—all regarded science as the only valid model for correct thinking and all claimed that their thought rested on a scientific foundation. They struggled with some of the crucial problems of modern society. How can society achieve coherence and stability when religion no longer unites people? What are the implications of the nonrational for political life? How can people preserve their individuality in a society that is becoming increasingly regimented?

Durkheim

Émile Durkheim (1858–1917), a French sociologist of Jewish background, was heir to Comte's positivism. Like Comte, he considered scientific thought the only valid model for modern society. A crucial element of Durkheim's thought was the effort to show that the essential ingredients of modern times—secularism, rationalism, and individualism—threaten society with disintegration. In traditional society a person's place and function were determined by birth. Modern people, however, captivated by the principle of individualism, will not accept such restraints. They seek to uplift themselves and demand that society allow them the opportunity. In the process they reject or ignore the social restraints that society so desperately requires, thereby giving rise to a spirit of anarchy.

The weakening of those traditional ties that bind the individual to society constitutes for Durkheim the crisis of modern society. Without collective values and common beliefs society is threatened with disintegration and the individual with disorientation. To a Western world intrigued by scientific progress, Durkheim emphasized the spiritual malaise of modern society. Modern people, said Durkheim, suffer from *anomie*—a collapse of values. They do not feel integrated into a collective community and find no purpose in life. In *Suicide* (1897), Durkheim maintained that the pathology of modern society is demonstrated by the higher rate of suicide. Intense competition and the disappointment and dissatisfaction resulting from unfulfilled expectations and lack of commitment to moral principles drive modern people to suicide. People must limit their aspirations and exercise discipline over their desires and passions. They must stop wanting more. Religion once could force people to do these things but it no longer can.

Durkheim approved of modernity but he noted that modern ways have not brought happiness or satisfaction to the individual. Modern scientific and industrial society requires a new moral system that would bind together the various classes into a cohesive social order and help to overcome those feelings of restlessness and dissatisfaction that torment people. Like Saint-Simon, Durkheim called for a rational and secular system of morals to replace Christian dogma, which had lost its power to attract and to bind. If a rational and secular replacement for Christianity is not found society runs the risk of dispensing with moral beliefs altogether and this it could not endure. Like the positivists, Durkheim insisted that these new beliefs must be discovered through the methods of science.

Durkheim hoped that occupational and professional organizations—updated medieval guilds—would integrate the individual into society and provide the moral force capable of restraining the selfish interests of both employer and worker. By curbing egoism, fostering self-discipline, and promoting altruism, these organizations could provide substitutes for religion.

Pareto

Like Comte, Vilfredo Pareto (1848–1923), an Italian economist and sociologist, aimed to construct a system of sociology on the model of the physical sciences. His studies led him to conclude that social behavior does not rest primarily on reason but on nonrational instincts and sentiments. These deeply rooted and essentially changeless feelings are the fundamental elements in human behavior. While society may change, human nature remains essentially the same. Whoever aims to lead and to influence people must appeal not to logic but to elemental feelings. Most human behavior is nonrational; nonlogical considerations also determine the beliefs that people hold. Like Marx and Freud, Pareto believed that we cannot accept a person's word at face value; in human instincts and sentiments we find the real cause of human behavior. People do not act according to carefully thought-out theories; they act first from nonlogical motivations and then construct a rationalization to justify their behavior. Much of Pareto's work was devoted to studying the nonrational elements of human conduct and the various beliefs invented to give the appearance of rationality to behavior that derives from feeling and instinct.

Pareto divided society into two strata—an elite and the masses. In the tradition of Machiavelli, Pareto held that a successful ruling elite must, with cunning and if necessary violence, exploit the feelings and impulses of the masses to its own advantage. Democratic states, he said, delude themselves in thinking that the masses are really influenced by rational argument. Pareto predicted that new political leaders would emerge who would master the people through propaganda and force, appealing always to sentiment rather than reason. To this extent, Pareto was an intellectual forerunner of fascism.

Weber

To Max Weber (1864–1920), a German sociologist, Western civilization, unlike the other civilizations of the globe, had virtually eliminated myth, mystery, and magic from its conception of nature and society. This process of rationalization—the "disenchantment of the world," as Weber called it—was most conspicuous in Western science but it was also evident in politics and economics. Weber considered Western science an attempt to understand and master nature through reason and Western capitalism an attempt to organize work and production in a rational manner. The Western state has a rational written constitution, rationally formulated law, and a bureaucracy of trained government officials that administers the affairs of state according to rational rules and laws.

Why did the West and not China or India engage in this process of rationalization? This question intrigued Weber and much of his scholarly effort went into answering it. Weber showed how various religious beliefs have influenced people's understanding of nature and their economic behavior. Weber's most famous thesis is that Protestantism produced an outlook that was conducive to the requirements of capitalism (see pages 315–316). Weber also explained how religious values hindered the process of rationalism in China and India.

Weber understood the terrible paradox of reason. Reason accounts for brilliant achievements in science and economic life, but it also despiritualizes life by ruthlessly eliminating centuries-old traditions, denouncing deeply felt religious beliefs as superstition, and regarding human feelings and passions as impediments to clear thinking. The process of disenchantment has given people knowledge, but it has also made people soulless and life meaningless. This is the dilemma of modern individuals, said Weber. Science cannot give people a purpose for living and the burgeoning of bureaucracy in government, business, and education stifles individual autonomy. The bureaucratization of modern society carries with it a potential for dictatorship.

It is horrible to think that the world could one day be filled with nothing but those little cogs, little men clinging to little jobs and striving towards bigger ones. . . . This passion for bureaucracy . . . is enough to drive one to despair. . . . That the world should know no men but these: it is in such an evolution that we are already caught up, and the great question is, therefore, not how we can promote and hasten it, but what can we oppose to this machinery in order to keep a portion of mankind free from this parceling-out of the soul, from this supreme mastery of the bureaucratic way of life.[15]

Will people endure this violation of their spiritual needs or will they reverse the process of disenchantment and seek redemption in the irrational? Weber himself was committed to the ideals of the Enlightenment and to perpetuating the rational humanist tradition, which he felt was threatened by bureaucratic regimentation on the one hand and irrational human impulses on the other.

GEORGES SEURAT (1859–1891): SUNDAY AFTERNOON ON THE
ISLAND OF LA GRANDE JATTE, 1886 In the late 1800s
and early 1900s, Newtonian science and the Enlightenment tradition in general were in disarray. Durkheim said that people suffered from *anomie,* a
collapse of values. Einstein's theories altered "fixed"
rules and emphasized relativity. Seurat's pointillist
landscape fragments the real world into thousands
of dots of color and seems to capture visually the
intellectual fragmentation and scientific exploration
of this period. (Collection of The Art Institute of
Chicago; Helen Birch Bartlett Memorial Collection)

ALTERING THE NEWTONIAN UNIVERSE

By the first decades of the twentieth century
the familiar philosophy of the Enlightenment
was in disarray. Doubts about human rationality, human goodness, and the progress of
civilization had undermined the Enlighten-

ment tradition. Human nature seemed far
more complex and the future far more uncertain than the philosophes had imagined. A
similar dissolution of Enlightenment certainties occurred with respect to people's view of
the physical universe.

According to classical physics, which
emerged during the seventeenth century, the

universe was a giant machine whose parts all functioned with perfect harmony and precision; objects followed strict laws of cause and effect; it was possible to compute the exact speed and exact position of a particle. Nature was an objective reality that existed independently of the observer. Through further knowledge it would be possible to fill in imperfectly understood parts of the machine and gain a complete understanding of nature.

The discoveries of Max Planck, Albert Einstein, and Werner Heisenberg upset the mechanistic conception of nature held by classical physics. The emergence of a new or modern physics (in contrast to the classical physics of Galileo and Newton) forced scientists to question, modify, and sometimes abandon traditional notions of matter, motion, light, space, time, cause and effect, and the meaning of scientific truth.

According to modern physics, the law of cause and effect does not operate in the small-scale world of electrons. For example, over a period of 1,622 years half the atoms of the element radium will have decayed and become transformed into atoms of another element. There are billions of atoms in a small lump of elemental radium and it is impossible to predict when a particular atom in the lump will decay and change into something else. The individual electron does not behave according to fixed laws.

The nature of electrons also makes it impossible to determine both their position and speed at the same time. If we calculate the exact speed of an electron we cannot at the same time locate precisely its exact position; if we pin down the exact position we cannot at the same time calculate its speed. When we attempt to examine the electron we alter its position. In dealing with elementary particles the laws of cause and effect cannot apply; in dealing with behavior of electrons we must speak of probability rather than certainty.

Albert Einstein (1879–1955), a German-Jewish scientist, was the principal architect of modern physics. According to Einstein's theory of relativity (1905–1916), Newton's laws must be modified when studying objects that move at great speeds. Einstein altered our conception of space and motion. For Einstein there is no motionless, absolute fixed frame of reference anywhere in the universe. All motion must be treated as relative to another moving body. Time is also relative, said Einstein; it is not a fixed and rigid measurement but differs for two observers traveling at different speeds.

For modern physics space and time no longer constitute an objective reality that exists independently of human beings. Our position in space and time determines what we mean by reality; our very presence affects what reality is. Nature cannot be fully intelligible to us. All the data collected by positivists cannot answer all the riddles of nature. Far from being a machine whose operations are fully knowable to the mind, the universe contains elements of uncertainty and mystery; it is governed by probability and relativity. This new awareness also contributed to that sense of disorientation and insecurity that characterizes the twentieth century.

Notes

1. Franklin L. Baumer, *Modern European Thought* (New York: Macmillan, 1977), p. 302.
2. Quoted in Ernst Cassirer, *The Problem of Knowledge* (New Haven: Yale University Press, 1950), p. 244.
3. Karl Pearson, *National Life from the Standpoint of Science* (London: Adam and Charles Black, 1905), pp. 21, 64.
4. Quoted in H. W. Koch, "Social Darwinism in the 'New Imperialism'," in H. W. Koch, ed., *The Origins of the First World War* (New York: Taplinger, 1972), p. 341.
5. Ibid., p. 345.
6. Quoted in John C. Greene, *The Death of Adam* (New York: Mentor Books, 1961), p. 313.
7. Friedrich Nietzsche, *The Will to Power*, trans. by A. M. Ludovici (New York: Rus-

sell & Russell, 1964), vol. 2, sec. 861–862, pp. 297–298.

8. Sigmund Freud, *Civilization and Its Discontents* (New York: W. W. Norton, 1961), p. 62.

9. Ibid., p. 58.

10. Ibid.

11. Ibid., p. 59.

12. Ibid., p. 61.

13. Ibid., p. 59.

14. Ibid., p. 69.

15. Quoted in Robert Nisbet, *The Social Philosophers* (New York: Thomas Y. Crowell, 1973), p. 441.

Suggested Reading

Baumer, Franklin, *Modern European Thought* (1977). A well-informed study of modern thought.

Coates, W. H., and White, H. V., *The Ordeal of Liberal Humanism*, vol. 2 (1970). A standard survey of intellectual history since the French Revolution.

Cruickshank, John, ed., *Aspects of the Modern European Mind* (1969). A useful collection of sources in modern intellectual history.

Farrington, Benjamin, *What Darwin Really Said* (1966). A brief study of Darwin's work.

Greene, J. C., *The Death of Adam* (1961). The impact of evolution on Western thought.

Hofstadter, Richard, *Social Darwinism in American Thought* (1955). A classic treatment of the impact of evolution on American conservatism, imperialism, and racism.

Hughes, H. Stuart, *Consciousness and Society* (1958). An excellent survey of thought from the 1890s to 1930.

Kaufmann, Walter, *Nietzsche* (1956). An excellent analysis of Nietzsche's thought.

Nelson, Benjamin, ed., *Freud and the Twentieth Century* (1957). A valuable collection of essays.

Rieff, Philip, *Freud: The Mind of the Moralist* (1961). A well-informed study of Freud's thought and influence.

Roazen, Paul, *Freud's Political and Social Thought* (1968). The wider implications of Freudian psychology.

Stromberg, Roland N., *An Intellectual History of Modern Europe* (1975). A fine text.

Zeitlin, I. M., *Ideology and the Development of Sociological Theory* (1968). Examines in detail the thought of major shapers of sociological theory.

Review Questions

1. How was the tradition of the Enlightenment carried forward in the nineteenth century?

2. What was Comte's law of the three stages?

3. The theory of evolution had revolutionary consequences in areas other than science. Discuss this statement.

4. What were Nietzsche's attitudes toward Christianity and democracy?

5. What was the significance of Nietzsche's thought?

6. How did Bergson reflect the growing irrationalism of the age?

7. How did Sorel show the political potential of the nonrational?

8. In what way was Freud a child of the Enlightenment? How did he differ from the philosophes?

9. What for Durkheim constituted the crisis of modern society? How did he attempt to cope with the crisis?

10. What do you think of Pareto's judgment that the masses in a democratic state are not really influenced by rational argument?

11. What for Weber was the terrible paradox of reason?

12. How did the new physics upset the classical physics of Newton?

PART V

World Wars and
Totalitarianism: The West
in Crisis / 1914–1945

CHAPTER 28

The Road to World War I:
Failure of the European
State System

PRIOR TO 1914 the dominant mood in Europe was one of pride in the accomplishments of Western civilization and confidence in its future progress. Advances in science and technology, the rising standard of living, the spread of democratic institutions, the expansion of social reform, the increase in literacy for the masses, Europe's position of power in the world—all contributed to a sense of optimism. Another reason for optimism was that since the defeat of Napoleon, Europe had avoided a general war, and that since the Franco-Prussian War (1870–1871), the Great Powers had not fought each other. Reflecting on the world he knew before World War I, Arnold Toynbee recalled that his generation

expected that life throughout the World would become more rational, more humane, and more democratic and that, slowly, but surely, political democracy would produce greater social justice. We had also expected that the progress of science and technology would make mankind richer, and that this increasing wealth would gradually spread from a minority to a majority. We had expected that all this would happen peacefully. In fact we thought that mankind's course was set for an earthly paradise, and that our approach towards this goal was predestined for us by historical necessity.[1]

Few people recognized that these achievements masked an inner turbulence that was propelling Western civilization toward a cataclysm. The European state system was failing. In the early nineteenth century, liberals had believed that the redrawing of the political map of Europe on the basis of nationality would promote peaceful relations among nations. But quite the reverse occurred. By 1914, national states, answering to no higher power, were fueled by an explosive nationalism, and were grouped into alliances that faced each other with ever-mounting hostility. Nationalist passions, overheated by the popular press and expansionist societies, poisoned international relations. Nationalist thinkers propagated pseudoscientific racial and Social Darwinist doctrines that glorified conflict and justified the subjugation of other peoples. Committed to enhancing national power, statesmen lost sight of Europe as a community of nations sharing a common civilization. Caution and restraint gave way to belligerency in foreign relations.

The failure of the European state system was paralleled by a cultural crisis. Some European intellectuals attacked the rational tradition of the Enlightenment and celebrated the primitive, the instinctual, and the irrational. Increasingly young people grew attracted to philosophies of action that ridiculed liberal bourgeois values and viewed war as a purifying and ennobling experience. Colonial wars, colorfully portrayed in the popular press, ignited the imagination of bored factory workers and daydreaming students and reinforced a sense of duty and an urge for gallantry among soldiers and aristocrats. These "splendid" little colonial wars helped fashion an attitude that made war acceptable, if not laudable. Yearning to break loose from their ordinary lives and to embrace heroic values, many Europeans regarded violent conflict as the highest expression of individual and national life. "Even if we end in ruin it was beautiful," exclaimed General Erich von Falkenhayn, the future Chief of the German General Staff, at the outbreak of World War I.[2] Though technology was making warfare more brutal and dangerous, Europe retained a romantic illusion about combat.

While Europe was seemingly progressing in the art of civilization, the mythic power of nationalism and the primitive appeal of conflict were driving European civilization to the abyss. Few people recognized the potential crisis, including the statesmen whose blunders and recklessness allowed the Continent to stumble into war.

NATIONALITY PROBLEMS IN AUSTRIA-HUNGARY

On June 28, 1914, a young terrorist with the support of The Black Hand, a secret Serbian nationalist society, murdered Archduke Francis Ferdinand, heir to the throne of Austria-Hungary. Six weeks later the armies of Europe were on the march; an incident in the Balkans had sparked a world war. An analysis of why Austria-Hungary felt compelled to attack Serbia, and why the other powers became enmeshed in the conflict, shows how explosive Europe was in 1914. And nowhere were conditions more volatile than in Austria-Hungary, the scene of the assassination.

Composed of several nationalities, each with its own national history and traditions and often conflicting aspirations, Austria-Hungary stood in opposition to nationalism, the most powerful spiritual force of the age. Was the supranational Austrian Empire obsolete in a world of states based on the principle of nationality? Dominated by Germans and Hungarians, the Empire could neither satisfy the grievances nor contain the nationalist aims of its minorities, particularly the Czechs and South Slavs (Croats, Slovenes, Serbs).

Failure of the Austrian Empire to solve its minority problems had significant repercussions for international relations. The more moderate leaders of the ethnic minorities did not call for secession from the Empire. Nevertheless, heightened agitation among the several nationalities, which worsened in the decade before 1914, created terrible anxieties among Austrian leaders. The fear that the Empire would be torn apart by rebellion caused Austria to pursue a more forceful policy against any nation that fanned the nationalist feelings of its Slavic minorities. In particular, this policy meant a worsening of tensions between Austria and small Serbia, independent of the Ottoman Empire since 1878.

Captivated by Western ideas of nationalism, the Serbs sought to create a Greater

Serbia by uniting with their racial kin, the South Slavs who dwelt in Austria-Hungary. Since some 7 million South Slavs lived in the Hapsburg Empire, the dream of a Greater Serbia, shrilly expressed by Serbian nationalists, caused nightmares in Austria. Austrian leaders feared that continued Serbian agitation would encourage the South Slavs to press for secession. Regarding Serbia as a grave threat to Austria's existence, such leaders as Foreign Minister Count Leopold von Berchtold and Field Marshal Franz Conrad von Hötzendorf urged the destruction of the Serbian menace.

Another irritant to Austria-Hungary was Russian Pan-Slavism, which called for the solidarity of Russians with their Slavic cousins in eastern Europe—Poles, Czechs, Slovaks, South Slavs, Bulgarians. Pan-Slavism was based on a mystic conception of the superiority of Slavic civilization to Western civilization and of Russia's special historical mission to liberate its kin from Austrian and Turkish rule. Although Russian Pan-Slavists were few and did not dictate foreign policy, they constituted a significant pressure group. Moreover, their provocative and semireligious proclamations frightened Austria-Hungary, which did not draw a sharp line between Pan-Slavic aspirations and official Russian policy.

The tensions arising out of the multinational character of the Austro-Hungarian Empire in an age of heightened nationalist feeling set off the explosion in 1914. Unable to solve its minority problems and fearful of Pan-Slavism and Pan-Serbism, Austria-Hungary felt itself in a life-or-death situation. This sense of desperation led it to lash out at Serbia after the assassination of Archduke Francis Ferdinand.

THE GERMAN SYSTEM OF ALLIANCES

But the war might have been avoided or might have remained limited to Austria and Serbia had Europe in 1914 not been divided into two hostile alliance systems. Such a situation contains inherent dangers. For example, knowing that it has the support of allies, a country may pursue a more provocative and reckless course and be less conciliatory during a crisis. Second, a conflict between two states may spark a chain reaction that would draw in the other powers, thereby transforming a limited war into a general war. This course is precisely what followed the assassination. The origins of this dangerous alliance system go back to Bismarck and the Franco-Prussian War.

The New German Nation

The unification of Germany in 1870–1871 turned the new state into an international power of the first rank, upsetting the balance of power in Europe. For the first time since the wars of the French Revolution, a nation was in a position to dominate the European continent. What would be the place of a united and powerful Germany in European life? This was the crucial problem in the decades following the Franco-Prussian War.

To German nationalists, the unification of Germany was both the fulfillment of a national dream and the starting point of an even more ambitious goal—the extension of German power in Europe and the world. As the nineteenth century drew to a close, German nationalism grew more extreme. Believing that Germany must either grow or die, nationalists pressed the government to build a powerful navy, acquire colonies, gain a much greater share of the world's markets, and expand German interests and influences in Europe. Sometimes these goals were expressed in the language of Social Darwinism—nations are engaged in an eternal struggle for survival and domination.

MAP 28.1 ETHNIC GROUPS IN GERMANY, AUSTRIA, AND THE BALKANS BEFORE WORLD WAR I ▶

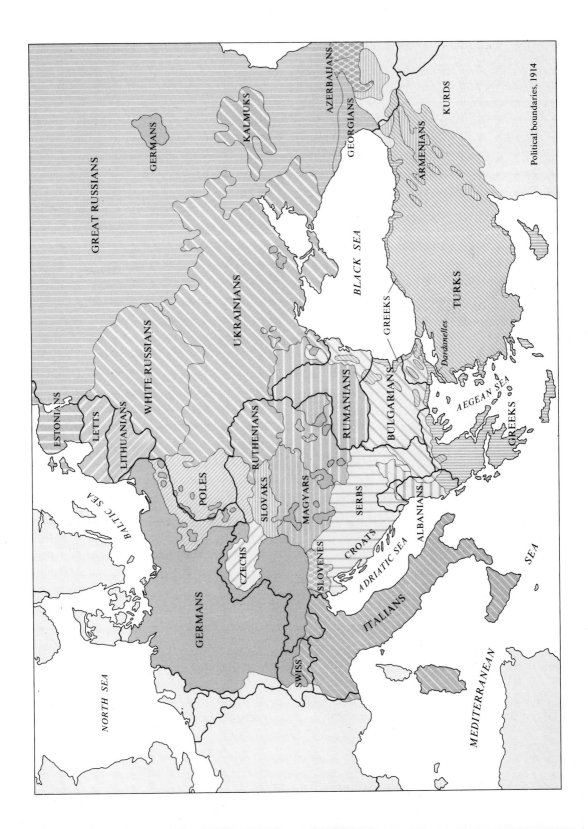

Political boundaries, 1914

GREAT RUSSIANS

GERMANS

KALMUKS

AZERBAIJANS

GEORGIANS

KURDS

ARMENIANS

BLACK SEA

UKRAINIANS

WHITE RUSSIANS

TURKS

ESTONIANS

LETTS

LITHUANIANS

RUTHENIANS

RUMANIANS

BULGARIANS

GREEKS

Dardanelles

AEGEAN SEA

GREEKS

POLES

SLOVAKS

MAGYARS

SERBS

ALBANIANS

BALTIC SEA

CZECHS

SLOVENES

CROATS

ADRIATIC SEA

ITALIANS

GERMANS

SWISS

NORTH SEA

MEDITERRANEAN

SEA

The Pan-German Association, which included among its membership some prominent intellectuals, journalists, and politicians, preached the special destiny of the German race and advocated German expansion in Europe and overseas. Pan-Germans probably had less power than Russian Pan-Slavs. Nevertheless, like their Pan-Slav counterparts, they included people of influence, engaged in shrill propaganda, and frightened observers in other countries. Decisive victories against Austria (1866) and France (1871), the formation of the German Reich, rapid industrialization, and the impressive achievements of German science and scholarship had molded a powerful and dynamic nation imbued with great expectations for the future. Germans became increasingly impatient to see the fatherland gain its "rightful" place in world affairs, an attitude that frightened non-Germans.

Bismarck's Goals

Under Bismarck, who did not seek additional territory but wanted only to preserve the recently achieved unification, Germany pursued a moderate and cautious foreign policy. One of Bismarck's principal goals was to keep France isolated and friendless. France suffered a deep humiliation as a result of its defeat in the Franco-Prussian War. Prussia's quick and decisive victory shocked the French, who had entered the war brimming with confidence. Compounding French humiliation was the loss of Alsace and Lorraine to Germany. Victor Hugo expressed the "sacred anger" of the French: "France will have but one thought: to reconstitute her forces, gather her energy . . . raise her young generation to form an army of the whole people . . . to become again a great France, the France of 1792, the France of an idea with a sword. Then one day she will be irresistible. Then she will take back Alsace-Lorraine."[3] While French nationalists yearned for a war of revenge against Germany, the

government, aware of Germany's strength, was unlikely to initiate such a conflict. Nevertheless, the issue of Alsace-Lorraine increased tensions between France and Germany. Germany's annexation of the French provinces of Alsace and Lorraine proved to be a serious blunder, for it precluded any reconciliation between Germany and France.

Bismarck also hoped to prevent a war between Russia and Austria-Hungary, for such a conflict could lead to German involvement, to the breakup of Austria-Hungary, and to Russian expansion in eastern Europe. To maintain peace and Germany's existing borders, Bismarck forged complex alliances. In the decade of the 1880s Bismarck created the Triple Alliance—consisting of Germany, Austria-Hungary, and Italy—and an alliance with Russia.

There was one major weakness to Germany's alliance system. How could Germany remain allied to both Austria and Russia when these two nations were potential enemies? Austria feared Russian ambitions in the Balkans and felt threatened by Russian Pan-Slavs who sought union with the Slavs under Austrian rule. Bismarck knew that an alliance with Austria was essentially incompatible with Germany's treaty obligations to Russia, but he hoped that these treaties would enable him to exercise a moderating influence over both eastern powers, thereby forestalling a war that would upset the status quo. An additional reason for the treaty with Russia was that it denied France a valuable ally.

Bismarck conducted foreign policy with restraint. He formed alliances not to conquer new lands but to protect Germany from aggression from either France or Russia, not to launch war but to preserve order and stability in Europe. In 1888 a new emperor ascended the throne in Germany; the young Kaiser Wilhelm II (1888–1918) clashed with his aging prime minister, and in 1890 Bismarck was forced to resign. Lacking Bismarck's diplomatic skills, his cool restraint, and his determination to keep peace in Europe, the new leaders

KAISER WILLIAM II Many historians debate whether the Germany of William II should bear the principal blame for World War I; other historians, dismissing the question of responsibility, hold that the war resulted from dangerous forces in European civilization. William II has been criticized for supporting a belligerent foreign policy. (Brown Brothers)

would pursue a belligerent and imperialistic foreign policy in the following decades that would frighten other states, particularly Britain. Whereas Bismarck considered Germany a satiated power, these men insisted that Germany must have its place in the sun.

The first act of the new leadership was to permit the treaty with Russia to lapse, thereby allowing Germany to give full support to Austria, which was considered a more reliable ally. Whereas Bismarck had warned Austria to act with moderation and caution in the Balkans, his successors not only failed to hold

Austria in check but actually encouraged Austrian aggression. This proved fatal to the peace of Europe.

THE TRIPLE ENTENTE

Fear of Germany

When Germany broke with Russia in 1890, France was quick to take advantage of the situation. Frightened by Germany's increasing military strength, expanding industries, growing population, and alliance with Austria and Italy, France eagerly coveted Russia as an ally. The French government urged its bankers to invest in Russia, supplied weapons to the tsar, and arranged for the French and Russian fleets to exchange visits. In 1894, France and Russia entered into an alliance; the isolation forced on France by Bismarck had ended.

Like France and Russia, Great Britain was alarmed by Germany's growing military might. Furthermore, because of its spectacular industrial growth, Germany had become a potent trade rival of England. Britain was also distressed by Germany's increased efforts to acquire colonies. But most alarming was Germany's decision to build a great navy, for it could interfere with British overseas trade or even blockade the British Isles. Germany's naval program was the single most important reason that Britain moved closer first to France and then to Russia. Germany's naval construction, designed to increase its stature as a Great Power but not really necessary for its security, was one indication that Germany had abandoned Bismarck's policy of good sense. Eager to add Britain as an ally, France, demonstrating superb diplomatic skill, moved to end long-standing colonial disputes with Britain. This was accomplished by the Entente Cordiale of 1904. England had emerged from self-imposed isolation.

The Franco-British understanding increased German anxiety, but Germany also doubted that France and England, who had almost gone to war in 1898 over regions in the Sudan, had overcome their deep animosities. Consequently, Chancellor Bernhard von Bülow (1849–1929) decided to provoke a crisis in Morocco that would sever the Anglo-French Entente Cordiale. Von Bülow chose Morocco because earlier the British had resisted French imperialist designs there. He prodded a reluctant Kaiser William II to visit the Moroccan port of Tangier, a sign that Germany would support the Moroccan sultan against France; von Bülow had his crisis. In January 1906, a conference was held in Algeciras, Spain, to resolve the crisis; it was a defeat for Germany, for Britain sided with France, which was given special rights in Morocco. Germany's efforts to disrupt the Anglo-French Entente Cordiale had failed; the two former enemies had demonstrated their solidarity.

Eager to erect a strong alliance to counter Germany's Triple Alliance, French diplomats now sought to ease tensions between their Russian ally and their new British friend. Two events convinced Russia to adopt a more conciliatory attitude toward Britain: a disastrous and unexpected defeat in the Russo-Japanese War of 1904–1905 and a working-class revolution in 1905. Shocked by defeat, its army bordering on disintegration, its workers restive, Russia was now receptive to settling its imperial disputes with Britain over Persia, Tibet, and Afghanistan, a decision encouraged by France. In the Anglo-Russian Entente of 1907, as in the Anglo-French Entente Cordiale of 1904, the former rivals conducted themselves in a conciliatory if not friendly manner. In both instances, what engendered this spirit of cooperation was fear of Germany; both agreements represented a triumph for French diplomacy. The Triple Entente, however, was not a firm alliance, for there was no certainty that Britain, traditionally reluctant to send its troops to the Continent, would give any more than diplomatic support to France and Russia in case there was a showdown with Germany.

Europe was now broken into two hostile camps: the Triple Entente of France, Russia, and Britain and the Triple Alliance of Germany, Austria-Hungary, and Italy. Serving to increase fear and suspicion between the alliances was the costly arms race and the maintenance of large standing armies by all the states except Britain.

German Reactions

Germany denounced the Triple Entente as a hostile anti-German coalition designed to encircle and crush Germany. If Germany were to survive, it must break this ring. In the past, German arms had achieved unification; German military might would also end this threat to the fatherland. Considering Austria-Hungary as its only reliable ally, Germany resolved to preserve the power and dignity of the Hapsburg Empire. If Austria-Hungary fell from the ranks of Great Powers, Germany would have to stand alone against its enemies. At all costs Austria-Hungary must not be weakened.

But this assessment suffered from dangerous miscalculations. First, Germany overstressed the hostile nature of the Triple Entente. In reality, France, Russia, and Britain drew closer together not to wage aggressive war against Germany but to protect themselves against burgeoning German military, industrial, and diplomatic power. Second, by linking German security to Austria, Germany greatly increased the chance of war. Becoming increasingly fearful of Pan-Serbism and Pan-Slavism, Austria might well decide that only a war could prevent its empire from disintegrating. Confident of German support, Austria would be more likely to resort to force; fearful of any diminution of Austrian power, Germany would be more likely to give Austria that support. Unlike Bismarck, the new leadership did not think in terms of restraining Austria but of strengthening it, by war if necessary.

THE DRIFT TOWARD WAR

The Bosnian Crisis

After 1908, several crises tested the competing alliances, pushing Europe closer to war. Particularly significant was the Bosnian affair, for it contained many of the ingredients that eventually ignited the war in 1914. The humiliating defeat by Japan in 1905 had diminished Russia's stature as a Great Power and an abortive revolution in the same year had weakened the government's authority at home. The new Russian foreign minister, Alexander Izvolsky, hoped to gain a diplomatic triumph by compelling Turkey to allow Russian warships to pass through the Dardanelles, fulfilling a centuries-old dream of extending Russian power into the Mediterranean.

Izvolsky hoped that England and France, traditional opponents of Russia's Mediterranean ambitions but now allies, would not block Russia. But certainly Austria would regard this as a hostile act. Perhaps a bargain could be struck with the Hapsburg monarchy, which desired the annexation of the provinces of Bosnia and Herzegovina. Officially a part of the Ottoman Empire, these provinces had been administered by Austria-Hungary since 1878. The population consisted mainly of ethnic cousins of the Serbs. A formal annexation would certainly infuriate the Serbs, who hoped one day to make the region part of a Greater Serbia. Russia and Austria made a deal. Russia would permit Austrian annexation of Bosnia and Herzegovina, and Austria would support Russia's move to open the Dardanelles. In 1908 Austria proceeded to annex the provinces, but Russia met stiff resistance from England and France when it presented its case for opening the Straits to Russian warships.

Austria had gained a diplomatic victory while Russia suffered another humiliation. Even more enraged than Russia was Serbia, which threatened to invade Bosnia to liberate its cousins from Austrian oppression. The Serbian press openly declared that Austria-Hungary must perish if the South Slavs were to achieve liberty and unity. A fiery attitude also prevailed in Vienna—Austria-Hungary cannot survive unless Serbia is destroyed. During this period of intense hostility between Austria-Hungary and Serbia, Germany supported its Austrian ally. To keep Austria strong, Germany would even agree to the dismemberment of Serbia and to its incorporation into Austria. As a result of this crisis, Austria and Germany coordinated battle plans in case a conflict between Austria and Serbia involved Russia and France. Unlike Bismarck, who tried to hold Austria in check, German leadership now coolly envisioned an Austrian attack on Serbia and coolly offered German support if Russia intervened.

Balkan Wars

The Bosnian crisis pushed Germany and Austria closer together, brought relations between Austria and Serbia to the breaking point, and inflicted another humiliation on Russia. The first Balkan War (1912) continued these trends. The Balkan states of Montenegro, Serbia, Bulgaria, and Greece attacked a dying Ottoman Empire. In a brief campaign, the Balkan armies captured the Turkish empire's European territory with the exception of Constantinople. Because it was on the victorious side, landlocked Serbia gained the Albanian coast, which gave it a long-desired outlet to the sea. Austria was determined to keep its enemy from reaping this reward, and Germany, as in the Bosnian crisis, supported its ally, Austria. Unable to secure Russian support, an enraged Serbia was forced to surrender the territory, which became the state of Albania.

Thus, during a five-year period, Austria-Hungary inflicted on Serbia two terrible humiliations. Russia shared these humiliations, for it had twice failed to help its small Slavic

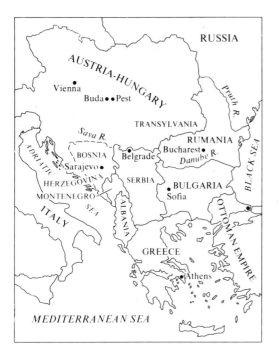

MAP 28.2   THE BALKANS, 1914

tary visit to Sarajevo, capital of Bosnia, when Bosnian territorists assassinated him. The conspiracy was supported by the chief of intelligence of the Serbian army, who was linked to a Serbian nationalist society, the Black Hand. Francis Ferdinand was sympathetic to the grievances of the South Slavs and favored a policy that would place the Slavs on equal footing with Hungarians and Germans within the Hapsburg Empire. If such a policy succeeded, it could soothe the feelings of the Austrian· Slavs and reduce the appeal of a Greater Serbia, the aim of the Black Hand.

By killing the archduke, the terrorists hoped to bring to a boiling point tensions within the Hapsburg Empire and to prepare the way for revolution. On June 28, 1914, young Gavrilo Princip, part of the terrorist team, fired two shots at close distance into the archduke's car. Francis Ferdinand and his wife died within fifteen minutes.

Feeling that Austria's prestige as a Great Power, indeed its very survival as a supranational empire, was at stake, key officials, led by Count Leopold von Berchtold, the foreign minister, decided to use the assassination as a pretext to crush Serbia. For many years leaders of Austria had yearned for war with Serbia in order to end the agitation for the union of the South Slavs. Now, they reasoned, the hour had struck. But war with Serbia would require the approval of Germany, Austria's ally. Holding that Austria was Germany's only reliable ally and that a diminution of Austrian power and prestige threatened German security, German statesmen decided to support Austria. Consequently, Germany did not urge a peaceful settlement of the issue but encouraged its ally to take up arms against Serbia. Germany and Austria wanted a quick strike to overwhelm Serbia before other countries were drawn in.

friend. Incensed Serbian nationalists accelerated their campaign of propaganda and terrorism against Austria. Believing that another humiliation would irreparably damage its prestige, Russia vowed to back Serbia in its next confrontation with Austria. And Austria had reached the end of its patience with Serbia. Emboldened by German encouragement, Austria would end the Serbian threat once and for all. Thus the ingredients for war between Austria and Serbia, a war that might easily draw in Russia and Germany, were present. Another incident might well start a war; it came on June 28, 1914.

Assassination of Francis Ferdinand

Archduke Francis Ferdinand (1863–1914) heir to the throne of Austria, was making a mili-

Germany Encourages Austria

Confident of German backing, on July 23 Austria presented Serbia with an ultimatum

THE ASSASSINS OF THE ARCHDUKE FRANZ FERDINAND AND
HIS WIFE BEING CAPTURED IN SARAJEVO, JUNE 28, 1914
The assassination of the Archduke and his wife was
the spark that ignited World War I. The adversaries
looked forward to a short, decisive conflict. Emotions ran high with visions of gallantry. Only a few
foresaw the collapse of a Western ideal: a world ruled
by reason and morality. (The Granger Collection,
New York)

and demanded a response within forty-eight
hours. The terms of the ultimatum were so
harsh that it was next to impossible for Serbia
to accept them. This reaction was the one that
Austria intended, as it sought a military and
not a diplomatic solution to the crisis. But
Russia would not remain indifferent to an
Austro-German effort to liquidate Serbia. Russia feared that an Austrian conquest of Serbia
was just the first step of an Austro-German

plan to dominate the Balkans. Such an extension of German and Austrian power in a region
bordering Russia was unthinkable to the tsar's
government. Moreover, after suffering repeated reverses in foreign affairs, Russia would not
tolerate another humiliation. As Germany had
resolved to back its Austrian ally, Russia
determined not to abandon Serbia.

Serbia responded to Austria's ultimatum in
a conciliatory manner, agreeing to virtually all

Austria's demands. But Serbia would not allow Austrian officials into Serbia to investigate the assassination. Having already decided against a peaceful settlement, Austria insisted that Serbia's failure to accept one provision meant that the entire ultimatum had been rejected and ordered mobilization of the Austrian army.

This was a crucial moment for Germany. Would it continue to support Austria, knowing that an Austrian attack on Serbia would most likely bring Russia into the conflict? Determined not to desert Austria and believing that a showdown with Russia was inevitable, the German war party continued to urge Austrian action against Serbia. They argued that it was better to fight Russia now than a few years later when the tsar's empire would be stronger. Confident of the superiority of the German army, the war party held that Germany could defeat both Russia and France, that Britain's army was too weak to make a difference, and that, in any case, Britain might remain neutral. While Germany would have preferred a limited war involving only Austria and Serbia, it was not dismayed by the idea of a general war. Indeed, some military leaders and statesmen were exhilarated by the prospect of a war with Russia and France. The defeat of Germany's enemies would break the ring of encirclement, would increase German territory, and would establish Germany as the foremost power in the world.

On July 28, 1914, Austria declared war on Serbia; Russia, with the assurance of French support, proclaimed partial mobilization aimed at Austria alone. But the military warned that partial mobilization would throw the slow-moving Russian war machine into total confusion if the order had to be changed suddenly to full mobilization. Moreover, the only plans the Russian general staff had drawn up called for full mobilization, that is, for war against both Austria and Germany. To facilitate military efficiency, the tsar agreed to general rather than partial mobilization and gave the order on July 30. This meant that

Russian forces would be arrayed against Germany as well as Austria.

Since German military plans called for fighting a two-front war against both France and Russia, it could not allow Russia the advantage of mobilizing first. Thus the prevailing military theory worked against peace. Battle plans, worked out years in advance, required the mobilization of huge numbers of soldiers and were geared to tight railroad timetables. Because the country that struck first had the advantage of fighting according to its own plans rather than having to improvise in response to the enemy's attack, generals regarded mobilization by the enemy as an act of war. Therefore, when Russia refused a German warning to halt mobilization, Germany, on August 1, ordered a general mobilization and declared war on Russia. Two days later Germany also declared war on France, believing that France would most likely support its Russian ally. Moreover, German battle plans called for a war with both Russia and France. Thus a war between Germany and Russia automatically meant a German attack on France.

When Belgium refused to allow German troops to march through Belgian territory into France, Germany invaded the small nation, an act that brought Britain into the war, for Britain was pledged to guarantee Belgian neutrality. Furthermore, Britain could never tolerate German troops directly across the English Channel, a position which, combined with a German victory over France, would make Germany master of western Europe. A century before, Britain had fought Napoleon to prevent France from becoming master of Europe. Now it would fight Germany for the same reason.

Responsibility

Was any one power mainly responsible for the war? This question has intrigued historians. In assessing blame, historians have been principally concerned with Germany's role. German historian Fritz Fischer argues that Germany's ambition to dominate Europe was the underlying cause of the war. Germany encouraged Austria to strike at Serbia knowing that an attack on Serbia could mean war with Russia and its French ally. Believing that it had the military advantage, Germany was willing to risk such a war. "As Germany willed and coveted the Austro-Serbian war and, in her confidence in her military superiority, deliberately faced the risk of a conflict with Russia and France, her leaders must bear a substantial share of the historical responsibility for the outbreak of general war in 1914."[4]

Attracted by Social Darwinist and militarist doctrines, continues Fischer, Germany aimed to become the foremost economic and political power in Europe and to play a far greater role in world politics; to achieve this goal Germany was willing to go to war. Critics of Fischer point out that other nations, not merely Germany, were enthralled by Social Darwinism and militarism, that this was not a particularly German mode of thinking but part of a general European sickness. They argue further that Germany would have preferred a limited war between Austria and Serbia and in 1914 had no plans to dominate Europe.

The other powers have also come in for a share of the blame. Austria bears responsibility for its determination to crush Serbia and its insistence on avoiding a negotiated settlement; Russia for instituting general mobilization, thereby turning a limited war between Austria-Hungary and Serbia into a European war; France for failing to restrain Russia and indeed for encouraging its ally to mobilize; England for failing to make clear that it would support its allies, for had Germany seen clearly that Britain would intervene it might have been more cautious.

Other historians, dismissing the question of responsibility, regard the war as a clear sign that European civilization was in deep trouble. Viewed in the broad perspective of European history, the war marked a culmination of dangerous forces in European life: the glorification of power, the fascination for violence, the celebration of the nonrational, the diminishing confidence in the capacity of reason to solve the problems created by the Industrial Revolution, the general dissatisfaction and disillusionment with bourgeois society, the alliance system, and, above all, an explosive nationalism.

WAR AS CELEBRATION

When war was certain, an extraordinary phenomenon occurred. Crowds gathered in capital cities and expressed loyalty to the fatherland and their readiness to fight. Even socialists, whose loyalty was supposed to be given to an international movement, devoted themselves to their respective nations. It seemed as if people wanted violence for its own sake. It was as if war provided an escape from the dull routine of classroom, job, and home, from the emptiness, drabness, mediocrity, and pointlessness of bourgeois society, from "a world grown old and cold and weary," said Rupert Brooke, a young British poet.[5] To some, war was a "beautiful . . . sacred moment" that satisfied an "ethical yearning."[6] But more significantly, the outpouring of patriotic sentiments demonstrated the immense power that nationalism exercised over the European mind. With extraordinary success, nationalism welded millions of people into a collectivity ready to devote body and soul to the nation, especially during its hour of need.

In Paris, men marched down the boulevards singing the stirring words of the French national anthem, the Marseillaise, while women showered young soldiers with flowers. "Young and old, civilians and military men burned with the same excitement. . . . Beginning the next day, thousands of men eager to fight would jostle one another outside recruiting offices, waiting to join up. . . . The word 'duty' had a meaning for them, and the word 'coun-

TROOPS LEAVING BERLIN, 1914 "The sword has been forced into our hand," said Germans at the outbreak of war. German troops mobilized eagerly and efficiently; here a trainload is leaving for the western front. (Historical Pictures Service, Inc., Chicago)

try' had regained its splendor."[7] Similar scenes occurred in Berlin. "It is a joy to be alive," editorialized one newspaper. "We wished so much for this hour. . . . The sword which has been forced into our hand will not be sheathed until our aims are won and our territory extended as far as necessity demands."[8]

Soliders bound for battle acted as if they were going off on a great adventure. "My dear ones, be proud that you live in such a time and in such a nation and that you . . . have the privilege of sending those you love into so glorious a battle," wrote a young German law student to his family.[9] The young warriors yearned to do something noble and altruistic, to win glory, and to experience life at its most intense moments.

Many of Europe's most distinguished intellectuals were also captivated by the martial mood. To the prominent German historian, Friedrich Meinecke, August 1914 was "one of the great moments of my life which suddenly filled my soul with the deepest confidence in our people and the profoundest joy."[10] Besides being gripped by a thirst for violent adventure, a quest for the heroic, some intellectuals welcomed the war because it unified the nation in a spirit of fraternity and self-sacrifice. It was a return, some felt, to the organic roots of human existence, a way of overcoming a sense of individual isolation. To some intellectuals the war would spiritually regenerate a sick European society. It would cleanse Europe of its spiritual and racial impurities. It would serve as a prelude to rebirth; from it would emerge a higher civilization and a higher type of person endowed with a Nietzschean spirit.

But it must be emphasized that the soldiers who went off to war singing and the statesmen and generals who welcomed war or did not try hard enough to prevent it expected a short, decisive, gallant conflict. Virtually no one envisioned what the First World War turned out to be—four years of frightful, barbaric, indecisive, senseless bloodletting. There were prophets who realized that Europe was stumbling into darkness, but their gloomy words were drowned out by the cheers of chauvinists and fools. "The lamps are going out all over Europe," said British Foreign Secretary Edward Grey. "We shall never see them lit again in our lifetime."

Notes

1. Arnold Toynbee, *Surviving the Future* (New York: Oxford University Press, 1971), pp. 106–107.
2. Quoted in James Joll, "The Unspoken Assumptions," in H. W. Koch, ed., *The Origins of the First World War* (New York: Taplinger, 1972), p. 325.
3. Quoted in Barbara Tuchman, *The Guns of August* (New York: Dell, 1962), pp. 46–47.
4. Fritz Fischer, *Germany's Aims in the First World War* (New York: W. W. Norton, 1967), p. 88.
5. Rupert Brooke, *1914*.

6. Quoted in Joachim C. Fest, *Hitler* (New York: Harcourt Brace Jovanovich, 1973), p. 66.
7. George A. Panichas, ed., *Promise of Greatness* (New York: John Day, 1968), pp. 14–15.
8. Quoted in Tuchman, *The Guns of August*, p. 145.
9. Quoted in Robert G. L. Waite, *Vanguard of Nazism* (New York: W. W. Norton, 1969), p. 22.
10. Quoted in Koch, *The Origins of the First World War*, p. 318.

Suggested Reading

Berghahn, V. R., *Germany and the Approach of War in 1914* (1975). Relates German foreign policy to domestic problems.

Fay, Sidney, *The Origins of the World War*, 2 vols. (1966). A comprehensive study of the underlying and immediate causes of the war.

Fischer, Fritz, *Germany's Aims in the First World War* (1967). A controversial work, stressing Germany's responsibility for the war.

Geiss, Imanuel, ed., *July 1914* (1967). Selected documents.

Koch, H. W., ed., *The Origins of the First World War* (1972). Useful essays, particularly those dealing with the glorification of war before 1914.

Lafore, Laurence, *The Long Fuse* (1971). A beautifully written study of the causes of the conflict.

Langer, W. L., *European Alliances and Alignments* (1964). Originally published in 1931, this now-classic work treats the major international issues between 1871 and 1890.

Laqueur, Walter, and George Mosse, eds., *1914* (1966). A valuable collection of essays on the coming of war.

Remak, Joachim, *The Origins of World War I* (1967). A fine introduction.

Thomson, G. M., *The Twelve Days* (1964). An account of the twelve days preceding the outbreak of war.

Review Questions

1. How did the nationality problems in Austria-Hungary contribute to the outbreak of World War I?

2. What were the principal purposes of Bismarck's system of alliances?

3. What conditions led to the formation of the Triple Entente? How did Germany respond to it?

4. After the assassination of Archduke Francis Ferdinand, what policies were pursued by Austria-Hungary, Germany, Russia?

5. Was World War I inevitable?

6. Why did many Europeans welcome the war?

CHAPTER 29

World War I: The West
in Despair

THERE WILL BE wars as never before on earth," predicted Nietzsche. World War I was just such a war. Modern technology enabled the combatants to kill with unprecedented efficiency; modern nationalism infused both civilians and soldiers with the determination to fight until the enemy was totally beaten. The modern state, exercising wide control over its citizens, mobilized its human, material, and spiritual resources to wage total war. As the war hardened into a savage and grueling fight, the statesmen did not press for a compromise peace, but demanded ever more mobilization, ever more escalation, and ever more sacrifices. The Great War profoundly altered the course of Western civilization. It deepened the spiritual crisis that had produced the war. How could one speak of the inviolability of the individual when Europe had become a slaughterhouse? Or of the primacy of reason when nations permitted slaughter to go unabated for four years? Now only the naive could believe in continuous progress. Western civilization had entered an age of violence, anxiety, and doubt that still persists.

STALEMATE IN THE WEST

On August 4, 1914, the German army invaded Belgium. German war plans, drawn up years earlier principally by General Alfred von Schlieffen, called for the German army to swing through Belgium to outflank French border defenses and then race on to Paris. After Paris was captured and the French army smashed, German railroads would rush the victorious troops to the eastern front to augment the small force that had been assigned to hold off the Russians. The German military felt certain that the spirit and skill of the German army would ensure victory over the much larger Russian forces. But everything depended on speed. Paris must be taken before the Russians could mobilize sufficient numbers to invade Germany. The Germans were confident that they would capture Paris in two months or less.

French strategy called for a headlong attack into Alsace and Lorraine. Believing that French strength lay in the spiritual qualities of the French soldier, in the will to victory that had inspired Republican arms in 1792, the French generals completely embraced an offensive strategy. "The French Army returning to its tradition henceforth admits no law but the offensive," began the field regulations drawn up in 1913. Inspired by Napoleon's stress on attack strategy and convinced that French soldiers possessed an unconquerable will and an irresistible nerve, the French army prepared its soldiers only for offensive warfare. The field regulations proclaimed: "Battles are beyond anything else struggles of morale. Defeat is inevitable as soon as the hope of conquering ceases to exist. Success comes not to him who has suffered the least but to him whose will is firmest and morale strongest."[1]

The French doctrine proved an instant failure. Though bayonet charges against machine-gun emplacements demonstrated the valor of French soldiers, they also revealed the incompetence of French generals. Making no effort at concealment or surprise and wearing striking red and blue uniforms, French soldiers were perfect targets. Marching into concentrated fire, they fell like pins. Everywhere the audacious attack was failing, but French generals, beguiled by the mystique of the offensive, would not change their strategy.

But the German success was not complete. Moving faster than anticipated, the Russians invaded East Prussia. This forced General Helmuth von Moltke to transfer troops from the French front, hampering the German advance. By early September the Germans had reached the Marne River, forty miles from Paris. With their capital at their backs, the regrouped French forces, aided by the British, fought with astounding courage. Meanwhile the Germans were exhausted by long marches and had outrun their supplies. Moreover, in their rush toward Paris, they had unknowingly

ON LES AURA! (WE'LL WIN), FRENCH WARBOND APPEAL, 1916 In the first months of the war, the French talked only of offensive. This lithograph (44½ ×31¼") by Jules-Abel Faivre exudes confidence. Bayonets, however, were no match for German machine guns. (Collection, The Museum of Modern Art, New York)

exposed their flanks, which the French attacked. The British then penetrated a gap that opened up between the German armies, forcing the Germans to retreat. Paris was saved, and the war entered a new and unexpected phase—the deadlock of trench warfare.

For four hundred miles, from the Alps to the North Sea across northern France, the opposing sides both constructed a vast network of trenches. These trenches had underground dugouts and barbed wire stretched for yards before the front trenches as a barrier to attack. Behind the front trenches were other lines to which soldiers could retreat and from which support could be sent. Between the opposing armies lay "no man's land," a waste-

BRITISH MUNITIONS WORKERS With millions of men in the military, women took jobs formerly held only by men. Women drove trucks and buses, operated cranes, and worked in armament factories. Resistance to granting them equal rights diminished, as politicians recognized the essential contribution of women to the war effort. (Brown Brothers)

land of mud, shattered trees, torn earth, and broken bodies. Trench warfare was a battle of nerves, endurance, and courage, waged to the constant thunder of heavy artillery. It was also butchery. As attacking troops climbed over their trenches and advanced across no man's land, they were decimated by heavy artillery and chewed up by machine-gun fire. If they did penetrate the front-line trenches of the enemy, they would soon be thrown back by a counter-attack.

Despite the frightful loss of life entailed by trench warfare, little land changed hands. So much heriosm, sacrifice, and death achieved nothing. The generals ordered still greater attacks to end the stalemate; this only increased the death toll, for the advantage was always with the defense, which possessed machine guns, magazine rifles, and barbed wire. Tanks could redress the balance, but the generals committed to old concepts, did not make effective use of tanks. Moreover, the technology of the machine gun had been perfected but the motorized tanks often broke down.

Gains and losses of land were measured in yards, but the lives of Europe's youth were squandered by the hundreds of thousands. In 1915, for example, France launched numerous attacks against German lines but never gained more than three miles in any one place. Yet these small gains cost France 1,430,000 casualties. Against artillery, barbed wire, and machine guns, human courage had no chance; the generals, uncomprehending, unfeeling, and incompetent, persisted in their massed attacks. This futile effort at a breakthrough wasted hundreds of thousands of lives.

In 1915, neither side could break the deadlock. Hoping to bleed the French army and force its surrender, the Germans in February 1916 attacked the town of Verdun, which was protected by a ring of forts. They chose Verdun because they knew the French could never permit a retreat from this ancient fortress. Compelled to pour more and more troops into battle, France would suffer such a loss of manpower that it would be unable to continue the war. Verdun was the bloodiest battle of the war. The leadership of General Henri Philippe Pétain, the tenacity of the French infantry, and the well-constructed concrete and steel forts enabled the French to hold on. When the British opened a major offensive on July 1, the Germans had to channel their reserves to the new front, relieving the pressure on Verdun.

France and Germany suffered more than a million casualties at Verdun, which one military historian calls "the greatest battle in world history."[2] No longer was the war a

WAR IN FRANCE Entrenched Allied troops met the entrenched German army. Stalemate resulted. In 1915, despite many assaults and shockingly high casualty rates, no more than a total of three miles was ever gained in any one place. (BBC Hulton Picture Library, London)

romantic adventure. A young French soldier, shortly before he was killed, expressed the mood of disillusionment that gripped the survivors of trench warfare: "Humanity is mad! It must be mad to do what it is doing. What a massacre! What scenes of horror and carnage. I cannot find words to translate my impressions. Hell cannot be so terrible. Men are mad!"[3]

At the end of June 1916 the British, assisted by the French, attempted a breakthrough at the Somme River. After five days of intense bombardment intended to destroy German defenses, the British on July 1 climbed out of their trenches and ventured into no man's land. But German positions had not been destroyed. Marching into concentrated machine-gun fire, the British troops never made it across no man's land. Sixty thousand Britons fell dead or wounded, "the heaviest loss ever suffered in a single day by a British army or by any army in the First World War," observes British historian A. J. P. Taylor.[4] Some reached the German wire, only to become entangled in it. The Germans killed them with rifle fire and bayonets. After this initial disaster, common sense and a concern for human life demanded that the attack be called off, but the generals continued to feed the soldiers to the German guns. When the battle of the Somme ended in mid-November, Britain and France had lost over 600,000 men. And the military situation remained essentially unchanged.

In December 1916, General Robert Nivelle was appointed Commander-in-Chief of the French forces. Having learned little from past French failures to achieve a breakthrough, Nivelle ordered another massed attack for April 1917. The Germans discovered the battle plans on the body of a French officer and withdrew to a shorter line on high ground, constructing the strongest defense network of the war. Knowing that they had lost the element of surprise and pushing aside the warnings of leading statesmen and military men, Nivelle went ahead with the attack. "The offensive alone gives victory; the defensive gives only defeat and shame," he told the president and the minister of war.[5]

The battle, which began on April 16, was another blood bath. In many places French artillery had not cut the German barbed wire. As the soldiers tried to grope their way through, they were chewed up by German machine-gun fire. Sometimes the fire was so intense that the French could not make it out of their own trenches. Although French soldiers fought with courage, the situation was hopeless. Still Nivelle persisted with the attack; after ten days French casualties numbered 187,000.

The soldiers could endure no more. Spontaneous revolts, born of despair and military failure, broke out in rest areas as soldiers refused to return to the slaughter ground. In some instances they shouted "Peace" and "To hell with the War." Mobs of soldiers seized trains in order to reach Paris and stir up the population against the war. Mutineers took control of barracks and threatened to fire on officers who interfered. The mutiny spread to the front lines as soldiers told their officers they would defend the trenches but not attack. The French army was disintegrating. "The slightest German attack would have sufficed to tumble down our house of cards and bring the enemy to Paris," recalled a French officer.[6]

General Pétain, the hero of Verdun, replaced the disgraced Nivelle. To restore morale, Pétain granted more leave, improved the quality of food, made the rest areas more comfortable, and ordered officers to demonstrate a personal concern for their men. He visited the troops, listened to their complaints, and told them that France would engage in only limited offensives until American reinforcements arrived in large numbers. These measures, combined with imprisonments and executions, restored discipline. The Germans, unaware of the full magnitude of the mutiny, had not put pressure on the front; by the time the Germans attacked, Pétain had revitalized the army.

OTHER FRONTS

While the western front hardened into a stalemate, what was happening on the eastern front? In August 1914, according to plan, the bulk of the German army invaded France hoping for a knockout blow, while a small force defended the eastern frontier against Russia. Responding to French requests to put pressure on Germany, the Russians, with insufficient preparation, invaded East Prussia. After some initial successes, which sent a scare into the German general staff, the Russians were soundly defeated at the battle of Tannenberg (August 26–30, 1914) and forced to withdraw from German territory, which remained inviolate for the rest of the war.

Meanwhile Germany's ally Austria was having no success against Serbia and Russia. An invasion of Serbia was thrown back, and an ill-conceived offensive against Russia cost Austria its Galician provinces. Germany had to come to Austria's rescue. In the spring of 1915 the Germans made a breakthrough that forced the Russians to abandon Galicia and most of Poland. Outrunning their supplies, the Ger-

MAP 29.1   WORLD WAR I, 1914–1918 ▶

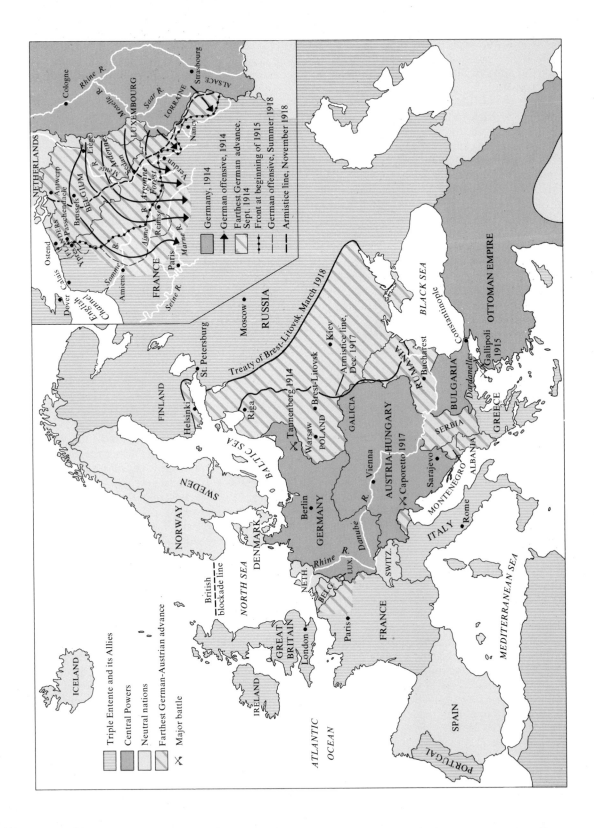

Germany, 1914

German offensive, 1914

Farthest German advance, Sept. 1914

Front at beginning of 1915

German offensive, Summer 1918

Armistice line, November 1918

Triple Entente and its Allies

Central Powers

Neutral nations

Farthest German-Austrian advance

✕ Major battle

British blockade line

Treaty of Brest-Litovsk, March 1918

Armistice line, Dec. 1917

ICELAND

ATLANTIC OCEAN

IRELAND

GREAT BRITAIN

London

NORTH SEA

NORWAY

SWEDEN

DENMARK

BALTIC SEA

FINLAND

Helsinki

St. Petersburg

Moscow

RUSSIA

Riga

✕ Tannenberg 1914

Warsaw

POLAND

Brest-Litovsk

Kiev

GALICIA

Berlin

GERMANY

Rhine R.

Danube R.

AUSTRIA-HUNGARY

Vienna

R.

✕ Caporetto 1917

NETH.

BELG.

LUX.

SWITZ.

FRANCE

Paris

ITALY

Rome

SPAIN

PORTUGAL

MEDITERRANEAN SEA

MONTENEGRO

ALBANIA

SERBIA

Sarajevo

RUMANIA

Bucharest

BULGARIA

GREECE

BLACK SEA

Constantinople

Dardanelles

Gallipoli 1915

OTTOMAN EMPIRE

Cologne

Rhine R.

R.

Moselle R.

Saar R.

LUXEMBOURG

LORRAINE

Strasbourg

ALSACE

Nancy

NETHERLANDS

Antwerp

Liège

BELGIUM

Brussels

Meuse R.

Sedan

Argonne Forest

Verdun

FLANDERS

Passchendaele

Ostend

Yser R.

Aisne R.

Remy

Marne R.

Calais

Dover

English Channel

Somme R.

Amiens

FRANCE

Paris

Seine R.

mans and Austrians had to slow down their pursuit of the retreating Russians, who were able to build a new line. Germany did not gain the decisive victory it had sought; although badly battered, Russia remained in the war, forcing Germany to fight a two-front war.

In June 1916 the Russians launched an offensive under General Aleksei Brusilov that opened a wide breach in the Austrian lines. Brusilov proved to be a brilliant commander but he did not get sufficient aid from other Russian armies. Hampered by this lack of support and by the inability of the Russian railways to transport his reserves, Brusilov could not maintain the offensive. A German counteroffensive forced a retreat that cost the Russians over a million casualties. After the winding down of the Brusilov offensive, Russia's military position deteriorated and domestic unrest worsened.

The Ottoman Empire joined the war as an ally of Germany. Prior to the war, Germany had cultivated the Ottoman Empire's friendship by training the Turkish army; on its part, the Ottoman Empire wanted German help in case Russia attempted to seize the Dardanelles. To relieve the pressure on Russia caused by an Ottoman invasion of the Caucasus, the British planned to seize the Dardanelles and Constantinople. Although the Turks retreated from the Caucasus, Britain persisted with the plan. Supporters of the plan, including Winston Churchill, First Lord of the Admiralty, argued that the opening of another front in the Balkans might compel Germany to withdraw forces from the west. Even more important, the capture of the Dardanelles would enable the Allies to supply Russia and, in turn, obtain badly needed Russian grain.

In April 1915, a combined force of British, French, Australian, and New Zealander troops stormed the Gallipoli Peninsula on the European side of the Dardanelles. Ignorance of amphibious warfare, poor intelligence, and the fierce resistance of the Turks prevented the Allies from getting off the beaches and taking the heights. Some of the hardest fighting of the war took place on the beaches and cliffs of Gallipoli. The Gallipoli campaign cost the Allies 252,000 casualties, and they had gained nothing.

Although a member of the Triple Alliance, Italy remained neutral when war broke out. In 1915, on the promise of receiving Austrian territory, Italy entered the war on the side of the Allies. The Austrians repulsed a number of Italian offensives along the frontier and in 1916 took the offensive against Italy. A combined German and Austrian force finally broke through the Italian lines in the fall of 1917 at Caporetto and the Italians retreated in disorder, leaving behind huge quantities of weapons. Germany and Austria took some 275,000 prisoners.

THE COLLAPSE OF THE CENTRAL POWERS

American Entry

The year 1917 seemed disastrous for the Allies. The Nivelle offensive had failed, the French army had mutinied, the British attack at Passchendaele did not bring the expected breakthrough and only added some 300,000 casualties to the butchery list, and the Russians, torn by revolution and gripped by war weariness, were close to withdrawing from the war. But there was one encouraging development for the Allies. In April 1917 the United States had declared war on Germany.

From the outset America's sympathies lay with the Allies. To most Americans, Britain and France were democracies, threatened by an autocratic and militaristic Germany. These sentiments were reinforced by British propaganda that depicted the Germans as cruel "Huns." Since most war news came to the United States from Britain, anti-German feeling gained momentum. What precipitated American entry was the German decision of January 1917 to launch a campaign of unrestricted submarine warfare in a determined effort to deprive Britain of war supplies and to starve it into submission. This meant that German U-boats would torpedo both enemy and neutral ships in the war zone around the British Isles. Since the United States was Britain's principal supplier, American ships became a target of German submarines.

Angered by American loss of life and material and by the violation of the doctrine of freedom of the seas, and fearful of a diminution of prestige if the United States took no action, President Woodrow Wilson (1856–1924) pressed for American entry. Also at stake was American security, which would be jeopardized by German domination of western Europe. Leading American statesmen and diplomats feared that such a radical change in the balance of power threatened American national interests. Some argued that a Germany bloated with victory in Europe might one day seek conquests in the Western Hemisphere. As Secretary of State Robert Lansing wrote in a private memorandum just prior to American entry into the war: "The Allies must *not* be beaten. It would mean the triumph of Autocracy over Democracy; the shattering of all our moral standards; and a real, though it may seem remote, peril to our independence and institutions."[7] Not only would a German triumph destroy the balance of power and foment German expansion in Europe and other parts of the world, it would also shatter any hopes of building a peaceful and democratic world after the war, which was a principal hope of the idealistic Wilson.

In initiating unrestricted submarine warfare, Germany gambled that the United States would continue to maintain a neutral policy. But the United States immediately broke diplomatic relations with Germany. Three weeks later the British turned over to the United States a message sent by Berlin to the German ambassador in Mexico City and deciphered by British code experts. Germany proposed that in case of war between Germany and the United States, Mexico should join Germany as an ally; in return Mexico would receive Texas, New Mexico, and Arizona. This fantastic proposal further exacerbated anti-German feeling in the United States. As German submarines continued to attack neutral shipping, President Wilson, on April 2, 1917, urged Congress to declare war on Germany, which it did, on April 6.

Although the United States may have entered the war to protect its own security, President Wilson told the American people and the world that the United States was fighting "to make the world safe for democracy." With America's entry, the war had been transformed into a moral crusade, an ideological conflict between democracy and autocracy. In January 1918, Wilson enunciated American war aims in the Fourteen Points, which called for territorial changes based on nationality and the application of democratic principles to international relations. An association of nations would be established to preserve peace; it would conduct international relations with the same respect for law evidenced in democratic states. In nationalism and democracy, the two great legacies of the nineteenth century, Wilson placed his hope for the future peace of the world.

Germany's Last Offensive

With Russia out of the war, General Erich von Ludendorff prepared for a decisive offensive before the Americans could land sufficient troops in France. A war of attrition now favored the Allies, who could count on American supplies and manpower. Without an immediate and decisive victory, Germany could not hope to win the war. Ludendorff hoped to drive the British forces back to the sea, forcing them to withdraw from the Continent. Then he would turn his full might against the French. Just before dawn on March 21, 1918, the Germans began the bombardment against the British lines. After hitting the British with artillery, gas, and mortar shells, the Germans climbed out of their trenches and moved across a no man's land enveloped by fog; the attackers could not be seen as they advanced toward the British trenches. The British retreated. Expanding their offensive, the Germans now sought to split the British and French forces by capturing Amiens, the major communications center, and to drive the British back to the channel ports.

Suddenly the deadlock had been broken; it was now a war of movement. Within two weeks the Germans had taken some 1,250 square miles. But British resistance stiffened and the Germans, exhausted and short of ammunition and food, called off the drive. A second offensive against the British in April also had to be called off as the British contested every foot of ground. Both campaigns depleted German manpower while the Americans were arriving in great numbers to strengthen Allied lines and to uplift Allied morale.

At the end of May, Ludendorff resumed his offensive against the French. Attacking unexpectedly, the Germans broke through and advanced to within thirty-seven miles of Paris by early June. General John Pershing, head of the American forces, cabled Washington that "the possibility of losing Paris has become apparent."[8] But in the battle of Belleau Wood (June 6–25, 1918), the Americans checked the Germans, depriving them of an open road to Paris.

In mid-July the Germans tried again, crossing the Marne River in small boats. Although in one area they advanced nine miles, the offensive failed against determined opposition by the Americans and French. Unable to widen the *salient* (battle line), Ludendorff ordered a pullback. The Germans had thrown everything they had into their spring and summer offensive, but it was not enough. The Allies had bent, but reinforced and encouraged by American arms, did not break. Now they began to counterattack.

On August 8 the British, assisted by the French and using tanks to great advantage,

broke through east of Amiens. Ludendorff called this battle the Black Day. Aware that victory was now impossible, he sought an immediate armistice, lest the Allies invade the fatherland and shatter the reputation of the German army. Hoping to obtain more favorable armistice terms from President Wilson, and to shift the blame for the lost war away from the military and the Kaiser to civilian leadership, Ludendorff cynically urged the creation of a popular parliamentary government in Germany.

Meanwhile Germany's military position was deteriorating rapidly. British successes in the Near East compelled the Ottoman Empire to withdraw from the war; rebellions by the various Slavic nationalities and the virtual disintegration of the empire forced Austria to agree to an armistice. And events in Germany went further than Ludendorff had anticipated. Whereas Ludendorff sought a limited monarchy, the shock of defeat and hunger sparked a revolution that forced the Kaiser to abdicate. On November 11, the new German Republic signed an armistice ending the hostilities. At 11 A.M. the soldiers from both sides walked into no man's land and into the daylight. A newspaper correspondent with the British army in France wrote: "Last night for the first time since August in the first year of the war, there was no light of gunfire in the sky, no sudden stabs of flame through darkness, no spreading glow above black trees where for four years of nights human beings were smashed to death. The Fires of Hell had been put out."[9]

THE PEACE CONFERENCE

Wilson's Hope for a New World

In January 1919, representatives of the Allied Powers assembled in Paris to draw up peace terms; President Wilson was also there. The war-weary masses turned to Wilson as the

WILSON'S WELCOME TO EUROPE Woodrow Wilson was greeted as the bringer of peace. His presence at the peace conference, where he haggled over points, and the Republican victory in the U.S. presidential election in November 1918 soon tarnished that image. (The National Archives)

prophet who would have the nations beat their swords into plowshares. In Paris, two million people lined the streets to cheer Wilson and throw bouquets; his carriage passed under a huge banner on which was written "Honor to Wilson the Just." In Rome, hysterical crowds called him the god of peace; in Milan, wounded soldiers sought to kiss his clothes; in Poland, university students spoke his name when they shook hands.

For Wilson the war had been fought to "make the world safe for democracy"; it was a war of the people against absolutism. A peace settlement based on liberal-democratic ideals, he hoped, would sweep away the foundations of war. Wilson proclaimed his message with a spiritual zeal that expressed his Presbyterian background and his faith in American democracy.

None of Wilson's principles seemed more just than the idea of self-determination—the right of a people to have its own state free of foreign domination. In particular, this meant (or was interpreted to mean) the return of

Alsace and Lorraine to France, the creation of an independent Poland, a readjustment of the frontiers of Italy to incorporate Austrian lands inhabited by Italians, and an opportunity for Slavs of the Austrian Empire to form their own states. While Wilson did not demand the liberation of all colonies, the Fourteen Points did call for "a free, open-minded and absolutely impartial adjustment of all colonial claims," and a territorial settlement "made in the interest and for the benefit of the population concerned."

Aware that a harshly treated Germany might well seek revenge, thereby engulfing the world in another cataclysm, Wilson insisted that there should be a "peace without victory." A just settlement would encourage a defeated Germany to work with the victorious Allies in building a new Europe. But on one point he was adamant: Prussian militarism, which he viewed as a principal cause of the war, must be eliminated.

To preserve peace and to help remake the world, Wilson urged the formation of a League of Nations, an international parliament to settle disputes and discourage aggression. Wilson wanted a peace of justice in order to preserve Western civilization in its democratic and Christian form.

Obstacles to Wilson's Program

But how could such high-sounding, moralistic proclamations be translated into concrete peace provisions? "Obviously no mortal man this side of the millennium could have hoped to bring about all the things that the world came to expect of Wilson," concludes American historian Thomas A. Bailey. "Wilson's own people were bound to feel disillusioned; the peoples of the neutral and Allied countries were bound to feel deceived; and the peoples of the enemy countries were bound to feel betrayed."[10]

Wilson's negotiating position was under-mined by the Republican party's victory in the Congressional elections of November 1918. Before the election, Wilson appealed to the American people to vote for Democrats as a vote of confidence in his diplomacy. But Americans elected twenty-five Republicans and fifteen Democrats to the Senate. Whatever the motives of the American people in voting Republican—apparently their decision rested on local and national, not international, issues—the outcome hurt Wilson's prestige at the conference table. To his fellow negotiators, Wilson was trying to preach to Europe when he could not command the support of his own country. Since the Senate must ratify a treaty, European diplomats had the terrible fear that what Wilson agreed to the Senate might reject—which is precisely what happened.

It has been suggested that Wilson's very presence at the conference table also diminished his prestige. As president of the nation that had rescued the Allies and as initiator of a peace program that held the promise of a new world, Wilson occupied a position of honor from which he could exact considerable influence and authority. But by attending the conference in person, by haggling with the other representatives, he was knocked from his lofty pedestal and became all too human. "Messiahs tend to arouse less enthusiasm the more they show themselves," observes Bailey; "the role requires aloofness and the spell of mystery."[11]

Another obstacle to Wilson's peace program was the French demand for security and revenge. Nearly the entire war on the Western front had been fought in French territory. French industries and farms had been ruined; the French people mourned their dead. To many French the Germans were savages, vandals, assassins. The French people were skeptical of Wilson's idealism. "Let us try out the new order," said a French editorial in the *Echo de Paris*, "but so long as we are not assured of its absolute success . . . let us maintain . . . unsatisfactory though they may be, the pillars of the old order . . . which will seek to maintain peace by the aid of military, political and economic guarantees."[12]

Representing France at the conference table was Georges Clemenceau (1841–1929), nicknamed "the Tiger." Nobody loved France more or hated Germany more. Cynical, suspicious of idealism, and not sharing Wilson's hope for a new world or his confidence in the future League of Nations, Clemenceau demanded that Germany be severely punished and German capacity to wage war destroyed. Fearful of Germany's superior manpower and industrial strength, and its military tradition that would not resign itself to defeat, Clemenceau wanted guarantees that the wars of 1870–1871 and 1914–1918 would not be repeated. The war had shown that, without the help of Britain and the United States, France would have been at the mercy of Germany. Because there was no certainty that these states would again aid France, Clemenceau wanted to use France's present advantage to cripple Germany.

The intermingling of European nationalities was another barrier to Wilson's program. Because in so many regions of Central Europe there was a mixture of nationalities, no one could create a Europe completely free of minority problems; some nationalities would always feel that they had been treated shabbily. And the various nationalities were not willing to moderate their demands or lower their aspirations. "To most Europeans," states German-American historian Hajo Holborn, "the satisfaction of their national dreams was an absolute end even when their realization violated the national determination of others."[13] For example, the Fourteen Points called for the creation of an independent Poland with a secure access to the sea. But between Poland and the sea lay territory populated by Germans. Giving this land to Poland would violate German self-determination; denying it to Poland would mean that the new country had little chance of developing a sound economy. No matter what the decision, one people would regard it

as unjust. Similarly, to provide the new Czechoslovakia with defensible borders, it would be necessary to give it territory inhabited principally by Germans. This too could be viewed as a denial of German self-determination, but not granting it to Czechoslovakia would mean that the new state would not be able to defend itself against Germany.

Also serving as a barrier to Wilson's program were the secret treaties drawn up by the Allies during the war. These agreements, dividing up German, Austrian, and Ottoman territory, did not square with the principle of self-determination. For example, to entice Italy into entering the war, the Allies had promised it Austrian lands that were inhabited predominantly by Germans and Slavs. Italy was not about to repudiate its prize because of Wilson's principles.

Finally, the war had aroused great bitterness that persisted after the guns had been silenced. Both the masses and their leaders demanded retribution and held exaggerated hopes for territory and reparations. In such an atmosphere of postwar enmity, the spirit of compromise and moderation could not overcome the desire for spoils and punishment. A century earlier, when the monarchs had defeated Napoleon they sought a peace of reconciliation with France. But democratic statesmen and nations found it harder to set aside their hatreds than had despotic monarchs and aristocratic diplomats.

The Settlement

After months of negotiations, punctured often by acrimony, the peacemakers hammered out a settlement. Five treaties made up the Peace of Paris, one each with Germany, Austria, Hungary, Bulgaria, and Turkey. Of the five, the Treaty of Versailles, which Germany signed on June 28, 1919, was the most significant. France regained Alsace and Lorraine, lost to Germany in the Franco-Prussian War of 1870–1871.

Germany was barred from placing fortifications in the Rhineland.

The French military had wanted to take the Rhineland from Germany and break it up into one or more republics under French suzerainty. The Rhine River was a natural defensive border; one had only to destroy the bridges to prevent a German invasion of France. With Germany deprived of this springboard for invasion, French security would be immensely improved. Recognizing that the German people would never permanently submit to the amputation of the Rhineland, which was inhabited by more than 5 million Germans and contained key industries, Wilson and British Prime Minister David Lloyd George (1863–1945) resisted these French demands. They did not want to create an Alsace and Lorraine in reverse by awarding France a region that was overwhelmingly German. Nor could Wilson ever agree to such a glaring violation of the principle of self-determination.

But Clemenceau did not willingly agree to give up France's demand for control of the Rhineland. The confrontation between Wilson and Clemenceau was so bitter that the president made plans to return to the United States, threatening to disrupt the conference. Faced with the opposition of Wilson and Lloyd George, Clemenceau backed down and agreed instead to Allied occupation of the Rhineland for fifteen years, the demilitarization of the region, and an Anglo-American promise of assistance if Germany violated these arrangements. This last point, considered vital by France, proved useless. The alliance only went into effect if both the United States and Britain ratified it. Since the Security Treaty did not get past the United States Senate, Britain also refused to sign it. France had made a great concession on the Rhineland issue but received nothing in exchange; the French people felt that they had been wronged and duped.

A related issue concerned French demands for annexation of the coal-rich Saar Basin, which adjoined Lorraine. By obtaining this region, France would weaken Germany's military potential and strengthen its own. France argued that this would be just compensation for the deliberate destruction of the French coal mines by the retreating German army at the end of the war. But here too France was disappointed. The final compromise called for a League of Nations commission to govern the Saar Basin for fifteen years, after which the inhabitants would decide whether the territory would be ceded to France or returned to Germany.

In eastern Germany, in certain districts of Silesia that had a large Polish population, a plebiscite would be held to determine the future of the region. As a result, part of Upper Silesia was ceded to Poland. A corridor terminating in the Baltic port of Danzig was cut through West Prussia and given to Poland, and Danzig was declared an international city to be administered by a commission appointed by the League of Nations. The Germans would never resign themselves to this loss of territory that separated East Prussia from the rest of Germany, especially since it was awarded to the Poles, whom many Germans viewed as cultural and racial inferiors.

Regarding the Germans as unfit to care for colonial peoples, Wilson supported stripping Germany of its overseas possessions, all of which had been seized by the Allies during the war. But instead of the outright annexation of German colonies by the victorious powers, Wilson proposed the mandate system, whereby small nations would be entrusted with the administration of the colonies under the guidance of the League of Nations. Such an arrangement would accord with the spirit of the Fourteen Points. Here too, Wilson's proposal conflicted with secret agreements made by Britain to its dominions—the Union of South Africa, Australia, New Zealand—and to Japan.

Backing down from his position that the German colonies be mandated to small nations, Wilson permitted the victorious nations to be awarded control. However, these nations

MAP 29.2 POST–WORLD WAR I: BROKEN EMPIRES AND CHANGED BOUNDARIES▶

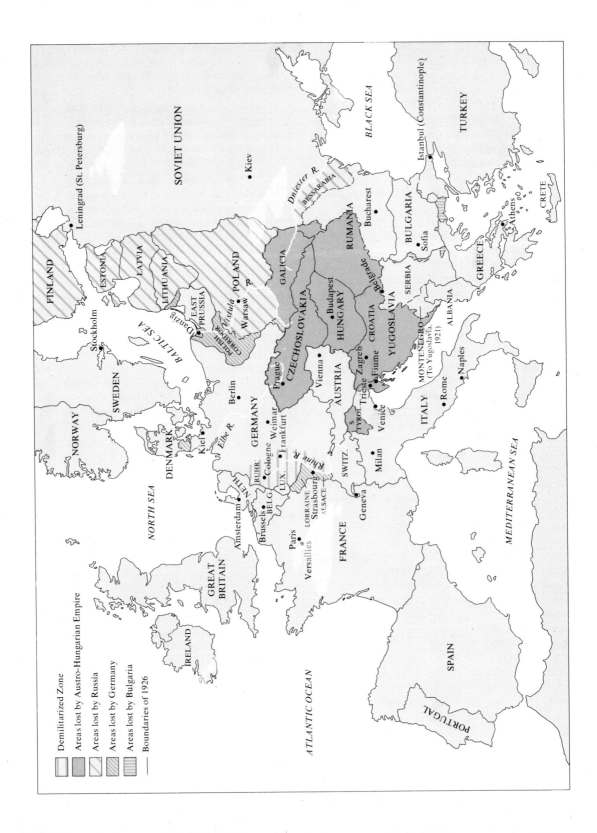

FINLAND

SOVIET UNION

Leningrad (St. Petersburg)

Kiev

ESTONIA

LATVIA

LITHUANIA

BALTIC SEA

Stockholm

SWEDEN

NORWAY

DENMARK

Kiel

NORTH SEA

NETH.

Amsterdam

GREAT BRITAIN

IRELAND

ATLANTIC OCEAN

Berlin

GERMANY

Weimar

Cologne
RUHR
Frankfurt
Elbe R.
Rhine R.

Brussels
BELG.
LUX.
Paris
Versailles
LORRAINE
Strasbourg
ALSACE

FRANCE

SWITZ.

Geneva

SPAIN

PORTUGAL

Danzig
EAST PRUSSIA
POLISH CORRIDOR
Vistula R.
Warsaw
POLAND

GALICIA

Dniester R.
BESSARABIA

CZECHOSLOVAKIA

Prague

Vienna

AUSTRIA

S. TYROL

Venice

Milan

ITALY

Rome

Naples

Budapest

HUNGARY

CROATIA

Zagreb

Trieste
Fiume

YUGOSLAVIA

MONTENEGRO
(To Yugoslavia,
1921)

Belgrade

SERBIA

ALBANIA

RUMANIA

Bucharest

BULGARIA

Sofia

GREECE

Athens

Istanbul (Constantinople)

TURKEY

BLACK SEA

CRETE

MEDITERRANEAN SEA

Demilitarized Zone

Areas lost by Austro-Hungarian Empire

Areas lost by Russia

Areas lost by Germany

Areas lost by Bulgaria

Boundaries of 1926

held the former German and Ottoman colonies not outright but as mandates under the supervision of the League, which would protect the interests of the native peoples. Thus the division of Ottoman and German colonies represented a compromise between traditional imperialism and Wilsonian idealism. The mandate system implied the ultimate end of colonialism, for it clearly opposed the exploitation of colonial peoples and asserted independence as the rightful goal for subject nations.

To prevent a resurgence of militarism, the German general staff was abolished and military conscription forbidden. The German army was limited to 100,000 volunteers and deprived of heavy artillery, tanks, and warplanes. The German navy was limited to a token force that did not include submarines.

The issue of reparations (compensation) aroused terrible bitterness between Wilson and his French and British adversaries. Goaded by public opinion and enticed by a helpless Germany, Lloyd George and Clemenceau sought to make Germany pay the total costs of the war. While Wilson resisted such an impossible demand, he did make considerable concessions to Anglo-French insistence on exacting vast reparations from the defeated army. Wilson agreed that the costs of Allied pensions paid to veterans and their families should be borne by Germany, an inclusion that nearly tripled the bill. The American delegation wanted the Treaty to fix a reasonable sum that Germany would have to pay and specify the period of years allotted for payment. But no such items were contained in the Treaty; they were left for future consideration. When Germany signed the Treaty, it was left with an open-ended bill that would probably take generations to pay. The Allies had not considered Germany's capacity to pay, and Wilson had lost on the issue of reasonable reparations.

Moreover, Article 231, which preceded the reparation clauses, placed sole responsibility for the war on Germany and its allies. The Germans responded to this accusation with contempt. Clearly the German government would feel little incentive to pay the reparations and considerable moral justification in evading them.

In separate treaties the conference dealt with the liquidation of the Hapsburg Empire. In the closing weeks of the war, the Austro-Hungarian Empire had crumbled as the various nationalities proclaimed their independence from Hapsburg rule. In most cases the peacemakers put into a treaty what the nationalities had already accomplished in fact. Serbia joined with Austrian lands inhabited by Croats and Slovens to become Yugoslavia. Czechoslovakia arose from the predominantly Czech and Slovak regions of Austria. Hungary, which broke away from Austria to become a separate country, had to concede considerable land to Rumania and Yugoslavia. Austria had to turn over to Italy the South Tyrol, which was inhabited by 200,000 Austrian Germans, a clear violation of the principle of self-determination that greatly offended liberal opinion. Deprived of its vast territories and prohibited from union with Germany, the new Austria was now a third-rate power.

Assessment and Problems

The Germans unanimously denounced the Treaty, for in their minds the war had ended not in German defeat but in a stalemate. They regarded the armistice as the prelude to a negotiated settlement among equals based on Wilson's call for a peace of justice. Instead the Germans were barred from participating in the negotiations. And they viewed the terms of the Treaty as humiliating and vindictive, designed to keep Germany militarily and economically weak. What standard of justice, they asked, allowed the Allies to take the German colonies for themselves, to reduce the German military to a pitiful size without themselves disarming, to ban Germany from the League of Nations, to saddle Germany with impossible reparations, to amputate approximately one-eighth of German territory and deprive it of one-tenth of its population, to blame the war on Germany alone, to provide for the self-determination of Poles while precluding the union of German-speaking Austria with Germany, to hand over to Italy some 200,000 Austrian Germans, to place Germans under Polish rule and declare the German port of Danzig a free city?

When the United States entered the war, the Germans protested, Wilson had stated that the enemy was not the German people but their government. Surely, the Germans now argued, the new German democracy should not be punished for the sins of the monarchy and the military. To the Germans the Treaty of Versailles was not the dawning of the new world that Wilson had promised, but an abomination, a vile crime.

War weary, torn by revolutionary unrest, desperately short of food, its economy in disarray, and with the Allies poised to invade, the new German Republic had no choice but to sign the Treaty. However, the sentiments of the German people were clearly and prophetically expressed by the Berlin *Vorwärts*, the influential Social Democratic newspaper. "We must never forget it is only a scrap of paper. Treaties based on violence can keep their validity only so long as force exists. Do not lose hope. The resurrection day comes."[14]

Critics in other lands also condemned the Treaty as a punitive settlement in flagrant violation of Wilsonian idealism. The peacemakers, they argued, should have set aside past hatreds and, in cooperation with the new democratic German Republic, forged a just settlement that would serve as the foundation of a new world. Instead they burdened the fledgling German democracy with reparations that were impossible to pay, insulted it with the accusation of war guilt, and deprived it of territory in violation of the principle of self-determination. All these provisions, said the critics, would only exacerbate old hatreds and fan the flames of German nationalism. This was a poor beginning for democracy in Germany and for Wilson's new world.

Defenders of the peace settlement insisted that had Germany won the war it would have imposed a far harsher settlement on the Allies. They pointed to German war aims, which called for the annexation of parts of France and Poland, the reduction of Belgium and Rumania to satellites, and German expansion in central Africa. They pointed also to the Treaty of Brest-Litovsk (see page 680), which Germany compelled Russia to sign in 1918, as an example of Germany's ruthlessness and appetite. Moreover, they insisted that the peace settlement was by no means a repudiation of Wilson's principles. The new map of Europe was the closest approximation to the ethnic distribution of peoples that Europe had ever known.

What is most significant about the Treaty of Versailles is that it did not solve the German problem. Germany was left weak but unbroken, its industrial and military power only temporarily contained, its nationalist fervor undimmed. The real problem was not the severity of the Treaty but German unwillingness to accept defeat or surrender the dream of expansion.

Would France, Britain, and the United States enforce the Treaty against a resurgent Germany? The war had demonstrated that an Allied victory depended on American intervention. But in 1920 the U.S. Senate, angry that Wilson had not taken Republicans with him to Paris and fearing that membership in the League of Nations would involve America in future wars, refused to ratify the Treaty of Versailles. Britain, feeling guilty over the treatment of Germany, lacked the will for enforcement and even came to favor treaty revision. The responsibility for preserving the settlement therefore rested primarily with France, which was not encouraging. The Paris peace settlement left Germany resentful but potentially powerful, and to the east lay small and weak states, some of them with sizable German minorities, which could not check a rearmed Germany.

THE WAR AND EUROPEAN CONSCIOUSNESS

World War I was a great turning point in the history of the West. The war left many with the gnawing feeling that Western civilization had lost its vitality and was caught in a rhythm of breakdown and disintegration. It seemed that Western civilization was fragile and perishable, that Western people, despite their extraordinary accomplishments, were never more than a step or two away from barbarism. Surely any civilization that could allow such senseless slaughter to last four years had entered its decline and could look forward to only the darkest of futures.

European intellectuals were demoralized and disillusioned. The orderly, peaceful, rational world of their youth had been destroyed. The world-view of the Enlightenment, weakened in the nineteenth century by the assault of romantics, race mystics, extreme nationalists, Social Darwinists, and glorifiers of the irrational, was now in disarray. The enormity of the war had shattered faith in the capacities of reason to deal with crucial social and political questions. It seemed that civilization was fighting an unending and seemingly hopeless battle against the irrational elements in human nature.

Confidence in the future gave way to doubt. The old beliefs in the perfectibility of humanity, the blessings of science, and linear progress now seemed an expression of naive optimism. A. J. P. Taylor concludes:

The First World War was difficult to fit into the picture of a rational civilization advancing by ordered stages. The civilized men of the twentieth century had outdone in savagery the barbarians of all preceding ages, and their civilized virtues—organization, mechanical skill, self-sacrifice—had made war's savagery all the more terrible. Modern man had developed powers which he was not fit to use. European civilization had been weighed in the balance and found wanting.[15]

Western civilization had lost its spiritual center. Paul Valéry summed up the mood of a troubled generation for whom the sun seemed to be setting on the Enlightenment.

The storm has died away, and still we are restless, uneasy as if the storm were about to break. Almost all the affairs of men remain in a terrible uncertainty. We think of what has disappeared, and we are almost destroyed by what has been destroyed; we do not know what will be born, and we fear the future, not without reason. We hope vaguely, we dread precisely; our fears are infinitely more precise than our hopes; we confess that the charm of life is behind us. There is no thinking man . . . who can hope to dominate this anxiety, to escape from this impression of darkness. . . . But among all these injured things is the Mind. The Mind has indeed been cruelly wounded; its complaint is heard in the hearts of intellectual men; it passes a mournful judgment on itself. It doubts itself profoundly.[16]

This disillusionment with liberal-democratic values contributed to the widespread popularity of fascist ideologies in the postwar world. Having lost confidence in the power of reason to solve the problems of the human community, in liberal doctrines of individual freedom, and in the institutions of parliamentary democracy, many people turned to fascism as a simple saving faith. Far from making the world safe for democracy as Wilson and other liberals had hoped, World War I gave rise to totalitarian movements that would nearly destroy democracy.

The war produced a generation of young people who had reached their maturity in combat. Violence had become a way of life for millions of soldiers hardened by battle and for millions of civilians aroused by four years of propaganda. The astronomical casualty figures—some 10 million dead and 21 million wounded—had a brutalizing effect. Violence, cruelty, suffering, and even wholesale death seemed to be natural and acceptable compo-

KÄTHE KOLLWITZ: THE SURVIVORS With an estimated 10 million dead and 21 million wounded, World War I shattered the hope that western Europe had been making continuous progress toward universal peace and a rational and enlightened civilization. (National Gallery of Art, Washington, D.C.; Rosenwald Collection)

nents of human existence; the sanctity of the individual seemed to be liberal and Christian claptrap. This fascination for violence and contempt for life lived on in the postwar world. Many returned veterans yearned for the excitement of battle and the fellowship of the trenches.

The brutalizing effect of the war is seen in the following statement by a German soldier for whom the war never ended:

People told us that the War was over. That made us laugh. We ourselves are the War. Its flame burns strongly in us. It envelopes our

CHRONOLOGY 29.1   WORLD WAR I

June 28, 1914	Archduke Ferdinand of Austria is assassinated at Sarajevo
August 4, 1914	The Germans invade Belgium
August–September 1914	The Russians invade East Prussia; the battle of Tannenberg (Russians are defeated by the Germans)
September 1914	The battle of the Marne (Germans retreat)
April 1915	The Allies storm Gallipoli Peninsula, withdrawing after 252,000 casualties are suffered
May 1915	Italy enters the war on the Allies' side
1915	Germany forces Russia to abandon Galicia and most of Poland
February 1916	General Pétain leads French forces at Verdun (Germans are defeated)
June 1916	General Brusilov leads a Russian offensive against Austrian lines with a million casualties
July–November 1916	The battle of the Somme—high casualties on both sides
January 1917	Germany resumes unrestricted submarine warfare
April 6, 1917	The United States declares war on Germany

whole being and fascinates us with the enticing urge to destroy. We . . . marched onto the battlefields of the postwar world just as we had gone into battle on the Western Front: singing, reckless, and filled with the joy of adventure as we marched to the attack; silent, deadly, remorseless in battle.[17]

These veterans made ideal recruits for extremist political movements that glorified action and promised to rescue society from a decadent liberalism.

Both Hitler and Mussolini, themselves ex-soldiers imbued with the ferocity of the front, knew how to appeal to veterans. The lovers of violence and the harbingers of hate who became the leaders of fascist parties would come within a hairsbreadth of destroying Western civilization. The intensified nationalist hatreds following World War I also helped to fuel the fires of World War II. The Germans swore to regain lands lost to the Poles; some Germans dreamed of a war of revenge. Italy, too, felt aggrieved because it had not received more territory from the dismembered Austro-Hungarian Empire.

World War I was total war—it encompassed the entire nation and was without limits.

CHRONOLOGY 29.1 continued

May 1917	General Pétain restores morale and discipline
July–November 1917	Britain is defeated at Passchendale
Fall 1917	The Italians are defeated at Caporetto
November 1917	The Bolsheviks take power in Russia
January 1918	U.S. President Woodrow Wilson announces his Fourteen Points
March 1918	Russia signs Treaty of Brest-Litovsk, losing territory to Germany and withdrawing from the war.
May–June 1918	General Ludendorff leads German forces to within 37 miles of Paris; Americans stop the Germans in the battle of Belleau Wood
August 1918	The British win the battle of Amiens
October 1918	Turkey is forced to withdraw from the war after several British successes
November 3, 1918	Austria-Hungary signs an armistice with the Allies
November 11, 1918	Germany signs an armistice with the Allies, ending World War I
January 1919	Paris Peace Conference
June 28, 1919	Germany signs the Treaty of Versailles

States demanded total victory and total commitment from their citizens. They regulated industrial production, developed sophisticated propaganda techniques to strengthen morale, and exercised ever greater control over the lives of their people, organizing and disciplining them like soldiers. This total mobilization of nations' human and material resources provided a model for future dictators. With ever greater effectiveness and ruthlessness, dictators would centralize power and manipulate thinking. The first indication that the world would never be the same again, and the most important consequence of the war, was the Russian Revolution in 1917, when the Bolsheviks seized control.

Notes

1. Quoted in Barbara Tuchman, *The Guns of August* (New York: Dell, 1962), p. 51.
2. S. L. A. Marshall, *The American Heritage History of World War I* (New York: Dell, 1966), p. 215.
3. Quoted in Alistair Horne, *The Price of Glory* (New York: Harper, 1967), p. 240.

4. A. J. P. Taylor, *A History of the First World War* (New York: Berkley, 1966), p. 84.

5. Quoted in Richard M. Watt, *Dare Call It Treason* (New York: Simon & Schuster, 1963), p. 169.

6. Quoted in Watt, *Dare Call It Treason*, p. 215.

7. Quoted in Daniel M. Smith, *The Great Departure* (New York: Wiley, 1965), p. 20.

8. Quoted in Marshall, *The American Heritage History of World War I*, p. 334.

9. Excerpted in Louis L. Snyder, ed., *Historic Documents of World War I* (Princeton: D. Van Nostrand, 1958), p. 183.

10. Thomas A. Bailey, *Woodrow Wilson and the Lost Peace* (Chicago: Quadrangle Books, 1963), p. 29.

11. Bailey, *Woodrow Wilson and the Lost Peace*, p. 209.

12. Quoted in *The Nation*, 108 (January 18, 1919): 86.

13. Hajo Holborn, *The Political Collapse of Europe* (New York: Alfred A. Knopf, 1966), p. 102.

14. Quoted in Bailey, *Woodrow Wilson and the Lost Peace*, p. 303.

15. A. J. P. Taylor, *From Sarajevo to Potsdam* (New York: Harcourt, Brace and World, 1966), pp. 55–56.

16. Paul Valéry, *Variety* (New York: Harcourt, Brace, 1927), pp. 27–28.

17. Quoted in Robert G. L. Waite, *Vanguard of Nazism* (New York: W. W. Norton, 1969), p. 42.

Suggested Reading

Albrecht-Carrie, René, *The Meaning of the First World War* (1965). How the war upset the delicate equilibrium of Europe.

Bailey, Thomas, *Woodrow Wilson and the Lost Peace* (1963). A critical interpretation of the role of the United States at the peace conference.

Falls, Cyril, *The Great War* (1961). A good narrative of the war.

Fussell, Paul, *The Great War and Modern Memory* (1977). The influence of the Great War on British writers.

Horne, Alistair, *The Price of Glory* (1967). Brilliantly recaptures the Battle of Verdun.

Marshall, S. L. A., *The American Heritage History of World War I* (1966). Probably the best account available.

Panichas, George A., ed. *Promise of Greatness* (1968). Recollections of the war by people of prominence.

Tuchman, Barbara, *The Guns of August* (1963). A beautifully written account of the opening weeks of the Great War.

Watt, R. M., *Dare Call It Treason* (1963). A brilliant study of the French Army mutinies of 1917.

Williams, John, *The Other Battleground* (1972). A comparison of the home fronts in Britain, France, and Germany.

Review Questions

1. What battle plans did Germany and France implement in 1914?

2. Describe trench warfare.

3. Why did the United States enter the war?

4. Why did General Ludendorff seek an armistice?

5. What was Wilson's peace program? What obstacles did he face?

6. What were the provisions of the Treaty of Versailles regarding Germany? How was Austria-Hungary affected by the war?

7. Why was World War I a great turning point in the history of the West?

CHAPTER 30

The Soviet Union: Modernization and Totalitarianism

A FATEFUL consequence of World War I, even before its final battles were fought, was the Russian Revolution of 1917. The revolution occurred in two stages. In March the tsarist regime was overthrown, ushering in a period of liberal government and freedom. But the weakness of leadership, the war, the divisions among the Russian people, and the inexperience of the masses in dealing with freedom and parliamentary institutions, combined with their ingrained suspicion of government—all these factors caused freedom to degenerate into anarchy. Taking advantage of the chaos, the Bolsheviks seized power in November 1917 and established a communist dictatorship.

These events were fateful not only for Russia, but also for Europe and the world, and foreshadowed basic trends of the twentieth century. The overthrow of the tsar showed that governments without a base of support among the mass of their people were unable to survive the heightened tensions of social change and the requirements of international power politics. The collapse of Russian liberalism in the first stage of the revolution demonstrated the difficulty of establishing Western liberal-democratic forms of government in countries lacking a sense of unity, a strong middle class, and a tradition of freedom and responsible participation in government affairs. After World War I the weaknesses of liberal government became more glaring, and in one country after another liberal governments were replaced with authoritarian regimes. European dictators copied the Russian communists, who pioneered the essential traits of the mass-oriented totalitarian state.

THE RUSSIAN REVOLUTION OF 1917

The Collapse of Autocracy

In the spring of 1914, Peter N. Durnovo, a retired minister of the interior and a prominent supporter of the tsarist regime, warned that in case of a major war Russia would suffer worse than in the late Japanese conflict. Russian industry was unprepared for the test, the railroads were insufficient, and the administration was disorganized. What the country needed was peace for the sake of letting the internal reforms started after 1905 (see page 584) take effect. War would lead to defeat, and defeat to revolution, as in 1905—only worse, for the enemy was more powerful and closer to the Russian heartlands. Durnovo prophesied that "social revolution in its most extreme form is inevitable. . . . The defeated army, having lost its most dependable men and carried away by the tide of primitive peasant desire for land, will find itself too demoralized to serve as a bulwark of law and order. The legislative institutions and the intellectual opposition parties, lacking real authority in the eyes of the people, will be powerless to stem the popular tide aroused by themselves, and Russia will be flung into hopeless anarchy, the issue of which cannot be foreseen."[1] Durnovo anticipated that after the fall of tsarism a liberal-democratic regime had no chance; it would be swept aside by a tide of peasant anarchy.

And indeed, after the outbreak of the war, the curtain did come down on the tsarist era. On the western front the Russian armies, ill-equipped, poorly led, and suffering huge losses, were soon defeated and began a long retreat to the east, giving high hopes to the German government with its plans ready for dismembering the Russian Empire. By 1916 the calamity predicted by Durnovo had begun. The home front fell apart. Shops were empty, money valueless, and hunger and cold stalked the working quarters of cities and towns. But the tsar, Nicholas II (1868–1918), who was determined to preserve autocracy, resisted any suggestion that he liberalize the regime for the sake of the war effort.

The people of Russia had initially responded to the war as tradition demanded: with a show of patriotic fervor and love for the tsar. But by January 1917, virtually all Russians, and foremost the soldiers, despaired of autoc-

racy: it had failed to protect the country from the enemy and economic conditions had deteriorated. Autocracy was ready to collapse at the slightest adversity. In early March (February 23 by the Julian calendar then in use) a strike, riots in the food lines, and street demonstrations in Petrograd, as the capital was then called, flared into sudden unpremeditated revolution. The soldiers, who in 1905 had stood by the tsar, now rushed over to the striking workers. The Romanov dynasty, after three hundred years of rule (1613–1917), came to a petty and inglorious end, a month before the United States entered the war "to make the world safe for democracy."

Even before the tsar had abdicated, two rival centers of government sprang up in Petrograd, first a council of soldiers and workers called the Petrograd *Soviet (council)*, representing those who had fought in the street and risked their lives; and soon thereafter a committee of various liberals afraid of revolution and the soviet. The latter claimed office as the Provisional Government, provisional until a representative Constituent Assembly (to be elected as soon as possible) could establish a permanent regime. Both the Petrograd Soviet and the Provisional Government agreed that henceforth all Russians should enjoy full freedom.

Thus, at the height of a disastrous war, under mounting hardships which mobilized the unresolved social and political tensions of many centuries, liberty at last came to Russia, suddenly and without preparation. Liberal democrats in Western countries had never experienced conditions like those now emerging in Russia.

The Problems of the Provisional Government

The collapse of autocracy was followed by what supporters in Russia and the West hoped would be a liberal-democratic regime pledged to give Russia a constitution. In reality, however, the course of events from March to November 1917 resembled a free-for-all, no-holds-barred fight for the succession to autocracy, with only the fittest surviving. It also demonstrated, under conditions of exceptional popular agitation and mobility, the desperate state of the Russian Empire, its internal disunity, and the furies of the accumulated resentments. Freedom soon degenerated into anarchy. Both Germany and national minorities in Russia took advantage of the anarchy to dismember the country.

Among the potential successors to the tsars, the liberals of various shades seemed to enjoy the best chances. Representing the educated and forward-looking elements in Russian society that had arisen after the reforms of the 1860s—lawyers, doctors, professional people of all kinds, intellectuals, businesspeople and industrialists, many landowners and even some bureaucrats—they had opposed autocracy and earned a reputation for leadership. Their strength lay in the Party of Popular Freedom, generally known by its previous name as Constitutional Democrats (or Cadets), led by the historian Paul Miliukov. The liberals had joined the March revolution only reluctantly, for they were afraid of the masses and the violence of the streets, and dreaded social revolution, which could result in seizure of factories, dispossession of landowners, and tampering with property rights. Although most leaders of the Provisional Government had only modest means, they were "capitalists," believing in private enterprise as the source of economic progress. Their ideal was a constitutional monarchy, its leadership entrusted to the educated and propertied elite familiar with the essentials of statecraft. For them freedom meant rule by the educated minority.

Unfortunately, the liberals deceived themselves about the mood of the majority of the people. Looking to the Western democracies—including, after April 1917, the United States—for political and financial support, they were eager to continue the war on the side of the Allies; as Russian nationalists,

they also stuck to the war aims of the tsar. These war policies discredited them among the war-weary masses. The liberals also antagonized the peasants by not giving them landlords' lands free of charge as the peasants had long demanded. As nationalists the liberals also opposed the self-determination sought by national minorities; their Russia was to remain whole and undivided.

In all their plans, the liberals acted as if conditions were normal and Russia still had a chance of winning the war. In fact, not enough steel was produced for supplying both the railroads with rails and the army with artillery shells. Almost 2 million soldiers had deserted, "voting for peace with their legs," as Lenin, the Bolshevik leader, said; more were to be demobilized for lack of food. It was the liberals' misfortune that they belonged to the Europeanized elite, whom the peasants ever since the time of Peter the Great had feared and hated. Freedom to workers, soldiers, and peasants—all classified as peasants before 1917—meant for once speaking their own untrained minds and having their own kind of government.

Because of the talents it commanded and the moderation still prevailing in the first months, the Provisional Government's legislative achievement was considerable. It dismantled the tsarist regime and introduced a liberal and humane legal system. It could not, however, create an administrative network capable of taking the place of the tsarist bureaucracy. Consequently the Russian Empire ceased to function as a state, and the masses resorted to direct action. More soviets of workers and soldiers sprang up; some villages even declared themselves independent. In the face of the rising chaos, many liberals gave up all hope for a free Russia; said one of them in early May: ". . . on the day of the revolution Russia received more liberty than she could take, and the revolution has destroyed Russia. Those who made it will be cursed. . . ."[2]

The government created by the soldiers and workers after their own liking was the Petrograd Soviet. Representing the peasant soldiers in the city's garrison even more than the workers, and self-consciously excluding all nonpeasant elements except for a few socialist intellectuals, the Petrograd Soviet spoke for the Russian masses. Feeling incapable with their untrained constituency to take the lead in guiding the country through its crisis, they tolerated the Provisional Government as long as it respected the sentiments of the Soviet. Some Soviet leaders eventually joined the Provisional Government in a series of coalitions between "capitalists" and "socialists." In July, Aleksandr Kerensky (1881–1970), a radical lawyer of great eloquence who from the start had belonged to both camps, became the leader of the Provisional Government, the symbol of a liberal-democratic Russia determined to continue the war. These coalitions, however, did not halt the drift toward soviet democracy.

The drift, swelling to a mighty tide of spontaneous social revolution in midsummer, was fed from many sources. The war brought further disasters; the army disintegrated, sending its deserters into the countryside as armed agitators. The peasants began to divide the landlords' land among themselves, which encouraged more soldiers to desert in order to claim a share of the land. The breakdown of the railways stopped factory production; enraged workers ousted factory managers and owners. Because consumer goods grew scarce and prices soared, the peasants could see no reason to sell their crops if they could buy nothing in return. Thus arose the specter of famine in the cities. Hardships mounted and tempers flared.

The suffering of the people was blamed on the *burzhui*. The *burzhui* (bourgeoisie) was taken to mean all the "capitalists," all those who had been associated with the Europeanized elite, under the tsars or now the Provisional Government—bureaucrats, landlords, merchants, manufacturers, teachers, doctors—anybody with clean fingernails and soft hands. The popular mood turned ugly; now at last was the time to settle age-old scores. Among the groups carried away by the

tide were the non-Russian nationalities—Finns, Ukrainians, Georgians, and others. Sometimes supported by German money, they demanded self-determination and even secession. Freedom obviously was not leading to a grand upsurge of patriotic resolve to drive out the enemy, as had happened in the course of the French Revolution, but rather to dissolution and chaos, as Durnovo had foreseen.

By July 1917, it had become clear that law and order could be upheld only by brute force. But who could marshal such force? In late August and early September, a conspiracy led by an energetic young general, Lavr Kornilov, aimed at setting up a military dictatorship. Kornilov had the support not only of the officer corps and the tsarist officials, but also of many liberals fed up with anarchy. What stopped the general was not Kerensky's government (which had no troops), but the workers of Petrograd. Their agitators demoralized the soldiers sent to suppress the Soviet, thereby proving that a dictatorship of the right had no mass support. The workers also repudiated Kerensky and the Provisional Government as well as their moderate leaders; henceforth they voted for the Bolsheviks.

In this setting the Bolsheviks, under their leader Lenin, were ready to attempt their solution for Russia's supreme crisis: a dictatorship of the left exclusively based on the soviets, with mass support from the peasants in uniform, the peasants at the factory, and to some extent, even from the peasants in the villages. Thus entered the Bolsheviks, communists as they soon called themselves, a small band of unknown but surprisingly well prepared political soldiers.

THE BOLSHEVIK REVOLUTION

Lenin and the Rise of Bolshevism

By the fall of 1917, revolutionary Bolshevism had a long history. Rooted in the Russian revolutionary tradition, it harked back to the early nineteenth century when educated Russians began to compare their country unfavorably with western Europe. They too wanted constitutional liberty, the rights to free speech and political agitation, in order to make their country modern. Prohibited from speaking out in public, the critics went underground, giving up their original liberalism as too pacifist and narrow for their ends. Revolutionary socialism, with its idealistic vision and compassion for the multitude, was a better ideology in the harsh struggle with the police. By the 1870s these socialists had evolved the type of the austere and self-denying professional revolutionary who, in the service of the cause, had no scruples, just as the police had no moral scruples in the defense of the tsars. Bank robbery, murder, assassination, treachery, and terror were not immoral if they served the revolutionary cause.

In the 1880s and 1890s, the most alert of these hardened revolutionaries learned industrial economics and sociology from Marx; from Marxism they also acquired a vision of a universal and inevitable progression toward socialism and communism which satisfied their semireligious craving for salvation in this world, not the next. Marxism also allied them with socialist movements in other lands, giving them an internationalist outlook. History, they believed, was on their side, as it was for all the proletarians and oppressed peoples in the world.

By 1900 a number of able young Russians had rallied to revolutionary Marxism, almost all of them from privileged families or favored by education. The most promising was Vladimir Ilyich Ulyanov, known as Lenin (1870–1924), the son of a teacher and school administrator who had attained the rank of a nobleman. Lenin was trained as a lawyer, but he practiced revolution instead. His first contribution to the revolution lay in adapting Marxism to Russian conditions, taking considerable liberties with the master's teaching. His second followed from the first: outlining the organization of an underground party capable of survival against the tsarist police. It was to be a tightly knit conspiratorial elite of professional revolutionaries, its headquarters safely abroad, with close ties to the masses, that is, the workers and other potentially revolutionary elements. For protection against police infiltration, Lenin rejected formal democracy within the party after the manner of Western Marxist parties. He trusted that an informal give-and-take among comrades would occur, never suspecting that the lack of checks and balances promoted abuses of personal power.

Two prominent Marxists close to Lenin were Leon Trotsky (1879–1940) and Joseph Stalin (1879–1953). Trotsky, whose original name was Lev Bronstein, was the son of a prosperous Jewish farmer from southern Russia and was soon known for his brilliant pen. Stalin (the man of steel), was originally named Iosif Dzhugashvili; he was the son of a poor cobbler from Georgia beyond the Caucasus mountains, bright enough to be sent to the best school in the area, yet he dropped out for a revolutionary career. While they were still young, all three of them were hardened by arrest, lengthy imprisonments, and exile to Siberia. Lenin and Trotsky later lived abroad, while Stalin, following a harsher life, stayed in Russia; for four years before 1917 he was banished to bleakest northern Siberia.

In 1903, the Russian Marxists had split into two factions, the moderate Mensheviks, so named after finding themselves in a minority (menshinstvo) at a rather unrepresentative vote at the Second Party Congress, and the extremist Bolsheviks, who at that moment were in the majority (bolshinstvo). They might more accurately have been called the "softs" and the "hards." The "softs" (Mensheviks) preserved basic moral scruples; they would not stoop to crime or undemocratic methods for the sake of political success. For that the "hards" (Bolsheviks) ridiculed them: what use, they asked, was a dead, imprisoned, or unsuccessful revolutionary?

Meanwhile Lenin perfected Bolshevik revolutionary theory. He violated Marxist tradition by paying close attention to the revolutionary potential of peasants (thereby anticipating Mao Tse-tung). Lenin also looked closely at the numerous peoples in Asia who had recently fallen under Western imperialist domination. These people, he sensed, constituted a potential revolutionary force. In alliance with the Western—and Russian—proletariat, they might overthrow the worldwide capitalist order. Imperialism, he said, was caused by the giant monopolies of the Great Powers. Driven by their rivalry for profits, they had pushed their countries into colonial expansion and now into suicidal war. Lenin overlooked the fact that the financing of colonial ventures was but a minute part of capitalist enterprise and that the international monopolies, handling business in many different states, were bound to suffer by war. He did, however, anticipate the anti-Western groundswell that arose from the great outpouring of European power and culture in the decades before the war; he saw that that tide might rise to a mighty world revolution. The Bolsheviks, the most militant of all revolutionary socialists, were ready to assist in that gigantic struggle.

Lenin's Opportunity

On April 16, 1917, Lenin, with German help, arrived in Petrograd from Switzerland where he had been living. Of all Russian political leaders, Lenin possessed the clearest insight into his country's condition. Russia was, he said, the freest country in the world, but the Provisional Government could not possibly preserve Russia from disintegration. The bulk of the soldiers, workers, and peasants would repudiate the Provisional Government's cautious liberalism in favor of a regime expressing their demand for peace and land. Nothing would stop them from avenging themselves for centuries of oppression. Lenin also felt that only complete state control of the economy

THE PROCLAMATION OF SOVIET POWER BY LENIN, PAINTING BY V. A. KUZNETSOV The Bolsheviks' assumption of power was, in fact, not as dramatic as painted. Nevertheless, Lenin's discipline, intelligence, and dedication to his goals are suggested by the messianic pose. (Sovfoto)

could rescue the country from disaster. The sole way out, he insisted, was the "dictatorship of the proletariat" backed by the soviets of soldiers, workers, and peasants, particularly the poorer peasants.

Lenin was a Russian nationalist as well as a socialist internationalist; he stepped forward with a vision of a modern and powerful Russian state destined to be a model in world affairs. As he boasted in October 1917: "The [March] revolution has resulted in Russia catching up with the advanced countries in a few months, as far as her political system is concerned. But that is not enough. The war is inexorable; it puts the alternative with ruthless severity; either perish or overtake and outstrip the advanced countries *economically* as well."[3] Russia, he implied, was fully capable of overtaking and outstripping even the most advanced countries. Russian communism was thus nationalist communism; the Bolsheviks saw the abolition of income-producing property by the dictatorship of the proletariat as the most effective way of mobilizing the resources of the country, like Peter the Great's service state two centuries earlier (see pages 376–378). Yet in twentieth-century style, the Bolshevik mission was also internationalist. The Russian Revolution was to set off a world revolution, liberating all oppressed classes and peoples around the world, thereby achieving a higher stage of civilization.

With arguments like these, Lenin prepared his party for the second revolution of 1917, the seizure of power by the Bolsheviks. Conditions favored him, as he had predicted. The Bolsheviks obtained majorities in the soviets everywhere. The peasants were in active revolt, seizing the land themselves. The Provisional Government lost all control over the course of events. The planning and execution of the Bolshevik coup was in the hands of Trotsky, who carried out his task with exceptional skill. The Bolshevik Revolution required little force; it lacked the drama of massed action. Even more than the tsarist regime in March, Kerensky's in November was a hollow shell.

On November 6/7 (October 24/25 by the old calendar), the Bolsheviks hardly seized power; it almost fell into their laps. The Bolsheviks quickly organized a government in the name of the Second All-Russian Congress of Soviets just assembling in Petrograd, proclaiming "soviet democracy" but determined to establish a dictatorship. Only a dictatorship of the left, they said, had any chance of restoring governmental authority. How little Americans understood the significance of these events was revealed by an editorial in the *New York Times* published on November 10. It called the Bolsheviks "political children,

without the slightest understanding of the vast forces they are playing with, men without a single qualification for prominence but the gift of gab."

Thus a twentieth-century version of Peter the Great's service state was launched, the first of the new single-party dictatorships born of national humiliation and internal disintegration. Its hero was Lenin, who escalated Russian nationalism into revolutionary internationalism.

THE EARLY YEARS OF THE BOLSHEVIK REGIME

Lenin is most commonly remembered in Soviet Russia from the ever-present, eye-catching posters framed with slogans addressed to the masses. The posters show Lenin in a dark business suit and sport cap, addressing a spellbound audience of workers and soldiers with sweeping gestures, right arm outstretched as if to drive home his point, not commanding like Peter the Great, but pleading, persuading, cajoling, and sometimes threatening, a symbol to idolize. Lenin looked like a source of inexhaustible energy and confidence—he alone had grasped the opportunity for a socialist revolution; he had sustained a wavering, uncertain party and had led the advance into a totally unknown and risky future.

Lenin was guiding the Russian proletariat and all humanity toward a higher social order, symbolizing—in Russia and much of the world—the rebellion of the disadvantaged against Western (or "capitalist") superiority. That is why in 1918 he changed the name of his party from Bolshevik to Communist. For Lenin, as for Marx, a world without exploitation was humanity's noblest ideal. Under this creed he matched his mission against that of

MAP 30.1 RUSSIAN CIVIL WAR, 1918–1920 ▶

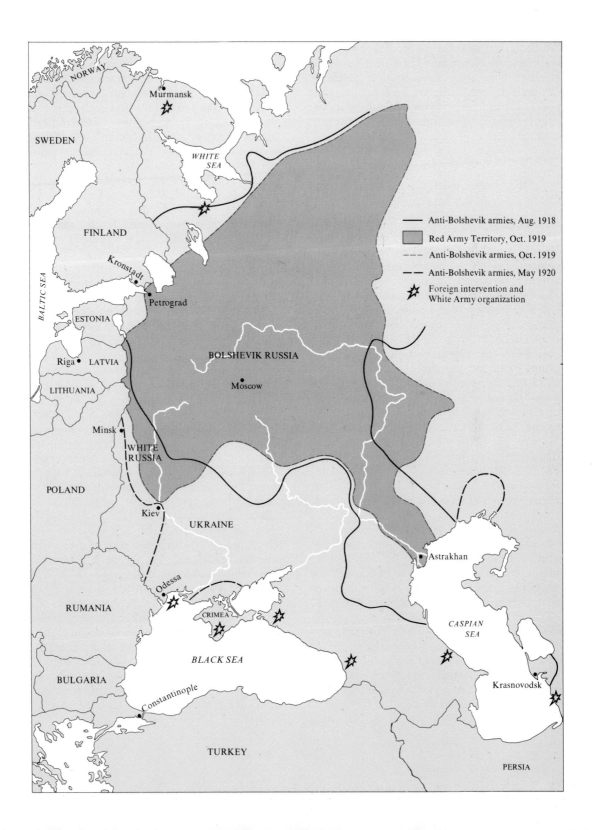

NORWAY

SWEDEN

Murmansk

WHITE SEA

FINLAND

BALTIC SEA

Kronstadt

Petrograd

ESTONIA

Riga   LATVIA

LITHUANIA

Minsk

WHITE RUSSIA

POLAND

Kiev

UKRAINE

RUMANIA

Odessa

CRIMEA

BULGARIA

BLACK SEA

Constantinople

TURKEY

BOLSHEVIK RUSSIA

Moscow

Astrakhan

CASPIAN SEA

Krasnovodsk

PERSIA

⸻⸻ Anti-Bolshevik armies, Aug. 1918

▓ Red Army Territory, Oct. 1919

– – – Anti-Bolshevik armies, Oct. 1919

— — Anti-Bolshevik armies, May 1920

✦ Foreign intervention and White Army organization

Woodrow Wilson, who wanted to make the world safe for democracy. There were now two ideals of democracy—soviet style and American style. If individuals can be taken as symbols of historic turning points, Lenin must be counted among the greatest in the twentieth century.

Dismemberment, Civil War, and Foreign Intervention

The adversity confronting Lenin after his seizure of power was staggering. In the prevailing anarchy, Russia lay open to the German armies. The German government invoked the plea for national self-determination and was quick to take advantage of its appeal. Under the Treaty of Brest-Litovsk, signed in March 1918, the lowest point in Russian history for over two hundred years, Russia lost Finland, Poland, the Baltic provinces—regions inhabited largely by non-Russians—plus the rebellious Ukraine, its chief industrial base and breadbasket. Yet Lenin had no choice but to accept the humiliating terms.

After the Treaty of Brest-Litovsk was signed, the civil war that had been brewing since the summer of 1917 escalated. In the winter of 1917–1918, tsarist officers had been gathering troops in the south, counting on the loyalty of the Cossacks; other anticommunist centers rose in Siberia, still others in the extreme north and along the Baltic coast. The political orientation of these anticommunist groups, generally called Whites in contrast to the Communist Reds, combined all shades of opinion from moderate socialist to reactionary, the latter usually predominating. All received support from foreign governments that freely intervened in Russia's agony. The Germans, until their own revolution in November 1918, occupied much of southern Russia. England, France, and the United States sent troops to points in northern and southern European Russia; England, Japan, and the United States also sent troops to Siberia. At first they hoped to offset German expansion, later to overthrow the communist regime, which tried to provoke revolution around the world. In May and June 1918, Czech prisoners of war, about to be evacuated, precipitated anticommunist uprisings along the Siberian railway, bringing the civil war to fever pitch.

On July 16, 1918, Nicholas II and his entire family were murdered by communists. Under Trotsky's command, the communists had built up their own armed forces, the Red Army. Recruited from the remnants of the tsarist army and its officer corps, the Red Army was reinforced by compulsory military service and strict discipline; Trotsky reintroduced the death penalty outlawed by the provisional government. Patriotism prompted many tsarist officers to continue serving their country, even though their loyalty was often severely strained. As a check on them, Trotsky appointed political commissars responsible for the political reliability and morale of the troops. Despite these measures the Red Army, like the armies of the Whites, lacked discipline. While assembling their army, the communists faced a severe crisis in August 1918, when a noncommunist socialist nearly assassinated Lenin, and the Whites in the south moved to cut off central Russia from its food supply. Both Trotsky and Stalin ruthlessly stopped that threat.

In 1919, thanks to the Allied victory and the American contribution to it, the German menace was ended. Yet foreign intervention was stepped up in response to the formation of the Communist International (Comintern), an organization founded by Lenin to guide the international revolutionary movement that he expected to issue from the World War. Lenin sought revolutionary support from abroad for strengthening his hand at home; his enemies reached into Russia to defeat at its source the revolution that they feared in their own countries. At the same time the civil war rose to its climax.

In the spring of 1919, the White forces in Siberia marched west. Too late to prevent their defeat, other White units advanced from the south to a point 250 miles from Moscow, where Lenin had moved his capital in early 1918. Meanwhile, on the Baltic coast, still other White troops came within thirty miles of Petrograd. Yet having the advantage of interior communications and greater popular support, the Red Army gradually prevailed over its enemies. The last White forces, entrenched on the Crimean peninsula, were evacuated with British help in November 1920. At the same time, foreign intervention was called off. War-weariness and communist propaganda undermined the morale of Allied soldiers, and public opinion at home demanded their return.

Before winning the civil war, the communists faced a sudden invasion from Poland. In April 1920, the government of the newly liberated Poland under General Józef Piłsudski advanced its army into the Ukraine. After initial victories, the Red Army was routed and Lenin was forced to accept a new Polish-Russian boundary running deep inside Russian territory. By 1921, Soviet Russia had been virtually ejected from eastern Europe, yet the major parts of Russia had at last been brought under communist control. Faced with the utter exhaustion of the country, Lenin called for a retreat from the impetuous revolutionary advance he had advocated in 1917.

Under the blows of adversity between 1917 and 1921, the communist regime barely survived, improvising its policies from one emergency to the next and calling its severe measures "war communism." Threatened with starvation in the cities, it took food from the peasants at the point of the gun; it supplied the Red Army with weapons and uniforms as best it could from shattered industries. In these years the country passed through unspeakable tragedies, some of them described by Russian novelist Boris Pasternak in *Doctor Zhivago*. The human toll ran into several million lives, as World War I, the civil war, and foreign intervention ended, and effective government, under communist authority, was restored.

The Revolutionary Dictatorship

Lenin succeeded in establishing a communist regime because the communists possessed a more disciplined and reliable party organization than their opponents and with its help at once imposed a ruthless dictatorship. Almost immediately after the seizure of power, the communists, in a temporary coalition with radical peasant-oriented socialists, outlawed all other political parties and suppressed their newspapers. In January 1918, they dispersed the Constituent Assembly, the last vestige of the Provisional Government. Losing their peasant-socialist partners after the Treaty of Brest-Litovsk, the communists established a full-blown one-party state. Already in November, they had set up a commission (called *Cheka*) to ferret out all counterrevolutionary activity. Staffed with hardened revolutionaries, the Cheka soon became a dreaded secret police.

The communists felt no moral objection to the use of force or even of stark terror. As Lenin admonished his followers: "cleanse the land of Russia of all sorts of harmful insects, of crook-fleas, and bedbugs," by which he meant "the rich, the rogues, and the idlers." He even suggested that "one out of every ten idlers be shot on the spot."[4] Those not shot found themselves, with Lenin's blessings, in forced labor camps directed by the Cheka. In the unrestrained violence of the civil war, the communists surpassed all rivals in brutality in order to build up their own power.

The communists also made sure of continued popular support. Caught between Red and White, most of the people tended to favor the Reds because they offered more. Out of respect for the ideal of self-determination among the non-Russian nationalities (and in violation of their Marxist belief in centralization), the communists adopted a federal constitution, granting at least cultural and administrative autonomy to non-Russian areas. At the same time, they pleased Russian nationalists by bringing back and forcibly holding most of those nationalities that had tried to escape from the empire. By warding off foreign intervention, the communists also claimed credit for defending the fatherland.

More important, the communists gave land to the peasants, although with mental reservations about the peasants' capitalist instincts. They reluctantly allowed workers to control factories, gradually strengthening the more enlightened authority of the trade unions. They separated church and state, more ruthlessly than had been done in western Europe over the centuries. They also simplified the alphabet, changed the calendar to the Gregorian system prevailing in the capitalist West, and brought theater and all arts, hitherto reserved for the elite, to the masses. Above all, they wiped out—by expropriation of property and discrimination, expulsion, and execution—the educated upper class of bureaucrats, landowners, professional people, and industrialists.

The Russia of the communists was "Soviet" Russia, led by Westernized revolutionaries who were the first rulers in Russian history to derive their power and legitimacy from below, from the toiling masses, talking their rough language and expressing their crude sense of social justice. Their constituency was both men and women. They promised "to liberate woman from all the burdens of antiquated methods of housekeeping, by replacing them by house-communes, public kitchens, central laundries, nurseries, etc."[5] Traditional values, particularly in the Asian parts of the Soviet Union, hardly favored equality between the sexes, especially in political work. The practical necessity of combining work with family responsibility, moreover, also tended to keep women out of managerial positions in the party and the organizations of the state, but the ideal remained alive.

The Bolsheviks derived much acclaim from their emphasis on redistributing scarce resources like housing, food, and clothing, taking from the rich and giving to the poor, and making education available to the masses. They were not opposed to all forms of private property; they allowed items for personal use, provided they were in keeping with the standards of the common people. But in nationalizing industry and finance, they outlawed income-producing private property, which enabled capitalists to employ (or exploit, as the communists said) others for their own profit. With the disappearance of private enterprise, the state gradually became the sole employer, thereby gaining unprecedented power over the individual, forcefully integrating him or her into the common social efforts for the reconstruction of the country. Socialism permitted a far more intense mobilization of the country than a system based on private property. The Bolsheviks never ceased to stress that they worked strenuously for the welfare of the proletarians and peasantry, the vast majority of the population.

The latter point, unfortunately, was not easily proved, for Lenin's views of the country's needs differed sharply from common opinion. The working people wanted democracy, by which they meant governing themselves in their own customary ways. Lenin, on the other hand, wanted socialism, reeducating the masses to a higher standard of individual conduct and social responsibility, and economic productivity that would be superior even to capitalism. In the spring of 1918, he argued that the Russian workers had not yet matched capitalist performance: "The Russian worker is a bad worker compared with the workers of the advanced, i.e., western countries." To overcome this fatal handicap, Lenin urged competition—socialist competition— and gave some stern advice: "The revolution demands in the interest of socialism that the masses unquestioningly obey the single will of the leaders of the labor process." Relentlessly he hammered home the need for "iron discipline at work, unquestioning obedience to the will of a single person, the Soviet leader," by which he meant the Communist Party. There was no alternative: "Large-scale machinery calls for absolute and strict unity of will, which directs the joint labors of hundreds and thousands and tens of thousands of people. A thousand wills are subordinated to one will. . . ."[6]

In these words lay the essence of subsequent Soviet industrialization. The entire economy was to be monolithic, rationally planned in its complex interdependence, and pursuing a single goal: overcoming the weaknesses of Russia, so disastrously demonstrated in the war, whatever the price in terms of individual freedom and dignity. Leaving the workers to their own spontaneity, Lenin realized, merely perpetuated Russian backwardness; it might lead to a foreign oppression worse than domestic tyranny. Instead he called for a new "consciousness," a hard-driving work ethic expressed in the Russian Marxist revolutionary vocabulary.

Lenin's words showed that the Bolsheviks led a double revolution. The first was the elemental revolution from below, overthrowing the Europeanized elite, both tsarist and liberal-democratic, making the ordinary people of Russia feel more at ease in their country. That revolution, one could argue, resembled the great French Revolution, which ended royal prerogative and aristocratic privilege. The second revolution was of a different kind; it subjected Russia to a new autocracy. The new leadership, even more authoritarian than the old, told the Russian people that their country would not stand up to the times unless it were rebuilt after an alien and uncongenial design, against their will, if necessary.

The second revolution, in short, was yet another revolution from above. It was imposed by a revolutionary elite in close touch with the masses, using their language and stooping to their ignorance and hardened instincts and yet also working for their long-range betterment. The new revolution—the revolution of high-speed modernization—began an experiment of social engineering on the grandest scale and with hitherto unimagined tragedies.

The One-Party State

The new elite, numbering about 500,000 in 1921, was indeed remarkable. It consisted of a small, close-knit party of professional political leaders, the best of them unusually disciplined in personal dedication and endowed with organizational skills permitting them to preserve their original revolutionary drive in the face of both failure and success. From the start, those who did not pull their weight were purged. The Communist Party was more adaptable, energetic, and effective than the tsarist bureaucracy.

The onerous duties of good communists did not sit lightly on easygoing but stubborn Russians. According to the official rules, party members had to

observe strict party discipline, to take an active part in the political life of the party and of the country, and to carry out in practice the policy of the party and the decision of the party organs; to work untiringly to raise their ideological equipment, to master the principles of Marxism-Leninism and the important political and organizational decisions of the party and to explain these to the non-party masses; as members of the ruling party in the Soviet state to set an example in the observances of labor and state discipline, to master the techniques of their work and continually raise their production and work qualifications.[7]

The party leaders also embodied both a long experience of working with the masses and a fierce patriotic ambition to rescue their country from defeat and backwardness. They were inexperienced in statecraft, but ready to learn, and explosively energetic.

Under its constitution, the "Russian Communist Party (Bolshevik)," as its formal title read, was a democratic body, its members electing delegates to periodic party congresses, which in turn elected the membership of the central committee, where leadership was originally centered. From there, however, power soon shifted to a smaller and more intimate group, the *politburo* (political bureau). Here the key leaders, Lenin, Trotsky, Stalin, and a few others, determined policy, assigned tasks, and appointed key officials. Ideally their leadership was collective, based on consensus; ideally too, the party was democratic, in the sense that the flow of decisions from the top down was matched by an upward flow of information and opinion, in a system called "democratic centralism." In the face of continuing crises, however, individual leaders like Lenin or later Stalin dominated their associates. And as the party grew, so did the need for centralization and bureaucratic organization; the higher echelons controlled the lower; there was never time for extensive consultation.

Thus the conditions favoring the one-party dictatorship in Russia also shaped the Communist Party. In order to guarantee the unity of the country, it had to be monolithic itself. For that reason, the party's central committee, and soon the politburo, assumed a dictatorial role. Impatient with unending disputes among righteous and strong-willed old revolutionaries, Lenin, in full agreement with other top leaders, demanded unconditional submission to his decisions. He even ordered the Cheka to discipline the dissidents; no price was too high for the sake of unity.

The party dominated all public agencies, and its key leaders held the chief positions in government. No other political parties were tolerated, and trade unions became agents of the regime, enforcing Leninist consciousness rather than defending workers' interests. Never before had the people of Russia come to depend so abjectly on their government.

The minds of the people, too, came under the control of the party-state. The Communist Party undertook to fashion people's thoughts in order to create the proper "consciousness." It made Marxism-Leninism the sole source of inspiration, eliminating as best it could all rival creeds, religious, liberal-democratic, or philosophical. Minds were to be as reliably uniform as machine processes, and totally committed to the party and its vision of the socialist future. Moreover, they were to be protected against all subversive capitalist influences. Soviet Russia, so the party explained, had risen to a superior plane of social existence; the Bolshevik Revolution had put all capitalist countries behind. Soviet Russia, a party document predicted, would attract other soviet socialist states to its federal union, until eventually it covered the entire world. Lest Soviet citizens doubt their new superiority, the party prohibited all uncontrolled comparison with other countries.

An Ideology for World Revolution

In one respect, Lenin was far bolder than any tsar: he turned Russian state ambition into an international revolutionary force, making Russian Marxism an inflammatory worldwide ideology and thereby creating new allies for a Soviet Russia totally bereft of military or industrial power. As he had observed already before 1914, the nascent nationalism of non-European peoples living under European domination, especially in Asia, was a promising revolutionary force. Seeing the revolutionary movement in Europe lag, he had talked of "progressive Asia" and "backward Europe."

The Russian Revolution deeply touched hitherto suppressed ambitions for political self-determination and cultural self-assertion among a growing number of peoples around the world. It appealed particularly to intellectuals educated in the West (or in Westernized schools) yet identifying themselves with their downtrodden compatriots. Taught to worship the ideals of the French Revolution—liberty, equality, and fraternity—they noted that the Europeans (or white people everywhere) did not apply these ideals to people of different cultures and colors (if indeed they applied them among themselves). These intellectuals were determined to turn these ideals to their own advantage, if necessary by revolution. Like Lenin, they were of a double mind: they spoke for their own countries and cultures, but also were eager to make them modern, that is, reshape them in some form after the model of Western power. They included moderates like Gandhi and Nehru in India, who soon repudiated Lenin, and radicals like Ho Chi Minh in Vietnam, and Chou En-lai and Mao Tse-tung in China, who became his disciples. Lenin made himself the spokesman for the rising tide of anti-Westernism, soliciting support for the common aim of unhinging the capitalist world order based on Western superiority.

As a political tool for this purpose, Lenin used the Communist—or Third—International (Comintern), the most radical successor to earlier socialist international associations. It helped to create small communist parties in western Europe which, in time, became dependable, although rather powerless, agents of Soviet Russia. In Asia, where no proletariat existed, Lenin tried to work closely with incipient nationalist movements and even envisaged setting up peasant soviets. He also held out the possibility that backward countries might skip the hated capitalist phase altogether, provided they allied themselves with the "leading socialist country," namely the Soviet Union.* It was soon clear that the anti-Western agitation of the twentieth century would not follow the path of world revolution as predicted by Lenin. Yet

Lenin and the Bolshevik Revolution had inspired admiration and instinctive loyalty among the colonial and semi-colonial peoples in what was later called *the Third World.*

Unwittingly Lenin also contributed to a novel division in the world. In the uncertainties following the First World War, the specter of world revolution created extravagant hopes and fears. Some bewildered people believed in the communist vision; others were thrown into a panic by it. The spread of communism was more than matched, in western and central Europe and the Americas as well, by a vigorous anticommunism which, in turn, contributed to the rise of right-wing or fascist movements. Propertied and patriotic men and women had good reason to be scared; world revolution threatened their sense of security, their religion, their very sanity. World opinion became polarized: fear of communism became an obsession in the West as did the fear of capitalism in Russia and many poor countries around the world.

World revolution was never a realistic fear, however. The tide of Western ascendancy was still running strong. Moreover, the Comintern was never a truly international force; it remained a tool of the Russian Communist Party. Yet the fear it aroused served Lenin well: it made Soviet Russia appear strong when in fact it was totally exhausted. At very little cost, the Comintern put Russia back on the map of world politics, under a red flag. Prestige-conscious Russians had cause for rejoicing. Never before had their country so captured the attention of the world; now it stood out as the communist alternative to the capitalist West.

---

*Western Marxists believed that in the progression from feudalism to capitalism, and from capitalism to socialism and communism, no stage could be omitted. A country could start on a higher stage of development only if it had acquired all the social and technical skills of the preceding stage. Having argued, by contrast, that Russia could advance to socialism even though it had not matched the achievements of capitalism, Lenin advocated an even quicker shortcut for underdeveloped (later called Third World) countries under Soviet leadership. He argued this case in his "Theses on the National and Colonial Question" (1920).

THE STALIN REVOLUTION

Stalin's Rise to Power

Having set forth in his domestic and foreign policy a master plan for reviving Russian power, Lenin was not destined to see it carried

IDEALIZED PORTRAIT OF STALIN Like Lenin, Stalin's public image was idealized, but the real man was ruthless. He was determined to reshape the Soviet people's consciousness through the revolution of totalitarianism. His purges, which killed millions, nonetheless laid the foundation for Russia's emergence as a superpower. (Sovfoto)

In 1921 the Communist Party adopted the New Economic Policy, generally called NEP, which lasted until 1928. Under a system that Lenin characterized as "state socialism" the government retained control of finance, industry, and transportation, "the commanding heights" of the economy, but allowed the rest of the economy to return to private enterprise. The peasants, after giving part of their crops to the government, were free to sell the rest in the open market; traders could buy and sell as they pleased. With the resumption of small-scale capitalism, an air of prewar freedom returned, making the NEP era a paradoxical mixture of the old and the new Russia.

Lenin himself, incapacitated by strokes soon after the NEP was adopted, relinquished control of the party. In the leisure of his sickroom Lenin began to realize how little his backward country was prepared for building a superior society. His last words urged patient hard work in learning from capitalism.

The completion of the goal Lenin had set in his prime fell to Stalin, the man of steel, a high-ranking Bolshevik whom nobody in 1917 would have foreseen as Lenin's successor. Steadfast and efficient but relatively inconspicuous among the more temperamental and intellectual key Bolsheviks, Stalin was given in 1922 the unwanted and seemingly routine task of general secretary of the party. It became his responsibility, in the chaotic aftermath of the Revolution and the civil war, to give reality to the Leninist vision of the monolithic party. This he did to his own eventual advantage, building up and supervising a reliable party cadre—apparatus men, as they came to be called—and dominating the party as not even Lenin had. When in the struggle for the succession to Lenin he was challenged, particularly by Trotsky and his associates, it was too late to unseat him. None of Stalin's rivals could rally the necessary majorities at the party congresses.

Stalin, like Lenin, is best known from his poster image. Soviet citizens saw him as an energetic man clad in a simple military tunic, devoid of show or pomp, a fatherly figure, a

into action. He himself called for a retreat from his ambitious vision when in 1921 the country's exhaustion and an uprising of sailors at the Kronstadt naval base and of workers in nearby Petrograd indicated the need for a sharp change of course. In March 1921 the people who in 1917 had been ready to give their lives for the revolution now rose against the repression that had been introduced during the civil war; they called for a restoration of soviet democracy. Trotsky ruthlessly suppressed that uprising, but the lesson was clear: the communist regime had to grant some measure of freedom for the resumption of normal life.

good chairman, calm, benign, conciliatory, promoting consensus, signifying a new mood of quiet bureaucratic control suitable to the industrial era. Yet the image was a façade. Behind it lay an untamed, vindictive, impatient temperament cast in pre-industrial times, surcharged with the furies of a raw and brutal society in headlong change. The real Stalin was an appalling mixture of good and evil, each raised to superhuman proportions by his office as the dictator of Soviet Russia, upon whom, so the posters indicated, history had laid the challenge of introducing a new age of human progress. Nobody has ever suggested that he took that task lightly.

Modernizing Russia: Industrialization and Collectivization

To Stalin, Russia's most pressing need was not world revolution but the fastest possible build-up of Soviet power through industrialization. Bolshevik pride dictated that this must be done not with the help of foreign capital, as under the tsars, but as much as possible by purely Russian efforts. Stalin's slogan was "socialism in one country," which signified that Soviet Russia by itself possessed all the necessary resources for "surpassing and overtaking" capitalism in the shortest time possible. It was a staggering job.

Stalin decided to go all out for industrialization at the expense of the toiling masses. Peasants and workers, already poor, would be required to make tremendous sacrifices of body and spirit in order to overcome the nation's weaknesses. Stalin's decision to proceed regardless of the feelings of the masses recaptured the brutal impetuousness of Lenin and of Peter the Great; it completed the ambition of Witte (see page 584). The Bolshevik Revolution had cleared the way for decisive action. Dependent as never before on their government, the Russian people could offer little resistance.

Stalin decided to end the NEP and implement a series of Five-Year Plans, the first and most experimental one commencing in 1928. The industrialization drive was heralded as a vast economic and social revolution, undertaken by the state on a rational plan set forth with much fanfare and a glittering show of statistics. The emphasis lay on heavy industry, the construction of railroads, power plants, steel mills, and military hardware like tanks and warplanes. Production of consumer goods was cut down to the barest minimum. All small-scale private trading, revived under NEP, came to an end; the state shops and cooperatives were bare, the service in them poor. Russians who had just come within sight of their pre-1914 standard of living now found their expectations dashed for decades to come.

Thus a new grim age began with drastic material hardships and profound mental anguish. Few Soviet citizens understood the necessities of the Five-Year Plan, but in the early years young people particularly were fired into heroic exertions. They were proud to sacrifice themselves for the building of a superior society and they had good reasons to be proud. When the Great Depression in the capitalist countries put millions out of work, no Soviet citizen suffered from unemployment; gloom pervaded the West, but confidence and hope artificially fostered by the party buoyed up Soviet Russia. The first Five-Year Plan did not live up to its promise and had to be scrapped before running its course. Subsequent Five-Year Plans, however, gradually improved the quality of planning as well as of production.

Meanwhile, a second and even more brutal revolution overtook Soviet agriculture, for the peasants had to be forcibly integrated into the planned economy through collectivization. Agriculture—the peasants, their animals, their fields—had to submit to the same rational control as industry. Collectivization meant the pooling of farmlands, animals, and equipment for the sake of more efficient large-scale production. The Bolshevik solution for the backwardness of Russian agriculture had long

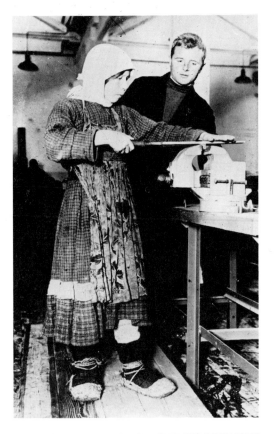

FOREMAN TEACHING A YOUNG PEASANT GIRL AT THE GORKI AUTO WORKS, 1931 The task of industrializing the Soviet Union was staggering. The subsequent hardships endured by its people during the 1920s and 1930s are hard to imagine. For decades, the working masses were rewarded with nothing more than hope for a vague future success. (Tass from Sovfoto)

size and quality at planned times. With collectivization, the ascendancy of the party over the people of Russia became almost complete.

But at what price! The *kulaks* (rich peasants) and even their poorest fellow villagers who might have gained from collectivization defended their customary life with a spite matching Bolshevik ruthlessness. In many cases, rather than surrender their animals they slaughtered them, gorging themselves in drunken orgies against the days of inevitable famine. Whether by design or accident, the country's cattle herds declined to one-half, inflicting irreparable secondary losses as well. The number of horses, crucial for rural transport and farm work, fell by one-third. Crops were not planted or not harvested, the Five-Year Plan was disrupted, and in 1931–33 untold millions starved to death. In the face of such resistance, the party used terror, killing ringleaders by the thousands, separating families, marching the men off to hard labor for industrial construction or into forced labor camps, wiping out the kulaks as a class, and eventually forcing the villagers to submit to party rule.

By 1935, practically all farming in Russia was collectivized. In theory, the collective farms were run democratically, under an elected chairman; in practice, they followed as best they could the directives handed down from the nearest party office. People grumbled about the rise of a new serfdom; deep in their hearts they were bound to resist it.

Total Control

In order to quash resistance and mold a new type of suitably motivated and disciplined citizen, Stalin unleashed a third revolution, the revolution of totalitarianism. It aimed at a total reconstruction of state and society down to the innermost recesses of human consciousness. It called for "a new man," suited to the needs of Soviet industrialism. Society was

been that the peasants should become like workers. But knowing the peasants' distaste for the factory, their attachment to their own land, and their stubbornness, the party had hesitated to carry out its ambition. In 1929, however, Stalin realized that for the sake of industrialization he had no choice. If the Five-Year Plan were to succeed, the government had to receive planned crops of planned reshaped for the utmost productivity. The hallowed revolutionary ideal of equality was denounced as petty bourgeois.

Soviet citizens had to work as hard as they could, with the rewards going to those who made special contributions toward plan fulfillment, to engineers, scientists, managers, and certain heroes of labor, like the famous miner Stakhanov, who set records of output. Workers were paid by piece wages; the trade unions henceforth became tools of the state, enforcing work discipline. A new elite of party-trained industrial managers rose. In addition, family discipline and sexual mores, exceedingly lax after the Revolution, were tightened by decree into a new work-oriented ethic.

In 1935 Stalin, summing up these changes, officially declared socialism to have been achieved in the Soviet Union. The Soviet Constitution of 1936 set forth major institutions and principles guiding the new society; it left no doubt as to what was expected of soviet citizens. They must "abide by the Constitution, observe the laws, maintain labor discipline, honestly perform public duties, respect the rules of socialist intercourse, and safeguard and strengthen public property" (theft of state property was a widespread practice). All offenders were called "enemies of the people" and threatened with dire punishment. The list of duties ended with the words "treason is the most heinous of crimes. The defense of the Fatherland is the most sacred duty of every citizen"—ominous words indeed.

The revolution of totalitarianism extended even further. All media of communications, literature, the arts, music, the stage, were forced into subservience to the Five-Year Plan. No Soviet citizen was allowed to think or feel other than to help industrial or agricultural output. In literature, as in all art, an official style was promulgated called *Socialist Realism*. It was to fill with human detail the realities of Soviet life as Stalin wished them to be set before the people.

In response to Stalin's request for Socialist Realism in art, a genre of Five-Year-Plan novels appeared. Such novels told how the romances of tractor drivers and milkmaids, or of lathe operators and office secretaries, led to new victories of production under the Five-Year Plan. Composers found their music examined for remnants of bourgeois spirit; they were to write simple tunes suitable for heroic times. Everywhere huge high-color posters showed men and women hard at work with radiant faces calling others to join them; often Stalin, the wise father and leader, was shown taking the salute among them. In this manner artistic creativity was put into a dull, utilitarian straitjacket of official cheerfulness; creativity was allowed only in order to boost industrial productivity. Behind the scenes, all artists were disciplined to conform to the will of the party or be crushed.

But still the Russian masses clung to their pre-industrial mode of life. The untamed Russian temperament, hardened for centuries by exhausting toil on the land and resentful of authority, resisted the enforced change to the large-scale cooperation of modern industrialism. Against that stubborn resistance, Stalin unleashed raw terror in order to break stubborn wills and compel conformity. Terror had been used as a tool of government ever since the Revolution (and the tsars had also used it, moderately and intermittently). After the start of the first Five-Year Plan, show trials were staged denouncing as saboteurs the engineers who found Stalin's tempo counterproductive. The state used large-scale terror to herd the peasants onto collective farms. Stalin also used terror to crush the opposition, within the party and throughout Soviet society, to instill an abject fear not only into the ranks of the party, but into Russian society at large.

Purges had long been used to rid the party of weaklings. After 1934 purges became instruments of Stalin's ruthless drive for unchallenged personal power. The world watched the great show trials with amazement and horror as Stalin intimidated his people. In 1936 the first batch of victims, including many founders of the Communist Party, was accused of conspiring with the exiled Trotsky to set up a "terrorist center" and of scheming to terrorize the party; they were blamed for the murder of Sergei Kirov, Stalin's aide, in 1934. After being sentenced to death, the first group was immediately executed. In 1937 the next group, including prominent communists of Lenin's day, was charged with cooperating with foreign intelligence agencies and wrecking "socialist reconstruction," the term for Stalin's revolution; they too were executed. Shortly afterward a secret purge wiped out the military high command, leaving the Soviet army without effective leadership for years.

In 1938 the last and biggest show trial advanced the most monstrous accusation of all: sabotage, espionage, and attempting to dismember the Soviet Union and kill all its leaders (including Lenin in 1918). In the public hearings some defendants refuted the public prosecutor, but in the end all confessed before being executed. Western observers were aghast at the cynical charges and the tortures used to obtain the confessions. But the mass of Russians meekly accepted the evidence and agreed with the death sentences, which deepened Stalin's authority.

The great trials, however, involved only a small minority of Stalin's victims; many more perished in silence. The terror hit first of all members of the party, especially the Old Bolsheviks, who had joined before the Revolution; they were the most independent-minded and therefore the most dangerous to Stalin. But it also diminished the cultural elite that had survived the Lenin revolution. Thousands of engineers, scientists, industrial managers, scholars, and artists disappeared; they were shot or sent to forced-labor camps where most of them perished. No one was safe. To frighten the common people in all walks of life among Russians and the other nationalities, men, women, and even children were dragged into the net of Stalin's secret police, a soul-killing reminder to the survivors: submit or else.

The toll of the purges is reckoned in the millions; it included Trotsky, who in 1940 was murdered in Mexico. The bloodletting was ghastly, as Stalin's purge officials themselves followed each other into death and ignominy. Such was the price which Soviet Russia paid for Stalin's effort to wipe out his country's inferiority in the shortest time possible. Yet in his eyes there was always new talent available; he provided opportunities for spectacular careers. And he got results: productivity, especially of armaments, did increase.

Stalin never left any doubt about his ultimate justification. In 1931, bluntly disregarding Marxist-Leninist jargon and forgetting about Russian expansion into Asia, he said:

Those who fall behind get beaten. But we do not want to be beaten. No, we refuse to be beaten. One feature of the history of old Russia was the continual beatings she suffered for falling behind, for her backwardness. All beat her—for her backwardness, for military backwardness, cultural backwardness, political backwardness, for industrial backwardness, for agricultural backwardness. She was beaten because to do so was profitable and could be done with impunity. . . . You are backward, you are weak—therefore you are wrong, hence you can be beaten and enslaved. You are mighty, therefore you are right, hence we must be wary of you. Such is the law of the exploiters. . . . That is why we must no longer lag behind.[8]

He set forth the stark reckoning of Russian history: the cost of foreign enslavement against the costs of a terror-driven mobilization for greater power. As a Polish historian said of Peter the Great, long before Stalin was heard of: "There will be an enormous squandering of resources, of labor, and even of human lives. But Russia's strength and the secret of her destiny have always in great part consisted in the will and in the power to disregard costs in view of the results to be achieved."[9] The gigantic power conflicts of the twentieth century had raised the scale of human sacrifice far beyond nineteenth-century practice, both inside Russia and in the world at large.

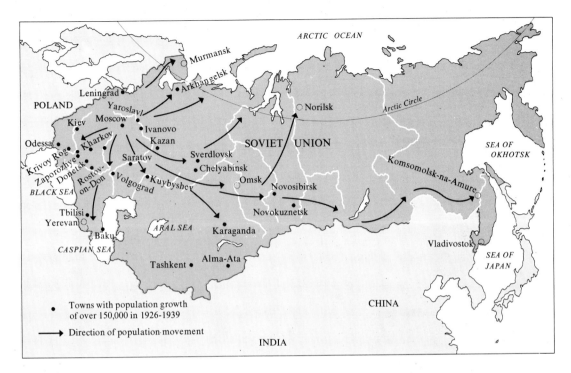

MAP 30.2 SOVIET POPULATION GROWTH AND MOVEMENT,
1926–1939

In foreign even more than in internal affairs, Stalin's policy was marked by fear; the
danger of war was always uppermost in his
mind. It was to Soviet advantage to make a
show of strength, but underneath this façade
Stalin played a cautious hand, husbanding
Russia's resources for internal reconstruction
and hoping that the capitalist states would fall
out among themselves, allowing him the role
of the happy bystander entering the fray only
for the kill. The preoccupation with internal
development made Soviet foreign policy conservative; Stalin did not follow up Lenin's
teaching about world revolution. He realized
that the key to the future of Soviet communism lay in the power of the Soviet Union and
that its power was never sufficient amid the
dangers it confronted in the world. His personal sense of insecurity reflected the persistent
insecurity of his country. By the end of the

1930s, after the second Russian revolution—
the Stalin revolution—yet another era of profound and cruel perils began for his country,
the Second World War and the battle with Nazi
Germany, followed by the cold war.

SOVIET COMMUNISM IN
PERSPECTIVE

Those fateful events in Russia from the end of
World War I to the late 1930s profoundly
excited opinion everywhere. Some Marxists
saw their ideals realized; others felt that Stalin
had betrayed the cause of socialism. Some
disillusioned Western liberals agreed with the
American visitor to the Soviet Union who said
that he "had seen the future and it worked."[10]

CHRONOLOGY 30.1   THE RISE OF THE SOVIET UNION

March 1917	The Bolsheviks take power, led by Lenin
1917–1920	Civil War
January 1918	The communists disband the Constituent Assembly
May–June 1918	Nicholas II and his family are executed
1919	Lenin moves the capital to Moscow; Lenin forms the Comintern
March 1919	The Treaty of Brest-Litovsk
April 1920	Russia loses eastern European territory to Poland
November 1920	The last remnants of the White Army's forces evacuate from the Crimean Peninsula
1921–1928	The New Economic Policy is implemented
1922	Stalin becomes General Secretary of the Communist party
1928	Stalin's first Five-Year Plan begins
1936	Stalin's purges begin
1940	Trotsky is murdered in Mexico

But most Westerners were appalled with Stalin's deeds, although for profit or political expediency some cooperated with the Soviet regime. In the face of the Great Depression and Japanese expansion, for instance, the United States officially recognized the Soviet Union in 1933. The purges disenchanted many early communist sympathizers, including George Orwell, who in revulsion wrote *Animal Farm* and *1984.* Many years later Aleksandr Solzhenitsyn described the horror and the tragedies of Stalin's terror in *The Gulag Archipelago.* In the countries of Asia, the progress of the Five-Year Plans was watched with envy and admiration: if Russia could

raise itself by its bootstraps, why could others not follow its example?

In retrospect, Nikita Khrushchev's attack (see page 777) on "the cult of personality" (as the glorification of Stalin came to be called after his death) and the works of Solzhenitsyn have driven home Stalin's inhumanity. At the same time, the continuity from Lenin to Stalin and their places in both the course of Russian history and the contexts of their times are clearer. Both men, but Stalin especially, fitted into the tradition of cruel and overbearing state-building tsars like Peter the Great.

To this setting the people themselves added their share of inhumanity. Given the age-old hardships of Russian peasants, one could hardly expect moderation. As the writer Maxim Gorki (1868–1936), one of the closest observers of the common people in Russia, commented in 1922: "Russians have a special gift for cruelty. It is a peculiar, cold-blooded cruelty which tests the limits of human endurance for suffering, cruelty which imparts a sense of tenacity and solidity to life."[11] The communist leaders, themselves exceptionally brutalized by their revolutionary experience, had to rebuild their state and society with people who had also been brutalized by hardship. They were eager to set an example, under the ideology of Marxism-Leninism, for all humanity suffering from the humiliations of inequality.

Under these circumstances, Stalin laid the foundations for the rise of Soviet Russia into a superpower, more secure and respected in the world than any previous Russian regime. For this historic success he could claim the same moral justification by which Western statesmen had sent millions of people to their deaths in World War I. Monstrous indeed are the stakes of twentieth-century power politics, down to the arms race of intercontinental ballistic missiles and the ever-threatening nuclear holocaust. It is in these perspectives, so alien to past American experience, that Stalin must be understood.

Notes

1. "Memorandum to Nicholas II, by Peter Durnovo," *Readings in Russian Civilization* II (1900–1917), ed., Thomas Riha (Chicago: University of Chicago Press, 1964), p. 469.

2. V. A. Maklakov, quoted in *The Russian Provisional Government 1917*, III, documents selected and edited by Robert Paul Browder and Alexander F. Kerensky (Stanford, California: Stanford University Press, 1961), p. 1276.

3. V. I. Lenin, "The Impending Catastrophe and How to Combat It," *Lenin on Politics and Revolution*, selected writings, ed., James E. Connor (New York: Pegasus, 1968), p. 183.

4. V. I. Lenin, "On Revolutionary Violence and Terror," *The Lenin Anthology*, ed., R. C. Tucker (New York: Norton, 1975), p. 432.

5. All-Russian Communist Party (Bolsheviks), 1919, in *Soviet Communism: Programs and Rules. Official Texts of 1919, 1952, (1956), 1961*, ed. Jan F. Triska (San Francisco: Chandler, 1962), p. 23.

6. V. I. Lenin, "The Immediate Tasks of the Soviet Government," *The Lenin Anthology*, pp. 448ff.

7. Quoted from the Rules of the Communist Party (December 1919). On the obligations of the party member see Merle Fainsod, *How Russia Is Ruled* (Cambridge, Mass.: Harvard University Press, 1964), p. 213.

8. J. V. Stalin, "Speech to Business Executives" (1931), in *A Documentary History of Communism from Lenin to Mao*, ed. Robert V. Daniels (New York: Random House, 1960), 2:22.

9. A. Walewski, quoted in A. Brueckner, *Peter der Grosse* (Berlin, 1897), p. 241.

10. Lincoln Steffens, "I have been over into the future, and it works." In *Autobiography* (New York: Harcourt, Brace, 1931), p. 799.

11. Quoted by Adam B. Ulam, *Stalin: The Man and His Era* (New York: Viking Press, 1973), p. 22.

Suggested Reading

Carr, E. H., *The Russian Revolution from Lenin to Stalin* (1970). A brief summary based on the author's multivolume study of the years 1917–1929.

Cohen, Stephen, *Bukharin and the Bolshevik Revolution* (1971–1980). Argues that there existed more moderate alternatives to Stalin's policies.

Deutscher, Isaac, *Trotsky: 1879–1940*, 3 vol., *The Prophet Armed* (1954), *The Prophet*

Unarmed (1959), *The Prophet Outcast* (1963). The classic work on Trotsky.

Koestler, Arthur, *Darkness at Noon* (1941). A revealing novel about the fate of an Old Bolshevik in the terror purge.

Nove, Alec, *Stalinism and After* (1975). An excellent short work from an economist's perspective.

Pasternak, Boris, *Doctor Zhivago* (1958). The tragedies of Russian life from Nicholas II to Stalin as seen through the eyes of a superbly sensitive and observant poet.

Scott, John, *Behind the Urals, An American Worker in Russia's City of Steel* (1942, reprint 1973). A firsthand account of life under the first Five-Year Plan.

Sholokhov, Mikhail, *And Quiet Flows the Don; The Don Flows Home to the Sea,* 2 vols. (1934–1940). A Nobel Prize–winning novel on the brutalizing effects of war, revolution, and civil war.

Trotsky, Leon, *The Russian Revolution: The Overthrow of Tzarism and the Triumph of the Soviets* (1932). A classic account of the Bolshevik Revolution by its chief organizer.

Tucker, Robert C., *Stalin as a Revolutionary* (1973). A psychological study of the young Stalin.

———, *The Lenin Anthology* (1975). For those who want a taste of Lenin's writings.

Ulam, Adam B., *The Bolsheviks: The Intellectual and Political History of the Triumph of Communism in Russia* (1965). A full account built around Lenin.

———, *Stalin: The Man and His Era* (1973). The best biography to date.

Von Laue, Theodore H., *Why Lenin? Why Stalin?* (1970). A readable survey emphasizing the global contexts.

Review Questions

1. Why did the Provisional Government and liberal democracy fail in 1917?

2. Why, by contrast, were the Bolsheviks successful in seizing and holding power from 1917 to 1921?

3. By what institutions and methods did Lenin build the Soviet state? What innovations did he introduce after the collapse of the tsarist regime and the failure of the provisional government?

4. How did the peasants fare through war, revolution, and the rise of the Soviet state? Why did Stalin collectivize agriculture?

5. How did the Soviet leaders view the position of Russia in the world? What were their aims and ambitions? How did their goals compare with those of other states?

6. What were Stalin's motives and justifications for the terror purge?

7. How do you explain the fact that the communist regime was far more ruthless in its methods of government than the tsarist regime? Which regime accomplished more for the power of Russia?

CHAPTER 31

The Rise of Fascism:
The Attack on Democracy

LIBERALS VIEWED the Great War as a conflict between freedom and autocracy and expected an Allied victory to accelerate the spread of democracy throughout Europe. In the immediate aftermath of the war it seemed that liberalism would continue to advance as it had in the nineteenth century. Had not the collapse of the autocratic German and Austrian empires led to the formation of parliamentary governments throughout eastern and central Europe? Yet within two decades, in an extraordinary turn of events, democracy seemed in its death throes. In Spain, Portugal, Italy, and Germany, and in all the newly created states of central and eastern Europe, with the exception of Czechoslovakia, democracy collapsed and various forms of authoritarian governments emerged. The retreat of democracy and the surge of authoritarianism was best exemplified by the triumph of totalitarian fascist movements in Italy and Germany.

The emergence of fascist movements in more than twenty European lands after World War I was a sign that liberal society was in a state of disorientation and dissolution. Fascism was a response to a postwar society afflicted by spiritual disintegration, economic dislocation, political instability, and thwarted nationalist hopes. It was an expression of fear that the Bolshevik Revolution would spread westward. It was also an expression of hostility to democratic values and a reaction to the failure of liberal institutions to solve crushing problems of modern industrial society. To fascists and their sympathizers, democracy seemed an ineffective, spiritless, and enfeebled old regime ready to be toppled. In their struggle to bring down the liberal state, fascist leaders aroused primitive impulses, resurrected ancient folkways and tribal loyalties, and made use of myths and rituals to mobilize and manipulate the masses.

The proliferation of fascist movements demonstrated that the habits of democracy are not quickly learned or easily retained. Particularly during times of crisis people lose patience with parliamentary discussion and constitutional procedures, sink into nonrational modes of thought and behavior, and are easily manipulated by unscrupulous politicians. For the sake of economic or emotional security and national grandeur they will often willingly sacrifice political freedom. Fascism brought into stark relief the immense power of the irrational; it humbled liberals, making them permanently aware of the limitations of reason and the fragility of freedom.

ELEMENTS OF FASCISM

Fascist movements were marked by an extreme nationalism and a determination to eradicate liberalism and Marxism, to undo the legacy of the French Revolution of 1789 and the Bolshevik Revolution of 1917. Fascists believed that theirs was a spiritual revolution, that they were initiating a new era in history, that they were building a new civilization on the ruins of liberal democracy. "We stand for a new principle in the world," said Mussolini. "We stand for sheer categorical, definitive, antithesis to the world of democracy . . . to the world which still abides by the fundamental principles laid down in 1789."[1] The chief principle of Nazism, said Hitler, "is to abolish the liberal concept of the individual and the Marxist concept of humanity, and to substitute for them the *Volk* community, rooted in the soil and united by the bond of its common blood."[2]

Fascists accused liberal society of despiritualizing human beings, of transforming them into materialistic creatures who knew no higher ideal than profit, whose souls were deadened to noble causes, heroic deeds, and self-sacrifice. Idealistic youth and intellectuals rejoiced in fascism's activism; they saw it as a revolt against the mediocrity of mass society, as a reaffirmation of the highest human spiritual qualities, an answer to despair.

Fascists regarded Marxism as another enemy, for class conflict divided the nation. Did not the Marxist call for workers of the world to unite mean the death of the national community? Fascism, in contrast, would reintegrate the proletariat into the nation and end class hostilities that divide and weaken the nation. By making people of all classes feel that they were a needed part of the nation, fascism offered a solution to the problem of insecurity, atomization, and isolation in modern industrial society.

In contrast to liberalism and Marxism, fascism attacked the rational tradition of the Enlightenment and exalted will, blood, feeling, and instinct. Intellectual discussion and critical analysis, said fascists, cause national divisiveness; reason promotes doubt, enfeebles the will, and hinders instinctive, aggressive action. Glorifying action for its own sake, fascists aroused and manipulated brutal and primitive impulses and carried into politics the combative spirit of the trenches. They formed private armies that attracted veterans, many of them rootless, brutal, and maladjusted men who sought to preserve the loyalty, camaraderie, and violence of the front.

Fascism exalted the leader who intuitively grasped what was best for the nation, and called for rule by an elite of dedicated party members. The leader and the party would relieve the individual of the need to make decisions. Holding that the liberal stress on individual freedom promoted competition and conflict that shattered national unity, fascists pressed for monolithic unity—one party and one national will.

Fascism drew its mass support from the lower middle class—small merchants, artisans, white-collar workers, civil servants, peasants of moderate means—who were frightened by both big capitalism and socialism. They hoped that fascism would protect them from the competition of big business and prevent the hated working class from establishing a Marxist state that would threaten their property. The lower middle class saw in fascism a noncommunist way of overcoming economic crises and restoring traditional respect for family, native soil, and nation. Many of these people also saw in fascism a way of attacking the existing social order, which denied them opportunities for economic advancement and social prestige. Having no patience for parliamentary procedures or sympathy for democratic principles they were drawn to demagogues who exuded confidence and promised direct action.

While a radicalized middle class gave fascist movements their mass support, the fascists could not have captured the state without the aid of existing ruling elites—landed aristocrats, industrialists, and army leaders. In Russia the Bolsheviks had to fight their way into power; in Italy and Germany the old ruling order virtually handed power to the fascists. In both Italy and Germany fascist leaders succeeded in reassuring the conservative elite that they would not institute widespread social reforms or interfere with private property and would protect the nation from communism. The old elite abhorred the violent activism and demagoguery of fascism and had contempt for fascist leaders, often brutal men without breeding or culture. Yet to protect their interests they entered into an alliance with the fascists.

THE RISE OF FASCISM IN ITALY

Postwar Unrest

Though Italy had been on the winning side of World War I, it had the appearance of a defeated nation. Food shortages, rising prices, massive unemployment, violent strikes, workers occupying factories, and peasants squatting on the uncultivated periphery of large estates created a climate of crisis. These dismal conditions contrasted sharply with the vision of a postwar world painted by politicians during the war. Italy required effective leadership and a reform program but the liberal government was paralyzed by party disputes; with several competing parties the liberals could not organize a solid majority that could cope with the domestic crisis.

The middle class was severely hurt. To meet its accelerating expenses, the government had increased taxes, but the burden fell unevenly on small landowners, small-businessowners, civil-service workers, and professionals. Moreover, the value of war bonds, purchased primarily by the middle class, had declined considerably because of inflation. Instead of a return to the good days and their former status once the war ended, these solid citizens found their economic position continuing to deteriorate.

Large landowners and industrialists feared that their nation was on the verge of a Bolshevik-style revolution. They took seriously the proclamations of the socialists: "The proletariat must be incited to the violent seizure of political and economic power and this must be handed over entirely and exclusively to the Workers' and Peasants' Councils."[3] In truth, Italian socialists had no master plan to seize power. Peasant squatters and urban strikers were responding to the distress in their own regions and did not significantly coordinate their efforts with those in other localities. Moreover, when the workers realized that they could not keep the factories operating, their revolutionary zeal waned and they started to abandon the plants. These poorly led and futile struggles of workers and peasants did not portend a Red Revolution. Nevertheless the industrialists and landlords, with the Bolshevik Revolution still vivid in their minds, were taking no chances.

Adding to the unrest was national outrage at the terms of the peace settlement. Italians felt that despite their sacrifices—500,000 dead and one million wounded—they had been robbed of the fruits of victory. While Italy had received the Brenner Pass and Trieste, it had been denied the Dalmatian coast, the Adriatic port of Fiume, and territory in Africa and the Near East. Nationalists blamed the liberal government for what they called a "mutilated victory." In 1919, a force of war veterans led by the poet and adventurer Gabriele D'Annunzio (1863–1938) seized Fiume, to the delirious joy of Italian nationalists and the embarrassment of the government. D'Annunzio's occupation of the port lasted more than a year, adding fuel to the flames of Italian nationalism and demonstrating the weakness of the liberal regime in imposing its authority on rightist opponents.

Mussolini's Seizure of Power

Benito Mussolini (1883–1945) was born in a small village in east central Italy. Proud, quarrelsome, violent, and resentful of the humiliation he suffered for being poor, Mussolini was a troublemaker and was often in trouble with the school authorities. But he was also intelligent, ranking first on final examinations in four subjects. After graduation, Mussolini taught in an elementary school, but this did not suit his passionate temperament. From 1902 to 1904 he lived in Switzerland, where he broadened his reading, lectured, and wrote. He also came under the influence of anarchist and socialist revolutionaries. Returning to Italy, he was labeled a dangerous revolutionary by the police. As a reward for his zeal and political agitation, which led to five months in prison for inciting riots, Mussolini in 1912 was made editor of *Avanti*, the principal socialist newspaper. During the early days of World War I he was expelled from the Socialist party for advocating Italian intervention in the war. After Italy entered the war, Mussolini served at the front and suffered a serious wound during firing practice for which he was hospitalized.

In 1919 Mussolini organized the Fascist party in order to realize his immense will to power; this quest for power, more than a set of coherent doctrines, characterized the young movement. A supreme opportunist rather than an ideologist, Mussolini exploited the unrest in postwar Italy in order to capture control of the state. He attracted converts from the discontented, disillusioned, and uprooted. Many Italians, particularly the educated bourgeoisie who had been inspired by the unification movement of the nineteenth century, viewed Mussolini as the leader who would gain Fiume, Dalmatia, and colonies and win for Italy a place of honor in international affairs. Hardened battle veterans joined the Fascist movement to escape the boredom and idleness of civilian life. They welcomed an opportunity to wear the uniforms of the Fascist militia (Black Shirts), parade in the streets, and do battle with socialist and labor union opponents. Squads of Fascist Black Shirts *(squadristi)* raided socialist and trade-union offices, destroying property and inflicting beatings. It soon appeared that Italy was drifting toward civil war as socialist Red Shirts responded in kind.

Industrialists and landowners, hoping that Mussolini would rescue Italy from Bolshevism, contributed large sums to the Fascist party. The lower-middle class, fearful that the growing power of labor unions and the Socialist party threatened their property and social prestige, viewed Mussolini as a protector. Middle-class university students, searching for adventure and an ideal, and army officers, dreaming of an Italian empire and hateful of parliamentary government, also were receptive to Mussolini's party. Intellectuals disenchanted with liberal politics and parliamentary democracy were intrigued by Mussolini's philosophy of action. Mussolini's nationalism, activism, and anticommunism gradually seduced elements of the power structure— capitalists, aristocrats, army officers, the royal family, the church. Regarding liberalism as bankrupt and parliamentary government as futile, many of these people yearned for a military dictatorship.

In 1922 Mussolini made his bid for power. Speaking at a giant rally of his followers in late October, he declared: "Either they will give us the government or we shall take it by descending on Rome. It is now a matter of days, perhaps hours." A few days later thousands of Fascists began the March on Rome. Some members of parliament demanded that the army defend the government against a Fascist coup. It would have been a relatively simple matter to crush the 20,000 Fascist marchers armed with little more than pistols and rifles, but King Victor Emmanuel III (1869–1947) refused to act. The king's advisors, some of them sympathetic to Mussolini, exaggerated the strength of the Fascists. Believing that he was rescuing Italy from terrible violence, the king appointed Mussolini prime minister.

Mussolini had bluffed his way into power. Fascism had triumphed not because of its own strength—the Fascists had only 35 of 535 seats in parliament—but because the liberal regime, irresolute and indecisive, did not counter force with force. In the past the liberal state had not challenged Fascist acts of terror; now it feebly surrendered to Fascist blustering and threats. No doubt liberals hoped that once in power the Fascists would forsake terror, pursue moderate aims, and act within the constitution. But the liberals were wrong; they had completely misjudged the antidemocratic character of Fascism.

THE FASCIST STATE IN ITALY

Consolidation of Power

In October 1922, when the liberal regime in Italy capitulated, the Fascists by no means held total power. Anti-Fascists still sat in parliament and only four ministers of Mussolini's cabinet of fourteen were Fascists. Cautious and shrewd, Mussolini resisted the extremists in his party who demanded a second revolution, the immediate and preferably violent destruction of the old order. In this early stage of Fascist rule when his position was still tenuous, Mussolini sought to maintain an image of respectability and moderation. He tried to convince the power structure that he intended to operate within the constitution, that he did not seek dictatorial power. At the same time he gradually secured his position and turned Italy into a one-party state. In 1923, an electoral law, approved by both chambers of

parliament, decreed that the party with the most votes in a national election (provided that the figure was not less than 25 percent of the total votes cast) would be granted two-thirds of the seats in the Chamber of Deputies. In the elections of 1924, marred by Fascist terrorism, Mussolini's supporters received 65 percent of the vote. Without having to use the new electoral law, the opponents of Fascism had been enfeebled and Mussolini had consolidated his power.

When socialist leader Giacomo Matteotti protested Fascist terror tactics, Fascist thugs killed him (in 1924). Although Mussolini had not ordered Matteotti's murder, his vicious attacks against his socialist opponent inspired the assassins. Repelled by the murder, some sincere democrats withdrew from the Chamber of Deputies in protest and some influential Italians called for Mussolini's dismissal. But the majority of liberals, including the leadership, continued to support Mussolini. And the king, the papacy, the army, large landowners, and industrialists, still regarding Mussolini as the best defense against internal disorder and socialism, did not lend their support to an anti-Fascist movement.

Pressed by the radicals within the Fascist party, Mussolini moved to establish a dictatorship. In 1925–1926 he eliminated non-Fascists from his cabinet, dissolved opposition parties, smashed the independent trade unions, suppressed opposition newspapers, replaced local mayors with Fascist officials, and organized a secret police to round up troublemakers. Many anti-Fascists fled the country or were deported.

Mussolini then turned on the extremist Fascists, the local chieftains (ras) who had led squadristi in the early days of the movement. Lauding violence, daring deeds, and the dangerous life, the ras were indispensable during the party's formative stage. But Mussolini feared that the radical adventurism of the ras posed a threat to his personal rule. And their desire to replace the traditional power structure with people drawn from their own ranks

MUSSOLINI AT ROME, CELEBRATING THE TENTH ANNIVERSA-RY OF THE FASCIST GATHERING IN MILAN FOR THE MARCH ON ROME Initially Mussolini was able to bluff his way to power because an indecisive liberal regime did not counter force with force. Ten years later, after making Italy a one-party nation and by switching ideologies at times for the sake of respectability, Mussolini appeared secure in the support of the Italian people. (Wide World Photos)

could block his efforts to cooperate with the established elite—industrialists, aristocratic landowners, and army leaders. Mussolini therefore expelled some squadristi leaders from the party and gave others positions in the bureaucracy in order to tame them.

Mussolini was less successful than Hitler and Stalin in fashioning a totalitarian state. The industrialists, the large landowners, the church, and to some extent even the army, never fell under the complete domination of the party. Nor did the regime possess the mind of its subjects with the same thoroughness as Nazi Germany. Life in Italy was less regimented and the individual less fearful than in

Nazi Germany or Communist Russia. The Italian people might cheer Mussolini, but few were willing to die for him.

Control of the Masses

Like Communist Russia and Nazi Germany, Fascist Italy used mass organizations and mass media to control minds and regulate behavior. As in the Soviet Union and the Third Reich, the Fascist regime created a cult of the leader. "Mussolini goes forward with confidence, in a halo of myth, almost chosen by God, indefatigable and infallible, the instrument employed by Providence for the creation of a new civilization," wrote the philosopher Giovanni Gentile.[4] To convey the image of a virile leader, Mussolini had himself photographed barechested or in a uniform with a steel helmet. Other photographs showed him riding horses, driving fast cars, flying planes, and playing with lion cubs. Mussolini frequently addressed huge throngs of admirers from his balcony. His tenor voice, grandiloquent phrases, and posturing—jaw thrust out, hands on hips—captivated audiences; idolatry from the masses, in turn, intensified Mussolini's feelings of grandeur. Elementary school textbooks depicted Mussolini as the savior of the nation, a modern-day Julius Caesar.

Fascist propaganda inculcated habits of discipline and obedience: "Mussolini is always right." "Believe! Obey! Fight!" Propaganda also glorified war: "A minute on the battlefield is worth a lifetime of peace." The press, radio, and cinema idealized life under Fascism, implying that Fascism had eradicated crime, poverty, and social tensions. Schoolteachers and university professors were compelled to swear allegiance to the Fascist government and to propagate Fascist ideals, while students were urged to criticize instructors who harbored liberal attitudes. Millions of youths belonged to Fascist organizations in which they participated in patriotic ceremonies and social functions, sang Fascist hymns, and wore Fascist uniforms. They submerged their own identity into the group.

Economic Policies

Fascists denounced economic liberalism for promoting individual self-interest, and socialism for instigating conflicts between workers and capitalists that divided and weakened the nation. The Fascist way of resolving tensions between workers and employers was to abolish independent labor unions, prohibit strikes,

and establish associations or corporations that included both the workers and employers within a given industry. In theory, representatives of labor and capital would cooperatively solve labor problems in a particular industry. In practice the representatives of labor turned out to be Fascists who protected the interests of the industrialists. Although the Fascists lauded the corporative system as a creative approach to modern economic problems, in reality it played a minor role in Italian economic life. Big business continued to make its own decisions, paying scant attention to the corporations.

Nor did the Fascist government solve Italy's long-standing economic problems. In order to curtail the export of capital and to reduce the nation's dependency on imports in case of war, Mussolini sought to make Italy self-sufficient. To win the "battle of grain," the Fascist regime brought marginal lands under cultivation and urged farmers to concentrate on wheat rather than other crops. While wheat production increased substantially, total agricultural output declined because wheat had been planted on land more suited to animal husbandry and fruit cultivation. In order to make Italy industrially self-sufficient, the regime limited imports of foreign goods, with the result that Italian consumers paid higher prices for Italian manufactured goods. Mussolini posed as the protector of the little people but under his regime the power and profits of big business grew and the standard of living of small farmers and urban workers declined. Government attempts to grapple with the Depression were half-hearted. Aside from providing family allowances—an increase in income with the birth of each child—the Fascist regime did little in the way of social welfare.

The Church and the Fascist Regime

Although anticlerical since his youth, Mussolini was also expedient. He recognized that coming to terms with the church would improve his image with Catholic public opinion. The Vatican regarded Mussolini's regime as a barrier against communism and less hostile to church interests and more amenable to church direction than a liberal government. Pope Pius XI (1922–1939) was an ultraconservative whose hatred of liberalism and secularism led him to believe that the Fascists would increase the influence of the church in the nation.

In 1929 the Lateran Accords recognized the independence of Vatican City, repealed many of the anticlerical laws passed under the liberal government, and made religious instruction compulsory in all secondary schools. The papal state, Vatican City, a small enclave within Rome over which the Italian government had no authority, was established. Relations between the Vatican and the Fascist government remained fairly good throughout the decade of the 1930s. One crisis arose in 1931 when Mussolini, pushed by militant anticlericals within his party, dissolved certain Catholic youth groups as rivals to Fascist youth associations, but a compromise that permitted the Catholic organizations to function within certain limits eased tensions. The church supported Mussolini's invasion of Ethiopia and his intervention in the Spanish Civil War. Although the papacy criticized Mussolini for drawing closer to Hitler and introducing anti-Jewish legislation, it never broke with the Fascist regime.

THE NEW GERMAN REPUBLIC

In the last days of World War I, a revolution brought down the German imperial government and led to the creation of a democratic republic. The German admirals had in October 1918 ordered the German navy to engage the British in the English Channel, but the sailors,

anticipating peace and resentful of their officers (who commonly resorted to cruel discipline), refused to obey. Joined by sympathetic soldiers, the mutineers raised the Red Flag of revolution. The revolt soon spread, as military men and workers demonstrated for peace and reform and in some regions seized authority. Reluctant to fire on their comrades and also fed up with the war, German troops did not move to crush the revolutionaries. On November 9, 1918, the leaders of the government announced the end of the monarchy and Kaiser William II fled to Holland. Two days later, the new German Republic, headed by Chancellor Friedrich Ebert (1871–1925), a Social Democrat, signed an armistice agreement ending the war. In the eyes of many Germans, the new democratic leadership was responsible for the defeat.

In February 1919 the recently elected National Assembly met at Weimar and proceeded to draw up a constitution for the new state. The Weimar Republic—born in revolution, which most Germans detested, and military defeat, which many attributed to the new government—faced an uncertain future.

Threats from Left and Right

The infant republic, dominated by moderate socialists, faced internal threats from both the radical left and the radical right. In January 1919 the newly established German Communist party, or Spartacists, disregarding the advice of their leaders Rosa Luxemburg and Karl Liebknecht, took to the streets of Berlin and declared the government of Ebert deposed. To crush the revolution, Ebert turned to the Free Corps—volunteer brigades of ex-soldiers and adventurers, led by officers loyal to the emperor, who had been fighting to protect the eastern borders from encroachments by the new states of Poland, Estonia, and Latvia. The men of the Free Corps relished action and despised Bolshevism. They suppressed the revolution and murdered Luxemburg and Liebknecht on January 15. In May 1919 the Free Corps also marched into Munich to overthrow the Soviet Republic set up there by communists a few weeks earlier.

The Spartacist revolt and the short-lived Soviet Republic in Munich (and others in Baden and Brunswick) had profound effects on the German psyche. The communists had been easily subdued, but fear of a communist insurrection remained deeply embedded in the middle and upper classes, a fear that drove many of them into the ranks of the right-wing opponents of the Weimar Republic.

The Spartacist revolt was an attempt of the radical left to overthrow the republic; in March 1920, the republic was threatened by the radical right. Refusing to disband as the government ordered, detachments of the right-wing Free Corps marched into Berlin and declared a new government headed by Wolfgang von Kapp, a staunch nationalist. President Ebert and most members of the cabinet and National Assembly fled to Stuttgart. Insisting that it could not fire on fellow soldiers, the German army, the Reichswehr, made no move to defend the republic. A general strike called by the labor unions prevented Kapp from governing and the coup collapsed. Although the Kapp Putsch failed, it demonstrated that the loyalty of the army to the republic was doubtful.

Economic Crisis

In addition to uprisings by the left and right, the republic was burdened by economic crisis. During the war, Germany financed its military expenditures not by increasing taxation but through short-term loans, thereby accumulating a huge debt that now had to be paid. A trade deficit and enormous reparation payments worsened the nation's economic plight. Unable to meet the deficit in the national budget, the government simply printed more money, causing the value of the German mark to decline precipitously. In 1914, the mark stood at 4.2 to the dollar; in 1919, 8.9 to the dollar; in early 1923, 18,000 to the dollar. In August 1923 a dollar could be exchanged for 4.6 million marks, and in November for 4 billion marks! Bank savings, war bonds, and pensions, representing years of toil and thrift, became worthless. Blaming the republic for this disaster, the ruined middle class became more receptive to rightist movements that aimed to bring down the republic.

With the economy in shambles, the republic defaulted on reparation payments. Premier Raymond Poincaré (1860–1934) of France took a hard line and in January 1923 ordered French troops into the Ruhr, the nerve center of German industry. Responding to the republic's call for passive resistance, factory workers, miners, and railroad workers in the Ruhr refused to work for the French. To provide strike benefits for the Ruhr workers, the government printed yet more money, making inflation even worse.

In August 1923, Gustav Stresemann became chancellor. The new government lasted only until November 1923, but during those one hundred days Stresemann skillfully placed the republic on the path to recovery. Warned by German industrialists that the economy was at the breaking point, Stresemann abandoned the policy of passive resistance in the Ruhr and declared Germany's willingness to make reparation payments. Stresemann issued a new currency, backed by a mortgage on German real estate. To reduce public expenditures that contributed to inflation, the government fired some civil-service workers and lowered salaries; to get additional funds, it raised taxes; to protect the value of the new currency, it did not print another issue. Inflation receded and confidence was restored.

A new arrangement regarding reparations also contributed to the economic recovery. Recognizing that in its present economic straits Germany could not meet its obligations to the Allies or secure the investment of foreign capitalists, Britain and the United States pressured France to allow a reparation commission to make new proposals. In 1924 the parties accepted the Dawes Plan, which reduced reparations and based them on Germany's economic capacity. During the negotiations France agreed to withdraw its troops from the Ruhr, another step toward easing tensions for the republic.

From 1924 to 1929 economic conditions improved. Attracted by high interest rates and the low cost of labor, foreign capitalists, particularly Americans, invested in German businesses, stimulating the economy. By 1929 iron, steel, coal, and chemical production exceeded prewar levels. The value of German exports also surpassed that of 1913. This spectacular boom was due in part to more effective methods of production and management and the concentration of related industries in giant trusts. Real wages were higher than before the war and improved unemployment benefits also made life better for the workers. It appeared that Germany had also achieved political stability as threats from the extremist parties of the left and the right subsided. Given time and economic stability, democracy might have taken firmer root in Germany. But then came the Great Depression (see page 710). The global economic crisis that began in October 1929 brought into stark relief the fundamental weaknesses of the Weimar Republic.

Fundamental Weaknesses of the Weimar Republic

German political experience provided poor soil for the transplanting of an Anglo-Saxon democratic parliamentary system. Imperial Germany had been a semiautocratic state ruled by an emperor who commanded the armed forces, controlled foreign policy, appointed the chancellor, and called and dismissed parliament. This authoritarian system blocked the German people from acquiring democratic habits and attitudes; still accustomed to rule from above, still in adoration of the power-state, many Germans sought the destruction of the Weimar Republic.

Traditional conservatives—the upper echelons of the civil service, judges, industrialists, large landowners, army leaders—were contemptuous of democracy and were avowed enemies of the republic. They wanted to restore a pre-1914 Prussian-type government that would fight liberal ideals and protect the fatherland from Bolshevism. Nor did the middle class feel a commitment to the liberal-democratic principles on which the republic rested. The traditionally nationalistic middle class identified the republic with the defeat in war and the humiliation of the Versailles Treaty; rabidly antisocialist, this class saw the leaders of the republic as Marxists who would impose on Germany a working-class state. Some intellectuals attacked democracy as a barrier to the true unity of the German nation. In doing so, they turned many Germans against the republic, thereby eroding the popular support on which democracy depends.

The Weimar Republic also showed the weaknesses of the multiparty system. With the vote spread over a number of parties, no one party held a majority of seats in the Reichstag, so the republic was governed by a coalition of several parties. But because of ideological differences, the coalition was always unstable and in danger of failing to function. This is precisely what happened during the Great Depression. When effective leadership was imperative, the government could not act. Political deadlock caused Germans to lose what little confidence they had in the democratic system. Support for the parties that wanted to preserve democracy dwindled, and extremist parties that aimed to topple the republic gained in strength. Supporting the republic were Social Democrats, Catholic Centrists, and German Democrats.* Seeking to bring down the republic were the Communists, on the left, and two rightist parties, the Nationalists and the National Socialist German Workers party led by Adolf Hitler.

THE RISE OF HITLER

The Early Years

Adolf Hitler (1889–1945) was born in the town of Braunau am Inn, Austria, on April 20, 1889, the fourth child of a minor civil servant. Much of his youth was spent in Linz, a major city in Upper Austria. A poor student at secondary school, although by no means unintelligent, Hitler left high school and lived idly for more than two years. In 1907 the Vienna Academy of Arts rejected his application for admission. With the death of his mother in December 1907, the nineteen-year-old orphan (his father had died in 1903) drifted around Vienna viewing himself as an art student. Contrary to his later description of these years, Hitler did not suffer great poverty, for he received an orphan's allowance from the state and an inheritance from his mother and an aunt. When the Vienna Academy again refused him admission

---

*The coalition that governed the republic during the 1920s consisted of Social Democrats, Catholic Centrists, and German Democrats. While the Social Democrats hoped one day to transform Germany into a Marxist society, they had abandoned revolutionary means and pursued a policy of moderate social reform. The largest party until the closing months of the Weimar Republic, the Social Democrats were committed to democratic principles and parliamentary government. The Catholic Center party opposed socialism and protected Catholic interests, but like the Social Democrats supported the republic. The German Democratic party consisted of middle-class liberals who also opposed socialism and supported the republic. Although the right-wing German People's party was more monarchist than republican, on occasion it joined the coalition of parties that sought to preserve the republic.

in 1908, he did not seek to learn a trade or to work steadily, but earned some money by painting picture postcards.

Hitler was a loner, often given to brooding and self-pity. He found some solace by regularly attending Wagnerian operas, by fantasizing about great architectural projects that he would someday initiate, and by reading. He read a lot, especially in art, history, and military affairs. He also read the racial, nationalist, anti-Semitic, and Pan-German literature that abounded in multinational Vienna. This literature introduced Hitler to a bizarre racial mythology: a heroic race of blond, blue-eyed Aryans battling for survival against inferior races, the danger posed by mixing races, the liquidation of racial inferiors, the Jew as the embodiment of evil and the source of all misfortune.

In Vienna, Hitler came into contact with Georg von Schönerer's Pan-German movement. For Schönerer, the Jews were evil not because of their religion, not because they rejected Christ, but because they possessed evil racial qualities. Schönerer's followers wore watch chains etched with pictures of hanged Jews. Hitler was particularly impressed with Dr. Karl Lueger, the mayor of Vienna, a clever demagogue who skillfully manipulated the anti-Semitic feelings of the Viennese for his own political advantage. In Vienna Hitler also acquired a hatred for Marxism and democracy and the conviction that the struggle for existence and the survival of the fittest are the essential facts of the social world. His years in Vienna emptied Hitler of all compassion and scruples and filled him with a fierce resentment of the social order that he felt ignored him, cheated him, and condemned him to a wretched existence.

When World War I began, Hitler was in Munich. He welcomed the war as a relief from his daily life, which had been devoid of purpose and excitement. Volunteering for the German army, Hitler found battle exhilarating and he fought bravely, twice receiving the Iron Cross.

The experience of battle taught Hitler to value discipline, regimentation, leadership, authority, struggle, ruthlessness—values that he carried with him into the politics of the postwar world. The shock of Germany's defeat and revolution intensified his commitment to racial nationalism. To lead Germany to total victory over its racial enemies became his obsession. Like many returning soldiers, he demanded explanations for lost victories. His answer was simple and demagogic: Germany's shame was due to the creators of the republic, the "November criminals." And behind them was a Jewish-Bolshevik world conspiracy.

The Nazi Party

In 1919, Hitler joined the German Worker's Party, a small right-wing group, one of the more than seventy extremist military-political-Volkish organizations that sprang up in postwar Germany. Displaying fantastic energy and extraordinary ability as a demagogic orator, propagandist, and organizer, Hitler quickly became the leader of the party, whose name was changed to National Socialist German Workers party (NAZI). As leader, Hitler insisted on absolute authority and total allegiance, a demand that coincided with the postwar longing for a strong leader who would set right a shattered nation. Without Hitler the National Socialist German Workers party would have remained an insignificant group of discontents and outcasts. Demonstrating a Machiavellian cunning for politics, Hitler tightened the party organization and perfected the techniques of mass propaganda.

Like Mussolini, Hitler incorporated military attitudes and techniques into politics. Uniforms, salutes, emblems, flags, and other symbols infused party members with a sense of solidarity and camaraderie. At mass meetings, Hitler was a spellbinder who gave stunning performances. His pounding fists, throbbing body, wild gesticulations, hypnotic eyes, rage-swollen face, and repeated, frenzied denunciations of the Versailles Treaty, Marxism, the republic, and Jews inflamed and mesmerized the audience, which became transformed into a single mass. Hitler's torrent of words, impassioned conviction, and extraordinary self-confidence swept away all doubt, all rational judgment, all critical faculties. Hitler instinctively grasped the innermost feelings of his audience, its resentments and longings. "The intense will of the man, the passion of his sincerity seemed to flow from him into me. I experienced an exaltation that could be likened only to religious conversion," said one early admirer.[5]

In November 1923, Hitler attempted to seize power (the Munich or "Beer Hall" Putsch) in the state of Bavaria as a prelude to toppling the republic. Ironically, despite the failure of the putsch and the poor showing of the Nazis—they quickly scattered when the Bavarian police opened fire—Hitler's prestige increased, for when he was put on trial, he used it as an opportunity to denounce the republic and the Versailles Treaty and to proclaim his philosophy of racial nationalism. His impassioned speeches, publicized by the press, earned Hitler a nationwide reputation and a light sentence—five years imprisonment with the promise of quick parole. While in prison Hitler dictated *Mein Kampf*, a rambling and turgid work that contained the essence of his world-view.

The unsuccessful Munich Putsch taught Hitler a valuable lesson: armed insurrection against superior might fails. He would gain power not by force but by exploiting the instruments of democracy—elections and party politics. He would use apparently legal means to destroy the Weimar Republic and impose a dictatorship. As Nazi propaganda expert Joseph Goebbels would later express it: "We have openly declared that we use democratic methods only to gain power and that once we had it we would ruthlessly deny our opponents all those chances we had been granted when we were in the opposition."[6]

Hitler's World-View

Some historians view Hitler as an unprincipled opportunist and a brilliant tactician who believed in nothing, but cleverly manufactured and manipulated ideas that were politically useful in his drive for power. To be sure Hitler certainly was not concerned with the objective truth of an idea but with its potential political usefulness. He was not a systematic thinker like Marx. Whereas communism claimed the certainty of science and held that it would reform the world in accordance with rational principles, Hitler proclaimed the higher validity of blood, instinct, and will and regarded the intellect as an enemy of the soul. Hitler nevertheless possessed a remarkably consistent ideology, as Hajo Holborn concludes:

Hitler was a great opportunist and tactician, but it would be quite wrong to think that ideology was for him a mere instrumentality for gaining power. On the contrary, Hitler was a doctrinaire of the first order. Throughout his political career he was guided by an ideology . . . which from 1926 onward [did] not show any change whatsoever.[7]

Hitler's thought comprised a patchwork of nineteenth-century anti-Semitic, Volkish, Social Darwinist, antidemocratic, and anti-Marxist ideas. From these ideas, many of them enjoying wide popularity, Hitler constructed a world-view rooted in myth and ritual. Given to excessive daydreaming and never managing to "overcome his youth with its dreams, injuries, and resentments,"[8] Hitler sought to make the world accord with his fantasies— struggles to the death between races, a vast empire ruled by a master race, a thousand-year Reich.

Racial Nationalism

Nazism rejected both the Judeo-Christian and the Enlightenment traditions and sought to found a new world order based on racial nationalism. For Hitler, race was the key to understanding world history. He believed that Western civilization was at a critical juncture. Liberalism was dying, and Marxism, that "Jewish invention," as he called it, would inherit the future unless it was opposed by an even more powerful world-view. "With the conception of race National Socialism will carry its revolution and recast the world," said Hitler.[9] As the German barbarians had overwhelmed a disintegrating Roman Empire, a reawakened, racially united Germany, led by men of iron will, would carve out a vast European empire and would deal a decadent liberal civilization its deathblow. It would conquer Russia, eradicate communism, and reduce to serfdom the subhuman Slavs, "a mass of born slaves who feel the need of a master."[10]

In the tradition of Volkish thinkers, Hitler divided the world into superior and inferior races and pitted them against each other in a struggle for survival. This fight for life was a law of nature, a law of history. The Germans, descendants of ancient Aryans, possessed superior racial characteristics; a nation degenerates and perishes if it allows its blood to be contaminated by intermingling with lower races. Conflict between races was desirable for it strengthened and hardened racial superiors; it made them ruthless, a necessary quality in this Darwinian world. As a higher race, the Germans were entitled to conquer and subjugate other races. Germany must acquire *Lebensraum* ("living space") by expanding eastward at the expense of the racially inferior Slavs.

The Jew as Devil

An obsessive and virulent anti-Semitism dominated Hitler's mental outlook (see pages 531–534 on anti-Semitism). In waging war against the Jews, Hitler believed that he was defending Germany from its worst enemy. In Hitler's mental picture the Aryan was the originator and carrier of civilization. As descendants of the Aryans, the Germans embodied creativity, bravery, and loyalty. As the counterpart of the Aryan, the Jew was stained with the vilest qualities. "Two worlds face one another," said Hitler, "the men of God and the men of Satan! The Jew is the anti-man, the creature of another god. He must have come from another root of the human race. I set the Aryan and the Jew over and against each other."[11] Everything Hitler despised— liberalism, intellectualism, pacifism, parliamentarism, internationalism, communism, modern art, individualism—he attributed to the Jew.

For Hitler, the Jew was the mortal enemy of racial nationalism. The moral outlook of the ancient Hebrew prophets, which affirmed individual worth and made individuals morally responsible for their actions, was totally in opposition to Hitler's morality which subordinated the individual to the national community. He once called conscience a Jewish invention. The prophetic vision of the unity of humanity under God, equality, justice, and peace were also in opposition to Hitler's belief that all history is a pitiless struggle between races and that only the strongest and most ruthless deserve to survive.

Hitler's anti-Semitism served a functional purpose. By concentrating all evil in one enemy, "the conspirator and demonic" Jew, Hitler provided the masses with a simple, consistent, and emotionally satisfying explanation for all their misery. By defining themselves as the racial and spiritual opposites of Jews, Germans of all classes felt joined together in a Volkish union. Even failures and misfits gained self-respect. By seeing themselves engaged in a heroic battle against a single enemy who embodied evil, their will was strengthened. Anti-Semitism provided insecure and hostile people with powerless but recognizable targets on whom to focus their antisocial feelings.

The surrender to myth served also to disorient the German intellect. When the mind accepts an image such as Hitler's image of Jews as vermin, germs, and satanic conspirators, it has lost all sense of balance and

THE FLAGBEARER Hitler knew the value of propaganda. In this poster, he appears as a knight from medieval myth and bears the flag of the nation against all enemies. (U.S. Army)

objectivity. Such a disoriented mind is ready to believe and to obey, to be manipulated and led; it is ready to brutalize and to tolerate brutality.

The Importance of Propaganda

Hitler understood that in an age of political parties, universal suffrage, and a popular press—the legacies of the French and Industrial revolutions—the successful leader must win the support of the masses. To do this, Hitler consciously applied and perfected elements of circus showmanship, church pageantry, American advertising, and the techniques of propaganda that the Allies had effectively used to stir the civilian population during the war. To be effective, said Hitler, propaganda must be aimed principally at the emotions. The masses are not moved by scientific ideas or by objective and abstract knowledge, but by primitive feelings, terror, force, discipline. Propaganda must reduce everything to simple slogans incessantly repeated and concentrate on one enemy. The masses are aroused by the spoken, not the written word, by a storm of hot passion erupting from the speaker "which like hammer blows can open the gates to the heart of the people."[12]

The most effective means of stirring the masses and strengthening them for the struggle ahead, said Hitler, is the mass meeting. Surrounded by tens of thousands of people, individuals lose their sense of individuality and no longer see themselves as isolated atoms. They become members of a community bound together by an esprit de corps reminiscent of the trenches during the Great War. Bombarded by the cheers of thousands of voices, by marching units, by banners, by explosive oratory, individuals become convinced of the truth of the party's message and the determination of the movement. Their intellects overwhelmed, their resistance lowered, they doubt their previous beliefs and are carried along on a wave of enthusiasm. "The man who enters such a meeting doubting and wavering leaves it inwardly reinforced; he has become a link to the community."[13]

Hitler Gains Power

When Hitler left prison in December 1924, after serving nine months, he proceeded to tighten his hold over the Nazi party. He relentlessly used his genius for propaganda and organization to strengthen the loyalty of his cadres and to instill in them a sense of mission. In 1925, the Nazi party counted about 27,000 members; in 1929, it had grown to 178,000 with units throughout Germany. But its prospects seemed dim, for since 1925 economic conditions had improved and the

republic seemed politically stable. In 1928 the National Socialists (Nazis) received only 2.6 percent of the vote. Nevertheless, Hitler never lost faith in his own capacities or his destiny; he continued to build his party and waited for a crisis that would rock the republic and make his movement a force in national politics.

The Great Depression, which began in the United States at the end of 1929, provided that crisis. As Germany's economic plight worsened, the Nazis tirelessly expanded their efforts. Everywhere they staged mass rallies, plastered walls with posters, distributed leaflets, and engaged in street battles with their opponents of the left. Hitler promised all things to all groups, avoided debates, provided simple explanations for Germany's misfortunes, and insisted that only the Nazis could rescue Germany. Nazi propaganda attacked the communists, the "November criminals," the democratic system, the Versailles Treaty, reparations, and, above all, the Jews. It depicted Hitler as a savior. Hitler would rescue Germany from chaos; he understood the real needs of the Volk; he was sent by destiny to lead Germany in its hour of greatest need. These propaganda techniques worked. The Nazi party went from 810,000 votes in 1928 to 6,400,000 in 1930 and its representation in the Reichstag soared from 12 to 107.

The Social Democrats (SPD), the principal defenders of democracy, could draw support only from the working class; to the middle class, the SPD were hated Marxists. Moreover, in the eyes of many Germans the SPD were identified with the status quo, that is, with economic misery and national humiliation. The SPD simply had no program that could attract the middle class or arouse their hope for a better future.

To the lower-middle class the Nazis promised effective leadership and a solution to the economic crisis. To them the Great Depression was the last straw, final evidence that the republic had failed and should be supplanted by a different kind of regime. They craved order, authority, and leadership and abhorred the disputes of political parties that provided neither. They wanted Hitler to protect Germany from the communists and organized labor. The traumatic experience of the Great Depression caused many bourgeois, hitherto apathetic about voting, politically immature, impatient, and easily excitable, to cast ballots. The depression was also severe in England and the United States, but the liberal foundations of these countries were strong; in Germany they were not because the middle class had never committed itself to democracy or indeed had any liking for it. Democracy endured in Britain and the United States; in Germany it collapsed.

But Nazism was more than a class movement. It appealed to the discontented and disillusioned from all segments of the population—embittered veterans, romantic nationalists, idealistic intellectuals, industrialists and large landowners frightened by communism and social democracy, rootless and resentful people who felt they had no place in the existing society, the unemployed, lovers of violence, and newly enfranchised youth yearning for a cause. The Social Democrats spoke the rational language of European democracy. The Communists addressed themselves to only a part of the nation, the proletariat, and were linked to a foreign country, the Soviet Union. The Nazis reached a wider spectrum of the population and touched deeper feelings.

And always there was the immense attraction of Hitler. Many Germans were won over by his fanatic sincerity, his iron will, and his conviction that he was chosen by fate to rescue Germany. No doubt many Germans voted for Hitler not because they approved of him or his ideas, but because he was a strong opponent of the Weimar Republic. What these people wanted, above all, was the end of the republic they hated.

Meanwhile the parliamentary regime failed to function effectively. President Paul von Hindenburg (1847–1934), the aging field marshall, exercised his emergency powers. According to Article 48 of the constitution, during times of emergency the president was empowered to govern by decree, that is, without parliament. In effect, the responsibility for governing Germany had been transferred from the political parties and parliament to the president and chancellor. Rule by the president, instead of by parliament, meant also that Germany had already taken a giant step away from parliamentary government in the direction of authoritarianism.

In the election of July 31, 1932, the Nazis received 37.3 percent of the vote and won 230 seats, far more than any other party but still not a majority. Determined to become chancellor, Hitler refused to take a subordinate position in a coalition government. Meanwhile, Franz von Papen, who had recently resigned as chancellor, persuaded Hindenburg, whose judgment was distorted by old age, to appoint Hitler chancellor. In this decision Papen had the support of German industrialists, aristocratic landowners, and the Nationalist party.

As in Italy, the members of the ruling elite were frightened by internal violence, unrest, and the specter of communism. They thought Hitler a vulgar man and abhorred his demagogic incitement of the masses. But they regarded him as a useful instrument to fight communism, block social reform, break the backs of organized labor, and rebuild the armament industry. Hitler had cleverly reassured these traditional conservatives that the Nazis would protect private property and business and go slow with social reform. Like the Italian upper class, which had assisted Mussolini in his rise to power, the old conservative ruling elite intrigued to put Hitler in power. Ironically, this decision was made when Nazi strength at the polls was beginning to ebb. Expecting to control Hitler, conservatives calculated badly, for Hitler could not be tamed. They had underestimated his skill as a politician, his ruthlessness, and his obsession with racial nationalism. Hitler had not sought power to restore the old order but to fashion a new one. The new leadership would be drawn not from the traditional ruling segments, but from the most dedicated Nazis, regardless of their social background.

When Hitler became chancellor on January 30, 1933, the army, fearing that the country was heading for civil war, did not offer any resistance. Nor did the Social Democratic and trade-union leaders rally the working class against the Nazis. Never intending to rule within the spirit of the constitution, Hitler quickly moved to assume dictatorial powers. Taking advantage of a fire set in the Reichstag in February 1933 by a Dutch drifter with communist leanings, Hitler urged Hindenburg to sign an emergency decree suspending civil rights on the pretext that the state was threatened by internal subversion. Hitler used these emergency powers to arrest, without due process, Communist and Social Democratic deputies.

In the elections of March 1933, Nazi thugs broke up Communist party meetings and Hitler called for a Nazi victory at the polls in order to save Europe from Bolshevism. Intimidated by street violence and captivated by Nazi mass demonstrations and relentless propaganda, the German people elected 288 Nazi deputies in a Reichstag of 647 seats. With the support of 52 deputies of the National party and the absence of Communist deputies who were under arrest, the Nazis now had a secure majority. Hitler then bullied the Reichstag into passing the Enabling Act (in March 1933), which permitted the chancellor to enact legislation independent of the Reichstag. With astonishing passivity the political parties had allowed the Nazis to dismantle the government and make Hitler a dictator with unlimited power. Hitler had used the instruments of democracy to destroy the republic and create a dictatorship. And he did it far more thoroughly and quickly than Mussolini.

NAZI GERMANY

Mussolini's Fascism exhibited much bluster and bragging, but Fascist Italy did not have the industrial and military strength or the total commitment of the people necessary to threaten the peace of Europe. Nazism, on the other hand, demonstrated a demonic quality that nearly destroyed Western civilization. The impact of Hitler's sinister, fanatic, and obsessive personality was far greater on the German movement than was Mussolini's character on Italian Fascism. Also contributing to the demonic radicalism of Nazism were certain deeply rooted German traditions that were absent in Italy—Prussian militarism, adoration of the power-state, belief in the special destiny of the German Volk. These traditions made the German people's attachment to Hitler and Nazi ideology much stronger than the Italian people's devotion to Mussolini and his party.

The Leader-State

The Nazis moved to subjugate all political and economic institutions and all culture to the will of the party. There could be no separation between the private life and politics; ideology must pervade every phase of daily life; all organizations must come under party control; there could be no rights of the individual that must be respected by the state. The party became the state, its teachings the soul of the German nation.

Unlike absolute monarchies of the past, a totalitarian regime requires more than outward obedience to its commands; it seeks to control the inner person, to shape thoughts, feelings, and attitudes in accordance with the party ideology. It demands total allegiance and submission. An anonymous Nazi poet succinctly expressed the totalitarian goal:

We have captured all the positions
And on the heights we have planted
The banners of our revolution.
You had imagined that that was all that we
*   wanted*
We want more
We want all
Your hearts are our goal,
It is your souls we want.[14]

The Third Reich was organized as a leader-state in which Hitler, the *Fuehrer* (leader), embodied and expressed the real will of the German people, commanded the supreme loyalty of the nation, and held omnipotent power. As a Nazi political theorist stated: "The authority of the Fuehrer is total and all-embracing . . . it embraces all members of the German community. . . . The Fuehrer's authority is subject to no checks or controls; it is circumscribed by no . . . individual rights; it is . . . overriding and unfettered."[15] To the Fuehrer the German people owed complete loyalty.

To strengthen the power of the central government and coordinate the nation under Nazism, the regime abolished parliaments in the various German states and appointed governors who made certain that Nazi directives were carried out throughout the country. The Nazis took over the civil service and used its machinery to enforce Nazi decrees. In this process of *Gleichschaltung* (coordination), the Nazis encountered little opposition. The political parties and the trade unions collapsed without a struggle.

In June 1933, the Social Democratic party was outlawed and within a few weeks the other political parties simply disbanded. In May 1933, the Nazis seized the property of the trade unions, arrested the leaders, and ended collective bargaining and strikes. The newly established German Labor Front, an instrument of the party, became the official organization of the working class. While there is evidence that the working class in 1933 would have resisted the Nazis, the leadership never mobilized proletarian organizations. With astonishing ease the Nazis had imposed their will over the nation.

Hitler made strategic but temporary concessions to the traditional ruling elite. On June 30, 1934, Nazi executioners swiftly murdered the leaders of the SA (the storm troopers who had battled political opponents) to eliminate any potential opposition to Hitler from within the party. With this move, Hitler also relieved the anxieties of industrialists and landowners, who feared that Ernst Röhm, the leader of the SA, would persuade Hitler to remove them from positions of power and to implement a program of radical social reform that would threaten their property.

The execution of the SA leaders (including Ernst Röhm) was also approved by the generals, for they regarded the SA as a rival to the army. In August, all German soldiers swore an oath of unconditional allegiance to the Fuehrer, cementing the alliance of the army to National Socialism. The army tied itself to the Nazi regime because it valued the resurgence of militaristic values and applauded the death of the Weimar Republic. German historian Karl Dietrich Bracher concludes: "Without the assistance of the Army, at first through its toleration and later through its active cooperation, the country's rapid and final restructuring into the total leader state could not have come about."[16]

Economic Life

Hitler had not sought power in order to improve the living standards of the masses but to convert Germany into a powerful war machine. Economic problems held little interest for this dreamer in whose mind danced images of a vast German empire. For him the "socialism" in National Socialism did not mean a comprehensive program of social welfare but the elimination of the class antagonisms that divided and weakened the fatherland. Radicals within the party wanted to deprive the industrialists and landowners of power and social dignity and expropriate their property. The more pragmatic Hitler wanted only to deprive them of freedom of action; they were to serve, not control, the state. Germany remained capitalist, but the state had unlimited power to intervene in the economy. Unlike the Bolsheviks, the Nazis did not destroy the upper classes of the Old Regime. Hitler made no war against the industrialists. From them he wanted loyalty, obedience, and a war machine. German businessmen prospered, but exercised no influence on political decisions. The profits of industry rose, but the real wages of German workers did not improve although rearmament did end the unemployment crisis.

Nazism and the Churches

Nazism conflicted with the core values of Christianity. "The heaviest blow that ever struck humanity was the coming of Christianity," said Hitler to intimates during World War II.[17] Had Germany won World War II, the Nazis would no doubt have tried to root out Christianity from German life. In 1937 the bishop of Berlin defined the essential conflict between Christianity and Nazism: "The question at stake is whether there is an authority that stands above all earthly power, the authority of God, Whose commandments are valid independent of space and time, country and race. The question at stake is whether individual man possesses personal rights that no community and no state may take from him; whether the free exercise of his conscience may be prevented and forbidden by the state."[18]

Nazism could tolerate no other faith alongside itself. Recognizing that Christianity was a rival claimant for the German soul, the Nazis moved to repress the Protestant and Catholic churches. In the public schools religious instruction was cut back and the syllabus changed to omit the Hebrew origins of Christianity. Christ was depicted not as a Jew, heir to the prophetic tradition of Hebrew monotheism, but as a Nordic hero. The *Gestapo* (secret state police) censored church newspapers, scrutinized sermons and church activities, forbade some clergymen to preach, dismissed the opponents of Nazism from theological schools, and arrested some clerical critics of the regime.

The clergy are well represented among those Germans who resisted Nazism; some were sent to concentration camps or were executed. But these courageous clergy were not representative of the German churches which, as organized institutions, capitulated to and cooperated with the Nazi regime. Both the German Evangelical and German Catholic churches demanded that their faithful render loyalty to Hitler; both turned a blind eye to Nazi persecution of Jews; both condemned resistance and found much in the Third Reich to admire; both supported Hitler's war. When Germany attacked Poland starting World War II, the Catholic bishops declared: "In this decisive hour we encourage and admonish our Catholic soldiers, in obedience to the Fuehrer, to do their duty and to be ready to sacrifice their whole existence."[19] Both churches urged their faithful to fight for fatherland and Fuehrer, pressured conscientious objectors to serve, and celebrated Nazi victories.

Why did the German churches, which preached Christ's message of humanity, fail to take a stand against Nazi inhumanity? The reasons are varied. Many German church leaders feared that resistance would lead to even more severe measures against their churches. Traditionally the German churches had bowed to state authority and detested revolution. These church leaders also found some Nazi ideas appealing. Intensely nationalistic, antiliberal, antirepublican, and anti-Semitic, many members of the clergy were filled with hope when Hitler came to power. The prominent Lutheran theologian who "welcomed that change that came to Germany in 1933 as a divine gift and miracle,"[20] voiced the sentiments of many members of the clergy. Such feelings encouraged prolonged moral myopia, not a revolt of Christian conscience. When the war ended the German Evangelical church leaders lamented:

. . . we know ourselves to be one with our people in a great company of suffering and in a great solidarity of guilt. With great pain do we say: Through us endless suffering has been brought to many people and countries. . . . We accuse ourselves for not witnessing more courageously, for not praying more faithfully, for not loving more ardently.[21]

Shaping the "New Man"

Propaganda had helped the Nazis come to power. Now it would be used to consolidate their hold on the German nation and to shape a "new man" committed to Hitler, race, and Volk. Hitler was a radical revolutionary who desired not only the outward form of power but also control over the inner man—his thoughts and feelings. Nazi propaganda conditioned the mind to revere the Fuehrer and to obey the new regime. It intended to deprive individuals of their capacity for independent thought. By concentrating on the myth of the race and the infallibility of the Fuehrer, Nazi propaganda disoriented the rational mind and gave the individual new standards to believe and to obey. The entire nation must be molded to think and respond as the leader-state directed; all the people must be culturally conditioned to feel and express the Germandom within themselves.

The Ministry of Popular Enlightenment, headed by Dr. Joseph Goebbels (1897–1945), controlled the press, book publishing, the radio, the theater, and the cinema. Goebbels, holder of a doctorate degree in the humanities, was intelligent and a master in the art of propaganda; he was also vain, cynical, and contemptuous of the very masses whom he manipulated. But the German people were not merely passive victims of clever and ruthless leaders. "The effective spread of propaganda and the rapid regimentation of cultural life," says Bracher, "would not have been possible without the invaluable help eagerly tendered by writers and artists, professors and churchmen." And the manipulation of the minds of the German people "would not have been effective had it not been for profound historically conditioned relations based . . . on a pseudoreligious exaggerated nationalism and on the idea of the German mission."[22] While some intellectuals showed their abhorrence of the Nazi regime by emigrating, the great majority gave their support, often with overt enthusiasm, to Nazism and Hitler. While some individuals rejected Nazi propaganda, the masses of German people came to regard Nazism as the fulfillment of their nationalist longings.

The Nazis kept the emotions in a state of permanent mobilization, for Hitler understood that the emotionally aroused are most amenable to manipulation. Goose-stepping SA (storm troopers) and SS (elite military and police) battalions paraded in the streets; martial music quickened the pulsebeat; Nazi flags decorated public buildings; loud-speakers installed in offices and factories blared the Nazi message, and all work stopped for important broadcasts. Citizens were ordered to greet each other with "Heil Hitler," a potent sign of reverence and submission. The regime made a special effort to reach young people. All youths between the ages of ten and eighteen were required to join the Hitler Youth, and all other youth organizations were dissolved. At camps and rallies, young people paraded, sang, saluted, and chanted: "we were slaves; we were outsiders in our own country. So were we before Hitler united us. Now we would fight against Hell itself for our leader."[23]

Nazification of Education

The schools, long breeding grounds of nationalism, militarism, antiliberalism, and anti-Semitism, now indoctrinated the young in Nazi ideology. The Nazis instructed teachers how certain subjects were to be taught; and to insure obedience, members of the Hitler Youth were asked to report suspicious teachers. Portraits of Hitler and Nazi banners were displayed in classrooms. War stories, adventures of the Hitler Youth, and ancient Nordic legends replaced fairy tales and animal stories in reading material for the young. The curriculum upgraded physical training and sports, curtailed religious instruction, and introduced many courses in racial science. Decidedly anti-intellectual, the Nazis stressed character building over book learning. They intended to train young people to serve the leader and the racial community, to imbue them with a sense

STORMTROOPERS AT NUREMBERG Parades and rallies whipped nationalistic sentiment to fever pitch during the 1930s. Hitler was presented as the savior of the German people amid a delirium of salutes and ear-shattering cheers. Individual conscience was abandoned. (Wide World Photos)

of fellowship for their Volkish kin, that sense of camaraderie found on the battlefield. Expressions of individualism and independence must be checked.

The universities quickly abandoned freedom of the mind, scientific objectivity, and humanist values. "We repudiate international science, we repudiate the international community of scholars, we repudiate research for the sake of research. Sieg Heil!"[24] declared one historian. Even before the Nazi takeover, many university students and professors had embraced Volkish nationalism and right-wing radicalism. Two years before Hitler came to power, for example, 60 percent of all undergraduates supported the Nazi student organi-

zation and anti-Semitic riots broke out at several universities.

For seventy years or more, the professors had preached aggressive nationalism, the German destiny of power, hero worship, irrational political Romanticism, and so forth, and had increasingly deemphasized, if not eliminated, the teachings of ethical and humanist principles. . . . Essentially neither [professors nor students] wanted to have anything to do with democracy. In the Weimar Republic . . . both groups, on the whole, seemed equally determined to tear down that Republic. The professors did their part by fiery lectures, speeches, and writings; the students did theirs in noisy demonstrations, torch-light parades, vandalism, and physical violence. . . . When Hitler came to power, both professors and students fell all over themselves to demonstrate their allegiance.[25]

In May 1933, professors and students proudly burned books considered a threat to Nazi ideology. Many academics praised Hitler and the new regime. Some 10 percent of the university faculty, principally Jews, Social Democrats, and liberals, were dismissed, often with the approval of their colleagues. "From now on it will not be your job to determine whether something is true but whether it is in the spirit of the National Socialist revolution," the new minister of culture told university professors.[26] Numerous courses on racial science and Nazi ideology were introduced into the curriculum.

Giant Rallies

Symbolic of the Nazi regime were the monster rallies staged at Nuremberg. Scores of thousands roared, marched, and worshiped at their leader's feet. In a delirium of thoughtlessness, they celebrated Hitler's achievements and demonstrated their loyalty to their savior. Everything was brilliantly orchestrated to impress Germans and the world with the irresistible power, determination, and unity of the Nazi movement and the greatness of the Fuehrer. Armies of youths waving flags, storm troopers bearing weapons, and workers shouldering long-handled spades paraded past Hitler, who stood at attention, his arm extended in the Nazi salute. The endless columns of marchers, the stirring martial music played by huge bands, the forest of flags, the chanting and cheering of spectators, and the burning torches and beaming spotlights united the participants into a racial community. "Wherever Hitler leads we follow," thundered thousands of Germans in a giant chorus. The Nuremberg rallies were among the greatest theatrical performances of the twentieth century.

Terror

Terror was another means of insuring compliance and obedience. The instrument of terror was the SS, which was organized in 1925 in order to protect Hitler and other party leaders and to stand guard at party meetings. Under the leadership of Heinrich Himmler (1900–1945), a fanatic believer in Hitler's racial theories, the SS was molded into an elite force of disciplined, dedicated, and utterly ruthless men. Myopic, narrow chested, and sexually prudish, Himmler cultivated a cult of manliness. He envisioned the SS, who were specially selected for their racial purity and physical fitness, as a new breed of knights and Nietzschean supermen who would lead the new Germany.

The SS staffed the concentration camps established to deal with political prisoners. Through systematic terror and torture, the SS sought to deprive the inmates of their human dignity and to harden themselves for the struggles that lay ahead. Knowledge that these camps existed and that some prisoners were never heard from again was a strong inducement for Germans to remain obedient.

Anti-Semitic Legislation

The Nazis instituted many anti-Jewish measures designed to make outcasts of the Jews. Thousands of Jewish doctors, lawyers, musicians, artists, and professors were barred from practicing their professions and members of the civil service were dismissed. A series of laws tightened the screws of humiliation and persecution. Marriage or sexual encounters between Germans and Jews were forbidden. Universities, schools, restaurants, pharmacies, hospitals, theaters, museums, and athletic fields were gradually closed to Jews.

Using as a pretext the assassination of a German diplomat by a Jewish youth, the Nazis organized an extensive pogrom in November 1938. Nazi gangs murdered scores of Jews and burned and looted thousands of Jewish homes and synagogues. The Reich then imposed on the Jewish community a fine of one billion marks. These measures were a prelude to the physical extermination of European Jewry which became a cardinal Nazi objective during World War II.

Mass Support

The Nazi regime increasingly became a police state symbolized by mass arrests, the persecution of Jews, and concentration camps that institutionalized terror. The Nazis skillfully established the totalitarian state without upsetting the daily life of the great majority of the population. Moreover, Hitler, like Mussolini, was careful to maintain the appearance of legality. By not abolishing parliament or repealing the constitution, he could claim that his was a legitimate government. By consolidating power in stages and retaining the institutions of the republic, the Nazis lulled both Germans and people in other countries into believing that legitimate statesmen, not gangsters, governed Germany.

To people concerned with little else but family, job, and friends—and this includes most people in any country—life in the first few years of the Third Reich seemed quite satisfying. People believed that the new government was trying to solve Germany's problems in a vigorous and sensible manner, in contrast to the ineffectiveness of the Weimar leadership. Had not Hitler's rearmament program virtually eliminated unemployment and restored German might? Had not Hitler awakened a sense of self-sacrifice and national dedication among a people dispirited by defeat and depression? Had he not united a country torn by class antagonisms and social distinctions and given the little people a sense of pride? Workers had jobs, businessmen profits, and generals troops—what could be wrong?

Many intellectuals, viewing Hitlerism as the victory of idealism over materialism and community over selfish individualism, lent their talents to the regime and endorsed the burning of books and suppression of freedom. To them, Hitler was a visionary who had shown Germany and the world a new way of life, a new creed.

Hitler's spectacular foreign policy successes made the world take notice of the new Germany. Having regained confidence in themselves and their nation, Germans rejoiced in Hitler's leadership, regretted not at all the loss of political freedom, and remained indifferent to the plight of the persecuted, particularly Jews. Hitler's popularity and mass support rested on something far stronger than propaganda and terror. The simple truth is that he had won the hearts of a sizable proportion of the German people. To many Germans, Hitler was exactly as Nazi propaganda had depicted him: "He stands like a statue grown beyond the measure of earthly man."[27]

There was some opposition and resistance to the Hitler regime. Social Democrats and communists in particular organized small cells. Conservatives, who considered Hitler a threat to traditional German values, and the clergy, who saw Nazism as a pagan religion, also formed small opposition groups. But only resistance from the army could have toppled Hitler. Some generals, even before World War II, urged such resistance, but the overwhelming majority of German officers either preferred the new regime, were concerned about their careers, or considered it dishonorable to break their oath of loyalty to Hitler. These officers would remain loyal until the bitter end. Very few Germans realized that their country was passing through a long night of barbarism, and still fewer considered resistance.

LIBERALISM AND AUTHORITARIANISM IN OTHER LANDS

The Spread of Authoritarianism

After World War I, in country after country, parliamentary democracy collapsed and authoritarian leaders came to power. In most of these countries, liberal ideals had not penetrated deeply; liberalism met resistance by conservative elites.

Spain and Portugal

In both Spain and Portugal, parliamentary regimes faced strong opposition from the church, the army, and large landowners. In 1926, army officers overthrew the Portuguese Republic that had been created in 1910, and gradually Antonio de Oliveira Salazar (1889–1970), a professor of economics, emerged as dictator. In Spain, after antimonarchist forces won the election of 1931, King Alfonso XIII (1902–1931) left the country and Spain was proclaimed a republic. But the new government, led by socialists and liberals, faced the determined opposition of the ruling elite. The reforms introduced by the republic—expropriation of large estates, reduction of the number of army officers, dissolution of the Jesuit order, and the closing of church schools—only intensified the hatred by the old order.

The difficulties of the Spanish Republic mounted: workers near starvation rioted and engaged in violent strikes; the military attempted a coup; Catalonia, with its long tradition of separatism, tried to establish its autonomy. Imitating the example of France (see page 722), the parties of the left, including the communists, united in the Popular Front, which came to power in February 1936. In July 1936 General Francisco Franco (1892–1975), stationed in Spanish Morocco, led a revolt against the republic. He was supported by army leaders, the church, monarchists, landlords, industrialists, and the Falange, a newly formed fascist party. Spain was torn by a bloody civil war. Aided by Fascist Italy and Nazi Germany (see pages 729–730), Franco won in 1939 and established a dictatorship.

Eastern and Central Europe

Parliamentary government in eastern Europe rested on weak foundations. Predominantly rural, these countries lacked the sizable professional and commercial class that had promoted liberalism in western Europe. Only Czechoslovakia had a substantial native middle class with a strong liberal tradition. The rural masses of eastern Europe, traditionally subjected to monarchical and aristocratic authority, were not used to political thinking or civic responsibility. Students and intellectuals, often gripped by a romantic nationalism, were drawn to antidemocratic movements. Right-wing leaders also played on the fear of communism. When parliamentary government failed to solve internal problems, especially after the Great Depression, people soured on democracy. Fascist movements, however, had little success in eastern Europe. It was authoritarian regimes headed by traditional ruling elites, army leaders or kings, that put an end to democracy there.

With the dissolution of the Hapsburg Empire at the end of World War I, Austria became a democratic republic. From the start, it suffered from severe economic problems. The Hapsburg Empire had been a huge free-trade area, permitting food and raw materials to circulate unimpeded throughout the Empire. The new Austria lacked sufficient food to feed the population of Vienna and needed raw materials for its industries. Worsening its plight was the erection of tariff barriers by each of the successor states to the Hapsburg Empire. Between 1922 and 1926, the League of Nations had to rescue Austria from bankruptcy. The Great Depression aggravated Austria's economic position. Many Austrians believed that only an *Anschluss* (union) with Germany could solve Austria's problems.

Austria was also burdened by a conflict between the industrial region, including Vienna, and the agricultural provinces. Factory workers were generally socialists and anticlerical; the peasants were strongly Catholic and antisocialist. The Social Democrats controlled Vienna, but the rural population gave its support to the Christian Social party. Each party had its own private army: the workers had the *Schutzbund* and the provincials the *Heimwehr*. During the Great Depression, Chancellor Engelbert Dollfuss (1892–1934) sought to turn the country into a one-party state. In February 1934, police and Heimwehr contingents raided Social Democratic headquarters. When the Social Democrats called a general strike, Dollfuss bombarded a workers' housing project, killing 193 civilians, and suppressed the Social Democrat party. Austria had joined the ranks of authoritarian states.

When Hitler came to power in Germany, Austrian Nazis pressed for Anschluss. In July 1934, a band of Austrian Nazis assassinated Dollfuss, but a Nazi plot to capture the government failed. Four years later, however, Hitler would march into Austria, bringing about the Anschluss desired by many.

The new Hungary that emerged at the end of World War I faced an uprising by communists inspired by the success of the Bolsheviks in Russia. Béla Kun (1885–1937), supported by Russian money, established a soviet regime in Budapest in March 1919. But Kun could not win the support of the peasants and was opposed by the Allies, who helped Rumania crush the revolutionary government. In 1920 power passed to Admiral Miklós Horthy (1868–1957), who instituted a white terror that exceeded the red terror of the Kun regime. During the Great Depression, the Horthy government, which favored the large landholders, was challenged by the radical right, which preached racial nationalism, anti-Semitism, and anticapitalism and sought to win mass

support through land reform. Its leader, Gyula Gömbös (1886–1936), who served as prime minister from 1932 to 1936, sought to align Hungary with Nazi Germany. Seeking to regain territories lost in World War I and aware of Hitler's growing might, Hungary drew closer to Germany in the late 1930s.

Poland, Greece, Bulgaria, and Rumania became either royal or military dictatorships. The new state of Czechoslovakia, guided by President Tomáš Masaryk (1850–1937) and Foreign Minister Eduard Beneš (1884–1948), both committed to the liberal-humanist tradition of the West, preserved parliamentary democracy. Its most serious problem came from the 3.1 million Germans living primarily in the Sudetenland (see pages 527–528). The German minority founded the Sudetenland German party, which modeled itself after Hitler's Nazi party. Hitler later exploited the issue of the Sudetenland Germans to dismember Czechoslovakia.

The Western Democracies

While liberal governments were everywhere failing, the great Western democracies—the United States, Britain, and France—continued to preserve democratic institutions. In Britain and the United States, fascist movements were no more than a nuisance. In France, fascism was more of a threat because it exploited a deeply ingrained hostility to the liberal ideals of the French Revolution.

The United States

The central problem faced by the Western democracies was the Great Depression, which started in the United States. In the 1920s hundreds of thousands of Americans had bought stock on credit; this buying spree sent the prices of stocks soaring well beyond what they were actually worth. In late October 1929, the stock market was hit by a wave of panic selling, and prices plummeted. Within a few weeks, the value of stocks listed on the New York Stock Exchange fell by some 26 billion dollars. A terrible chain reaction followed over the next few years. Businesses cut production and unemployment soared; farmers unable to meet mortgage payments lost their land; banks that had made poor investments closed down. American investors withdrew the capital they had invested in Europe, causing European banks and businesses to fail. Throughout the world, trade declined and unemployment rose.

When President Franklin Delano Roosevelt (1882–1945) took office in 1933, over 13 million Americans—one-quarter of the labor force—were out of work. Hunger and despair showed on the faces of the American people. Moving away from laissez faire, Roosevelt instituted a comprehensive program of national planning, experimentation, and reform known as the New Deal. Although the American political and economic system faced a severe test, few Americans turned to fascism or communism, and the government, while engaging in national planning, did not break with democratic values and procedures.

Britain

Even before the Great Depression, Britain faced severe economic problems. Loss of markets to foreign competitors hurt British manufacturing, mining, and shipbuilding; rapid development of waterpower and oil reduced the demand for British coal, and outdated mining equipment put Britain in a poor competitive position. To reduce costs, mine owners in 1926 called for salary cuts; the coal miners countered with a strike and were joined by workers in other industries. To many Englishmen the workers were leftist radicals trying to overthrow the government. Many people wanted the state to break the strike. After nine days, workers called off the strike, but the miners held out for another six months; they returned to work with longer

hours and lower pay. Although the General Strike had failed, it did improve relations between the classes, for the workers had not called for revolution and they refrained from violence. The fear that British workers would follow the Bolshevik path abated.

The Great Depression cast a pall of gloom over Britain. The Conservative party leadership tried to stimulate exports by devaluing the pound and to encourage industry by providing loans at lower interest rates, but in the main it left the task of recovery to industry itself. Not until Britain began to rearm did unemployment decline significantly. Despite the economic slump of the 1920s and the Great Depression, Britain remained politically stable, a testament to the strength of its parliamentary tradition. Neither the communists nor the newly formed British Fascist party gained mass support.

France

In the early 1920s, France was concerned with restoring villages, railroads, mines, and forests that had been ruined by the war. From 1926 to 1929 France was relatively prosperous; industrial and agricultural production expanded, tourism increased, and the currency was stable. Although France did not feel the Great Depression as painfully as did the United States and Germany, the nation was hurt by the decline in trade and production and the rise in unemployment.

The political instability that had beset the Third Republic virtually since its inception continued, and hostility to the republic mounted. As the leading parties failed to solve the nation's problems, a number of fascist-type groups gained in strength. On February 6, 1934, right-wing gangs threatened to invade the Chamber of Deputies. What brought on the crisis was the exposure of the shady dealings of Alexander Stavisky, a financial manipulator with high government connections. The resultant violence left hundreds wounded and several dead. The whole affair was too poorly organized to constitute a serious threat to the government. But to the parties of the left—socialists, communists, and radicals—the events of February 6–7 constituted a rightist attempt to establish a fascist regime.

Fear of growing fascist strength at home and in Italy and Germany led the parties of the left to form the Popular Front. In 1936 Léon Blum (1872–1950), a socialist and a Jew, became premier. Blum's Popular Front government instituted more reforms than any other ministry in the history of the Third Republic. To end a wave of strikes that tied up production, Blum gave workers a forty-hour week and holidays with pay and guaranteed them the right to collective bargaining. He took steps to nationalize the armaments and aircraft industries. To reduce the influence of the wealthiest families, he put the Bank of France under government control. By raising prices and buying wheat, he aided farmers. Conservatives and fascists denounced Blum as a Jewish socialist who was converting the fatherland into a communist state. "Better Hitler than Blum," grumbled French rightists.

Despite significant reforms, the Popular Front could not revitalize the economy. In 1937 the Blum ministry was overthrown and the Popular Front, always a tenuous alliance, fell apart. Through democratic means the Blum government had tried to give France a "New Deal," but the social reforms passed by the Popular Front only intensified hatreds between the working classes and the rest of the nation. France had preserved democracy against the onslaught of domestic fascists, but it was a demoralized and divided nation that confronted a united and dynamic Nazi Germany.

Notes

1. Quoted in Zeev Sternhill, "Fascist Ideology," in Walter Laqueur, *Fascism: A Reader's Guide* (Berkeley: University of California Press, 1976), p. 338.

2. Quoted in John Weiss, *The Fascist Tradition* (New York: Harper & Row, 1967), p. 9.

3. F. L. Carsten, *The Rise of Fascism* (Berkeley: University of California Press, 1969), p. 53.

4. Quoted in Max Gallo, *Mussolini's Italy* (New York: Macmillan, 1973), p. 218.

5. Quoted in Joachim C. Fest, *Hitler* (New York: Harcourt Brace Jovanovich, 1974), p. 162.

6. Quoted in Karl J. Newman, *European Democracy between the Wars* (Notre Dame, Indiana: University of Notre Dame Press, 1971), p. 276.

7. Hajo Holborn, *Germany and Europe* (Garden City, N.Y.: Doubleday, Anchor Books, 1971), p. 215.

8. Fest, *Hitler*, p. 548.

9. Quoted in Alan Bullock, *Hitler: A Study in Tyranny* (New York: Harper Torchbooks, 1964), p. 400.

10. *Hitler's Secret Conversations, 1941–1944,* with an introductory essay by H. R. Trevor Roper (New York: Farrar, Straus & Young, 1953), p. 28.

11. Quoted in Lucy S. Dawidowicz, *The War Against the Jews 1933–1945* (New York: Holt, Rinehart and Winston, 1975), p. 21.

12. Adolf Hitler, *Mein Kampf* (Boston: Houghton Mifflin, 1962), p. 107.

13. Ibid., p. 479.

14. Quoted in J. S. Conway, *The Nazi Persecution of the Churches* (New York: Basic Books, 1968), p. 202.

15. Quoted in Helmut Krausnick, Hans Buchheim, Martin Broszart, and Hans-Adolf Jacobsen, *Anatomy of the SS State* (London: Collins, 1968), p. 128.

16. Karl Dietrich Bracher, *The German Dictatorship* (New York: Praeger, 1970), p. 243.

17. *Hitler's Secret Conversations,* p. 6.

18. Quoted in Hans Rothfels, "Resistance Begins," in John Conway, ed., *The Path to Dictatorship* (Garden City, N.Y.: Doubleday, Anchor Books, 1966), pp. 160–161.

19. Quoted in Guenter Lewy, *The Catholic*

Church and Nazi Germany (New York: McGraw-Hill, 1965), p. 226.

20. Quoted in Hermann Graml, et al., The German Resistance to Hitler (Berkeley: University of California Press, 1970), p. 206.

21. Quoted in Conway, The Nazi Persecution of the Churches, p. 332.

22. Bracher, The German Dictatorship, pp. 248, 251.

23. Quoted in T. L. Jarman, The Rise and Fall of Nazi Germany (New York: New York University Press, 1956), p. 182.

24. Quoted in Horst von Maltitz, The Evolution of Hitler's Germany (New York: McGraw-Hill, 1973), pp. 433–434.

25. Ibid., pp. 438–439.

26. Quoted in Bracher, The German Dictatorship, p. 268.

27. Quoted in Fest, Hitler, p. 532.

Suggested Reading

Bracher, Karl Dietrich, The German Dictatorship (1970). A highly regarded analysis of all phases of the Nazi state.

Bullock, Alan, Hitler: A Study in Tyranny (1964). An excellent biography.

Cassels, Alan, Fascist Italy (1968). A clearly written introduction.

Conway, J. S., The Nazi Persecution of the Churches (1968). Nazi persecution of the churches and the capitulation of the clergy.

Fest, Joachim C., Hitler (1974). An excellent biography.

Haffner, Sebastian, The Meaning of Hitler (1979). A German journalist's inquiry into Hitler's successes and failures.

Jäckel, Eberhard, Hitler's Weltanschauung (1972). An analysis of Hitler's world-view.

Kirkpatick, Ivone, Mussolini, A Study in Power (1964). A solid biography.

Laqueur, Walter, ed. Fascism, A Reader's Guide (1976). A superb collection of essays.

Maltitz, Horst von, The Evolution of Hitler's Germany (1973). In trying to explain how it was possible, the author discusses the German roots of Nazism.

Mosse, George L., Nazi Culture (1966). A representative collection of Nazi writings with a fine introduction.

Paxton, Robert O., Europe in the Twentieth Century (1975). A first-rate text with an excellent bibliography.

Rogger, Hans, and Weber, Eugen, eds., The European Right (1966). A valuable collection of essays on right-wing movements in various European countries.

Review Questions

1. How did fascist principles "stand for the sheer, categorical, definitive antithesis to the world of democracy and the world which still abides by the fundamental principles laid down in 1789"?

2. Why did some Italians support Mussolini?

3. How did Mussolini bluff his way to power?

4. How did Mussolini try to extend his control over Italy?

5. What were Mussolini's policies toward the church? The economy?

6. In what ways was Mussolini less effective than Hitler in establishing a totalitarian state?

7. How was Hitler's outlook shaped by his experiences in Vienna?

8. What was the significance of the Munich Putsch of 1923?

9. What were Hitler's attitudes toward democracy, the masses, war, the Jews?

10. Why did Hitler's views prove attractive to Germans?

11. How was Hitler able to gain power?

12. How did the Nazis extend their control over Germany?

13. What lessons might democratic societies draw from the experience of fascist totalitarianism?

14. After World War I, in country after country, parliamentary democracy collapsed and authoritarian leaders came to power. Explain.

15. How did the United States, Britain, and France try to cope with the Great Depression?

CHAPTER 32

World War II: Western Civilization in the Balance

FROM THE EARLY DAYS of his political career, Hitler dreamed of forging a vast German empire in central and eastern Europe. He believed that only by waging a war of conquest against Russia could the German nation gain the living space and security it required and, as a superior race, deserved. War was an essential component of National Socialist ideology, and it accorded with Hitler's temperament. For the former corporal from the trenches, the war had never ended. Hitler aspired to political power in order to mobilize the material and human resources of the German nation for war and conquest. Though historians may debate the question of responsibility for World War I, few would deny that World War II was Hitler's war:

It appears to be an almost incontrovertible fact that the Second World War was brought on by the actions of the Hitler government, that these actions were the expression of a policy laid down well in advance in Mein Kampf, *and that this war could have been averted up until the last moment if the German government had so wished."*[1]

Western statesmen had sufficient warnings that Hitler was a threat to peace and the essential values of Western civilization, but they failed to rally their people and take a stand until Germany had greatly increased its capacity to wage aggressive war.

THE AFTERMATH OF WORLD WAR I

World War I had shown that Germany was the strongest power on the Continent. In the east, the German army had triumphed over Russia; in the west, Britain and France could have hoped for no more than a deadlock without the aid of the United States. The Treaty of Versailles had weakened Germany, but had not permanently crippled it.

In the decade after the war, responsibility for preserving the peace settlement rested essentially with France. The United States had rejected the treaty and withdrawn from European affairs; Soviet Russia was consolidating its revolution; Britain, burdened with severe economic problems, disarmed, and traditionally hostile to Continental alliances, did not want to join with France in holding Germany down. France sought to contain Germany by forging alliances with the new states of eastern Europe, which would serve as a substitute for alliance with a now untrustworthy communist Russia. So France entered into alliances with Poland, Czechoslovakia, Rumania, and Yugoslavia during the 1920s. But no combination of small eastern European states could replace Russia as a counterweight to Germany. Against Hitler's Germany, the French alliance system would prove useless.

A feeling of hope generally prevailed during the 1920s. The newly created League of Nations provided a supranational authority to which nations could submit their quarrels. At the Washington Naval Conference (1921–1922), the leading naval powers—the United States, Britain, France, Italy, and Japan—agreed not to construct new battleships or heavy cruisers for a ten-year period and established a ratio of capital ships between them. It was hoped that the ending of a naval arms race would promote international peace.

In the Locarno Pact (1925), Germany, France, and Belgium agreed not to change their existing borders. This meant, in effect, that Germany had accepted both the loss of Alsace and Lorraine to France and the demilitarization of the Rhineland, two provisions of the Versailles Treaty. The Locarno Pact held the promise of a détente between France and Germany. But it was only the illusion of peace, for Germany gave no such assurances for its eastern border with Czechoslovakia and Poland, France's allies.

Other gestures that promoted reconciliation followed the Locarno Pact. In 1926, Germany was admitted to the League of Nations, and in 1928 the Kellogg-Briand Pact renouncing war was signed by most nations. The signatories condemned war as a solution for international disputes and agreed to settle quarrels through peaceful means. Ordinary people welcomed the Kellogg-Briand Pact as the dawning of a new era of peace, but because the pact contained no clauses for enforcing the agreement, again it only fostered the illusion of peace.

Nevertheless, between 1925 and 1930, hopes for reconciliation and peace were high. Recovery from the war and increased prosperity coincided with the easing of international tensions. As evidence of the new spirit of conciliation, France and Britain withdrew their forces from the Rhineland in 1930, four years ahead of the time prescribed by the Versailles Treaty.

THE ROAD TO WAR

Hitler's Foreign Policy Aims

After consolidating his power and mobilizing the nation's will, Hitler moved to implement his foreign-policy objectives—the destruction of the Versailles Treaty, the conquest and colonization of eastern Europe, and the domination and exploitation of racial inferiors. In some respects, Hitler's foreign policy aims accorded with the goals of Germany's traditional rulers. Like them, Hitler sought to tear up the Versailles Treaty, rearm, and make Germany the pre-eminent power in Europe. During World War I, German statesmen and generals had sought to conquer extensive regions of eastern Europe, and in the Treaty of Brest-Litovsk, Germany took Poland, the Ukraine, and the Baltic states from Russia. But Hitler's racial nationalism—the subjugation and annihilation of inferior races by a master German race—marked a break with the outlook of the old governing class. Germany's traditional conservative leaders had never restricted the civil rights of German Jews and had sought to Germanize, not enslave, the Poles living under the German flag.

In foreign affairs, Hitler demonstrated that same blend of opportunism and singleness of purpose that had brought him to power. He behaved like a man possessed, driven by a fanatical belief that his personal destiny was tied to Germany's future. Here, too, he made use of propaganda to undermine his opponents' will to resist. The Nazi propaganda machine, which had effectively won the minds of the German people, became an instrument of foreign policy. Nazi propaganda tried to win the support of the 27 million Germans living outside the borders of the Reich proper, to promote social and political disorientation in other lands by propagating anti-Semitism on a worldwide basis, and to draw international support for Hitler as Europe's best defense against the Soviet Union and Bolshevism. The Nazi anticommunist campaign "convinced many Europeans that Hitler's dictatorship was more acceptable than Stalin's and that Germany—'the bulwark against Bolshevism'—should be allowed to grow from strength to strength."[2]

As Hitler anticipated, Britain and France backed down when faced with his violations of the Versailles Treaty and threats of war. Haunted by the memory of World War I, Britain and France went to great lengths to avoid another catastrophe. Moreover, Britain suffered from a bad conscience regarding the Versailles Treaty. Believing that Germany had been treated too severely and woefully unprepared for war from 1933 to 1939, Britain was amenable to making concessions to Hitler. Although France had the strongest army on the Continent, it was prepared to fight only a defensive war, the reverse of its World War I strategy. France built immense fortifications, called the Maginot Line, to protect its borders from a German invasion, but it lacked a mobile striking force that could punish an aggressive Germany. The United States, concerned with the problems of the Great Depression and standing aloof from Europe's troubles, was not there to strengthen the resolve of France and Britain. Since both France and Britain feared and mistrusted the Soviet Union, the grand alliance of World War I was not renewed. There was an added factor. Suffering from a failure of leadership and political and economic unrest that eroded national unity, France was experiencing a decline in morale and a loss of nerve. It persistently turned to Britain for direction.

British statesmen championed a policy of appeasement—giving in to Germany in the hope that a satisfied Hitler would not drag Europe through another world war. British policy rested on the disastrous illusion that Hitler, like his Weimar predecessors, sought peaceful revision of the Versailles Treaty and that he could be contained through concessions. This perception was as misguided as the expectation of Weimar conservatives that the responsibility of power would compel Hitler to abandon his National Socialist radicalism. Some British appeasers also regarded Hitler as a defender of European civilization and the capitalist economic order against Soviet communism—a view that Nazi propaganda cleverly propagated and exploited.

In *Mein Kampf*, Hitler had explicitly laid out his philosophy of racial nationalism and *Lebensraum* (living space), and as dictator, he had established a one-party state, confined political opponents to concentration camps, and persecuted Jews. But the proponents of appeasement did not properly assess these signs. They still believed that Hitler could be reasoned with. Appeasement, which in the end was capitulation to blackmail, failed. Germany grew stronger, and the German people more devoted to the Fuehrer. Hitler did not moderate his ambitions and war was not averted.

Breakdown of Peace

To realize his foreign-policy aims, Hitler required a formidable military machine; Germany had to rearm. The Treaty of Versailles had limited the size of the German army to 100,000 volunteers, restricted the navy's size, forbidden the production of military aircraft, heavy artillery, and tanks, and disbanded the general staff. Throughout the 1920s, Germany had evaded these provisions, even entering into a secret arrangement with the Soviet Union to establish training schools for German pilots and tank corpsmen on Russian soil.

In March 1935, Hitler declared that Germany was no longer bound by the Versailles Treaty. Germany would restore conscription, build an air force (which it had been doing secretly), and strengthen its navy. The German people were ecstatic over Hitler's boldness. France protested, but offered no resistance, and Britain negotiated a naval agreement with Germany, thus tacitly accepting Hitler's rearmament.

A decisive event in the breakdown of peace was Italy's invasion of Ethiopia in October 1935. Mussolini sought colonial expansion and revenge for a defeat the African kingdom had inflicted on Italian troops in 1896. The League of Nations called for economic sanctions against Italy, and most League members restricted trade with the aggressor. But Italy continued to receive oil, particularly from American suppliers. Believing that the conquest of Ethiopia did not affect their vital interests and hoping to keep Italy friendly in the event of a clash with Germany, neither Britain nor France sought to restrain Italy, despite its act of aggression against another member of the League of Nations.

Mussolini's subjugation of Ethiopia discredited the League of Nations, which had already been weakened by its failure to deal effectively with Japan's invasion of the mineral-rich Chinese province of Manchuria in 1931. At that time the League formed a commission of inquiry and urged nonrecognition of the puppet state of Manchukuo created by Japan, but the member states did not restrain Japan. Ethiopia, like Manchuria, showed that the League was reluctant to use force to resist aggression.

On March 7, 1936, Hitler marched troops into the Rhineland, violating both the Versailles Treaty and the Locarno Pact. German generals had cautioned Hitler that such a move would provoke a French invasion of Germany and reoccupation of the Rhineland, which the German army, still in the first stages of rearmament, could not repulse. But Hitler gambled that France and Britain, lacking the will to fight, would take no action.

Hitler had correctly assessed the mood of Britain and France. Britain was not greatly alarmed by the remilitarization of the Rhineland. Hitler, after all, was not expanding the borders of Germany, but was only sending soldiers to Germany's frontier. Such a move, reasoned British officials, did not warrant risking a war. France regarded the remilitarization of the Rhineland as a grave threat. It deprived France of the one tangible advantage that it had obtained from the Treaty of Versailles—a buffer area. Now German forces could concentrate in strength on the French frontier, either to invade France or to discourage a French assault if Germany attacked Czechoslovakia or Poland, France's eastern allies. France lost the advantages of being able to retaliate by invading a demilitarized zone.

If the consequences for France were so significant, why did it not try to expel the 22,000 German troops that occupied the zone? First, France would not act alone, and Britain could not be persuaded to use force. Second, the French general staff overestimated German military strength and thought only of defending French soil from a German attack, not of initiating a strike against Germany. Third, French public opinion showed no enthusiasm for a confrontation with Hitler.

The Spanish Civil War of 1936–1939 (see page 719) was another victory for fascism. Nazi Germany and Fascist Italy aided Franco; the Soviet Union supplied the Spanish Republic. The republic appealed to France for help, but the French government feared that the civil war would expand into a European war. With Britain's approval, France proposed the

MAP 32.1 GERMAN AND ITALIAN AGGRESSIONS, 1935–1939 ▶

ICELAND

Germany and Italy
Italian possessions in Africa before 1935
German aggressions, 1935–1939
Italian aggressions, 1935–1939

NORWAY

SWEDEN

FINLAND

BALTIC SEA

ESTONIA

• Moscow

LATVIA

NORTH SEA

DENMARK

Memel • LITHUANIA

SOVIET UNION

IRELAND

NETHERLANDS

Danzig •

EAST
PRUSSIA

GREAT
BRITAIN
• London

Brussels •
BELGIUM

Berlin •

POLISH
CORRIDOR

• Warsaw

POLAND

GERMANY

SUDETENLAND
1938

ATLANTIC
OCEAN

Paris •
LUXEMBOURG

RHINELAND
1936

• Weimar

• Prague

• Nuremberg
Munich •

CZECHOSLOVAKIA
1939

FRANCE

SWITZERLAND

Vienna •
AUSTRIA
1938

HUNGARY

RUMANIA

BLACK
SEA

YUGOSLAVIA

BULGARIA

PORTUGAL

• Madrid

SPAIN
(Civil War, 1936-1939)

• Barcelona

ITALY

• Rome

ALBANIA
1939

GREECE

TURKEY

MEDITERRANEAN SEA

AFRICA

LIBYA

ERITREA

ETHIOPIA
1935-1936

IT. SOMALILAND

A F R I C A

Nonintervention Agreement. Italy, Germany, and the Soviet Union signed the agreement, but continued to supply the warring parties. By October 1937, some 60,000 Italian "volunteers" were fighting in Spain. Hitler sent from 5,000 to 6,000 men and hundreds of planes, which proved decisive. By comparison, the Soviet Union's aid was meager.

Without considerable help from France, the Spanish Republic was doomed, but Prime Minister Léon Blum continued to support nonintervention. He feared that French intervention would cause Germany and Italy to escalate their involvement, bringing Europe to the edge of a general war. Moreover, supplying the republic would have dangerous consequences at home, because French rightists were sympathetic to General Francisco Franco.

In 1939, the republic fell, and Franco established a dictatorship. The Spanish Civil War drew Mussolini and Hitler closer together, provided Germany with an opportunity to test weapons and troops, and demonstrated again that France and Britain lacked the determination to fight fascism.

One of Hitler's aims was incorporation of Austria into the Third Reich. The Treaty of Versailles had expressly prohibited the union of the two countries. But in *Mein Kampf*, Hitler had insisted that such an *Anschluss* (union) was necessary for German Lebensraum. In February 1938, under intense pressure from Hitler, Austrian Chancellor Kurt von Schuschnigg promised to accept Austrian Nazis in his cabinet and agreed to closer relations with Germany. Austrian independence was slipping away, and increasingly, Austrian Nazis undermined Schuschnigg's authority. Seeking to gain the support of his people, Schuschnigg made plans for a plebiscite on the issue of preserving Austrian independence. An enraged Hitler ordered his generals to draw up plans for an invasion of Austria. Hitler then demanded Schuschnigg's resignation and the formation of a new government headed by Arthur Seyss-Inquart, an Austrian Nazi.

Believing that Austria was not worth a war, Britain and France informed the embattled chancellor that they would not help in the event of a German invasion. Schuschnigg then resigned, and Austrian Nazis began to take control of the government. Under the pretext of preventing violence, Hitler ordered his troops to cross into Austria, and on March 13, 1938, Austrian leaders declared that Austria was a province of the German Reich. The Austrians celebrated by ringing church bells, waving swastika banners, and attacking Jews and looting their property.

Czechoslovakia: The Apex of Appeasement

Hitler had obtained Austria merely by threatening force. Another threat would give him the Sudetenland of Czechoslovakia. Of the 3.5 million people living in the Sudetenland, some 2.8 million were ethnic Germans. The Sudetenland contained key industries and strong fortifications; since it bordered Germany, it was also vital to Czech security. Deprived of the Sudetenland, Czechoslovakia could not defend itself against a German attack. Encouraged and instructed by Germany, the Sudeten Germans, led by Konrad Henlein, shrilly denounced the Czech government for "persecuting" its German minority and depriving it of its right to self-determination. The Sudeten Germans agitated for local autonomy and the right to profess the National Socialist ideology. Behind this demand was the goal of German annexation of the Sudetenland.

While negotiations between the Sudeten Germans and the Czech government proceeded, Hitler's propaganda machine accused the Czechs of hideous crimes against the German minority and warned of retribution. Hitler also ordered his generals to prepare for an invasion of Czechoslovakia and to complete the fortifications on the French border. Fighting between Czechs and Sudeten Germans heightened the tensions. Seeking to preserve peace,

PABLO PICASSO (1881–1973): GUERNICA (MURAL), 1937.
Eager to test their military might, the Germans
leveled the town of Guernica in an air raid. These
strikes would become the blitzkrieg of World War II.
Picasso's *Guernica* (oil on canvas; 11′ 5½″ x 25′ 5¾″)
captures the barbarism of all wars. The Spanish
Civil War was another defeat for democracy. Aided
by Hitler and Mussolini, Franco overcame the forces
of the Republic. (On extended loan to the Museum
of Modern Art, New York, from the estate of the
artist)

Prime Minister Neville Chamberlain (1869–
1940) of Britain offered to confer with Hitler,
who then extended an invitation.

What was the position of Britain and France
toward Czechoslovakia, the only democracy in
eastern Europe? In 1924, France and Czechoslovakia had concluded an agreement of mutual assistance in the event either was attacked
by Germany. Czechoslovakia had a similar
agreement with Russia, but with the provision
that Russian assistance depended on France's
first fulfilling the terms of its agreement with
Czechoslovakia. Britain had no commitment
to Czechoslovakia. Some of the British officials, swallowing Hitler's propaganda, believed that the Sudeten Germans were indeed
a suppressed minority entitled to self-
determination and that the Sudetenland, like

Austria, was not worth a war that could
destroy Western civilization. Hitler, they said,
only wanted to incorporate Germans living
outside of Germany; he was only carrying the
principle of self-determination to its logical
conclusion. Once these Germans lived under
the German flag, argued these British officials,
Hitler would be satisfied. In any case, Britain's
failure to rearm between 1933 and 1938 weakened its position. The British chiefs of staff
believed that the nation was not prepared to
fight, that it was necessary to sacrifice Czechoslovakia in order to buy time.

Czechoslovakia'a fate was decided at the
Munich Conference (September 1938) attended by Chamberlain, Hitler, Mussolini, and
Prime Minister Édouard Daladier (1884–1970)
of France. The Munich Agreement called for

the immediate evacuation of Czech troops from the Sudetenland and its occupation by German forces. Britain and France then promised to guarantee the territorial integrity of the truncated Czechoslovakia. Both Chamberlain and Daladier were showered with praise by the people of Britain and France for keeping the peace.

Critics of Chamberlain have insisted that the Munich Agreement was an enormous blunder and tragedy. Chamberlain, they say, was a fool to believe that Hitler, who sought domination over Europe, could be bought off with the Sudetenland. Hitler regarded concessions by Britain and France as signs of weakness; they only increased his appetite for more territory. Second, argue the critics, it would have been better to fight Hitler in 1938 than a year later when war actually did break out. To be sure, in the year following the Munich Agreement, Britain increased its military arsenal, but so did Germany, which built submarines and heavy tanks, strengthened western border defenses, and trained more pilots.

Had Britain and France resisted Hitler at Munich, it is likely that the Fuehrer would have attacked Czechoslovakia. But Czechoslovakia would not have lain down and died. The Czech border defenses, which had been built on the model of the French Maginot line, were formidable. The Czechs had a sizable number of good tanks and the Czech people were willing to fight to preserve their nation's territorial integrity. By itself the Czech army could not have defeated Germany. But while the main elements of the German army were battling the Czechs, the French, who could mobilize a hundred divisions, could have broken through the German West Wall, which was defended by only five regular and four reserve divisions, invaded the Rhineland, and devastated German industrial centers in the Ruhr. And there was always the possibility that the Soviet Union would have come to Czechoslovakia's aid in fulfillment of its agreement.

After the annexation of the Sudetenland, the Fuehrer plotted to extinguish Czechoslo-vakia's existence. He encouraged the Slovak minority in Czechoslovakia, led by a fascist priest, Josef Tiso, to demand complete separation from Czechoslovakia. On the pretext of protecting the rights of the Slovak people to self-determination, Hitler ordered his troops to enter Prague. In March 1939, Czech independence came to an end.

The destruction of Czechoslovakia was of a different character from the remilitarization of the Rhineland, the Anschluss with Austria, and the annexation of the Sudetenland. In all these previous cases, Hitler could claim the right of self-determination, Woodrow Wilson's grand principle. The occupation of Prague and the end of Czech independence, though, showed that Hitler really sought European hegemony. Outraged statesmen now demanded that the Fuehrer be deterred from further aggresssion. Chamberlain, however, did not completely abandon appeasement; he still thought that war was not inevitable and that Germany's claims could be dealt with through negotiations.

Poland: The Final Crisis

After Czechoslovakia, Hitler turned to Poland, demanding that the free city of Danzig be returned to Germany and that railways and roads, over which Germans would enjoy extraterritorial rights, be built across the Polish Corridor, linking East Prussia with the rest of Germany. Poland refused to restore the port of Danzig, which was vital to its economy, to Germany. Poland would allow a German highway through the Polish Corridor, but it would not permit Germany extraterritorial rights. France informed the German government that it would fulfill its treaty obligations to Poland. Chamberlain also warned that Britain would assist Poland.

On May 22, 1939, Hitler and Mussolini entered into the Pact of Steel, promising mutual aid in the event of war. The following day, Hitler told his officers that Germany's

CHRONOLOGY 32.1 ROAD TO WORLD WAR II

1931	Japan invades Manchuria
March 1935	Hitler announces German rearmament
October 1935	Italy invades Ethiopia
1936–1939	The Spanish Civil War
March 7, 1936	Germany reoccupies the Rhineland
October 1936	Berlin-Rome Axis is formed
November 1936	German-Japanese anticommunist pact
July 1937	Japan invades China
March 13, 1938	Austria becomes a German province
September 1938	Munich Agreement—Germany's annexation of Sudetenland is approved by Britain and France
1939	Franco establishes a dictatorship in Spain
March 1939	Germany invades Czechoslovakia
April 1939	Italy invades Albania
May 22, 1939	Pact of Steel between Hitler and Mussolini
August 23, 1939	Nonaggression pact between Germany and Russia
September 1, 1939	Germany invades Poland; Britain and France declare war

real goal was the destruction of Poland. "Danzig is not the objective. It is a matter of expanding our living space in the east, of making our food supplies secure. . . . There is therefore no question of sparing Poland, and the decision remains to attack Poland at the first suitable opportunity."[3] In the middle of June, the army presented Hitler with battle plans for an invasion of Poland.

Britain, France, and the Soviet Union had been engaged in negotiations since April. The Soviet Union wanted a mutual-assistance pact including joint military planning, and demanded bases in Poland and Rumania in preparation for a German attack. Britain was reluctant to endorse these demands, fearing that a mutual assistance pact with Russia might cause Hitler to embark on a mad adventure that would drag Britain into war. Moreover, Poland would not allow Russian troops on its soil, fearing Russian expansion.

At the same time, Russia was conducting secret talks with Nazi Germany, and on August 23, 1939, the two totalitarian states signed a nonaggression pact that stunned the world. A secret annex called for the partition of Poland between the two parties and Russian control over Latvia and Estonia. By signing a pact with his enemy, Hitler had pulled off an extraordinary diplomatic coup: he blocked the Soviet Union, Britain, and France from duplicating their World War I grand alliance against Germany. The Nazi-Soviet Pact was the green light for an invasion of Poland, and at dawn on September 1, 1939, German troops crossed the frontier. When Germany did not respond to their demand for a halt to the invasion, Britain and France declared war.

THE NAZI BLITZKRIEG

Germany struck at Poland with speed and power. The German air force, the Luftwaffe, destroyed Polish planes on the ground, attacked tanks, pounded defense networks, and bombed Warsaw, terrorizing the population. Tanks opened up breaches in the Polish defenses, and paratroopers, dropped behind Polish lines, captured important positions. Ethnic Germans living in Poland sabotaged factories. By September 8, the Germans had advanced to the outskirts of Warsaw. On September 17, Soviet troops invaded Poland from the east. On September 27, Poland surrendered. In less than a month the Nazi *blitzkrieg* (lightning war) had vanquished Poland.

The Fall of France

For Hitler the conquest of Poland was only the prelude to a German empire stretching from the Atlantic to the Urals. When weather conditions were right, he would unleash a great offensive in the west. Meanwhile, the six-month period following the defeat of Poland was nicknamed the "phony war," for the fighting on land consisted only of a few skirmishes on the French-German border. Then, in early April 1940, the Germans struck at Denmark and Norway. Hitler wanted to insure access to Swedish iron ore that reached

Germany through Norwegian territorial waters. He knew that Britain and France had plans to occupy the mining region and the key Swedish and Norwegian ports. In addition, Hitler expected to establish naval bases on the Norwegian coast from which to wage submarine warfare against Britain.

Denmark surrendered within hours. A British-French force assisted the Norwegians, but the landings, badly coordinated and lacking in air support, failed. The Germans won the battle of Norway. But the Norwegian campaign produced two positive results for the Allies: Norwegian merchant ships escaped to Britain to be put into service; and Winston Churchill (1874–1965), who had opposed appeasement, replaced Chamberlain as British prime minister. Dynamic, courageous, and eloquent, Churchill had the capacity to stir and lead his people in the struggle against Nazism.

On May 10, 1940, Hitler lauched his offensive in the west with an invasion of neutral Belgium, Holland, and Luxembourg. While armored forces penetrated Dutch frontier defenses, airborne units seized strategic airfields and bridges. On May 14, after the Luftwaffe bombed Rotterdam, destroying the center of the city and killing many people, the Dutch surrendered.

A daring attack by glider-borne troops gave Germany possession of two crucial Belgian bridges, opening the plains of Belgium to German *Panzer* (tank) divisions. Believing that this was the main German attack, French troops rushed to Belgium to prevent a German breakthrough, but the greater menace lay to the south on the French frontier. Meeting almost no resistance, German Panzer divisions had moved through the narrow mountain passes of Luxembourg and the heavily wooded Forest of Ardennes in southern Belgium. On May 12, German units were on French soil

MAP 32.2 WORLD WAR II: THE EUROPEAN THEATER ▶

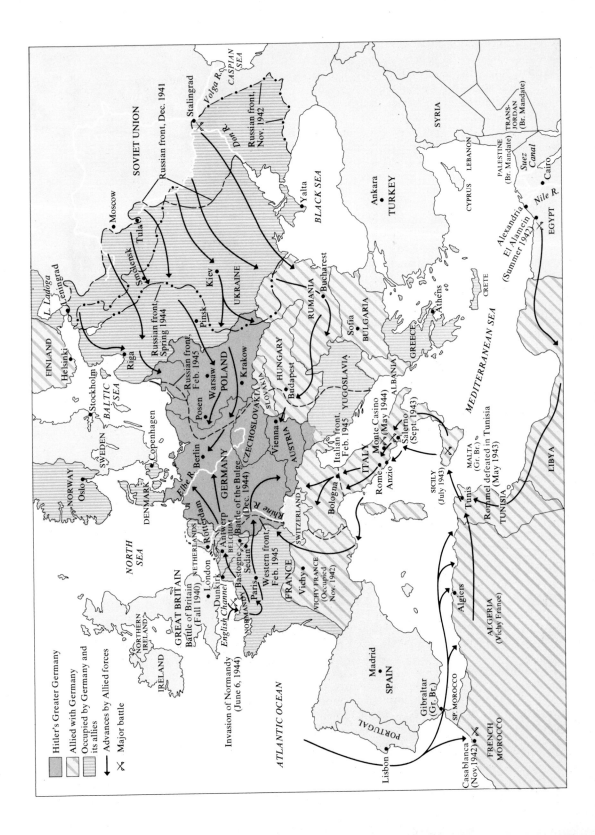

CASPIAN
SEA

Volga R.

Russian front, Dec. 1941

SOVIET UNION

Stalingrad

Russian front,
Nov. 1942

Don R.

Moscow

Russian front,
Spring 1944

Tula

Smolensk

Kiev

UKRAINE

Yalta

BLACK SEA

L. Ladoga

Leningrad

Riga

Pinsk

Russian front,
Feb. 1945

Warsaw

POLAND

Krakow

Posen

SLOVAKIA

HUNGARY

Budapest

RUMANIA

Bucharest

Sofia

BULGARIA

Ankara

TURKEY

SYRIA

TRANS-
JORDAN
(Br. Mandate)

PALESTINE
(Br. Mandate)

LEBANON

CYPRUS

*Suez
Canal*

Nile R.

Cairo

Alexandria
El Alamein
(Summer 1942)

EGYPT

FINLAND

Helsinki

Stockholm

BALTIC
SEA

SWEDEN

Copenhagen

NORWAY

Oslo

DENMARK

Elbe R.

Berlin

GERMANY

CZECHOSLOVAKIA

Vienna

AUSTRIA

Battle of the Bulge
(Dec. 1944)

Italian front,
Feb. 1945

YUGOSLAVIA

ALBANIA

Rome

Monte Casino

Anzio

(May 1944)

Salerno
(Sept. 1943)

ITALY

Bologna

GREECE

Athens

CRETE

MEDITERRANEAN SEA

MALTA
(Gr. Br.)

Rommel defeated in Tunisia
(May 1943)

LIBYA

NORTH
SEA

GREAT BRITAIN

Battle of Britain
(Fall 1940)

London

NETHERLANDS

Rotterdam

Antwerp

BELGIUM

Bastogne

Sedan

English Channel

Dunkirk

NORTHERN
IRELAND

IRELAND

Paris

NORMANDY

Western front,
Feb. 1945

Rhine R.

SWITZERLAND

FRANCE

Vichy

VICHY FRANCE
(Occupied
Nov. 1942)

Invasion of Normandy
(June 6, 1944)

SICILY
(July 1943)

Tunis

TUNISIA

Algiers

ALGERIA
(Vichy France)

ATLANTIC OCEAN

Madrid

SPAIN

PORTUGAL

Lisbon

Gibraltar
(Gr. Br.)

SP. MOROCCO

Casablanca
(Nov. 1942)

FRENCH
MOROCCO

Hitler's Greater Germany

Allied with Germany

Occupied by Germany and
its allies

Advances by Allied forces

Major battle

near Sedan. Thinking that the Forest of Ardennes could not be penetrated by a major German force, the French had only lightly fortified the western extension of the Maginot Line; the failure to counterattack swiftly was a second mistake. The best elements of the Anglo-French forces were in Belgium, but the Germans were racing across northern France to the sea, which they reached on May 20, cutting the Anglo-French forces in two.

The Germans now sought to surround and annihilate the Allied forces converging on the French seaport of Dunkirk, the last port of escape. But inexplicably Hitler called off his tanks just as they prepared to take Dunkirk; instead he ordered the Luftwaffe to finish off the Allied troops, but fog and rain prevented German planes from operating at full strength. Taking advantage of this breathing space, the Allies tightened their defenses and prepared for a massive evacuation. While the Luftwaffe bombed the beaches, some 338,000 British and French troops were ferried across the English Channel by destroyers, merchant ships, motorboats, fishing boats, tugboats, and private yachts. The British left all their equipment on the beaches but saved their armies to fight another day. Hitler's personal decision to hold back his tanks made the miracle of Dunkirk possible.

Meanwhile the battle for France was turning into a disaster. Whole divisions were cut off or in retreat and millions of refugees in cars and carts, on motorcycles and bicycles fled south to escape the advancing Germans. On June 10, Mussolini also declared war on France. With authority breaking down, demoralization spreading, and resistance dying, the French cabinet appealed for an armistice, which was signed on June 22 in the same railway car in which Germany had agreed to the armistice ending World War I.

How can the collapse of France be explained? The French had fewer planes than the Germans and were deficient in antiaircraft artillery, but they had as many tanks, some even superior in quality. Nor was German manpower overwhelming. France met disaster

THE FALL OF FRANCE   French civilians show the shock of defeat. Hitler's army accomplished what the German generals of World War I had planned but not brought about: the capture of Paris and the fall of France. The might of motorized warfare had prevailed over the French army and its outmoded World War I methods. (United Press International)

largely because its military leaders, unlike the German command, had not mastered the psychology and technology of motorized warfare. "The French commanders, trained in the slow-motion methods of 1918, were mentally unfitted to cope with panzer pace, and it produced a spreading paralysis among them," says British military expert Sir Basil Liddell Hart.[4] One senses also a loss of will among the French people, a product of internal political disputes that divided the nation, poor leadership, the years of appeasement and lost opportunities, and German propaganda, which depicted Nazism as irresistible and the Fuehrer as a man of destiny. It was France's darkest hour.

According to the terms of the armistice, Germany occupied northern France and the coast. The French military was demobilized and the French government, now located at Vichy in the south and headed by Marshall Pétain, the hero of World War I, would collaborate with the German authorities in occupied France. Refusing to recognize defeat, General Charles de Gaulle (1890–1970) escaped to London and organized the Free French forces. The Germans gloried in their revenge; the French wept in their humiliation; the British gathered their courage, for they now stood alone.

The Battle of Britain

Hitler expected that after his stunning victories in the west, Britain would make peace. The British, however, continued to reject Hitler's peace overtures, for they envisioned only a bleak future if Hitler dominated the Continent. "The Battle of Britain is about to begin," Churchill told the people of Britain. "Upon this battle depends the survival of Christian civilization. . . . if we fail, then . . . all we have known and cared for will sink into the abyss of a new Dark Age."[5]

With Britain unwilling to come to terms, Hitler proceeded in earnest with invasion plans. But a successful crossing of the English Channel and the establishment of beachheads on the English coast depended on the crippling of British air and sea power. Early in August 1940, the Luftwaffe began its attack on British naval and air bases; to damage production and weaken morale, they also bombed industrial and population centers. Air battles were waged daily in the sky above Britain; every night for weeks the inhabitants of London sought shelter in subways and cellars to escape German bombs. But English morale never broke. The development of radar by British scientists, the skill and courage of British fighter pilots, and the inability of Germany to make up heavy losses in aircraft saved Britain in its struggle for survival. By September 17, Hitler had to postpone indefinitely his plan for the invasion of Britain.

Invasion of Russia

The obliteration of Bolshevism and the conquest, exploitation, and colonization of Russia were cardinal elements of Hitler's ideology. From Russia the Nazi empire would obtain wheat, oil, manganese, and other raw materials, and the fertile Russian plains would be settled by the master race. German expansion in the east could not wait for the final defeat of Britain. In July 1940, Hitler instructed his generals to formulate plans for an invasion of Russia. On December 18, Hitler set May 15, 1941, for the beginning of Operation Barbarossa, the code name assigned for the blitzkrieg against the Soviet Union. But events in the Balkans forced Hitler to postpone the date to the latter part of June.

Seeking to make Italy a Mediterranean power and to win glory for himself, Mussolini had ordered an invasion of Greece. In late October 1940, Italian troops stationed in Albania—which Italy had occupied in 1939—crossed into Greece. The poorly planned operation was an instant failure; within a week, the counterattacking Greeks advanced into Albania. Hitler feared that Britain, which was encouraging and aiding the Greeks, would use Greece to attack the oil fields of Rumania, vital to the German war effort, and to interfere with the forthcoming invasion of Russia. Another problem emerged when a military coup overthrew the government of Prince Paul in Yugoslavia, which two days earlier had signed a pact with Germany and Italy. Hitler feared that the new Yugoslav government might gravitate toward Britain. To prevent any interference with Operation Barbarossa, the Balkan flank had to be secured. On April 6, 1941, the Germans struck at both Greece and Yugoslavia. Yugoslavia was quickly overrun and Greece, which was aided by 50,000 British, New Zealand, and Australian troops, fell at the end of April.

For the war against Russia, Hitler had assembled a massive force—some 4 million men, 3,300 tanks, 5,000 planes. In the early hours of June 22, 1941, the Germans launched their offensive over a wide front. Raiding Russian airfields, the Luftwaffe destroyed 1,200 aircraft on the first day. The Germans drove deeply into Russia, cutting up and surrounding the disorganized and unprepared Russian forces. The Russians suffered terrible losses. In a little more than three months, 2.5 million Russian soldiers had been killed, wounded, or captured and 14,000 tanks destroyed. Describing the war as a crusade to save Europe from "Jewish Bolshevism," German propaganda claimed that victory had been assured.

But there were also disquieting signs for the Nazi invaders. The Russians, who had a proven capacity to endure hardships, fought doggedly and courageously, and the government would not consider capitulation. Russian reserve strength was far greater than the Germans had estimated. The Wehrmacht, far from its supply lines, was running short of fuel, and trucks and cars had to contend with primitive roads that turned into a sea of mud when the autumn rains came. One German general described the ordeal: "The infantryman slithers in the mud, while many teams of horses are needed to drag each gun forward. All wheeled vehicles sink up to their axles in the slime. Even tractors can only move with great difficulty. A large portion of our heavy artillery was soon stuck fast. . . . The strain that all this caused our already exhausted troops can perhaps be imagined."[6] Conditions no longer favored the blitzkrieg.

An early and bitter cold hampered the German attempt to capture Moscow. Without warm uniforms, tens of thousands of Germans suffered from frostbite; without antifreeze, guns did not fire. The Germans advanced within twenty miles of Moscow, but on December 6 a Red Army counterattack forced a postponement of the assault on the Russian capital. The Germans were also denied Leningrad, which since September had been completely surrounded, except for one outlet onto Lake Ladoga, and under constant bombardment. During this epic siege, the citizens of Leningrad displayed extraordinary courage in the face of famine, disease, and shelling that cost nearly one million lives.

By the end of 1941, Germany had conquered vast regions of Russia but had failed to bring it to its knees. There would be no repetition of the collapse of France. The Russian campaign demonstrated that the Russian people would make incredible sacrifices for their motherland and that the Nazis were not invincible.

THE NEW ORDER

By 1942, Germany ruled virtually all of Europe from the Atlantic to deep into Russia. Some conquered territory was annexed outright; other lands were administered by German officials; in still other countries, the Germans ruled through local officials sympathetic to Nazism or willing to collaborate with the Germans. Over this vast empire Hitler and his henchmen imposed a New Order.

Exploitation and Terror

"The real profiteers of this war are ourselves, and out of it we shall come bursting with fat," said Hitler. "We will give back nothing and will take everything we can make use of."[7] The Germans systematically looted the conquered lands, taking gold, art treasures, machinery, and food supplies back to Germany and utilizing the industrial and agricultural potential of non-German lands to aid the German war economy. Some foreign businesses and factories were confiscated by the German Reich; others produced what the Germans demanded. Germany also requisitioned food from the conquered regions, significantly reducing the quantity available for civilian consumption. German soldiers were fed with food harvested in occupied France and Russia;

they fought with weapons produced in Czech factories; German tanks ran on oil delivered by Rumania, Germany's satellite. The Nazis also made slave laborers of conquered peoples. Some 7 million people from all over Europe were wrested from their homes and transported to Germany. These forced laborers, particularly Russians and Poles, whom Nazi ideology classified as subhumans, lived in wretched, unheated barracks and were poorly fed and overworked; many died of disease, hunger, and exhaustion.

The Nazis ruled by force and terror. The prison cell, the torture room, the firing squad, and the concentration camp symbolized the New Order. In the Polish province annexed to Germany, the Nazis jailed and executed intellectuals and priests, closed all schools and most churches, and forbade Poles from holding professional positions. In the region of Poland administered by German officials, most schools above the fourth grade were shut down. Himmler insisted that it was sufficient for Polish children to learn "simple arithmetic up to five hundred at the most; writing of one's name; a doctrine that it is a divine law to obey the Germans and to be honest, industrious, and good."[8] The Germans were particularly ruthless toward the Russians, whom they regarded as an especially low form of humanity. Soviet political officials were immediately executed; many prisoners of war were herded into camps and deliberately starved to death. The Germans took some 5.5 million Russian prisoners, of whom more than 3.5 million perished.

Extermination

Against the Jews of Europe the Germans waged a war of extermination. The task of imposing the "Final Solution of the Jewish Problem" was given to the SS headed by Heinrich Himmler, who fulfilled his grisly duties with fanaticism and bureaucratic efficiency. Seized by a mass psychosis akin to the witchcraft hysteria of the sixteenth century, Himmler and the SS believed that they had a holy mission to rid the world of a satanic foe and the lowest species of humanity that was plotting to destroy Germany. Regarding themselves as idealists who were writing a glorious chapter in the history of Germany, the SS tortured and murdered with immense dedication. The mind of the SS was dominated by the mythical world-view of Nazism, as the following tract issued by SS headquarters reveals:

Just as night rises up against the day, just as light and darkness are eternal enemies, so the greatest enemy of world-dominating man is man himself. The subman—that creature which looks as though biologically it were of absolutely the same kind, endowed by Nature with hands, feet and a sort of brain, with eyes and mouth—is nevertheless a totally different, a fearful creature, is only an attempt at a human being, with a quasi-human face, yet in mind and spirit lower than any animal. Inside this being a cruel chaos of wild, unchecked passions: a nameless will to destruction, the most primitive lusts, the most undisguised vileness. A sub-man—nothing else! . . . Never has the sub-man granted peace, never has he permitted rest. . . . To preserve himself he needed mud, he needed hell, but not the sun. And this underworld of sub-men found its leader: the eternal Jew![9]

Special squads of SS, the *Einsatzgruppen*, trained for mass murder, followed on the heels of the German army into Russia. Entering captured villages and cities, they rounded up Jewish men, women, and children, herded them to execution grounds, and slaughtered them with machine gun and rifle fire. Aided by Ukrainian, Lithuanian, and Latvian auxiliaries, the Einsatzgruppen massacred some two million Russian Jews.

To speed up the Final Solution, concentration camps, originally established for political prisoners, were transformed into killing centers and new ones were built for that purpose.

Jews from all over Europe were rounded up—for "resettlement," they were told. The victims dismissed rumors that the Germans were engaged in genocide. They simply could not believe that any nation in the twentieth century was capable of such evil. "Why did we not fight back? . . . I know why. Because we had faith in humanity. Because we did not really think that human beings were capable of committing such crimes," declared one survivor.[10] Jammed into sealed cattle cars, eighty or ninety to a car, the victims traveled sometimes for days without food or water, choking from the stench of vomit and excrement, and shattered by the crying of children. Disgorged at the concentration camps, they entered another planet.

Corpses were strewn all over the road; bodies were hanging from the barbed-wire fence; the sound of shots rang in the air continuously. Blazing flames shot into the sky; a giant smoke cloud ascended about them. Starving, emaciated human skeletons stumbled forward toward us, uttering incoherent sounds. They fell down right in front of our eyes gasping out their last breath.

Here and there a hand tried to reach up, but when this happened an SS man came right away and stepped on it. Those who were merely exhausted were simply thrown on the dead pile. . . . Every night a truck came by, and all of them, dead or not, were thrown on it and taken to the crematory.[11]

SS doctors quickly inspected the new arrivals, "the freight," as they referred to them. Rudolf Hoess, commandant of Auschwitz, the most notorious of the murder factories, described the procedure:

[I] estimate that at least 2,500,000 victims were executed and exterminated [at Auschwitz] by gassing and burning, and at least another half million succumbed to starvation and disease, making a total dead of about 3,000,000. This figure represents about 70 per cent or 80 per cent of all persons sent to Auschwitz as prisoners, the remainder having

been selected and used for slave labor in the concentration camp industries. . . .

The "final solution" of the Jewish question meant the complete extermination of all Jews in Europe. I was ordered to establish extermination facilities at Auschwitz in June, 1941. . . . It took from three to fifteen minutes to kill people in the death chamber, depending upon climatic conditions. We knew when the people were dead because their screaming stopped. We usually waited about one-half hour before we opened the doors and removed the bodies. After the bodies were removed our special commandos took off the rings and extracted the gold from the teeth of the corpses. . . .

The way we selected our victims was as follows . . . Those who were fit to work were sent into the camp. Others were sent immediately to the extermination plants. Children of tender years were invariably exterminated since by reason of their youth they were unable to work. . . . We endeavored to fool the victims into thinking that they were to go through a delousing process. Of course, frequently they realized our true intentions, and we sometimes had riots and difficulties due to that fact. Very frequently women would hide their children under clothes, but of course when we found them we would send the children in to be exterminated.[12]

The naked bodies, covered with blood and defecation and intertwined with each other, were piled high to the ceiling. To make way for the next group, a squad of Jewish prisoners emptied the gas chambers of the corpses and removed the gold teeth, which along with the victims' hair, eyeglasses, and clothing, were carefully collected and catalogued for the war effort. Later the bodies were burned in crematoria specially constructed by I. A. Topf and Sons of Erfurt. The chimneys vomited black smoke and the stench of burning flesh permeated the entire region.

Auschwitz was more than a murder factory. It also provided the German industrial giant,

JEWS BEING ROUNDED UP TO ENTER CONCENTRATION CAMPS As Germans overran Europe, Hitler broadened his campaign against the Jews; it was no longer confined to Germany. He sought the "final solution of the Jewish problem" through genocide. (Collection Viollet, Paris)

I. G. Farben, which operated a factory adjoining the camp, with slave laborers, both Jews and non-Jews. The working pace at the factory and the ill treatment by guards was so brutal, reported a physician and inmate, that "while working many prisoners suddenly stretched out flat, turned blue, gasped for breath, and died like beasts."[13]

Auschwitz also allowed the SS, the elite of the master race, to shape and harden themselves according to the National Socialist creed. This they did. A survivor recalls seeing SS men and women amuse themselves with pregnant inmates. The unfortunate women were "beaten with clubs and whips, torn by dogs, dragged by the hair, and kicked in the stomach with heavy German boots. Then, when they collapsed, they were thrown into the crematory—alive."[14] By systematically overworking, beating, terrorizing, and degrading the inmates, by making them live in filth and sleep sprawled all over each other in tiny cubicles, the SS deliberately sought to strip prisoners of all human dignity, to make them appear, behave, and believe that they were indeed "sub-man," as National Socialist ideology viewed them. When prisoners, exhausted, starved, diseased, and beaten, became unfit for work, generally within a few months, they were sent to the gas chambers. Many went mad or committed suicide; some struggled desperately, defiantly, and heroically to maintain their humanity. Auschwitz, the vilest assault on human dignity ever conceived, was the true legacy of National Socialism and the SS the true end product of National Socialist indoctrination and idealism.

The systematic extermination of European Jewry was the terrible fulfillment of Nazi racial theories. Believing that they were cleansing Europe of a lower and dangerous race that threatened the German people, Nazi executioners performed their evil work with dedication and resourcefulness, with precision and moral indifference, an astonishing testament to the power of mythical thinking. Utilizing the technology and bureaucracy of a modern state, the Germans killed some 6 million Jews, two-thirds of the Jewish population of Europe. Some 1.5 million of the murdered were children. Tens of thousands of entire families were wiped out without a trace. Centuries-old Jewish community life vanished, never to be restored. Burned into the soul of the Jewish people was a wound that could never entirely heal. Written into the history of Western civilization was an episode that would forever cast doubt on the Enlightenment conception of human goodness, rationality, and the progress of civilization.

Resistance

Each occupied country had its collaborators who welcomed the demise of democracy, saw Hitler as Europe's best defense against communism, and profited from the sale of war material. Each country also produced a resistance movement that grew stronger as Nazi barbarism became more visible, and prospects of a German defeat more likely. The Nazis retaliated by torturing and executing captured resistance fighters and killing hostages, generally fifty for every German killed.

In western Europe the resistance rescued Allied airmen, radioed military intelligence to Britain, and sabotaged installations. Norwegians blew up the German stock of heavy water needed for atomic research. The Danish underground sabotaged railways and smuggled into neutral Sweden almost all of Denmark's 8,000 Jews just before they were to be deported to the death camps. The Greek resistance blew up a vital viaduct, interrupting the movement of supplies to German troops in North Africa. After the Allies landed on the coast of France in June 1944, the French resistance delayed the movement of German reinforcements and liberated sections of the country. Belgian resistance fighters captured the vital port of Antwerp.

The Polish resistance, numbering some 300,000 at its height, reported on German troop movements and interfered with supplies destined for the eastern front. In August 1944, with Soviet forces approaching Warsaw, the Poles staged a full-scale revolt against the German occupiers. The Poles appealed to the Soviets, camped ten miles away, for help. Thinking about a future Russian-dominated Poland, the Soviets did not move. After sixty-three days of street fighting, remnants of the Polish underground surrendered and the Germans destroyed what was left of Warsaw.

Russian partisans numbered several hundred thousand men and women. Operating behind the German lines, they sabotaged railways, destroyed trucks, and killed scores of thousands of German soldiers in hit-and-run attacks.

The mountains and forests of Yugoslavia provided an excellent terrain for guerrilla warfare. The leading Yugoslav resistance army was headed by Josip Broz (1892–1980), better known as Tito. Moscow-trained, intelligent, and courageous, Tito organized the partisans into a disciplined fighting force that tied down a huge German army and ultimately liberated the country from German rule.

Jews participated in the resistance movement in all countries and were particularly prominent in the French resistance. Specifically Jewish resistance organizations emerged in Eastern Europe, but they suffered from shattering handicaps. Poles, Ukrainians, Lithuanians, and other East European peoples with a long history of anti-Semitism gave little or no support to Jewish resisters and, at times, even denounced them to the Nazis. For centuries, European Jews had dealt with persecution by complying with their oppressors and had unlearned the habit of armed resistance that their ancestors had demonstrated against the Romans. Nevertheless, revolts did take place in the ghettos and concentration camps. They were acts of great courage, particularly the uprising in the Warsaw ghetto during April–May 1943.

Italy and Germany also had resistance movements. After the Allies landed in Italy in 1943, bands of Italian partisans helped to liberate Italy from fascism and the German occupation. In Germany, army officers plotted to assassinate the Fuehrer. On July 20, 1944, Colonel Claus von Stauffenberg planted a bomb at a staff conference attended by Hitler, but the Fuehrer escaped serious injury. In retaliation, some 5,000 suspected anti-Nazis were tortured and executed in exceptionally barbarous fashion.

THE TURN OF THE TIDE

The Japanese Offensive

At the same time that Germany was subduing Europe, its ally, Japan, was extending its dominion over areas of Asia. Seeking raw materials, assured markets for Japanese goods, and driven by a xenophobic nationalism, Japan in 1931 had attacked Manchuria in northern China. Quickly overrunning the province, the Japanese established the puppet state of Manchukuo in 1932. After a period of truce, the war against China was renewed in July 1937. Japan captured leading cities, including China's principal seaports, and inflicted heavy casualties on the poorly organized Chinese forces, forcing the government of Chiang Kai-shek (1887–1975) to withdraw to Chungking in the interior.

In 1940, after the defeat of France and with Britain standing alone against Nazi Germany, Japan eyed southeast Asia—French Indochina, British Burma and Malaya, and the Dutch East Indies. From these lands Japan hoped to obtain the oil, rubber, and tin vitally needed by Japanese industry and enough rice to feed the nation. Japan hoped that a quick strike against the American fleet in the Pacific would give it time to enlarge and consolidate its empire. On December 7, 1941, the Japanese struck with carrier-based planes at Pearl Harbor in Hawaii. Taken by surprise, the Americans suffered a total defeat: seventeen ships were sunk, including seven of eight battleships; 188 airplanes destroyed, and 159 others damaged; and 2,403 men killed. The Japanese lost only 29 planes. After the attack on Pearl Harbor, Germany declared war on the United States. Now the immense industrial capacity of the United States could be used against the Axis.

By the spring of 1942, the Axis powers held the upper hand. The Japanese empire included the coast of China, Indochina, Thailand, Burma, Malaya, the Dutch East Indies, the Philippines, and other islands in the Pacific. Germany controlled Europe almost to Moscow. When the year ended, however, the Allies seemed assured of victory. Three decisive battles—Midway, Stalingrad, and El Alamein—reversed the tide of battle.

At Pearl Harbor the Japanese had destroyed much of the American fleet. Assembling a mighty flotilla (8 aircraft carriers, 11 battleships, 22 cruisers, and 65 destroyers), Japan now sought to annihilate the rest of the United States Pacific fleet. In June 1942 the main body of the Japanese fleet headed for Midway, 1,100 miles northwest of Pearl Harbor; another section sailed toward the Aleutian Islands in an attempt to divide the American fleet. But the Americans had broken the

Japanese naval code and were aware of the Japanese plan. On June 4, 1942, the two navies fought a strange naval battle, waged entirely by carrier-based planes, for the two fleets were too far from each other to use their big guns. Demonstrating marked superiority over their opponents and extraordinary courage, American pilots destroyed 4 aircraft carriers; 322 Japanese planes were also downed. The battle of Midway cost Japan the initiative. With American industrial production accelerating, the opportunity for a Japanese victory had passed.

Defeat of the Axis Powers

After being stymied at the outskirts of Moscow in December 1941, the Germans renewed their offensive in the spring and summer of 1942. Hitler's goal was Stalingrad, the great industrial center located on the Volga River; control of Stalingrad would give Germany command of vital rail transportation. The battle of Stalingrad was an epic struggle in which Russian soldiers and civilians contested for every building and street of the city. So brutal was the fighting that at night half-crazed dogs sought to escape the city by swimming across the river. A Russian counterattack in November caught the Germans in a trap. Exhausted and short of food, medical supplies, weapons, and ammunition, Friedrich Paulus, Commander of the Sixth Army, urged Hitler to order a withdrawal before the Russians closed the ring. The Fuehrer refused. After suffering tens of thousands of additional casualties, their position hopeless, the remnants of the Sixth Army surrendered on February 2, 1943. Some 260,000 German soldiers had perished in the battle of Stalingrad and another 110,000 were taken prisoner.

In January 1941, the British were routing the Italians in northern Africa. Hitler assigned General Erwin Rommel (1891–1944) the task of halting the British advance. Rommel drove the British out of Libya and with strong reinforcements might have taken Egypt and the Suez Canal. But Hitler's concern was with seizing Yugoslavia and Greece and preparing for the invasion of Russia. In the beginning of 1942, Rommel resumed his advance, intending to conquer Egypt. The British Eighth Army, commanded by General Bernard L. Montgomery, stopped him at the battle of El Alamein in October 1942. The victory of El Alamein was followed by an Anglo-American invasion of northwest Africa in November 1942. By May 1943, the Germans and Italians were defeated in North Africa.

After securing North Africa, the Allies, seeking complete control of the Mediterranean, invaded Sicily in July 1943 and quickly conquered the island. Mussolini's fellow fascist leaders turned against the Duce and the king dismissed him as prime minister. In September, the new government surrendered to the Allies and in the following month Italy declared war on Germany.

Italian partisans, whose number would grow to 300,000, resisted the Germans, who were determined to hold on to central and northern Italy. At the same time, the Allies fought their way up the peninsula. The fighting in Italy would last until the very end of the war. Captured by partisans, Mussolini was executed (April 28, 1945) and his dead body, hanging upside-down, was publicly displayed.

On June 6, 1944—D-Day—the Allies landed on Normandy in France. For the invasion they had assembled a massive force—2 million men and 5,000 vessels. Although suspecting an imminent invasion, the Germans did not think that it would occur in Normandy and they dismissed June 6 because weather conditions were unfavorable. The success of D-Day depended on securing the beaches and marching inland, which the Allies did despite stubborn German resistance on some beaches. By the end of July, the Allies had built up their strength in France to a million and a half. In

MAP 32.3 WORLD WAR II: THE PACIFIC THEATER ▶

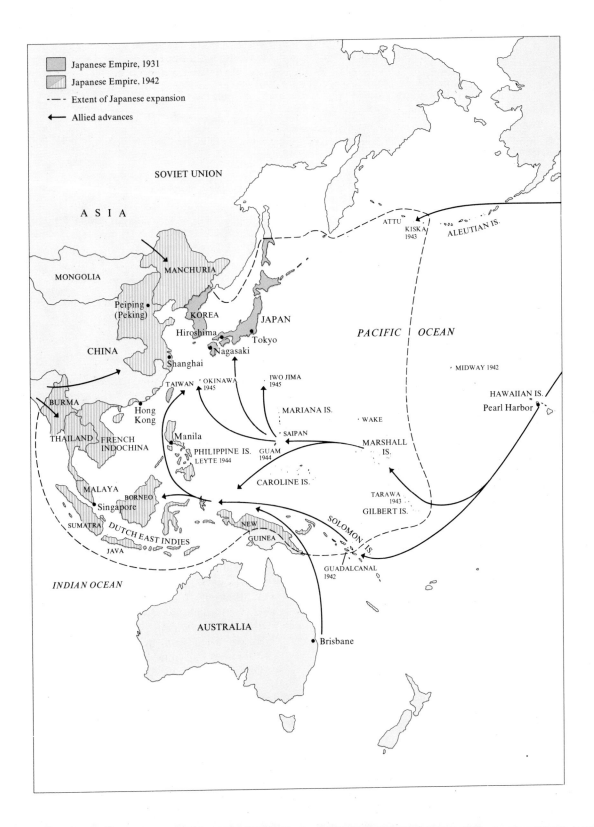

Japanese Empire, 1931
Japanese Empire, 1942
Extent of Japanese expansion
Allied advances

SOVIET UNION

A S I A

MONGOLIA

MANCHURIA

ATTU
KISKA 1943
ALEUTIAN IS.

Peiping (Peking)

KOREA

JAPAN

PACIFIC OCEAN

Hiroshima
Nagasaki
Tokyo

CHINA

Shanghai

MIDWAY 1942

TAIWAN

OKINAWA 1945

IWO JIMA 1945

HAWAIIAN IS.
Pearl Harbor

BURMA

Hong Kong

MARIANA IS.

WAKE

THAILAND   FRENCH INDOCHINA

Manila

PHILIPPINE IS.
LEYTE 1944

SAIPAN

GUAM 1944

MARSHALL IS.

MALAYA

BORNEO

Singapore

CAROLINE IS.

TARAWA 1943
GILBERT IS.

SUMATRA   DUTCH EAST INDIES

NEW GUINEA

SOLOMON IS.

JAVA

GUADALCANAL 1942

INDIAN OCEAN

AUSTRALIA

Brisbane

AMERICANS LANDING IN THE PACIFIC The bombing of Pearl Harbor on December 7, 1941, led the United States into war with Japan and Germany. Almost four years later, the United States brought World War II to a close with the dropping of the second atomic bomb on Nagasaki on August 9, 1945. (United Press International)

the middle of August, Paris rose up against the German occupiers and was soon liberated.

As winter approached, the situation looked hopeless for Germany. Brussels and Antwerp fell to the Allies; Allied bombers were striking German factories and mass bombing German cities in terror raids that took a terrible toll of life; the desperate Hitler made one last gamble. In mid-December 1944 he launched an offensive to split the Allied forces and regain the vital port of Antwerp. The Allies were taken by surprise in the Battle of the Bulge, but

a heroic defense by the Americans at Bastogne stopped the German offensive.

While the Allies were advancing in the west, the Russians were continuing their drive in the east, advancing into the Baltic states, Poland, and Hungary. By February 1945, they stood within one hundred miles of Berlin.

On March 7, 1945, American soldiers, seizing a bridge that the Germans had failed to destroy, crossed the Rhine into Germany. By April 1945, British, American, and Russian troops were penetrating into Germany from east and west. From his underground bunker near the chancellery in Berlin, Hitler, physically exhausted and embittered, engaged in wild fantasies about new German victories. On April 30, 1945, with the Russians only blocks away, the Fuehrer took his own life. In his last will and testament, Hitler insisted: "It is not true that I or anybody else in Germany wanted war in 1939. It was wanted and provoked exclusively by those international statesmen who either were of Jewish origin or worked for Jewish interests."[15] On May 7, 1945, a demoralized and devastated Germany surrendered unconditionally.

After the victory at Midway in June 1942, American forces attacked strategic islands held by Japan. American troops had to battle their way up the beaches and through the jungles tenaciously defended by Japanese soldiers, who believed that death was preferable to the disgrace of surrender. In March 1945, 21,000 Japanese perished on Iwo Jima; another 100,000 died on Okinawa in April 1945 as they contested for every inch of the island. On August 6, 1945, the United States dropped an atomic bomb on Hiroshima, killing more than 78,000 people and demolishing 60 percent of the city. President Truman ordered the atomic attack in order to avoid an American invasion of the Japanese homeland that would have cost hundreds of thousands of lives. On August 8, Russia entered the war against Japan, invading Manchuria. After a second atomic bomb was dropped on Nagasaki on August 9, the Japanese asked for peace.

THE LEGACY OF WORLD WAR II

World War II was the most destructive war in history. Estimates for the number of dead range as high as 50 million, including 20 million Russians, who sacrificed both in population and material resources more than the other participants. The war produced a vast migration of peoples unparalleled in modern European history. The Soviet Union annexed the Baltic lands of Latvia, Lithuania, and Estonia, forcibly deporting many of the native inhabitants into central Russia. The bulk of East Prussia was taken over by Poland, and Russia annexed the eastern portion. Millions of Germans fled or were forced out of Prussia and regions of Czechoslovakia, Rumania, Yugoslavia, and Hungary, places where their ancestors had lived for centuries. Material costs were staggering. Everywhere cities were in rubble; bridges, railway systems, waterways, and harbors destroyed; farmlands laid waste; livestock killed; coal mines wrecked. Homeless and hungry people wandered the streets and roads. Europe faced a gigantic rebuilding. Yet Europe did recover from this material blight, and with astonishing speed.

World War II produced a shift in power arrangements. The United States and the Soviet Union emerged as the two most powerful states in the world; the traditional Great Powers—Britain, France, Germany—were now dwarfed by these *superpowers*. The United States had the atomic bomb and immense industrial might; the Soviet Union had the largest army in the world and was extending its dominion over eastern Europe. With Germany prostrate and occupied, the principal incentive for Soviet-American cooperation had evaporated.

Whereas World War I was followed by an intensification of nationalist passions, after World War II western Europeans progressed toward cooperation and unity. The Hitler years had convinced many Europeans of the dangers inherent in extreme nationalism, and the fear of the Soviet Union fortified the need for greater cooperation.

World War II accelerated the disintegration of Europe's overseas empires. How could the European states justify ruling Africans and Asians after they had fought to liberate European lands from German imperialism? How could they ask their peoples, exhausted by the Hitler years and concentrating all their energies on reconstruction, to fight new wars against Africans and Asians pressing for inde-

CHRONOLOGY 32.2   WORLD WAR II

September 27, 1939	Poland surrenders
November 1939	Russia invades Finland
April 1940	Germany attacks Denmark and Norway
May 10, 1940	Germany invades Belgium, Holland, and Luxembourg
May 14, 1940	The Dutch surrender
May 20, 1940	British and French forces are evacuated from Dunkirk
June 1940	Fall of France
June 22, 1940	German Luftwaffe begins to attack Britain
September 1940	Japan begins conquest of Southeast Asia
October 1940	Italian troops cross into Greece
April 6, 1941	Germany attacks Greece and Yugoslavia
June 22, 1941	Germany launches offensive against Russia
December 7, 1941	Japan attacks Pearl Harbor; United States enters the war against Japan and Germany
1942	The tide of battle turns in the Allies' favor: Midway (Pacific), Stalingrad (Soviet Union), and El Alamein (North Africa)
September 1943	Italy surrenders to Allies, following invasion
June 6, 1944	D-Day—Allies land in Normandy, France
August 1944	Paris is liberated; Poles revolt against German occupiers
January 1945	Soviet troops invade Germany
March–April 1945	Allies penetrate Germany
May 7, 1945	Germany surrenders unconditionally
August 1945	United States drops atomic bombs on Hiroshima and Nagasaki; Soviet Union invades Manchuria; Japan surrenders

pendence? Immediately after the war, Great Britain surrendered India, France lost Lebanon and Syria, and the Dutch departed from Indonesia. In the 1950s and 1960s, virtually every colonial territory gained independence. In those instances where the colonial power resisted independence for the colony, the price was bloodshed.

The consciousness of Europe, profoundly damaged by World War I, was again grievously wounded. Nazi racial theories showed that in an age of sophisticated science the mind remains attracted to irrational beliefs and mythical imagery; Nazi atrocities demonstrated that people will torture and kill with religious zeal and machinelike indifference. The Nazi assault on reason and freedom demonstrated anew the precariousness of Western civilization. Both the Christian and Enlightenment traditions had failed the West. Some thinkers, shocked by the irrationality and horrors of the Hitler era, drifted into despair. To these thinkers, life was absurd, without meaning; human beings could neither comprehend nor control it. In 1945 only the naive could have faith in continuous progress or believe in the essential goodness of the individual. The future envisioned by the philosophes seemed further away than ever.

World War II ushered in the atomic age. At the end of the war, only the United States had the atomic bomb, but soon the Soviet Union and other states acquired an arsenal of atomic weapons. That people now possess the weapons to destroy themselves and their planet is the ever-present, ever-terrifying, and ultimately most significant legacy of World War II.

Notes

1. Pierre Renouvin, *World War II and Its Origins* (New York: Harper & Row, 1969), p. 167.
2. Z. A. B. Zeman, *Nazi Propaganda* (New York: Oxford University Press, 1973), p. 109.
3. *Documents on German Foreign Policy, 1918–1945*, vol. VI (London: Her Majesty's Stationery Office, 1956), series D, no. 433.
4. Basil H. Liddell Hart, *History of the Second World War* (New York: G. P. Putnam's Sons, 1970), pp. 73–74.
5. Winston S. Churchill, *The Second World War: Their Finest Hour* (Boston: Houghton Mifflin, 1949), 2:225–226.
6. Quoted in William L. Shirer, *The Rise and Fall of the Third Reich* (New York: Simon & Schuster, 1960), p. 860.
7. *Hitler's Secret Conversations, 1941–1944*, with an introductory essay by H. R. Trevor Roper (New York: Farrar, Straus, Young, 1953), p. 508.
8. Quoted in Gordon Wright, *The Ordeal of Total War* (New York: Harper Torchbooks, 1968), p. 124.
9. Quoted in Norman Cohn, *Warrant for Genocide* (New York: Harper Torchbooks, 1969), p. 188.
10. Gerda Weissman Klein, *All But My Life* (New York: Hill & Wang, 1957), p. 89.
11. Judith Sternberg Newman, *In the Hell of Auschwitz* (New York: Exposition, 1964), p. 18.
12. *Nazi Conspiracy and Aggression* VI (Washington, D.C.: United States Government Printing Office, 1964), pp. 787–789.
13. Quoted in Joseph Borkin, *The Crime and Punishment of I. G. Farben* (New York: The Free Press, 1978), p. 143.
14. Gisella Perl, *I Was a Doctor in Auschwitz* (New York: International Universities Press, 1948), p. 80.
15. Excerpted in George H. Stein, *Hitler* (Englewood Cliffs, N.J.: Prentice-Hall, 1968), p. 84.

Suggested Reading

Baumont, Maurice, *The Origins of the Second World War* (1978). A brief work by a distinguished French scholar.

Calvocoressi, Peter, and Wint, Guy, *Total War* (1972). A good account of World War II.

Cohn, Norman, *Warrant for Genocide* (1966). An astute analysis of the mythical components of modern anti-Semitism.

Des Pres, Terrence, *The Survivors* (1976). A sensitive analysis of life in the death camp.

Eubank, Keith, *The Origins of World War II* (1969). A brief introduction, with a good bibliographical essay.

Gilbert, Martin, and Gott, Martin, *The Appeasers* (1963). A study of British weakness in the face of Hitler's threats.

Hilberg, Raul, *The Destruction of the European Jews* (1967). A monumental study of the Holocaust.

Hildebrand, Klaus, *The Foreign Policy of the Third Reich* (1973). A brief assessment of Nazi foreign policy.

Marks, Sally, *The Illusion of Peace* (1976). The failure to establish peace in the period 1918–1933.

Michel, Henri, *The Shadow War* (1972). An analysis of the European resistance movement, 1939–1945.

———, *The Second World War*, 2 vols. (1975). Translation of an important study by a prominent French historian.

Remak, Joachim, *The Origins of the Second World War* (1976). A useful essay followed by documents.

Review Questions

1. What efforts promoted reconciliation during the 1920s? How did these efforts only foster the illusion of peace?

2. What were Hitler's foreign-policy aims?

3. Why did Britain and France practice a policy of appeasement?

4. Discuss the significance of each of the following: Italy's invasion of Ethiopia (1935); Germany's remilitarization of the Rhineland (1936); the Spanish Civil War (1936–1939); Germany's union with Austria (1938); the occupation of Prague (1939); and the Nazi-Soviet Pact (1939).

5. What factors made possible the quick fall of France?

6. What problems did the German army face in Russia?

7. Describe the New Order the Nazis established in Europe.

8. Discuss the significance of each of the following battles: Midway (1942); Stalingrad (1942–1943); El Alamein (1942); and D-Day (1944).

9. What was the legacy of World War II?

PART VI

The Contemporary World:
The Global Age
Since 1945

CHAPTER 33

Western Europe Since 1945:
Recovery and Realignment

THE COLD WAR

WESTERN EUROPE SINCE 1949
ECONOMIC DEVELOPMENTS
POLITICAL DEVELOPMENTS
PROBLEMS AND TENSIONS

THE LEADING WESTERN EUROPEAN STATES
FRANCE
WEST GERMANY
GREAT BRITAIN
ITALY

EUROPEAN UNITY

A T THE END of World War II, Winston Churchill lamented: "What is Europe now? A rubble heap, a charnel house, a breeding ground for pestilence and hate."[1] Everywhere the survivors counted their dead. War casualties had been relatively light in western Europe. England and the Commonwealth suffered 460,000 casualties; France, 570,000; and Italy, 450,000. War casualties were heavier in the east—5 million people in Germany, one in every five persons in the total population of Poland (largely because of the extermination of 3 million Polish Jews), one in every ten in Yugoslavia, and over 20 million in the Soviet Union. The material destruction had been unprecedentedly heavy in the battle zones of northwestern Europe, northern Italy, and Germany, growing worse farther east where Hitler's and Stalin's armies had fought without mercy to people, animals, or the environment. Industry, transportation, and communication had come to a virtual standstill; bridges, canals, dikes, and farmlands were ruined. Ragged, worn people picked among the rubble and bartered their valuables for food, while strangers straggled by. Members of families looked for each other; prisoners of war made their way home; Jews from extermination camps or from hiding places returned to life; displaced persons by the millions sought refuge.

An estimated 40 to 50 million people in central and eastern Europe (as much as the entire population of France) were driven from their homes as part of the boundary changes imposed by the Red Army, or fled in order to escape from Stalin's terror. They included Finns, Estonians, Latvians, Lithuanians, Poles, Czechs, Rumanians, Ukrainians, and above all Germans—an enforced *Völkerwanderung* ("migration of nations") of people too exhausted to complain, their suffering on a scale with the human sacrifices of the war itself. In France, some collaborators were lynched before courts could be set up. In western Germany, citizens were paraded past piles of skeletonlike corpses from concentration camps.

THE COLD WAR

Among the heavy anxieties of those days one stood out: what was to be the future order of Europe? Having escaped from German tyranny, would Soviet communism now swallow up Europe? One great conflict having just ended, another one, called the *cold war* (in a phrase coined in 1947 by American financier Bernard Baruch), immediately took its place. Would the contest between the United States and the Soviet Union, the two superpowers, erupt into still another world war?

The causes of the cold war were embedded in the divergent historical experience and the incompatible universal aims of the United States and the Soviet Union, which clashed head-on as a new global order took shape. Hitler's empire in Europe had collapsed and left a vacuum: which superpower was to fill it? In the world at large the overseas empires of Britain, France, and other western European nations were dissolving: which superpower was to become the predominant influence?

During the war the incompatibility of basic aims had been glossed over. Western self-interest had dictated giving the utmost support to the Red Army—the more powerful it was, the easier would be the western onslaught against Hitler. Stalin, however, had never shed his Bolshevik fear of capitalist superiority. Once the common danger receded, the underlying incompatibility pushed again to the fore, aggravated by the flush of victory and current conditions.

The incompatibility of objectives became clear even before the armistice. As the Red Army moved west, the fate of the peoples of eastern Europe hung in the balance. Would they be able to determine their own future as promised in the Atlantic Charter of 1941, which outlined English and American war aims? Or would Stalin treat them as conquered peoples, knowing that left to their own devices they would return to their traditional anti-Soviet orientation?

Attention first focused on Poland. At the Yalta Conference in early 1945 the nature of the new Polish government had also become controversial: was it to be a Soviet puppet or a pro-Western democracy? Whatever the diplomats said, the answer was provided when the Red Army occupied Poland; Stalin did as he wished. Were the Americans to endanger postwar cooperation with the Soviet Union, or even to start World War III in order to "liberate" Poland? It was the same with all the other eastern European countries overrun by the Red Army. Stalin was not yet able to introduce the full rigor of Soviet rule, but the Soviet occupation of eastern Europe was considered a dire calamity by westerners who could do nothing to prevent the extension of Soviet power.

The fate of Germany became an even more crucial bone of contention. The division of Germany into zones of occupation had been agreed to in 1944. The capital, Berlin, located within the Soviet zone, was to be the seat of the joint Allied Control Commission. A permanent partition of Germany was ruled out at the Potsdam Conference in July–August 1945 and joint reparations imposed in principle. Yet from the start the Soviets proceeded on their own, removing from their zone all portable resources and taking them to their own ravaged territories. The Soviets also brought a planeload of docile German communists under Walter Ulbricht (1893–1973) to take charge of political reconstruction. But the Soviets kept out observers from the other occupying powers—the United States, Britain, and later France.

The foreign ministers of the four occupying powers kept trying—in Paris, Moscow, and London—to arrive at common conditions for a peace treaty with Germany, but each time they drifted further apart. In 1947 England and the United States joined their zones and in 1949 the West German Federal Republic was established. Stalin matched every step of the Western powers by formally consolidating communist rule in his zone, thus adding

Legend:
- Territory lost by Germany
- Communist countries
- "Iron Curtain" after 1950
- NATO members
- Nonallied Western countries
- □ Original Common Market members
- △ Subsequent Common Market members

NORWAY
Oslo
SWEDEN
Stockholm
BALTIC SEA
SCOTLAND
NORTH SEA
DENMARK
Copenhagen
Incorporated into U.S.S.R., 1945
N. IRELAND
Belfast
Dublin
GREAT BRITAIN
IRELAND
WALES
ENGLAND
London
Gdansk (Danzig)
Hamburg
Szczecin (Stettin)
Berlin
Warsaw
POLAND
NETHERLANDS
Amsterdam
Antwerp
The Hague
Allied occupation, 1945-1955
E. GERMANY
Established, 1949
Dresden
Vistula R.
U.S.A.
Canada
Iceland
Brussels
BELGIUM
Bonn
Frankfurt
Ruhr R.
Elbe R.
Prague
CZECHOSLOVAKIA
ATLANTIC OCEAN
Paris
LUX.
W. GERMANY
Established, 1949
Nuremberg
Seine R.
Strasbourg
Rhine R.
Danube R.
Vienna
Budapest
HUNGARY
FRANCE
Loire R.
Munich
Salzburg
AUSTRIA
Allied occupa-tion, 1945-1955
Zagreb
Belgrade
SWITZERLAND
Geneva
Lyons
Milan
Trieste
Bordeaux
Garonne R.
Rhone R.
Po R.
ADRIATIC SEA
YUGOSLAVIA
BASQUE
Marseilles
Toulouse
Ebro R.
Barcelona
CORSICA
ELBA
ITALY
VATICAN CITY
Rome
Naples
Tirane
ALBANIA
Madrid
Lisbon
PORTUGAL
Tagus R.
SPAIN
Defense Treaty with U.S.A., 1953
SARDINIA
MEDITERRANEAN SEA
SICILY
Gibraltar (Gr. Br.)

MAP 33.1 WESTERN EUROPE AFTER 1945

anguish over the partition of Germany to the mounting fear of oppression in eastern Europe.

Not content with entrenching himself in eastern and central Europe, Stalin—so it seemed to alarmed Americans—tried to inter-

fere in the affairs of the western zone of Germany as well as in the internal affairs of France and Italy, where after the war communist parties participated in government coalitions. In the eastern Mediterranean Stalin was

Truman Doctrine

blamed for the Greek Civil War of 1946, in which communist partisans fought the monarchists. Stalin was also accused of claiming The Straits of Constantinople and he prolonged the Soviet wartime occupation of northern Iran.

The United States responded to these Soviet threats. Public opinion had at first favored "bringing the boys home" as soon as the war was over. In late 1946, however, it seemed better to continue to occupy Germany as long as the Soviets did. At the same time, Churchill warned of the "iron curtain" that Stalin had drawn from the Baltic Sea to the Adriatic, cutting Europe in half. In March 1947, alarmed by the threat of Soviet penetration into the eastern Mediterranean and by British weakness in that area, President Truman proclaimed the Truman Doctrine: "it must be the policy of the United States to support free people who are resisting attempted subjugation by armed minorities or by outside pressures." American military and economic support soon went to Greece and Turkey. In order to drive home to the American electorate the urgency of economic and military aid, Truman warned of the danger of world revolution.

In June 1947, Secretary of State George Marshall announced an impressive scheme of economic aid to Europe (the European Recovery Program) for rebuilding prosperity and stability. By December 1959, the Marshall Plan had supplied Europe with a total of over 74 billion dollars, a modest pump priming for the subsequent record upswing in American, European, and even global prosperity. Western Europe recovered and the United States gained economically strong allies.

Marshall Plan

The Marshall Plan, the product of apprehension over Soviet expansion, in turn forced Stalin to intensify his control over eastern Europe. In February 1948 he replaced, with couplike suddenness, the mildly procommunist coalition government of Czechoslovakia by an outright Stalinist clique. Stalin also promoted a Communist Information Bureau (Cominform) to subject communist parties in eastern and western Europe to tighter obedi-

ence. By these and similar actions he profoundly alarmed western Europeans who, three years after the end of the war, redoubled their search for military security.

The most spectacular test between the two superpowers took place from June 1948 to May 1949 when the Soviet authorities severed all overland access to the western sectors of Berlin (occupied by French, British, and American troops), expecting to starve into submission a half-city of about 2 million inhabitants who, because of their freedom, were "a bone in the communist throat" (as Khrushchev later put it). West Berlin was saved by a massive airlift, as the French, British, and Americans under American direction heroically flew in supplies around the clock in all kinds of weather. During the agonies of the airlift the outline of the present European order became visible.

It was clear by 1949 that the Soviet Union through the presence of the Red Army was entrenched in eastern Europe. Europe was now divided, its division marked at the center by the division of Germany, and the division of Germany by the division of Berlin, each half oriented toward one or the other of the superpowers, each consolidating its unity under the continuing tensions of the cold war. Few Europeans at the time were reconciled to the division of Europe. Not all of them are even now (although the partition of Germany caused little regret to non-Germans).

For their protection against the Soviet armed presence in central Europe, Great Britain, France, and the Benelux countries (Belgium, the Netherlands, and Luxembourg) in 1948 drew up a military alliance called the Brussels Pact. Aware of the inadequacy of the Brussels Pact they joined, in 1949, the United States and Canada, as well as Portugal, Norway, Iceland, Denmark, Greece, and Turkey in the North Atlantic Treaty Organization (NATO) for military security. NATO offered a shield under which political and economic life could return to normal. By 1949 Stalin's satellites in what is now called *Eastern Europe* had become sovietized as "peoples republics," but

Brussels Pact →

NATO

GERMANY'S POSTWAR RUBBLE: DRESDEN, 1946 Civilization seemed at a standstill in Western Europe at the war's end. The end of the military war, however, was not the end of international conflict. The cold war soon replaced the war of tanks and bombers. (United Press International)

the core countries of what is now called *Western Europe* had returned to democratic constitutions. Government in Western Europe rested in the hands of moderate parties setting the course for social democracy and re-establishing, after an initial preference for nationalization and state planning, the pre-eminence of private enterprise (although under strengthened public supervision).

WESTERN EUROPE SINCE 1949

Economic Developments

The most striking fact of recent history in the West, as in the world generally, is the unprece-dented economic advance. Between the end of the war and the late 1970s production in Western Europe and the United States, as elsewhere, surpassed all previous records. The ascent was marred by a few temporary slow-downs; by the late 1960s it had begun to level off. By the time the economic advance came to an end, it had created a new world economic order requiring adjustments in Western Europe, the United States, and around the world. In Western Europe the standard of living increased dramatically. Health service, housing, and educational opportunities were provided for nearly everyone. Never in all history have the world's peoples multiplied so rapidly and increased their material fortunes so markedly as in the years since the end of World War II.

The miraculous economic recovery of Western Europe is sometimes reckoned as a triumph of capitalism. But the term "capitalism" is an oversimplification. The Western European economy has always been the product of a fluctuating interaction between diverse public and private interests. The state has always been present, prodding, controlling, and directing, with an eye to the survival of the country as a whole.

In the immediate aftermath of the war the necessities of reconstruction demanded the fullest use of state authority. Following long-standing tradition most European governments extended their control over essential economic functions. Nearly everywhere the biggest banks were nationalized, together with key industries and public utilities; nationwide economic planning was harnessed to the same purpose. Social welfare was also extended. With the arrival of Marshall Plan aid and under American prodding the trend swung back toward private initiative working together with public authority. All national economies in Western Europe thus became "mixed" economies, combining public and private enterprises in complex interlocking arrangements.

The increase in the public sector everywhere, however, has been offset in recent years in the private sector by mergers, consolidations, and the rise of large holding corporations often with monopoly or near-monopoly standing. Under the stimulus of the expansion of American business and capital into Western Europe (particularly in the computer field), many European companies have become multinational and grown bigger than any nationalized industry. The Western European economy is now dominated by gigantic private and public enterprises that are tied to other parts of the world and subject to a growing volume of transnational regulation and guidance.

At the same time the huge burst of productivity and affluence has created an intense dependence on essential outside raw materials, chiefly oil from the Middle East. Like the United States and Japan—and most Third World countries—Western Europe after 1973 found itself at the mercy of the Organization of Petroleum Exporting Countries (OPEC) and therefore searched for substitute sources of energy, including nuclear power.

As in all industrialized societies, the percentage of the agricultural population has continued to shrink, ranging in the early 1970s from 2 percent in England to 15 percent in France and 19 percent in Italy, without loss of agricultural productivity. On the contrary, Western European farms, rapidly modernized after the war, are producing surpluses in meat, dairy products, and wines. Except for Great Britain, Western Europe is almost self-sufficient in foodstuffs.

Political Developments

Under conditions of record prosperity, the overall trend of political life in the West since World War II has been toward constitutional democracy. Although Spain and Portugal retained their prewar dictatorships until the mid-1970s and Greece for a time wavered between democracy and dictatorship, by the late 1970s even the fringe countries had conformed to the common pattern. Membership in the European Economic Community, or Common Market (see page 768), requires democratic government; as the Common Market expands, it confirms the liberal-democratic tradition.

Popular political allegiance remained scattered among parties spread over the spectrum of political creeds (yet somewhat to the left by American standards). Communists and various factions of socialism constituted the left. The center claimed the largest support. Lacking clear formulations, the center relied on traditional convictions and proceeded pragmatically, steering a cautious course between state control and free enterprise. Depending on circumstances it might ally itself with the moderate left or the moderate right, with socialists or conservatives. The conservatives, on the whole, adhered to nineteenth-century liberalism and to laissez-faire economics. Authoritarian or protofascist right-wing movements periodically rose and waned; they never had a serious chance; nor did the terrorists, who came to the fore in the early 1970s. Terrorism stood to the left of communism or to the extreme right; militant regionalism also spawned terrorism.

Political power essentially lay with the center parties which, recovering from the destruction of the constitutional regimes before and during the war, reconstituted their political platforms around the established traditions of Western Europe: Christianity and liberal democracy. In continental Western Europe the political and economic reconstruction after the war was largely the work of Christian Democratic parties, in France known as Mouvement Républicain Populaire (MRP)—rather shortlived under the conditions of French politics; in West Germany as Christian Democratic Union (CDU), which has lasted to the present; and in Italy perennially as Christian Democrats. Great Britain, whose constitution remained intact throughout the great wars, retained its traditional two-party system. But here, too, the winning majorities for both parties came from center votes shifting either toward the Conservatives or the Labour party.

It was a sign of the times that ideologically oriented moderate socialist parties did poorly at the polls. Strong immediately after the war, they lost support the longer they adhered to their doctrines. They were hurt by the new social awareness in private enterprise, the rise of the welfare state, and the complexity of modern life. Dogmatic socialists quarreled, splintered, and declined, or else they created reformist mass parties slightly left of center. For example, the West German Social Democratic party (SPD) and the British Labour party supported a number of mildly socialist policies but avoided a socialist program.

The major communist parties of Western Europe, especially those of Italy and France, could not escape the temper of the times. Dropped from the government coalitions in 1947, communists steadily held their own in the next three decades, polling in France between one-fifth and one-fourth of the total vote, and in Italy up to one-third. Yet in national politics communists were condemned to frustrating ineffectual opposition, even in Italy. Barred from national leadership, communists have been effective in local government, especially in Italy where they run the administration of most communities, including big cities.

Yet patriotism, prosperity, the brutality of the Soviet system, and the complexity of all things modern eroded the dogmatism of Western European communists as well as their dependence on the Kremlin. By the mid-1970s a new variety of communism called *Eurocommunism* emerged. Eurocommunism still cherished the communist tradition (thereby keeping alive traditional anticommunism), but was determined to prove itself under the established democratic ground rules as a mass party dedicated to better government, without rigid ideological commitment to the Soviet party line. But Eurocommunism was beset by internal contradictions; although critical of the Soviet Union, it could not free itself from association with it.

Problems and Tensions

Western Europe has not escaped serious problems and tensions. With the rise of the public sector and the increase in social services, government and bureaucracy grew huge and more impersonal. Individuals felt dwarfed by the state and lost in a complex interdependent society.

Youths especially were in ferment, tending to repudiate the new affluence and the complexity on which it was based. They also emphasized its drawbacks: stark inequality in the world, social callousness at home, the breakdown of human intimacy and community, and the mounting strain on human energy and integrity. In their protest they sided with a romantic and ostensibly antimodern counterculture which, paradoxically, was ultramodern in its disdain for traditional middle-class restraints, above all in sex, and also in its sense of solidarity with all oppressed peoples around the world. On the whole, the protest was nonpolitical, a part of the new "youth culture" that—an illustration of the new complexity—had split off from the dominant culture of adult society.

In 1968 youthful frustration for a time broke into politics, angrily and sometimes destructively, foremost in France and slightly less drastically throughout Western Europe (as it did, more mildly, in the anti–Vietnam War agitation in the United States). During May 1968, a spontaneous and embittered demonstration of students and workers in Paris set off a massive general strike such as France had not seen since 1936. Yet no revolution followed, no sudden social change, only a conservative backlash at the next national election. The majority of the French people, like their contemporaries elsewhere, realized that they cannot escape from the burden of complexity and bigness in contemporary state and society. The events of 1968, however, made them more aware of the need for the human touch in all official business.

Some impatient young protesters meanwhile turned to outright terrorism, especially in West Germany and Italy. In their eyes, the entire system of state and society was inhumane and deserved destruction by any means available. The targets of their attacks were leading representatives of "the system": politicians, industrialists, judges, and the police. After a few spectacular assassinations public opinion began to favor more effective countermeasures, thus curtailing terrorist violence, at least in West Germany.

Tensions in the body politic were also reflected in the rise of separatist and nationalist movements within well-established nation-states. Great Britain was troubled by nationalist movements in Wales, Scotland, and Northern Ireland, where Catholics and Protestants, driven by long-standing political and religious differences, continued to murder and maim each other; the violence occasionally spilled over into England. France suffered from separatist movements in the northwest and southwest. In Belgium, Walloons and Flemings strained their country's unity. In Spain the restoration of constitutional government after the death of General Franco in 1975 was marred by the terrorism of Basque extremists hoping to create a Basque state. Terrorists of all kinds established links with their counterparts in other troubled areas of the world, creating a sort of international terrorist movement. Although raw violence provided no answer to the intricate problems of modern society, it did offer opportunities for politically aware and self-denying heroism lacking in contemporary life.

The massive spurt of affluence had an unsettling effect on culture as well. Although prosperity provided more people with more material goods, it also encouraged a hedonistic self-indulgence that was contrary to the ascetic strain in Western tradition. Material security and abundance undermined the bourgeois work ethic; life became too easy. Intellectual and artistic life was both stimulated and fragmented by the influx of people, goods, and human values from around the world. In its new wealth and immense diversity of stimuli Western Europe was increasingly caught up in the cultural ferment of the new globalism.

The guardians of traditional religion were among the chief victims of cultural diversity and the easy life. The Catholic church passed through much collective soul-searching during the great council of Vatican II (1962–1965), asking how traditional dogma and pastoral care could be reconciled to modern conditions. Earnestly searching for answers, it infused new vitality into the worldwide church. Among Protestants, whether in the established state churches (as in West Germany, the

Scandinavian countries, or Great Britain), or in free churches, confusion also reigned. Church membership generally declined, especially among established (or state) churches; some fundamentalist churches and sects like Jehovah's Witnesses gained members, as did non-Western world religions like Bahai. Underneath the outward conformity and ready acceptance of the material boons of contemporary society many people in Western Europe lived in spiritual doubt, their inner lives out of tune with their outward existence; they lacked a clear vision for the future. Like their American counterparts most Western Europeans accepted the Now Age.

By 1980, however, there seemed to be cause for apprehension. After a full generation of unprecedented economic growth the economy of Western Europe was faced with staggering difficulties. The pressures for an even higher standard of living had for some time exceeded gains in productivity, driving up wages and prices, in Europe and around the world. Costs kept rising as more marginal resources were tapped and services became more extensive. Inflation increased, at various rates depending on social and political conditions in each country. England in 1974–1975 recorded the highest annual rate of inflation (28 percent), with Italy next; only the West German mark (and the Swiss franc) remained relatively stable. Different rates of inflation in turn created serious imbalances in currency relations between the chief trading partners within Western Europe and around the world, which affected their competitive position, increasing unemployment and promoting domestic discord.

A prominent source of economic adversity was the constantly rising price of oil controlled after 1973 by OPEC; Western Europe was dangerously dependent on non-Europeans for its energy. It also found its economy strained by the economic slowdown in the United States and other parts of the world. In addition it faced the mounting pressure of the world's fast-growing population on the earth's resources.

THE LEADING WESTERN EUROPEAN STATES

France

After 1945 France quickly laid the foundation for its subsequent rapid economic advance. Under the leadership of Jean Monnet, an able group of economists and planners mapped out strategies and institutions that have become models of state guidance in a mixed economy of public and private enterprise. During the 1950s the French economy grew at a very respectable rate. In national politics the sense of common purpose was less evident. In 1946 a new constitution created the Fourth Republic, following the pattern of the Third. The center of power rested in the Chamber of Deputies controlled by ever-shifting and unstable coalitions of parties.

The twenty-six short-lived governments of the Fourth Republic were weak. Between 1945 and 1958, though, they valiantly coped with a number of grave problems, putting down communist-led strikes in 1947 and 1948, assisting in the organization of Western European defense, laying the groundwork for the European Economic Community, and promoting political reconciliation with Germany.

The biggest problem France faced was decolonization. For the most part relations between France and its colonies and dependencies remained peaceful; Morocco, for instance, quietly attained independence. Yet in two areas the French army fought colonial liberation movements to the bitter end. In Indochina the French army in 1954 suffered a resounding defeat. In Algeria, administratively a part of France proper, French settlers and soldiers were determined to thwart demands for independence.

The long and bloody Algerian conflict had serious repercussions for French political life. In 1958 the insubordination of army leaders brought down the Fourth Republic with a resounding call for the return of General de Gaulle. De Gaulle then wrote the constitution of the Fifth Republic, largely to suit his own style as president. Elections were held regularly, reinforced by referendums, but they were manipulated to give support to the president; in emergencies the president could even claim dictatorial powers. Though De Gaulle thought of himself as towering above political parties, his political instincts remained moderate.

De Gaulle's grand design was simple enough: to restore France to its rightful place in Europe and the world. At home this meant that France had to make itself dynamic, modernize its economy, encourage science and technology, and regain a common will. Abroad it had to assert its presence by all means available—cultural, economic, political, and even military. De Gaulle insisted that France have its own nuclear force, and he pulled France out of the NATO high command. He increased French prestige among Third World Countries, consenting to Algerian independence over the protest of the army and retaining the good will of the new African states formerly under French rule. But his France, a mere middle-size state in the global world, was too small for De Gaulle's ambition; his grand style in foreign policy did not survive him. Under his successors, Georges Pompidou and Valéry Giscard d'Estaing, the power of the presidency has lost some luster. Yet the Fifth Republic built around a strong president has proved a suitable instrument of national advance and economic planning.

Over the years the Fifth Republic has followed a moderately conservative course. It has been held back by the forces of tradition. The French distrust their government as well as impersonal large-scale industrial or commercial organizations. Many French peasants have failed to become efficient farmers; French countryside in the west and southwest is drained of people. Society is localized and divided by social status. The political parties on which the government relies are unstable and shifting, centered more on personalities than issues. Deeply patriotic, the French people fear that becoming modern means becoming less French.

West Germany

Defeated, occupied, its cities in ruins, and branded as a moral outcast for the horrors that Nazi rule had brought to Europe, Germany in 1945 was a dispirited nation. Divided at first among four occupying powers, it was also politically ineffectual. The state of Prussia was declared dissolved; extensive eastern lands were handed to Poland and the Soviet Union; some territory also was lost to France. The dream of national glory that had provided the chief momentum in German life for over a century was ended. The German people had been torn apart, their national ambition crushed.

By 1949 the Federal Republic of Germany, formed from the three Western zones of occupation, faced a hostile Soviet-dominated German Democratic Republic in the East. The partition of Germany signified not only the destruction of Germany's traditional political identity, but also a personal tragedy for almost all Germans: families were split as communication between the two Germanies was interrupted. The national trauma reached a peak in August 1961 when the East German government suddenly threw up a wall dividing the city of Berlin and for years tightly sealed off East from West Germany.

By 1949 the cold war began to work to West Germany's advantage. Feared and despised though they were, the West Germans were needed. Located next door to the Red Army they possessed valuable manpower for the defense of Western Europe. Even more important, German industry and expertise were indispensable for a revived Western Europe and the success of the Marshall Plan. Finally, a democratic West Germany would aid the course of Western European unity.

On this basis the Federal Republic of Germany (far larger than its Soviet counterpart in the East and the most populous of all Western European countries) began to build a political identity of its own. The new West Germany was a demilitarized and decentralized federal

CHARLES DE GAULLE (right) AND KONRAD ADENAUER *Adolf Eichner* De Gaulle's Fifth Republic restored France to a respected position among nations, though not to such a grand one as De Gaulle had envisioned. Konrad Adenauer similarly guided the Federal Republic of Germany toward a remarkable economic recovery, as well as a position of trust among the European community and world nations. (United Press International)

state consisting of ten member states (plus West Berlin, which continued to exist under a special status). Under its constitution the executive power was held by the chancellor, who was checked by both a democratically elected parliament and the representatives of the member states. Because of constitutional precautions against the proliferation of parties, only three emerged: two dominant parties, the Christian-Democratic Union (CDU), the Socialist party of Germany (SPD), and a minor one: the Free Democratic party (FPD); the latter enjoyed the advantage of being indispensable to either of the major parties for a parliamentary majority. The CDU was the dominant party under the long chancellorship

(1949–1963) of Konrad Adenauer. In 1966 the CDU entered into a "grand coalition" with the SPD, its archopponent, from which the latter—now a nonideological mass party—emerged as the leader (under Chancellors Willy Brandt and Helmut Schmidt). In all these years German political life remained remarkably calm, without challenge to the constitution. Neither radical intellectuals nor terrorists gained influence.

The Nazi past remains a moral embarrassment and a source of anxiety to West Germany. The Nuremberg trials of the major war criminals were followed by de-Nazification under West German courts. Members of Nazi elite organizations were barred from public office and higher education. Many people guilty of atrocities were prosecuted; others went into hiding in Germany or abroad; Jews themselves tracked down some notable fugitives like Adolf Eichmann and brought them to justice. The search and the trials still continue, the West German Parliament having consistently refused to enact a statute of limitations on crimes committed under the Nazis. The government also has paid restitution to Israel and to survivors among Nazi victims and their kin.

Most older Germans have tried to forget the past and not ask hard questions. Even young people were undecided, caught between the democratic values introduced after the war and the national heritage; the schools often sidetracked discussion. Since the 1960s, however, the major aspects of Nazi rule have been openly aired; Nazi anti-Semitism has been dramatized by the showing on German television of an American program called *Holocaust*. Yet German minds are still troubled by the Nazi years.

Among the Germans who had shown moral courage under the Nazi regime, Konrad Adenauer (1876–1967) stood out. More than anyone else he therefore shaped the character of the new West Germany. A vigorous old-timer—he was seventy-five when he became chancellor—Adenauer represented the pro-

Western liberal-democratic tradition of the Weimar Republic. His policy was simple: to restore respect for Germany in cooperation with the United States and the leading states of Western Europe. Never giving up hope for the reunification of Germany, Adenauer worked foremost for the integration of West Germany into the emerging Western Europe community. Yet while boycotting all relations with the communist German Democratic Republic, Adenauer also promoted normal relations with Moscow. As a patriot he rebuilt a cautious continuity with the German past, courageously shouldering responsibility for the crimes of the Nazi regime.

Adenauer's political style, not unlike that of De Gaulle, showed at times scant regard for the fine points of the constitution. But his chancellorship proved popular, for it provided the stability and order required for West Germany's spectacular economic advance. Adenauer's economic policy was conducted by Minister of Finance Ludwig Erhard, who distrusted all large-scale planning. Erhard preferred private enterprise in a liberal market economy safeguarded from monopolies and made socially responsible through the extensive participation of labor unions. Labor representatives now sit on the boards of directors in major corporations. Given the opportunity, West Germans threw themselves into rebuilding their economy and their country, quickly creating a citadel of economic strength, their exports famous throughout the world and their currency the soundest in Western Europe. The whole world admired the West German "economic miracle."

Adenauer's policy paid off within a few years; West Germany regained its sovereignty. In 1955 a cautiously remilitarized West Germany became a member of NATO and in 1957 a founding member of the European Economic Community (EEC). Banking on their good relations with Western Europe and the United States, the SPD chancellors since 1968 have pursued a cautious policy of restoring normal relations with their Eastern European neighbors, including the German Democratic Republic. After 1972 both Germanies accepted the partition of their once-common fatherland as permanent; they began to conduct normal diplomatic relations.

Since 1945 the West Germans have undergone a remarkable transformation. Working together under an imposed democratic constitution, they have found prosperity a superior substitute for military might. They are now leaders within the European Economic Community, a mainstay even in the world economy.

Great Britain

In 1945 Britain was a member of the victorious alliance. It had escaped foreign occupation and suffered less physical damage than any other European belligerent; its political institutions were intact, its prestige and democratic convictions riding high. Yet after this moment of glory it passed through a steady decline, requiring of its people a drastic reassessment of their place in the world, without the happy ending of an economic boom.

World War II compounded Britain's long-standing economic woes, leaving the country impoverished and highly vulnerable in its dependence on imported food and raw materials. The British Empire was gradually and peaceably dismantled. Unlike the French, the English fought no last-ditch wars for retaining colonial control. British sea power waned, replaced by the American navy and air force. Confronted with the choice between maintaining a global military presence and building a welfare state at home, the British people clearly preferred the latter. Though still enjoying a special relationship with the United States, the British were thrown back on themselves and their neighbors in continental Europe. Among themselves they quarreled over autonomy for Scotland and Wales. In the late 1960s the ever-simmering conflict between

Protestants and the large Catholic minority in Northern Ireland broke into open and often vicious violence.

In their association with Western Europe the British also fared poorly. Their first application for membership to the EEC made in 1961, was vetoed by De Gaulle. Twelve years later, in 1973, another application was successful. But it soon became apparent that Britain not only constituted an economic liability rather than an asset to the other members, but it gained no immediate benefit for itself. Poor, insular, and hesitant about merging its fortune with Western Europe, the United Kingdom still glories in the traditions of empire, but by current standards of power and productivity it has become second-rate.

Under these circumstances successive British governments have done well in holding the ship of state together. A Labour government under Clement Attlee (1883–1967), elected immediately after the war, carried out the wartime promises of increased social services. Health care for the British people, traditionally deficient by comparison with Western Europe, was particularly improved. For better control over the national economy the Labour government also nationalized the Bank of England, public transport, and the coal mines; eventually even the iron and steel industries came under government ownership.

The Labour government, which lost the 1951 election largely because it seemed to have prolonged the postwar austerity unnecessarily, was succeeded by the Conservatives. With Winston Churchill as prime minister, the Conservatives ushered in a period of prosperity. In 1959, under Harold Macmillan, the Conservatives successfully campaigned for re-election under the slogan: "You've never had it so good." They favored private enterprise but continued the extension of the welfare state, most notably by an ambitious public construction program that greatly improved British housing. The Conservatives also modernized railway transport and expanded higher education.

Economic setbacks, scandal, failure in for-

eign policy, and indifferent leadership among the Conservatives brought the Labour Party back into power from 1964 to 1970, with the promise of boosting the lagging economy. That, however, proved an impossible task. British industry had not modernized itself as rapidly as its chief competitors. It was hampered by poor management and frequent strikes, many of them caused by disputes among rival labor unions. British exports were lagging while imports soared, causing perennial balance-of-payment deficits; the value of the pound continued to decline. Costly imports and pressures for higher wages and welfare benefits produced a high inflation rate.

Behind the economic ills lay a political problem: how to restrain the demands of British labor for a higher income and how to counter the strikes by which the workers backed up their demands. On this ground, the Labour party was weak, since it depended on worker support. Under the strain it even proved difficult to keep peace between the pragmatic majority and the socialist left wing. Yet when the Conservatives returned to power in 1970, they were equally powerless to restrain the unions. Were they to use force against coal miners on strike during the energy crisis of 1973? Prime Minister Edward Heath declared a state of emergency and soon called a general election over the question: who rules Britain, the government or the unions? The voters preferred the Labour party, by a small margin. Reversing themselves in 1979, the voters threw out the weak Labour government that had proved unable to hold the labor unions to its wage policy. They elected a Conservative government under Margaret Thatcher, the first British woman prime minister.

Ahead lies a full range of problems. The deepening economic crisis, barely stemmed by North Sea oil, necessitates willingness to tighten belts now for a better income later. British society must surmount its surviving class distinctions and its division into an impoverished industrial north and a more prosperous metropolitan south.

Italy

A country half the size of France yet with a population larger by several million, Italy has always occupied an ambiguous position in Europe. It has been respected, even revered, for its illustrious Roman past. Italy has also been condemned or even ridiculed for its backwardness in modern times, for its shaky or dubious liberal democracy, for its penchant for living beyond its means, for its me-too desire for power culminating in Mussolini's theatrical bid for empire. The victory of the Anglo-American countries allied with the Soviet Union had a sobering effect. Fascism was refuted, its chief henchman punished. In 1946 even the monarchy, discredited by its subservience to Mussolini, was rejected. Italy was humbled and ravaged by war.

After the war, Italy was a democratic republic that even the communists were pledged to uphold. The constitution, approved in 1947, resembled that of the French Fourth Republic, which meant that Italy would suffer from weak and unstable government. The average span of Italian cabinets to the present has been less than a year.

Hopeful for the future, the new republic could not escape the past. Italy has always been divided by internal cleavages, the chief of which is the contrast between north and south, each worlds apart from the other. A lively localism impeded national unity; so did an anarchical individualism. Far from forming an organic whole, the state and the individual were in continuous tension and conflict. The political parties, scattered over a wide spectrum of opinion from communism to neofascism, likewise enjoyed little cohesion, except for the communists. The socialists were ceaselessly in agitation among themselves, without, however, losing their following. The Christian Democrats were the leading party, polling around 40 percent of the vote and closely associated with the Catholic church. They have contributed continuity to Italian politics, supplying the prime ministers and forming and reforming coalitions with lesser parties. From 1976 to 1978 they even enjoyed the tacit support of the communists. But the Christian Democrats were only a loose alliance of Catholics split into right, center, and left, forever wrangling among themselves. In short, the parties as well as the national temperament accentuated the weakness of the constitution.

Spurred by the new postwar opportunities, Italian enterprise produced a striking economic advance. Its rate of growth culminating in the years 1958–1962, the country passed through an economic transformation that put it into the ranks of the ten leading industrial nations of the world. Private corporations (like Fiat) and industries under large government holding companies led the way in introducing an efficiency that unfortunately had no parallel in the civil service or the government. The boom was aided by cheap and abundant labor, by high profits reinvested in innovation; and by the timely discovery of natural gas and some oil in the Po Valley. As a result personal incomes, particularly in northern Italy, have come to resemble those of the richer European countries. Italy seemed to have caught up.

The sudden spurt of industrialization inevitably aggravated the traditional weaknesses in Italian society. The economic advance remained incomplete, merely superimposing a layer of progressive prosperity on a backward and divided country. In their eagerness to catch up, most Italians preferred to live well now rather than save for the future. The contradiction led to a deterioration in Italy's position in the European Economic Community and to widespread apathy in the face of mounting terrorist violence. Terrorists (not counting the criminal elements) come from the extremes at both ends of the political spectrum. The neofascists, however, have been less active than the Red Brigades, who stand to the left of the law-abiding communists. Trying to create conditions favoring the overthrow of the ineffectual democratic constitution, the terrorists have resorted to bombings, kidnapings, maimings, and political murders, not sparing in 1978 the much-respected

Moro

Aldo Moro, leader of the Christian Democratic party.

What form of government can provide better leadership? A presidential republic like De Gaulle's? A "historic compromise" between the communists and the Christian Democrats as once advocated by Enrico Berlinguer, the secretary of the Italian Communist party and leading Eurocommunist? Or a neofascist regime supported by the army? Given the strong democratic pull exerted by the European Economic Community and NATO, extreme solutions are unlikely. Yet can the Italians be persuaded to undertake the personal sacrifices and self-discipline necessary to build a vigorous administration and an economy able to strengthen the European Economic Community?

Common Market Spaak

EUROPEAN UNITY

Although Europeans share a common cultural heritage, the diversity of their history and national temperaments has burdened them in the past with incessant warfare. After two ruinous world wars many people at last began to feel that the price of violent conflict had become excessive; war no longer served any national interest. In addition, the extension of Soviet power made some form of unity imperative for all states not under Soviet domination. The first call for a united Europe was sounded by Winston Churchill who, reviving a project first launched in the seventeenth century, declared in 1946: "We must build a kind of United States of Europe."[2]

Despite such hopes the major governments of Western Europe and their peoples were unprepared suddenly to submerge their separate national traditions in a common government empowered to regulate their internal affairs. Political unity was not forthcoming, but in the field of economics the movement for unity made headway.

Western European economic cooperation began rather modestly with the creation of the European Coal and Steel Community (ECSC) in 1951. It drew together the chief Continental consumers and producers of coal and steel, the two items most essential for the rebuilding of Western Europe. Its members were France, West Germany, the three Benelux countries, and Italy, the six countries that thus became the core countries of Western European unity. Their design was to put the Ruhr industrial complex, the heart of German industrial power, under international control, thereby promoting cooperation and reconciliation as well. Their project was endorsed by Konrad Adenauer, who expected it to restore confidence in Germany. West Germany has stood in the forefront of European integration since then.

Emboldened by the success of the ECSC, the Six soon pressed forward. "In order to maintain Europe's place in the world, to restore her influence and prestige, and to ensure a continuous rise in the living standards of her people," their foreign ministers, led by Paul-Henri Spaak, prepared two treaties, signed in Rome in March 1957. One treaty created a European Atomic Energy Community (called Euratom) for joint research on nuclear energy, and the other establishing the Common Market or European Economic Community. Euratom did not flourish, but the EEC has become the focus of the European search for unity, prosperity, and power.

Minimally, the EEC was to be a customs union, creating a free market among the Six, with a common external tariff for protection from the rest of the world, yet pledged to participate in the worldwide reduction of trade barriers. At the same time the EEC aimed higher: it was to improve living conditions among the people, help reduce "the differences existing between the various regions" and countries, and mitigate "the backwardness of the less favored" among themselves. It also promised to confirm "the solidarity which binds together Europe and overseas countries" in the spirit of the United Nations. Finally, it called on the other states of Europe to join the Six "in an ever closer union."[3] Toward the outside world the EEC was empowered to act as agent for its members in all commercial transactions. It has negotiated a great variety of special agreements with an ever-widening circle of Western European states and Third World countries.

It was clear from the outset that free trade within the EEC called for increasing uniformity among all the factors affecting the marketplace. The free movement of goods and people encouraged standardization and cooperation in every aspect of the economy. For that reason, the "Eurocrats" in Brussels, the headquarters of the European Economic Community, were forever eager to extend their authority. They and the governments of the Six also worked hard to make the Common Market more inclusive. In 1973 the original Six were joined by three new members, Great Britain, Ireland, and Denmark. The Nine, calling themselves simply the European Community (EC), began to work for greater political integration. By 1979 three more states had applied for membership: Spain, Portugal, and Greece. Only Switzerland, Austria, Norway, Sweden, and Finland remain outside the EC, Finland because of its proximity to the Soviet Union; yet all of them benefit from the EC.

With the inclusion of Greece, Spain, and Portugal, the EC will face profound challenges. Apart from working with notoriously unstable governments, it must harmonize competition among Western Europe's farmers raising similar crops. Even more ominous is the challenge posed by the rising prices of oil and energy. Meanwhile political integration among the Nine has made good progress. In June 1979 direct elections were held for the delegates to the European Parliament sitting at Strasbourg. Although possessing only advisory power, the Strasbourg Assembly provides the first transnational representative forum for the discussion of common concerns. The Nine also have kept up the momentum toward cooperation in

their foreign policy. Their foreign ministers meet for regular consultation, trying to head off any conflicts among themselves or with outside powers. In order to negotiate effectively with the Soviet Union they presented a common front in 1973–1975 at the Helsinki Conference on Security and Cooperation in Europe—the larger Europe that includes the Soviet Union and its Eastern European satellites. Favoring relaxation of tension between the superpowers and welcoming negotiations for arms limitations, they joined the United States in signing the Helsinki Agreement, thereby accepting as permanent the division of Europe produced by World War II. The hopes of 1975, however, were not fulfilled; tension continued, keeping NATO a major concern in the European Community as well as across the North Atlantic. It is NATO, of which the United States is a member, and not the European Community, that provides the ultimate guarantee of the survival of Western Europe.

Seen in the larger context, the groping search for Western European unity is one of the many interlacing and crisscrossing contemporary experiments in international and transnational cooperation. Alongside their efforts to overcome the historical differences among themselves and to create a common European identity, the peoples of Western Europe are laced into global interdependence. Western Europeans now occupy one of the several key centers of the world community, irreversibly tied, like all others, to the unpredictable interaction of all with all, and overburdened by the consequences.

Notes

1. Quoted in Walter Laqueur, *Europe Since Hitler* (Baltimore: Penguin Books, 1970), p. 118.
2. Quoted in Roger Morton, *West European Politics Since 1945* (London: P. T. Botsford, 1972), p. 91.

3. Preamble to Treaty of Rome, 1958, in ibid., pp. 132–133.

Suggested Reading

Becker, Jillian, *Hitler's Children: The Story of the Baader-Meinhof Terrorist Gang* (1977). Good insights into the terrorist state of mind.

Böll, Heinrich, *Group Portrait with Lady* (1973). The foremost West German novelist looks back at the last years of the Nazi regime.

De Gaulle, Charles, *Memoirs of Hope, Renewal and Endeavor* (1971). An autobiographical account of his work after 1958, reflecting the grandeur of the man.

Dornberg, John, *The New Germans, Thirty Years After* (1975). A German-born American journalist looks at the many faces of contemporary Germany.

Periodicals providing current analyses of European developments. *Europe, Magazine of the European Community* (Washington, D.C.); *Current History* (Philadelphia), and *Foreign Affairs* (New York).

Servan-Schreiber, Jean-Jacques, *The American Challenge* (1969). A famous treatise on European reaction to American influence.

Wilson, Harold, *The Labour Government, 1964–1970: A Personal Record* (1971). Crucial years in Britain as viewed by the Labour leader who then was Prime Minister.

Wiskeman, Elizabeth, *Italy since 1945* (1971). A brief survey by an English specialist on Italian history.

Wylie, Lawrence, *Village in the Vaucluse* (1974). A well-written glimpse of French peasant life through the eyes of an American anthropologist.

Yergin, Daniel, *The Shattered Peace* (1977). The most balanced and readable of the analyses of the cold war.

Review Questions

1. How did the cold war affect the reorganization of Europe from 1945 to 1958?

2. Trace the evolution of the European Economic Community. What information about its current activities do you find in the current news?

3. Which of the major peoples of Western Europe faced the greatest adjustments after World War II? What reasons do you give for your choice?

4. France and Italy are often compared because of their common Latin heritage. Do you see any similarities in their histories after 1945?

5. What have been the major problems of government in Great Britain since 1945? What has been the recent news about Britain?

6. How, after the partition of Germany in 1945, did West Germany rise to its present pre-eminence in the European Community and in world affairs?

7. How do you account for the rise of terrorism in postwar Europe? What about European terrorists in the recent news?

8. What have been the major aspects of Western Europe's relations with the United States since 1945? What is the current state of American relations with the countries of Western Europe?

CHAPTER 34

Eastern Europe Since 1945:
Extension of Soviet Power

F OUR TRENDS have dominated the evolution of the Soviet Union since 1945: the continuing increase in Soviet military power matched by caution in foreign policy; the gradual relaxation of the extreme measures of national mobilization designed by Stalin; the marked improvement in the material condition of the people; and the normalization of party rule.

Until Stalin's death in 1953, Stalinism grew more burdensome and rigid. Yet it laid the groundwork for the production of atomic weapons and space rockets. Stalinism also consolidated communist rule in the postwar period within the Soviet Union and among the countries conquered by the Red Army. Stalin's successors continued to build up Soviet power, achieving parity with the United States in nuclear weapons and space exploration by the mid-1970s. They also raised the material well-being of their peoples; Soviet Russia shared in the worldwide economic upswing of the postwar decades.

To increase productivity the Soviet rulers loosened the extreme controls of the Stalin era without endangering the pre-eminence of the Communist party or weakening the country's unity. They changed the form of government from the "dictatorship of the proletariat" to "the state of all the people," sponsoring controlled public participation in running the country. They also eased their hold over their Eastern European satellites, allowing them, within the limits of military security and communist unity, to find their own way toward a standard of living higher than that of the Soviet Union.

Contrary to expectation abroad, the problem of succession in the Communist party dictatorship was handled smoothly. Within two years of Stalin's death, Nikita Khrushchev peacefully emerged as leader, boldly revealing the excesses of Stalinism, but impatient and erratic in remedying them. Quietly retiring him in 1964, his more practical successors— among whom Leonid Brezhnev gradually rose to pre-eminence—continued in his spirit, introducing a sense of orderliness and routine that the country had lacked since 1914 and adding an assurance of power and accomplishment unprecedented in Russian history.

STALIN'S LAST YEARS

In Soviet experience, World War II was but another cruel landmark in the long succession of wars, revolutions, and crises that had started in 1914; nothing basically changed after 1945. The liberation from terror and dictatorship, which many soldiers had hoped for as a reward for their heroism, never occurred. Stalin viewed the postwar scene in the light of his life's lessons. He had helped Lenin seize power and fight the cruel civil war in fear and hatred of the capitalist world. As Lenin's successor, he had demanded unprecedentedly brutal efforts from his people to strengthen Soviet Russia against its enemies. The epic struggle against the Nazi invaders had further hardened him. Was he now to deny his past? Sixty-six years old in 1945, corrupted by unlimited power and unrestrained adulation, Stalin displayed in his last years an unrelenting ruthlessness and a suspiciousness raised to the pitch of paranoia.

Stalin's assessment of Soviet Russia's condition at the end of the war was consistent with his previous thinking. He saw no ground for rejoicing or relaxing control, for the country still had immense problems: the large anti-Soviet populations in Eastern Europe; the lack of atomic weapons; the traditional poverty and additional destruction wrought by the war; the political unreliability of returning soldiers and prisoners of war; and the unimpaired strength of the United States. Wherever he looked, Stalin saw cause for concern. The government, the party, communist ideology, the economy—all were in disarray. The generals were riding high, threatening his own supremacy and that of the party. Ideological control had slackened during the war. The exhausted people were in danger of falling into a postwar slump, yearning for normality and greater freedom in their personal lives. Tired and hungry as they were, how could they be goaded to work for the speedy reconstruction of their country? How could the party be reinvigorated? Communist parties in other lands not directly under his thumb were to be trusted even less. Against these threats, Stalin had to exercise full Bolshevik vigilance. His indomitable ambition, undiminished by age, was to build up Soviet power in his lifetime, whatever the human cost. More Five-Year Plans were needed.

On this familiar note the Soviet Union changed from war to peace, staggering through the hardships and hunger of the war's aftermath, deprived of the flower of its manhood. As before, the peasants were squeezed to the utmost, furnishing the state with food without receiving more than the barest minimum in return. The urban-industrial population fared slightly better. With planning, manpower released from the army, much selfless hard work, and resources requisitioned from all occupied territories, industrial production was back to prewar levels within three years— no mean achievement. Thereafter, consumer prices were gradually reduced. Yet the government's concern remained concentrated on heavy industry and defense.

With the return to Five-Year Plans came a deliberate tightening of ideological control. The party boss of Leningrad, Andrei Zhdanov (1896–1948), lashed out against well-known literary figures for their "escapist, unorthodox, and un-Soviet" thinking. His target was any form of Western influence and personal withdrawal from the tasks set by the party. Thus, thousands of returning soldiers and prisoners of war, who had seen too much in the West, were sent to forced-labor camps; the Soviet intelligentsia was terrorized into compliance with the party line.

A shrill, dogmatic superpatriotism became mandatory for all Soviet citizens. This patriotism extolled Russia's achievements past and present over those of the West. Even scientists had to submit, at a fearful cost to research (except in nuclear physics). Zhdanov singled

Zhdovoursin

out the most famous composers, Dmitri Shostakovich and Sergei Prokofiev, whom he accused of "bourgeois formalism," a derogatory term for refined artistic standards. The intellectual tenor of Stalin's last years was antiforeign and shallow, an affront to artistic and intellectual creativity. It suited a society of rank-conscious officials regimented by fear and routine. Zhdanovism, as the anti-intellectual campaign was called, was accompanied by renewed political terror, again centered on Leningrad. In 1948 in Leningrad the chief leaders of the heroic struggle against the Nazi siege were arrested and shot.

The cold war drove Stalin to further ruthlessness; Eastern Europe had to be brought under a tight rein. He set a lesson by overthrowing (in 1948) the moderately procommunist democracy of Czechoslovakia and instituting cruel purges. He tried to oust Marshal Tito of Yugoslavia but failed. Misjudging Tito's determination, Stalin committed a profound mistake: after 1948 the unity of world communism under Soviet leadership, a central dogma in Soviet ideology, was broken; Tito proclaimed a rival communist creed. In East Asia in 1949 Stalin had to accept, though he did not welcome, the victory of the Chinese communists. The "fraternal" relations between the Russian and Chinese communist parties were decidedly cool. Mao's China diminished rather than enhanced Stalin's power; Mao was destined to establish a third variant of communist ideology. In 1950 the North Korean communists, possibly with Stalin's approval, attacked South Korea, which further intensified the cold war.

In his last years Stalin withdrew into virtual isolation, surrounded by a few fawning and fearful subordinates, and his sickly suspicion worsened. Before he died, he "recognized" a plot among the doctors who treated him and personally issued orders for torturing them (which killed one of them). When on March 5, 1953, the failing dictator died of a stroke, his advisers sighed with relief, but many people cried: to them Stalin was the godlike leader and savior of the nation.

One of the most remarkable people of the twentieth century, Stalin was a towering figure in the Russian mold of Ivan the Terrible or Peter the Great. Like them he had stirred popular imagination at the deepest layers of human consciousness. For those whom he had made tremble a thousand times for their lives, his death was a cosmic event. The human costs of his labor had been immense, but of his achievements in raising Soviet power there can be no doubt. By 1949 (sooner than expected) Soviet Russia possessed the atomic bomb (A-bomb). By 1953 (at the same time as the United States) it had the hydrogen bomb (H-bomb) as well. Stalin also helped lay the foundation for *Sputnik I* (see page 777), the first artificial terrestrial satellite in the world's history. Undeniably, Stalin had taken gigantic strides toward his goal of making Soviet Russia secure against all rivals.

More important perhaps, Stalin also bequeathed to his successors a tamed and even cowed population, more malleable and cooperative than any previous generation. Stalin himself was the last of the self-willed, self-centered revolutionaries who had nearly torn the country apart in the 1920s. His successors were masterful organization men ruling over obedient and hard-driven subjects; Soviet society still suffered the strains of excessive diversity and backwardness, but the party could now count on a growing number of people with a personal stake in the regime and its institutions.

THE KHRUSHCHEV YEARS

The chief question after Stalin's death was: who would succeed him and in what manner? The succession struggles of the 1920s and their bloody aftermath in the terror purges were still on everybody's mind. How would the issues be settled this time? Could the new

MAP 34.1 EASTERN EUROPE AFTER 1945

German territory to Poland

Acquired by Soviet Union, 1939-1945

Soviet satellites

Communist, nonsatellite nation

"Iron Curtain" after 1950

NORWAY

SWEDEN

FINLAND

Helsinki

G. of Finland

Leningrad

Stockholm

ESTONIA

BALTIC SEA

LATVIA

DENMARK

Copenhagen

LITHUANIA

SOVIET UNION

Moscow

Gdansk (Danzig)

Hamburg

Elbe R.

Berlin

NETHERLANDS

Vistula R.

Warsaw

WHITE RUSSIA

EAST GERMANY

POLAND

WEST GERMANY

Kiev

Bonn

Rhine R.

Prague

UKRAINE

Dnieper R.

CZECHOSLOVAKIA

Dniester R.

Munich

Vienna

BESSARABIA

SWITZERLAND

AUSTRIA

Budapest

HUNGARY

CRIMEA

RUMANIA

Po R.

Bucharest

BLACK SEA

Belgrade

Danube R.

YUGOSLAVIA

ITALY

ADRIATIC SEA

BULGARIA

Sofia

Istanbul

CORSICA

Rome

Ankara

Tirane

ALBANIA

TURKEY

SARDINIA

GREECE

AEGEAN SEA

Athens

SICILY

CYPRUS

MEDITERRANEAN SEA

THE LENIN SQUARE, VOLGOGRAD At the conclusion of World War II, Stalin found the U.S.S.R. threatened by a capitalist West. The country had been ravaged by the war with disastrous results to populace, agriculture, and industry. Taking a tougher stance than ever, Stalin glorified the Soviet Union and its achievements and bolstered his nation's military power with the development of the atomic and hydrogen bombs. (Tass from Sovfoto)

leadership cope with Russia's difficult problems?

The economy required overhauling; people demanded more consumer goods and services. Yet how could they be satisfied without undercutting the growth of the heavy industry that most communists still considered central? Consumer demand also called for a new approach to agriculture, which had been neglected under Stalin to the point of endangering the country's food supply. In addition, central planning had to be adjusted to a more diversified and complex economy. In foreign policy the emergence of nuclear weaponry required special caution; tension had to be reduced and

contact with the non-Soviet world increased. Finally, how were the new leaders to deal with Stalin, whose body was now resting next to Lenin's in the mausoleum on Red Square? The tactics of terror and repression had to be modified, yet how much change could the regime withstand?

In addition to debate on these issues, Stalin's heirs also competed for leadership. Feared if not hated by all, Laurentia Beria, who headed the secret police and the vast empire of forced labor camps, was executed in December 1953, together with his chief henchmen, for having been a "foreign spy." As it turned out, these cynical accusations and subsequent exe-

Laurenti Beria

Krushchev

cutions were the last gasp of Stalinism; since then the rivals for supreme leadership have died of natural causes. Gradually leadership was assumed by a team headed by Nikita Khrushchev (1894–1971), the new first secretary of the party.

After Stalin's death Khrushchev was the driving force behind the "thaw" that emptied the forced-labor camps and allowed the return of most nationalities that had been forcibly resettled during the war. Khruschchev also relaxed censorship, although he repressed religion, which during and after the war had enjoyed a limited freedom. And Khrushchev dared to attack Stalin himself.

After 1953 Stalin had been cautiously downgraded and even denounced under the cover of charges against "the cult of personality." In a speech at the Twentieth Party Congress in February 1956 Khrushchev brought the issue to a head. His audience gasped with horror and indignation as he recited the facts: "Of the 139 members and candidates of the Party Central Committee who were elected at the 17th congress, 98 persons, i.e., 70%, were arrested . . . and shot. . . ." Or, "Comrade Eikhe, a highly esteemed communist, was shot. . . . It has been definitely established that Eikhe's case was fabricated." In this vein Khrushchev cited example after example of Stalin's terror, summing up with the charge that "the accusations were wild, absurd, and contrary to common sense" and the tortures used to extract confessions "barbaric, cruel, and inhuman." He also enumerated Stalin's mistakes, as for instance in not sufficiently preparing for Hitler's attack in 1941. Throughout, he revealed, Stalin had "discarded the Leninist methods of convincing and educating" and "abandoned the method of ideological struggle for that of administrative violence, mass repression, and terror. . . ."[1] Three years after Stalin's death these were potent and unsettling revelations; yet they were needed. They lifted (though did not eliminate) from Soviet politics—and from people's consciences—an intolerable burden of crime

and complicity, restoring a modicum of honesty and humaneness.

Khrushchev's revelations created a profound stir around the world and promoted defection from communist ranks everywhere. Among the Soviet satellite countries, Poland in 1956 was on the brink of rebellion; a workers' uprising forced a change of leadership. In Hungary in 1956 the entire communist regime was overthrown before the Red Army reoccupied the country. Only Mao objected to the downgrading of Stalinism.

After the stormy events of 1956 Khrushchev's standing temporarily declined; in June 1957 his opponents in the politburo even forced a showdown. Yet unexpectedly he rallied the central committee and the army to his support and then ousted what he called "the anti-party group." Khrushchev's enemies were relegated to minor jobs and soon disappeared from public view. In 1958, at the height of his power, Khrushchev occupied, as Stalin had, the leading posts in both the party and the state administration.

Personable and approachable, Khrushchev talked to all and sundry in his folksy, unceremonious manner that occasionally bordered on bad taste, admonishing officials high and low and pushing his rapidly changing projects. He was excitable and carried away by visions of Soviet superiority, particularly after the launching of *Sputnik I* in early October 1957. *Sputnik I* (meaning "fellow traveler" [of earth]), an artificial earth satellite, opened the space age and boosted Khrushchev's pride beyond bounds. Eager to prod his country toward a higher state in Marxist-Leninist ideology, he presented a new party program and impatiently pressed for reforms in industry, agriculture, and party organization. An idealist of sorts, he called for wider public participation in the administration of the country, holding more frequent and longer sessions of the central committee, extending freedom of public discussion, and encouraging individual initiative. Khrushchev also allowed the publication of Aleksandr Solzhenitsyn's short novel, *One*

A. Solzhenitsyn

Day in the Life of Ivan Denisovich, which offered a first public glimpse into life at a forced-labor camp. He permitted the public showing of abstract art. He tried to curb the privileges of the well-entrenched upper layers of bureaucrats and went so far as to declare the dictatorship of the proletariat ended and replaced by "the state of all the people." The people responded with increased restlessness.

In foreign policy, Khrushchev professed to promote peace. He made some provocative moves, though, by threatening Western access to West Berlin and placing missiles in Cuba; American pressure forced him to withdraw in both cases. In 1956 Khrushchev dissolved the Cominform (founded in 1947 for controlling Eastern European communists) for the sake of a reconciliation with Marshal Tito, whose good will he subsequently lost again. Not wishing to help communist China build atomic weapons, he withdrew, after mutual recrimination, all Soviet advisers in 1960, causing a break between two communist nations. Mao then charged him with "revisionism" as well as imperialism; as a sequel Khrushchev also had to accept the defection of Albania from Soviet to Chinese allegiance. Among the satellites the Kremlin's control lessened.

In whatever he undertook Khrushchev could not deny his Stalinist training; arbitrariness and impetuosity counteracted his good intentions. Increasingly his ceaseless reorganizations and impatient manner antagonized wide sections of state and party administration. In October 1964, while he was on vacation, his comrades on the politburo unceremoniously voted him out for ill health or, as they later added, his "hare-brained schemes." He was retired, leaving to his successors the task of finding a steadier middle course between Stalinist tradition and creative innovation.

Khrushchev's years in power, however, marked some very basic changes in Soviet and even in Russian history. The Soviet regime proved that it could settle the succession from one leader to another in a peaceful manner, without the benefit of written constitutional procedure. Infinitely more important, Soviet

NIKITA KHRUSHCHEV Contrary to expectations, the succession after Stalin's death was relatively bloodless. Khrushchev emerged in a peaceful transference of leadership. He denounced Stalin's crimes and excesses. An approachable man, Khrushchev restored a touch of humanity to a political system that had long seemed paranoid and militaristic. (United Press International)

Russia acquired protection from foreign attack as never before in Russian history. Thanks to the efforts of its leaders and the labors of its citizens the country was able to build the weapons and delivery system that essentially put it on a par with the United States. Henceforth, the Soviet Union was as invulnerable—or as vulnerable—as its chief opponent. A huge stride forward had been made in the age-long Russian quest for external security.

BREZHNEV AND KOSYGIN

Khrushchev was succeeded, as was Stalin, by a group of leaders acting in common: Nikolai V.

Podgorny (1903–1977), the official president of the Soviet Union (the least significant office), Aleksei Kosygin (born 1904) as prime minister heading the state organization, and Leonid Brezhnev (born 1906) directing the party; all of them had worked closely with Khrushchev. While they reversed his hasty reforms, they undertook no notable changes of policy or personnel. Raised within the party, associated with the key industries of space and defense, the new leaders were pragmatic bureaucrats, cautious, aware of the need for smooth cooperation among the many interlacing administrative agencies of the party and the government, and mellowed by age and experience. After Khrushchev's personalism they deemphasized personality as well as personal power. Brezhnev gradually rose to prominence as first secretary of the party, but Kosygin remained prime minister. Under him the government of the U.S.S.R. turned from a personal dictatorship into an oligarchy, the collective rule of a privileged minority. Brezhnev's style stressed reasoned agreement rather than command and security of office, status, and autonomy within their various jurisdictions for the rank and file. Soviet officials breathed more easily.

Brezchnev

Domestic Policies

In internal affairs the long-range trend was toward cautiously reducing traditional restrictions; by the mid-1970s for instance, Soviet young people were allowed generous access to Western styles of music and dress. More issues of state policy were opened to public debate, more latitude granted to artistic expression. The lifeless stereotypes of social realism gave way to more candid treatment of human reality and even tragedy; art moved closer to actual experience, although in a running battle with censorship. Interest in religion revived. More significantly, Russian nationalism, anti-Western and even anti-Marxist, reappeared from the pre-Soviet past. In part it responded to the marked increase in the non-Russian population of the Soviet Union; in part it replaced Marxist-Leninist ideology, which, as one communist admitted, had turned into "stale bread." Even the party seemed sympathetic to the new nationalism.

Dissent, furthermore, was treated with greater circumspection. Since the country was no longer poor and weak, dissent seemed less dangerous. Surfacing with confidence as never before, protest literature, ranging from anti-regime Leninism to fascist racism, received wide attention even abroad. Born of the "thaw" under Khrushchev in revulsion against Stalinism in all its forms, the protest enlisted a tiny and splintered but heroic nucleus of the literary, artistic, and scientific elite; some people called it *the democratic movement*. Dissenters distributed a variety of protest writings known by their mode of production as *samizdat* (self-published), some of it of high artistic or scholarly quality.

thaw

For a while the dissenters, including Andrei Sakharov who developed the Soviet H-bomb, were treated leniently, in part because their cases received much attention abroad and partly because of the moral authority they enjoyed at home. The most adamant critics like Aleksandr Solzhenitsyn or Andrei Amalrik were expelled (or allowed to emigrate) rather than shot or worked to death. Other critics who stayed were declared insane, following a practice begun under Nicholas I, and kept drugged. The secret police (KGB) remained as powerful as ever, its head a member of the politburo. It practiced more discretion and less terror, closely watching the trends of Soviet opinion and the impact of external hostility, ever ready to resume overt repression.

Under Brezhnev, the life of the Soviet elite became more abundant and secure; Soviet power also was more visible and respected in the world. Technicians, scientists, and managers, the country's most crucial asset, felt committed to order and continuity by their self-interest. Imperial Russia had rendered few if any services to the majority of its subjects.

By contrast, contemporary Soviet Russia has become a full-fledged welfare state.

The party under Brezhnev and Kosygin stepped up its policy of providing more consumer goods, falling in with the worldwide trend toward affluence. Soviet citizens now received household appliances and television sets. Housing improved. The greatest concession to consumerism was the production of automobiles for private use, at least among the privileged, although services and road facilities remained limited. Soviet consumers still cannot compare with their Western European contemporaries, but the standard of living has improved.

The party continued to devote much attention to agriculture, channeling heavy investments into fertilizers, farm machinery, and farm welfare, yet it could not raise output in proportion to this attention. Soviet agriculture remains the least productive sector of the economy. The motivation of collective farmers remains poor. They still prefer to work the private plots (which often produce a good income) allowed to them on their collective farms rather than in the collective work brigades. The young people drift to the cities, which offer more amenities. Two bad harvests in the early 1970s forced the government to import large quantities of grain (mostly from the United States), thereby increasing Soviet dependence on capitalist countries. Agriculture remains a costly problem in the Soviet economy, an impediment to economic growth.

Top priority still lies with heavy industry and capital construction. Roads, bridges, railways, pipelines for gas and oil, mines and oilwells, steel mills and power plants are necessary to give the huge country an adequate infrastructure. The U.S.S.R. forged ahead of the smaller and better-equipped United States in the production of iron, steel, coal, and cement; it preserved its self-sufficiency in fossil fuels longer than the United States. The center of industrial activity is gradually shifting eastward, into western Siberia, with careful planning of new integrated industrial regions. Soviet planners pay special attention to the defense and space industries, both crucial to the country's prestige in the world. By the mid-1970s the Soviet Union achieved parity in weapons production and defense capacity with the United States.

Apart from a very small sector limited to farmers' markets and to an unofficial black market (or "underground capitalism"), all economic activity is subject to vigorous central planning. One of the key features of the Soviet economy, planning now has grown to an unimagined complexity that belies the claim of rational control. Regulations designed to increase output reduce it instead. Secure in their jobs, workers lack incentives. Rather than maximize production according to socialist theory, the huge regimented economy suffers from a counterproductive inflexibility. Soviet planners have tried to keep up with the demands made on them by introducing new management procedures, better computer systems, and tighter techniques of control without being able to offset the inherent conservatism of huge, interdependent bureaucracies. Inventors have been known to land in jail rather than earn promotions—innovation upsets too many routines.

Yet the call for planning never ceases. Facing a growing manpower shortage, rising costs of production, and even reduction of their oil supply, Soviet leaders, like industrial entrepreneurs elsewhere, must pay more attention to making more with less. They can look back with pride over the fast growth of their economy in the recent past: setting the base rate at 100 in 1950, the gross national product (GNP) rose to 435 in 1970, the fastest growth taking place in the 1950s. The Soviet growth rate outpaced that of the United States, yet without producing anywhere near the American standard of living. By comparison to the United States, the Soviet Union is still a poor country. The high growth rates, already flattening, are bound to level off in the future. The Soviet Union, like the United States, faces growing scarcities. Even with planning the

Soviet Union cannot raise the standard of living to the abundance required for full communism as defined by the Marxist vision.

In their efforts to increase productivity the Soviet leaders have not hesitated to establish closer economic ties with capitalist countries around the world; their dependence on Germany, both East and West, is particularly marked. Although stressing self-sufficiency, the Soviet Union like every other nation is living in an age of global interdependence that has gained momentum since 1948.

Foreign Policy

The needs of domestic policy helped to determine the character of foreign policy during the 1970s. More than under Khrushchev the course was set toward a reduction of international tension and peaceful coexistence with capitalism. No more confrontations with the United States were staged; the Soviet government took no advantage of American setbacks in Vietnam. The leaders of the politburo pressed for *détente* (the diplomatic term for the relaxation of political tension). The leaders admitted more Western visitors and were less secretive.

In Europe the Soviet Union achieved a major goal in the Helsinki Agreements on Security and Cooperation, signed August 1, 1975, in which the NATO powers formally gave up any territorial claim to Eastern Europe by recognizing the boundaries established in 1945. In return, the governments of the Soviet bloc promised to relax internal controls for the sake of better cultural relations with the West; the promise included easier emigration from the U.S.S.R. for Jews. Because of the danger to their regimes resulting from greater contact with the West, the governments of the Soviet bloc, however, have not lived up to the expectations aroused among the noncommunist nations that signed the Helsinki Agreement.

Tensions with the West eased somewhat until late 1979, but the Soviet Union has never ceased to fear the awesome power of the United States, the other superpower. The Soviet Union is also increasingly troubled by communist China, a potential ally of the United States and troublemaker in communist ranks, especially in Eastern Europe. Its long boundary with China and the pressure of the Chinese population on its underpopulated eastern territories make the Soviet Union feel vulnerable in the Far East and central Asia.

In 1979, while the United States was embroiled with the Islamic revolution after the ouster of the shah of Iran, a crisis broke out in neighboring Afghanistan, a hitherto quiet sector on the Soviet borders. Relying on a mildly pro-Soviet regime, the Soviet government had assisted in the modernization of Afghanistan. Would the U.S.S.R. then allow a hostile Afghan regime, guided by the new Islamic militancy, to take over the country, possibly even affecting the Soviet Union's own Muslim minorities? Unwilling to face the risk and unable to support the government of its forever-feuding Marxist friends by peaceful means, the Soviet army in late 1979 recklessly overran Afghanistan to the Pakistan border. Interpreted as another case of communist aggression and as a threat to vital oil supplies from the Persian Gulf, the Soviet move set off a massive alarm in the United States, reviving, after a decade of détente, the hostility of the cold war. The nuclear arms race escalated as well.

In the wider world Soviet Russia pressed its self-appointed role as leader of all anti-imperialist forces with uncertain results. After initial successes in the Mideast, for example, Soviet influence in the area drastically declined again. Soviet Russia remains the main source of support, directly or indirectly through its satellites (including Cuba), for indigenous challengers of white supremacy in southern Africa. But the long-range effects are uncertain, for Africans are not interested in Soviet domination. Soviet aid to developing countries is decidedly meager, the bulk going to countries nearest the U.S.S.R. like India, and the rest to others, Cuba foremost, who loudly subscribe to Marxist ideology. In no case has Soviet economic or military assistance created a dependable ally anywhere in the world. International communism, once firmly under Kremlin control, has been fragmented by nationalism and lost its compelling ideological force; it is a poor match for the global internationalism of capitalist influence.

Although the Soviet Union has steadily increased its naval presence on the high seas, the center of Soviet power continues to lie in the country's capacity to sustain the nuclear-arms race. Soviet military power now equals that of the United States. ?

THE SATELLITE COUNTRIES

Soviet Russia's power is closely tied to its relations with its *satellite* countries (nations that it dominates politically) within the Soviet bloc in eastern and southeastern Europe. Eastern Europe (Poland, East Germany, Czechoslovakia, and Hungary) and southeastern Europe (the Balkan countries: Yugoslavia, Albania, Bulgaria, and Rumania) have been a long-standing concern of Russian and Soviet leaders. When in 1944 and 1945 the Red Armies poured into these lands on their way to Germany, Stalin was faced with a historically unique opportunity—Soviet Russia now controlled the entire area as a huge territorial buffer against invasion from the West. Would it be able to continue its domination in peacetime?

Conditions both favored and opposed Soviet rule. The Baltic peoples and the inhabitants of Eastern Europe (the Finns and the Hungarians excepted) for the most part were fellow Slavs, even the Rumanians who boasted a strong Latin strain. Many Eastern Europeans belonged to the Eastern Orthodox church, another tie, at least to traditional Russia. At the same time, they shared a common suspi-

cion or even hostility toward the giant to the east. Some among them, Poles and Czechs foremost, saw themselves as representatives of the superior culture of the West and wanted to strengthen ties with Western Europe rather than Russia. All, remembering centuries of foreign domination, were passionately nationalist. The majority, moreover, were of peasant stock, opposed to collectivization and socialism. Under any regime the peoples of these countries (now counting about 100 million) would have been difficult to govern. They were split into innumerable groups (many of them sporting their own separatist movements though intermingling in the same territory), most of them were stubborn, suspicious of government, and prone to violence. National independence between the First and Second World Wars had not been a happy experience.

The Stalinization of Eastern Europe

Whatever the prospects, Stalin seized the opportunity. As the Red Armies fought their way west, Eastern European communists, trained in the Soviet Union, followed behind them. The Baltic States (Lithuania, Latvia, Estonia), seized after the Nazi-Soviet Pact of 1939 and then lost to Hitler, were reincorporated into the Soviet Union as "soviet socialist republics." Elsewhere Stalin respected, outwardly at least, the national sovereignty of the occupied countries by ruling through returned communists and whatever sympathizers he could find.

At first the imported communists worked, under the umbrella of the Red Army, through a coalition of "antifascist" parties—all political groupings not guilty of collaborating with the Germans or Italians. As the cold war progressed, Stalin had these puppet communist parties destroy the other parties by trickery, fraud, or violence.

In the fateful year of 1948 a third stage was reached: full Stalinization. The tottering coalition governments were replaced by one-party regimes led by newly formed "workers' unity" parties, patterned after the Communist party of the Soviet Union but containing other socialist elements made pliant by threats or bribes. The most dramatic transition took place in Czechoslovakia in February 1948, when the government of President Eduard Benes (1884–1948) and Foreign Minister Jan Masaryk (1886–1948) was overthrown by the Stalinist hard-liner Klement Gottwald.

By the end of 1948 the countries of eastern and southeastern Europe emerged as "peoples democracies," distinct both from the "bourgeois democracies" of the West and from the "soviet socialist republics" of the U.S.S.R. The latter title would have smacked of open annexation by the Soviet Union. Eventual incorporation into the Union of Soviet Socialist Republics remained a theoretical possibility, however. Whatever their names, the Soviet Union continued to claim the right, based on conquest, of intervening at will in the internal affairs of its satellites.

Thus, although civic initiative and confidence gradually returned to Western Europe, the pall of Stalinism hung over war-torn and impoverished Eastern Europe. The formerly privileged classes, like the scattered German minorities, were liquidated. Private enterprise was curtailed or abolished. The socialized economy was placed under the rigid and hasty plans of industrialization and the collectivization of agriculture. Religion and the churches were repressed and political liberty and free speech stamped out. Even the "proletarian masses" derived few benefits from the artificial revolution engineered from Moscow, because Stalin drained Eastern Europe of its resources for the sake of rebuilding the Soviet Union. All contact with Western Europe or the United States was banned; even travel within the Soviet bloc suffered. Each satellite existed in isolation, surrounded by borders fortified with barbed wire and watch towers set along mined corridors cut through the landscape. Fear and terror reached deep into every house and individual soul, as Stalin's style was copied by little Stalins in East Berlin, Warsaw, Prague, Budapest, Sofia, and Bucharest.

Two exceptions to that trend emerged; Albania and Yugoslavia, located on the flanks of the Soviet westward surge. During the war indigenous communist parties had conducted successful guerrilla wars; they rose to power when the Germans withdrew, each under the leadership of a strong man: Enver Hoxha in Albania, and Josip Broz, known as Marshal Tito, in Yugoslavia. A Stalinist even after Stalin's death, Hoxha turned against Moscow in 1961, making Albania a satellite of Mao's China. Tito (1892–1980), by contrast, became a symbol of defiance to Stalin. The child of Croatian peasants, Tito showed his mettle in a tough succession of careers. Starting as a mechanic, Tito became a sergeant in the Austro-Hungarian army. A prisoner of war in Russia during World War I, Tito learned his communism from the Bolshevik Revolution and the Russian Civil War. After his return to Yugoslavia, Tito became a communist organizer and was soon condemned to spend many years in jail. In 1937 Stalin chose him to reorganize the Yugoslav Communist party. During World War II he led the Yugoslav resistance movement against Nazi occupation. A convinced and hardened communist, Tito was also a Yugoslav patriot committed to rebuilding and unifying his country.

Yugoslavia escaped Soviet occupation, but Stalin did not ignore it. Arrogant Soviet advisers descended on Belgrade, determined to bend Tito's policies to Stalin's bidding, but Tito warded off Soviet domination. In June 1948, Stalin commanded the expulsion of the Yugoslav communists from the Cominform, expecting the party would obediently drop its leader and beg readmission. Stalin's words recalled by Khrushchev were: "I will shake my little finger and there will be no more Tito; he will fall."

To Stalin's dismay, Tito did not fall. On the contrary, backed by his party and his people, Tito pioneered, with increasing confidence, his own brand of communism. Tito accused Stalin of betraying true Marxism-Leninism by establishing an imperialist and bureaucratic dictatorship. He also boldly attempted a more democratic communist regime based on workers' participation in industry. Tito's communism has served as a model of socialist ownership of production combined with workers' control and, more broadly, with extensive participation in the administration of the entire state. While he was alive, Stalin ruthlessly purged all potential Titos in other communist parties, everywhere suspecting "bourgeois nationalism," his pet phrase for Titoism.

The satellite countries bore the marks of Soviet control. All communist parties (by whatever name) were guided by Moscow; Soviet troops remained strategically stationed in the area; Comecon attempted to integrate the area's economy with the Soviet economy. In 1955 a further bond was created in the Warsaw Pact or Warsaw Treaty Organization (WTO). It coordinated the armies of the satellite countries with the Red Army as a military instrument for preserving the ideological and political unity of the bloc and as a counterbalance to NATO (which respected Soviet control over its satellites); like Comecon the WTO decentralized and disguised the preponderance of Soviet power.

A New Era of Permissiveness and Reprisals

Stalin's successors, realizing that continued repression among the satellites would provoke trouble, began to relax their controls. A new era began for eastern and southeastern Europe. The Soviet satellites began to move toward greater national self-determination, searching for their own forms of industrialization, collectivization of agriculture, and communist dictatorship. The history of eastern and southeastern Europe since 1953 thus presents a series of experiments: What deviations from Soviet practice in domestic politics would the Kremlin tolerate? What measure of self-assertion in foreign policy was compatible with Soviet control over the entire bloc?

No event proved more crucial than Khrushchev's attack on Stalin in 1956. It set off a political earthquake throughout the bloc, discrediting the Stalinists and encouraging the moderates among the communist parties, reviving cautious discussion among intellectuals, and even emboldening public opinion with visions of national self-determination. The first rumble of protest was heard in June 1956 in the Polish city of Poznan, where workers took to the street protesting low wages and high prices. Their anger brought to the fore Wladyslaw Gomulka (born 1905), a staunch anti-Stalinist communist once imprisoned for his moderation. In order to retain control, Gomulka sided with the rapidly growing anti-Russian agitation, carefully preserving the ascendancy of the communist party.

In October 1956 popular agitation in Poland came to a climax. A Soviet delegation under Khrushchev rushed to Warsaw while preparations were being made for a national uprising. On the night of October 19, the outcome hung in the balance: would there be a revolt, to be crushed by the Red Army, or would the Soviet leaders accede to Gomulka's request for the withdrawal of Soviet officers from the Polish army and a reduced Soviet presence in general? Rather than tarnish his reputation, Khrushchev gave way in return for Gomulka's promise of continued loyalty to Soviet leadership. The Polish Communist party subsequently entered on a course of cautious if uncertain liberalization, virtually ending collectivization in agriculture and lifting its tight censorship. Thereafter, Poland breathed more freely, reconciled to the continued presence of Soviet troops as a protection against a revival of German nationalism and clinging to its Catholic faith as a guarantee of its national identity.

Although "the Polish October" ended peacefully, events moved to a brutal showdown in Hungary. The Stalinists had suppressed national pride in Hungary for too long. No Gomulka was available, either, to contain

NAGY

protest within communist ranks. On October 20, 1956, an uprising took place in Budapest that brought the anti-Soviet feeling to fever pitch and forced Soviet troops to withdraw from the country. Next, the Hungarian government under Imre Nagy (1896–1958), a communist moderate eager to capture popular sentiment, called for political democracy in the Western manner and Hungary's withdrawal from the Warsaw Pact, hoping to win neutrality like Finland. Thoroughly alarmed, and with the backing of Mao Tse-tung and even Tito, the Soviet leaders struck back. On November 4, 1956, Soviet troops re-entered the country and crushed all opposition. The NATO countries stood by helplessly. Imre Nagy was executed in 1958, yet the bold uprising had left its mark.

KADAR

The new communist leader of Hungary, János Kádár (born 1912), was a moderate who with Khrushchev's approval built a pragmatic regime of consumer-oriented "goulash communism." Kádár's regime allowed extensive participation in public affairs to noncommunists and, through relaxation and decentralization of planning, made possible in the 1960s a remarkable increase in popular prosperity and individual freedom that became the envy of all other Soviet-bloc countries. In return for this privilege the Hungarians resumed their membership in the Warsaw Pact and excelled in their demonstration of loyalty to the Soviet leadership.

The Soviet Union also had to pay a price for crushing the revolts in its satellite countries. Its bloody reoccupation of Hungary was a blow to its reputation as a peace-loving, anti-imperialist force; it lost many hitherto loyal supporters around the world. Thus in 1956, the Soviet leaders were made aware of the political liabilities they had acquired by Stalin's conquests.

As a result, the Soviet leaders began to approach the internal affairs in the satellite countries with greater circumspection, allowing increasing diversity of political development. The stereotyped supranational socialism of Stalin's era was gradually replaced by a socialist nationalism, each country stressing its own heritage as proof of its freedom from Soviet domination. None went further in this than Rumania, which was given special leeway by the Kremlin because it was surrounded on all sides by other Soviet-bloc countries and preserved a tight dictatorship of its own. Yet the new permissiveness was never without risks, even under the milder regime of Brezhnev and Kosygin.

CZECKSLOVAK

In 1968, it was Czechoslovakia's turn to face the consequences of liberating innovation. A new group of communist leaders under Alexander Dubček (born 1921) sought to broaden their regime so as to include noncommunists, allow greater freedom of speech, and rid the economy of the rigidities that for so long had prevented prosperity. Their goal was a "humanist democratic socialism" or "socialism with a human face," a communist party supported by public good will rather than by the secret police.

Dubček's program enjoyed the full support of the Czech and Slovak communists as well as Tito, but it panicked the governments of East Germany, Poland, and the Soviet Union, which did not appreciate lectures about humaneness toward their subjects. On August 21 East German, Polish, Hungarian, and Soviet troops, under the provisions of the Warsaw Pact, carried out a swift and well-prepared occupation of Czechoslovakia, yet without breaking the rebellious will of its communists. While Soviet tanks rumbled through Prague, an extraordinary Czechoslovak party congress secretly met in choked fury. Never had the Soviet leaders encountered such a united resistance by a communist party! Moderating their tactics, the Soviets restored Dubček, previously arrested, to his office while recruiting a more pliant successor.

Dubček was ultimately stripped of political power but he was not executed. The purge of his followers was also mild by previous standards. His successor, Gustav Husak (born 1913), acceded to Soviet demands that Soviet troops be stationed near the German border and scrapped the reforms, reducing the country to abject hopelessness for years to come. But again the Soviet Union paid a high price: a cry of moral outrage resounded around the world; protests were even heard in Moscow.

Although there have been many liabilities, Soviet leaders can also point to positive results from their rule over eastern and southeastern Europe. They have instituted an orderly process of industrialization in predominantly agrarian and backward countries. They have minimized the gap between rich and poor. They have substantially promoted education and cultural opportunity for the bulk of the population and made great strides toward social integration and consolidation among fragmented and divided peoples. The standard of living has greatly risen, although not as much as in Western Europe; it still slopes downward from West to East, the German Democratic Republic enjoying the highest levels in the entire Soviet bloc (its per capita gross national product matching that of the United Kingdom). As in the Soviet Union, agricultural production has not kept pace with industrial growth, and the latter was often achieved at unnecessarily high social costs.

Western observers have protested that freedom and all its benefits are missing from the Soviet bloc. Over the years the Soviet Union has grudgingly permitted a larger measure of personal liberty to its satellites than it has granted to its own peoples. Soviet Russia is still far from enjoying the good will of its satellites. They continue to be a source of unrest and weakness, but large-scale uprisings are unlikely. Recognizing Soviet power, the people are cautious. Moreover, less repression from above is likely to be met with more acceptance from below.

THE SOVIET UNION IN AN AGE OF GLOBALISM

A measure of security has come at last to Russia in the mid-twentieth century, partly because of the exertions and sacrifices exacted by the Stalin revolution in the 1930s and the Great Fatherland War (1941–1945), and partly as a result of external factors. Soviet Russia moved into the political vacuum created in eastern and central Europe by the German defeat; its landlocked empire held together by force while the overseas empires of Western Europe fell apart. It now possesses nuclear weapons equal to those of the United States. As long as the balance of terror prevents a nuclear war, it is militarily more secure than ever before in Russia's entire history. Yet its rulers still have reason to be afraid, for their empire is still based more on compulsion and indoctrination than on spontaneous loyalty, and their prestige in the world more on raw power and deliberate manipulation than on the natural persuasiveness of a respected model. It is still only the second superpower, negotiating with the first from weakness rather than strength in everything but nuclear weapons.

The Soviet Union makes its presence felt over the entire world, strengthening its borders, seeking out its opportunities, tightly holding on to its gains, and with imposing moral righteousness advertising its achievements as examples for all. It follows its long-range goal, hoping, like the United States, to reshape the world in its own interest. National liberation movements directed against Western nations find a willing ally in Moscow. Still feeling humiliated by Western superiority, Moscow represents the natural antithesis to Western ascendancy. It also tries to outdo the West on its own terms, in space exploration and other spectacular technological feats, in setting up bases around the world, or in the ultimate promise of the best society.

In world affairs, the Soviet Union's role is ambiguous. The Leninist dream of world revolution has faded. The Kremlin now conducts its foreign relations pragmatically, guided by a sober sense of self-interest. Trying to expand its power at the expense of the other superpower, it is also dependent on the Western world in the widening network of global interdependence. Soviet Russia still needs to draw on Western know-how (along with Japan's), to satisfy the material wishes of its subjects (whom it cannot entirely insulate from the outside). Having neglected its agriculture, it must buy food abroad. No less than the United States, it must avoid a nuclear confrontation. The politburo is still determined to protect the country's security at any point where it seems threatened and to manipulate the world balance of power in the Soviets' favor.

Notes

1. Nikita S. Khrushchev's speech (in translation) in *The Crimes of the Stalin Era: Special Report to the 20th Congress of the Communist Party of the Soviet Union,* annotated by Boris I. Nicolaevsky, *The New Leader* (New York), 1956.

Suggested Reading

Berliner, Joseph S., *Innovation Decision in Soviet Industry* (1976). A scholarly study of the vital question: how innovative is the Soviet planned economy?

Hough, Jerry F., and Merle Fainsod, *How the Soviet Union Is Governed* (1979). The updated version of a classic study of the Soviet system.

Khrushchev, Nikita S., *Khrushchev Remembers* (1974). Although its authenticity has been questioned, this autobiography is alive with his personality.

Matthews, Mervyn, *Privilege in the Soviet Union: A Study of Elite Life Styles under Communism* (1978). An analysis of how an egalitarian ideology need not always mean egalitarianism in practice.

Periodicals specializing in Soviet and Soviet-related subjects: *Problems of Communism* (Washington, D.C.), a journal of East and West studies (London); and the *Current Digest of the Soviet Press* (Columbus, Ohio), which provides weekly translations from the most significant latest items in the Soviet press.

Smith, Hedrick, *The Russians* (1976). The best account by an American journalist in recent years of everyday life in the Soviet Union.

Solzhenitsyn, Aleksandr, *One Day in the Life of Ivan Denisovich* (1963); *The First Circle* (1968); *Cancer Ward* (1968); *The Gulag Archipelago* (3 vols, 1973–1979). The major works dealing with terror under the Soviet system.

Ulam, Adam B., *The Rivals: America and Russia Since World War II* (1972). A stimulating essay on American-Soviet relations to the beginning of détente.

Werth, Alexander, *Russia: The Post-War Years* (1972). A firsthand account by an experienced journalist who had watched the Soviet Union throughout the war.

Review Questions

1. What problems in the Soviet Union did Stalin face after the end of World War II? How did he try to cope with them?

2. What happened to Stalinism after Stalin's death? What was Khrushchev's role? What was the role of Khrushchev's successors?

3. Imagine that you are a member of the politburo. What would be your major anxieties? What would be your sources of pride?

4. How do Soviet leaders view their Eastern European satellites? How do these satellite countries view the Soviet Union?

5. How has the Soviet system of government handled the problem of succession in the top leadership? How does the Soviet system of choosing political leaders compare with the American system?

6. What are the aims of Soviet foreign policy? How do Soviet foreign-policy aims compare with those of the United States?

CHAPTER 35

Globalism: The Stresses
of Interdependency

WORLDWIDE WESTERNIZATION
BEFORE WORLD WAR II

WORLDWIDE WESTERNIZATION
AFTER WORLD WAR II

DECOLONIZATION

EXPERIMENTS IN MODERNIZATION

GLOBAL PERSPECTIVES

A T THIS POINT in its long history, Western civilization has entered the age of
globalism, an age of its own making. For better
or worse, the peoples of Europe and of European descent took the initiative in creating the
single, irreversibly interdependent world with
which the present and all future generations of
humanity must cope. No other civilization in
human history has managed to so universalize
itself by imposing its achievements and its
spirit on all others. Penetrating into all lands,
the West has transformed a fragmented world
of villages and loosely related communities
into an emerging "global city" linked by
instant telecommunications. Never before
have so many human beings—there are now
over 4.5 billion people alive—from so many
different cultural backgrounds been brought
into such close association.

Interaction between incompatible ways of
life is inescapable. European—or Western—
culture is challenging all others and being
increasingly challenged in turn. The gravest
threats posed by the future, nuclear war and
destruction of the world's biosphere, can be
averted—or their consequences mended—
only by large-scale human cooperation across
inherited cultural boundaries. Survival demands a heightened awareness of the genesis
and nature of the new globalism.

At the beginning of the twentieth century,
the West was far in advance of the other
civilizations of the world in science and technology. No other civilization had given rise to
a Scientific Revolution or an Industrial Revolution. No other civilization had produced
such self-assertive people determined to
achieve worldly success through individual
initiative and enterprise. Europeans had developed an elaborate industrial system that relied
on factories, mills, and innumerable small
shops with a well-apprenticed, industrial labor
force and a disciplined and knowledgeable
elite of managers and entrepreneurs. From
their factories came advanced weapons, the
foundation of Western power in the modern
world, and goods that raised Europe and Amer-

ica to unrivaled material welfare and affluence.

By the opening of the twentieth century the
European mode of production was typically set
into a parliamentary system of government.
Drawing on the good will of its citizens, the
liberal state granted all adult males the right to
vote, protected individual rights and liberties,
enacted social legislation to combat human
misery, and fostered education, achieving almost universal literacy. Despite incessant
wrangling, occasional bloodshed, and persistent inequality, millions of citizens cooperated in order to improve their standard of living
and to preserve law and order, as well as to
keep their particular country strong.

Western society had never been at peace
with itself; the major countries of Europe had
constantly prepared for war or waged war. Yet
despite their conflicts, Europeans adhered
to common values stemming ultimately
from Greco-Roman civilization and a Judeo-
Christian tradition. Reliance on reason fostered the systematic and critical examination
of nature and society, producing astounding
discoveries in science. Respect for the individual produced a high level of individual initiative and political liberty. Faith in progress
facilitated reform movements that aspired to
improve the conditions of human existence.

Most Europeans relished their remarkable
pace of innovation, priding themselves on the
inquiring spirit that propelled them to unravel
nature's mysteries and explore the universe.
With their ever-increasing knowledge of
nature, society, and the individual human
being, most Europeans were confident of their
capacity to make life more secure and comfortable for all. Convinced, like members of
other proud civilizations, that theirs was history's finest achievement, they also uniquely
possessed the means to prove it. They therefore sought to shape the rest of the world in
their own image.

Yet their experience had not prepared them
for the different conditions in the rest of the
world. How were the essentials of modern
power—industrialism, democracy, private initiative, social mobility, literacy, the rational
outlook, the whole package, in short, of Western civilization—to be transferred to lands
where natural circumstances, institutions,
skills, attitudes, and human values were entirely different and where poverty constricted
all opportunity?

WORLDWIDE WESTERNIZATION
BEFORE WORLD WAR II

At the time of the First World War the transfer
of Western ideas and institutions beyond Europe's boundaries was well under way. At the
height of European imperialism, aspiring
young non-Western men, commonly from
privileged families, went to study in Europe or
the United States. Westerners themselves established Western schools in lands under their
domination. There arose a non-Western intelligentsia, its members prompted by the most
advanced Western ideals and equipped with
Western learning. Their sense of human dignity was patterned after that of their teachers,
yet stunted because the Westerners treated
them as inferior. Copying their Western masters, these uprooted and inwardly divided
intellectuals became nationalists. Western-
educated, they wanted to be "modern" Turks,
Arabs, Indians, Chinese, or Africans. They
wanted their nations to be respected.

These educated nationalists soon became
revolutionaries as well, because colonial officials or traditional rulers generally suppressed
open resistance. As revolutionaries they
turned elitist and socialist. They believed that
their people did not know how to make
themselves strong; that they had to be led and
firmly organized for the purpose of liberation;
that leaving people to their own devices merely meant perpetuating their weakness. Yet the
Western-trained, non-Western intelligentsia
also remained dedicated—at least in the
abstract—to the democratic ideal. How its
elitism and pro-Western orientation could be
reconciled with its faith in the common peo-

ple and its attachment to indigenous culture remained an unresolved problem for the future.

The progress of this intelligentsia varied from one non-Western country to the next. In the dying Ottoman Empire, for instance, the Western-trained Young Turks seized power in 1908. After the collapse of their ramshackle state at the end of World War I, they created a reasonably modern and stable Turkey under the leadership of Kemal Atatürk. The transformation was achieved in relatively short order and has endured to the present.

The experience in India, though, was more representative of non-Western trends. British-educated Indians, with the help of a British civil servant, established in 1885 the Indian National Congress and made it the instrument of a moderate Indian nationalism. Radicalized by World War I, the Indian National Congress fell under the sway of Mohandas Gandhi (1869–1948), one of the most remarkable of the Westernized anticolonial leaders. Born into a prominent family, Gandhi completed his legal training in England. He spent twenty years in South Africa defending its large Indian population against discrimination. Under the influence of European anti-industrialism, Gandhi glorified—in English—the ascetic, antimaterialist Hindu tradition in which he had been raised.

After his return to India, British brutality in repressing a postwar nationalist demonstration turned Gandhi into a political activist who used his religious convictions for a mass campaign of nonviolent resistance. He himself set a heroic example of nonviolent protest by his fasting. His resolve to fast as long as he was in jail—even if he died—endeared him to the Indian masses and established his worldwide reputation as a modern saint.

Gandhi considered himself a representative of the best qualities in Indian tradition, but he and his work were also the product of intensive Westernization. Nationalism and political mass movements were not part of the Indian past. His anti-industrialism, moreover, did not stop the further industrialization of India, nor

was his pacifism shared by Jawaharlal Nehru (1889–1964), a relatively more Westernized Indian, who guided India after independence.

Under British rule for over 150 years, India developed effective nationalist leadership and administrative, legal, and economic structures suitable for nationhood. Its Westernization proceeded from both above and below: from British rule and native resistance to it. The chief flaw in Indian nationalism lay in the insurmountable religious division between Muslims and Hindus. When independence came in 1947, the Indian subcontinent was split into two states: India and Pakistan. Independence was followed by a wave of communal riots that took many hundreds of thousands of lives.

Westernization in China took an even more tormented turn. Through repeated defeats by the European powers after 1839 the imperial Chinese government lost control over its major seaboard cities and its foreign trade. It surrendered territory to Russia, Britain, Germany, and France. The interior was divided into foreign spheres of influence and opened to unwanted Christian missionaries. After a futile uprising—the Boxer Rebellion of 1900—the government was saddled with a heavy indemnity for the damage done to Europeans and Americans. Against such continued humiliation, Chinese patriots trained in Japan, Western Europe, or the United States began to repudiate the imperial heritage and its Confucian roots. In 1911 the imperial government was overthrown.

Raised in the belief that China represented the center of the world, the Chinese had to accept the Western view that it was merely one country among many, and weak and poor, at that. They studied the victorious Western democracies and after 1919 also the Soviet Union for lessons on how to stop the ruin of China, which was ruled by rival warlords. From their studies came two major political experiments.

The first experiment was the Kuomintang (Nationalist party), founded in 1911 by a Western-trained physician and ardent patriot,

Chiang-She k

Sun Yat-sen (1866–1925), one of the revolutionaries responsible for the revolution of 1911. After his death, the Kuomintang was led by General Chiang Kai-shek (1887–1975) who, although Soviet-trained, rejected communism. He vainly tried to fuse the Confucian heritage with Western innovations in military power, state organization, and the economy. His authoritarian regime began to crumble when it failed to enlist the support of the peasants, who were the bulk of the population.

MAO Tse Tung

Peasants played a key role in the second political experiment, that of the Chinese communists. The Chinese Communist party was founded in 1921 and led, after 1935, by Mao Tse-tung (1893–1976). Mao's leadership combined the elitism of the Communist party with close support from the peasants. A mass-oriented nationalism within communist internationalism replaced the Confucian heritage, putting the Chinese communists under a tighter discipline than China had ever known. From a peasant family somewhat better off than the rest, Mao was a member of the generation most humiliated by the collapse of imperial China. Mao became a student of Western learning. He then went into politics with the Chinese Communist party, risking his life and living under worse hardships than those experienced by most other revolutionaries. He tried to win the peasants over to the demanding routines of guerrilla warfare, political agitation, and more efficient agriculture. His success came because he stayed close to the people and, unlike other rulers of China, showed genuine concern for their needs.

MAO

To Mao, Chinese tradition mixed uneasily with the teachings of Marx, Lenin, and Stalin. His close comrade, Chou En-lai (1898–1976), who had studied in France, was more open to Western ideas than Mao, who had never left China. Their Marxism was less doctrinaire and rigid than Lenin's or Stalin's. They put pragmatic experience—Chinese experience—before theory. They were ardent patriots; the Chinese communists fought the Japanese invaders more vigorously than did Chiang's forces. After World War II the communists fought Chiang's Kuomintang. In 1949, with superior organization and purpose, as well as with peasant support, the communists became masters of a new China, reunited and rid of unwanted foreign influence.

The communist victory was dearly bought. The Chinese people had suffered brutally from the war with Japan and the civil war that restored their unity. Nor was the communist victory the end of their trials. Although poor, internally disorganized, and externally weak, communist China was ambitious—by virtue of both its Maoist Marxism and the imperial heritage of Old China—to be a leader in human progress. After 1949 a new experience began, the recasting of China, the most populous state in the world, into a modern form. It has been a tortured and protracted process.

In contrast, the rapid modernization of its small insular neighbor, Japan, was a profound cultural miracle, unique in the world. Forced in the 1850s by Western guns to open their islands to foreigners, the Japanese after a brief civil war turned their humiliation into a radical collective effort to copy all that had made the foreigners victorious. Under the *Meiji* emperor (1868–1912), the Japanese rebuilt their army and navy after the best Western models, created a constitutional monarchy, and instituted a Western system of universal education. Their new code of law embodied the Western concept of individual rights. At the same time they overhauled their economy, adapting the semifeudal social order to the needs of industrial production.

Meiji

In 1911 Japan threw off the last of the foreign controls and faced the Westerners as equals, the first non-Western people to do so. The fusion of Western and Japanese cultures achieved under the Meiji emperor was strengthened by Japanese military victories—over the Chinese, the Koreans, and, in 1905, the Russians. At the end of World War I, Japan was the most powerful state in Asia, challenging not only China but, more cautiously, the Soviet Union, Great Britain, and the United States. Japan championed racial and cultural equality against Western superiority, but at the same time remained highly exclusive within its own boundaries. In the 1930s and early 1940s, driven by nationalist fervor in search of markets and badly needed resources, Japan tried to extend its hegemony over much of eastern Asia until defeated in World War II.

In sub-Saharan Africa—to complete this survey of Western expansion before World War II—Western penetration was much slower and infinitely more troubled than it had been even in China. Here the accidents of climate, geography, and history had produced ways of life and cultural skills very different from those of Europe or Asia. African society had evolved no enduring strong states similar to those of Europe or China or Japan. Many Africans lived in societies without formal government. Most Africans were also strangers to the mechanical arts and the literacy common in Asia and Europe. Medieval Arab travelers, like later Europeans, ignorantly comparing their own more powerful societies with those of Africa, considered themselves superior and regarded the tropical black skins of Africans as a sign of inferiority. The issue of color and racial discrimination, aggravated by the sharp contrast of culture between blacks and whites, especially in America, thus became a major source of conflict for centuries to come.

Western fortified trading bases had spread along the African coast after the sixteenth century, doing business largely on African terms. After the mid-nineteenth century, however, European power increased. By 1900, virtually all of black Africa was partitioned among European states, all resistance crushed. Under colonial rule, Western-trained Africans, especially along the west coast, rose to prominence through trade and the practice of law or medicine; they fumed at the inferiority assigned to colonial subjects. From their anger a West African nationalism was born; it was reinforced by a new Pan-Africanism brought from the Americas by descendants of African slaves. Before World War I political protests multiplied. In the aftermath of the war, a Pan-African congress met alongside the Paris Peace conference.

While black intellectuals and business leaders were learning Western skills and attitudes, European missionaries and colonial officials introduced Western institutions and habits into Africa. They built churches, schools, hospitals, railroads, telegraph lines, harbors, and roads. They established administrative services. They began what later became known as "development," although still uncertain whether to preserve or to change indigenous institutions. For European benefit more than their own, Africans were drawn into varying amounts of contact with the wider world. At the same time, an increasing number of Westernized Africans participated in the colonial government, though never enough to satisfy the nationalists.

On the eve of World War II, Western ambitions, ideas, and institutions had everywhere been imposed on culturally unprepared non-Western people. Such Westernization was imposed either by Europeans eager to extend their domain or by indigenous leaders who learned Western skills in order to escape inequality and permanent domination. The painful and disorienting process of Westernization was inevitably blamed on the colonial powers and Western culture itself.

WORLDWIDE WESTERNIZATION AFTER WORLD WAR II

After the Second World War a new phase in the relationship between the West and non-Western peoples began. It gave vent to the accumulated resentment of previous generations. The rising militancy of the Western-trained anti-Western nationalist movements collided with the declining resources of the colonial empires. The political agitation of the war, in which many colonial soldiers had loyally fought, fired the desire for political independence. After all, freedom and self-determination had been prominent Allied war slogans. France and Holland had been overrun by Nazi Germany, their Asian colonies by the

Japanese; they had no strength left for colonial rule. Great Britain, exhausted by the war, also was ready to let its colonies go as soon as it could responsibly do so. Equally important, the United States, in its new superpower role, took a decidedly anti-imperialist stand. The Soviet Union, although it tightened control over its Asian subject nationalities with whom it shared the geographic insecurity and backwardness of Eurasia, also affirmed its customary moral support for all oppressed peoples. Too weak to provide aid, the Soviet Union nevertheless furnished a heroic model of rapid mobilization (see Chapter 30) for ambitious leaders in non-Western countries.

Decolonization

Thus began the mighty groundswell of decolonization that after 1946 abolished all overseas empires and propelled their former subjects into independent statehood. At best, the colonial powers, under the threat of violence, relinquished their control quietly. At worst, they were driven out by embittered wars of liberation. Sometimes independence was followed by civil war. Whatever the course of events, decolonization profoundly altered the political landscape of the world, giving the non-Western states a worldwide numerical superiority over their former masters and ending for good the political ascendancy of the West. Great was the jubilation in Asia and Africa.

Decolonization began when in 1946 the United States granted independence to the Philippines. In 1947 India and Pakistan attained sovereign statehood. In 1948 Burma, Ceylon (later renamed Sri Lanka), and an independent Israel emerged. In 1949 it was the turn of the Dutch possessions in Indonesia. In 1954 the French quit Laos, Cambodia, and Vietnam (leaving the Americans to defend South Vietnam against North Vietnam until 1973). In 1956 France's northern African colonies, Morocco and Tunisia, were freed (but not Algeria, which attained independence in 1962 after a cruel revolutionary war).

Ghana's much-hailed independence came in 1957. After 1959 virtually all French and English possessions in Africa were decolonized. In 1960 the Belgians reluctantly left the Congo (now called Zaire), which started independence amidst a civil war. By 1975 even the Portuguese, determined to the last to keep their African colonies, were driven out. In 1980 white-ruled Rhodesia changed into the African state of Zimbabwe. Only in South Africa and Southwest Africa (renamed Namibia) did white settlers, including the long-established Afrikaners, continue to defy black majority rule.

In the Mideast, Egypt and Saudi Arabia, which had become independent before World War II, were joined between 1951 and 1971 by other free Arab states. By the mid-1970s Western colonialism had formally come to an end. But the accumulated resentments of colonial rule and the struggle for independence remained a potent political legacy.

The newly independent states lost no time in taking advantage of their political freedom. They captured the voting power in the General Assembly of the United Nations, and dominated the UN agencies of use to them. They staged political demonstrations (such as the Afro-Asian Solidarity Congresses) to announce their arrival in world affairs. The African states in 1963 created the Organization of African Unity (OAU). At every opportunity the newcomers pressed the separate claims of a Third World, unaligned with the power blocs of the United States or the Soviet Union. They used every means available to increase their share of the world's resources. To that end the Organization of Petroleum Exporting Countries (OPEC), formed in 1960, proved an unrivaled weapon after 1973 for at least some members of the Third World. Expectations ran high that the days of humiliation had ended and that indigenous building of a society free of exploitation and inhumanity had begun.

The new governments ruled over nations patterned after European models. They adopted both the ambitions and the trappings of European rule. National anthems, flags, armies, navies, and air forces all proclaimed national power. Putting forth the most advanced ideals of democracy, socialism, and the welfare state, the new constitutions were paper models of enlightened governments. Moreover, they put the most Westernized and cosmopolitan elements in the population into the seats of power where they had so long yearned to be. But disillusionment arrived swiftly. After independence the new masters discovered that their countries, often excruciatingly poor, composed of quarreling ethnic groups that felt no attachment to the new nation, and crowded with illiterate, disease-ridden, stubborn peasants, were unprepared for achieving the global respectability that they craved.

Another round of cruel political, social, economic, and cultural experimentation in search of wealth and power began. The key in all these experiments was a further transfer of cultural skills, in the broadest sense, from the Western countries as in the past and in addition from countries like Japan or the Soviet bloc. Such cultural transfer, designed to raise Third World countries to greater equality, came to be called "development." By common usage the world was hierarchically divided into "developing" and "developed" (or "leading") countries. At the bottom stood the "least developed" or most backward countries, sometimes called the Fourth World. At the top stood the United States, Western Europe, the Soviet Union, and Japan. Between the extremes ranged the intermediate countries, some of them like South Korea or India moving upward, many barely holding their own, and some in desperate trouble.

The excolonial countries were often joined now by the countries of Latin America, whose cultural evolution had lagged after they had attained independence in the wake of the American revolution. With their often sizable Indian (and sometimes African) populations they found themselves, in their relative poverty, their helplessness toward foreign business,

HENRY MOORE (b. 1898): NUCLEAR ENERGY, SCULPTURE COMMEMORATING THE TWENTY-FIFTH ANNIVERSARY OF THE FIRST CONTROLLED NUCLEAR CHAIN REACTION Nuclear power may help solve the problem of decreasing resources of natural energy. Used in military weapons, nuclear energy may also put a permanent end to a long tradition of Western civilization. (Photo courtesy of The University of Chicago)

their political instability, and their sense of frustration, closer to the developing countries. Among them Brazil proved the most successful in industrializing its economy. A spectacular experiment in revolutionary mobilization was carried out in Cuba by Fidel Castro (born 1927), who with the help of the Soviet Union made his country a force among anti-Western countries, especially in Africa.

The gap between the "developed" and the "developing" countries has widened over the years despite all efforts to narrow it. The task of creating equality among the diverse and incompatible cultures developed in the past history of mankind turned out to be infinitely more difficult than expected.

Experiments in Modernization

The experiments of mobilizing a country's resources by the use of Western or Western-derived cultural skills are too numerous to be recounted; each country conducted its own. All such experiments were based on a particular country's resources and history. In Asia after World War II, the most spectacular regime was that of Chairman Mao who thought of his work as a continuing cultural revolution carrying China to the glory of full communism. It proved to be an endless and discouraging ascent.

How was Mao to move the huge population in his vast country, still suffering from decades of war and civil war, into the superior order of socialism, let alone communism? He could adopt the Stalinist model and put the mobilization of China into the hands of a dictatorial bureaucracy of administrators and experts, for quick results. The flaw in using the Stalinist approach was that it would condemn the Chinese masses to the sullen passivity that had ruined the empire; it would restore the elitism of the imperial regime. Or, deviating from Stalinism, Mao could follow the "mass line" and take the slow road of liberating the creative energies of the peasants—at the price of letting China fall further behind in acquiring the latest methods of economic productivity. By temperament Mao inclined toward the latter solution. He hated the presumption of bureaucrats and experts, trusting that the creativity of the masses, once liberated, would conquer all obstacles. Yet many of his ablest comrades remained unconvinced.

Mao also oversimplified the complexities of industrial society. This trait showed up disastrously when in 1958 he staked his leadership on a campaign of creating giant communes engaged in agriculture, industry, education, defense, and administration. As his Soviet critics had predicted, this Great Leap Forward into communism proved a catastrophe, and Mao for a time retired from the limelight. At the same time the Chinese communists, angered by Soviet arrogance and traditionally suspicious of Russian territorial ambition at China's expense, broke away from Moscow's leadership. The Sino-Soviet rift inflicted a serious blow to the unity of world communism.

Great Pro-Cult Rev

China's isolation was greatest in 1965, when Mao, with the help of the army, staged the Great Proletarian Cultural Revolution. It was directed at entrenched and autocratic bureaucrats and experts, and at any lingering veneration of the Chinese past or foreign models. The agents of this new revolution were young zealots carrying a little red book of *Quotations from Chairman Mao.* In these years Chairman Mao was God; never was the cult of personality carried to greater extremes. The revolution closed universities and institutes of scientific research for many years and carried the country to the verge of economic and civil chaos. The only experts spared were those working on nuclear weapons, the most prestigious instruments of national security. Four years later Mao, having purged potential rivals, returned to a calmer course. Yet he laid down no firm guidelines. At his death in 1976, at the age of eighty-three, it was clear that success had escaped him.

Yet Mao still stands out as one of the greatest political leaders of the twentieth century. He had, at a heroic personal risk and a high price for his people, restored unity and a common purpose to China. He also had pioneered a valiant effort to relate China's heritage to the harsh demands of an interdependent and competitive world. If the political experiments he undertook to make China a worldwide model proved inconclusive, the flaw did not lie in his lack of ingenuity or daring, but in the magnitude and novelty of the task: recasting an ancient and deeply rooted culture into an alien modern mold.

Expecting the Chinese revolution to continue long into the future, he left his country a troubled and still backward giant.

Throughout these hectic years, the bulk of the Chinese people, dressed alike in padded cotton, seemed to work in austere disciplined harmony. Foreigners called them the "blue ants." Yet industrial and agricultural productivity remained low, scientific research lagged, hunger and poverty persisted despite the egalitarian regimentation. The isolation from the outside world decreed by Mao as a protection against foreign contamination also undercut progress, as Mao's successors had to acknowledge. From behind the Maoist façade, evidence of dissent and corruption crept into the open when political controls were eased. Mao's teachings had not taken root. Thus began still another round of learning from more advanced foreigners; it favored the experts rather than the creativity of the masses.

After World War II Japan continued its phenomenal progress with relatively minor disorientation. Its social, economic, and political order was further Westernized by the American occupation (1945–1952). Currently it is one of the most productive industrial nations in the world, its pace sustained by the voluntary cooperation of its well-trained citizens. Japan's prosperity depends on world peace and continued access to raw materials.

A somewhat similar economic boom, spurred by American investments, occurred on the Chinese island of Taiwan, which was occupied by the remaining forces of the defeated General Chiang Kai-shek. South Korea too began to prosper, as did Hong Kong and Singapore.

In India, the most populous nation in the world after China, British political tradition and the diversity of people have helped to preserve a pluralist democratic order, protected by a federal constitution. India has made considerable economic development, with assistance from both Western countries and the Soviet Union. But economic development has created two Indias living side by side in stark contrast. Modern and industrialized India is capable even of exporting industrial equipment and living in reasonable comfort. The other India is poor, traditional, caste-ridden, with little hope for improvement. Tension runs high between the two elements of Indian society. India also fears its neighbor, Pakistan.

The greatest tragedies in the relations between traditional cultures and the realities of modern life have taken place in Southeast Asia, especially in Vietnam and Cambodia, an area idyllically untouched by modernization until the 1950s. Thereafter it was plunged, utterly unprepared, into the vortex of world politics. In North Vietnam a liberation movement under Ho Chi Minh (1890–1969) ousted the French colonialists in 1954 and set up a communist regime. Noncommunist South Vietnam came under American protection and was defended, in the devastating war waged over the issue of Vietnamese unification, by American troops using the most modern weapons short of atomic bombs. The war brought cruel destruction and poverty to the civilian population. Virtually all Vietnamese saw members of their families killed or maimed, their farms and livelihood ruined for decades to come. Unable to prevail among an alien people in a tropical battleground, the United States withdrew in 1973, acquiescing in the creation of a unified communist Vietnam.

The Vietnam War brought unspeakable misery to neighboring Cambodia, now called the Khmer Republic. In the wake of the American withdrawal, Cambodian communists, called the Khmer Rouge, seized power under their leader Pol Pot, an enraged patriot radicalized in Left-Bank Paris and fanatically determined to avenge the brutalities committed in his country by both Vietnamese and Americans. He drove over 2 million people from the capital city of Phnom Penh. He hated the city that had harbored so many foreign agents and tried to establish a new order based on ideologically regimented rural communes. Hundreds of thousands of people died in the evacuation and more died later in the countryside. In 1979 the bloodstained and starving country was occupied by Vietnamese troops, visiting further catastrophe on its people. The communist government of Vietnam, resuming an age-old hostility toward China, began to eject Chinese residents of Vietnam, putting them out to sea without a place to land—a shocking reminder that nationalist passion outbids communist solidarity and human decency.

Everywhere in Asia, the experiments in modernization were painful, violent, and marred by adversity. In both India and Sri Lanka, democratic forms of government inherited from British ideals were progressively eroded. Elsewhere dictatorship in one form or another was the rule, procommunist and more often anticommunist, all dependent on outside aid. Although crucial for the regimes in power, such aid rarely reached the bulk of the population. In the continuous unrest, tradition everywhere crumbled under foreign innovations.

A particularly striking experiment of modernization took place in Iran. The shah of Iran, Mohammed Riza Pahlavi (1919–1980), was the son of an illiterate army sergeant who had risen to be Iran's ruler for a time. In 1941, Riza Pahlavi succeeded his father after the latter's abdication, but it was not until 1953 that he consolidated his power with American help. Relying on traditional forms and symbols artificially but grandly updated, he pressed a precipitous revolution of Westernization from above. With the help of his country's oil riches, Western investments, and American weapons, the shah attempted to build a modern state and economy. The shah disregarded his country's religious leaders and savagely repressed all resistance. Yet the forces of tradition, threatened with extinction, struck back. Deeply stirred, Shiite Muslim fundamentalists, basing their creed on the Koran and moving the mass of people to acts of bravery and martyrdom, staged a revolution that drove out the shah in early 1979.

Then began a new experiment, as extreme as that of the shah, under Ayatollah (the highest rank of religious leader) Ruholla Khomeini (born 1902), an unbending and puritanical Muslim nearly eighty years old who rules from the holy city of Qum. He decries all Western influences, trying to make his Iran, half modern and half traditional, conform to the simple teachings of the prophet Muhammad. Yet Khomeini and his supporters cannot escape modernity. They proclaimed a constitution and held elections. They must collect taxes to run the government and buy weapons to fight secessionist Kurds and Arabs. They must satisfy the expectations of their people for a better life, give jobs to the unemployed, conduct foreign relations, import food, and sell oil. Although they denounce the materialist immorality of the West and rage against the United States for its support of the shah, they must come to terms with the complex Western instruments of power if their revolution is to survive.

No experiment of modernization or of protest against it has yet proved conclusive; experimentation continues everywhere. It continues in the Arab states where immense oil wealth, suddenly descended on ancient desert kingdoms, calls for equally immense adjustments. Here too the Koran is the guide to life. Yet is the spiritual ascendance and the social and political order built under the inspiration of the Koran compatible with oil money?

Nearby in the tiny state of Israel yet another experiment is underway. Israel is a state starting afresh after long centuries of exile and bringing together Jews from many lands, under embittered conflict with displaced Arab neighbors. Israel has great assets. Bound together by a common religion and living under daily threat of attack from without, it can count on the loyalty of its citizens. It also has free access to Western capital and knowledge. In some ways, it is part of the West; yet it also is a hazardous long-range experiment. Can it fuse together its heterogeneous Jewish peoples, many from non-Western countries? Can it evolve a constructive relationship with its Arab neighbors, above all the Palestinians, many of whom were displaced from their homesteads? Can it harmonize the demands of religious tradition with the requirements of a modern state?

The African experience of decolonization is well illustrated by the example of Ghana. The hero of African liberation was Kwame Nkrumah (1909–1972), who transformed the small but comparatively advanced British colony of the Gold Coast into the independent country of Ghana, named after a fabled medieval empire in the western Sahel. From Ghana, Nkrumah wanted to advance to a powerful united Africa. As spokesman for a distinct African personality he symbolized the promise of the new Africa. After World War II he emerged in England as a prominent West African nationalist with Pan-African aspirations. Back in the Gold Coast in 1947 he soon became the charismatic leader of the most Westernized elements among the mass of the population. Jailed for incitement to violence, Nkrumah stepped directly into the top post in the government created by the colonial administration in preparation for full self-government. He joyfully presided over the celebration of independence in 1957.

Democratic at the outset, Nkrumah's regime turned into a personal dictatorship and his one-party state into an instrument for the personal enrichment of his lieutenants, despite its increasingly socialist ideology. Nkrumah took Ghana out of the British Commonwealth, spent the financial reserves left from British rule on hasty and overambitious ventures of economic development, and antagonized the leaders of other newly independent African states. He soon lost the confidence of his people. Exiled in 1966 by a military coup, he died a spokesman of a Soviet-oriented scientific socialism that allowed little room for the glorification of African tradition. His successors, both military and civilian, have failed, however, to restore the promise or even the prosperity with which Ghanaian independence began. For that reason Ghanaians remember Nkrumah with renewed affection.

The tribulations of Ghana were shared by most of the other newly created African states.

Starting with democratic constitutions, they changed into one-party states, military dictatorships, or personal regimes, some of them benevolent like those of Jomo Kenyatta of Kenya or Julius Nyerere of Tanzania, desperately trying to hold their multiethnic states together while also paying lip service to African unity. In their countries, as throughout sub-Saharan Africa, loyalty still centers on family, lineage, and ethnic groups. Only the most uprooted foreign-educated Africans put their country first.

Unity often was preserved by compulsion and repression, sometimes degenerating into genocidal violence. In a few lands time-honored African forms of government were perverted by the demands of statehood into unbridled personal rule, rendered murderous by imported Western techniques, as in the case of Idi Amin Dada of Uganda. Some lands, like Senegal and the Ivory Coast, remained closely associated with their former colonial master. Economic conditions thus improved and governments remained stable. Among the former English colonies, Nigeria was rent by a destructive civil war, barely preventing secession of a large section of the country. By 1979 the most powerful of the sub-Saharan states, its economy buoyed by large exports of oil, Nigeria changed from a military to a civilian regime, beginning a new experiment of democratic rule.

As for economic conditions, the testimony (in 1979) of the Executive Secretary of the United Nations' Economic Commission for Africa, a Nigerian, speaks for itself. "The reality is that after two decades of political independence . . . the economic emancipation which had been expected to follow closely upon the heels of independence has still remained a hope." The UN secretary found Africa "basically undeveloped," with low per-capita incomes, a high percentage of the population in subsistence farming, a narrow industrial base, insufficient enterprise, low productivity in all branches of the economy, its most modern sectors dominated by foreigners. He concluded that "the very strategies of development which African governments have been pursuing . . . have come from outside." But how are Africans going to help themselves when the sources of capital, knowledge, and technology and the markets for African goods continue to lie in the developed industrial countries?

The experiments in Westernization exacted an excruciating human toll from societies unprepared for the adjustments required of them. Breaking with tradition and acquiring new ways of thinking and acting left people uncertain of their bearings. Societies once reasonably in harmony with themselves are now torn between incompatible ways of life. No convincing and successful new order has taken the place of tradition (except in Japan). Despite its unprecedented opportunities, the global order is burdened for generations to come with a huge legacy of frustration and disorientation.

GLOBAL PERSPECTIVES

Yet there is another, more positive and elemental side to global Westernization: the preservation and increase of human life. The Westernized world not only sustains a larger population than ever existed before but also endows it with more control over its survival. People, on the average, have a longer life expectancy; they live more securely. They have more opportunity to sharpen their wits, to develop their potential, and to see more of the world that shapes their destiny. They are filled with new expectations and aspirations, too high for immediate satisfaction. Indeed, the rising expectations cause even more frustrations and more articulate protest. But in their struggles the dissatisfied also can draw on a vastly enlarged store of skills in every field of human endeavor. The massive spurt of

material productivity released in the twentieth century has been accompanied by a worldwide knowledge explosion.

But what of the long-run future of Western civilization? No doubt, having universalized itself, it has passed its zenith. Westernization is being supplanted by modernization, by keeping up with other people around the world who have come from cultures other than the West. The talent pool on which human progress now depends includes people of all races and colors.

A Westernized world, moreover, is no longer a Western-controlled world. Westerners now deal in formal equality not only with Westernized, but also with less Westernized peoples in settings barely comprehensible to them (as in Iran). They cannot even avoid the unsettling subversive influence of non-Western cultures on their own. All countries are now vulnerable to the complexity and diversity of the world. Like non-Western peoples in the age of imperialism, every nation today is confronted by conditions for which its past evolution has not prepared it. And worse, the uncompromising hostility of the two superpowers may utterly destroy Western civilization and the lands from which it rose.

Out of their privileged past, Westerners carry forward into their troubled future one major advantage: Western society, still a sizable portion of the world's population, continues to enjoy a reasonable harmony between its institutions and its underlying values. It possesses a capacity for combining freedom with political responsibility, equal protection under the law with effective state power, human dignity with the inescapable personal discipline of work in a complex and demanding industrial society. If Western society can enlarge its tradition of reason and freedom to the requirements of the global age, it may still serve as an example and guide to the peoples of the world.

Index

Charles IV, king of Spain, 463
Charter of Nobility, 419
Chartist movement, 567–568
Cheka, 681
Chénier, André, 428
Chiang Kai-shek, 743, 792, 797
China: European imperialism in, 599–600; Sino-Japanese War, 599; overthrow of Manchu dynasty, 600; war with Japan, 743; relations with Soviet Union, 778, 781; Westernization before World War II, 791; Chiang Kai-shek's Kuomintang vs. Mao's Communism, 791–792; modernization under Mao's leadership, 796–797
Chou En-lai, 685, 792
Christian Democratic Union (CDU), 760, 764
Christian Democrats (Italy), 767–768
Christianity: under challenge by Enlightenment, 401–406; as basis of society for Conservatives, 481; attacked by Nietzsche, 620–621; conflict with Nazism, 714. See also Protestantism; Roman Catholic Church
Churchill, Winston, 570, 656, 734, 737, 757, 766, 768
Class struggle, in Marxism, 556–558
Clemenceau, Georges, 576, 661–664
Clergy, as French First Estate, 428
Cobenzl, comte du, 418
Code Napoléon, 458, 462
Colbert, Jean Baptiste, 353
Cold War, 755–758, 774
Collins, Anthony, 403
Colonialism: German, 579–580; contrasted with imperialism, 590; World War II ends European, 747–748; Algerian war ends France's colonialism, 762–763; westernization of, before World War II, 790–793; decolonization and Third World emergence after World War II, 794–796. See also Imperialism
Columbus, Christopher, 363
Comecon, 784
Cominform, 757, 778
Comintern, see Communist International
Committee of Public Safety, 443–444
Common law, English, 356
Common Market, see European Economic Community
Communards, Parisian, 574–575
Communism: Bolsheviks change name to Communist Party, 678; International (Comintern), 680–681; as one-party dictatorship in Russia, 683–684; Spartacists in Germany, 703–704; in post-World War II Europe, 756–757; major parties

in Western Europe since 1949, 760; break between Tito and Stalin, 777–784; break between Mao and Stalin, 778, 781; in China, Mao's brand of, 792; Sino-Soviet rift, 796. See also Leninism; Marxism; Soviet Union
Communist International, 680–685
Communist Manifesto, 555–557
Comte, Auguste, 616–617, 625
Concert of Europe, 494, 497
Concordat of Bologna, 349
Condillac, Étienne, 409, 476
Congo, 594, 598
Congress of Vienna, 490–494, 497
Conservatism, 479–481, 522–523
Conservative Party, British, 568–570, 766
Constable, John, 478
Constitutional Democrats (Russian), 674
Continental System, 463
Copernicus, Nicolaus, 385, 387–388, 393
Corn Laws, 567
Cortés, Hernando, 363
Cosmology, medieval, 383–385
Counter Reformation, 371, 397
Crime and Punishment (Beccaria), 410–411
Crimean War, 516, 568, 582, 605
Criminal justice system, Enlightenment views on, 410–411
Crompton, Samuel, 542
Cromwell, Oliver, 358–360
Cuba: relations with Soviets, 781–782; revolutionary mobilization, 795
Czechoslovakia: creation of, 664; middle class in, 719; democracy in, 720; British and French appease Hitler on issue of Sudetenland, Germans march into, 730–732; as a Soviet satellite, 782–783
Czechs: in Bohemia, crushed by Hapsburgs, 505–506; conflict with Germans in Austro-Hungarian Empire, 527–528

Daladier, Édouard, 731–732
D'Alembert, Jean, 421
D'Annunzio, Gabriele, 698–699
Danzig, 732–733
Darby, Abraham, 542
Dardanelles, 641, 656
Darwin, Charles, 617–619
Darwin, Erasmus, 617
David, Jacques Louis, 435, 440, 455
Dawes Plan, 705
D-Day, 744–745
Declaration of Independence, 482

Muslim League, 602

Muslims: reconquest of Spain from, 362–363; rivalry with Hindus in India, 599, 602–603. *See also* Arab world

Mussolini, Benito, 668, 697–703, 729–732, 736–737, 744

Nagasaki, 747

Nagy, Imre, 785

Namibia, 794

Napoleon I, emperor of France, 447, 453–471

Napoleon III (Louis Napoleon), emperor of France, 500, 507, 516–518, 523–525, 571–574, 608

National Assembly of France, 435–440

Nationalism: birth in French Revolution, 449–450; emergence of modern, 484–487; and revolutions of 1820–1848, 490–510; 19th-century surge of, 512–535; unification of Italy, 512–518; Prussia agent of German unification, 519–525; conservatism triumphs over liberalism, 522–523; causes problems in Hapsburg Empire, 525–528; and racism, especially in Germany, 528–534; and anti-Semitism, 531–534; new imperialism as accelerating, 592; as fuel for World War I, 634–647; and racism of Nazism, 708–711; separatist movements in Western Europe since 1949, 761; and Third World modernization, 790–796

National Socialist German Workers Party, *see* Nazism

Nation-states, growth of, 346–380

NATO, *see* North Atlantic Treaty Organization

Natural religion, 402

Natural selection, 618

Nature, Scientific Revolution alters view of, 385–387

Nazism: principle of, 697; Nazi Party as Hitler's creation, 707; Munich Putsch, racial nationalism, 708; anti-Semitism, 708–709, 717–718; propaganda, 709; power gains, 710–712; party as state, 712–718; and churches, 714; shaping "New Man" thru propaganda, education, rallies, terror, anti-Semitism, 715–718; German mass support for, 718; German postwar guilt for, 764

Nehru, Jawaharlal, 685, 791

Nelson, Horatio, 454, 463

Neo-Platonism, 385–387

Netherlands: revolt against Spain, 365–366; bourgeois republic free from Spain, capitalism and Protestantism in, 367–369; Enlightenment in, 401–403. *See also* Belgium; Holland

New Deal, 720–721

New Enlightenment, 616–620

Newton, Isaac, 383–391, 396, 397, 404, 407

Nicholas I, tsar of Russia, 495, 506, 582

Nicholas II, tsar of Russia, 584, 586, 673, 680

Nietzsche, Friedrich, 620, 624, 650

Nigeria, 799

Nihilism, 620

Nile, battle of the, 454

"Nine, the," 769

1984 (Orwell), 692

Nivelle, Robert, 654

Nkrumah, Kwame, 799

Nobility, French, 429–430

Nonconformists, 552, 567

North African Campaign, 744

North Atlantic Treaty Organization (NATO), 757, 763, 765, 768, 769, 781, 785

North Korea, 774

Norway: Germans conquer, 734; resistance movement, 742

Nuclear weapons, 747, 749, 774, 786

Nuremberg rallies, 716–717

Nuremberg trials, 764

Nyerere, Julius, 799

O'Connor, Feargus, 568

Olivares, count of (Gaspar de Guzmán), 366–367

Omdurman, battle of, 596

One Day in the Life of Ivan Denisovich (Solzhenitsyn), 777–778

On the Revolution of the Heavenly Spheres (Copernicus), 387

OPEC, *see* Organization of Petroleum Exporting Countries

Operation Barbarossa, 737

Opium Wars, 599

Opticks (Newton), 391

Orange, House of, 369

Organization of African Unity (OAU), 794

Organization of Petroleum Exporting Countries (OPEC), 759, 762, 794

Origin of Species (Darwin), 617–618

Orleanists, 575

Orwell, George, 692

Otto I (the Great), Holy Roman Emperor, 369

Ottoman Empire: Hapsburg warfare against, 372–373; Anglo-Russian rivalry over, 605–606; in World War I, 656; modernization of, 791. *See also* Turkey

Owen, Robert, 555

Pact of Steel, 732–733

Pahlavi, Mohammed Riza, 798

Saar Basin, 662
St. Bartholomew's Day Massacre, 350
St. Helena, 468
Saint-Just, Louis, 450
Saint-Simon, Henri de, 553–554, 574, 616, 625
Sakharov, Andrei, 779
Salazar, Antonio de Oliveira, 719
Salons of the Enlightenment, 403
Samizdat, 779
Samurai, 600
Sans-culottes, 440–442, 445–447
San Stefano, Treaty of, 605
Sarajevo, 642–643
Sardinia, 516–518
Satellite countries of Soviet Union, 782–786
Schlegel, Friedrich, 465, 476
Schleswig-Holstein, 522
Schlieffen, Alfred von, 650
Schmidt, Helmut, 764
Scholasticism, 385
Schönerer, Georg von, 528, 706
Schopenhauer, Arthur, 621
Schusnigg, Kurt, 730
Science: Scientific Revolution, 382–400; medieval
    cosmology, 383–385; new view of nature, 385–
    387; Copernicus and Neo-Platonism, 387; laws
    of planetary motion, 388; physics, 388–390;
    Newton, 390–391; Bruno, Bacon, and Descartes,
    393–395; and English Revolution, 395–396;
    meaning of, 396–398; in Catholic vs. Protestant
    countries, 397–398; influence on Enlightenment,
    400; New Enlightenment and irrationalism as
    affecting views on, 616–620; positivism and so-
    ciology, 616–617; evolution and Social Darwin-
    ism, 617–620; Freud's theory of human nature,
    623–625; discoveries of modern physics change
    views of nature, 628–629
Scotland, education in, 409
Second World War, *see* World War II
Self-determination principle, 659, 661, 662
Sepoy Mutiny, 599, 602
Serbia: conflict with Austria-Hungary, 528; and
    World War I, 635–636, 641–644, 654
Serfdom, 373, 374, 419, 519, 583
Seton-Watson, Hugh, 506
Settlement of 1867, 526, 527
Seurat, Georges, 628
Seven Week's War, 522
Seven Year's War, 418, 420
Seyss-Inquart, Arthur, 730
Shostakovich, Dmitri, 774

Siam, 604
Sicily, and unification of Italy, 516–518
Siemens, William, 542
Sieyès, Abbé, 434
Sigismund, Holy Roman Emperor, 373
Silesia, 418, 420
Sino-Japanese War, 599
"Six, the," 768–769
Skepticism, 402
Slavery: Enlightenment view of, 411–412; abol-
    ished in Africa, 594
Slavs: in Austro-Hungarian Empire, 527–528; Pan-
    Slavism, 636–640
Smith, Adam, 414–416, 483, 551
Soboul, Albert, 441
Social classes: Three Estates in France, 428–434;
    changes due to industrialization, 548–550; in
    Marxism, 556–558
Social Contract (Rousseau), 406, 408, 413
Social Darwinism, 591, 618–619, 636
Socialism: of French workers and revolutions of
    1848, 498; as early protest movement created by
    industrialization, 553–555; Bismarck attacks in
    Germany, 578–579; in Russia becomes Marx-
    ism-Leninism, 676; in Western Europe since
    1949, 760
Socialist Party of Germany (SPD), 710–713, 760,
    764
Socialist Realism, 689
Sociology: Comte's positivism as founding of,
    616–617; of modern society, 620–627; Nie-
    tzsche, 620–623; Durkheim, 625–626; Pareto,
    626–627; Weber, 627
Solzhenitsyn, Aleksandr, 692, 777, 779
Somme, battle of the, 653–654
Sorel, Georges, 622–623
South Africa: British imperialism, 597–598; mod-
    ernization, 744
South America: western imperialism in, 608–610;
    developing countries in, 795
Southeast Asia, 604, 797
Sovereignty concept, 378. *See also* Monarchy
Soviet Union: beginnings in Revolution of 1917,
    672–675; Petrograd Soviet, 673–678; Lenin's
    leadership of Bolshevism (Communism), 675–
    678; formation of Comintern, 680–681; em-
    phasizes industrialization, 681–684; Stalin's
    totalitarian power, 685–693; New Economic
    Policies (NEPs), Five-Year Plans, 686–687;
    collectivization of peasantry, 687–688; purges,
    689–691; chronology of rise, 692; nonaggression

Tzu Hsi, Chinese empress, 599

Ulbricht, Walter, 755
Union of Utrecht, 369
Unions, labor, *see* Trade unionism
United Nations, Third World power in, 794
United States: imperialism in Latin America, 608–610; role in World War I, 656–658; Wilson's leadership at Peace Conference, 658–661; Senate refuses to ratify Treaty of Versailles, 665; Great Depression, Franklin Roosevelt's New Deal, 720–721; isolationism from Europe, 727; Japan attacks Pearl Harbor, destroys U.S. fleet, 743; Germany declares war on, 743; battle of Midway turns tide in Pacific, 744; D-Day invasion of Normandy begins defeat of Axis powers, Bastogne defense, 744–746; drops atomic bombs on Japan, 747; emergence as superpower, 747; Cold War with Russia, 755–758; Marshall Plan aid to Germany, Berlin airlift, 757; in Vietnam War, 797
Universe, Enlightenment vs. modern views on, 628–629
University of France, 458
Urbanization, and industrialization, 547–548
U.S.S.R., *see* Soviet Union
Utilitarians, 552

Valéry, Paul, 666
Valmy, battle of, 442
Valois dynasty, 350
Van de Velde, Jan, 367
Van Dyck, Anthony, 359
Van Swieten, Gerard, 418
Vatican, *see* Papacy
Vendée insurrection, 443, 446
Venetia, 518
Venice, republic of 1848, 507
Verdun, battle of, 652
Vermeer, Jan, 369
Versailles, 352
Versailles Treaty, *see* Treaty of Versailles
Vesalius, Andreas, 392
Vichy government, 737
Victor Emmanuel I, king of Italy, 516–518, 580
Victor Emmanuel III, king of Italy, 700
Victoria, queen of England, 574
Vietnam, 794, 797–798
Villa, Francisco (Pancho), 610
Vinci, Leonardo da, 349
Vindication of the Rights of Women (Wollstonecraft), 414

Vindiciae contra Tyrannos, 350
Volkish movement, 529–534, 706–712
Volksgeist, 485
Voltaire (François Marie Arouet), 403–404, 409–412

Wagner, Richard, 530
Wallace, Alfred Russel, 619
Warfare: total, in French Revolution, 449; Napoleon's art of, 459–460
War of the Spanish Succession, 367, 373
Warsaw, 742, 743
Warsaw Treaty Organization (WTO), 784, 785
Wars of the Roses, 356
Washington Naval Conference, 726
Waterloo, battle of, 468
Watt, James, 542
Wealth of Nations (Smith), 414–416
Weber, Max, 627
Weimar Republic, 703–707, 711
Wellesley, Arthur (duke of Wellington), 465, 466, 567
Western Europe: since 1945, 754–770; Cold War, 755–758; economy, 758–759; political developments, 759–760; problems, 760–762; leading states, 762–768; unity attempts, 768–769. *See also* Europe
Westernization of world, *see* Globalism
West German Federal Republic, 755–756. *See also* Federal Republic of Germany
West German Social Democratic Party, *see* Socialist Party of Germany
West Germany: since 1949, political identity, Adenauer's leadership, economic prosperity, 763–765. *See also* Germany
Whig party, 565–568
William I (of Prussia), German kaiser, 520, 523–525, 579
William II, German kaiser, 580, 597, 598, 638, 640, 658, 703
William I (the Conqueror), king of England, 354
William III (of Orange), king of England, 360–361, 369
William IV, king of England, 567
Wilson, Woodrow, 610, 657–665, 680
Winstanley, Gerrard, 360
Witte, Sergei, 584
Wollstonecraft, Mary, 414
Women: in Enlightenment, 406, 412–414; in Soviet Union, 682

Wordsworth, William, 476

World War I, 634–669; antecedents of, 634–647; minority problems in Austria-Hungary, 635–636; German-Austrian-Italian alliances, 636–639; Triple Entente (France, Russia, Britain), 639–640; Bosnian crisis, 641; Balkan Wars, 641–642; assassination of Francis Ferdinand, 642–643; declarations of war, 644; war as celebration, joy, 645–647; western trench warfare deadlock 650–654; Verdun, 652; Pétain restores French morale after Nivelle defeats soldiers' mutiny, 654; eastern front, 654, 656; Gallipoli campaign, 656; American entry follows German submarine warfare, 656–657; Ludendorff's last German offensive, 657–658; Germany signs armistice, 658; Peace Conference, Wilson's principles of self-determination, 658–661; Treaty of Versailles, other treaties, 661–664; European disillusionment as aftermath of war, 666–669; chronology of, 668–669; aftermath of, as leading to World War II, 725–726

World War II, 725–750; conciliatory spirit after World War I, 725–726; Hitler's foreign policy, British appeasement, 726–727; Mussolini invades Ethiopia, 729; Hitler occupies Rhineland, 729; Spanish Civil War, 729–730; Hitler takes Austria, 730; Munich Conference gives up Czechoslovakia to Germany, 730–731; Hitler-Mussolini pact, 732; chronology of road to war, 733; German-Russian nonaggression pact, 733–734; Britain and France declare war after invasion of Poland, 734; Nazi blitzkrieg, 734–738; fall of France, 734–737; Battle of Britain, 737; invasion of Russia, 737–738; Hitler's rule of terror, exploitation of Europe, 738–743; extermination of Jews, 739–742; resistance movements, 742–743; Japan attacks Pearl Harbor, U.S. victories in Pacific, 743–744; North African campaigns, D-Day invasion, Battle of Bulge lead to German surrender, 744–747; Japanese surrender after atom bomb attacks, 747; legacy of, 747–749; chronology of, 748; total casualties, 754

Worldwide westernization, *see* Globalism

WTO, *see* Warsaw Treaty Organization

Yalta Conference, 755

Youth culture, post-World War II, 760–761

Yugoslavia: creation of, 664; German invasion, 737; guerrilla resistance, 742–743; resistance to Stalinization, 783–784

Zaire, 794

Zapata, Emiliano, 610

Zhdanov, Andrei, 773–774

Zimbabwe, 794

Zionism, 606

Zola, Émile, 576

Zollverein, 519–520